# APPLIED
# EDUCATIONAL
# ASSESSMENT

**Second Edition**

David Allen Payne
*University of Georgia*

**WADSWORTH**

**THOMSON LEARNING**   Australia • Canada • Mexico • Singapore • Spain • United Kingdom • United States

Education Editor: Dan Alpert
Development Editor: Tangelique Williams
Editorial Assistant: Lilah Johnson
Technology Project Manager: Jeanette Wiseman
Marketing Manager: Beverly Dunn
Marketing Assistant: Dory Schaeffer
Advertising Project Manager: Bryan Vann
Project Manager, Editorial Production: Trudy Brown
Print/Media Buyer: Rebecca Cross

Permissions Editor: Bob Kauser
Production Service: Bookcomp, Inc./Nighthawk Design
Copy Editor: Maria denBoer
Illustrator: Bookcomp, Inc./Nighthawk Design
Cover Designer: Belinda Fernandez
Cover Image: Tony Stone
Compositor: Bookcomp, Inc./Nighthawk Design
Text and Cover Printer: Transcontinental

COPYRIGHT © 2003 Wadsworth Group. Wadsworth
is an imprint of the Wadsworth Group, a division
of Thomson Learning, Inc. Thomson Learning™
is a trademark used herein under license.

ALL RIGHTS RESERVED. No part of this work covered by the copyright hereon may be reproduced
or used in any form or by any means—graphic,
electronic, or mechanical, including but not limited to photocopying, recording, taping, Web distribution, information networks, or information stor-
age and retrieval systems—without the written
permission of the publisher.

Printed in Canada
1  2  3  4  5  6  7  06  05  04  03  02

For more information about our products, contact us at:
**Thomson Learning Academic Resource Center**
**1-800-423-0563**
For permission to use material from this text,
contact us by: **Phone:** 1-800-730-2214
**Fax:** 1-800-730-2215
**Web:** http://www.thomsonrights.com

**Library of Congress Cataloging-in-Publication Data**

Payne, David A.
   Applied educational assessment / David Allen Payne.—
2nd ed.
      p. cm.
   Includes bibliographical references and index.
   ISBN 0-534-60282-7 (alk. paper)
   1. Educational tests and measurements—United States. 2.
Educational tests and measurements—United States—
Design and construction. 3. Academic achievement—
United States—Testing. 4. Education—Aims and objec-
tives—United States. I. Title.

LB3051 .P3342002
371.26—dc21                                    2001056776

**Wadsworth/Thomson Learning**
**10 Davis Drive**
**Belmont, CA 94002-3098**
**USA**

**Asia**
Thomson Learning
60 Albert Street, #15-01
Albert Complex
Singapore 189969

**Australia**
Nelson Thomson Learning
102 Dodds Street
South Melbourne, Victoria 3205
Australia

**Canada**
Nelson Thomson Learning
1120 Birchmount Road
Toronto, Ontario M1K 5G4
Canada

**Europe/Middle East/Africa**
Thomson Learning
Berkshire House
168-173 High Holborn
London WC1V 7AA
United Kingdom

**Latin America**
Thomson Learning
Seneca, 53
Colonia Polanco
11560 Mexico D.F.
Mexico

**Spain**
Paraninfo Thomson Learning
Calle/Magallanes, 25
28015 Madrid, Spain

# Family is the Essence of Happiness

**FOR**

**BEVERLY** (Amore, cuare e felicita)

Karen, *Steve,* Jeff, Mike, Beth, *Dad, Mom*

———■———

# Contents

## PART V Summarizing Assessment Data                            **373**

# Preface

The perspective and philosophy of this second edition is the same as that of its predecessor, namely, that the considered, insightful, and appropriate use of measurement and assessment data can significantly enhance the educational experience. The educational experience might be viewed from the classroom, school, or system level. Although the focus is primarily on the development of classroom assessments, appropriate space is given to the consideration of "high-stakes" and standardized testing that has become such a part of the educational reform movement. There will hopefully be much of interest and value here for both pre-service and in-service educators. The term *educator* is used in a very generic sense. In addition to teachers, administrators, curriculum directors, and superintendents should have a working knowledge of measurement and assessment whether at the data generation level or interpretation of results level.

## WHAT'S NEW ABOUT THIS EDITION

Among new features are:

- *Standards Alert*. Sprinkled throughout the text are excerpts from the new *Standards for Educational and Psychological Testing* published by the American Educational Research Association, American Psychological Association, and the National Council on Measurement in Education (1999). These excerpts are included to sensitize the reader to what is considered "best professional practice" and to alert the developers and users of educational and psychological measures to what criteria should be used in evaluating such measures.

- *Portfolio Assessment.* The increasing emphasis on authentic assessments requires significant separate-chapter attention to the development and use of portfolio and performance assessment.

- *Instructional Materials Assessment.* This highly important but frequently overlooked task faced by educators at all levels is addressed in a chapter of its own.

- *Revised Taxonomy of Educational Objectives.* It has been over 45 years since the classic work of Benjamin Bloom and others was published. This completely revised classification system by Anderson and Krathwohl should find acceptance by both teacher and test developer. The cognitive domain is given meaningful coverage.

New topics addressed include dangers in using tests to evaluate teaching performance; methods to control cheating on tests; student-led conferences; recommendations for using tests in tracking, promotion, and graduation; writing prompt development; and guidelines for preparing reports of student test scores.

Updated illustrations and references are also included.

## ORGANIZATION OF THE BOOK

The book's 18 chapters are divided into six broad groupings, as follows:

| Part | | Chapters |
|------|------|----------|
| 1. | Overview of Concepts and Issues in Educational Assessment | 1–4 |
| 2. | Planning Assessments | 5–6 |
| 3. | Creating Traditional Assessments | 7–9 |
| 4. | Constructing Modern Assessments | 10–12 |
| 5. | Summarizing Assessment Data | 13–14 |
| 6. | Application of Assessment Data | 15–18 |

An overview of the concept of traditional and modern educational assessment, with heavy emphasis on the teaching-learning process in today's culturally diverse classrooms, together with consideration of professional standards are topics treated in the first four chapters. Chapters 5 and 6 focus on specifying expected outcomes and the all-important activity of planning the assessment blueprint. Six chapters are next devoted to actually constructing assessments, three to traditional approaches and three to modern approaches. Summarizing data, along with how to measure reliability and validity, are topics treated in chapters 13 and 14. The final four chapters address the increasingly important topics of how to deal with standardized measures, grading and reporting, and the infrequently considered topic of assessing educational materials.

## RETAINED FEATURES OF THE BOOK

Among the major features of the book are the following:

- An *Integrated Case Study*. Each relevant chapter has an integrated case study. Case studies are sequenced and build on the previous studies, and focus on the development, analysis, and application of an assessment in a college reading education course.

- *Speculations*. A set of thought-provoking questions that can be used for initiating classroom discussions are included in each chapter.

- *Content Review Statements*. Each chapter contains a summary of major content topics presented and discussed. These summaries could be used for review or preview. Instructional objectives are implied.

- *Suggested Readings*. A list of both contemporary and classic references are to be found at the conclusion of each chapter.

- *Glossary*. An up-to-date 200-item glossary of key terms and concepts can be found at the end of the book.

- *Focus Concepts and Key Terms for Study*. At the beginning of each chapter key concepts and terms are highlighted to serve as advance organizers to guide study.

## Accompanying Student CD-ROM

A CD-ROM (see inside back cover), linked to a companion Web site, contains the following instructional materials:

- *Illustrative Responses to Integrated Case Study*. Each relevant chapter has an integrated case study. Case studies are sequenced with each building on the previous studies and focus on the development, analysis, and application of an assessment in a college reading education course.

- *Sample Assessments.* Sample elementary and high school assessments are presented with task requirements and scoring directions.
- *Study Guide.* A basic lecture outline for each chapter is presented to assist student study efforts.
- *Sample Exam Questions.* Sample exam questions covering the text in a variety of formats are included to again aid student study efforts.

## ACKNOWLEDGMENTS

"It takes a village full of helpers to produce a book." In addition to the expert reviewers of the manuscript many "significant others" contributed to the creation of this book. The author is indebted to Dr. Jeanne Swafford of Texas Tech University for preparation of materials on which the case studies materials contained in the student instructional disk are based. Alice Tam and Lisa Garberson provided additional assistance and instructional materials. Many colleagues throughout the country, especially users of the previous edition of the book, contributed valuable ideas.

Thank you to the following reviewers: Jane Abraham, Virginia Tech University; Marlaine Chase, University of Southern Indiana; Alan Cohen, Adelpi University; Anthony Gabriele, University of Northern Iowa; Jay Graening, University of Arkansas; Margaret Laughlin, University of Wisconsin-Green Bay; Mary Ellen Levin, Fairleigh Dickinson University; Maria Medina-Diaz, University of Puerto Rico; Monika Schafener, Bowling Green State University; Suzanne Tochterman, Colorado State University; Luis G. Valerio, University of Southern Colorado; and Kimberly Williams, State University of New York, Cortland.

The author, of course, takes all responsibility for any erroneous misinterpretations.

*A special acknowledgment and dedication is hereby made to Janet Goetz, my right-hand person, friend, colleague, CPA, and communications expert for her assistance with this and other books, and my career.*

And when all is said and done don't forget Sandra Schurr's *Ten Commandments of Testing in Middle Grades* (or anywhere else).

# Ten Commandments of Testing in Middle Grades

1. Thou shalt not overuse any one testing strategy.

2. Thou shalt not spring surprise tests on students.

3. Thou shalt not administer tests without adequate preparation on the part of students.

4. Thou shalt not use tests as a threat to motivate or discipline students.

5. Thou shalt not avoid using tests as feedback to teachers on the effectiveness of classroom delivery systems.

6. Thou shalt not use paper and pencil tests as the only means for student evaluation.

7. Thou shalt not overlook the importance of measuring growth in both affective and cognitive areas of student development.

8. Thou shalt not fail to provide adequate feedback to students on test results.

9. Thou shalt not neglect to reduce test anxiety among students.

10. Thou shalt not limit test questions to the lower levels of Bloom's Taxonomy.

Used with permission from National Middle School Association. Materials originally appeared in *The ABCs of Evaluation* by Sandra Schurr, 1992.

# PART One

# Overview of Concepts and Issues in Educational Assessment

*Beverly's Journal* _____

It's been six years since my daughter Chelsea began teaching high school English. Although she still loves the students, the job itself has become quite stressful. There are the seemingly endless paper tasks, teacher meetings, parent meetings, fund-raisers, and all forms of intrusions into the ongoing classroom program. There are special projects for reading and math, character education, and safety, and in-service programs (at night or on weekends) about everything from nutrition to new methods of teaching shoelace tying. There doesn't seem to be enough time to actually teach. No wonder the onset of teacher burnout gets earlier every year. But despite all these pressures, stresses, and clock-robbing activities, Chelsea and I still love our profession. The salaries are getting a little better (if inflation and taxes would leave them alone), and there is a definite general realization that education is the key to a viable and productive society. To keep our schools productive and truly centers of learning will take constant vigilance. Unfortunately, too many policy-makers see accountability as the primary means of reform. We have become a test-obsessed educational profession. Assessment of student and institutional progress is necessary, but it must be conducted in a supportive atmosphere. We must be open to new ideas about people and how the world works. Some of that information can be quantified, some of it cannot.

Dear Journal: I'm afraid I got carried away—a mother's prerogative. Assessing students can be a very meaningful activity for both teacher and learner. I learn how well I've done, and they learn how well they have done. Creating an effective assessment takes considerable effort. It can and should be a meaningful activity.

# 1

# A Perspective on Educational Assessment

---

## FOCUS CONCEPTS AND KEY TERMS FOR STUDY

**Accountability**

**Context**

**Criterion-Referenced**

**Domain**

**Educational Assessment**

**Evaluation**

**Formative Evaluation**

**Measurement**

**Norm-Referenced**

**Performance Assessment**

**Portfolio Assessment**

**Summative Evaluation**

**Test**

---

## STANDARDS ALERT

### Standard 1.2          Interpretation

The test developer should set forth clearly how test scores are intended to be interpreted and used. The population(s) for which a test is appropriate should be clearly delimited, and the construct that the test is intended to assess should be clearly described.

### Taking It to the Classroom

Assessments, classroom or standardized, are not valid or invalid in general but for a particular purpose or application. The teacher should have specific purposes in mind when constructing and interpreting the resulting data.

---

Reprinted with permission from the *Standards for Educational and Psychological Testing.* Copyright © 1999 by the American Educational Research Association, the American Psychological Association, and the National Council on Measurement in Education.

"How'm I doin'?" is a frequently heard question in school, in the workplace, and at home. It is natural to want to know how well you did or are doing on a task or lesson, whether you are learning in school, being productive on the job, or participating in family life at home.

To make judgments about performance or progress, relevant information is needed. This information can be gathered using formal or informal assessments. Formal assessments, such as a science experiment, usually involve structural tasks to be accomplished or questions to be answered. Informal assessments, such as observing a cooperative elementary school map project, can involve individuals or groups carrying out assigned or routine tasks.

In public schools the demand for data is ever-increasing. Hundreds of decisions in and about school and schooling are made each day. We need the best information available, but technical adequacy must be balanced by practical considerations. If assessments, particularly state or federally mandated tests, are abandoned, as some critics would have it, negative consequences could result (for example, the distinction between competent and less competent individuals would be very difficult to make). Our society needs as many competent individuals as possible if we are to compete successfully with other countries in business, research, and education. If we did not assess, evaluation of achievement would be based on influence or background rather than on performance and aptitude; programs would be evaluated on appearance rather than on efficiency and effectiveness.

Granted, preparing relevant assessments requires expending considerable time, effort, and resources, but considering the importance of the data, such expenditures are justified.

The thoughtful and intelligent application of educational assessment principles and devices can profoundly improve the quality of education. Measurement's primary relevance is, of course, to the activities of student and instructor, but its applicability to administration, curriculum development, counseling, and supervision should not be overlooked. Measurement provides data for assessment.

The kinds of questions that can be addressed are many and varied. For example:

- How did Kisha do on her human physiology exam?
- Can Paul solve simple three-digit division problems?
- Did Kim and Raul work together effectively in creating the drug abuse poster?
- Can Chloe and Cheddar create an experiment to identify the density of an unknown object?
- Has the class achieved an understanding of how World War II started?
- Can our eighth-graders write a coherent two-page narrative essay?

To these examples could be added more broadly based questions such as the following:

- What effect has implementing a new way of organizing the language arts curriculum had on student achievement?
- Is the drug abuse video program more effective than the current combination of lecture and programmed materials?
- Is our current performance and records system adequate in identifying those students in need of academic counseling?
- Has the tracking system based on post–high school aspirations resulted in changes in learner motivation?

This is all well and good, but what does it mean to assess in an educational setting?

## THE CONCEPT OF EDUCATIONAL ASSESSMENT

**Educational assessment** is difficult to define. A. English and H. B. English (1958) define assessment as "a method of evaluating personality in which an individual, living in a group under partly controlled physical and social conditions, meets and solves a variety of lifelike problems, including stress problems, and is observed and rated" (p. 44). Sounds like a school setting, doesn't it? This statement describes the procedures the military used to select staff for the Office of Strategic Services (a forerunner of the Central Intelligence Agency) during World War II. This intense process involved a variety of data-gathering techniques, such as observations, stress interviews, performance measures, group discussions, individual and group tasks, peer ratings, projective techniques, and various kinds of structured tests. Lee J. Cronbach (1960) notes three principal features of assessment: (1) the use of a variety of techniques, (2) reliance on observations in structured and unstructured situations, and (3) integration of information.

These characteristics and the Englishes' definition are readily applicable to a classroom situation. Educators are, of course, concerned with the totality of an individual's characteristics—cognitive, affective, and psychomotor. The classroom setting is social and provides both structured and unstructured phases. Problem solving is a major learning task. Obviously, a variety of instruments are needed to measure the myriad of relevant variables. Appraising the totality of the student, his or her environment, and his or her accomplishments is the objective of educational assessment.

The following statement by Benjamin Bloom (1970, p. 31) admirably summarizes the process of educational assessment:

> Assessment characteristically begins with an analysis of the criterion and the environment in which the individual lives, learns, and works. It attempts to determine the psychological pressures the environment creates, the roles expected, and the demands and pressures—their hierarchical arrangement, consistency, as well as conflict. It then proceeds to the determination of the kinds of evidence that are appropriate about the individuals who are placed in this environment, such as their relevant strengths and weaknesses, their needs and personality characteristics, their skills and abilities.

Assessment concerns itself with the totality of the educational setting and is the more inclusive term, that is, it subsumes measurement and evaluation. Assessment focuses not only on the nature of the learner, but also on what is to be learned and how. Robert Stake (1967) has drawn attention to the importance of what he calls the "transactions" of the classroom: the countless interactions between student and teacher, student and instructional material, and student and student that constitute the education process. In a very real sense, educational assessment is diagnostic in intent. Those with responsibility for overseeing education are concerned not only with the strengths and weaknesses of an individual learner, but also with the effectiveness of the instructional materials and curriculum.

We can differentiate between assessment and measurement and testing. **Measurement** is concerned with the systematic collection, quantification, and ordering of information. It implies both the process or quantification and the result. Measurement can take many forms, ranging from the application of very elaborate and complex electronic devices, to paper-and-pencil exams, to rating scales or checklists. **Testing** is a particular form of measurement. Implicit in the term's current usage is the notion of a formal, standardized procedure in which the examinee is aware that she or he is being tested for a particular purpose at a specified time. Normative data also tend to be presented along with raw scores. A test might be defined as a systematic method of gathering data for the purpose of making intra- or interindividual comparisons. A test is a sample of behavior. **Evaluation** describes a general process for making judgments and decisions. The data used to make evaluations can be quantitative, qualitative, or both. A teacher can draw on classroom exams, anecdotal material, scores from standardized tests, and informal observations in arriving at a decision on the promotion of a student. **Formative evaluation** can improve a program by using information gathered along the way as the student progresses or the curriculum unfolds. **Summative evaluation** can be used in making terminal end-of-experience judgments of worth, value, appropriateness, or goodness (for example, as summarized in a final course grade). A more visual comparison of assessment and testing can be seen in Figure 1-1.

Assessments are made continuously in educational settings. For example, decisions are made about content and specific objectives (inputs); the nature of student, faculty, and staff morale or attitudes (context); and the extent to which student performances meet standards (outputs). A typical example of how assessments can be used in decision making is described by Gilbert Guerin and Arlee Maier (1983):

1. The teacher reviews a work sample, which shows that some column additions are incorrect and there are frequent carrying errors.

2. The teacher assigns simple problems focused on the student's consistent addition errors in some number combinations, as well as repeated errors in carrying from one column to another.

3. The teacher gives instruction through verbal explanation, demonstration, trial, and practice.

4. The student is successful in calculations made in each preparation step after direct teacher instruction.

**Figure 1-1**  *Springtime—Time to stop and smell the flowers*

Reprinted by permission of R. C. Harvey and the National Council of Teachers of English from the *Council Chronicle*.

**5.** The student returns to the original page, completes it correctly, and is monitored closely when new processes are introduced.

This example illustrates the intimate association of assessment and instruction. The data useful in decision making can be related from informal assessments (for example, brief observations from interactions) or from teacher-made or selected commercial standardized tests.

The benefits of informed decision making in education are obvious. Enhancing student learning and development is foremost. Evaluating feelings of competence about academic skill and one's perception about functioning effectively in society is mandatory. The affective side of development is equally important. Such personal dimensions as feelings of self-worth and mental health lead to better overall life adjustment.

### The Nature and Place of Measurement in Assessment

The primary component of educational assessment is data collection—specifically, data collection through measurement. Measurement is the backbone of any educational process, as it provides information for decision making. Decisions are made continually about objectives, materials, the cost-effectiveness of the instructional system, student progress, and other similarly important questions.

Educational measurement is a process of gathering data that provides a more precise and objective appraisal of learning outcomes than could be accomplished by less formal and systematic procedures. But why be concerned with precision at all? Precise information is desirable because it can be applied to a wide variety of problems and decision-making activities.

There are probably as many definitions of measurement as there are measurers and testers. All definitions, although qualitatively different, involve systematically assigning numerals to objects, events, places, processes, or phenomena. Such a definition is not sufficient, however, because it allows enumeration and classification to be considered aspects of measurement. Measurement is more than counting or sorting. Measurement compares something with a unit or standard amount or quantity of that same thing, to represent the magnitude of the variable being measured. Data can be gathered, however, by either quantitative or qualitative means. A synonym for measurement might be quantification, specifically, the quantification of *properties* of objects, not the objects themselves or the assignment of numerals to represent objects, properties, individuals, performance, dimension, variables, and so forth. Quantification is both the process and the result of measurement. The alternative to measurement is verbal description, but attempts—however systematic—to describe phenomena verbally tend to be laborious and inefficient, and the results tend to be rather vague and inexact. We still need a working definition of educational assessment. Considering our previous discussions of assessment, tests, measurements, and evaluation, the following working definition of assessment is proposed:

■ **Educational Assessment**
*The interpretive integration of application tasks (procedures) to collect objectives-relevant information for educational decision making and communication about the impact of the teaching-learning process.*

ASSESSMENT = MEASUREMENT + EVALUATION

It is obvious from this somewhat academic definition that educational assessment is more than just collecting information. The information must have meaning. Meaning can be derived from the task itself (for example, a student can build a birdhouse according to a specific blueprint), or it can come from some manipulation of the score reporting scale, that is, using norms. The following example shows how measurement is different from an assessment.

> Rick, an eighth-grader, is administered the science subtest of the Stanford Achievement Test and obtains a grade-equivalent score of 6.4. He also obtains 23 correct on a 75-item comprehensive teacher-made final exam in biology, a *measurement*. The *assessment* would be that Rick is a candidate for remediation in science. An *evaluation* might be a failing course grade or a failure to be promoted to the next grade.

The main thing is that this student needs help.

## EDUCATIONAL ASSESSMENT AND THE TEACHING-LEARNING PROCESS

The major area of application for educational assessment data is with regard to classroom evaluation. It is here where there is much potential and promise. Unfortunately, neither have been fully realized. Sheppard (2000) has commented on how research, knowledge, and instructional bases have changed over many decades and how these should bring about a new conceptualization of the interrelationships of teaching, learning, and assessment. The dominant learning theory has changed from a primarily behaviorist view, with its emphasis on stimulus-response learning and the teaching of relatively independent objectives, to a more integrated approach based on social constructivism (see Chapter 3). The curriculum paradigm has moved from an emphasis on scientific management of schools and specified objectives toward an integrated model that emphasizes higher-order thinking skills and real-life relevance. If teaching and learning have changed, so must assessment. Forward-looking schools no longer focus on assessment with objective tests of limited scope but on authentic, student-constructed, and formative student evaluation where the concern is that assessment be used to improve the teaching-learning process.

The essence of Sheppard's conceptualization has been captured in the form of three interlocking circles representing the three elements in the educational process: teaching/learning, the curriculum, and classroom assessment. Figure 1-2 presents a graphic representation of these three interrelationships.

The most important contribution assessment can make in education is in the service and support of learning. Research on the teaching—learning suggests that one of the most viable models is social constructivism. This approach harkens back to the philosophy of John Dewey (1916), who suggested that children learn best by doing. Teachers work with students to

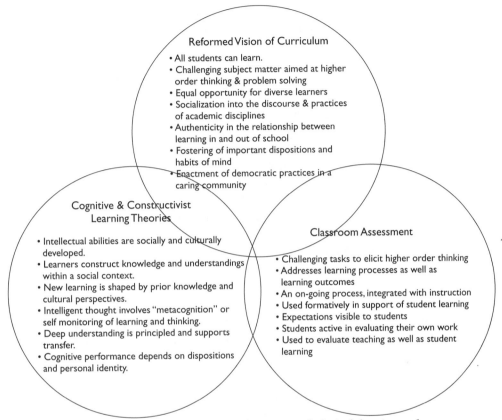

**Figure 1-2** *Shared principles of curriculum theories, psychological theories, and assessment theory characterizing an emergent, constructivist paradigm. (Sheppard, 2000).*

Reprinted by permission of the American Educational Research Association.

find activities which link knowledge and action. Enhancing and nurturing this relationship leads to longer lasting skill development and problem solving. This hands-on approach to the curriculum requires modification in the way in which we assess. The result is something generally referred to as *modern educational assessment*.

## CHARACTERISTICS OF MODERN EDUCATIONAL ASSESSMENT

Over the past several years, we have seen movement toward a somewhat nontraditional philosophy about educational measurement. Although the basic elements are not new, they are being organized in a new way that—

it is hoped—will provide stronger links among instruction, learning, and measurement. This approach has been variously termed as authentic assessment, direct assessment, alternative assessment, or **performance assessment**. The umbrella term *modern assessment* will be used in this book. What is desired is a more operational definition of what students can do, what skills they possess, and what problems they can solve. Definite emphasis is placed on higher-order thinking skills. This philosophy developed in partial response to dissatisfactions expressed about some current testing practices, especially multiple-choice tests. Dissatisfaction has been expressed particularly concerning state-mandated testing programs established for accountability, with their predominant emphasis on minimum competencies and basic skills, and norm-referenced interpretations. There is a desire to reduce the "inference gap" between assessment and criterion, in order to yield better validity.

The notion and practice of modern assessment is not new; we have been doing it for many years. Assessments of writing skills, typing, computer applications, science laboratory skills, foreign language learning, and a variety of physical education, art, and music outcomes all qualify as performance assessments. Educators appear to want more hands-on assessment in which actual student behaviors as well as products can be examined.

Among the more important general characteristics of modern assessment are the following:

1. *Value beyond the assessment itself*. The assessment task should be meaningful in and of itself and not derive value from being a "test."

2. *Student-constructed response*. Having a record of an actual student behavior or product observed and evaluated brings criterion and assessment closer together.

3. *Realistic focus*. This characteristic relates to the contemporary need to show students that they are involved in "meaningful" (real-world) learning that will have an ultimate tangible payoff.

4. *Application of knowledge*. The need to measure problem-solving and critical thinking skills results in educational outcomes being reemphasized.

5. *Multiple data sources*. A variety of approaches will enhance validity and reliability and allow greater adaptability to individual student differences. This characteristic obviously represents a desire to address the increasing diversity in our classrooms.

6. *Objectives-based and criterion-referenced*. Having objectives to guide development *and* interpretation contributes to the relevance of the

assessment and thereby its validity. Having this characteristic allows the assessment to meet both summative and formative goals.

7. *Reliability*. Consistency is a requisite in any assessment, from administration to performance and scoring.

8. *Multiple approaches*. The student, with advance notice, should have some latitude in determining how the assessment will be documented.

9. *Multidimensional in structure*. This characteristic addresses the comprehensive integration and combination of skills and knowledge.

10. *Multidimensional scores*. A single summative score is less meaningful and has less diagnostic value than several subscores.

Implied in this list of characteristics are criteria for instrument development. Particularly important is the concept of reliability, or the consistency with which results are obtained. The terms *instrument, task, procedure,* and *method* will be used interchangeably in this book because they all imply a process for collecting information. The list also suggests that we are attempting to do things differently today.

One example of trying to do things differently with modern authentic assessment in the elementary grades is **portfolio assessment**. A portfolio is a collection of student products intentionally selected to represent a variety of achievements over a specified period of time, usually a school year. The portfolio must include the actual student productions, a statement of why each was included, and the criteria used in evaluating them. A final item sometimes included is a student self-evaluation of selected products or the portfolio as a whole. Student progress can therefore be documented and evaluated over time. The opportunity for student creativity—for example, in writing—is significant. In addition, this approach creates a real sense of ownership and investment in assessment. Of course, good teachers have been doing this kind of thing for a long time. Assessment definitely gets integrated into learning when approached in this manner. The aggregation of portfolio data useful in evaluation at other than the student level is difficult if not impossible because of the very idiosyncratic nature of the portfolios. Creative methods for identifying and synthesizing themes and trends across portfolios are needed.

Despite obvious advantages, several disadvantages are evident. The first relates to time. Developing and evaluating a representative authentic assessment, particularly portfolios, is labor-intensive. Just from a physical standpoint, only a limited and therefore selected number of objectives can be documented to any depth. If we are focusing on numerous respondents, time and cost can be very significant factors indeed.

Table 1-1 compares some of the advantages and disadvantages of both current educational assessment approaches and traditional approaches.

The educational information questions at the beginning of this chapter suggest a variety of applications of assessment data. The following section discusses six major areas in which educational assessment data can make significant contributions.

## APPLICATIONS OF EDUCATIONAL ASSESSMENT DATA

The kinds of outcomes considered important in American schools appear to be ever-changing. Several different emphases or trends are currently evident. On the one hand, society appears to be pushing schools to engage exclusively in a basic skills and fact acquisition development orientation. The heated rhetoric about reading and mathematics and minimum com-

**Table 1-1** *Comparison of Characteristics of Modern Educational Assessment and Traditional Educational Measurement*

| Characteristic | Modern Assessment | Traditional Measurement |
|---|---|---|
| Intent | Emphasis on improvement | Focus on accountability |
| Nature of Objectives | Integrated sets of objectives Higher-order outcomes | Tending to isolate lower-level and separate objectives |
| Nature of Task(s) | Variety of methods, especially open-ended | Tends to be structured |
| Administration | Can be time-consuming | Efficient |
| Nature of Response | Usually student-constructed response, supply | Fixed-response, selection |
| | Oral, process, written, product, observation of performance | |
| Scoring and Reporting | Can be complex, multidimensional | Objective, efficient machine-scorable |
| | | Single global score |
| Reliability | Can reach acceptable levels with training | Almost always high |
| Cost | Can be very high | Per unit cost is modest |
| Impact on Student | Less threatening | Can be anxiety-provoking, especially with high-stakes tests |

petencies attests to this concern. On the other hand, schools also appear to be assuming many educational responsibilities that were historically considered the prerogative of parents and other socializing segments of society. Such areas as sex education, human relations (including marriage), values, morality, and ethics are now addressed in schools. These affective concerns require evaluation, but they pose many methodological problems. There also exists a need to develop and assess problem-solving skills to help students make applications of their knowledge.

Perhaps assessment has made its greatest contributions to education in the understanding of the teaching-learning process. In particular, assessment data have been found useful in diagnosing learning difficulties and evaluating their treatments. The use of broadband survey batteries, particularly the achievement variety, has experienced both historic and contemporary acceptance in public schools. These tests are useful in directing curriculum emphasis, providing valuable information for a variety of administrative decisions, stimulating and motivating student learning, and aiding in the academic and vocational guidance of students.

On the contemporary education scene, assessments, although different in form and output, continue to be used in traditional ways. Achievement tests are being applied throughout the grade range, and diagnostic tests are applied in the early grades and in special education settings. Selection and admission tests are used at institutions of higher education with undergraduate, graduate, and professional school students.

An increasing use of assessments is found in program and project evaluation. Large numbers of educational and psychological assessments are being made because of accountability issues and because virtually all funding agencies, especially at the state and federal levels, require documentation of program effectiveness.

Six broad-use categories can be identified for educational assessments:

1. selecting, appraising, and clarifying instructional objectives
2. determining and reporting student achievement of educational objectives
3. planning, directing, and improving learning experiences
4. evaluating accountability and programs
5. counseling
6. selecting students for special programs

### Selecting, Appraising, and Clarifying Instructional Objectives

Achievement in school involves movement toward a specified set of objectives. When teachers develop an instrument to collect data to be used in evaluating progress toward these objectives, they are forced by the very nature of the task to define and review this instruction. Ideally, specifying objectives will be accomplished before instruction begins and will continue as the curriculum is modified to meet individual student needs. Administering an achievement test to reveal deficiencies may be useful at the beginning of a course of study. The original objectives can then be modified, expanded, or discarded, as the data dictate. The more comprehensive, complex, and higher-order outcomes being addressed in schools bring the need for a similar kind of assessment.

## Determining and Reporting Student Achievement of Educational Objectives

Educational assessment is most frequently used to assess the level of student achievement in school subjects. Applying assessment procedures yields more objective data on achievement than does subjective appraisal. Such information is obviously critically important to the student, as it provides some perspective on the student's position relative to acceptable educational standards (those of the school, society, or teacher, or the student's own standards).

Many other individuals, in addition to instructor, student, and parent, are interested in individual student learning status. School administrators are obviously concerned. College admissions personnel find high school grades useful in making decisions. Despite the proliferation of national admissions and scholarship testing programs and grade inflation, previous academic performance remains the single best predictor of future performance.

## Planning, Directing, and Improving Learning Experiences

The diagnostic use of assessment data can be extremely helpful. Tests can serve a valuable function by identifying strengths and weaknesses in the achievement of individual students or classes. If the teacher and student can identify the areas in which achievement is less than adequate, individual learning efforts—and, for that matter, teaching—can be directed more efficiently.

Data on the sequence, continuity, and integration of learning experiences can be valuable in improving and facilitating learning. For example, the requisite skills and knowledge for certain courses or units can be identified. The effectiveness of selected instructional practices can also be evaluated. This use of assessment is becoming more important each year with the appearance of new curricula, particularly in language arts, science, mathematics, and social studies. This essentially involves using tests for research. A teacher might engage in an action research study of a new device or program compared with previous educational outcomes from the same class, from control groups, or from similar classes.

## Evaluating Accountability and Programs

Educational assessment can make a significant contribution to today's schools in the area of accountability. Marvin Alkin (1972) has defined accountability as "a negotiated relationship in which the participants agree in advance to accept specified rewards and costs on the basis of evaluation findings as to the attainment of specified ends." The key is the term *negotiated*, which suggests a dialogue among teachers, parents, administrators, and students. One common type of negotiated relationship is a contract, and the performance contract has already emerged as a frequently used method of implementing accountability. A performance contract is, basically, an agreement to bring about specified changes in individuals or groups. Criteria are detailed and the "level of payment" is correlated with performance. Obviously, assessing performance is critical. Several technical problems are, however, associated with performance contracts—for example, regression effects and unreliable gain scores.

Another dimension of accountability comes from the many innovative programs and projects that are continually being implemented in schools. Implementation requires evaluation—evaluation in the formative sense (data are used to improve the program or project) and also in the summative sense (an overall judgment of worth is made and reported to the responsible funding agency or institution).

## Counseling

With increasing frequency public schools are emphasizing a "human resource development" educational goal. There is a desire to help the individual student assess his or her strengths and weaknesses in the context of academic and vocational guidance and personal growth. A variety of measures from all three human resource domains (cognitive, affective, and psychomotor) are available. In particular, specialized aptitude measures and self-report personality and adjustment inventories are valuable sources of information. More and more elementary schools are developing counseling programs to help students build psychological adjustment mechanisms that will be useful throughout the developmental years and over the entire life span.

## Selecting Students for Special Programs

Whether for academic or vocational purposes, assessment can provide information that will aid individual and institutional decision making. Schools, colleges, and universities must select those students most likely to benefit and succeed in their programs. Vocational training institutions are forced to make similar decisions. Assessment can help delineate general individual differences in ability and the extent of mastery of basic knowledge and skills. Special education programs frequently use extensive assessment data.

## DANGERS IN USING STUDENT TEST DATA TO INFER TEACHER AND SCHOOL EFFECTIVENESS

During the past several decades, administrators and policy-makers have been seeking systems of teacher and school accountability. A central component in those systems is reliance on student test data. These data may be from classroom tests, or more likely from nationally normed standardized tests or state-created/mandated curricular-based assessments. There are many problems that could mitigate against accepting such data as evidence of teacher effectiveness. "Standardized" high-stakes student test data have been proposed to be used for annual teacher evaluations, for career ladder decisions, and for school evaluations (aggregated across classrooms). In many instances aggregated student test performances at the school level are used to either reward or punish the school. One of the unfortunate consequences of this school reform improvement model is excessive test preparation activities in classrooms (McColskey & McMunn, 2000). Among the many dangers inherent in this approach are:

- reduced emphasis on nontested objectives
- allowing test preparation materials (text or computer software) to drive the instructional program
- reduction of availability and participation of students in extracurricular activities
- reliance on external rewards (such as cash) to motivate learning
- failure to provide instruction in question formats not on the high-stakes tests
- creating an emotionally charged and test-anxious environment
- failure to emphasize higher-order thinking skills
- restricted reliance on staff development activities focused on improving test performances
- differential effects of test preparation, that is, greater impact on low-ability students to the detriment of better students

A significant danger for teachers in having student test data form the basis of the evaluative criteria rests on the assumption that teachers have total and complete control of student learning. Obviously there is a meaningful direct influence, but there are many factors that impact learning that are beyond the control of the teacher. There are a number of factors which operate against the total reliance on student test scores to evaluate teachers. Among these are:

- lack of universally appropriate measures for all of the important educational outcomes

- lack of uniformity in opportunities to learn within and between schools

- the differential effect of home and parental variables on learning

- lack of uniformity in opportunity to teach, that is, subject-area teachers have differing amounts of contact time

- lack of uniformity in assignment of students with regard to ability level

- the likelihood that teachers will focus on students most likely to show gains

- the potential for the development of destructive teacher attitudes toward teaching, school, and education

- the disproportionate allocation of resources and personnel across schools (this is the most important factor, perhaps)

The above represent just some of the potential dangers in using student test data to evaluate teaching effectiveness. Not to be overlooked is the trade-off of cost-benefit and effectiveness gains versus the cost of data collection. Is it worth the cost to collect all these possibly flawed data? Despite many decades of instructional research we are no closer to being able to completely define effective teaching. We have some pretty good ideas about what constitutes "best professional practice," but lack prescriptions that will work for most students. The increasing diversity in classrooms represents an even greater obstacle to the identification of a uniformly effective teaching methodology. Much research remains to be done. More important, what is needed is a uniformly supportive environment in the schools with local leadership, including parents, teachers, students, support staff, and the community, devoted to nurturing the educational process. A continuing and informed dialogue needs to be maintained among all stakeholders.

We must be careful not to fall into the trap suggested by an analogy attributed to Linda Darling-Hammond (Culkins, Montgomery, & Santman, 1998). A hospital is interested in assessing the overall level of health care.

It decides to gather temperatures on all patients at the same time. The hospital staff, in an effort to project a uniform "good health impression," plies patients with aspirin and cold drinks just before temperatures are taken. Lo and behold, everybody's temperature is down, indicating a healthy hospital. Just because test scores are up due to quick-fix test practices does not mean that all is well with education.

## TWO APPROACHES TO ASSESSMENT: CRITERION-REFERENCED AND NORM-REFERENCED

The multiple purposes of assessment mentioned previously require different methodologies. The term *methodology* as used here includes everything from specifying objectives, to construction, to analysis and interpretation. For monitoring individual student progress in a course of study, we might want a limited sample of objectives that are similar in content or process. If we were interested in surveying the math achievement of all tenth-graders in the school system in a variety of skills (for example, basic skills, algebra, geometry, and so on), a heterogeneous sample of various outcomes with different kinds of questions might be desired.

In 1963 an essay by Robert Glaser paved the way for the formal differentiation of two general approaches to test construction and interpretation. These methodologies are referred to as criterion-referenced and norm-referenced. Jimmy Popham (2002) suggests the following general definitions:

■ **Criterion-Referenced Measurement (CRM)**
*A criterion-referenced measure is used to ascertain an individual's status in a defined assessment domain. (p. 85)*

■ **Norm-Referenced Measurement (NRM)**
*A norm-referenced measure is used to ascertain an individual's status compared with the performance of other individuals on that measure. (p. 86)*

One important distinction between these two approaches to interpretation rests on the specification and description of the **domain** to be sampled. The concept of domain is broadly described by learner behaviors. Specifying the instructional objectives associated with these behaviors is central to criterion-referenced measurement. The criterion is "performance with regard to the domain." In some respects, the current classroom testing practice of writing items for objectives is like a CRM. The difference rests on a tighter, more complete definition of the domains being sampled, and in some cases a specification of a performance standard. The performance standard can take the form of specifying the number of items to be answered correctly or the number of objectives to be mastered (which usually refers to the number or percentage of correctly answered items).

Popham (2002) sees two major differences between CRM and NRM. The first relates to the previous discussion of domain, with CRM focusing mostly on relatively homogeneous sets of objectives (words spelled, problems solved, periods of history, species of trees, and so forth) and NRM focusing more on general content or process domains (such as reading comprehension or knowledge about elements of biology or geography).

The second major difference relates to interpretation. CRM usually employs percentages (of items or objectives) achieved or an absolute standard; NRM uses scoring that compares an examinee's performance with that of other examinees who have been assessed. In NRM, percentiles and standard scores are used in conjunction with tables of norms (numerical collections or summaries of the performances of specified groups of individuals, such as a national sample of fifth-graders). In this regard classroom tests are most like CRM and standardized tests are like NRM. The distinction, however, is not pure: Classroom tests can be, but are usually not, norm-referenced.

### Areas of Application for CRM and NRM

Six broad-use categories have been described previously in this chapter. The following list indicates whether a particular measurement approach—CRM or NRM—is predominantly relevant (+) to a given test purpose or application.

| Purpose | CRM | NRM |
|---|---|---|
| Clarifying instructional goals and objectives | + | |
| Determining and reporting student achievement | + | |
| Planning, directing, and improving learning experiences | + | |
| Accountability/program evaluation | + | + |
| Counseling | | + |
| Selection | + | + |

The first three classifications are self-evident. CRM is a better approach for assessing individual instructional treatment effectiveness and progress. Accountability, however, can be oriented toward individual students, teachers, schools, or systems. We frequently engage in program or project evaluation and, depending on the nature of the activities, we may therefore desire CRM or NRM. We cannot make, however, very solid inferences regarding teaching quality from student achievement data aggregated at the classroom level, particularly at the upper end of teacher performance levels (Millman & Darling-Hammond, 1990). Counseling applications are primarily made in the areas of personality/mental health and vocation/career guidance. Measures in these areas are primarily available from commercial publishers, and therefore NRM applies. Selecting individuals for programs, projects, or training can be on the basis of meeting a minimum knowledge or performance standard or discrimination among members of a qualified group. When minimum standard selection is used, such as meeting licensure or certification requirements, a CRM would be most appropriate. If one must fill a limited number of openings, positions, or slots, then spreading the qualified applicants out to spot the best is most effectively accomplished with NRM.

How does one develop measures to meet the projected applications? CRM and NRM approaches have unique and common requirements, adjustments, modifications, and embellishments, which are highlighted throughout the remainder of this book.

These two major approaches to measurement, with their different emphases on the source of standards, imply different kinds of tests. These tests vary in the nature of the benchmarks they use to help interpret the resulting scores.

## OUTLINE OF THE ASSESSMENT TASK DEVELOPMENT PROCESS

The term *education*, as used throughout this book, is defined as the process of creating changes in the cognitive, affective, and psychomotor characteristics of individuals. How does this process relate to *assessment?* How does the developer begin to construct the instrument or task? Presumably, one could simply sit down and begin writing questions about the material that has been taught. If the instructor is creating the assessment, the types of questions that easily come to mind are those that address outcomes high on his or her list of priorities. If the assessment is to be fair, the instructor will have to examine the task to be sure that content and behavioral applications are covered in the proportion intended. This is the beginning of a deliberate, analytic approach to development, whose sequence of steps is approximately as follows:

1. Specify the ultimate goals of the education process.
2. Derive from these the goals of the portion of the system under study, for example, a math class or social studies curriculum.

3. Specify these goals as expected student outcomes. If relevant, articulate the acceptable level of successful performance.

4. Determine the relative emphasis or importance of various objectives, their content, and their behaviors.

5. Select or develop situations that will elicit the desired behavior in the appropriate context or environment, assuming the student has mastered it.

6. Assemble a sample of such situations that together represent accurately the emphasis on content and behavior previously determined.

7. Record responses in a form that will facilitate scoring but will not so distort the nature of the behavior elicited that it is no longer a true sample or index of the behavior desired.

8. Establish scoring criteria and guides to provide objective and unbiased judgments.

9. Try out the instrument in preliminary form.

10. Revise the sample of situations on the basis of tryout information.

11. Analyze reliability, validity, and score distribution in accordance with the projected use of scores.

12. Integrate information into assessment.

This sequence of steps describes the ideal process usually followed in developing standardized measures. The intent if not the letter of the recommendations implicit in the steps should be adhered to when you are constructing any custom-made assessment instrument, whether for classroom or commercial purposes.

The importance of educational objectives in the first stages of test construction cannot be overemphasized. Objectives, ideally in behavioral form, guide and shape the total process. Developing and applying educationally relevant assessments can be a revealing and professionally satisfying activity. But, like most worthwhile activities, it requires concentrated time, effort, and patience.

## GENERAL CRITERIA FOR EVALUATING ASSESSMENT INSTRUMENTS

How does one judge the quality of a classroom assessment? This question frequently goes unanswered due to lack of knowledge about standards and criteria for evaluation, or lack of effort. If either of these conditions exists, the assessment activity cannot be a meaningful one for student or instructor, both of whom should profit from the experience. The student profits because the process of preparing for the assessment causes him or her to review and interrelate the material. We might call this learning experience a *motivational effect*. Upon completion of the assessment, assuming close proximity between it and knowledge of the results, a *learning effect* should also be noted. The instructor should not only profit from the experience of reviewing his or her instruction, but also from the significant data about student learning he or she derives. In constructing an assessment, a teacher is asked to summarize the salient elements of instruction in terms of content, student behavior, and classroom activity. The instructor then summarizes these elements in the form of questions or tasks to be presented to students. Instructors are next, obviously, forced to "think through" their instruction and thus gain perspective on their teaching and insight into the organization of the material that should prove beneficial to themselves and their students.

Because of their intimate association we will discuss data and measurements as one. Measurements yield data. Measurements are evaluated and become the assessment. If the measures are good, the data will be good. Data become "informative" only after they are communicated. But what constitutes a "good" measurement? Following are 10 desirable characteristics to be sought in a measuring instrument, whether it is to be used to collect data on achievement, aptitude, or attitudes.

1. **Relevance**. Relevance is the correspondence between the data and the intent or objective in gathering the data. It might be the match between a test question or task and a behavioral objective, or the match between a series of planned observations and projected teacher-student or student-student interactions. In the measurement sense, relevance is the primary contributor to validity or the degree to which the measurement is a true and accurate reflection of the variable of interest.

2. **Balance**. Any assessment needs a framework or plan for its development. The extent to which the developed measure corresponds to the ideal measure reflects balance. In developing an achievement test, for example, a blueprint of specifications is created whereby content and outcomes are summarized in a $2 \times 2$ table. Entries in the cells reflect the proportion of instructional time devoted to those objectives. The test is then built according to those proportions, resulting in a balanced measure. Any multidimensional instrument can benefit from the application of this concept.

3. **Efficiency**. Basically, we are looking for the greatest number of meaningful responses per unit of time. Gathering data costs time and money,

so we want to conserve our resources. A balance between time available to collect the data, cost, requirements for scoring and summarization, and relevance should be sought.

4. *Objectivity.* Do experts agree on the interpretation of the data? With regard to paper-and-pencil exams, for example, do different scorers or raters come up with the same results? If behavioral observations are involved, will different observers "see" the same thing? Along the same line, given a series of extensive field notes from participant-observers, will different ethnographers evolve the same interpretation? Objectivity, then, is a characteristic of the "scoring" or the assignment of meaning to the data, rather than a description of the method of data collection.

5. *Reliability.* Reliability is a complex characteristic, but generally involves consistency of measurement. Consistency of measurement might be judged in terms of time, items, scorers, examinees, examiners, or accuracy of classifications. It also has important applications when dealing with qualitative data. These might relate to such activities as interobserver agreement and consistency in drawing inferences from observational data or written descriptions.

6. *Fairness.* The criterion of fairness relates to a wide range of data characteristics, from freedom from bias (gender, ethnic, or racial) to the administration of a test in a manner that allows all students an equal chance to demonstrate their knowledge or skill. Everybody should play by the same rules, and the rules should be the same for everybody.

7. *Specificity.* If subject-matter experts should receive perfect scores, test-wise but course-naive students should receive near-chance scores, indicating that course-specific learnings are being measured. Another way of looking at specificity would be if a large proportion of students fail a question or have low scores before instruction, but significantly improve their scores after instruction. This means the assessment device was obviously "sensitive" to instruction. This rationale would also hold for an attitude change program or performance training program.

8. *Difficulty.* The questions should be appropriate in difficulty level to the students and the group being assessed. In general, for a norm-referenced test, a maximally reliable test is one in which each item is passed by about half of the students. For a criterion-referenced test, difficulty could be judged relative to the percentage passing before and after instruction. Difficulty will be dictated by skill and knowledge measured and the ability of students (see Chapter 9).

9. *Discrimination.* For norm-referenced tests, the ability of a question to discriminate is generally indexed by the difference between the proportion of

good (or more knowledgeable) and poor (or less able) students who respond correctly. For a criterion-referenced test we tend to think of discrimination in terms of pre-post differences (see Chapter 9) or the ability of the test or item to differentiate the competent (masters) from the less competent (nonmasters). (*Note:* Taken together, difficulty and discrimination describe the influence of the "complexity" of a task. Complexity might be inherent in the question or skill being assessed or the way in which it is asked. Reading level, for example, can have a dramatic effect on the difficulty level of a question.)

10. ***Speededness***. To what degree are scores on the test influenced by speed of response? For most achievement tests, speed should generally not be allowed to play a significant role in determining a score, and sufficient time should generally be allowed for all or most examinees to finish the test.

Taken together, these 10 characteristics spell "validity" as, in the aggregate, they determine what the test measures and how these scores should be interpreted.

For the most part, a test constructor or user may evaluate the instrument in light of the foregoing 10 factors by careful examination of the test and/or the data it yields. Obviously, consideration should be given to these factors before, during, and after test development and administration. The refinement of a test is a continuous and ongoing process.

The characteristics are not mutually exclusive. Lack of "balance," for example, would be an unfair assessment.

The characteristics of difficulty and discrimination have greatest relevance if one's intent is to maximize the measurement of inter- or intraindividual differences. If the intent is to assess progress toward a specific set of objectives, they may have less applicability in instrument development.

Wall and Summerlin (1972) have completed an interesting and useful comparative application of the characteristics of a good measuring instrument. They examine teacher-made and standardized tests in light of each of the 10 characteristics. The results of their analysis are shown in Table 1-2.

## WEB SITES FOR EDUCATIONAL ASSESSMENT INFORMATION

The Internet has become a powerful force in the information-producing and -transmitting industry. Such technology comes with a caution about accuracy, particularly data from commercial vendors. Nowhere is that

**Table 1-2** *Relative Merits of Teacher-Made and Standardized Tests*

| Characteristic | Teacher-Made | Standardized |
|---|---|---|
| Relevance | Measures objectives for the class | Measures achievement for typical classes |
| Balance | Measures objectives in same proportion as time spent on instruction | Measures a large variety of objectives |
| Difficulty | Is geared to the group being tested | May vary; usually averages around 50 percent passing for all items |
| Reliability | Usually not calculated; normally very low but can be as high as standardized tests if carefully planned | Usually high; normally 0.85 and above |
| Speededness | Sufficient time is usually given for completion of test | Strict time limits are typical |
| Discrimination | Each question helps to differentiate between high- and low-scoring students if differentiation is goal; if testing for mastery, this characteristic is meaningless | Attempts to find individual differences between students, with each question contributing to differentiation of those scoring high and low |
| Specificity | Measures specific learnings | Attempts to measure specific learning |
| Objectivity | There is agreement among experts on answers to items chosen | Answers have usually been checked by subject-matter experts |

more true than with regard to educational assessment information (Bennett, 2001). The following Web sites are offered only as starting points for the initial collection of information. Most have links to other valuable sites.

| Professional Organization | Location |
|---|---|
| American Psychological Association | *http://www.apa.org/science/test.html* |
| Association of Test Publishers | *http://www.testpublishers.org* |
| Buros Institute of Mental Measurements | *http://www.UNL.edu:80/buros/* |
| Center for Research on Evaluation, Standards & Student Testing (CRESST) | *http://www.CSE.ucla.edu* |
| ERIC Clearinghouse on Assessment and Evaluation | *http://www.ericae.net* |
| National Assessment of Educational Progress | *http://www.nces.ed.gov/NAEP/* |
| National Association of Test Directors | *http://www.natd.org* |
| National Council on Measurement in Education | *http://www.ncme.org* |

| Test Publishers | Location |
| --- | --- |
| American College Testing | http://www.act.org |
| American Guidance Service | http://www.agsnet.com |
| California Test Bureau | http://www.ctb.com |
| College Board (SAT) | http://www.collegeboard.com |
| Educational & Industrial Testing Service | http://www.edits.net |
| Educational Testing Service | http://www.ets.org |
| Graduate Record Examination | http://www.gre.org |
| Harcourt Brace Educational Measurement (Stanford 9) | http://www.hblem.com |
| Institute for Personality & Ability Testing | http://www.epat.com |
| Psychological Corporation | http://www.hbtpr.com |
| Psychological Test Publishers PRO-ED | http://www.preedinc.com |
| Riverside Publishing (ITBS) | http://www.riverpub.com |
| Western Psychological Services | http://www.wpspublish.com |

## Content Review Statements

1. Educational assessment is a very powerful force that can be used to improve the effectiveness of teaching-learning situations.

2. Educational assessment involves collecting and integrating data involving inputs to, transactions within, and outputs from an educational system.

3. Diagnosing learning difficulties and their implications for remedial procedures is one major intent of educational assessment.

4. Significant inputs to an educational assessment decision-making system derive from measurement and evaluation procedures.

5. Measurement is the process of collecting, quantifying, and ordering information on an individual, attribute, or object.

6. A test is a means of measurement characterized by systematic administration and scoring procedures, formalized objectives, and applications aimed at intra- or interindividual comparisons.

7. Evaluation is the process of making value judgments about measurement data.

8. Assessments are the collective interpretations of the evaluations of measurement and test data.

9. Assessment data can be used to help
   a. select, appraise, and clarify instructional objectives.
   b. describe and report student progress toward, or achievement of, educational objectives.
   c. plan, direct, and improve learning experiences.
   d. provide a basis for assessing accountability.
   e. counsel students.
   f. select students.

10. Norm-referenced measures have *relative* interpretation.

11. Criterion-referenced measures have *absolute* interpretation.

12. The processes of instruction and evaluation are intimately related.

13. An educational assessment system should be responsive to relevant cognitive, affective, and psychomotor educational objectives.

14. Creating an educational assessment involves the following stages:
    a. specifying goals and objectives
    b. designing the assessment system
    c. selecting data-gathering methods
    d. collecting relevant data
    e. analyzing and summarizing data
    f. contrasting data and objectives
    g. feeding back results

15. Educational assessments should be specifically applicable to the instructional field, area, discipline, or course in which they are used.

16. Educational assessments should yield reliable, consistent, and replicable results.

17. A good assessment instrument should, as a rule, be
    a. relevant
    b. balanced
    c. efficient
    d. objective
    e. specific
    f. appropriately difficult and discriminating
    g. reliable

    h. fair

    i. unspeeded

**18.** When tests are used to assess the effectiveness of teachers and schools, misevaluation can come about due to

    a. deemphasized nontested objectives

    b. the test to drive the curriculum

    c. creating a debilitating, test-dominated environment

    d. deemphasis on higher-order thinking skills

    e. differential effects of test preparation activities

    f. focusing on students most likely to perform well or show gain

    g. uneven distribution of student ability across classrooms

    h. differential allocation of teaching time to different content areas

**19.** The Internet can provide extremely valuable information about assessment to the critical consumer.

## SPECULATIONS

**1.** In what ways does the concept of educational assessment make more sense than the individual process of measurement and testing?

**2.** How have particular assessments or tests influenced your life?

**3.** What are the essential ways in which criterion-referenced and norm-referenced measurement are different? In what ways are they alike?

**4.** What is the relationship of the terms *test, measurement, evaluation,* and *assessment?*

**5.** What kinds of decisions can assessments help us make?

**6.** Would you want your neurosurgeon to be a graduate of the Norm-Referenced College of Hard Knocks or the Criterion-Referenced University of Competencies? Why?

## SUGGESTED READINGS

Airasian, P. W. (2001). *Classroom assessment.* 4th ed. Boston: McGraw-Hill.

Cangelosi, J. S. (2000). *Assessment strategies for monitoring student learning.* New York: Longman.

Gifford, B. R., & O'Connor, M. C. (Eds.). (1992). *Changing assessments: Alternative views of aptitude, achievement and instruction.* Boston: Kluwer.

Hakel, M. D. (Ed.). (1998). *Beyond multiple choice: Evaluating alternatives to traditional testing for selection.* Mahwah, NJ: Erlbaum.

Kohn, A. (2000). *The case against standardized testing.* Portsmouth, NH: Heinemann.

Nuttall, E. V., Romero, I., & Kalesnik, J. (1992). *Assessing and screening preschoolers.* Boston: Allyn & Bacon.

Popham, W. James. (1999). Why standardized tests don't measure educational quality. *Educational Leadership, 56*(6), 8–15.

Rothman, R. (1995). *Measuring up (Standards, assessment, and school reform).* San Francisco: Jossey-Bass.

Smith, J. K., Smith, L. F., & DeLisi, R. (2001). *Natural classroom assessment (Designing seamless instruction and assessment).* Thousand Oaks, CA: Corwin.

Stiggins, R. J., Conklin, N. F., & Bridgeford, N. J. (1986). Classroom assessment: A key to effective education. *Educational Measurement: Issues and Practice, 5*(2), 5–17.

Tanner, D. E. (2001). *Assessing academic achievement.* Boston: Allyn & Bacon.

Willingham, W. W., & Cole, N. C. (Eds.). (1997). *Gender and fair assessment.* Hillsdale, NJ: Erlbaum.

Witt, J. C., Elliott, S. N., Kramer, J. J., & Gresham, F. M. (1994). *Assessment of children.* Madison, WI: WCB Brown & Benchmark.

# 2

## Assessment Standards and Concerns

---

### FOCUS CONCEPTS AND KEY TERMS FOR STUDY

| | |
|---|---|
| **Assessment Standards** | **Fair Testing Code** |
| **Bias** | **Legal Standards** |
| **Ethical Principles** | **Testing Standards** |
| **External Tests** | |

---

## STANDARDS ALERT

**Standard 2.12**                    **Reliability**

If a test is proposed for use in several grades or over a range of chronological age groups and if separate norms are provided for each grade or each age group, reliability data should be provided for each age or grade population, not solely for all grades or ages combined.

### Taking It to the Classroom

A reliability coefficient for a standardized assessment if it is based on a sample of examinees spanning several grades or a broad range of ages in which average scores are steadily increasing may give a spuriously inflated impression of reliability. When a test is intended to discriminate within age or grade populations, reliability coefficients should be reported separately for each population. It is surprising how much difference a year can make in the reliability of an assessment.

---

Reprinted with permission from the Standards for Educational and Psychological Testing. Copyright © 1999 by the American Educational Research Association, the American Psychological Association, and the National Council on Measurement in Education.

Assessment practices, particularly as implemented in public schools, are undergoing real and meaningful changes. These changes are evident in both why and how assessment is done, and are evident not only in the United States but elsewhere in the world as well.

## TRENDS IN STUDENT ASSESSMENT

The forces that bring about change stem primarily from efforts toward educational reform. Not to be overlooked is the influence of politics and economics. The public, parents, and employers want more informed and competent graduates of our schools. State and local legislators are concerned about spending hard-earned dollars for education that may be less than optimal. One attempt to "control" education and establish accountability is through student assessment.

Student assessment is big business. The National Association of State Boards of Education estimated that states spend $423 million per year on average on assessment. A recent Harris Poll supports these expenditures, as it reports that 87 percent of Americans favor testing students in grades 3 through 8 annually in reading and math. In addition, they report that 78 percent favor making principals and teachers more accountable for how well or badly students do on tests. But, make no mistake, preparing for tests does take away from instructional time. Some balance is needed. But what does research say about the nature of student assessment, particularly "standardized testing" in schools?

The most up-to-date information on the state of external assessment systems is contained in a 1998 survey by the Council of Chief State School Officers (Olson, Bond, & Andrews, 1999). Their data reveal the following trends:

- All 50 states and three jurisdictions (Puerto Rico, Virgin Islands, and the Department of Defense) schools have some type of large-scale assessment program in place.

- The most frequently assessed grade levels are 4, 8, and 11.

- Test results are most frequently reported as being used in curriculum planning as can be seen with the data in the following graph.

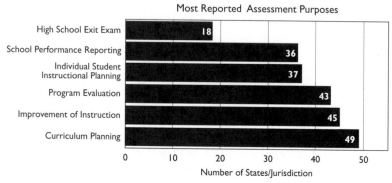

**Most Reported Assessment Purposes**

(Adapted from Olson, Bond, & Andrews, 1999)

- Not unexpectedly, the most frequently assessed subjects are mathematics and language arts/reading.

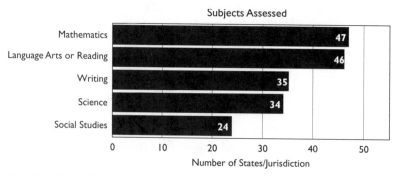

**Subjects Assessed**

(Adapted from Olson, Bond, & Andrews, 1999)

- A variety of methods are used to assess American students. Not unexpectedly, multiple-choice items are the most frequently used. The use of student-constructed assessments is on the increase, around the country, however.

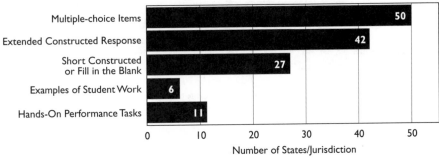

Types of Items in State Assessment Component

(Adapted from Olson, Bond, & Andrews, 1999)

- With regard to the growth of nontraditional assessment methods, the most popular are the extended response assessment techniques associated with writing. The use of such methods add greatly to the validity and credibility of large-scale state assessments. It also adds great cost.

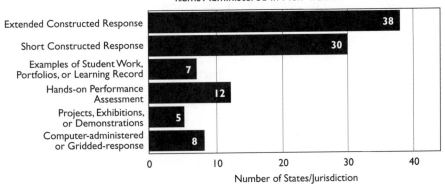

Items Administered In Non-Traditional Assessment

(Adapted from Olson, Bond, & Andrews, 1999)

- Special needs groups of students receive accommodations during large-scale state and most classroom assessments. Adjustments are sometimes made in presentation format, setting, timing or schedule, and response format. The following graph reflects these accommodations for disability and English-language learner groups.

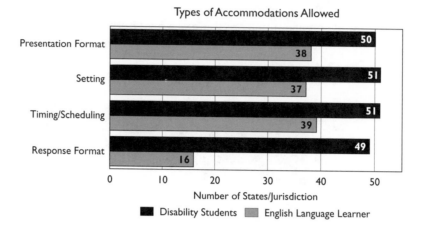

Although the use of alternative approaches to testing is increasing, it is costly. Teachers, of course, create and use the most assessments in classrooms. We want to be sure they are of the highest quality and are given greatest priority, for these tests are most closely aligned to instruction.

Public schools involve an estimated 20 million school days and require somewhere between $700 million and $900 million a year. Because of the amount of time, effort, and money expended on testing, a three-year study was undertaken of testing practices for the purpose of making recommendations for significant changes (National Commission on Testing and Public Policy [NCME], 1990). Among the major deficiencies identified in current testing practice were the following:

- Tests can mislead as indicators of performance.
- Testing can result in unfairness.
- There is too much educational testing.
- Testing practices can undermine social policies.
- Tests are subject to insufficient public accountability.

The recommended reforms are summarized in the following statements:

- Testing policies and practices must be reoriented to promote the development of all human talent.
- Testing programs should be redirected from overreliance on multiple-choice tests toward alternative forms of assessment.

- Test scores should be used only when they differentiate characteristics relevant to the opportunity being allocated.

- The more test scores disproportionately deny opportunities to minorities, the greater the need to show that the tests measure characteristics relevant to the opportunities being allocated.

- Test scores and implied measures should not be used alone to make important decisions about individuals, groups, or institutions; individuals' past performance and relevant experience must be considered when opportunities are allocated.

- More efficient and effective assessment strategies are needed to hold institutions accountable.

- The enterprise of testing must be subjected to greater public accountability.

- Research and development programs must be expanded to create assessments that promote developing the talents of all people.

The criticisms of student assessment are welcome, for they provide a major impetus for improvement. They reemphasize the inadequacy of certain testing practices. In addition, these critics' comments should caution both professionals and laypersons against the misuse of tests.

Critics have joined professional testers in demanding better training for those who administer, interpret, and use tests, and they have made a significant contribution by identifying issues that need research. The latter contribution is, however, directly related to a distinctly negative outcome: the critics, both directly by influencing professional educators and indirectly through parents, can tend to deter schools from participating in the much-needed research in testing. Furthermore, the brunt of criticism falls on the tests, instruments, methods, or devices themselves, when all too often the users are at fault.

Most observers would agree that the need to improve communications between the testing profession and the public is being acknowledged. Continued vigilance is necessary on the part of professional and lay groups to expose quacks and incompetents and to press for higher standards in the test-publishing industry and more intensive preservice and in-service training in measurement. Although politics is reality, let us not allow it to distort the educational process.

How have those who practice assessment on a day-to-day basis and those who engage in assessment as a primary occupation responded to the criticisms of assessment as it exists today?

## ASSESSMENT: QUESTIONS AND ANSWERS

Criticisms and controversies periodically draw attention to the many problems associated with educational and psychological assessment. Some of these are long-standing whereas others have arisen out of changes in society. Following is a list of questions and answers about a variety of aspects of student assessment.

Question: *Are educational and psychological assessments biased against some individuals?*

Answer: *Any* assessment can be biased. The **bias**, or discriminatory practice, might begin with the basic intent in even conducting the assessment, through specifying the objectives, writing the questions, and selecting the final questions for the assessment. If the assessment is to be a standardized test offered for commercial sale, then establishing norms represents a potentially significant source of bias in selecting groups to be included in the summary data. Both subject (content bias review panels) and empirical methods (differential item functioning) are available to help control bias during the developmental stages of assessment creation. Performance assessments can also be biased if all individuals do not approach this task with the same knowledge and skill background.

Question: *Can assessments control the school curriculum, inhibit change and reform, and become standards in and of themselves?*

Answer: There is a real danger that this can happen. Such an occurrence reflects a misuse of data, however, rather than a shortcoming of the assessments themselves. The critical question is whether or not the teachers' objectives are the same as those on the assessment. If they are, there is no problem. If, however, the content of the assessment becomes the determining criterion, the educational process can be seriously distorted.

Some uninformed users of educational assessments regard the distribution of scores derived from nationwide population samplings as goals to be achieved by each of their students. National norms can serve a useful function by providing "benchmarks" by which to judge students' overall progress, but they should never serve as the sole criterion of program effectiveness or student progress. Failure to consider the educational philosophy of local teachers, administrators, and the community as well as the socioeconomic and ability levels of the school population can lead to gross misevaluations. A related danger is that the tests begin to determine the nature of the instructional program. A school and its teachers should not be evaluated exclusively by students' performance on any external assessment. Nor should standards for a local school district be determined by blind application of norms tables. Furthermore, a standardized achievement test should never be the sole source of data for marking or promotional decisions.

**Question:** *Do intelligence and achievement tests measure the same thing?*

**Answer:** In a very real sense, intelligence and achievement tests measure the same thing: the ability to perform selected tasks at a specified point in time. Although achievement tests measure abilities acquired under relatively controlled conditions, and intelligence tests measure abilities acquired under relatively uncontrolled conditions, a cursory review of standardized achievement and intelligence tests reveals significant overlap. The content of the two types of tests is quite similar, and the correlations between scores are usually in the mid-0.50s and higher. The tests do differ, however, in how the results are used. We tend to use achievement tests to measure past performance or to describe how well certain learning tasks have been accomplished and intelligence tests to predict future performance. In schools and colleges today, however, achievement tests are playing an increasingly important role in prediction.

New data suggest that humans possess multiple intelligences, and that "intelligent" behavior is shown by an individual's ability to learn from experience and adapt successfully to the environment. We find ourselves in a variety of environments that require different adaptation mechanisms, which might range from information-processing skills to creativity and the ability to find practical solutions (Gardner, 1983; Sternberg, 1988). Tests do not directly measure innate characteristics!

**Question:** *Do standardized tests only measure recall of facts?*

**Answer:** Most standard achievement tests and a large part of classroom assessments do emphasize recall, but it can legitimately be argued that one must have a large fund of information at one's command to reason, argue, solve problems, or function effectively in society. Most reputable achievement tests can measure such higher-order abilities as comprehension, application, and problem solving. Test publishers, using performance and traditional approaches, are increasingly emphasizing the measurement of "higher-order" outcomes as curriculum emphases and instruction move in that direction. The user must remember that even the highest-quality achievement test cannot measure an entire subject-matter area. Such tests can only sample types of learning. Similarly, users should be very cautious in interpreting the multiscore profiles that many survey batteries provide. Test experts have demonstrated that, because of the high degree of relationship among subtests, the differences reflected in such profiles are highly unreliable.

**Question:** *Do tests predict imperfectly?*

**Answer:** Yes. All instruments are fallible, just as are test-takers. In many instances, however, the use of test data is preferable to reliance on subjective judgment alone. In most cases some data are better than none. In combination with other kinds of information, tests can do a very creditable job. The fallibility of test scores is partly because humans are fallible. People are inconsistent in responding to tests, which raises problems of measurement reliability. In addition, the criteria we use for test validation are less than perfect.

**Question:** *Do assessments, particularly tests-based assessments, harm students' cognitive style, self-concept, and aspirations?*

**Answer:** There is little or no evidence that exposure to particular kinds of tests, for example, multiple-choice or true-false, adversely affects the development of an individual's style of thinking or problem solving.

A comprehensive review of the literature has suggested some variables that can contribute, however, to testing's impact on students (Natriello, 1987):

**1.** Students who were provided information about the criteria for performance on their assignments showed the highest levels of skill, self-efficacy, and speed of problem solving.

2. Teachers who hold high standards for their students tend to find student effort and performance at a higher actual level.

3. Individual competitive (versus cooperative) standards tend to produce superior academic performance.

4. More frequent testing tends to yield better achievement.

5. If students do not perceive the evaluation as being credible, performance and acceptance of results are depressed.

6. Personalized feedback to students about their performance has a very positive effect on their acceptance of results and future performance.

It can be argued that tests help individuals to see themselves, their capacities, and their accomplishments more realistically. We strive to assure that the tests provide fair and valid results, which are communicated by a trained professional skilled in test interpretation. This is an area in which school guidance and counseling personnel can make a significant contribution.

## ETHICS AND ASSESSMENT

**Ethics** is the systematic study of human actions in terms of right or wrong. Morality is the pattern of behavior reflecting the impact of ethics. When applied to professional organizations, ethical codes set standards for members and regulate their actions. A code of ethics attempts to set high standards of competence, strengthen relationships among its constituents, and provide for the common good of society. Major organizations within the behavioral sciences have provided guidelines for the ethical practice of assessment and educational measurement.

The first set of principles, *Ethical Principles of Psychologists and Code of Conduct*, comes from the American Psychological Association (1992). In general, these principles deal with issues of competence, integrity, responsibility, and respect and concern for the rights, dignity, and welfare of others. Specifically, for evaluation and assessment, 10 standards are enumerated. These relate to

- evaluation, diagnosis, and interventions in professional contexts
- competence and appropriate use of assessments and interventions
- test construction
- use of assessment in general and with special populations

- interpreting assessment results
- unqualified persons
- obsolete tests and outdated test results
- test scoring and interpretation services
- explaining assessment results
- maintaining test security

The following excerpts from the *Ethical Principles of Psychologists and Code of Conduct* illustrate these standards:

> Psychologists attempt to identify situations in which particular interventions or assessment techniques or norms may not be applicable or may require adjustment in administration or interpretation because of factors such as individuals' gender, age, race, ethnicity, national origin, religion, sexual orientation, disability, language, or socioeconomic status. (2.04c)
>
> When interpreting assessment results, including automated interpretations, psychologists take into account the various test factors and characteristics of the person being assessed that might affect psychologists' judgments or reduce the accuracy of their interpretations. They indicate any significant reservations they have about the accuracy or limitations of their interpretations. (2.05)
>
> Psychologists do not promote the use of psychological assessment techniques by unqualified persons. (2.06)
>
> Unless the nature of the relationship is clearly explained to the person being assessed in advance and precludes provision of an explanation of results (such as in some organizational consulting, preemployment or security screenings, and forensic evaluations), psychologists must ensure that an explanation of the results is provided using language that is reasonably understandable to the person assessed or to another legally authorized person on behalf of the client. Regardless of whether the scoring and interpretation are done by the psychologist, by assistants, or by automated or other outside services, psychologists take reasonable steps to ensure that appropriate explanations of results are given. (2.09)
>
> Psychologists make reasonable efforts to maintain the integrity and security of tests and other assessment techniques consistent with law, contractual obligations, and in a manner that permits compliance with the requirements of this Ethics Code. (2.10)

A second set of principles has been declared by the National Council on Measurement in Education in the *Code of Professional Responsibilities in Educational Measurement* (1995). The 78 specific responsibilities are extremely relevant. But, perhaps of equal interest are the eight assumptions underlying their development. These assumptions should be considered by all who develop assessments, not just teachers.

1. Hold paramount the safety, health, and welfare of all students being assessed.

2. Be knowledgeable about, and behave in compliance with, the law in the conduct of professional activities.

3. Maintain and improve professional competence in educational assessment.

4. Provide assessment services only in areas of one's competence and experience, affording full disclosure of one's professional qualifications.

5. Strive to improve the assessment literacy of the public by promoting sound assessment practices in education.

6. Adhere to the highest standards of conduct and promote professionally responsible conduct within educational institutions and agencies that provide educational services.

7. Perform all professional responsibilities with honesty, integrity, due care, and fairness.

8. Avoid the use of professional roles for fraudulent or improper purposes.

These commonsense principles are another example of the Golden Rule: Assess As Ye Would Be Assessed.

### Legally Mandated Ethical Standards

Thus far, we have considered voluntary ethical guidelines for assessment practice. The emphasis on educational accountability has caused some states to pass laws that require adherence to practices that attempt to control unethical or inappropriate activities within the assessment context. One such state is Ohio. In October 1994, a set of standards (R.C. 3301-7-01) for ethical test use was adopted by the state board of education and sanctions were specified. Among the specific practices considered to be unethical are the following:

- any practice that results solely in raising scores or performance levels on a specific assessment instrument, without simultaneously increasing the student's achievement level as measured by other tasks and/or instruments designed to assess the same content domain;

- any practice involving the reproduction of actual assessment materials, through any medium, for use in preparing students for an assessment;

- any preparation activity that includes questions, tasks, graphs, charts, passages, or other materials included in the assessment instrument or in a parallel form of the instrument, and/or materials that are paraphrases or highly similar in content to those in actual use;

- any preparation for the assessment that focuses primarily on the assessment instrument or a parallel form of the instrument, including its format, rather than on the objectives being assessed;

- any modification in procedures for administering and/or scoring the assessment that results in nonstandard and/or delimiting conditions for one or more students;

- any practice that allows persons without sufficient and appropriate knowledge and skills to administer and/or score the assessment;

- any administration or scoring practice that produces results contaminated by factors not relevant to the purpose(s) of the assessment;

- any practice of excluding one or more students from an assessment solely because the student has not performed well, or may not perform well, on the assessment and/or because the aggregate performance of the group may be affected;

- any practice such as a gesture, facial expression, use of body language, comment, or any other action that guides students' responses during an assessment;

- any practice such as providing to students, either immediately preceding or during administration of an assessment, any definitions of words or terms contained in the actual assessment instrument;

- any practice such as erasing, darkening, rewriting, or in any other way correcting or altering student responses to an assessment task either during or following the administration of an assessment.

The serious intent to ensure fair, valid, and reliable assessment cannot be underestimated. If professionals are lax in establishing, implementing, and maintaining ethical assessment practices, others will step in to protect consumers and clients.

The foregoing general principles have been expanded and refined for specific groups associated with assessment.

## TECHNICAL STANDARDS AND CODES OF PROFESSIONAL PRACTICE

A variety of professional organizations, both those affiliated with a subject-matter discipline (for example, the National Council of Teachers of Mathematics), as well as measurement organizations have created useful assessment guidelines.

## Measurement Competencies Needed by Teachers

The roles played by teachers are varied and significant. Their instructional and interpersonal skills are vital to the educational development of today's youth. Many of their instructional skills are related to assessing student progress, both formally and informally. These competencies are critical because they relate directly to gathering the information needed to make rational instructional decisions.

A committee of representatives of four professional organizations (the American Association of Colleges of Teacher Education, the American Federation of Teachers, the National Council on Measurement in Education, and the National Education Association) has recommended seven general assessment competencies an effective teacher must have (National Council on Measurement in Education, 1990). Table 2-1 contains comparisons of the *Standards for Teacher Competence in Educational Assessment of Students* and some comments.

## Measurement Competencies Needed by Educational Administrators

Educational administrators are also involved in assessment, although primarily as consumers of information. The National Council on Measurement in Education in collaboration with the American Association of School Administrators, the National Association of Elementary School Principals, and the National Association of Secondary School Principals has also developed a set of competency standards for school administrators (NCME, 1994). These guidelines are called the *Competency Standards in Student Assessment for Educational Administration*. Administrators here obviously include school principals, but also include superintendents and selected central office personnel. The recommended competencies deal with basic concepts, applications, and management responsibilities. The educational administrator must demonstrate 10 competencies:

1. Demonstrate a working level of competence in the *Standards for Teacher Competence in Educational Assessment of Students*. (See previous section.)

2. Understand and be able to apply the basic precepts of assessment and measurement theory.

3. Understand the purposes of different kinds of assessment (for example, ability, achievement, diagnostic).

4. Understand measurement terminology and be able to express that terminology in nontechnical terms.

**Table 2-1** *Comparison of Standards for Teacher Competence in Educational Assessment of Students*

| Standard | Comment |
|---|---|
| *Teachers should be skilled in* | |
| 1. Choosing assessment methods appropriate for instructional decisions. | 1. Criteria that should be considered are technical adequacy, usefulness, convenience, and fairness. A variety of methods should be used, and a teacher should know where to obtain information about them. |
| 2. Developing assessment methods appropriate for instructional decisions. | 2. If high-quality commercial methods are not available, teachers must create them. Methods include classroom tests, oral exams, rating scales, performance assessments, observation schedules, and questionnaires. |
| 3. Administering, scoring, and interpreting the results of both commercially produced and teacher-produced assessment methods. | 3. Knowledge about the common methods of expressing assessments is essential. Numerous quantitative concepts need to be assimilated (for example, descriptive statistical methods, reliability, validity, and so on). |
| 4. Using assessment results in making decisions about individual students, planning instruction, developing curriculum, and improving schools. | 4. Assessments are valueless unless they are applied at both group and individual levels. Planning is a vital part of the educational process. |
| 5. Developing student grading procedures that use student assessments. | 5. Grades and marks should be data-based. Grading, although subjective to a great extent, can be rational, justifiable, and fair. The rules must be the same for everyone. |
| 6. Communicating assessment results to students, parents, other lay audiences, and educators. | 6. An effective communication should include the facts and an indication of the limitations and implications. In addition, everyone involved must use terminology in the same way. |
| 7. Recognizing and having knowledge about unethical, illegal, and inappropriate assessment. | 7. Potential dangers of invasion of privacy and discrimination exist, and these—together with legal and professional ethics—should always be in the forefront of a teacher's mind while planning and implementing assessment tasks. |

5. Recognize appropriate and inappropriate uses of assessment techniques on results and understand and follow ethical guidelines for assessment.

6. Know the mechanics of constructing various assessments that are both appropriate and useful.

7. Interpret and use assessment information appropriately.

8. Know how interpretations of assessments can be moderated by students' socioeconomic, cultural, linguistic, and other background factors.

9. Be able to evaluate an assessment strategy or program.

10. Use computer-based assessment tools that collect input and mediating and outcome variables that relate to student learning, instruction, and performance.

All the foregoing competencies represent commonsense behaviors, but it is good to have them codified. As useful as these standards are for administrators, they might not be much help to a general population of users or developers.

### A Code of Fair Testing Practices in Education

In 1986 a Joint Committee on Testing Practices (JCTP) was formed with representatives from the American Educational Research Association, the American Psychological Association, the National Council on Measurement in Education, the American Association for Counseling and Development, and the American Speech-Language-Hearing Association. JCTP was to develop guidelines for use in protecting the rights of test takers of standardized tests. The resulting *Code* of the Joint Committee on Testing Practices specified essential principles of good practice and the obligations of those who develop, administer, and use educational tests. The *Code* amplifies and supplements the *Standards*, and was created to meet the needs of the professional *and* the general public. (See box for the *Code* in its entirety.)

The concern about developing competent training in constructing and responsibly using tests is not new. The recommendations reinforce the need to maintain vigilance in such problem areas as the abuse and misuse of tests, lack of criterion-related validity, bias, measurement fallibility, and lack of accountability. If the profession doesn't take the responsibility and leadership for accountability, the public will. The cry for renewed energies and resources to be focused on important testing issues should be heeded around the country.

### Technical Standards for Educational and Psychological Assessment

Another more technical set of guidelines has been developed to help both the producer and the consumer of educational and psychological tests. The *Standards for Educational and Psychological Testing* first appeared in 1954 and is now available in extended and extensively revised form (Joint Committee, 1999). "The intent of the *Standards* is to promote the sound and ethical use of tests and to provide a basis for evaluating the quality of testing

# CODE OF FAIR TESTING PRACTICES IN EDUCATION

## A. Developing/Selecting Appropriate Tests*

Test developers should provide the information that test users need to select appropriate tests.

*Test Developers Should:*

1. Define what each test measures and what the test should be used for. Describe the population(s) for which the test is appropriate.

2. Accurately represent the characteristics, usefulness, and limitations of tests for their intended purposes.

3. Explain relevant measurement concepts as necessary for clarity at the level of detail that is appropriate for the intended audience(s).

4. Describe the process of test development. Explain how the content and skills to be tested were selected.

5. Provide evidence that the test meets its intended purpose(s).

6. Provide either representative samples or complete copies of test questions, directions, answer sheets, manuals, and score reports to qualified users.

7. Indicate the nature of the evidence obtained concerning the appropriateness of each test for groups of different racial, ethnic, or linguistic backgrounds who are likely to be tested.

Test users should select tests that meet the purpose for which they are to be used and that are appropriate for the intended test-taking populations.

*Test Users Should:*

1. First define the purpose for testing and the population to be tested. Then, select a test for that purpose and that population based on a thorough review of the available information.

2. Investigate potentially useful sources of information, in addition to test scores, to corroborate the information provided by tests.

3. Read the materials provided by test developers and avoid using tests for which unclear or incomplete information is provided.

4. Become familiar with how and when the test was developed and tried out.

5. Read independent evaluations of a test and of possible alternative measures. Look for evidence required to support the claims of test developers.

6. Examine specimen sets, disclosed tests or samples of questions, directions, answer sheets, manuals, and score reports before selecting a test.

7. Ascertain whether the test content and norms group(s) or comparison group(s) are appropriate for the intended test takers.

*(continued)*

*Code of Fair Testing Practices in Education.* (1988) Washington, D.C.: Joint Committee on Testing Practices, American Psychological Association, 1200 17th Street, NW, Washington, D.C. 20036.

### A. Developing/Selecting Appropriate Tests (continued)

**Test Developers Should:**

8. Identify and publish any specialized skills needed to administer each test and to interpret scores correctly.

**Test Users Should:**

8. Select and use only those tests for which the skills needed to administer the test and interpret scores correctly are available.

*Many of the statements in the Code refer to the selection of existing tests. However, in customized testing programs test developers are engaged to construct new tests. In those situations, the test development process should be designed to help ensure that the completed tests will be in compliance with the Code.

### B. Interpreting Scores

Test developers should help users interpret scores correctly.

Test users should interpret scores correctly.

**Test Developers Should:**

9. Provide timely and easily understood score reports that describe test performance clearly and accurately. Also explain the meaning and limitations of reported scores.

10. Describe the population(s) represented by any norms or comparison group(s), the dates the data were gathered, and the process used to select the samples of test takers.

11. Warn users to avoid specific, reasonably anticipated misuses of test scores.

12. Provide information that will help users follow reasonable procedures for setting passing scores when it is appropriate to use such scores with the test.

13. Provide information that will help users gather evidence to show that the test is meeting its intended purpose(s).

**Test Users Should:**

9. Obtain information about the scale used for reporting scores, the characteristics of any norms or comparison group(s), and the limitations of the scores.

10. Interpret scores taking into account any major differences between the norms or comparison groups and the actual test takers. Also take into account any differences in test administration practices or familiarity with the specific questions in the test.

11. Avoid using tests for purposes not specifically recommended by the test developer unless evidence is obtained to support the intended use.

12. Explain how any passing scores were set and gather evidence to support the appropriateness of the scores.

13. Obtain evidence to help show that the test is meeting its intended purpose(s).

(continued)

### C. Striving for Fairness

Test developers should strive to make tests that are as fair as possible for test takers of different races, gender, ethnic backgrounds, or handicapping conditions.

Test users should select tests that have been developed in ways that attempt to make them as fair as possible for test takers of different races, gender, ethnic backgrounds, or handicapping conditions.

*Test Developers Should:*

14. Review and revise test questions and related materials to avoid potentially insensitive content or language.

15. Investigate the performance of test takers of different races, gender, and ethnic backgrounds when samples of sufficient size are available. Enact procedures that help to ensure that differences in performance are related primarily to the skills under assessment rather than to irrelevant factors.

16. When feasible, make appropriately modified forms of tests or administration procedures available for test takers with handicapping conditions. Warn test users of potential problems in using standard norms with modified tests or administration procedures that result in non-comparable scores.

*Test Users Should:*

14. Evaluate the procedures used by test developers to avoid potentially insensitive content or language.

15. Review the performance of test takers of different races, gender, and ethnic backgrounds when samples of sufficient size are available. Evaluate the extent to which performance differences may have been caused by inappropriate characteristics of the test.

16. When necessary and feasible, use appropriately modified forms of tests or administration procedures for test takers with handicapping conditions. Interpret standard norms with care in the light of the modifications that were made.

### D. Informing Test Takers

Under some circumstances, test developers have direct communication with test takers. Under other circumstances, test users communicate directly with test takers. Whichever group communicates directly with test takers should provide the information described below.

*Test Developers or Test Users Should:*

17. When a test is optional, provide test takers or their parents/guardians with information to help them judge whether the test should be taken, or if an available alternative to the test should be used.

*(continued)*

---

**D.   Informing Test Takers** (continued)

---

18. Provide test takers the information they need to be familiar with the coverage of the test, the types of question formats, the directions, and appropriate test-taking strategies. Strive to make such information equally available to all test takers.

Under some circumstances, test developers have direct control of tests and test scores. Under other circumstances, test users have such control. Whichever group has direct control of tests and test scores should take the steps described below.

**Test Developers or Test Users Should:**

19. Provide test takers or their parents/guardians with information about rights test takers may have to obtain copies of tests and completed answer sheets, retake tests, have tests rescored, or cancel scores.

20. Tell test takers or their parents/guardians how long scores will be kept on file and indicate to whom and under what circumstances test scores will or will not be released.

21. Describe the procedures that test takers or their parents/guardians may use to register complaints and have problems resolved.

---

practices" (p. 1). The *Standards* is an outstanding example of how a professional organization can develop the criteria to monitor itself and have a demonstrably positive influence on practice. The *Standards* provides technical criteria and policy that are in keeping with best professional practice. Although it lacks the mechanism for enforcement and cannot mandate sanctions, the *Standards* by sheer force of its presence can influence the profession. Following is an outline of the *Standards* categories.

*Part I Test Construction, Evaluation, and Documentation*

1. Validity
2. Reliability and errors of measurement
3. Test development and revision
4. Scaling, norms, and score comparability
5. Test administration, scoring, and reporting
6. Supporting documentation for tests

*Part II Fairness in Testing*

7. Fairness in testing and test use
8. The rights and responsibilities of test takers

9. Testing individuals of diverse linguistic backgrounds

10. Testing individuals with disabilities

*Part III Testing Applications*

11. The responsibilities of test users

12. Psychological testing and assessment

13. Educational testing and assessment

14. Testing in employment and credentialing

15. Testing in program evaluation and public policy

Although aimed primarily at commercially available, so-called standardized tests, the *Standards* has many applications to classroom teacher-made tests, particularly concerning the development process. Following is a sample "standard."

---

### STANDARDS ALERT

#### Standard 2.12 — Reliability

If a test is proposed for use in several grades or over a range of chronological age groups and if separate norms are provided for each grade or each age group, reliability data should be provided for each age or grade population, not solely for all grades or ages combined.

*Comment:* A reliability coefficient based on a sample of examinees spanning several grades or a broad range of ages in which average scores are steadily increasing will generally give a spuriously inflated impression of reliability. When a test is intended to discriminate within age or grade populations, reliability coefficients and standard errors should be reported separately for each population.

---

Reprinted from the *Standards for Educational and Psychological Testing.* Copyright © 1999 by the American Educational Research Association, the American Psychological Association, and the National Council on Measurement in Education.

## HIGH-STAKES TESTING

Many states and school districts have mandated assessment at a number of grade levels in a variety of content areas. Typical grade levels might be 4–5, 8, and 10–11–12. In addition, some data are periodically gathered, even at the kindergarten and primary school levels. The usual content areas are mathematics and language arts, specifically reading and writing. Such data are usually considered "high-stakes" because of the consequences attached to the use of the data in making promotion, certification, and selection decisions. The potential for significant public consumption of the results of such assessments is considerable. Potential dangers abound.

The American Educational Research Association (AERA), in a position statement adopted in July 2000, notes that

> The various high-stakes testing applications are enacted by policy makers with the intention of improving education. For example, it is hoped that setting standards of achievement will inspire greater effort on the part of students, teachers, and educational administrators. Reporting of test results may also be beneficial in directing public attention to gross achievement disparities among schools or among student groups. However, if high-stakes testing programs are implemented in circumstances where educational resources are inadequate or where tests lack sufficient reliability and validity for their intended purposes, there is potential for serious harm. Policy makers and the public may be misled by spurious test score increases unrelated to any fundamental educational improvement; students may be placed at increased risk of educational failure and dropping out; teachers may be blamed or punished for inequitable resources over which they have no control; and curriculum and instruction may be severely distorted if high test scores per se, rather than learning, become the overriding goal of classroom instruction.

The new *Standards for Educational and Psychological Testing* (Joint Committee, 1999) represents the most comprehensive set of technical and policy guidelines available. AERA has recast 11 of these *Standards* into guides for the development and use of high-stakes tests. They are:

| Standard Condition | Description |
|---|---|
| **Alignment Between the Test and the Curriculum** | Assessments should be specific to all dimensions of the instructional treatment and have multiple forms. |
| **Validity of Passing Scores and Achievement Levels** | Standard-setting procedures must accompany the use of any "cut-scores" or proficiency categories. |
| **Opportunities for Meaningful Remediation for Examinees Who Fail High-Stakes Tests** | Remediation should focus on the knowledge skills assessed. Reasonable time should exist between retests. |
| **Appropriate Attention to Language Differences Among Examinees** | If the student lacks proficiency in the language used in the assessment, the assessment becomes a language test. Accommodations may be necessary for English spoken as second language (ESL) students. |

*continued*

| Standard Condition | Description |
|---|---|
| Careful Adherence to Explicit Rules for Determining Which Students Are to Be Tested | Uniformity in inclusion rules relates to comparability in meaningfulness of data. |
| Protection Against High-Stakes Decisions Based on a Single Test | No life-determining decision should be made on the basis of test data alone. There are multiple opportunities to perform well and, when necessary, alternate assessment approaches should be taken. |
| Adequate Resources and Opportunity to Learn | Particularly when testing for accountability and certification, ensure that students have had equal opportunity to learn and that the curriculum is relevant. |
| Validation for Each Separate Use | Assessments and their interpretations are not valid in general but for specific applications. The projected use needs to be "validated." |
| Full Disclosure of Likely Negative Consequences of High-Stakes Testing Programs | All consequences of test use need to be made known to the public. |
| Sufficient Reliability for Each Intended Use | Acceptable reliability is necessary for all groups and scores used to report results about individual students, classrooms, schools, or districts. |
| Ongoing Evaluation of Intended and Unintended Effects of High-Stakes Testing | It is necessary to monitor the extent to which assessment meets user needs as well as what might be some unintended effects, if any. |

The making of important educational and life decisions requires that we use the most reliable and relevant information. Data from the early part of a student's life need to be gathered in an environment that affords him or her opportunities to maximize the results.

### National Recommendations for Using Tests in Tracking, Promotion, and Graduation

High-stakes testing has received both criticism and support over the past several years. High-stakes tests might be commercially available standards of measure, but are usually custom-made for state programs. The application of such assessments has significant educational, social, and economic implications. Congress and President Clinton commissioned a study of this hotly debated proposal. The publication that resulted, *High Stakes Testing for Tracking, Promotion, and Graduation* (Heubert & Hauser, 1999), contains some important recommendations that make both practical and common sense. The intent of the tests is to support educational reform without losing sight of the fact that they should follow changes in teaching and curriculum. Sudden adoption of "world-class" standards without extensive preparation would undoubtedly result in extremely high failure rates. Following are recommendations that cut across applications for purposes of tracking, promotion, and the certification for graduation.

- Accountability for educational outcome should be considered the shared responsibility of states, school districts, public officials, educators, parents, and students.

- Information about the nature and interpretation of tests and test scores should be available to all and incorporated in all educational programs.

- Tests should not be used for individual student decision making until they have been proven to be valid.

- High-stakes tests should be used continuously and in combination with other information in making instructional and administrative decisions.

- Large-scale assessments should not be used to make high-stakes decisions about students who are less than eight years old or enrolled below grade 3.

- All students must receive adequate test preparation in test-taking skills.

- Large-scale testing programs should be monitored continuously and evaluated periodically.

These recommendations make common sense but also technical sense in that they help create an environment that protects the student and yields maximally useful information. In particular, protection is needed for minorities, English-language learners, and special needs students.

## CONCERNS ABOUT LARGE-SCALE ASSESSMENT PROGRAMS

Within the past few decades the number of external tests administered to high school students has spiraled dramatically. Explanations for this phenomenon are varied, but primarily involve college admissions and the granting of scholarships. Objections to external tests are voiced by many local school administrators, because the burden of proving the legitimacy and validity of such programs frequently falls on their shoulders. External tests are characterized by three distinctive features: (1) their results are used primarily by an institution or organization other than the high school, (2) the local school is unable to choose whether or not their students take such tests, and (3) responsibility for security of the tests is assumed by the test publisher. Two tests widely used for selection purposes are the College Entrance Examination Board's Scholastic Assessment Tests and the American College Testing Program Tests.

Administering of these tests to hundreds of thousands of students each year has generated considerable controversy. Table 2-2 contains a list of major criticisms of external testing programs and possible responses or solutions to each.

Efforts are under way to revise external tests used for college admissions. Such innovations are the (1) inclusion of writing samples, (2) application of computerized adaptive testing (see Chapter 6), (3) inclusion of problem-solving and critical-thinking measures as part of the regular testing program, (4) use of specific subject area tests, and (5) student-constructed response items.

The overall positive contribution of external testing programs is evident. In addition to the potential advantages to the individual, society benefits by identifying and training those students best qualified to make contributions. The voluntary nature of the testing system is another point in its favor. It promotes initiative. Problems within the system should be worked out cooperatively by test specialists, college faculties and admissions officers, test publishers, and school administrators.

We can see that the profession is concerned about the many issues surrounding the development and use of tests in all areas of human endeavor. Despite the shortcomings of some tests and users, tests have proven to be valuable educational tools. As William Angoff and Scarvia Anderson (1963) noted:

> For both human and practical reasons, the standardized text is a necessary outcome of the philosophy of a modern democratic society in which large masses of individuals, competing for educational awards or simply seeking better self-understanding, assemble for an objective, unbiased evaluation of their abilities. No other method that we know of today can provide measurement for the tremendous numbers of individuals who demand objective consideration of their talents. Certainly no other method that we know of today can accomplish this measurement as equitably as the standardized test.

**Table 2-2**  *External Testing Programs: Criticisms and Solutions*

| Criticism of External Testing | Response or Possible Solution |
| --- | --- |
| 1. Not all important outcomes are measured. | 1. Those variables of primary importance to college work are assessed. If important variables are ignored, they may not have been defined clearly enough. |
| 2. Only facts and knowledge are measured. | 2. Within the past several years external tests have stressed the ability to use information. Command of useful knowledge is important |
| 3. External tests are unfair to some students. | 3. Measuring instruments are fallible. Common essential outcomes are emphasized. Great care is made to control bias. |
| 4. The use of objective (for example, multiple-choice) items is discriminatory. | 4. If these items are relevant to the criterion of college success, they are valid. Choice making is an aspect of all human activities. |
| 5. External tests adversely influence curriculum innovation and educational change. | 5. There is danger that this will be the case. Test developers work with curriculum experts and educators in establishing objectives. |
| 6. Tests do not predict perfectly. | 6. Tests, as well as individuals, are fallible. Successful predictions far outnumber mispredictions. It is impossible to assess all relevant variables in advance. |
| 7. There is too much duplication of testing. | 7. Development of general-purpose equivalency tables that allow equating of results from different tests would help. |
| 8. Too much time and money are expended on tests. | 8. Considering the potential payoff and the importance of the decisions to be made, the investment is minimal. |
| 9. The advantaged can secure coaching that helps ensure success on tests. | 9. Research indicates that coaching has, on the whole, only a modest effect If coaching also improves school performance, so much the better. The validity of the test is not undermined. The opportunity for coaching should be made available to all. |
| 10. The use of external tests invites invidious comparisons between schools. | 10. Scores should be reported only to target institutions and individual students. |
| 11. Exposure to external testing situations adversely affects students' emotional stability and mental health. | 11. There is little or no evidence that this is true. |
| 12. External test scores determine college entrance. | 12. Nothing could be further from the truth. An entrance decision is made on the basis of a collection of a variety of relevant data, never on a single test score. |

## Content Review Statements

1. The testing profession is continually subject to criticism, some of which is justified and some of which is not.

2. Many criticisms leveled at tests and testing would be more appropriate if aimed at the users of tests.

3. Criticisms of school assessments, particularly use of standardized measures, revolve around the issues of

   a. discrimination against minority and disadvantaged groups

   b. imperfect predictability

   c. potentially harmful social, educational, and psychological effects

   d. potential dangers in controlling curricula

4. The majority of the problems posed by using educational and psychological tests can be overcome with common sense, intelligent application of professional guidelines, establishment of standards, and education.

5. Criticisms of external tests can be addressed by the cooperative efforts of the testing profession, school administrators, college faculties, test publishers, and admissions officers.

6. Common misapprehensions about tests rest on the false beliefs that

   a. Tests are perfectly reliable.

   b. Test norms constitute standards and can determine curricula.

   c. Intelligence and achievement are separable.

   d. Tests measure only recall of specific facts.

7. College admission and scholarship testing programs have been criticized for their

   a. duplication

   b. lack of demonstrated relevance

   c. cost

   d. susceptibility to coaching

   e. susceptibility to invidious interschool comparisons

   f. possible adverse psychological effects on examinees

8. Detailed guidelines are available for teachers, educational administrators, and other professionals regarding assessment development and use.

9. Assessment reform centers around the development and application of alternative methods.

10. Among the most influential standards for assessment development and use are the following:
    a. *Ethical Principles of Psychologists and Code of Conduct*
    b. *NCME Code of Professional Responsibility in Educational Measurement*
    c. *Standards for Teacher Competence in Educational Assessment of Students*
    d. *Competency Standards in Student Assessment for Educational Administration*
    e. *Code of Fair Testing Practices in Education*
    f. *Standards for Educational and Psychological Testing*

11. Through the development of guidelines, codes, and ethical standards, professional organizations are making great strides toward eliminating the unethical practices associated with assessment use.

12. Professional organizations have established important guidelines and standards for test developers to protect users.

13. Individuals involved in test administration should maintain a respectful attitude toward test instruments, individuals, and the setting in which the tests are to be applied.

14. The intelligent use of assessments constitutes one of the most powerful, fair, comprehensive, and democratic methods of improving the quality of life for individuals and society.

## SPECULATIONS

1. What way could the *Code of Fair Testing Practices* have an impact on your professional life?

2. Do you feel the testing profession is adequately monitoring itself? If yes, how; if not, how can it be improved?

3. Which criticisms of tests and testing are justified in your mind and which are not?

4. What are some ways tests and measurements can have positive influences in our schools?

5. What are some dangers that we have to watch for when using educational assessments?

**6.** What are some consequences of *not* using educational assessments in our schools?

**7.** What topics would you include in a speech to a group of parents on *The Importance of Educational Assessments in Our Schools?* How would it be different for a group of students? A group of teachers? A group of community business leaders? The board of education?

**8.** What role, if any, should the federal government have in controlling the testing industry?

**9.** Are the effects of professional and ethical standards diminished because there are no legal sanctions applied for violators?

## Suggested Readings

Corbett, H. D., & Wilson, B. L. (1991). *Testing, reform, and rebellion.* Norwood, NJ: Ablex.

Haney, W. M., Madaus, G. F., & Lyons, R. (1993). *The fractured marketplace for standardized testing.* Boston: Kluwer. A discussion of how commercial vendors influence and are influenced by assessment demands and the schools. Education, politics, and economics are indeed strange bedpersons.

Kellaghan, T., Madaus, G. F., & Airasian, P. W. (1982). *The effects of standardized testing.* Boston: Kluwer.

Kifer, E. (2001). *Large-scale assessment (Dimensions, dilemmas, and policy).* Thousand Oaks, CA: Corwin. Presentation of an 11-dimension grid facilitates planning and comparing assessments.

Kohn, A. (2000). *The case against standardized testing.* Portsmouth, NH: Heinemann.

Messick, S. (1981). Evidence and ethics in the evaluation of tests. *Educational Researcher, 10*(9), 9–20.

Mitchell, R. (1992). *Testing for learning: (How new approaches to evaluation can improve American schools).* New York: The Free Press.

Popham, W. J. (1999). Why standardized tests don't measure educational quality. *Educational Leadership,* March, 8–15.

Robinson, C. M. (1988). Improving education through the application of measurement and research: A practitioner's perspective. *Applied Measurement in Education, 1*(1), 53–65. A representative of the public schools calls for collaboration to improve the nation's schools.

# 3

## The Teaching-Learning Process, Diversity, and Assessment

### FOCUS CONCEPTS AND KEY TERMS FOR STUDY

| | |
|---|---|
| **Assessment Pitfalls** | **Learning Styles** |
| **Culture** | **Multicultural Education** |
| **Direct Instruction** | **Social Constructivism** |
| **Diversity** | **Summative Evaluation** |
| **Formative Evaluation** | **Teaching-Assessment Linkage** |
| **Instructional Development** | |

## STANDARDS ALERT

**Standard 7.1**          **Diversity Perspective**

When credible research reports that test scores differ in meaning across examinee subgroups for the type of test in question, then to the extent feasible, the same forms of validity evidence collected for the examinee population as a whole should also be collected for each relevant subgroup.

Subgroups may be found to differ with respect to appropriateness of test content, internal structure of test responses, the relation of test scores to other variables, or the response processes employed by individual examinees. Any such findings should receive due consideration in the interpretation and use of scores as well as in subsequent test revisions.

### Taking It to the Classroom

Drawing upon the diversity of backgrounds and experiences of students can enhance instruction. Using a variety of methods can also make assessment more attractive. Simply looking at descriptive data such as means and percentages can reveal possible assessment biases.

Reprinted with permission from the *Standards for Educational and Psychological Testing.* Copyright © 1999 by the American Educational Research Association, the American Psychological Association, and the National Council on Measurement in Education.

Teachers and educators are decision makers who decide what and how to teach, when to teach, and to whom to teach. A typical classroom teacher may make several hundred instructional decisions an hour. Rational decisions are based on relevant data. Using an integrated educational assessment system can provide that data.

In the beginning there were educational goals and objectives to be accomplished. Teacher and student work *together* to accomplish these objectives. The objectives may have come from a predetermined pool of outcomes specified by the school, system, or state, or they may have evolved out of an analysis of student interests and needs. In this case, they are negotiated objectives derived from mutual agreement between teacher and student. Both teacher and student need information on how well they are doing. They need to know if they have "arrived" or must change direction to continue on toward the desired educational destinations. There are alternative modes of educational travel. After many decades of research on the teaching-learning process no universal and definitive answers to the question, "What is the most effective way to teach?" are available—only tentative guidelines for general approaches.

## APPROACHES TO TEACHING: DIRECT AND CONSTRUCTIVIST

Two representative approaches to teaching have been selected for discussion—direct and constructivist. There are many other approaches, but they represent the two prevalent methods in today's schools. In some respect the *direct* approach is a kind of traditional approach. It has been around for a long time and most teachers use bits and pieces of it if they have been teaching for any length of time. This approach shares major philosophies with "mastery learning" (Kulik, Kulik, & Bangert-Downs, 1990; Popham, 1987a). The more contemporary approach is called **social constructivism** and is very compatible with the increasing diversity seen in classrooms.

### Direct Instruction

Based on their review of the relevant research literature Brophy and Good (1986) concluded that student achievement is significantly enhanced if:

**1.** The teacher is actively involved in actual teaching or supervising learning.

**2.** There are frequent lessons (for total class or individuals).

**3.** The teacher (a) presents information, (b) develops concepts through lecture, (c) requires students to recite or respond to questions, (d) provides feedback and reteaching as necessary.

Brophy and Good (1986) have found that although it is only one of several effective approaches, this kind of **direct instruction** is particularly helpful in increasing the achievement of low ability–low achievement students.

A similar set of teaching activities that has been shown to be effective in enhancing learning has been described by Rosenshine (1985). They include the following six functions: (a) daily review of previous day's work, (b) presentation of new content/skills, (c) student practice on new materials, (d) feedback and corrections, (e) independent practice, and (f) weekly and monthly review with reteaching as necessary. A detailed list of instructional functions that research and practice support as having a positive impact on student learning is presented in Table 3-1. Some experts refer to this approach as direct instruction. Another variation is **measurement-driven instruction** (MDI) (Popham, 1987a; Popham, Cruse, Smart, Sandifer, and Williams, 1985).

**Table 3-1** *Instructional Functions*

1. Daily review, checking previous day's work, and reteaching (if necessary):
   - Checking homework

2. Presenting new content/skills:
   - Providing overview
   - Proceeding in small steps (if necessary), but at a rapid pace
   - If necessary, giving detailed or redundant instructions and explanations
   - Phasing in new skills while old skills are being mastered

3. Initial student practice:
   - High frequency of questions and overt student practice (from teacher and materials)
   - Prompts are provided during initial learning (when appropriate)
   - All students have a chance to respond and receive feedback
   - Teacher checks for understanding by evaluating student responses
   - Continue practice until students are firm
   - Success rate of 80 percent or higher during initial learning

4. Feedback and correctives (and recycling of instruction, if necessary):
   - Feedback to students, particularly when they are correct but hesitant
   - Student errors provide feedback to the teacher that corrections and/or reteaching is necessary
   - Correction by simplifying questions, giving clues, explaining or reviewing steps, or reteaching last steps
   - When necessary, reteach using smaller steps

5. Independent practice so that students are firm and automatic:
   - Seatwork
   - Unitization and automaticity (practice to overlearning)
   - Need for procedure to ensure student engagement during seatwork (that is, teacher or aide monitoring)
   - 95 percent correct or higher

6. Weekly and monthly reviews:
   - Reteaching, if necessary

Rosenshine, B. (1985). Teaching functions in instructional programs. *The Elementary School Journal, 83*(4), 335–351.

### Social Constructivism

One of the foremost philosophers of education in the twentieth century was John Dewey (1916). His emphasis on "learn by doing" has received renewed attention on the part of teachers, theorists, and researchers. Figure 3-1 (the origin of which is unknown) underscores the importance of experience in the support of learning. Contemporary educational psychologists have drawn on the ideas of Dewey and the research and observations of Piaget (1970) to create a learning theory called social constructivism (Fosnot, 1996; Orlich, Harder, Callahan, & Gibson, 1998). This view of learning generally holds that students should be active learners who construct knowledge out of personal experiences. Knowledge does not exist outside the student, as objectivists claim, but is molded, modified, and

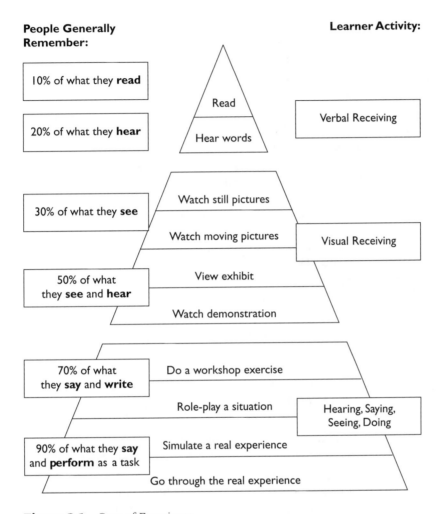

**People Generally Remember:**

**Learner Activity:**

10% of what they **read**

20% of what they **hear**

30% of what they **see**

50% of what they **see** and **hear**

70% of what they **say** and **write**

90% of what they **say** and **perform** as a task

Read

Hear words

Watch still pictures

Watch moving pictures

View exhibit

Watch demonstration

Do a workshop exercise

Role-play a situation

Simulate a real experience

Go through the real experience

Verbal Receiving

Visual Receiving

Hearing, Saying, Seeing, Doing

**Figure 3-1**   *Cone of Experience*

expanded by the student, depending on his or her experiences. The tenets of modern social constructivism are summarized in Table 3-2.

Whenever feedback is required, measurement and assessment can make a contribution. The direct instructional approach is usually associated with "traditional assessment" as discussed in Chapter 1 and social constructivism with "modern assessment" approaches. This is obviously not a strict dichotomy as all teachers are concerned with both acquisition of knowledge *and* application and problem solving. It may be formal or informal. The instructional approaches just described basically relate to day-to-day activity. Periodically the teacher (principal, superintendent) will also

**Table 3-2** *Tenets of Modern Social Constructivism*

- Learning is dependent on the prior conceptions the learner brings to the experience.
- The learner must construct his or her own meaning.
- Learning is contextual.
- Learning is dependent on the shared understandings learners negotiate with others.
- Effective teaching involves understanding students' existing cognitive structures and providing appropriate learning activities to assist them.
- Teachers can utilize one or more key strategies to facilitate conceptual change, depending on the congruence of the concepts with student understanding and conceptualization.
- The key elements of conceptual change can be addressed by specific teaching methods.
- Greater emphasis should be placed on "learning how to learn" than on accumulating facts. In terms of content, less is more.

After Anderson et al., 1994.

want to step back and take snapshots of the larger picture of learning. This might be at the individual, classroom, school, or system level.

## A MODEL FOR INSTRUCTIONAL DEVELOPMENT

If one is going to implement an instructional strategy, whether it is based on learning styles or another approach, extensive and thoughtful planning must take place. One simply does not walk into a classroom and begin teaching. As with any complex process, planning must precede implementation. Instructional planning tasks can and should be approached systematically. Many theories of teaching (Joyce & Weil, 1986; Snelbecker, 1985) and models for the design of instruction (Bass & Dills, 1984; Gagné & Briggs, 1979; Reigeluth, 1983) have been developed. Those readers who have gone through a teacher preparation program will undoubtedly recall coursework related to instructional strategies. If they were lucky enough to be at an "enlightened" school or college of education, they also would have taken coursework in educational measurement. A comprehensive model of the **instructional development** process should interrelate both teaching process skills and measurement. Such a system has been created by Dick and Carey (1990). The basic components of their system are graphically presented in Figure 3-2. The solid lines represent direct sequence or action, and the dotted lines represent the feedback process—feedback in the sense

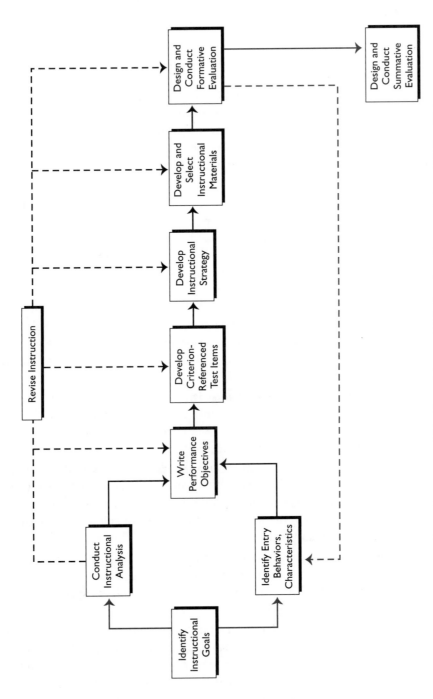

**Figure 3-2** *Instructional Development Model (Dick and Carey, 1990). Reprinted by permission of Walter Dick.*

that information (data, measurements) is used for decision making, that is, to revise an objective or learning experience.

It is interesting to note that the major concepts of assessment, measurement (tests), and evaluation discussed in Chapter 1 are prominently evident in the Dick–Carey model. Obviously, measures of expected outcomes need to be developed—in this case, criterion-referenced measures. In addition, a formative and summative evaluation of learning experience (unit or course) should be undertaken. Assessment is the integrating construct. Consideration is given to entry behaviors, together with measurement and evaluation of existing behaviors. Following are brief descriptions of the components of the Dick–Carey system.

- *Identifying Instructional Goals*. The old adage "If you don't know where you're going, you may end up somewhere else" is as true in education as it is in vacationing. We need maps to guide us. Instructional goals can serve as desired locations on that map. Each teacher must ask, "What do I want my students to be able to do at the end of this instructional experience?" It might be something as simple as being able to recognize and write the letters of the alphabet, or as complex as conducting a quantitative and qualitative analysis of an unknown chemical substance. A needs assessment may be undertaken, or goals may be "given" by the county or state curriculum guides. See Chapter 5 for an expanded discussion of this topic.

- *Conducting an Instructional Analysis*. Once you know where you want to go, or where you and your students will travel together, you need to assess what it will take to get there. Each learning task needs to have the appropriate subordinate skills identified.

- *Identifying Entry Behavior and Characteristics*. The subordinate skills may need to be developed or students may already possess them in varying degrees. This analysis is basically a "prerequisite" evaluation. Are there special needs of the learner that must be considered in designing the instructional activities?

- *Writing Performance Objectives*. It's time to get truly operational. The old-fashioned term for a performance objective is "behavioral objective" (BO). BOs have been around for a long time and help us specify exactly what changes we wish to bring about in students.

- *Developing Criterion-Referenced Test Items*. The key criterion for any assessment task is *relevance*, that is, the match between item (or task) and performance objective. Creating good measurements is a very difficult job!

- *Developing an Instructional Strategy*. Given goals and objectives, and taking into account student entry level, a decision is made as to what would be the most effective media to be used. Consideration must be given to the optional conditions for learning (Gagné, 1985). These would include pre-instruction activities, method of presentation, practice, feedback, and evaluation.

- *Developing and Selecting Instruction*. One may develop or create a new instructional method or technique, select one from commercial sources, or borrow from colleagues. Such factors as time, cost, number of students to be served, and (obviously) nature of behavior to be shaped will influence development versus selection decision.

- *Designing and Conducting a Formative Evaluation*. The focus here is on how to improve the instruction. The "instruction" might be as small as a unit on fractions, or as large as a curriculum. A variety of data-types should be used so as to reflect different aspects of the instruction (e.g., objectives [good-bad], instructional material [understandable-not understandable], instruction [effective-ineffective]).

- *Revise Instruction*. Here is the key to the process. Good instruction is iterative. Use data to make rational decisions about how to improve what you have already done. Gather data on how effective the instruction was, as well as how the students felt about the instruction. Did they like it in general? What in particular was satisfying? Revision could go all the way back to the objectives strategy selected, or focus only on the effectiveness of the materials.

- *Conduct a Summative Evaluation*. After revisions are made and the instruction is implemented, another evaluation can be undertaken. Although the evaluation is summative, the resulting data again could be used formatively, to compare and contrast this final version with a competing approach. Critical at this stage, as at the previous one, are applications of standards and criteria.

## Summative and Formative Evaluation

The focus on the relationship between instruction and evaluation, and on the potential contribution of evaluation to the improvement of quality and quantity in education as argued in the foregoing discussion, has been underscored by Scriven's (1967) distinction between "summative" and "formative" evaluation. He notes that the goal of evaluation is always the same, that is, to determine the worth and value of something. That "something" may be a microscope, a unit in biology, a science curriculum, or an entire educational system. Depending upon the role value judgments are to play, evaluation data may be used developmentally or in a summary way. In the case of an overall decision, the role of evaluation is summative. An end-of-course assessment would be considered summative. **Summative evaluation** may employ absolute or comparative standards and judgments.

**Formative evaluation**, on the other hand, is almost exclusively aimed at improving the educational experience or product during its developmental phases. A key element in the formative technique is feedback. Information is gathered during the developmental phase with an eye to improving the total product. The evaluation activities associated with the development of *Science—A Process Approach*, the elementary science curriculum supported by the National Science Foundation and managed by the American Association for the Advancement of Science during the program's development, were used in centers throughout the country. Summer writing sessions were then held at which tryout data were fed back to the developers. A superior product resulted. The summative-formative distinction among kinds of evaluation reflects differences in intent, rather than different methodologies.

The use of evaluation in this formative way almost implies that evaluation may be viewed as a kind of research effort, which it is. The importance of the use of measurement data is evident in the Dick–Carey model outlined in Figure 3-2. There is, of course, a danger that the measurement data may play too important a role in determining the content and methods of instruction.

## DIVERSITY AND THE TEACHING-LEARNING PROCESS

The enlightened conscience of society, changing demographics, and the courts have resulted in ever increasing diversity in classrooms. **Diversity** is typically described in terms of race and ethnicity (usually African Americans, Hispanic Americans, Native Americans, and Asian Americans), but might also include designations related to gender, age, religion, and disability. The presence of diversity in classrooms places even more demands on teachers to address all the individual differences that already exist in their classrooms. Attempts to deal fairly, effectively, and efficiently with diversity have led to the development of multicultural education (Banks & Banks, 1995).

### Multicultural Education

**Multicultural education** is a pervasive reform movement that aims to modify the content and processes within classrooms and schools to be more responsive to cultural diversity. (**Culture** is a complex of shared beliefs, values, language artifacts, and habits acquired by members of a particular group or society.)

Sleeter and Grant (1987) have observed five general approaches to multicultural education. Following is a very abbreviated description of the methods.

- *Human Relations Training*. The intent of this approach is to provide *all* students with the skills necessary to communicate, get along with others, and feel good about themselves. The affective component of education obviously has a strong influence. The study of values, and the inclusion of self-concept enhancing experiences, particularly at the elementary school level, is strongly objected to by certain political action groups. It is difficult sometimes to differentiate political from educational issues in contemporary America.

- *Single-Group Studies*. This approach focuses on the experiences and cultures of a specific group such as an ethnic, racial, or age group. Concern is for long-term social change and sensitization to the minority's victimization as well as accomplishments. The danger here is that the individual "studies" approach tends to promote the notion of differences among groups rather than common elements or the appreciation of both common and unique cultural elements. We as educators really should emphasize the commonalities in our society. We share a large number of values and the need for academic and vocational survival skills. Surely there exists a large pool of academic knowledge, skill, and competencies that are necessary for success and a satisfying lifestyle. Examples of the negative influence of the single-group study approach is to consider only Native Americans at Thanksgiving (The Three Little Indians Visit Plymouth Rock) or African Americans around Dr. Martin Luther King's birthday.

- *Teaching the Culturally Different*. It is assumed that by providing minority members with the necessary experiences, knowledges, and skills to compete with the majority that equity will be achieved. As laudable as the challenging of perceived cultural deficiency is, particularly through language bridge building, the danger remains that it is still minority-oriented and assumes that the dominant group doesn't need much reeducation.

- *Multicultural Education*. The major goals of this approach are to promote the (a) value and strength of cultural diversity, (b) respect for cultural diversity and human rights, (c) acceptability of alternative life choices, (d) concepts of social justice and equal opportunity, and (e) need for equity in the distribution of power. This is obviously a more comprehensive approach as it addresses *all* sources of diversity. There are some who fear the needed heavy emphasis on racial and ethnic issues will not receive a fair share of attention.

- *Global Multicultural and Social Reconstruction Education*. This approach prepares young people to "change" society. They are exposed to methods of social action that will fight against social structural inequality. Social and economic factors are very important in this approach. There is a danger that with the focus on the causes of oppression and inequality important academic goals may be overlooked.

Although the above approaches all seem to have a central thrust, how we practice them in schools is not pure. Local needs will influence the major emphasis to be taken, but some conscious and deliberate effort must be made to address the many and significant issues raised by diversity if we are to truly educate all students. But how can a teacher deal with such diversity?

## The Use of Learning Styles to Address Cultural Diversity

It's surely not "new" news that students learn in different ways and have selective preferences for how they are taught. Systematic research over the past several decades suggests that there may be some identifiable and consistent patterns in those learning preference experiences. These preferences are called **learning styles** and represent the aggregate influence of cognitive, affective, and psychomotor/physiological characteristics of the learner as she or he approaches an educational experience. Learning styles have a basis in brain density, personality, and acculturation process. Irvine and York (1995) suggest the following learning preferences:

*Cognitive*—Method preference for receiving and processing information and experiences, retrieving information, creating concepts.

*Affective*—Method preference for how an individual likes to interact interpersonally, be motivated, and have curiosity and attention stimulated.

*Psychomotor/Physiological*—Method preference based on gender, health and nutrition, and arcadian rhythms.

Following is a selected list of commercially available learning style measures. In making a selection be sure to undertake a critical evaluation. *Caveat emptor.*

*Group Embedded Figures Test* (Witkin, 1971)

*Learning Style Inventory* (Dunn, Dunn, & Price, 1978)

*Myers-Briggs Type Indicator* (Myers & Briggs, 1976)

*Locus of Control Scale for Children* (Nowicki & Strickland, 1972)

In common parlance, for example, do some students prefer to be lectured at or to "see" material presented? Do they prefer to have material presented in a context of common cultural experience or in a new and unique way that forces them to "discover" meaning? The presence of a variety of styles in a classroom poses a dilemma for teachers: "Should I try to find a teaching material that is most responsive to the majority of learning styles in the classroom, or try to individualize all my teaching?" Would that anyone could satisfactorily answer that question. At the very least, all students deserve to be exposed to a variety of teaching styles. The question is not just cultural diversity, but learning needs diversity.

## Student-Preferred Learning Styles and the Teaching-Learning Process

There are many advocates of the application of learning style data in the teaching-learning process (Cushner et al., 1990). The assumption is that the closer the fit or match between student-preferred learning style and the instructional method, the higher the likelihood that significant learning will take place. Domino (1971), for example, has experimentally demonstrated interaction among a student's achievement values, the instructor's teaching style, and the amount of—and the satisfaction with—learning. There are a variety of teaching modes. As noted earlier, these could be generally classified as visual, auditory, or tactile. Input could be accomplished in a variety of ways (Renzulli & Smith, 1978). These methods might involve projects, drill and recitation, peer tutoring, discussion, gaming, independent study, programmed instruction, lecture, or simulation. Given an **agreed-upon set of goals, objectives, and intents,** student learning style could be used to moderate the impact of instruction on learning. It follows that some adjustments would need to be made in the methods used to assess that learning. Figure 3-3 is a hypothetical representation of the moderation of teaching and learning by consideration of student learning style, that is, the extent of the use of alternative instructional approaches depending on the heterogeneity of the student body. Does this approach work? Slavin (1987) found that African American students' achievement is enhanced when cooperative learning groups incorporate group rewards based on individual student performance. In addition, it has been found that an impulsive learner is more likely to be inaccurate (Becker, Bender, & Morrison, 1978), and that field independence is positively related to reading achievement in a study of African American and white fifth-grade children (Blaha, 1982).

In addition, it was found that locus of control was related to mathematical computation. Achievement was measured with the *Iowa Tests of Basic Skills.* There is obviously a strong affective component in student-preferred learning style. Perhaps it is sufficient to say that students will be

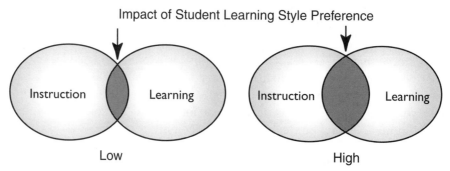

**Figure 3-3** *Moderation of Teaching-Learning Process by Student-Preferred Style of Learning*

happier, feel good about themselves, and have positive attitudes toward and interest in the subject content and school in general if they are instructed in a self-preferred method.

### Learning Styles and Cultural Diversity

Assuming moderate consistency in students' preferred learning style we can use research information to help teachers increase the correlation among learning style, instruction, and learning outcomes. A significant body of literature is being accumulated on learning styles and cultural diversity (Irvine & York, 1995). Table 3-3 contains a summary of trends in the research on cultural diversity and learning styles using ethnicity as the organizing category. It represents an oversimplified synthesis of a great deal of research (see Reiff, 1992, 1993; Smith, 1995; Dana, 1993; Baruth & Manning, 1992; Treuba, Cheng, & Ima, 1993). The summary should be considered tentative at this time. Generalizations should be made with caution. There is considerable variation within each cultural grouping. The table does, however, suggest that although there is uniqueness within groups there are also commonalities. The information is meant to provoke awareness and sensitivity. All that is being suggested here is that multiple approaches make sense both culturally and instructionally.

Not to be overlooked are gender differences in the classroom. Dunn and Dunn (1978) and Witkin and Goodenough (1981), for example, report data that suggest the following:

- Females prefer to learn alone in the early grades.
- There is an increase in male student preference for tactile and kinesthetic sense-based learning experiences from grades 5 to 8.
- Males tend to be more field independent.

**Table 3-3**  *Trends in Learning Style Preferences of Selected Ethnic Groups*

**AFRICAN AMERICAN**

Respond to things in terms of the whole instead of isolated parts

Prefer inferential reasoning as opposed to deductive or inductive reasoning

Approximate space and numbers rather than adhere to exactness or accuracy

Focus on people rather than things

Are more proficient in nonverbal than verbal communications

Prefer learning characterized by variation and freedom of movement

Prefer kinesthetic/active instructional activities

Prefer evening rather than morning learning

Choose social over nonsocial cues

Proceed from a top-down processing approach rather than a bottom-up approach

**NATIVE AMERICAN**

Have well-formed spatial ability

Learn best from nonverbal mechanisms rather than verbal

Learn experientially and in natural settings

Have a generalist orientation, interested in people and things

Value conciseness of speech, slightly varied intonation, and limited vocal range

Prefer small-group work

Favor holistic presentations and visual representations

Prefer visual, spatial, and perceptual information rather than verbal

Learn privately rather than in public

Use mental images to remember and understand words and concepts rather than word associations

Watch and then do rather than employ trial and error

**HISPANIC**

Prefer group learning situations

Are sensitive to the opinions of others

Remember faces and social words

Are extrinsically motivated

Learn by doing

Prefer concrete representations to abstract ones

Prefer people to ideas

**ASIAN AMERICAN**

Structured

Cooperative/group-oriented

Effort more important than ability

Drill and practice

Peer tutoring

Importance of homework

Tactile (esp. writing)

**ANGLO AMERICAN**

Prefer sequential presentation

Field independent

Analytical

Competitive

Individualistic

Visual

Like structured material

*Note:* Based for the most part on summaries contained in Irvine and York (1995).

- Females are more likely to use both hemispheres of the brain in problem solving and communicating.

Again, these trends are only suggestive of the diversity that exists and can be used to enrich learning experiences.

Whatever approach a teacher takes to instruction it should be systematic. Following is a description of one approach. While it is systematic, it is not rigid or inflexible. Provisions for individual differences are made at every step in the development process.

## TEACHING PRACTICES—ASSESSMENT PRACTICES

Most educators agree that assessment is an integral component of the instructional process. Progress toward the achievement of instructional goals must be periodically evaluated if effective teaching and learning are to be accomplished. Educators agree that educational objectives and learning experiences are intimately related. It is less apparent to many that objectives, learning experiences, *and* assessment activities are also intimately related. It is the interaction of these three elements in a well-planned program of education that best promote the desired changes in student behavior. The intimate relationship of instruction and assessment activities is contained in the following listing of the parallel elements in these two activities and illustrates their common objectives:

| Instruction | Assessment |
|---|---|
| 1. Instruction is effective to the degree that it leads to desired changes in students. | 1. Assessment is effective to the degree that it provides evidence of the extent of changes in students. |
| 2. New behavior patterns are best learned by students when the inadequacy of present behavior is understood and the significance of the new behavior patterns is thereby made clear. | 2. Assessment is most conducive to learning when it provides for and encourages self-evaluation. |
| 3. New behavior patterns can be more efficiently promoted by teachers who recognize the existing behavior patterns of individual students and the reasons for them. | 3. Assessment is conducive to good instruction when it reveals major types of inadequate behavior and the contributory causes. |
| 4. Learning is encouraged by problems and activities that require thought and/or action on the part of each individual student. | 4. Assessment is most significant in learning when it permits and encourages the exercise of individual initiative. |
| 5. Activities that provide the basis for the teaching and learning of specified behavior are also the most suitable for evoking and evaluating the adequacy of that behavior. | 5. Activities or exercises developed for the purpose of evaluating specified behavior are also useful in the teaching and learning of the behavior. |

After examining in detail the objectives of both activities it should be apparent that they do not really differ in methods or materials. This is particularly true when performance assessments are involved. They can be differentiated only when evaluating achievement at the close of a period of instruction (summative evaluation).

## TEACHING AND ASSESSMENT: SOME PITFALLS

As one approaches teaching and testing, there are some common dangers that must be avoided. To be forewarned is to be forearmed.

There is no doubt that a student feels tension and anxiety before, during, and after an assessment experience. This is particularly true if the assessment is of great consequence to the examinee, that is, is a high-stakes test. Midterms and finals, college entrance exams, and scholarship qualifying exams are examples of tests likely to evoke considerable test anxiety that can be potentially harmful to the student. Both internal and external tests may be high-stakes. In the classroom situation, improper tests and use of tests can damage the teacher-student relationship. The misuse of tests stems primarily from two sources: (a) misunderstanding of the proper role of tests, and (b) failure to appreciate the emotional problems posed for some students by any ego-threatening evaluation procedure. Among the potential problems are the following dangers.

1. If a teacher looks upon the norm on a standardized test as a goal to be reached by all children, and criticizes those who fail to meet this rigid standard, students will quite naturally come to think of tests as hurdles rather than as stepping stones to development.

2. If a teacher, in interpreting test results, fails to take into account other relevant information—ability differences, health status, home background, and the like—he or she is likely to render an unjust appraisal of a child's work, which may well have the effect of discouraging or antagonizing the child.

3. If teachers overemphasize tests in the assessment program, and fail to realize that they cover only part of the desired outcomes, they run the risk of placing undue emphasis on certain objectives and of confusing students as to what they are supposed to be learning.

4. If a teacher habitually uses test results as a basis for invidious comparisons among students, not only is the student-teacher relationship damaged, but also the relationships among the students.

5. If a teacher berates or scolds a child because of poor performance on a

test, the teacher may be building up unfavorable attitudes toward future testing and learning.

6. If teachers fail to let students know how they did on a test, or give any indication of how the testing is related to instructional purposes, it is hard for the students to make sense of the procedure.

7. If a teacher is insecure, and feels threatened by the tests, it is almost certain that this attitude will be communicated to the children. If a schoolwide or systemwide program is in operation, in the planning of which teachers have had no part, and the purposes of which they do not understand, they obviously will be in no position to make clear to students how the testing is likely to do them any good. If the test results are used as a means of appraising teacher competence, the temptation becomes very strong for the teacher to teach for the tests.

8. If a teacher is unsympathetic to a testing program in which he or she must participate, and makes derogatory or sarcastic reference to "these tests that we have to give again," he or she is certainly engendering a poor attitude among students; even they are shrewd enough to sense, however vaguely, that by such behavior the teacher is abdicating his or her rightful position.

Such commonsense procedures as returning test papers as soon as possible, discussing test items with the entire class, and demonstrating to the class the uses of test information help to develop proper student attitudes and a healthy perspective on the place and value of testing in the instructional program. There is no substitute for respect of students' needs and desires.

## CONTENT REVIEW STATEMENTS

1. Direct instruction can significantly promote achievement, particularly of low-ability students.

2. Social constructivism is based on hands-on and real-life experiences where the learner constructs the meaning.

3. Diversity in the classroom can be used to enhance learning experiences.

4. Learning style preferences can be characterized as visual, auditory, and tactile.

5. Both common and unique preferred learning styles exist within and across cultural groups.

**6.** The systematic development of instructional programs involves the:

    a. identification of goals

    b. identification of entry behavior and characteristics

    c. conducting of an instructional analysis of performance requirements

    d. writing of performance objectives

    e. writing of criterion-referenced test items

    f. development of an instructional strategy

    g. development and/or selection of instructional materials

    h. conducting of a formative evaluation

    i. revision of instruction based on formative evaluation data

    j. conducting of a summative evaluation

**7.** Summative evaluation refers to an end-of-experience assessment.

**8.** Formative evaluation refers to the use of data through feedback to improve a program during its development.

**9.** Measurement-driven instruction (MDI) involves the use of high-stakes tests of educational achievement to highlight student progress and curricular effectiveness.

**10.** If not properly monitored, measurement-driven instruction can result in fragmentation and trivialization of educational outcomes.

**11.** Measurement-driven instruction can result in focused, efficient, and effective instruction.

**12.** The processes of teaching and testing are intimately related.

**13.** In interpreting test scores for students, the teacher should carefully consider the potential psychological impact of such scores and the many related factors that bear on the meaning of the scores.

**14.** Students have inalienable rights to an interpretation of their assessments and the data collected.

**15.** Teachers need to master measurement competencies related to the following skills:

    a. selecting appropriate methods

    b. developing appropriate instructional assessment methods

    c. administering, scoring, and interpreting assessment

    d. applying measurement data in instructional decision making

  e. establishing student grading procedures

  f. communicating assessment results to relevant audiences

  g. approaching assessment in a legal and ethical manner

## SPECULATIONS

**1.** How can assessment enhance learning?

**2.** How are formative and summative evaluations different? How are they alike?

**3.** What are the advantages and disadvantages of direct instruction? Does one outweigh the other?

**4.** How would a teacher using a primarily direct approach to instruction behave differently from one using a social constructivist approach?

**5.** A parent has challenged the time you spend giving your tests as well as those mandated by the state. How would you respond?

**6.** What are some ways of using diversity in the classroom to enhance learning?

## SUGGESTED READINGS

Banks, J. A., & Banks, C. A. M. (Eds.). (1995). *Handbook of research on multicultural education*. New York: Macmillan.

Banks, J. A., & Banks, C. A. M. (Eds.). (1993). *Multicultural education (issues and perspectives)*. Boston: Allyn & Bacon.

Baruth, L. G., & Manning, M. L. (1992). *Multicultural education of children and adolescents*. Boston: Allyn & Bacon.

Bennett, C. I. (1995). *Comprehensive multicultural education*. Boston: Allyn & Bacon.

Crooks, T. J. (1988). The impact of classroom evaluation practices on students. *Review of Educational Research, 58*(4), 438–481. Research data from more than 14 fields reflected in 242 references provide nine categories of recommendations.

Cushner, K., McClelland, A., & Stafford, P. (1992). *Human diversity in education*, New York: McGraw-Hill.

Linn, R. L. (1983). Testing and instruction: Links and distinction. *Journal of Educational Measurement, 20*, 179–189.

Natriello, G. (1987). The impact of evaluation processes on students. *Educational Psychologist, 22*(2), 155–175. A conceptual framework presents the influence that a variety of elements have in the evaluation process.

Nitko, A. J. (1989). Designing tests that are integrated with instruction. In R. L. Linn (Ed.), *Educational measurement* (3rd ed., pp. 447–474). New York: Macmillan.

Salvia, J., & Hughes, C. (1990). *Curriculum-based assessment (Testing what is taught)*. New York: Macmillan.

Treuba, H. T., Cheng, L. R. L., & Ima, K. (1993). *Myth or reality (adaptive strategies of Asian Americans in California)*. Washington, DC: Falmer.

# 4

# Assessment and Cultural Diversity

## FOCUS CONCEPTS AND KEY TERMS FOR STUDY

| | |
|---|---|
| **Accommodation** | **Legal Considerations** |
| **Bias** | **Multicultural Validity** |
| **Cultural Diversity** | **Multicultural Assessment Standards** |
| **Culturally Assaultive Classrooms** | **Pluralistic Assessment** |
| **Empirical Bias Control** | **Responsive Assessment** |
| **Judgmental Bias Control** | |

> ## STANDARDS ALERT
>
> ### Standard 11.23    Testing Accommodations
>
> If a test is mandated for persons of a given age or all students in a particular grade, users should identify individuals whose disabilities or linguistic background indicates the need for special administration and ensure that these accommodations are employed.
>
> ### Taking It to the Classroom
>
> There are not only legal but ethical obligations to provide the student every opportunity to demonstrate what he or she knows and can do. Sometimes adjustments (e.g., in time or method of presentation) need to be made so that fair assessment results.

Reprinted with permission from the *Standards for Educational and Psychological Testing*. Copyright © 1999 by the American Educational Research Association, the American Psychological Association, and the National Council on Measurement in Education.

**Cultural diversity** in the classroom was described in the previous chapter as encompassing varieties of students with regard to race, ethnicity, gender, age, religion, disability, and, for that matter, social class. We might also include extremes of ability and behavior if represented in the same class. That includes just about everybody, doesn't it? It should, inasmuch as we as teachers are concerned with individual differences in general. Diversity is what we are about and what we encourage. Pushing students intellectually as far as they can go is one good example. Diversity in the classroom represents a challenge to education both instructionally and in regard to assessment.

## AVOIDING CULTURALLY ASSAULTIVE CLASSROOMS

Before valid assessment can take place we must create a receptive environment.

We have all been exposed to sexism and racism in everyday life. We have also addressed the divisive effects of these influences in schools. As teachers look toward structuring an environment free of negative influences, what are some commonsense things they can do to help build sensitivity and appreciation of diversity (Clark, DeWolf, & Clark, 1992)?

- Consider and discuss cultures not only from a historical context but also in terms of contemporary society.

- Don't consider culture only on special days (e.g., "holiday units," Cinco de Mayo, Martin Luther King's birthday) but throughout the school year.
- Use hands-on activities to develop both a cognitive and physical sense of cultural artifacts.
- Beware of using cultural stereotypes.
- Emphasize both similarities and differences of cultural varieties.
- Emphasize both group and individual characteristics of culture.
- Avoid token representation of particular cultures.

Educators must take the long view. In a very real sense they have in their grasp the power to influence social justice by creating understanding and sensitivity to the diversity in students' lives.

## ASSESSING THE EXTENT OF DIVERSITY IN THE CLASSROOM

After preliminary steps have been taken to avoid a culturally assaultive classroom, the teacher or building-level principal can engage in an assessment of the extent to which diversity has been identified and responded to in the classroom. The checklist in Table 4-1 by Karen Matsumoto-Grah (1992) provides a succinct summary of a variety of factors that educators need to be sensitive to if they are to deal with both instructional and assessment activities in the classroom.

## PLURALISTIC ASSESSMENT AND MULTICULTURAL VALIDITY

Garcia and Pearson (1994) note that the desire to see changes in the ways in which we assess educational outcomes, particularly at the individual student level in the classroom, has been motivated and stimulated by four major beliefs: (1) current assessment practices have caused today's educational ills; (2) tests have a pernicious effect on people; (3) the lack of a national accountability assessment system has inhibited the production of internationally competitive graduates; and (4) assessment practice has failed to keep step with recent research in language, learning, and cognition. Bits and pieces of all four of these beliefs are true and the cumulative effect has been, in fact, a trend toward the use of what were called in Chapter 1 more authentic assessments. Garcia and Pearson (1994) further note

**Table 4-1**   *Diversity in the Classroom: A Checklist*

### Teacher/Student Interactions

_____ Am I careful not to prejudice a student's performance based on cultural differences, socioeconomic status or gender?

_____ Do I promote high self-esteem for all children in my classroom? Do I help each child to feel good about who he or she is?

_____ Do I encourage students to understand and respect the feelings of others who are different from them?

_____ Do my students see me as actively confronting instances of stereotyping, bias, and discrimination when they occur?

_____ Given what I ask students to talk or write about, do I avoid placing value on having money, spending money, or major consumer products?

_____ Do I put myself in the place of the limited-English-proficient student and ask, "How would I feel in this classroom?"

_____ Do I make an effort to learn some words in the home languages that my limited-English-proficient students speak?

_____ Am I conscious of the degree and type of attention I am giving to members of each gender in classroom interactions? Do I have an equitable system for calling on students?

_____ Do I use gender-neutral language?

_____ Do I teach about religion, rather than teaching religion or ignoring religion altogether?

_____ When teaching about religion, do I

- Place religion within historical and cultural context?
- Use opportunities to include religion in history, literature, and music?
- Avoid making qualitative comparisons among religions?
- Avoid soliciting information about the religious affiliations or beliefs of my students?

### Teaching Children to Be Proactive

_____ Do I teach children to identify instances of prejudice and discrimination?

_____ Do I help my students develop proper responses to instances of prejudice and discrimination?

### General Strategies

_____ Do I involve parents and other community members to help children develop greater understanding of the benefits and challenges of living in a culturally diverse society?

_____ Do I inform parents of my multicultural, anti-bias curriculum?

_____ Do I support and encourage the hiring of minority teachers and staff?

_____ Do I build a secure and supportive atmosphere by creating a noncompetitive classroom environment?

(continued)

**Table 4.1** *Diversity in the Classroom: A Checklist (continued)*

### General Strategies

_____ Do I use opportunities such as current events to discuss different cultures and religions?

_____ Do I provide students with opportunities to problem-solve issues of inclusiveness?

_____ Do I use activities that demonstrate how the privilege of groups of higher economic status is directly connected to the lack of privilege of lower socioeconomic status people?

_____ Do I have students examine and analyze the representation of class, race, gender, ability, and language differences in media and their community?

_____ Do I recognize that tracking reinforces "classism" and is counterproductive to student learning at all ability levels?

_____ Do I utilize children's literature to help students understand and empathize with individuals who have experienced prejudice and discrimination and to discuss important social issues?

Reprinted by permission of Karen Matsumoto-Grah and the Association for Childhood Education International, 11501 Georgia Avenue, Suite 315, Wheaton, MD. Copyright 1992 by the Association.

that "African-American, Latino, and Native American students, as well as students for whom English is a second language, do not as a group, perform as well as Anglos on formal tests. . . . Differences between Anglo students and students of color are substantially reduced when comparison is limited to students from the same income levels and similar proficiency in standard English" (p. 340). Gender differences also exist and show, for example, a long-standing advantage for males on mechanical, physical, mathematical, scientific, and technical skills. If adjustments for democratic differences can take care of some of the formal performance discrepancies, perhaps teachers using appropriate techniques with an eye toward diversity of cultural experiences can further reduce performance divergence.

The key element in any assessment is the relevance of the task for the purpose and intended use of the data. The assessment task must be relevant to and for the person(s) being assessed. Are teachers then required to individualize their assessments relative to every member in a class? This obviously would be an impossible task! Great destruction of mental health has been wrought by lesser so-called solutions. What is proposed here is the use of a variety of tasks at a given point or points in time, which should allow for all students to, at some point, demonstrate what they have learned. This approach is consistent with the advocacy of "learning styles" in culturally diverse classrooms discussed previously in Chapter 3. Does the matching of learning style and assessment method make a difference? A good example of the positive benefit of that relationship can be found in a study by Lu and Suen (1995). Their investigation found that performance-based assessments (as opposed to a traditional multiple-choice test) tended to favor those students who had field-independent cognitive style.

There exists then a need to create a *pluralistic* assessment philosophy whereby diversity in learners is matched by diversity in the application of instructional methods, the results of which are assessed with a variety of techniques. These techniques and authentic or modern performance assessments are used both during instruction and at its conclusion. The distinction between formative and summative evaluation was noted earlier in Chapter 3. If we teach one way, we should assess in the same or similar way. Some of the authentic/alternative assessments that are available to be adapted to a diversity of learning styles include:

- portfolios (showcase, documentation of progress)
- research projects
- process assessments
- demonstrations
- simulations
- interviews/conferences
- product assessment
- oral presentations

The reader could add to this list. Do not overlook the very significant contributions that traditional assessments (e.g., multiple-choice exams, essay questions) can also make in measuring important knowledge and problem-solving educational outcomes.

The thrust of this section has been to build an argument for the judicious use of a variety of assessments such that diversity can be both included and used to demonstrate competence. If a variety of methods are used we can come closer to what Kirkhart (1995) has called **multicultural validity**. An educator focusing on multicultural validity would, in creating assessments, be concerned with how diversity influences the (a) way in which data are gathered, (b) reliability of the match between assessment task and the individual being assessed, and (c) consequences of the application of the assessment. "Consequential validity" is particularly important when considering the possible adverse impact of the failure to take account of cultural diversity on formal assessments of performance. The impact can be on how the assessment makes the student feel about himself or herself or the likelihood that he or she will be selected or nominated or hired. The interpersonal dimension is important in data collection, particularly where there is a one-on-one relationship. Is the "person environment" supportive of the student such that the most accurate information can be gathered? Using a variety of methods increases the likelihood of getting "good" data. Occasionally special provisions need to be made to accommodate diversity.

### Responsive Assessment

One of the exciting dimensions of today's classrooms is diversity. As exciting, stimulating, and challenging as that may be, it also can pose problems, in terms of both instruction and assessment. One of the major problems is the lack of common experiences students bring with them to the learning situation. That lack of commonality is a primary contributor to less than valid assessment. Learning takes place in a social environment and social influences, especially the home, impinge from outside. As noted previously, if an approach to teaching uses concepts, ideas, or materials alien to the student a barrier to learning and assessment have been erected. If learning and assessment has been identified, the teacher must first look to the context of learning.

An approach to assessment that appears to be particularly well suited to at-risk students has been documented by Mary Henning-Stout (1994). Figure 4-1 outlines the assessment framework. Two aspects of this approach to assessment set it apart from the usual methods: (1) the clarification and examination of the student's learning problems in a social context in consultation with all stakeholders (those with a vested interest in the student's progress), and (2) a negotiated solution. The involvement of many individuals allows for a more holistic approach to problem solving. Considering the student's home situation at least allows the teacher to attack one of the potentially significant barriers to academic progress.

### Accommodations During Assessment

Special groups sometimes request or require accommodations for the administration of tests or assessments. Students with physical disabilities in particular request adjustments, particularly for high-stakes tests (e.g., high school graduation). In addition to adaptations to the physical environment in the form of wheelchair accessibility, appropriate desks, restrooms, and parking, Phillips (1994) has noted requests are made for time extensions, frequent rest breaks, readers, sign language, interpreters, word processors, typewriters, cassette recorders, large-print or braille booklets, magnification apparatus, calculators, computers, and oral/interactive administration. In addition to the physically disabled making requests, those with some form of mental impairment (e.g., attention deficit disorder, dyslexia, dyscalculia, etc.) may do so. Following passage of the Americans

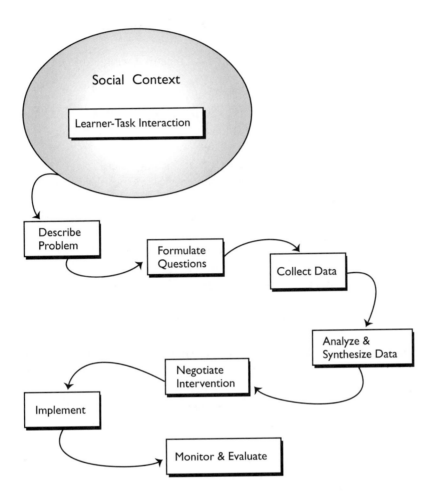

**Figure 4-1** *Responsive assessment framework (after Henning-Stout, 1994)*

with Disabilities Act and the Individuals with Disabilities Education Act, assessment experts have begun to wrestle with the problem of balancing the desirability of the social good with the need for valid data. The federal court, for example, has held in *Brookhart v. Illinois State Board of Education* (1983) that disabled students can be required to pass a graduation test if due process requirements are met. Decisions about what and how to test are based on an individual student's Individualized Educational Program (IEP).

# POTENTIAL SOURCES OF BIAS IN ASSESSMENT

What are some of the documented sources of bias that we need to be aware of and control?

Criticisms and controversies periodically draw attention to the many problems associated with educational and psychological assessment, especially standardized assessments. Some of these are long-standing, while others have arisen out of changes in society.

A growing body of literature suggests that tests are biased against some individuals or groups. In some cases, given tests work best with particular groups. It is argued by some that it is not the test but the unresponsive society that discriminates. It will be argued by all assessment professionals that the use of any instrument that has no demonstrable validity is inexcusable. There is evidence that certain tests are biased in selecting individuals, particularly in employment situations. If such differentiation can be shown to be a function of the relationship between test content and criterion performance, there are no grounds for objection. Such a test distinguishes between those who have and those who have not achieved, and between those who are and those who are not likely to be successful. If, on the other hand, the test discriminates on the basis of variables unrelated to validity, it should not be used. Cultural factors (e.g., socioeconomic condition) can operate to decrease the validity of any assessment. Some of the issues central to this problem have been highlighted by Cole and Moss (1989), Berk (1982), and Bond (1981).

**Bias**, as used in this context, refers to cultural or societal discrimination where factors *unrelated to the test* influence the scores. Such bias may operate to systematically inflate or decrease an individual's score. Quality of education could be used as an example. If quality of education is high and some individuals have access to it, bias may be positive. If the instruction is of inferior quality, then it may operate to depress an individual's scores. Reynolds and Brown (1984) have summarized six major types of objections to the use of educational and psychological tests (especially standardized commercial measures) with minorities because of the possible influence of potentially significant bias.

| Type of Objection | Description |
| --- | --- |
| Inappropriate content | Lack of background or experience inhibits performance. |
| Inappropriate standardization | Standardization samples do not reflect proportional representation in population with which test is used. |
| Examiner bias | Use of only standard English may operate to intimidate minority examinees. |

| Type of Objection | Description |
|---|---|
| Compounded consequences | Bias in test coupled with already existing disadvantages compound plight of minority test taker. |
| Construct validity error | Because of background differences and language problems, test may not measure same construct for majority and minority. |
| Predictive validity error | It may be the case that both test *and* criteria are biased. |

There are some very complex issues here and many legal challenges have been raised. A major concern of educators should be advocating research and validity studies into sound construction practices and applications of results.

## LEGAL CHALLENGES TO ASSESSMENT PRACTICES

We live in a litigious society so it is not surprising that when some individual or organization feels discriminated against by a test or application of test results the initial response is to go to court. The past several decades have seen a number of significant court cases where precedents have been set and the application of standard test development procedures reaffirmed. An overview of some of these landmark cases can be found in Table 4-2.

Whenever there is an apparent conflict between social policy objectives and accepted professional and administrative practices, governmental agencies increase their attacks. Nowhere is this more evident than in several employment selection discrimination cases that can be traced directly to Title VII of the 1964 Civil Rights Act, which requires employers to hire individuals without regard to race, religion, national origin, or sex. Title VII and the resulting Equal Employment Opportunity Commission Guidelines (1966, 1970, 1978) have resulted in clearer perspectives on what are acceptable testing practices under the law.

The history of the *Griggs v. Duke Power Company*, which spread over the 1968–1970 period, reflects the joint efforts of the testing profession and the court to find reasonable guidelines to help both test users and developers. The bottom line was that forevermore it is necessary to empirically demonstrate job-relatedness (usually in the form of criterion-related validity) of any test used for personnel selection or the evaluation of training.

Misapplication of any test can result in legal action. It was charged in *Griggs v. Duke Power Company*, and *United et al. v. Georgia Power Company*

**Table 4-2** *Summary of Court Cases Challenging Tests and Testing Procedures*

| Litigations | Result |
|---|---|
| *Griggs v. Duke Power Company* (1968) | Required test user to demonstrate job-relatedness of scores. |
| *Baker v. Columbus Municipal Separate School District* (1971) | National Teacher Examination (NTE) was held to be racially biased in terms of specifying a cutoff score. |
| *United States v. State of South Carolina* (1977) | Held NTE was acceptable measure of impact of academic training and could be used for certification and salary decisions. |
| *Debra P. v. Turlington* (1979, 1984) | Upheld instructional/content validity of Florida's minimum competency graduation test. |
| *Larry P. v. Riles et al.* (1979) | Placement in special education classes not allowed solely on basis of intelligence test if results in racial imbalance. |
| *Parents in Action on Special Education v. Hannon* (1980) | Upheld use of individually administered intelligence tests for placement purposes. |
| *Brookhart v. Illinois State Board of Education* (1983) | Held that if due process was given in form of IEP disabled students were accountable for graduation test. |
| *Golden Rule et al. v. Washburn et al.* (1984) | Procedure agreed upon in out-of-court settlement did not appreciably increase minority pass rate. |

that tests were used in discriminatory ways. Title VII of the 1964 Civil Rights Act, which requires employers to hire individuals without regard to their race, religion, national origin, or sex, led to the establishment of the Equal Employment Opportunity Commission (EEOC). EEOC has established guidelines for testing and other selection procedures. In writing the Supreme Court's unanimous opinion in *Griggs v. Duke Power Company*, Chief Justice Burger noted that

> The Act proscribes not only over discrimination but also practices that are fair in form, but discriminatory in operation. The touchstone is business necessity. If an employment practice which operates to exclude Negroes cannot be shown to be related to job performance, the practice is prohibited. . . . Nothing in the Act precludes the use of testing or measuring procedures; obviously they are useful. What Congress has forbidden is giving these devices and mechanisms controlling force unless they are demonstrably a reasonable measure of job performance. Congress has not commanded that the less qualified be preferred over the better qualified simply

because of minority origins. Far from disparaging job qualifications as such, Congress has made such qualifications the controlling factor, so that race, religion, nationality and sex become irrelevant. . . . Congress has placed on the employer the burden of showing that any given requirement must have a manifest relationship to the employment in question.

In an educational context the National Teacher Examination was also subjected to similar scrutiny with the decision being that it was not considered to be an acceptable measure of teaching effectiveness (*Baker v. Columbus Municipal Separate School District*, 1971), and did not reflect the impact of academic training (*United States v. South Carolina*, 1977).

Cultural bias was the basis for the *Larry P. v. Riles* case revolving around the assignment of students to classes for the educable mentally retarded. *Larry P.* defined an unbiased test as one that yields "the same pattern of scores when administered to different groups of people," an unreasonable criterion at best. It flies in the face of the whole notion of individual differences and their measurement. Fortunately, Judge Grady's decision in *Parents in Action on Special Education v. Hannon* (1980) upheld the use of individually administered intelligence tests for special education classification purposes.

The Golden Rule Insurance Company challenged the Illinois Department of Insurance and Educational Testing Service claiming racial bias in the licensing tests for insurance underwriters (*Golden Rule et al. v. Washburn et al.*, 1984). In an effort to work out a conciliation rather than force a confrontation, ETS President Anrig agreed to an out-of-court settlement, which was later renounced as unsound and ineffective (Anrig, 1987; Linn & Drasgow, 1987). The agreed-upon procedure required the selection of items where answer rates of black and white examinees differ by no more than 15 percent and exceed 40 percent of the items. The procedure did not improve pass rates. In addition, the exclusion of selected items may have had a detrimental effect on the exam's content validity. With the exception of applying the Golden Rule procedure in Illinois, ETS now uses a sophisticated item bias detection method (Mantel & Haenszel, 1959) with some success. The basis of the procedure rests on the assumption that test takers who have the same knowledge base should have equal or similar chances of responding correctly regardless of their race, sex, or ethnic background. The usual test/item review procedures are still employed.

It is frequently the case, however, that questions of test validity and use are overshadowed and subverted because of perceived adverse test effects on discriminated-against groups. The use of dual standards in making selection decisions is a case in point. The admission criteria for the dominant cultural group are ranked for each criterion, and a decision is made.

The same procedure is followed independently for minority group members. The *Bakke v. Regents of the University of California* (regarding nonminority admission to medical school) opinion pointed out the potential legal problems in using a quota system for making educational or training decisions. In addition to the need for guidelines for the use of tests in employment selection and admission decisions, additional measurement issues can be traced to the use of test data to allocate funds for educational programs. The economic implications of the "truth in testing" legislation now in effect in the state of New York with regard to tests used for college admission—where copies of the tests must be made available to examinees—are staggering. Beyond the obvious economic effect is the influence on the test security of external testing programs and test validity.

The spate of well-intentioned state and federal legislation is aimed at curbing abuses of tests. Some court cases related to accommodations for the physically disabled have arisen as a result of the Americans with Disabilities Act and the Individuals with Disabilities Education Act. In most instances the state and federal courts have sided with the academic defendants. It would probably be best if the testing profession could police its own ranks, but what procedures are available for curbing the misuses of educational and psychological tests? There is, of course, now a legal precedent requiring proof of validity for tests used for selection purposes. Tightening state licensing and certification laws for those who are charged with the responsibility of administering and scoring tests is another avenue for improvement. Voluntary restrictions on the sale and distribution of tests by test publishers is yet another possibility. Perhaps the most powerful pressure for improved testing practices can be exerted within the profession. Pre-service and in-service training programs should be expanded and updated.

Some redeeming social consequences have come from considerations of both legitimate and other legal issues. Public and professional awareness of sensitive testing issues has been addressed, accountability has been reaffirmed, and needed research has been stimulated. But perhaps more important is the underscoring of the use of already acceptable test development procedures and standards (see Chapter 2).

## DETECTING AND CONTROLLING MEASUREMENT BIAS

Ideally, once a test, measurement, or assessment has been created it should be checked for bias. Commercial test makers do this as a matter of course. There are some sophisticated statistical methods that can be used to assess the presence of bias, but informal procedures can yield very important data as well. Bias is always important but particularly so when high-stakes tests (e.g., promotion, scholarship, graduation) are involved. There are two major categories of methods for detecting item and thereby test bias. The first of these is basically **judgmental**. Systematically collected opinions of teachers or a group of students themselves could be asked to make evaluations of whether or not differences in gender or race, for example, could influence how a particular question was answered, or whether or not the content was in any way offensive. Parents might be sampled at the time of parent-teacher conferences or at a PTO(A) meeting. It could be a very positive public relations opportunity.

The second method is **empirical**. In this approach actual performance data are gathered from protected and unprotected groups. For example, a true-false item like the following could be given to a class:

A cross-cut saw has larger teeth than a ripsaw. (Answer: False)

This item yielded the following data in terms of who got the item right or wrong in a class of 30 students, comprised of 17 females and 13 males.

|  | PERCENT | |
|---|---|---|
|  | Correct | Incorrect |
| Male | 77 | 23 |
| Female | 35 | 65 |

These data obviously suggest that the item, perhaps because of gender-specific experiences, is biased toward males. How great the differences have to be, nobody really knows. A rule of thumb might be 25 percent. There are statistical methods for analyzing such data, but they are outside the purview of our discussion.

## Control of Evidential Bias

When establishing a plan to control bias in developing and applying educational assessments, whether using judgmental or empirical approaches, several factors must be kept in mind. Mehrens and Popham (1992) have identified some of these factors and how they might be controlled:

| Factor | Control |
|---|---|
| 1. Selection of bias review committee | 1. Include representatives of major protected groups |
| 2. Training of review committee | 2. Importance of documenting a highly relevant training program |
| 3. Criteria for item retention | 3. One rule of thumb is 80 percent agreement |
| 4. Groupings for statistical investigation of item bias | 4. At least 50 individuals should represent the protected group |
| 5. Statistical significance | 5. Practical consideration of greater concern than statistics |

What is being suggested with regard to the last item is that very often in statistical analyses the use of very large sample sizes can almost ensure "statistical significance." Of greater concern is the magnitude of the difference. Small may be significant but not meaningful.

## MULTICULTURAL ASSESSMENT STANDARDS

An overview of general guidelines for assessment instrument development, interpretation, and application developed by various professional organizations was presented in Chapter 2. The Association for Assessment in Counseling has recently published a set of 34 similar "standards" relevant to multicultural populations (Prediger, 1993). The following sources were used in the compilation:

*Code of Fair Testing Practices in Education* (CFTP)

*Responsibilities of Users of Standardized Tests* (RUST)

*Standards for Educational and Psychological Testing* (SEPT)

*Multicultural Counseling Competencies and Standards: A Call to the Profession* (MCCS)

*Ethical Standards of the American Counseling Association* (ESACA)

Seventeen of the "standards" judged most relevant to classroom teachers and the directors of school or system assessment programs and their sources are reproduced here. These "standards" are *in addition* to those already presented in Chapter 2.

**Selection of Assessment Instruments: Content Considerations**

- Determine the limitations to testing created by an individual's age, racial, sexual, ethnic, and cultural background; or other characteristics. (RUST)

- Give attention to how the test is designed to handle variation of motivation, working speed, language facility, and experiential background among persons taking it; [and] bias in response to its content. (RUST)

- Determine whether a common test or different tests are required for accurate measurement of groups with special characteristics. . . . Recognize that the use of different tests for cultural, ethnic, and racial groups may constitute ineffective means for making corrections for differences. (RUST)

- Determine whether persons or groups that use different languages should be tested in either or both languages and, in some instances, tested first for bilingualism or language dominance. (RUST)

- When a test is recommended for use with linguistically diverse test takers, test developers and publishers should provide the information necessary for appropriate test use and interpretation. (SEPT)

- When selecting the type and content of items for tests and inventories, . . . consider the content and type in relation to cultural backgrounds and prior experiences of the variety of ethnic, cultural, age, and gender groups represented in the intended population of test takers. (SEPT)

**Selection of Assessment Instruments: Norming, Reliability, and Validity Considerations**

- When a test is translated from one language or dialect to another, its reliability and validity for the uses intended in the linguistic groups to be tested should be established. (SEPT)

**Administration and Scoring of Assessment Instruments**

- Demonstrate verbal clarity, calmness, empathy for the examinees, and impartiality toward all being tested. . . . Taking a test may be a new and frightening experience or stimulate anxiety or frustration for some individuals. (RUST)

- Evaluate unusual circumstances peculiar to the administration and scoring of the test. . . . Consider potential effects of examiner-examinee differences in ethnic and cultural background, attitudes, and values based on available relevant research.

- For non-native English speakers or for speakers of some dialects of English, testing should be designed to minimize threats to test reliability and validity that may arise from language differences. (SEPT)

- Linguistic modifications recommended by test publishers should be described in detail in the test manual. (SEPT)

## Use/Interpretation of Assessment Results

- Examine the possibility that a client's group membership (socioeconomic status, gender, subculture, etc.) may affect test performance and, consequently, validity. (RUST)

- In educational, clinical, and counseling applications, test administrators and users should not attempt to evaluate test takers whose special characteristics—ages, handicapping conditions, or linguistic, generational, or cultural backgrounds—are outside the range of their academic training or supervised experience. A test user faced with a request to evaluate a test taker whose special characteristics are not within his or her range of professional experience should seek consultation regarding test selection, necessary modifications of testing procedures, and score interpretation from a professional who has had relevant experience. (SEPT)

- Culturally skilled counselors have training and experience in the use of traditional assessment and testing instruments. They not only understand the technical aspects of the instruments but are also aware of the cultural limitations. This allows them to use test instruments for the welfare of the diverse clients. (MCCS)

- The member must ensure that members of various ethnic, racial, religious, disability, and socioeconomic groups have equal access to computer applications used to support counseling services and that the content of available computer applications [e.g., a test interpretation] does not discriminate against the groups described above. (ESACA)

- The member must provide specific orientation or information to the examinee(s) prior to and following the test administration so that the results of testing may be placed in proper perspective with other relevant factors. In so doing, the member must recognize the effects of socioeconomic, ethnic, and cultural factors on test scores. (ESACA)

- The member must proceed with caution when attempting to evaluate and interpret the performance of minority group members or other persons who are not represented in the norm group on which the instrument was standardized. (ESACA)

Multicultural assessment is a complex topic requiring a great deal of thought, planning, and, most of all, common sense. It is a challenge to find the approach to assessment that will at once be fair to virtually all students and yet provide an authentic and valid picture of learning outcomes.

## CONTENT REVIEW STATEMENTS

1. Avoiding culturally assaultive classrooms involves conscious efforts to provide a variety of culturally linked experiences and the avoidance of stereotypes.

2. Consciousness about diversity in the classroom can be gauged by examining (a) teaching materials, (b) teacher modeling, and (c) the nature and character of teacher-student interactions.

3. Pluralistic assessment involves the use of a variety of assessment approaches so as to be responsive to a variety of learning styles related to diversity.

4. Multicultural validity focuses on the potential impact of differences in cultural background as it influences the validity of assessments.

5. The use of authentic or performance assessments is a major component in pluralistic assessment.

6. A "responsive assessment" framework allows all those interested in a given student's progress to look at learning problems holistically.

7. Ideally, the use of validated tests should reduce discrimination in employment and educational situations.

8. Recent court decisions have required that educational and psychological tests, particularly those bearing on employment, be of proven empirical validity.

9. *Debra P. v. Turlington* and *Larry P. v. Riles et al.* are landmark court decisions regarding high school graduation and the use of tests for student placement.

10. Bias during instrument development can be controlled by judgmental or empirical (statistical) means.

11. Commonsense procedures are available for establishing methods to control assessment bias.

12. Standards are available to guide the development, application, and interpretation of assessments with multicultural classes.

## SPECULATIONS

1. What "accommodations" are reasonable in assessing the culturally different?

2. What are the major sources of bias in educational assessment and how might they be controlled?

3. In what way have any of the legal challenges to assessment had an impact on your life?

4. What kinds of evidence can a teacher, school, or school system assemble to justify claims of assessment validity?

5. How can teachers avoid culturally assaultive classrooms?

6. What does the concept of *pluralistic assessment* mean to you?

7. Describe specific examples of a judgmental way and an empirical way to control for measurement bias.

8. Describe one multicultural assessment standard.

## SUGGESTED READINGS

Dana, R. H. (1993). *Multicultural assessment perspectives for professional psychology*. Boston: Allyn & Bacon. An in-depth survey of assessment practices in a multicultural environment. Extensive research base.

Educational Testing Service. (1980). *An approach for identifying and minimizing bias in standardized tests: A set of guidelines*. Princeton, NJ: Educational Testing Service. This excellent set of "standards" deals with all aspects of test development, from item writing to scoring. Language and cultural experience factors are of critical concern.

Garcia, G. E., & Pearson, P. D. (1994). Assessment and diversity. In L. Darling-Hammond (Ed.), *Review of research in education* (vol. 20, pp. 337–391). Washington, DC: American Educational Research Association. The most comprehensive overview available to date.

Geisinger, K. F. (Ed.). (1992). *Psychological testing of Hispanics*. Washington, DC: American Psychological Association. One of the very few scholarly treaties concerning the assessment of those of Hispanic extraction.

Rothman, R. (1994). *Assessment questions: Equity answers. Evaluation Comment,* Winter, 2–12. University of California at Los Angeles, Center for the Study of Evaluation and the National Center for Research on Evaluation, Standards and Student Testing.

Samuda, R. J. (1998). *Psychological testing of American minorities* (2nd ed.). Thousand Oaks, CA: Sage.

# PART Two

# Planning Assessments

*Beverly's Journal* ——————————————————————

It's easy to get lost trying to navigate through today's complex curricula. A good plan can really help both teaching and assessment. We have to know where we want to go and how we plan to get there. There can still be side trips along the way. We need to take advantage, however, of those spontaneous learning opportunities when they present themselves.

Technology has really helped teachers plan, teach, and assess. New software seems to appear almost daily. Now I've got to learn or relearn how to make the most effective use of the new media. The Internet is great, but with so much information one has to be careful. Of course, even without technology there are so many other ways to prepare for tests.

# 5

## Specifying Educational and Assessment Outcomes and Standards

---

### FOCUS CONCEPTS AND KEY TERMS FOR STUDY

| | |
|---|---|
| **Affective Objectives** | **Immediate Objectives** |
| **Cognitive Objectives** | **Mastery Objectives** |
| **Developmental Objectives** | **National Educational Goals** |
| **Educational Achievement** | **Specificity of Outcomes** |
| **Educational Objectives** | **Revised Taxonomy of Educational Objectives** |
| **Educational Outcomes** | **Ultimate Objectives** |

---

## STANDARDS ALERT

### Standard 13.3 — Test Blueprint

When a test is used as an indicator of achievement in an instructional domain or with respect to specified curriculum standards, evidence of the extent to which the test samples the range of knowledge and elicits the processes reflected in the target domain should be provided. Both tested and target domains should be described in sufficient detail so their relationship can be evaluated. The analyses should make explicit those aspects of the target domain that the test represents as well as those aspects that it fails to represent.

### Taking It to the Classroom

A valid assessment of knowledge acquisition or skill development is predicated on the assumption that the student has had the opportunity to learn the material or develop and practice the skill. The blueprint helps document these "opportunities." A *table of specifications* helps ensure balance between instruction and assessment.

---

Reprinted with permission from the *Standards for Educational and Psychological Testing*. Copyright © 1999 by the American Educational Research Association, the American Psychological Association, and the National Council on Measurement in Education.

Whether you are building a house or creating an educational test or an assessment, you need a set of plans. Solid construction and efficient operations require detailed blueprints. Because we make important decisions based on assessment data, we must make sure that the information is the best we can collect. The blueprint for an assessment device, traditional or performance, is comprised of many components, ranging from the number of questions, to the nature of administration, to the recording of responses, conditions, time, and scoring. Central to instruction *and* assessment is specifying expected outcomes: "If I teach this, I should observe this outcome."

Contemporary **educational outcomes** are different than those of several decades ago. Knowledge about the world—what it is made of and what is happening in it—increases geometrically each day. Just think about the complexity of so many jobs. Today's life-support skills require more integrative competencies. School curricula emphasize higher-order thinking and problem-solving skills. Where traditional measurements have emphasized information and facts, modern assessment requires both command of information *and* the ability to apply it.

**Educational achievement** can be defined as the extent to which specified objectives are accomplished by individual students or groups of students with common comparable instruction and goals. Most classroom assessment is objectives-referenced or criterion-referenced, although norm-referenced measurement also has its place. All approaches require objectives. In developing methods to measure the impact of instruction, the instrument developer for either a classroom or standardized test must specify a detailed set of objectives to guide development. A content domain must be specified. The statement of educational objectives (purposes or goals) for expected student changes and outcomes constitutes one of the most important elements in developing a sound classroom test. Objectives provide guidelines for both instruction and assessment. Objectives also serve as standards against which the final validity or relevance or the questions will be judged. (*Note:* The terms *objective, outcome, curriculum standards,* and *instructional intent* will be used interchangeably in this book.) The extent to which the test adequately samples from this domain of objectives is referred to as *content validity.*

An **educational objective** can be broadly defined as a statement of desired change in student behavior, knowledge, or affect. For example: students will be expected to evaluate newspapers, magazines, and television nutrition ads with respect to five principles of credibility. This middle school objective has both a content or knowledge base and a cognitive process base. In total it represents a "learning standard." Thus, an objective represents a value judgment and reflects the purposefulness of education. In another sense it represents a normative concept, a standard to be sought by all students. Some teachers rebel at the notion of "setting standards," but who is in a better position than the teacher to make judgments about what students should learn? It is part of the teacher's responsibility to delineate learning objectives and activities.

It is imperative that the teacher's instructional intent, however, be communicated to the student. The following anecdote illustrates a possible result of failure to communicate:

> At a parent-teacher conference the teacher complained to Mr. Bird about the foul language of his children. Mr. Bird decided to correct this behavior. At breakfast he asked his oldest son, "What will you have for breakfast?" The boy replied, "Gimme some of those damn cornflakes." Immediately Mr. Bird smashed the boy on the mouth. The boy's chair tumbled over and the boy rolled up against the wall. The father then turned to his second son and politely inquired, "What would you like for breakfast?" The boy hesitated, then said, "I don't know, but I sure as hell don't want any of those damn cornflakes!" (Yelon & Scott, 1970, p. 5)

Moral: If you want someone to change his or her behavior, tell that person your goals.

An acceptable objective has two components: a "content" or knowledge element and a "process" or behavioral element. Most educational objectives are found wanting in the process element. Instructional objectives are frequently couched in vague, ambiguous terms ("to know," "to appreciate," "to believe," "to have faith in," and the like), that have very little value in determining the processing units of instruction or in directing assessment efforts. A useful set of objectives is expressed as expected changes in overt student behavior.

## TYPES OF OUTCOMES

Many systems are available for classifying educational objectives and outcomes. Objectives can be characterized as (a) achievable or unachievable, (b) explicit or implicit, (c) intrinsic or transcendental, (d) individual or societal, (e) ultimate or immediate, and (f) general or specific. A detailed discussion of the last two types of objectives should help clarify the process of identifying and stating objectives and highlight the importance of objectives in developing assessments.

**Ultimate objectives** are behaviors ordinarily not observable under classroom conditions. They are important goals of education, but cannot, under normal circumstances, be directly evaluated. Ultimate objectives frequently refer to the projected adult behavior of children and adolescents. Examples of ultimate (broad goal) objectives are sound health habits, intelligent voting behavior, and critical attitudes about literature and the arts.

We must, therefore, approach the evaluation of ultimate objectives by way of immediate (intermediate, approximate) or short-range objectives. A teacher would specify a set of **immediate objectives** measurable under classroom conditions. Accomplishing these short-range objectives is assumed to be directly related to one or more ultimate objectives. Suppose, for example, that an instructor of a graduate-level course in educational tests and measurements adopted the following ultimate objective: "Upon completion of the course, the student will return to the classroom and write better tests." It is not feasible to gather data on the student's accomplishment of this objective. But data on such immediate objectives as recall of specific guidelines for constructing multiple-choice items, comprehension of the concept of reliability, and ability to apply methods of estimating validity can be used as approximate measures of the achievement of the ultimate objectives.

# GENERAL AND SPECIFIC OUTCOMES

General objectives or goals are similar to ultimate objectives, but often have some comparability over wide grade ranges (e.g., developing reading skills). Specific objectives are usually unique to particular courses and are stated as expected student behavior. Differences in specific objectives can be traced not only to variations in content but also to relative emphasis on similar objectives across grades or classes. General objectives can provide an overall framework within which the instructional program can be viewed. In addition, they serve as categories or rubrics under which specific objectives can be collected in efficient groupings, which in turn help direct assessment efforts.

There is a danger that general objectives can become too global and too influenced by Madison Avenue to be meaningful. Henry Dyer (1967, p. 9) cites the following paragraph from a report of the President's Commission on Higher Education as an example of "word magic":

> The first goal in education for democracy is the full, rounded, and continuing development of the person. The discovery, training, and utilization of individual talents is of fundamental importance in a free society. To liberate and perfect the intrinsic powers of every citizen is the central purpose of democracy, and its furtherance of individual self-realization is its greatest glory.

As Dyer noted, "it sings to our enthusiasms," but does not allow us to discern when educators have "liberated and perfected the intrinsic powers of a citizen." Nor does this kind of statement help explain how to calibrate the roundness of one's development. Some of us are easier to calibrate than others. But a statement at this level specifying, for instance, that "each student graduating from high school shall, if he or she desires it, be adequately prepared to enter a vocation" has very concrete implications for vocational education.

Some teachers argue that high-quality instruction can exist without explicit formal statements of the educational goals. This may be true, but assessment cannot be accomplished without a set of operational definitions of instruction. General objectives are usually dictated by community and societal needs, and the teacher is left with the task of translating these goals into specific objectives.

Frequently the list of specific objectives for a course of instruction becomes unmanageably long. Breaking down the instructional program into small but intelligible units has the overriding advantage of greatly facilitating test development. In practice, a compromise between an exhaustive list and a manageable one generally results.

### National Goals (Goals 2000)

The National Educational Goals Panel has declared hoped-for outcomes of public school education. These national goals are as follows:

- **Goal 1:** By the year 2000, all children in America will start school ready to learn.

- **Goal 2:** By the year 2000, the high school graduation rate will increase to at least 90 percent.

- **Goal 3:** By the year 2000, American students will leave grades 4, 8, and 12 having demonstrated competency in challenging subject matter including English, mathematics, science, foreign languages, civics and government, economics, arts, history, and geography, and every school in America will ensure that all students learn to use their minds well, so they may be prepared for responsible citizenship, further learning, and productive employment in our nation's modern economy.

- **Goal 4:** By the year 2000, the nation's teaching force will have access to programs for the continued improvement of their professional skills and the opportunity to acquire the knowledge and skills needed to instruct and prepare all American students for the next century.

- **Goal 5:** By the year 2000, U.S. students will be first in the world in mathematics and science achievement.

- **Goal 6:** By the year 2000, every adult American will be literate and will possess the knowledge and skills necessary to compete in a global economy and exercise the rights and responsibilities of citizenship.

- **Goal 7:** By the year 2000, every school in the United States will be free of drugs, violence, and the unauthorized presence of firearms and alcohol and will offer a disciplined environment conducive to learning.

- **Goal 8:** By the year 2000, every school will promote partnerships that will increase parental involvement and participation in promoting the social, emotional, and academic growth of children.

These general statements help us see broad-based intents and even have some implications for resource allocation. But something a little more specific is needed. We probably do not need, however, to go back to the 1960s and "behavioral objectives" when there was an effort to "behavioralize" everything short of respiration and blood flow in classrooms.

Examples of a general objective and related specific objectives are helpful at this point:

General Objective: The student will be able to evaluate a test he or she has constructed and administered.

Specific Objectives: The student will be able to

a. Determine the difficulty level of test items

b. Determine the discrimination power of items

c. Relate test items to the educational objectives

d. Estimate internal consistency reliability

This list of specific objectives is obviously not exhaustive, but it would make item writing (and instruction) much easier than would a simple general objective.

### Developmental and Mastery Objectives

Norman Gronlund and Robert Linn (1995) have proposed a somewhat different classification of objectives. They divide educational outcomes into **mastery** and **developmental** objectives. In a general sense these categories correspond to our immediate versus ultimate classification. At the mastery level are foundational or basic information and skill objectives. These objectives represent minimal essentials that must be mastered before moving to higher levels. The developmental objectives tend to be more complex and appear later in the study of a subject area or in life. In this regard they are ultimate because they tend not to be observed under classroom conditions. Both kinds of objectives are important, as are the related instructional experiences. Criterion-referenced measurement approaches are likely appropriate for mastery objectives and norm-referenced measurement approaches are likely appropriate for developmental objectives. A continuum is implied in the distinction. For example, at one end we have mastery of basic arithmetic operations, and at the developmental level, we require the solving of quadratic equations. In social studies, we might be interested in these objectives:

■ **Mastery**
*The ability to recall major sources of income for selected African countries.*

■ **Developmental**
*Describe current world problems resulting from recent political changes in Africa.*

The current minimum competency testing movement is based partly on legislators' desires to hold students and schools accountable for mastery objectives. All evaluation is not, however, objectives-based. Michael Scriven (1972) and Robert Stake (1975), for example, have described general approaches to evaluation that use an inductive rather than the usual deductive approach. Qualitative methods and naturalistic observation are used in these "goal-free" approaches. Objectives (in a sense, hypotheses) are inferred from observational data. Rather than evaluate from a prescribed framework, a description of ongoing activities is used to identify which objectives are being addressed.

In many instances you may not need or want to specify outcomes or behaviors, but simply wish to describe a situation to be experienced by the student. These "experiential objectives" are important because they provide opportunities for learning and appreciation. The exact nature of change will depend on the individual. Visits to a zoo, museum, botanical garden, stock exchange, manufacturing plant, or hospital allow cognitive and affective growth.

## Levels of Specificity in Educational Outcomes

Educational objectives, like people, come in all shapes and sizes. Big objectives can at times be so ponderous that they don't say anything and can't move anywhere. Others are so minuscule that you can't see them and are meaningless because they are so small, even nitpicky. "Truth," as so often is the case, is probably somewhere in the middle. Outcomes that are useful probably have enough bulk to render them visible and able to make a statement, but not be so small as to become intellectually invisible. We can conceive of outcomes as falling on a continuum of specificity. Figure 5-1 visualizes the individual differences in specificity. It contains a variety of terms that are frequently used to help focus and direct educational efforts. At the very general end we have educational goals like, "Become a good citizen." In the middle (*Revised Taxonomy of Educational Objectives*) we might have, "Applies Archimedes principles of specific gravity in problem solving." At the specific end we have test items: "What domestic animal is most closely related to the wolf?"

Note that the spacing of the outcome-related terms is not even, as objectives and categories of objectives are not all created equal. Figure 5-1 is not an equal interval scale. Goals like those from national educational commissions would be on the left—the *far* left—on our continuum, and the ultimate in specificity is the test or performance item, which would be on the right. The test task is an actual sample of what we want the student to know or to be able to do. If not an actual sample, it is as good an approximation as we can create.

The process of stating objectives is an iterative one; each level helps one understand the levels above and below it. There is lots of interaction. Developments at one level frequently have implications for other levels, and

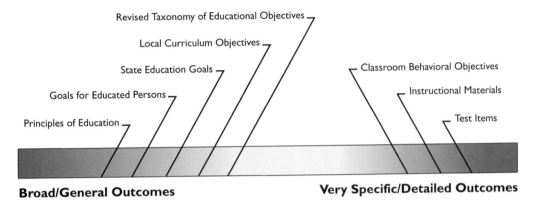

**Figure 5.1** *Degrees of specificity of educational outcomes*

one obtains the most complete understanding—particularly once the major developmental lines have become clear—by working back and forth among the various levels. Thus it is clear that objectives can and must be stated at a variety of levels of specificity, for both testing and curriculum building.

### Illustration of Relationship Among General Objectives, Specific Objectives, and Test Items

The basis of validity for an achievement test rests, for the most part, on the match between intended outcomes and the measures of those outcomes. Stated another way, the basis of validity (relevance) is the relationship of objective and item. The overall or sum total test validity (defined as a content domain, see Chapter 14) is an aggregate of the individual items. One approach to assessing test validity is to have experts make judgments about the number of items that match their respective objectives. All this assumes that everything is in balance—in other words, that there is symmetry and proportionality between instructional intent and actual instruction. (See Chapter 6 for a discussion of the concept of "test blueprint" or "table of specification," which relates very directly to balance.) Following are three sample objectives and items. (The idea of relevance is so important that an early introduction to item writing can't hurt.)

The examples are taken from a science report card of the National Assessment of Educational Progress (Mullis & Jenkins, 1988). Three levels of specificity are represented. The first level is the general objective or goal. Goals are useful because they help us focus on the appropriate instructional path to follow. Next come the specific objectives, detailing the content and processes to be measured. Finally, the test itself represents an operational definition of our objective.

**General Objective:** Knows everyday science facts

**Specific Objective:** Can read and interpret simple graphs

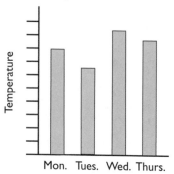

The graph above shows the high temperature on each day for four days. Which day was the hottest?

Monday

Tuesday

*Wednesday

Thursday

**General Objective:** Applies basic scientific information

**Specific Objective:** Can make inferences about the outcomes of experimental procedures

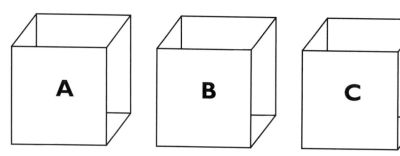

Blocks A, B, and C are the same size. Blocks B and C float on water. Block A sinks to the bottom. Which one of the following do you know is TRUE?

- ● Block A weighs more than block B.
- ○ Block B weighs more than block C.
- ○ Block C weighs more than block A.
- ○ Block B weighs more than block A.
- ○ I don't know.

General Objective: Integrates specialized scientific information

Specific Objective: Can apply basic principles of genetics

A female white rabbit and a male black rabbit mate and have a large number of baby rabbits. About half of the baby rabbits are black, and the other half are white. If black fur is the dominant color in rabbits, how can the appearance of white baby rabbits best be explained?

- ○ The female rabbit has one gene for black fur and one gene for white fur.
- ● The male rabbit has one gene for black fur and one gene for white fur.
- ○ The white baby rabbits received no genes for fur color from the father.
- ○ The white baby rabbits are the result of accidental mutations.

# THE REVISED TAXONOMY OF EDUCATIONAL OBJECTIVES

One attempt to provide a framework for the entire panorama of educational objectives is the *Taxonomy of Educational Objectives*—so-called because it is a hierarchical classification scheme. The *Taxonomy* authors were much concerned with the holistic nature of learning, so educational objectives are divided solely for convenience into three domains—cognitive, affective, and psychomotor. Most objectives for conventional courses are in the cognitive and affective domains, and a framework has been developed for each of these (Bloom, 1956; Krathwohl, Bloom, & Masia, 1964). The cognitive domain of the *Taxonomy* has recently been revised (Anderson & Krathwohl, 2001). From this point on in the book the cognitive domain will be referred to as the *Revised Taxonomy*. Tentative frameworks for the psychomotor domain also have been developed. These frameworks are hierarchical in nature, that is, the lowest level of behavior in the hierarchy is believed to be the least complex, and its achievement is presumed to be the key to successful achievement at the next higher level in the structure.

The structure proposed in the *Revised Taxonomy* is educationally, logically, and psychologically consistent. The *Revised Taxonomy* represents an educational system in that the categories correspond to a teacher's concerns in developing curricula and selecting learning experiences. This system is logical because its categories are precisely defined and can be subdivided. It is psychological because it is consistent with current thought and research in the psychological sciences, although it does not depend on any particular theory.

The *Revised Taxonomy* is not a traditional content classification scheme applicable in various subject-matter areas. Rather, it represents a set of cognitive goals per se, as well as a system for developing goals.

The major reason for developing the *Revised Taxonomy* was to facilitate communication among educational teachers, curriculum developers, and evaluators. The original *Taxonomy* has enjoyed its widest acceptance among educational testers and evaluators because of their need for explicit statements of objectives. The new form emphasizes the teaching-learning process and assessment of results.

### The Structure of the Revised Cognitive Domain

An extensive meta-analysis of the vast body of research on the *Taxonomy* was undertaken. On the basis of this synthesis a new structure was created which was a better fit with research findings and educational applications reported by a variety of audiences. The new structure involved breaking knowledge into four categories (running from concrete to abstract) and the process dimension into six categories (running from less to greater cognitive complexity). The process dimension employs 19 verbs to operationalize objectives. Following is a description of the new structure (these descriptions are mixtures of paraphrases and quotes):

### Knowledge Dimension

(a) Factual Knowledge—basic facts, terminology, and specific details and elements (e.g., statistical symbols)

(b) Conceptual Knowledge—knowledge about larger structures that describe interrelationships among elements, (e.g., periods of geological time)

(c) Procedural Knowledge—the steps involved in calculating a correlation coefficient

(d) Metacognitive Knowledge—knowledge of cognition in general (e.g., types of assessment tasks used by teachers and why)

### Process Dimension

**1. REMEMBER—Retrieve information from memory**

1.1 Recognizing (identifying), e.g., recognize names of famous composers

1.2 Recalling (retrieving), e.g., recall major U.S. wars

**2. UNDERSTAND—Construct meaning from a communication**

2.1 Interpreting (paraphrasing, clarifying, translating), e.g., a foreign language

2.2 Exemplifying (illustrating), e.g., finding a specific example

2.3 Classifying (Categorizing), e.g., classify types of motors

    2.4 Summarizing (abstracting), e.g., write summary of novel

    2.5 Inferring (predicting), e.g., extrapolate from number sequence

    2.6 Comparing (contrasting), e.g., compare antecedents of World War I with World War II

    2.7 Explaining (constructing models), e.g., account for the simultaneous rise of Protestantism and capitalism in the sixteenth century

**3. APPLY — Use a procedure in a particular situation**

    3.1 Executing (carrying out), e.g., multiplying two two-digit numbers

    3.2 Implementing (using), e.g., apply Bernoulli's law in a physics problem regarding conservation of energy

**4. ANALYZE — Dissect material into constituent elements and describe interrelationships**

    4.1 Differentiating (distinguishing), e.g., to discriminate relevant from irrelevant information in a math word problem

    4.2 Organizing (integrating), e.g., develop an argument for and against paying college athletes

    4.3 Attributing (deconstructing), e.g., determine religious values of author from essay on ethics

**5. EVALUATE — Make judgments using criteria/standards**

    5.1 Checking (testing), e.g., determine if conclusions follow from observed reported data

    5.2 Critiquing (judging), e.g., judge which of two statistical methods is best to analyze a particular data set

**6. CREATE — Put or reorganize elements into a new pattern or structure**

    6.1 Generating (hypothesizing), e.g., generate hypotheses to account for observed data

    6.2 Planning (designing), e.g., design a plan to evaluate a school's language arts program

    6.3 Producing (constructing), e.g., construct a third-grade social studies assessment

The *Revised Taxonomy* can be used in many productive ways, including assisting teachers with classroom instructional activity selection, curriculum planning, assessment planning, and analyzing sets of objectives. Figure 5-2 is based on a display in Anderson and Krathwohl (2001) showing how an objective can be classified in the knowledge-process matrix (taxonomy table).

| The Knowledge Dimension | The Cognitive Process Dimension | | | | | |
|---|---|---|---|---|---|---|
| | **1. Remember** | **2. Understand** | **3. Analyze** | **4. Apply** | **5. Evaluate** | **6. Create** |
| A. Factual | | | | Differentiate appropriate and inappropriate use of measurement terms | | |
| B. Conceptual | | Express in own words value of *Revised Taxonomy* | | | Judge two methods for writing analysis test items | |
| C. Procedural | Recall formula for Kuder-Richardson internal consistency reliability estimate | | | | | |
| D. Meta-cognitive | | | | | | Design a classroom assessment to meet particular teacher and student needs |

**Figure 5-2** *Sample Objectives in Revised Taxonomy Knowledge-Process Matrix*

## Useful Infinitives and Direct Objects for the *Revised Taxonomy*

Metfessel, Michael, and Kirsner (1969) have provided examples of verbs and direct objects useful in working with the original *Taxonomy*. Some of these are directly applicable to the *Revised Taxonomy*. The following categorizations are those of the author and not the originators Anderson and Krathwohl.

**Table 5-1**

| Category | Infinitive | Direct Object |
|---|---|---|
| **REMEMBER** | recall, identify, recognize, acquire | vocabulary, terminology, definitions, referents, names, sources, elements, properties, convention, ways, devices, forces, classes, categories, theories, formulas |
| **UNDERSTAND** | translate, paraphrase, represent, interpret, explain, estimate, differentiate, distinguish, transform, change, rephrase, restate | meanings, definitions, words, phrases, representations, theories, relationships, conclusions, effects |
| **APPLY** | generalize, use, employ, restructure, classify, transfer, organize, develop, relate | principles, laws, effects, conclusions, methods, theories, generalizations, procedures, phenomena, abstraction, situations |
| **ANALYZE** | distinguish, detect, discriminate, categorize, contract, deduce | hypotheses, conclusions, assumptions, arguments, relationships, themes, evidence, fallacies, patterns, structures, arrangements, organizations |
| **EVALUATE** | judge, assess, appraise, compare, contrast, argue, validate, decide | consistencies, fallacies, means, ends, courses, alternatives, standards, theories, generalizations, errors, exactness |
| **CREATE** | write, tell, relate, produce, document, plan, design, modify, derive, develop, synthesize, formulate, deduce | structure, pattern, product, performance, design, composition, plan, schematic, solution, specification, communication |

## The *Revised Taxonomy*, Objectives and Assessment

For the most part instructional and assessment objectives will be the same. This assumes that the objective specifies the expected actual performance or standard. This might be recalling last year's Oscar winners, identifying an unknown chemical, or building a birdhouse—better yet, designing a birdhouse with special attention to indoor plumbing, walk-in closets, dining area, and pool. Performance objectives by their very nature will be more complex, and therefore higher on a taxonomy scale. Performance assessment represents an opportunity to integrate the cognitive, affective, and psychomotor aspects of instruction. Let's design and build a functional economic birdhouse that looks good and makes birds happy. If the objective describes what we want the student to be able to do, then let's teach him or her to do it. Easier said than done!

Objectives derived using the *Revised Taxonomy* have direct implications for assessment. Anderson and Krathwohl (2001) suggest that most cognitive domain objectives can be assessed using either supply (constructed) or selection formats. They give an example for the following objective:

The student will be able to identify an author's point of view from a speech.

A supply item might be: "What is the author's purpose in writing the essay you read on the Amazon rainforests?" A parallel selection item might be:

"The author's purpose in writing the essay you read is to:

(a) provide factual information about the Amazon rainforests

(b) alert the readers to the need to protect rainforests

(c) demonstrate the economic advantages of developing rainforests

(d) describe the consequences to humans if rainforests are developed."

Anderson and Krathwohl (2001) also suggest that one might turn the objective into an "affective" item by using a degree of agreement continuum such as Strongly Agree-Agree-Don't Know-Disagree-Strongly Disagree to evaluate the statement "The rainforest is a unique type of ecological system."

Educational purposes are reflected in goals and objectives. The more detailed they are, the greater their usefulness for guiding instruction and evaluating the effectiveness of that instruction. Educators—for people other than teachers also use objectives—frequently adopt or adapt already existing objectives or sets of objectives for their own purposes. Whether creator or borrower, one must be sure that the objectives (a) are compatible with school and system goals; (b) are representative of best current pedagogical thought; (c) are compatible with student background, experience, and ability; (d) reflect the current state of knowledge; (e) describe expected student performances; and (f) contain a description of the conditions under which that behavior is to be observed.

### Illustrative Cognitive-Domain Objectives

The following list of objectives should illustrate the flavor of the *Taxonomy*.

- Recall of major facts about particular cultures (*Factual Knowledge*)
- Knowledge of scientific methods for evaluating health concepts (*Procedural Knowledge*)
- Skill in translating verbal mathematical material into symbolic statements, and vice versa (*Understanding*)

- Ability to predict the probable effect of a change in a factor on a biological situation previously at equilibrium (*Understand*)
- Ability to recognize form and pattern in literary and artistic works as a way of understanding their meaning (*Analyze*)
- Skill in distinguishing facts from hypotheses (*Analyze*)
- Ability to recount a personal experience effectively (*Synthesis*)
- Ability to plan a unit of instruction for a particular teaching situation (*Create*)
- Ability to compare a work with the highest known standards in its field, especially other works of recognized excellence (*Evaluate*)
- Ability to recognize logical fallacies in arguments (*Evaluate*)

**Illustrative Taxonomy Objectives for Elementary Students**

Higher-order outcomes can be stated and used with elementary students. The following summary illustrates that point and provides an overview of the modified *Taxonomy* (Reisman & Payne, 1987):

- *Knowledge*
  - To say the letters of the alphabet in order.
  - To point to all of the *e*'s in a word.
  - To state the definition of the word *mammal*.
- *Understand*
  - To translate a simple word sentence into a simple number sentence.
  - To summarize the main ideas of a paragraph.
  - To predict the ending of a story.
- *Apply*
  - To follow safety rules when the fire drill bell rings.
  - To make cookies using a recipe.
  - To compose a paragraph using proper usage and good sentence structure.
- *Analyze*
  - To recognize statements of fact and opinion in a short story.
  - To underline the main ideas in a letter.
  - To identify the parts of a sentence.
- *Evaluate*
  - To write a critique of a short story.
  - To draw a conclusion based on data.
- *Synthesis*
  - To write a poem.
  - To construct a collage.

## SPECIFYING COGNITIVE OUTCOMES

Two major factors must be considered in constructing statements of educational objectives: content and form. Objectives should be evaluated not only for subject matter (content), but also for how the subject matter is treated or expressed (form). These two dimensions are significantly related and can influence the utility of objectives and the quality of the resulting test and items. Desirable characteristics of objectives will be discussed in this section.

### Content

1. Objectives should be appropriate for level of difficulty and prior learning experiences. If the *Revised Taxonomy* was used as a guide, objectives encompassing all six major levels might be stated for a college-level course, but only the first three levels might be emphasized for a fifth-grade social studies unit. Higher-order outcomes—that is, problem solving and logical thinking—should be focused on in the early grades! For a fifth-grade social studies unit:

   **Unacceptable:** The student will trace the economic and philosophical origins of communism.

   **Acceptable:** The student will identify three European countries where peaceful changes were brought about in communist political organizations.

2. Objectives should be "real," in the sense that they describe behaviors the teacher actually intends to act on in the classroom situation. Frequently a teacher will state that he or she intends to bring about changes in the "attitudes" and "appreciations" of his or her students, but plans no specific learning experiences to achieve these kinds of objectives. These are, of course, useful or desirable objectives, but if you adopt an objective, you must evaluate progress toward it. Conversely, if an objective is not part of the actual instructional program, you shouldn't evaluate it.

   **Unacceptable:** Students will learn to love science.

   **Acceptable:** After a visit to a local hospital, pharmacy students will better appreciate the importance of scientific experimentation.

3. A useful objective will describe both the content and the mental process or behavior required for an appropriate response. A list of objectives should *not* become a "table of contents"—a list of topics to be covered in class. An objectives list should describe the overt behavior expected and the content vehicle (e.g., instructional procedure) that will be used to bring about change.

**Unacceptable:** Students will know world capitals.

**Acceptable:** Students will be able to recall the capitals of the countries in the North Atlantic Treaty Organization.

4. The content of the objectives should be responsive to the needs of both the individual and society.

   **Acceptable:** Students can describe the requirements for becoming registered voters in their states.

5. Generally, a variety of behaviors should be stated because most courses attempt to develop skills other than "recall." Only recently, however, have we made a concerted effort to abandon the stultifying emphasis on memorizing facts. This seems strange in light of the results of relevant research, which have been available for some time. Ralph Tyler (1933), for example, has shown that knowledge of specific information is not a lasting outcome of instruction. On the other hand, the higher-order mental abilities and skills (e.g., application and interpretation) show much greater stability.

## Form

1. Objectives should be stated in the form of expected student changes. They should *not* describe teacher activities. If we are to measure and evaluate validly, we must articulate precisely what we expect students to be able to do at the end of a course or unit of instruction.

   **Unacceptable:** The teacher will describe the major events in the United States Civil War.

   **Acceptable:** The student will recall the military event that directly led to the outbreak of hostilities at the beginning of the United States Civil War.

2. Objectives should be stated in behavioral or performance terms. The terms used should have the same meaning for student and instructor. Robert Mager (1962) points out that words such as *identify, differentiate, solve, construct, list, compare,* and *contrast* communicate more precisely and efficiently than do traditional educational terms. In general, the broad class of words called *action verbs* is preferred. Objectives must be stated operationally if we are to evaluate them adequately. Following is an example:

   **Unacceptable:** The student will see the importance of the Magna Carta.

   **Acceptable:** The student will be able to identify three major provisions of the Magna Carta that relate directly to the Constitution of the United States of America.

   Although wordier, the "Acceptable" objective better clarifies the task and surely gives the instructor more content and behavior guidance. See Tables 5-1 and 5-2 for a useful list of "behaviors" in the "Infinitives" column.

3. Objectives should be stated singly. Compound objectives are likely to lead to inconsistent measurement. At the beginning of a course, a teacher may have a particular objective, such as, "The student should be able to recall, comprehend, and apply the four major correction-for-guessing formulas." But any of three behaviors might measure the achievement of this objective. In addition, those selected may or may not be measured in proportion to the emphasis given them in class. If the resulting test is not responsive to the instruction objectives, it is invalid for determining whether these goals have been accomplished. Another shortcoming of compound objectives is that the easier portions of the objectives may be measured because it is easier to write recall (knowledge) items than application items. Again, the relevance of the test is destroyed.

4. Objectives should be parsimonious. Statements of instructional goals are easier to work with when trimmed of excess verbiage. Following is an example:

   **Unacceptable:** The student will be capable of establishing a quantitative chemistry design with which, when presented with an unknown compound, the student will thereafter correctly identify its constituent elements.

   **Acceptable:** The student will describe verbally a design for an experiment to test for an unknown chemical.

The streamlined version is clearer and communicates more effectively.

5. Objectives should be grouped logically, so they make sense in determining units of instruction and evaluation.

6. The conditions under which the expected student behavior will be observed should be specified. The objective "to be able to solve problems in algebra," although useful, could be improved as follows: "Given a linear algebraic equation with one unknown, the learner must be able to solve for the unknown without the aid of references, tables, or calculating devices" (Mager, 1962). Although a little more wordy, the objective more clearly delineates the instructor's intent and the expected student behavior.

7. If possible, the objective should contain a statement indicating the criteria for acceptable performance. Criteria might involve time limits or a minimum number of correct responses. Both student and instructor should know what is expected of them. Following is an example.

   **Unacceptable:** The student will be able to identify examples of each part of speech.

**Acceptable:** When presented with a grammatically correct paragraph of at least three sentences, the student will be able to identify examples of each part of speech.

How elaborately should objectives be specified? What degree of refinement is necessary? These questions do not have absolute answers, and they require decisions by the teacher-evaluator. The more refined the objectives are, the easier the task of measurement is. Obviously, there is a point of diminishing returns. The list could become so lengthy and involved that it would be unwieldy, confusing, and perhaps negatively reinforcing to the writer. Instructors are encouraged to consider the guidelines listed earlier in developing a suitable style to express their objectives.

Following are several specific objectives from a course in educational tests and measurements that illustrate many of the points in the foregoing discussion.

The student should be able to do the following:

1. Write a multiple-choice item free of grammatical errors.
2. Correctly classify a set of test items according to the six major process categories of the *Revised Taxonomy of Educational Objectives*.
3. Select the most important rule in constructing assessment exercises from a list of positive suggestions.
4. Construct a scoring rubric for an essay item.

Figure 5-3 contains the "World's Worst Specific Objective" to illustrate in summary form the problems that might be encountered in writing a good instructional objective. As it stands, the objective is beyond help. Probably five or six objectives are implied in this collection of words. It would be merciful to simply remove the life support system and begin anew.

## CONSIDERATIONS OF AFFECTIVE OUTCOMES

Although controversial, definite and somewhat pervasive evolutionary change is taking place in education. This change involves nurturing and naturalizing affective learning outcomes. The impact of affective outcomes is evident in the type and extent of research on affective outcomes published in the professional journals; the papers presented and discussed at professional, educational, and research meetings; the sensitizing experiences being introduced into teacher training programs; and the books published on humanizing the school curriculum. Nearly all teachers are aware

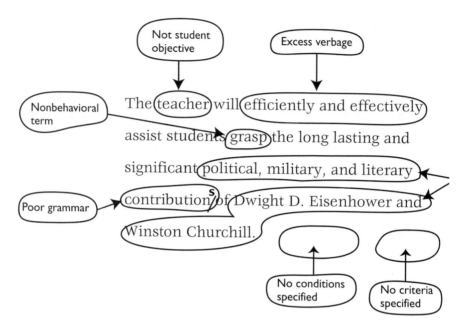

**Figure 5.3** *World's worst specific objective*

that, no matter what they do, affective learning takes place. Robert Gagné (1985), for example, noted that

> [T]here are many aspects of the personal interaction between a teacher and his students that do not pertain, in a strict sense, to the acquisition of skills and knowledges that typically form the content of a curriculum. These varieties of interaction include those of motivating, persuading, and the establishment of attitudes and values. The development of such human dispositions as these is of tremendous importance to education as a system of modern society. In the most comprehensive sense of the word "learning," motivations and attitudes must surely be considered to be learned.

Affective and cognitive phenomena are not separate. They develop together and influence one another. Concern with both kinds of outcomes, then, is evidence of concern for the "whole person."

Some educators are less than enthusiastic about accepting affective outcomes as part of their educational responsibility. They assume or wish that interests, values, and attitudes were developed at home or in the church. Considering the amount and nature of violence in today's society, as well as the general dilution of morality and values in government, students could well benefit from some attention to old-fashioned values. But those affective components that motivate us to learn the value "right" and feel good about ourselves are independent of citizenship values. If we expect certain value outcomes, we must provide relevant classroom experiences.

## The Need to Assess Affective Outcomes

There are four primary reasons affective outcomes need to be assessed:

- *Affective variables influence an individual's ability to participate effectively in a democratic society.* Attitudes toward institutions, practices, social groups, and the like are affected by society's efforts to maintain itself and meet the needs of its members. If for no other reason than this, affective objectives must be considered legitimate outcomes of concern to educators.

- *The development of skills and abilities related to the acquisition and growth of attitudes and values is necessary for a healthy and effective life.* The development of rational attitudes and values is the result of intelligent examination of society's needs and those of the individual. Affective skills are necessary to the overall effective functioning of the individual in society. This observation has many implications for mental health. Developing attitudes and values can be a rational process and is therefore amenable to modification. That affective variables can be manipulated and changed has been repeatedly demonstrated. The kinds of experiences an individual has with a variety of tasks have been shown to influence the kinds of attitudes he or she develops. Experimentally, for example, the experience of failure or success at a task has been shown to be causally related to a variety of beliefs and values associated with the concept of achievement. There is also evidence that tasks that are either too easy or too hard are less motivating than those of moderate difficulty.

- *Affective outcomes interact with occupational and vocational satisfaction.* In maintaining themselves economically, individuals must (a) relate effectively with their associates, (b) enjoy their work, (c) believe it is possible to make maximal use of their abilities, and (d) feel that they are making a contribution to society. Experts have reasoned that the values of mastery, activism, trust of others, and independence of family should be considered legitimate educational objectives, because they have been empirically related to socioeconomic achievement and upward mobility in our heavily industrialized society (Kahl, 1965).

- *Affective variables influence learning.* The interaction of teachers' and students' affective characteristics influences progress toward attaining classroom goals. Richard Ripple (1965), in summarizing research on the affective characteristics of the learning situation, concluded that the attainment of classroom objectives is facilitated by (a) a generalized feeling of warmth in the learning environment, (b) tolerance of emotional and feeling expressions on the part of students, (c) democratic group decision making leading to stimulating activities, (d) the use of nonpunitive control techniques of considerable clarity and firmness, (e) reduced frustration and anxiety in learning tasks, and (f) shifting states or order based on the organization of emotions toward the achievement of goals. More specifically, research has experimentally demonstrated interaction among a student's achievement values, the instructor's teaching style, and the amount of—and the satisfaction with—learning (Domino, 1971). If students are learning material that interests them, they are likely to develop positive attitudes toward it. Studies have demonstrated modest relationships between attitude toward school and specific subject matter and performance.

A cautionary note must be added. The desire to improve, modify, adjust, expand, or in some way influence and alter attitudes and values should not obscure the primary concern with learning. D. H. Heath suggests that "we need to educate youth, not just his head nor his heart. The promise of affective education is that it will stimulate us to recover the person lost among our abstractions; its danger is that it may devalue man's most promising adaptive and educable skill: a disciplined intellect" (1972, p. 371).

## Characteristics of Affective Outcomes

There are a number of levels of affective variables. Many terms have been used to describe these variables, including attitude, value, interest, opinion, appreciation, and motive. The concept of *attitude* holds a central position in research and literature on curriculum and instruction, so it will be the focus of this discussion of affective variables. The observations in this section draw primarily on material on attitudes, but these implications are germane to the entire affective domain.

The degree to which a feeling concept has been internalized is the factor that unifies the affective domain of the *Taxonomy*. Interests are considered more transitory and therefore less fully internalized. The development of a value system that strongly controls one's behavior is a relatively lasting general characteristic of the individual and is highly internalized. In the middle range of internalization we find attitudes that are somewhat internalized, and therefore influence behavior, but are not so rigidly set that they cannot be changed. Lewis Aiken (1988) has combined several definitions of attitude as follows:

An attitude is a learned predisposition to respond positively or negatively to a certain object, situation, or person. As such, it consists of cognitive (knowledge or intellective), affective (emotional and motivational), and performance (behavioral or action) components. (p. 303)

The major characteristics of the affective domain continuum are (a) increasing emotional quality of responses, (b) responses increasingly automatic as one progresses up the continuum, (c) increasing willingness to attend to a specific stimulus, and (d) developing integration of a value pattern at the upper levels of the continuum.

### Illustrative Affective Domain Objectives

Following are some sample objectives for the affective domain:

- Listens to music with some discrimination of mood and meaning and some recognition of the contribution of various musical instruments to the total effect.
- Contributes to group discussions by asking thought-provoking questions.
- Is willing to work for improvement of health regulations.
- Weighs alternative social policies and practices against the standards of the public welfare rather than against the advantage of specialized and narrow interest groups.
- Is ready to revise judgments and change behavior in the light of evidence.
- Decides to avoid trying new drugs as encouraged by peers.
- Does not drive a car after drinking two or more beers.
- Recycles aluminum cans and newspapers.

### Behavioral Affective Categories for the *Taxonomy* of Educational Objectives

One criticism frequently leveled at the *Taxonomy*, particularly by evaluators, is that it is not couched in behavioral terms. The possibility of some latitude in interpreting the various categories of the *Taxonomy* frequently makes the tasks of curriculum evaluation and test construction difficult. Newton Metfessel, William Michael, and Donald Kirsner (1969) have made a very practical contribution by listing infinitives and direct objects that can be used to operationalize the *Taxonomy*. Table 5-2 suggests many important objectives and assists in orienting the *Taxonomy* more toward behavioral objectives.

### Popham's Strategy for Specifying Affective Outcomes

In addition to Metfessel, Michael, and Kirsner's list of behavioral terms, the interested teacher can use W. James Popham's relatively simple strategy for

**Table 5-2** *Instrumentation of the Taxonomy of Educational Objectives: Affective Domain*

| | Taxonomy Classification | Key Words | |
|---|---|---|---|
| | | Examples of Infinitives | Examples of Direct Objects |
| 1.0 | Receiving | | |
| 1.1 | Awareness | to differentiate, to separate, to set apart, to share | sights, sounds, events, designs, arrangements |
| 1.2 | Willingness to Receive | to accumulate, to select, to combine, to accept | models, examples, shapes, sizes, meters, cadences |
| 1.3 | Controlled or Selected Attention | to select, to posturally respond to, to listen (for), to control | alternatives, answers, rhythms, nuances |
| 2.0 | Responding | | |
| 2.1 | Acquiescence in Responding | to comply (with), to follow, to commend, to approve | directions, instructions, laws, policies, demonstrations |
| 2.2 | Willingness to Respond | to volunteer, to discuss, to practice, to play | instruments, games, dramatic works, charades, burlesques |
| 2.3 | Satisfaction in Response | to applaud, to acclaim, to spend leisure time in, to augment | speeches, plays, presentations, writings |
| 3.0 | Valuing | | |
| 3.1 | Acceptance of a Value | to increase measured proficiency in, to increase numbers of, to relinquish, to specify | group membership(s), artistic production(s), musical productions, personal friendships |
| 3.2 | Preference for a Value | to assist, to subsidize, to help, to support | artists, projects, viewpoints, arguments |
| 3.3 | Commitment | to deny, to protest, to debate, to argue | deceptions, irrelevancies, abdications, irrationalities |
| 4.0 | Organization | | |
| 4.1 | Conceptualization of a Value | to discuss, to theorize (on), to abstract, to compare | parameters, codes, standards, goals |
| 4.2 | Organization of a Value System | to balance, to organize, to define, to formulate | systems, approaches, criteria, limits |
| 5.0 | Characterization by Value of Value Complex | | |
| 5.1 | Generalized Set | to revise, to change, to complete, to require | plans, behavior, methods, effort(s) |

| | Taxonomy Classification | Key Words | |
| --- | --- | --- | --- |
| | | Examples of Infinitives | Examples of Direct Objects |
| 5.2 | Characterization | to be rated high by peers in, to be rated high by superiors in, and to be rated high by subordinates in<br><br>and<br><br>to avoid, to manage, to resolve, to resist | humanitarianism, ethics, integrity, maturity<br><br><br><br>extravagance(s), excesses, conflicts, exorbitancy/exorbitancies |

Source: N. S. Metfessel, W. B. Michael, and D. A. Kirsner, Instrumentation of Bloom's and Krathwohl's taxonomies for the writing of educational objectives. *Psychology in the Schools* 6 (1969): 227–231. Copyright 1969 Clinical Psychology Publishing Co., Inc., Brandon, Vermont 05733. Reprinted by permission.

identifying and specifying affective learning outcomes. Popham's basic intent is to describe observable student behaviors that reflect attainment or nonattainment of these affective objectives. There are five general steps in the procedure (Popham, 1975):

1. Begin with a general statement of the broad affective objective.

     Example:    At the end of this course, students will have more favorable attitudes toward science.

2. Next, imagine a hypothetical student who personifies the objective. The intent is to describe the behavior likely to be exhibited by a possessor of this positive attitude.

     Example:    A student who has a positive attitude toward science is more likely to read scientific articles in popular magazines, attend science-fiction movies, and select science book titles.

3. Third, imagine a student who is a nonpossessor of the attitude or has a negative attitude toward the objective or stimulus.

     Example:    A student who has a negative attitude toward science would not choose magazine articles dealing with science, would not enjoy courses in science, and would not enjoy or choose to visit a science museum.

4. Describe a situation in which the attribute possessor and nonpossessor would respond differently. Define difference-producing situations in which the hypothetical individuals would behave differently. The situations might be contrived or occur naturally.

Example:     When put in a forced-choice situation, students majoring in science will select more hypothetical book titles dealing with scientific topics than will individuals not majoring in science.

It is of great importance that the situations chosen be free of behavior-inducing cues. There should be no external pressure to respond in a particular way. Do not ask for a show of hands to indicate interest or request that students sign a survey of attitudes toward a course. The teacher can, however, work out a code with students so that the teacher can keep track of individual student progress toward selected affective objectives.

Unobtrusive measures are particularly well suited to many kinds of affective outcomes (Webb, Campbell, Schwartz, Sechrest, & Grove, 1981). Such measures are considerably less influenced by the desire of students to please the teacher, unless they know they are observed and for what purpose. Observation during recess, free play, group activities, physical education activities, in homeroom, on the bus, and in the schoolyard before and after school can provide valuable insights into affective behavior.

5. Select those difference-producing situations that most effectively, efficiently, and practically define the intended outcomes.

(Some of the many methods that can be used to measure affective learning outcomes are described in Chapter 12.)

# CASE STUDY

The following series of exercises are presented to help students apply relevant materials from selected chapters. Obviously the responses to each case study exercise will be unique. Sample responses can be found on the Student Instructional Materials Disc.

## Introduction/Setting

The development of reading skills is central to virtually all aspects of an individual's academic and vocational pursuits. If we are to do anything about the very significant national and international literacy problem it must be through the improvement of reading skills. Each succeeding generation should be more literate than the previous one, or at least that would be a reasonable goal. We are called upon to read and understand large amounts of information every day. With the "knowledge explosion," the ability to input, comprehend, and integrate this information in an efficient and effective manner can often determine the difference between success and failure, passing or not passing, being promoted or not being promoted. The development of reading skills in students is very much contingent upon high-quality instruction. High-quality instruction in turn is dependent upon effective teacher training. We have now backtracked to the reason for offering a course in the teaching of reading for pre-service juniors in an early childhood education or elementary education college curriculum.

*Course and curriculum.* This is the first required five-credit-hour quarter-long course for junior pre-service students in early childhood or elementary education. Students generally spend six weeks learning about methods and materials used in the teaching of reading. They then spend three weeks in elementary classrooms, and they finish the quarter by spending the final week on campus after their field experiences to share and seek solutions and resolutions. A typical text for this course might be: Vacca, J., Vacca, R., & Gove, M. (2000). *Reading and learning to read* (4th ed.). New York: HarperCollins.

The major aims (goals) of the course are to provide pre-service teachers with declarative, procedural, and conditional knowledge in the following areas:

- reflection on the reading process and beliefs about teaching reading
- emerging literacy
- language experience activities
- decoding strategies
- comprehension strategies
- classroom discussion strategies
- basal reading lessons
- modifications of the reading program for bilingual learners
- modifications of the reading program for exceptional children
- evaluation of individual and group progress

Class activities include whole- and small-group discussions of assigned readings, teaching simulations by professors and students, mini-lectures, and audiovisual presentations.

The course grade is based on the midterm exam, final exam, and several other assignments: daily written journals, field-based teaching, written lesson plans, written assignments from course textbooks, and classroom observations. The present case study will focus on the midterm exam.

Following are 29 sample objectives for the first six weeks of the course. The original list contained 42 objectives. Six of these objectives (indicated with an asterisk*) would not become part of the midterm exam plan; they (a) related to activities that were part of later coursework, or (b) were performance objectives aimed at campus or field experience classroom activities.

Evaluate each objective in comparison to the guidelines presented in the chapter relative to content and form. Suggest improvements.

## Cognitive Objectives

### Reflection on the Reading Process and Beliefs About Teaching Reading

The student should be able to:

1. Associate different instructional practices with three conceptual frameworks (models) of the reading process.
2. Recognize the importance of automaticity in the reading process.

### Emerging Literacy

The student should be able to:

3. Recognize instructional activities that emphasize the uses of language.
* 4. Read two children's books aloud using appropriate voice inflections, introductory activities, and follow-up activities.
5. Identify ways to create a classroom environment where learning to read is supported.

### Language Experience Activity (LEA)

The student should be able to:

6. Identify the purposes of Language Experience Activity.
7. Recognize the characteristics of a particular Language Experience Activity.
* 8. Plan and teach two Language Experience Activities.

### Decoding Strategies

The student should be able to:

9. Identify the goal of decoding strategies.
10. Recognize three types of decoding strategies.
11. Apply phonics generalizations to decode nonsense words.
12. Apply syllabication rules.

## Comprehension Strategies

The student should be able to:

13. Recognize the purpose of Informed Strategies for Learning.
14. Recognize the characteristics of Informed Strategies for Learning.
15. Recognize the characteristics of Question-Answer-Relationships.

## Discussion Strategies

The student should be able to:

16. Identify three different types of discussion activities.
17. Recognize characteristics of three different types of discussion activities.
* 18. Participate in classroom discussions that use various formats.

## Basal Reading Lessons

The student should be able to:

19. Identify the basal reader's emphasis as skills instruction, vocabulary instruction, oral reading, silent reading, comprehension instruction, guided practice, evaluation and use of children's literature.
20. Recognize the purpose and function of a scope and sequence chart.
21. Identify alternatives to round-robin reading.
* 22. Plan and teach several basal reading lessons.

## The Reading Program and Exceptional Children

The student should be able to:

23. Recognize reading instructional activities that are appropriate for exceptional children (both hard-to-teach and gifted).
* 24. Modify a basal lesson so that it is appropriate for an exceptional student.

## The Reading Program and Bilingual Learners

The student should be able to:

25. Differentiate among the terms *bilingual learner, multicultural education, first language*, and *second language*.
26. Recognize instructional activities that are appropriate for bilingual learners and will increase multicultural appreciation in the classroom.
* 27. Modify a basal lesson so that it is appropriate for bilingual learners.

*Evaluation*

28. Recognize characteristics of norm-referenced and criterion-referenced tests.
29. Differentiate between characteristics of test reliability and validity.

### Affective Objectives

Cognitive outcomes have dominated the curricula of schools since their inception. This chapter has highlighted the important role that affective outcomes can play in developing a totally educated person—a person who is academically and occupationally competent, and who can function effectively in society; a person possessed of positive self-image and the ability to appreciate many and varied environments.

Take a few minutes and try your hand at creating some affective objectives for a reading education course. These would be objectives that a reading instructor would hold for undergraduate teachers-in-training. The instructor would like to see movement toward the objectives. Try two types of objectives. One type would be tied to the *Taxonomy of Educational Objectives*, perhaps using the behavioral infinitives contained in Table 5-2. Another route would be the use of Popham's five-step strategy useful in identifying difference-producing situations where people holding different attitudes and beliefs would act or react differentially.

Another source of ideas is the section of Chapter 12 entitled "Approaches to the Assessment of Affective Outcomes." Implied in every useful affective objective would be the germ of an idea as to how to measure it.

## CONTENT REVIEW STATEMENTS

1. Establishing educational goals, instructional objectives, and standards is a time-consuming, important, and often frustrating task.

2. Specifying outcomes is probably the single most important step in educational assessment.

3. An educational objective or standard is a statement of desired change in student behavior.

4. Objectives can be classified as

    a. ultimate or immediate.

    b. general or specific.

    c. cognitive, affective, or psychomotor.

    d. mastery or developmental.

5. Objectives can be classified at different levels of specificity, depending on their origin and projected method of application.

6. Objectives are derived from

    a. analysis of the needs of individuals and society.

    b. subject-matter experts.

    c. professional societies and commissions.

    d. analyses of the learning process itself.

7. In selecting an instructional objective, one must consider its consistency with the school's educational philosophy and with accepted knowledge and theories of learning and instruction.

8. Educators must accept that value judgments cannot be avoided when they select or specify educational objectives.

9. The *Taxonomy of Educational Objectives* is a nonsubject-matter classification of educational outcomes related to each other and to the teaching-learning process.

10. The *Taxonomy* considers cognitive (thinking), affective (feeling), and psychomotor (doing) kinds of school outcomes.

11. The major process categories of increasing complexity of the cognitive domain in the *Revised Taxonomy of Educational Objectives* are

    a. remember.

    b. understand

    c. apply

    d. analyze

    e. evaluate

    f. create

**12.** The knowledge dimension (from concrete to more complex) includes four major types: factual, conceptual, procedural, and metacognitive.

**13.** A good educational objective should

   a. deal with actual relevant classroom behaviors.

   b. be appropriate to the students involved.

   c. be stated in the form of expected change in individual student behaviors.

   d. have direct implications for modifying and assessing behavior.

**14.** Students learn attitudes, values, interests, and other affective characteristics in the classroom.

**15.** It is important for teachers to be concerned with affective learning outcomes, which influence the student's

   a. eventual ability to participate effectively in society.

   b. development of a healthy personality.

   c. occupational and vocational satisfaction.

   d. learning.

**16.** Specifying affective outcomes (e.g., attitudes, interests, values, and the like) can be as important, or more important, than specifying cognitive or psychomotor outcomes.

**17.** Cognitive and affective outcomes interact to the degree that they are virtually inseparable.

**18.** Affective outcomes directly influence learning and also constitute legitimate educational outcomes in themselves.

**19.** How an individual feels about subject matter, school, and learning can be as important as how much he or she achieves.

**20.** The major categories of the affective domain of the *Taxonomy of Educational Objectives* are

   a. receiving (attending and awareness)

   b. responding

   c. valuing

   d. organization

   e. characterization by a value or value complex

**21.** The organizing principle in the affective domain of the *Taxonomy of Educational Objectives* is *internalization*.

22. Internalization is the inner growth that occurs as the individual becomes aware of and then adopts attitudes, principles, codes, and sanctions that are basic to his or her value judgments and that guide the individual's behavior.

23. The hierarchical continua of the affective domain have the following characteristics:

    a. increasing emotionality of responses

    b. increasing automatic responses

    c. increasing willingness to attend to particular stimuli

    d. increasing integration of diverse values

24. Popham developed a method for specifying affective objectives that involves

    a. generating a general affective statement.

    b. imagining a hypothetical student who positively typifies the objective.

    c. imagining a hypothetical student who negatively typifies the objective.

    d. describing a situation in which these two individuals would respond differentially.

25. Providing students with a list of course objectives can enhance the learning experience.

## SPECULATIONS

1. What are the characteristics of a good instructional objective?

2. Does the *Revised Taxonomy of Educational Objectives: Cognitive Domain* make sense to you? Why or why not?

3. Can all educational outcomes be expressed as cognitive or behavioral objectives?

4. What are the advantages and disadvantages of objectives?

5. Which are more valuable from an educational standpoint, goals or objectives?

6. Is form or content more important in an instructional objective?

**7.** Are taxonomies really helpful?

**8.** Is it always necessary to have instructional objectives?

**9.** Are developmental or minimum competency objectives more important? Why?

**10.** Close your eyes and reminisce about the chapter you have just read. Now try to express your feelings using terms from the *Taxonomy of Educational Objectives: Affective Domain*.

**11.** Are we justified in including affective outcomes in schools? If so, which ones?

**12.** Why is it so difficult to express affective outcomes in behavioral terms?

**13.** What are some ways in which cognitive outcomes influence affective outcomes? And vice versa?

**14.** Using Popham's strategy, conceive an attribute possessor and nonpossessor relative to an attitude toward educational measurement. In what kinds of situations would they respond differentially?

**15.** Do psychomotor outcomes tend to get overlooked in public education? Why or why not?

## SUGGESTED READINGS

Fuchs, L. S., & Fuchs, D. (1986). Effects of systematic formative evaluation: A meta-analysis. *Exceptional Children, 53,* 199–208. A systematic review of 21 studies revealed that students of teachers who use objectives-based measurement performed better than those students of teachers who did not regularly use such procedures.

Gronlund, N. E. (1985). *Stating behavioral objectives for classroom instruction.* New York: Macmillan.

Harrow, A. J. (1972). *A taxonomy of the psychomotor domain.* New York: David McKay.

Mager, R. F. (1962). *Preparing objectives for programmed instruction.* San Francisco: Fearon. This brief (now classic) but excellent programmed text provides rationale and procedures for stating operational educational objectives.

Mager, R. F. (1968). *Developing attitude toward learning.* Palo Alto, CA: Fearon. This describes three principles that teachers can apply in nurturing favorable attitudes toward school subjects. Some consideration is also given to measurement.

Reisman, F. K., & Payne, B. D. (1987). *Elementary education: a basic text*. Columbus, OH: Charles E. Merrill.

Trecker, M. S., & Coddling, J. B. (1998). *Standards for our schools*. San Francisco: Jossey-Bass.

# 6

# Planning for the Development, Administration, and Scoring of the Assessment

---

## FOCUS CONCEPTS AND KEY TERMS FOR STUDY

| | |
|---|---|
| **Blueprint** | **Motivational Effect** |
| **Cheating** | **Optical Scanning** |
| **Coaching** | **Strip Key** |
| **Computer Application** | **Student Test Preparation** |
| **Cutout Key** | **Table of Specifications** |
| **Directions** | **Test Anxiety** |
| **Fan Key** | **Test-Wiseness** |
| **Guessing** | **Weighting** |
| **Learning Effect** | |

# STANDARDS ALERT

**Standard 3.3**          **Test Specifications**

The test specifications should be documented, along with their rationale and the process by which they were developed. The test specifications should define the content of the test, the proposed number of items, the item formats, the desired psychometric properties of the items, and the item and section arrangement. They should also specify the amount of time for testing, directions to the test takers, procedures to be used for test administration and scoring, and other relevant information.

## Taking It to the Classroom

The assessment blueprint, like an architect's rendering or an engineer's design, provides the required foundation for a valid and relevant assessment. A table of specifications is an important part of that blueprint.

**Standard 13.11**          **Test Preparation**

In educational settings, test users should ensure that any test preparation activities and materials provided to students will not adversely affect the validity of test score inferences.

## Taking It to the Classroom

Provide relevant practice on all types of outcomes likely to be assessed. Don't focus on just one type of task or question, as doing so could be a real disservice to the student.

Reprinted with permission from the *Standards for Educational and Psychological Testing*. Copyright © 1999 by the American Educational Research Association, the American Psychological Association, and the National Council on Measurement in Education.

To ensure the best possible assessment, you must plan for it. Appropriate planning involves considering numerous factors, including the type of procedure to be used, the length of the task, the type of task, the range and difficulty level of the task, the arrangement of the tasks within the assessment, the time limits, the scoring system, the manner of reporting results, the method of recording responses, and, most important of all, the subject matter, mental operation, process, or behavior to be sampled.

Several important decision points in test planning are discussed in this chapter. The term *task* is used here to represent a question, a problem to be solved, or a test item.

Just as a competent contractor and architect must have blueprints to erect buildings with functional integrity and stability, so must the test developer have a similar set of specifications. The blueprint includes many important components.

## COMPONENTS OF AN ASSESSMENT BLUEPRINT

Decisions must be made early in the development of the blueprint about a number of components of the assessment. All these decisions must flow from the purpose(s) of creating the instrument initially. Contemporary measurement practice tends to focus on two methodologies: criterion-referenced and norm-referenced. With these two general methods in mind, an overview of some major decision points in the test development process is in order.

### Development Should Flow Directly from Purpose

All decisions about how the instrument is created and applied should flow directly from the intent in creating the device. Jason Millman and Jennifer Greene (1989) have concisely summarized categories of the kinds of inferences that a teacher is likely to make with tests. Figure 6-1 is an adaptation of that classification system. The inferences described are for individuals, although data can be aggregated (e.g., across classes, grades, schools) for curriculum evaluation. *Assessments are only as valid as the inferences we can make from their scores.* Either norm-referenced or criterion-referenced

|  | Time in Curriculum | | |
|---|---|---|---|
|  | Before Instruction | During Instruction | After Instruction |
| Description of Attainments | Placement | Diagnosis | Grading |
| Mastery Decision | Selection | Instructional Guidance | Promotion |

(Application)

**Figure 6-1** *Kinds of classroom inferences made from tests (after Millman & Greene, 1989)*

methods can be used with either type of application. The choice depends on whether the inference or decision is based on absolute (criterion-referenced measurement [CRM]) or relative (norm-referenced measurement [NRM]) standards. The content basis of the inferences is the *curriculum*. The content domain can be expanded to include developing intellectual skills and abilities. If this content dimension is added to the curriculum, then our measurement intent moves from an achievement to an ability-testing orientation.

The intimate relationship between assessment development and data collection can be illustrated further by referring to the variety of decisions that educators must make which require a variety of data. Table 6-1 provides a summary of data requirements relative to three general categories of decisions. The similarity to the decision types in Figure 6-1 (before, during, and after instruction) is evident. Table 6-1 contains three important messages. The first relates to the value of pre-testing. The need, desire, and value of determining where a student "is" in an instructional plan is critical. Such information provides a more rational and helpful approach to teaching. Second, we need to know how we and the students are doing during instruction; relevant test results can help us monitor progress. Information about which students have not mastered projected objectives and where reteaching needs to take place are illustrative decisions to be made during instruction. A final "big picture" of the effect and impact of the learning experience can be a third area where measurement can contribute to decision making in the classroom. A "terminal" end-of-experience measurement can help both student and instructor see how all the pieces fit together. It can also help teachers see areas where they might need to change instruction next time. Teachers are basically being asked to make four kinds of decisions: placement, formative, diagnostic, and summative.

### Areas and Proportions of Content Should Be Specified

Content specification should reflect the purpose of assessment, curriculum, and instruction. Any of the three major categories of school outcomes can be included: cognitive, affective, or psychomotor (although the emphasis is usually on cognitive objectives). A listing of topics covered and the amount of time spent on each is a good place to begin clarifying the content dimension.

### The Categories and Nature of Process Objectives (Behaviors) in the Assessment Should Be Specified

Content or knowledge doesn't exist in and of itself; something must be done with them. Content must be recalled or manipulated in some way—

**Table 6-1** *Outline for Obtaining Information Needed in an Evaluation Program Designed to Aid Decision Making in All Phases of Instruction*

| | Phase I: Planning Instruction | Phase II: Guiding instruction | Phase III: Evaluating Results of Instruction |
|---|---|---|---|
| Major questions or decisions | What is to be studied? (What are the needs of these pupils with respect to this content?) Where should instruction start? | How should instruction be carried out? When is the class (or a student) ready to move on? | Have pupils mastered and retained important learning outcomes? |
| Basis for planning | Course outline. Specification of units and objectives. The textbook outline. Specification of prerequisite sequences. | Diagnostic outline of units or major topics. Identification of possible instructional alternatives. Specification of mastery criteria for objectives, units, topics. | Specification of essential content and skills (especially those needed as basis for subsequent courses). |
| Specific types of information needed | Do students already have mastery of any course content? What have students studied before? Do students have prerequisites for course? What is present student status in mastery within sequence? Do certain topics have special interest and meaningfulness for students? | Do students have mastery or partial mastery of some topics within units? What type of instruction is most effective for this class (or for this student)? Have students mastered what they have been studying (objective, topic, unit)? | Have students retained the essential content and skills? |
| Possible sources of information | Course pretest. Standardized achievement tests. Student records. Placement test. Readiness tests. Aptitude tests. | Unit pretest. Interview with student. Student records. Personal knowledge of student. Aptitude tests. Quiz covering a given objective or topic (CET).* Unit post-test. Student work. Observation. | End-of-course exam. Standardized achievement test. Projects. Observation. |

*Curriculum embedded test.

Source: From Measuring Pupil Achievement and Aptitude, Second Edition, p. 208, Table 10.1, by C M. Lindvall and A. J. Nitko, © 1975 by Harcourt Brace Jovanovich, Inc. Reprinted by permission of the authors.

for example, applied, used in problem solving, analyzed, and so forth. This dimension lends itself to classification according to the *Revised Taxonomy of Educational Objectives* (Anderson & Krathwohl, 2001) (see Chapter 5). Again, the nature of the instructional activities should be a helpful guide in describing the distribution of process outcomes. How much time the teacher spent in developing student understanding or application of a particular knowledge would be the typical kind of question asked. One device useful in bringing together the content and process dimensions is the *table of specifications*. The construction of this device is discussed in the next section.

### The Number and Type of Tasks Should Be Discussed

The term *task*, as used in this book, means a test question or task, problem, or stimulus that requires a response, either from examinees themselves or from observers. In an achievement testing context, *task* usually translates into multiple-choice, true-false, completion, or essay question. The number of items to be used will be a function of the objectives and time available, with higher-order problem solving and reasoning outcomes tending to require more time and to be more difficult than knowledge items. Bill Mehrens and Irv Lehmann (1991) summarized research suggesting that examinees can, on the average,

1. Answer one multiple-choice item every 75 seconds.

2. Answer a short-answer, completion, matching, or true-false item every 50 seconds.

3. Answer six restricted-response essay items (one-half page each) in one hour.

4. Respond to three extended-response essay items (two to three pages) per hour of testing time.

In most achievement assessment situations we do not want speed to be a factor; therefore we use sufficient items to measure the intended objectives that can be answered in the available time. Everyone should have fair and equitable time to finish the assessment. Do not hesitate to spread the assessment over several periods. The assessment will, in most cases, be timed but not speeded. A timed assessment is one for which a specified amount of time is allowed for completion. Usually 90 percent will finish. A speeded assessment is also timed, but speed influences scores because performance is based on number of completed tasks per unit of time. Obviously the more complex the task, the more time needed. The number of tasks per objective used will be a function of the weight given that objective in the table of specifications. Jim Popham (2002) suggests that a minimum of 10 items should be used for each major behavior assessed. Stated another way, each row or column in the table of specifications (see Table 6-2) should start with 10 items. Depending on the importance of the behavior or task, this figure might drop to five or increase to 15 to 20. The number and complexity of the task is also important because of their relationship to reliability. In general, the greater the number of questions there are, the more consistent the measurement is.

### Directions for Administration Need to Be Written

These directions are for both the person administering the assessment and the person taking the assessment. The conditions under which the assessment is to be administered must be specified along with the materials needed, (e.g., special answer sheets, and so on). Is the assessment group or individually administered? Is the assessment a pre-assessment, intermediate, or final exam? What are the time limits? Will a correction formula for guessing be applied? These are some important questions to be addressed about test administration.

### Scoring Criteria Should Be Specified

Each item, task, or question should have performance criteria described. Measurement is, after all, the comparison of "something" against a standard. The pre-specification of scoring criteria is particularly important for items requiring student-constructed responses. The responses can range from a numeral or word to complex and extended answers to essay items. If the task is a performance assessment, a rubric or scoring guide will have to be created and pilot-tested. Developing performance assessment rubrics will be considered in Chapter 10.

## CONSTRUCTING A TABLE OF SPECIFICATIONS

Ordinarily the first step to be taken in developing a measuring instrument would be to review the objectives of this instructional program, both those originally proposed and those actually used. This information basically describes and summarizes what content the examinee has had an opportunity to learn. A convenient way to conduct this review is through the use of a table of specifications (TOS). This table is simply a two-way grid or chart that relates the two major components of an educational objective: the knowledge or content element and the cognitive process outcome element. In addition, the table should contain percentages that reflect the relative emphases given each objective in the instructional situation. An example is presented in Table 6-2.

**Table 6-2** *Sample Abbreviated Table of Specifications for a Course in Educational Assessment Used in Developing a Midsemester Exam*

| Knowledge/ Content Dimension | Remember (BD₁) | | Understand (BD₂) | | Apply (BD₃) | | Analyze (BD₄) | | Total Content Dimension |
|---|---|---|---|---|---|---|---|---|---|
| | Cell # | % | Cell # | % | Cell # | % | Cell # | % | |
| History of Assessment ($C_1$) | (1) | 5 | (8) | | (15) | | (22) | | 5 |
| Uses of Assessment ($C_2$) | (2) | 3 | (9) | 4 | (16) | | (23) | | 7 |
| Assessment Terminology ($C_3$) | (3) | 3 | (10) | 2 | (17) | | (24) | | 5 |
| Planning the Assessment ($C_4$) | (4) | 1 | (11) | 6 | (18) | 3 | (25) | | 10 |
| Constructing Supply-Type Questions ($C_5$) | (5) | 2 | (12) | 11 | (19) | 8 | (26) | 3 | 24 |
| Constructing Selection-Type Questions ($C_6$) | (6) | 4 | (13) | 6 | (20) | 12 | (27) | 7 | 29 |
| Constructing and Scoring Writing Assessments ($C_7$) | (7) | 4 | (14) | 8 | (21) | 5 | (28) | 3 | 20 |
| Total Behavior Dimension | | 22 | | 37 | | 28 | | 13 | 100% |

Note that the process dimension (see Chapter 5) uses the first four categories of the *Revised Taxonomy of Educational Objectives*. There are, obviously, alternative ways of viewing this dimension. The categories selected for a table of specifications are heavily influenced by the student's level and the nature of the subject matter.

In practice the knowledge content categories will be more detailed than those in Table 6-2. The more detail the test blueprint and table of specifications contain, the easier item construction will be. Some compromise between the extremes of objectives—highly specific and highly general—will result in a reasonably balanced assessment.

Having developed a table of specifications, the teacher-evaluator now writes questions or tasks corresponding to each cell in the table. He or she writes a number of independent items in proportion to the representation of each objective in the table. Again, referring to Table 6-2, the teacher writes 5 percent of the items (assuming the use of short-answer varieties) on the midsemester exam to measure the objectives of cell 1, 3 percent of cell 2, and so on. If an instructor is using essay items as a performance assessment, the percentage might reflect the amount of time and scoring weight given to certain tasks, skills, or processes. In this way the evaluator ensures proportionality, or what is referred to as *balance* in the test. Balance is interpreted relative to the amount of time spent on certain topics and skills in class, which in turn reflects the importance of selected objectives.

One frequently encountered problem in constructing a table of specifications is knowing how to operationally allocate weights to the cells in the TOS. Two general approaches are possible. The first involves simply classifying each instructional objective into one of the cells of the TOS (using both dimensions) and then expressing that frequency as a percentage of the total number of objectives. You will have to spend more time on certain objectives than others; therefore, some adjustment in the percent-weights should be made to reflect the varying instructional emphases. A second approach is simply to distribute the percentages for each row total—for example, 5, 7, 5, 10, 10, 24, 29, and 20—over the columns. Connect the percentages to frequencies based on how many questions you are going to have, then cross-multiply the appropriate marginal totals and divide by the grand total to get cell frequencies. For example, in Table 6-2, all 5 percent for History of Testing went to the Remember cell, but only 3 percent of Uses of Assessments went to Remember whereas 4 percent went to Understanding.

*Tables of specification should be shared with students* because what an instructor has done is to condense a unit or course into a simple two-way grid. The percentages allow students to apportion their study time not only by content, but also by what kinds of tasks they will be asked to perform. Some sample test items would also help students prepare for the exam. The exam should have both a pre-test or motivational effect, as well as post-test or instructional effect.

In summary, the use of a table of specifications in test or assessment development will help ensure (a) that only those objectives actually pursued in instruction will be measured, (b) that each objective will receive the appropriate relative emphasis in the test, and (c) that, by using subdivisions based on content and cognitive process, no important objectives will be overlooked or misrepresented.

## ADMINISTRATIVE CONSIDERATIONS

What are the factors that need to be considered as we prepare to administer our instrument?

After deciding which measurement procedures should be used, you must make several important additional decisions. The teacher-evaluator must determine the administration procedures to be followed. If he or she has selected a standardized test, many decisions have already been made. The test manual will contain very detailed directions that must be followed precisely. If the scores are to be legitimately compared with those of the standardized group, an attempt to duplicate the standardization testing conditions must be made.

Controlled administration is just as important to a teacher-made test as to a standardized test. This is particularly true if a teacher anticipates combining the score distributions from several different tests or sections of the same course to arrive at evaluations.

Many factors are involved in conducting an assessment. How the tasks are presented, the preparation of the students, and the actual assessment conditions should be considered. Each student should have a copy of the assessment. Films, oral presentations, slides, and computers have been used to administer assessment with varying degrees of success. The most noteworthy characteristic of these methods, which is both an advantage and a drawback, is the control of presentation. The fixed rate, even if generous, does not allow all students to manifest their natural test-taking behavior or to review questions. The feeling of excessive pressure is not desirable, but concern and involvement in and focused attention on the test-taking task is necessary.

### General Guidelines for Administration

If assessments are to have any meaning, they must be gathered under uniform and optimal conditions. This is particularly true if the intent is to make comparisons between individuals or against an absolute scoring standard. Anyone who ever has been involved in large-scale assessment programs knows the importance of preparation. Administering any group test, particularly a standardized test, is a complex task. To facilitate administration, Prescott prepared a set of guidelines that, although most relevant to standardized tests, can be adapted to classroom tests and assessments as well. Prescott's suggestion that the examiner take the test is a very good one. The guidelines are as follows:[*]

---

**Before the Testing Date**

---

1. Understand nature and purpose of the testing:
    a. Tests to be given.
    b. Reasons for giving tests.

---

[*]From George A. Prescott, *Test Service Bulletin 102, Test Administration Guide.* Formerly issued by the Test Department of Harcourt, Brace, Jovanovich, undated.

2. Decide the number to be tested at one time.

3. Decide the seating arrangements.

4. Decide the exact time of testing.

   a. Avoid day before holiday.

   b. Avoid conflicts with recess of other groups.

   c. Make sure there is ample time.

5. Procure and check test materials:

   a. Directions for administering.

   b. Directions for scoring.

   c. Test booklets:

      (1) One for each student and examiner.

   d. Answer sheets:

      (1) One for each student and examiner.

   e. Pencils (regular or special).

   f. Stopwatch or other suitable timer.

   g. Scoring keys.

   h. "Testing—Do Not Disturb" sign.

   i. Other supplies (scratch paper, and so on).

6. Study test and directions carefully.

   a. Familiarize yourself with

      (1) General test makeup.

      (2) Time limits.

      (3) Directions (e.g., what students are to do about guessing).

      (4) Method of indicating answers.

   b. Take the test yourself.

7. Arrange materials for distribution.

   a. Count number needed.

8. Decide the order in which materials are to be distributed and collected.

9. Decide what students who finish early are to do.

## Just Before Testing

1. Make sure central loudspeaker is disconnected.

2. Put up "Testing—Do Not Disturb" sign.

3. See that desks are cleared.

4. See that pupils have sharpened pencils.

5. Attend to restroom needs of students.

6. Check lighting.

7. Check ventilation.

8. Make seating arrangements.

## During Testing

1. Distribute materials according to predetermined order.

2. Caution students not to begin until you tell them to do so.

3. Make sure that all identifying information is written on booklet or answer sheet.

4. Read directions exactly as given.

5. Give signal to start.

6. Write starting and finishing times on the chalkboard.

7. Move quickly about the room to:

    a. Make sure students are marking answers in the correct place.

    b. Make sure students are continuing to the next page after finishing the previous page.

    c. Make sure students stop at the end of the test.

    d. Replace broken pencils.

    e. Encourage students to keep working until time is called.

    f. Make sure there is no copying.

    g. Attend to students who finish early.

8. Permit no outside interruptions.

9. Stop at the proper time.

## Just After Testing

1. Collect materials according to predetermined order.

2. Count booklets and answer sheets.

3. Make a record of any incidents observed that tend to invalidate scores made by students.

The directions for taking a test or completing an assessment should be as complete, clear, and concise as possible. The student must be made aware of what is expected of him or her. The method of responding should be kept as simple as possible. Reducing the possible mechanical complexities involved in responding is very important for younger students. Instead of using one of the many convenient National Computer Systems, Scantron, or other preprinted answer sheets, the student (to grade 4) can respond in the test booklet. The directions should also contain instructions on guessing. (This problem will be discussed in greater detail in a later section.)

### Criteria for Preparing Directions

Following are some commonsense criteria that you should consider when writing the directions for a test or assessment:

- Assume that all involved are totally "ignorant" about what is to take place.

- In writing the directions, use a clear, succinct style. Be as explicit as possible, but avoid long, drawn-out explanations.

- Emphasize the more important directions and key activities through underlining, italics, or different type size or style.

- Give the examiner and each proctor full instructions on what is to be done before, during, and after the administration.

- Field or pre-test the directions with a sample of both examinees and examiners to identify possible misunderstandings and inconsistencies and gather suggestions for improvement.

- Keep the directions for different forms, subsections, or booklets as uniform as possible.

- Where necessary or helpful, give practice items (or, if possible, tests) before each regular section. This is particularly important when testing the young or those unfamiliar with objective tests or separate answer sheets (e.g., the educationally or culturally disadvantaged, foreign students, or special education students).

Any important assessment (e.g., final exam) should be announced well in advance; do not dangle the threat of a surprise test over the students' heads. Such an "announced test" procedure is more likely to result in effective study.

If possible, practice should be given in taking tests. This is very important if unusual items or ways of asking questions (e.g., analogy items) are to be used. Again, younger students will probably benefit most from this practice.

Obviously, the testing room should be as conducive as possible to concentration on the task at hand. Very little research has been done on the effect of distractions on test results. The results of the few investigations that have been undertaken seem to indicate that absolute quiet may not be as important as one might expect. The same general conclusion has been reached concerning the general physical health of a student at the time of testing. Nevertheless, freedom from distractions and a healthy examinee seem desirable.

Unless an instructor considers time a major factor in learning, achievement tests should be administered in a way that allows all, or nearly all, students enough time to finish. In general, speed of response is not a relevant variable; allowing sufficient time for the test tends to reduce wild guessing and results in a more reliable measure, particularly if one's concern is with relative achievement performance. There are, of course, situations in which speed alone or a combination of speed of response and level of performance is significant.

It is probably a sound idea to arrange items in order of increasing difficulty (actual or estimated). Locating easy items at the beginning of the test, thereby providing success experiences, makes good psychological sense. It is also desirable to group items requiring similar types of responses. Such a grouping tends to allow the students to develop a mental or mechanical set conducive to answering a particular type of item.

## METHODS AND CONTROL OF CHEATING

There is more to test administration than simple distribution and collection of the exam booklets and answer sheets.

Emphasis on "good" classroom and standardized test performances for purposes of assessing school/teacher effectiveness and student progress has brought about an increase in student cheating. A 1997 survey of Who's Who Among American High School Students revealed that 76 percent of the responding students admitted to having cheated at least once. Although copying a spelling word on a test may not be deemed as serious as plagiarizing or buying a term paper, both cheating activities nevertheless reflect the attitude that getting a good grade is worth violating any ethical or moral code. In summarizing his work on the research on correlates of cheating, Cizek (1999) concludes that "Research on correlates of cheating shows that children who break the rules in a maze game, medical students who are dishonest in their care of patients, and employees who admit to stealing office supplies are more likely to cheat on tests and have more lenient attitudes towards tests" (p. 104).

In his definitive book *Cheating on Tests*, Cizek (1999) classifies cheating methods into three major categories. These categories, together with examples, are as follows:

| Category | Examples |
| --- | --- |
| Taking, Giving, or Receiving Information from Others | Copying from another's test paper or answer sheet. Pointing to letters or predetermined locations with laser. Using sign language. |

| | |
|---|---|
| Using Forbidden Materials | Crib sheets (ties, skirts, Band-Aids, watchband, appendage, shoe, "extra blue book tissues"). Writing information on a blank sheet with White Out. Electronic calculator watches for storing data, and Walkmen. |
| Circumventing/Taking Advantage of the Testing Process | Changing answers after grading. Substitute test taker. Not turning in test—claiming teacher lost it. Obtaining extra copy of test. |

Needless to say, a great deal of creativity and effort has gone into creating ways to "cheat the test." Perhaps if that energy had been focused on preparation and study on the part of students, no cheating would have been perceived as necessary. But what is the beleaguered teacher to do? It is probably well to keep in mind the old adage about keeping an open eye and monitoring the ongoing assessment environment. Cizek (1999) has again contributed to our understanding of the problem by delineating the two major methods used to detect cheating. The first, and most prevalent is observation or proctoring. Although potentially unreliable, observation can occasionally yield hard evidence that cheating has taken place (e.g., finding cheat notes, or identifying behavior that might "trigger" further investigation). A second method relies on statistical procedures and the laws of probability. The search for answer patterns among student peers can be accomplished with computer programs, some of which are quite sophisticated. These procedures are more likely to be used with standardized measures than classroom assessments, although a program called Security! is available from Assessment Systems Corporation of St. Paul, Minnesota, for around $400 and can be used with any platform. The data from such statistical analysis are not conclusive, as false positives do occur (saying there was collusion when none occurred between a pair of students). The problem with both observation and statistical methods is that they are applied after the fact. What is needed are procedures that inhibit cheating in the first place.

There exists an obligation to protect those students who have prepared for assessments and have conducted themselves according to moral and ethical codes. Hollinger and Lanza-Kaduce (1996) report that the most frequently used "cheating prevention" strategies they found at the university level were:

- scrambled test forms (81.0 percent)
- using small classes (69.8 percent)
- using multiple proctors (68.4 percent)
- different makeup exams (68.4 percent)

Frequently used approaches that make sense educationally were to provide study guides (54.8 percent) and copies of old exams for review (52.4 percent). Suffice it to say that every school should have an "honor code" that addresses the definition and consequences of cheating.

## SCORING CONSIDERATIONS

Common sense probably yields more helpful suggestions for test scoring than does prolonged discussion. Obviously, responses must be recorded in a convenient form so that scoring can proceed efficiently. If scoring is done by hand, it should be checked. A number of devices and machines using mark-sensing methods of a mechanical, electrical, or optical nature are available to assist in test scoring. Their cost, however, is still beyond the budgets of most schools. Answer keys and scoring rules should be prepared before actual scoring. This is very important if supply questions, particularly extended-response essay questions, are used. (See Chapter 9 for suggestions on scoring essay items.) In addition, it is an excellent idea to have a colleague check the content, phrasing, and keying of the items. If a performance assessment is being used, rubrics or scoring guides should be developed, tried out, and revised as necessary.

### Optical Scanning

The development and application of optical scanning hardware and software, particularly with desktop scanners, has greatly increased the efficiency of information processing, not only in scoring test answer sheets but also in creating information on student schedules and registration, attendance, inventory control, personnel tracking and record keeping, health histories, food service reports, surveys, payroll preparations and financial accounting, and instructional management. A great variety of off-the-shelf forms (full- or half-sheet) are available. Response documents can also be created for a modest cost.

### Developing Hand-Scoring Answer Keys

If standard commercial or separate pre-printed answer documents are to be used, the punch-out overlay scoring template can be applied. These templates are available from most commercial test and answer sheet producers and service organizations. Many teachers, because of the peculiarities of the subject matter, behavior, or examinee involved must develop their own answer documents. Three major types of hand-scoring answer keys—the fan (or accordion), the strip, or the cutout key—can be developed by teachers.

- *Fan key*. This type of key consists of a series of columns, extending from the top to the bottom of the page, on which are recorded acceptable answers or directions scored for the individual items. The key and answer sheet are the same size and are identically spaced. Usually each column corresponds to a page of the test. The key is folded along vertical lines separating its columns and is superimposed on the appropriate page of the test or next to the appropriate column of the answer sheet and matched to the corresponding responses.

- *Strip key.* Similar to the fan key, this method employs separate columns, usually on cardboard.

- *Cutout key.* Windows are cut to reveal letters, numbers, words, or phrases on the answer sheet. The key is superimposed on a page of the test or answer sheet.

In addition to considerations of what kind of key to use, there are two more common problems encountered in making decisions about test scoring that involve the weighting of responses and corrections for guessing.

Teachers often believe—and it seems intuitively reasonable—that differential weighting of items, elements, or alternative answers provides more discriminating measures. To some extent this is true. If differential weights can be identified and applied on the basis of quality of response, difficulty level, or some other basis that is at least logically if not empirically justified, there is a tendency for the weighted items and tests to be more reliable. The difference in the reliabilities of weighted and unweighted items is a generally quite small, especially if the test is initially reliable. If a test is of moderate reliability, differential weighting can slightly increase the consistency of measurement. The scoring task is, of course, thereby made more complex.

For more than 35 years researchers have been investigating whether or not to correct for guessing. There is still no definite answer or argument among academic researchers (not that academic researchers can agree about anything). The main purpose of applying corrections is to discourage dishonest or "wild" guessing by exacting a penalty for it. Guessing's most important effect is not on individual scores, and how high or low they are, but on the reliability of the test. If the test is reliable to begin with, chance success is relatively unimportant and its effects are negligible.

Generally, directions concerning guessing like the following are sufficient: "Answer every item without omissions. Select the alternative you feel is best even though you are not absolutely sure." These directions are preferred not only because the effect of guessing is spread throughout the group, but because we then have a "complete" picture of the performance of all students on all items.

## TEST ANXIETY AND TEST PERFORMANCE

Every time we are evaluated, whether for a driving license or college admission, we have some degree of anxiety. It is natural to be self-protective and want positive assessments by others. Sometimes, especially in educational settings, anxiety can inhibit performance. Test anxiety is generally described as an uncomfortable feeling before, during, or after an examination or evaluation. It has cognitive, affective, and psychological components. In general, the greater the significance of the test results or the greater the importance of the decision to be made on the basis of the test results, the greater the test anxiety is. There are real and meaningful individual differences in test anxiety. Some students respond with memory blocks, others with increased heart rate or sweating. The anxiety can be present during any test (trait) or it can be specific to a particular situation (state). Research suggests that test anxiety might be associated with an aggregate of child-rearing techniques that do not provide the child with emotional support during problem-solving experiences. Whatever the origin, the teacher/test administrator must deal with the possible presence and effects of test anxiety.

The increasing reliance on test scores, particularly standardized test scores, to evaluate student performance and teacher and school effectiveness raises examinee anxiety about performance (Spielberger & Vagg, 1995). Research suggests that test anxiety increases dramatically between grades 3 and 5. The manifestation of test anxiety takes diverse forms, from inhibited memory to a variety of physical complaints such as upset stomach, profuse sweating, elevated blood pressure, and increased pulse. It is not surprising to find students wary of testing occasions, particularly those where significant consequences are associated with score level, (e.g., promotion, graduation, or admissions). After an extensive review of the literature, Wren (2000) concluded that authoritative child-rearing practices, the motive to avoid failure, and learned helplessness have been found to be correlated positively with test anxiety and children's self-efficacy, self-esteem, and achievement level.

In an effort to quantify test anxiety, Wren (2000) has created the *Children's Test Anxiety Scale*. (See box for a copy of the CTAS in its entirety.[*]) The 30 items contain assessments of three variables that have been demonstrated to influence test anxiety:

---

[*]Dr. Wren has agreed to allow use of this copyrighted material by any classroom teacher if results are shared with him. 1561 Tryon Road, Atlanta, GA, 30319.

# CHILDREN'S TEST ANXIETY SCALE

**SAMPLE**—Please read the following statement and decide if it describes the way you are while you are taking tests. If the statement is **almost never** or **never** like you, you should circle **1**. If the statement describes the way you are **some of the time**, circle **2**. If the statement describes the way you are **most of the time**, circle **3**. If the statement is **almost always** or **always** like you, circle **4**.

|  | ALMOST NEVER | SOME OF THE TIME | MOST OF THE TIME | ALMOST ALWAYS |
|---|---|---|---|---|
| **While I am taking tests . . .** |  |  |  |  |
| I think about doing other things | 1 | 2 | 3 | 4 |

The rest of the items describe how some students may think, feel, or act while they are taking tests. Please read each statement carefully and decide if the statement describes how you think, feel, or act during a test. Then circle the answer that best describes the way you are while you are taking a test. If you are not sure which answer to circle, read the statement again before circling your answer. Remember that there are no "right" or "wrong" answers on this survey. Please give truthful answers.

|  | ALMOST NEVER | SOME OF THE TIME | MOST OF THE TIME | ALMOST ALWAYS |
|---|---|---|---|---|
| **While I am taking tests . . .** |  |  |  |  |
| 1. I wonder if I will pass. | 1 | 2 | 3 | 4 |
| 2. My heart beats fast. | 1 | 2 | 3 | 4 |
| 3. I look around the room. | 1 | 2 | 3 | 4 |
| 4. I feel nervous. | 1 | 2 | 3 | 4 |
| 5. I think I am going to get a bad grade. | 1 | 2 | 3 | 4 |
| **While I am taking tests . . .** |  |  |  |  |
| 6. It is hard for me to remember the answers. | 1 | 2 | 3 | 4 |
| 7. I play with my pencil. | 1 | 2 | 3 | 4 |
| 8. My face feels hot. | 1 | 2 | 3 | 4 |
| 9. I worry about failing. | 1 | 2 | 3 | 4 |
| 10. My belly feels funny. | 1 | 2 | 3 | 4 |

Copyright Dr. Douglas G. Wren, Kittredge Elementary School, Atlanta, GA. Used by permission.

| | ALMOST NEVER | SOME OF THE TIME | MOST OF THE TIME | ALMOST ALWAYS |
|---|---|---|---|---|
| **While I am taking tests . . .** | | | | |
| 11. I worry about doing something wrong. | 1 | 2 | 3 | 4 |
| 12. I check the time. | 1 | 2 | 3 | 4 |
| 13. I think about what my grade will be. | 1 | 2 | 3 | 4 |
| 14. I find it hard to sit still. | 1 | 2 | 3 | 4 |
| 15. I wonder if my answers are right. | 1 | 2 | 3 | 4 |

| | ALMOST NEVER | SOME OF THE TIME | MOST OF THE TIME | ALMOST ALWAYS |
|---|---|---|---|---|
| **While I am taking tests . . .** | | | | |
| 16. I think that I should have studied more. | 1 | 2 | 3 | 4 |
| 17. My head hurts. | 1 | 2 | 3 | 4 |
| 18. I look at other people. | 1 | 2 | 3 | 4 |
| 19. I think most of my answers are wrong. | 1 | 2 | 3 | 4 |
| 20. I feel warm. | 1 | 2 | 3 | 4 |

| | ALMOST NEVER | SOME OF THE TIME | MOST OF THE TIME | ALMOST ALWAYS |
|---|---|---|---|---|
| **While I am taking tests . . .** | | | | |
| 21. I worry about how hard the test is. | 1 | 2 | 3 | 4 |
| 22. I try to finish up fast. | 1 | 2 | 3 | 4 |
| 23. My hand shakes. | 1 | 2 | 3 | 4 |
| 24. I think about what will happen if I fail. | 1 | 2 | 3 | 4 |
| 25. I have to go to the bathroom. | 1 | 2 | 3 | 4 |

| | ALMOST NEVER | SOME OF THE TIME | MOST OF THE TIME | ALMOST ALWAYS |
|---|---|---|---|---|
| **While I am taking tests . . .** | | | | |
| 26. I tap my feet. | 1 | 2 | 3 | 4 |
| 27. I think about how poorly I am doing. | 1 | 2 | 3 | 4 |
| 28. I feel scared. | 1 | 2 | 3 | 4 |

| | ALMOST NEVER | SOME OF THE TIME | MOST OF THE TIME | ALMOST ALWAYS |
|---|---|---|---|---|
| 29. I worry about what my parents will say. | 1 | 2 | 3 | 4 |
| 30. I stare. | 1 | 2 | 3 | 4 |

Circle the answers that best describe or tell about you.

1. I am a . . .    boy.    girl.

2. Circle your grade.    3rd    4th    5th    6th

3. I am . . .    Asian.    Black.    White.    Other.

**Thank you for your help!**

- autonomic reaction—"I feel warm"

- behavior tendencies—"I play with my pencil"

- negative thoughts—"I think most of my answers are wrong"

Data from over 230 students revealed a very high coefficient of internal consistency reliability of .92.

After lamenting the fact that grandmothers either become ill or expire at astronomical rates around exam time, John Chivdo (1987) suggests 10 activities that can significantly help reduce test anxiety:

**1.** Review the scope of the exam with the students.

**2.** If practical, use practice tests, and definitely use practice items.

**3.** Emphasize time limits.

**4.** Specify what can and cannot be brought to the exam.

**5.** Review grading procedures and point values.

**6.** Review policies on makeup tests and retakes.

**7.** Provide study help with instructors or form study groups.

**8.** Allow and encourage last-minute questions just before the exam.

**9.** Allow breaks as appropriate for long exams or very young examinees.

**10.** Coach students on test-taking techniques.

The last item, coaching of test-taking skills, is very important, particularly for young test takers. Practice really helps the potential examinee become familiar with the usual testing procedures. Both examinee and examiner must remember that a test is only one sample of behavior and does not represent a microcosm of one's life. Common sense by a test taker can make as important a contribution to preparing a class for testing and reducing test anxiety as any extended technical treatment: answer easy questions first, watch the clock, ask for clarification of questions, get rest before the test, eat a good meal (but not too much), practice filling in answer bubbles on machine-scored tests, and review to make sure you have answered each question. One must be careful about what kind of test preparation practices are used with students. Some are defensible and some are not.

## COACHING AND TEST PERFORMANCE

We have become a test-oriented society! We test for entry into first grade, college, and most professions. We certify the possession of semitechnical and technical skills and all sorts of competencies. Medicine, law enforcement, teaching, and many other careers are influenced by test scores. It is no wonder then that an examination of skills needed to take a test has come under the researchers' psychometric microscope.

The major contribution to the score on any test or assessment is the required knowledge or skill being measured. But other factors can also influence test scores. Among these are experience in taking tests, how to use special answer sheets, the physical testing environment, and the psychological state of the test taker.

*Test-wiseness* is a term sometimes used to describe a whole range of test-taking skills. There are two major types of contributors to test-wiseness. The first is basically examinee-controlled—for example, guessing strategy used, use of testing time, and so on. A second set of elements is controlled by the test constructor—for example, grammatical consistency in items, number of interrelated items, and so on. Both categories of test-wiseness are independent of the examinee's knowledge or academic ability. Test-wiseness is nevertheless a cognitive skill that an examinee can apply to a variety of tests and that can in fact be taught.

With the increased emphasis on test results, many schools are instituting programs aimed at enhancing student test-taking skills. Coaching, usually through the examination of old test items, is a frequently used method to try to improve student test scores and reduce test anxiety. Some research supports the benefits of coaching. Robert Bangert-Downs, James Kulik, and Chen-Lin Kulik (1983) found that for 25 of the 30 studies they reviewed, coaching showed a positive effect on test performance. In the typical study, coaching raised students' scores by 0.25 standard deviations. This effect would increase an average student's score from the 50th to 60th percentile, or by about 2.5 months on a grade-equivalent scale. The more elaborate and broadly based the educational experience—whereby academic skills and knowledge are, in fact, taught, rather than just test-taking skills—the greater the likelihood of score improvements.

Test-taking training programs sometimes address specific test-taking techniques such as guessing and answer changing. Research suggests that, contrary to folklore, if students have some information about what is being tested and can eliminate at least one alternative on a multiple-choice test, they will benefit from guessing. This is because they have ameliorated the probability estimates that were used to establish the correction-for-guessing formulas. Not to be overlooked is test anxiety. Beverly Payne (1984), for example, found significantly greater answer-changing behavior for black middle school students. In addition, black and female eighth-grade students had significantly higher test anxiety scores than did their counterparts. If the coaching and the teaching of test-taking skills only raise scores and do not improve the overall capacity of the student to perform better, then the validity of the test will have been violated.

### Effects of Coaching on College Admissions Tests

Beyond the technical and legal issues involved in using tests for making decisions, there exists an additional problem: the effect of public, private, and commercial coaching and training programs that have been developed to assist students to prepare for college admissions tests. It is very difficult to prepare a student for a particular secure test if training involves primarily examining old test items. If, however, coaching involves a more elaborate and broadly based educational experience whereby academic skills and knowledge are in fact taught, the likelihood of increasing test scores is improved. Such improvement is, however, very modest. A review of the literature by L.W. Pike (1978) revealed inconsistent results for the effect of coaching on both verbal and math tests, specifically the *Scholastic Aptitude Test—Verbal* and *Math*. Simply retaking the test, will, of course, result in some score gain, so that intentional gains or gains derived from coaching should be judged against these kinds of *practice* change scores. A reasonable estimate of overall math gain resulting from a short-term instructional program (e.g., one to six hours) has been found to be around 10 College Entrance Examination Board (CEEB) score units, and for intermediate-term instruction (50 hours), the gains are between 20 and 25 CEEB units (where the mean is 500 and the standard deviation is 100). Comparable results were found for SAT-V coaching programs. Two confounding factors in comparing coaching studies are the initial ability level of the subjects being coached and the similarity of the coaching materials to the criterion measure. The greater this similarity and the longer the period of instruction, the greater the positive impact. This impact, numerically, however, is quite small.

Confirmatory evidence has been reported by D. L. Alderman and Donald Powers (1979). These investigators found, after about 13 hours of instruction, a difference of only 8 CEEB units between the means of coached versus uncoached groups for the SAT-V. A review (Powers, 1993) confirms these findings. Increases, beyond expected growth gains, of 10 points on verbal and 20 points on math were observed. The crucial question here is not whether or not one can increase the scores but whether the increase (a) is worth the time and financial investment, and (b) helps the student perform better in college. The response to both questions is negative. Students might better spend their time being educated rather than coached. Samuel Messick and Ann Jungeblut (1981) have interpreted their extensive review data as suggesting that the student contact time necessary to achieve an average score increases much greater than 20 or 30 points and rapidly approaches that of full-time schooling. If significant gains had been observed, then a real question of test validity might have been raised. If coaching raised only the scores and did not improve the overall capacity of the student to perform better, then the validity of the test would have been destroyed. Because the score increases are small, the validity question is a moot one.

## APPROPRIATE AND INAPPROPRIATE TEST PREPARATION PRACTICES

Teachers always want students to do well on assessments. When those assessments involve external standardized tests applied in making high-stakes decisions (e.g., promotion, scholarships, school accountability, or graduation) maximizing student motivation is a great concern. Increasing numbers of teachers are relying on selected test preparation practices to help their students get ready for the challenge. W. Jimmy Popham (1991) has cautioned us to remember two evaluative standards when preparing students for high-stakes tests:

### ■ Professional Ethics
*No test-preparation practice should violate the ethical standard of the education profession.*

### Educational Defensibility

*No test-preparation practice should increase students' test scores without simultaneously increasing students' mastery of the assessment domain tested.*

Popham further elaborates five typical test preparation practices frequently encountered in the schools, as shown in Table 6-3.

Current form preparation is obviously unethical, whereas varied format preparation allows the student to be prepared for a variety of possible question types. Same and variety formats might be illustrated by language arts instruction where reading is taught by only doing reading, versus an approach where writing activities are incorporated with materials read. The student, for example, might make up a new ending for a story read in class or at home. How do these five preparation practices stack up against the two evaluative criteria? W. J. Popham (2002) presents the summary shown in Table 6-4.

Only preparation practices related to developing general test-taking skills and using a variety of instructional approaches meet both criteria and represent good instructional practice. The considerable reliance being placed on test scores puts pressure on teachers to make sure that their students do well. This goal can be attained by following accepted professional educational practice.

## TECHNOLOGY AND ASSESSMENT

We live in an age of technology, so it is not surprising that many of the mechanical tasks involved in test development, assembly, administration, scoring, and reporting can be handled very efficiently by computer.

**Table 6-3**  *Five Typical Test Preparation Practices*

| Type of Preparation | Example |
| --- | --- |
| Previous Form | An older form of the *Jefferson Law Enforcement Test* is used by a training officer to get cadets ready to take the state certification exam |
| Current Form | Actual items from the current form of the above test are used for practice |
| Generalized Test-Taking | Examinees are introduced to "test-wiseness" skills—for example, when to guess or when not to guess |
| Same Format | The same content is covered in preparation as is on the test, but only the same format as the test used is included in the practice |
| Varied Format | A variety of instructional and test formats are used, thus preparing the student for any assessment |

Computers have changed the lives of professionals and laypersons alike. Massive amounts of data can be accessed and processed to support development and decision making. Computer applications in educational measurement have the potential to drastically change the ways we create, assemble, administer, analyze, report, and interpret test results. It may be that simply the availability of a personal computer and word-processing and graphics software will turn out to be the greatest boon ever for the teacher-tester. Tests can be easily created, corrected, and printed. Computerized measurement systems can significantly facilitate the use of test data to serve education.

In their 1994 Board of Trustees' public accountability report, the Educational Testing Service noted seven reasons why computer-administered tests are proving to be popular, particularly with colleges and professional organizations and agencies involved with licensure and certification. These tests:

- Make it possible for students to schedule tests at their convenience, rather than limiting testing to a few unmovable dates.

- Can be taken in a more comfortable setting and with fewer people than in large, paper-and-pencil administrations.

- Allow faster score reporting. In some cases test takers can get the results as soon as they finish, compared with the four to six weeks that is usual for a national test.

- Permit sending scores electronically to colleges, schools, or licensing agencies.

- Offer a wider range of questions and test content. Computers have the capacity to provide simulations of real-life situations, three-dimensional graphics, voice-activated responses, on-screen calculators, and split screens

**Table 6-4**  *Preparation Practices versus Evaluative Criteria*

| Preparation Practice | Meets Professional Ethics Standard | Meets Educational Defensibility Standard |
|---|---|---|
| Previous Form | No | No |
| Current Form | No | No |
| Generalized Test-Taking | Yes | Yes |
| Same Format | Yes | No |
| Varied Format | Yes | Yes |

that show reading passages and questions at the same time, to name only a few of the possibilities.

- Improve the link between instruction and assessment by providing a profile of the strengths and weaknesses in students' performance in ways that can be helpful to both students and teachers.

- Save time by matching questions, and the order in which those questions are presented, to the ability of each test taker. Time isn't wasted on questions that are too easy or too hard, and tests that once took four or five hours may take only two or three.

Paper and pencils may be on their way out.

C. Victor Bunderson, Dillon Inouye, and James Olsen (1989) have described four "generations" of applications of computer technology. These applications are summarized in Table 6-5. Computerized testing (CT) is very prevalent today, particularly for test scoring. Collecting large item pools (including the necessary supporting graphics) and item banks provides the opportunity to create tests efficiently. Eventually there may be a computer on every teacher's desk to assist assembly and also to help deal with the paper blizzard that threatens to engulf us all. Computers have been used in test scoring for several decades and have more than realized their potential. Test administration can be more uniformly controlled through computer technology, and testing time is in fact reduced. A recently reported summary of the equivalence of computerized and paper-and-pencil aptitude tests showed a high degree of correspondence of results (Mead & Drasgow, 1993).

Computerized adaptive testing (CAT) has also been described as tailored or customized testing because the examinee's path through a set of

**Table 6-5** *Applications of Computer Technology in Educational Measurement*

| Category | Measurement Applications |
|---|---|
| Computerized Testing (CT) | Assembly |
| | Administration |
| | Scoring |
| | Reporting |
| Computer Adaptive Testing (CAT) | Modification of administration on basis of examinee responses |
| Continuous Measurement (CM) | Measurements embedded in curriculum dynamically monitor examinee progress |
| Intelligent Measurement (IM) | Data bases are used to create test interpretations |

Source: After Bunderson, Inouye, & Olsen, 1989.

tasks is determined by performance, response time, or both. In a real sense, each test is individualized. CAT is based on a psychometric theory called *item response theory*, which assumes that the likelihood of answering an item correctly is a function of examinee ability, guessing, item difficulty, and item discrimination. Testing time is significantly reduced through CAT.

The development of continuous measurement (CM) parallels that of computer-assisted instruction. The difference lies in the interaction of measurement and the treatment. Actual instructional decisions are assisted through test data use. Developing CM systems requires considerable expense and time for calibrating tests and instructional materials.

Intelligent measurement (IM) captures the knowledge of experts to create interpretation or prescriptive advice. Combinations of scores and data about the examinee are collected in an individualized but "standard" printout. Applications can be found in academic and vocational counseling, individually administered personality or intelligence tests, and tutoring. Theories of learning or personality can be incorporated into IM systems.

**Computer-Generated Interpretations**

With increasing frequency, test publishers and computer software vendors are making available programs that will "create" interpretations of test scores. Programs can be purchased separately or as part of the reporting service packages offered by the publisher. Intelligent measurement was previously referred to as test interpretation, in which extensive databases are combined with on-file expert judgment to generate representative printed narratives for different levels of performance and combinations of scores. These computer-generated narratives are available for measures in the affective domain (personality and interests) as well as in the cognitive domain (achievement, aptitude, and intelligence). The diagnostic use of the computer interpretations of such personality inventories as the *Minnesota Multiphasic Personality Inventory* is prevalent with clinicians. Figure 6-2 contains a sample individual student analysis of a hypothetical performance on Form J of the Intermediate 1 level of the *Stanford Achievement Test*. In addition to raw and standard scores, national grade percentile bands reflecting the "confidence range" for scores are presented (plus and minus one standard error of measurement). Also of interest are the Achievement/Ability Comparison (AAC) ranges. The AAC shows how well, within limits, a student has performed on a particular subtest or total score as predicted by the student's total score on the *Otis-Lennon School Ability Test*. Our hypothetical student is apparently not performing up to expectations because 13 of 19 SAT performances were below that which would have been projected on the basis of the *Otis-Lennon School Ability Test*. The

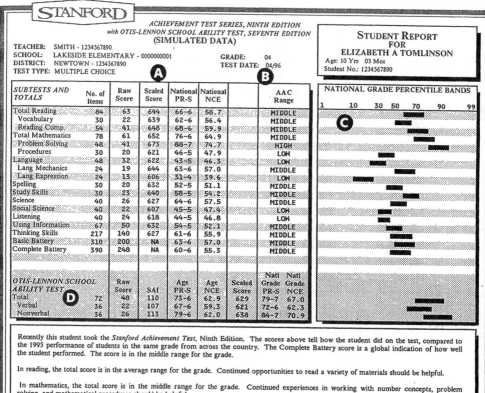

**STANFORD**

*ACHIEVEMENT TEST SERIES, NINTH EDITION*
*with OTIS-LENNON SCHOOL ABILITY TEST, SEVENTH EDITION*
**(SIMULATED DATA)**

TEACHER: SMITH - 1234567890
SCHOOL: LAKESIDE ELEMENTARY - 0000000001
DISTRICT: NEWTOWN - 1234567890
TEST TYPE: MULTIPLE CHOICE

GRADE: 04
TEST DATE: 04/96

**STUDENT REPORT FOR ELIZABETH A TOMLINSON**
Age: 10 Yrs 03 Mos
Student No.: 1234567890

| SUBTESTS AND TOTALS | No. of Items | Raw Score | Scaled Score | National PR-S | National NCE | AAC Range |
|---|---|---|---|---|---|---|
| Total Reading | 84 | 63 | 644 | 66-6 | 58.7 | MIDDLE |
| Vocabulary | 30 | 22 | 639 | 62-6 | 56.4 | MIDDLE |
| Reading Comp. | 54 | 41 | 648 | 68-6 | 59.9 | MIDDLE |
| Total Mathematics | 78 | 61 | 652 | 76-6 | 64.9 | MIDDLE |
| Problem Solving | 48 | 41 | 673 | 88-7 | 74.7 | HIGH |
| Procedures | 30 | 20 | 621 | 46-5 | 47.9 | LOW |
| Language | 48 | 32 | 622 | 43-5 | 46.3 | LOW |
| Lang Mechanics | 24 | 19 | 644 | 63-6 | 57.0 | MIDDLE |
| Lang Expression | 24 | 13 | 606 | 31-4 | 39.6 | LOW |
| Spelling | 30 | 20 | 632 | 52-5 | 51.1 | MIDDLE |
| Study Skills | 30 | 23 | 640 | 58-5 | 54.2 | MIDDLE |
| Science | 40 | 26 | 627 | 64-6 | 57.5 | MIDDLE |
| Social Science | 40 | 22 | 607 | 45-5 | 47.4 | LOW |
| Listening | 40 | 24 | 618 | 44-5 | 46.8 | LOW |
| Using Information | 67 | 50 | 632 | 54-5 | 52.1 | MIDDLE |
| Thinking Skills | 217 | 140 | 627 | 61-6 | 55.9 | MIDDLE |
| Basic Battery | 310 | 200 | NA | 63-6 | 57.0 | MIDDLE |
| Complete Battery | 390 | 248 | NA | 60-6 | 55.3 | MIDDLE |

NATIONAL GRADE PERCENTILE BANDS
1  10  30  50  70  90  99

| OTIS-LENNON SCHOOL ABILITY TEST | | Raw Score | SAI | Age PR-S | Age NCE | Scaled Score | Natl Grade PR-S | Natl Grade NCE |
|---|---|---|---|---|---|---|---|---|
| Total | 72 | 48 | 110 | 73-6 | 62.9 | 629 | 79-7 | 67.0 |
| Verbal | 36 | 22 | 107 | 67-6 | 59.3 | 621 | 72-6 | 62.3 |
| Nonverbal | 36 | 26 | 113 | 79-6 | 62.0 | 638 | 84-7 | 70.9 |

Recently this student took the *Stanford Achievement Test*, Ninth Edition. The scores above tell how the student did on the test, compared to the 1995 performance of students in the same grade from across the country. The Complete Battery score is a global indication of how well the student performed. The score is in the middle range for the grade.

In reading, the total score is in the average range for the grade. Continued opportunities to read a variety of materials should be helpful.

In mathematics, the total score is in the middle range for the grade. Continued experiences in working with number concepts, problem solving, and mathematical procedures should be helpful.

Performance on the language subtests was in the average range for the grade. Scores on Spelling and Study Skills subtests are also in the average range.

The Science and Social Science subtest scores are in the middle range for the grade. The student's understanding of the concepts in these two areas should continue to develop with future instruction.

Performance on the Listening subtest was within the middle range for this grade, indicating that the student can process information that is heard about as well as the typical student in the grade. ·

The *Otis-Lennon School Ability Test* (OLSAT) measures the student's ability to cope with school-learning tasks in verbal and nonverbal areas. The total score is the best overall indicator of that school-learning ability. The AAC (Achievement/Ability Comparison) describes how a student performed on Stanford relative to other students with similar OLSAT scores. The AAC is High (H) if the Stanford score is among the highest of the scores earned by students of the same measured ability; the AAC is Middle (M) if the Stanford scores is in the middle range of scores; the AAC is Low (L) if the Stanford score is among the lowest of the scores.

It is important to keep in mind that test scores give only one picture of how a student is doing in school and that many things can affect a student's test scores. Therefore it is important to consider other kinds of information as well. The school has more detailed information about how the student is doing.

**Figure 6-2** Computer-generated test interpretation for Stanford Achievement Test: *Ninth Edition. Level/Form: Intermediate/1/S. 1995 Norms-Spring. OLSAT Level/Form: E/3. Copyright © 1996 by Harcourt, Inc. Reproduced by permission. All rights reserved.*

narrative is based on accumulated experience with the test and student performances.

The computer can only do the operator's bidding: it is only as smart as we make it. Test development is a human activity, and to attempt to remove the human element would detract from the meaningfulness of the results of the activity. It is hard work, but it can be rewarding to both test developer and test taker.

Getting ready to test takes almost as much time as building the test (almost). Good planning will make the test not only easier, but also more meaningful to both teacher and student. Several important measurement issues were discussed in this chapter. Among these were: (a) How should I weigh and balance different content and process outcomes in my test blueprint? (b) How many items of what type can I use? (c) How should the directions for a test be stated? (d) What alternate modes of test administration are currently available? and (e) What should I do about the problem of guessing? If it's worth doing, it's worth doing right!

# CASE STUDY

The availability of objectives for the Reading Education exam (see Chapter 5) now allows us to create a table of specifications (TOS) for the midterm exam. The central problem to be addressed is what weights should be assigned to the cells of the TOS. One starting point is the amount of instructional time devoted to topics. Following is a summary of these data.

| Content area (Goals) | Class Time | Expected Relative Weights for Each Content Area | Actual Weight |
|---|---|---|---|
| Reflection on the reading process and beliefs about teaching reading | 4.5 hours | 13.00% | 14.00% |
| Emerging literacy | 6 hours | 17.00% | 20.00% |
| Language experience Activity (LEA) | 3 hours | 8.50% | 6.00% |
| Decoding strategies | 6 hours | 17.00% | 19.00% |

| Content area (Goals) | Class Time | Expected Relative Weights for Each Content Area | Actual Weight |
|---|---|---|---|
| Comprehension strategies | 1.5 hours | 4.30% | 5.00% |
| Discussion strategies | 1.5 hours | 4.30% | 4.00% |
| Basal reading lessons | 8 hours | 23.00% | 17.00% |
| Reading program and exceptional children | 1.5 hours | 4.30% | 5.00% |
| Reading program and bilingual learners | 1.5 hours | 4.30% | 4.00% |
| Evaluation | 1.5 hours | 4.30% | 6.00% |
| TOTAL | 35 hours | | |

After instruction took place the weights were adjusted to reflect the *actual* amount of time spent on each topic. The intended and actual weights are quite close.

The next decision relates to what kind and how much emphasis should be placed on the behaviors measured by the items. It was felt that 80 items would be sufficient for a 100-minute class period, and that the following weights should be placed on the respective behavioral outcomes:

| Behavioral Outcome | Weight |
|---|---|
| Knowledge | 65.00% |
| Comprehension | 25.00% |
| Application | 9.00% |
| Analysis | 1.00% |

The emphasis was on knowledge and comprehension outcomes because (a) the exam was a midterm and therefore concerned with "foundation" information, and (b) application outcomes were dealt with in the field-setting classrooms during the second half of the course.

With this available information create a TOS indicating the number of items in each cell. In addition, write a set of examinee directions for taking the test that would be in the test booklet. Remember one approach is to set the marginal totals in a behavioral outcome by content area table

$(4 \times 10)$. Multiplying the row by the appropriate column totals will give the expected cell entries without rounding error.

Create a set of directions for administration that details general procedural elements such as (a) distribution of testing materials, (b) how the answer sheet should be marked, (c) whether or not students may mark in the test booklets if they wish, (d) what the student should do about guessing, (e) the amount of time available, and (f) the different weighting or importance of parts of the test (if applicable). Student names are entered on both booklet and answer sheet. Social security numbers might be used in lieu of names to facilitate creating an instructor test score data file and for purposes of recording and reporting results.

## CONTENT REVIEW STATEMENTS

1. In planning the development of an assessment device, consider the following:
   a. type of measuring procedure used
   b. length of the instrument
   c. range of difficulty of items
   d. time limits
   e. objectives to be sampled
   f. arrangement of items
   g. scoring procedures
   h. method of recording and reporting results

2. The most important decision to be made during test development is what to measure.

3. Developing a table of specifications (a two-way grid contrasting content and behavioral outcomes) can greatly facilitate both the instructional process and the test development process.

4. The *Revised Taxonomy of Educational Objectives* provides very useful categories to help the tester develop a table of specifications.

5. Cheating on tests usually takes the form of one of the following:
   a. taking, giving, or receiving information from others
   b. using forbidden materials
   c. circumventing or taking advantage of the testing process

6. The most practical methods of controlling cheating on tests is to:
   a. proctor and monitor closely
   b. use scrambled forms

7. Test anxiety may manifest itself physiologically or psychologically.

8. The types of outcomes measured are not readily apparent from the format of the measurement procedure used.

9. Carefully controlled conditions should prevail when administering a test, particularly a standardized test.

10. The directions for taking a test should be as clear and concise as possible.

11. Great care needs to be taken in specifying test-scoring procedures.

12. Optical scanning is the most efficient method of collecting objective test responses in public schools.

13. Teachers can use fan, strip, or cutout keys in test scoring.

14. If all individuals attempt all items, a correction for guessing on objective tests is probably not needed.

15. The greater the variety of outcomes measured and the more frequent the measurement, the greater the reliability of the assessment will be.

16. The results of all tests should be discussed with individual students and the entire class.

17. The teacher should give students samples of the questions he or she will ask on tests and should allow practice on them to reduce test anxiety and make possible a fairer sampling of behavior.

18. Achieving a passing score by chance on a reliable classroom test is extremely unlikely.

19. The differential weighting of response alternatives on a multiple-choice exam rarely improves its measuring capacity.

20. Test-wiseness can interfere with what is being measured.

21. The effects of coaching on college admissions tests are probably not worth the effort or expense.

22. Test anxiety can be decreased by working with the examinee on the purposes and procedures of test taking.

**23.** Computer-generated test interpretations should be considered with caution.

**24.** Computer applications in test development include test

    a. assembly

    b. administration

    c. scoring

    d. analysis

    e. reporting or interpreting

**15.** Test preparation practices must be both professionally ethical and educationally defensible.

## SPECULATIONS

**1.** To correct-for-guessing or not to correct-for-guessing, that is the question. What is the answer?

**2.** Why is a table of specifications important in test development?

**3.** Describe some applications of computers in testing.

**4.** What are some ways in which arranging items in different ways within a test could influence performance?

**5.** Describe the optimal conditions under which either standardized or nonstandardized tests should be administered.

**6.** What testing conditions are best for you?

**7.** Is the differential weighting of (a) item alternatives or (b) items justified? Why?

**8.** Do you think the directions for taking a test are really all that important? In what way?

**9.** How do you personally deal with test anxiety? What can teachers do about test anxiety?

**10.** In what way might the results of the research on the effects of coaching influence your test-taking behavior?

**11.** What are some unethical and unprofessional test preparation practices?

**12.** What are three practical ways to control for potential cheating in classroom tests?

## Suggested Readings

Antes, R. L. (1989). *Preparing students for taking tests.* Bloomington, IN: Phi Delta Kappa. Contains advice on test-taking strategies for both standardized and teacher-made tests, and ways of dealing with test anxiety.

Drasgow, F., & Olson-Buchanan, J. B. (Eds.). (1999). *Innovations in computerized assessment.* Mahwah, NJ: Lawrence Erlbaum.

Fuchs, D., & Fuchs, L. S. (1986). Test procedure bias: A meta-analysis of examiner familiarity effects. *Review of Educational Research, 56*(2), 243–262. An analysis of 22 studies involving 1,489 subjects revealed high scores for students where the examiner was familiar and when subjects were of low socioeconomic status.

Linn, R. L. (Ed.). (1989). *Educational measurement* (3rd ed.). Washington, DC: American Council on Education and Macmillan. The following chapters represent current thought on the topics of this chapter: Chapter 8, "The Specifications and Development of Tests of Achievement and Ability," by Jason Millman and Jennifer Greene; Chapter 9, "The Four Generations of Computerized Educational Measurement," by C. Victor Bunderson, Dillon K. Inouye, and James B. Olsen; Chapter 10, "Computer Technology in Test Construction and Processing," by Frank B. Baker; and Chapter 12, "Designing Tests That Are Integrated with Instruction," by Anthony J. Nitko.

Woodtke, K. H., Harper, F., Schommer, M., & Brunelli, P. (1989). How standardized is school testing? An exploratory observational study of standardized group testing in kindergarten. *Educational Evaluation and Policy Analysis, 11*(3), 223–235.

# PART Three

# Creating Traditional Assessments

*Beverly's Journal* _____

Even after all these years I still can't believe that writing assessment questions doesn't get any easier. I guess because content changes, students are different, and since I teach differently than I used to I need to think of new ways to ask about new ideas. It's a lot of work! I see why my colleagues do so much sharing. It's amazing how often when we answer each other's questions we get things tripped up. But the best tripper-uppers are the students. You have to listen to what they say—they can really help you improve your tests.

Essay questions are really tough. You don't want to give the answer away but you want the student to think and have an opportunity to create his or her own personal response.

# 7

# The Development of Traditional Assessment Tasks

---

## FOCUS CONCEPTS AND KEY TERMS FOR STUDY

| | |
|---|---|
| **Constant Alternative (T-F) Questions** | **Selection (Multiple-Choice) Questions** |
| **Interrelated Questions** | **Specific Determiners** |
| **Matching Exercises** | **Supply/Completion Questions** |
| **Problem Solving** | |

---

# STANDARDS ALERT

### Standard 3.7          Format Relevance

The type of items, response formats, scoring procedures, and test administration procedures should be selected based on the purposes of the test, the domain to be measured, and the intended test takers. To the extent possible, test content should be chosen to ensure that intended inferences from test scores are equally valid for members of different groups of test takers. The test review process should include empirical analyses and, when appropriate, the use of expert judges to review items and response formats. The qualifications, relevant experiences, and demographic characteristics of expert judges should also be documented.

### Taking It to the Classroom

Fellow teachers, particularly if members of a minority group, can be invaluable evaluators of question appropriateness and relevance.

---

Reprinted with permission from the *Standards for Educational and Psychological Testing*. Copyright © 1999 by the American Educational Research Association, the American Psychological Association, and the National Council on Measurement in Education.

Consider the following assessment tasks.

---

## Language

---

"A man is coming down the hill; he is old; he is weak; he is ragged. The hill is steep; it is stony; it is slippery. The old man stumbles; he struggles; he falls; he does not rise; he is hurt."

- Retell this story in your own words.
- Write a story regarding the old man.

---

## Arithmetic

---

- What will 412 horses cost at 1/8 of $1,000 each?
- How much will 12 1/6 acres of land cost at $57.50 per acre?

---

## Geography

---

- Explain the value of commerce.
- Mention some proofs that the earth is round.

---

## General

---

- What is meant by "rotation of crops"?
- Mention the rulers of the European countries engaged in war.

---

These questions were taken from the statewide fall sixth-grade assessment mandated in the state of Michigan in 1914 (Research Concepts, 1978). Several things are suggested by the questions. How well would today's sixth-graders do with these questions? Obviously there was a heavy memory load although application skills were also required. Students had to construct their responses, and of course we still use supply and completion items. If alternative answers were provided for the student and selections were made among the alternatives we would have contemporary multiple-choice items. *No matter how much education changes, things tend to stay the same.* At least the good practices that work tend to be retained over time.

As opposed to a great deal of modern assessment, traditional measurement tends to rely on structured items, and teachers do a pretty good job of preparing them. McMorris and Boothroyd (1993) found only about 35 percent of teacher-made completion items and 25 percent of multiple-choice items were faulty. They also found in a survey of math and science teachers that 33 percent of the items they constructed were multiple-choice and 19 percent computation. One unfortunate additional finding was a mean score of about 50 percent on a competency test of measurement principles.

Effective educational assessment will result from planning, imaginative and skillful question writing, careful formulation of questions into a total test, and fair, proper administration and scoring. Effectiveness also depends on the quality of instruction preceding assessment and on the intelligent subsequent interpretation and use of scores. It was noted in previous chapters that planning, whose importance is often underestimated, involves decisions about learning outcomes, the contexts in which they are most likely to be demonstrated, and the kinds of stimuli necessary or likely to elicit them. Question or item writing would follow logically from the test development sequence outlined above, and—make no mistake—it is a difficult and time-consuming task. We do, however, make very important decisions about curricula, students, programs, and institutions on the basis of assessments that we have prepared. Therefore, maximum efforts are required. What follows are idealized guidelines. Don't be intimidated by them. Use them as standards along with common sense in writing questions.

Question writers need to keep one major principle in mind: the question needs to match the intent (objective). The previously discussed characteristic of *relevance* is of paramount concern. Do not forget that the kinds of tests we construct not only reflect on our teaching but can and do influence it. How we test, for example, will influence how students study.

The writing of test questions, items, or exercises basically involves finding the most suitable manner in which to pose problems to students. Sometimes this can result in some interesting challenges, as seen in the examples in Table 7-1. Such problems may involve the recall of learned

**Table 7-1** *Creative Measurement Approaches from America's Campuses*

HISTORY: Describe the history of the papacy from its origins to the present day, concentrating especially, but not exclusively, on it social, political, economic, religious, and philosophical aspects and impact on Europe, Asia, America, and Africa. Be brief, concise, and specific.

MEDICINE: You have been provided with a razor blade, a piece of gauze, and a bottle of Scotch. Remove your appendix. Do not suture your work until it has been inspected. You have 15 minutes.

PUBLIC SPEAKING: 2,600 riot-crazed aborigines are storming the test room. Calm them. You may use any ancient language except Latin or Greek.

MUSIC: Write a piano concerto. Orchestrate and perform it with flute and drum. You will find a piano under your chair.

EDUCATION: Develop a foolproof and inexpensive system of education that will meet the needs of all segments of society. Convince both the faculty and rioting students outside to accept it. Limit yourself to the vocabulary found in the Dick and Jane Reading Series.

PSYCHOLOGY: Based on your knowledge of their works, evaluate the emotional stability, degree of adjustment, and repressed frustrations of the following: Alexander of Aphrodisias, Rame-

ses II, Gregory of Nyssa, and Hammurabi. Support your evaluations with quotations from each man's works, making appropriate references. It is not necessary to translate.

SOCIOLOGY: Estimate the sociological problems that might accompany the end of the world. Construct an experiment to test your theory.

BIOLOGY: Create life. Estimate the differences in subsequent human culture if this form of life had been developed 500 million years ago, with special attention to the probable effect on the English parliamentary system. Prove your thesis.

ENGINEERING: The disassembled parts of a high-powered rifle have been placed in a box on your desk. You will also find an instruction manual printed in Swahili. In 10 minutes a hungry Bengal tiger will be admitted to the room. Take whatever action you feel appropriate. Be prepared to justify your decision.

POLITICAL SCIENCE: There is a red telephone on your desk. Start World War III. Report at length on its sociopolitical effects, if any.

EPISTEMOLOGY: Take a position for or against truth. Prove the validity of your position.

GENERAL KNOWLEDGE: Describe in detail your general knowledge. Be objective and specific.

Reprinted from "Capital M," a publication of MENSA.

information or the use of some higher-order mental abilities. This chapter contains guidelines and suggestions that have been found useful in constructing a variety of question types, ranging from completion to matching. The supply (student/respondent constructs response/answers) items examined will be simple direct questions and completion items. The selection items (choice among alternatives) discussed will be of the true-false, multiple-choice, and matching varieties. The essay question is considered by some experts to fall in the "supply" category, and a distinction is sometimes made between extended-response and restricted-response supply questions. We are here considering only the short-answer (e.g., a single word, phrase, or sentence) supply item. Essay or extended free-response items and large-scale writing assessment will be considered in Chapter 8.

Historically, supply items have been referred to as "recall" or short-answer items and selection items as "recognition" items. The distinction may not be warranted, implying as it does that we are only measuring qualitative differences in memory.

We refer here only to the *form in which the response* to a test question is to be made. The student either constructs her or his own response or identifies the correct answer in a list of alternatives. The instructional objective being measured (ability) depends upon the content and structure of the item itself, rather than on the form of the response. There are some data in the literature of experimental psychology which suggest that tests of recognition yield higher scores than tests of recall. If we can accept length of retention as a criterion of success, however, we also have evidence that recall and recognition activities are very highly correlated. Thus supply and selection items can measure related behavior, and the decision about the type to use may be dictated by such practical considerations as ease of scoring.

## PRELIMINARY CONSIDERATIONS

By way of preview, let us point out five principles that need to be considered as one prepares to construct items:

1. Adequate provision should be made for measuring all of the important outcomes of instruction.

2. The test and its items should reflect the approximate emphases given various objectives in the course.

3. The nature of the test and its items must take into account the nature of the group to be examined.

4. The nature of the test and its items must take into consideration the conditions under which the test is to be administered.

5. The nature of the test and its items must take into consideration the purpose it is to serve.

Implicit in these principles are several prerequisites for sound item construction. The first and probably most obvious prerequisite is competence in the subject matter to be examined. The test constructor should be a scholar in the broadest and finest sense of the word. The teacher-test constructor must have a grasp of the basic principles and knowledges, as well as the common fallacies.

Command of the subject matter is a necessary but not sufficient condition for writing effective questions, however. The test constructor must also possess skill in item writing. The item writer must be aware of the various ways in which questions can be asked and the kinds of objectives for which each is best suited. Some of these knowledges may be acquired in courses in test construction or from the references listed at the end of this chapter. The best approach is, of course, a combination of formal study and experience. One must actually write many items of various types and try them out with students before one can develop skill and perspective on the relative advantages and disadvantages of the various question forms.

An integral aspect of item-writing skill is, of course, mastery of verbal and written communication skills. The item writer must be able to apply the rules of grammar and rhetoric. Test items are probably read more closely than any other type of nonlegal written communication.

If item construction and test development do not proceed from a rational and well-developed philosophy of education, the resulting items are likely to treat only superficial aspects of instruction. The resulting test would be of variable quality. The specification of defensible instructional objectives is of paramount importance in test construction.

Finally, the item writer must be a kind of educational and developmental psychologist. Test constructors must possess knowledge of how students learn, think, and develop. Such knowledge of individual differences will allow them to accomplish an optimal matching of test questions and students. One would not, for example, use analogy items with third-grade students, because this mechanically contrived way of asking questions does not correspond to the way in which we teach at this level. Moreover, students are unfamiliar with the form. We do not want the mechanics of responding to the question to interfere with what it is we are trying to find out.

Let us now turn our attention to some guidelines for writing items. Many of the suggestions in the remainder of this chapter will be considered common sense. But, unfortunately, the application of commonsense principles in test development is often found wanting. If we can underscore the importance of common sense in item writing, we will have made a worthwhile contribution.

## GENERAL GUIDELINES FOR QUESTION WRITING

Before considering specific item types, it is profitable to consider some general principles applicable to all short-answer items:

1. *Avoid using items which, in terms of either content or structure, could be considered obvious, trivial, meaningless, or ambiguous.* If a test developer does not rely heavily upon a table of specifications to guide item and test development, these types of unsatisfactory items may result.

**2.** *Follow the rules of punctuation, grammar, and rhetoric.* Again, the importance of command of language and expressive skills in item development is emphasized.

**3.** *Use items that have a "right" or "definitely correct" answer, or at least an answer upon which experts agree.* This item characteristic was described in Chapter 1 as "objectivity."

**4.** *Avoid items that rely on obscure or esoteric language.* Unless one's intent is to test vocabulary, it is not desirable to elicit responses whose correctness depends upon size of vocabulary or reading ability. If key words are obscure, even the better students will fail to give them sufficient attention, and the items may become "trick" or "catch" questions.

**5.** *Avoid interrelated items.* This situation arises when the content of one item (e.g., the stem or alternatives in a multiple-choice item) furnishes the answer to other items. Inasmuch as we frequently test the same content area a number of times, it is difficult to avoid interrelated items, and only very careful inspection of the test will reveal them.

**6.** *Avoid items containing "irrelevant cues."* Irrelevant cues probably constitute the chief fault of most classroom tests. Irrelevant cues are a class of defects that leads a student to the correct answer independent of knowledge or skill. Such defects may take the form of grammatical clues, word associations or definitions, a systematic difference in the correct answer, or stereotyped language, to name only a few. The type of cue will vary with the type of item. A test that contains a large number of items with irrelevant cues is probably measuring nothing more than test-wiseness or intelligent test-taking behavior.

A general checklist of questions relating to the quality of item content and structure is presented in Table 7-2. It is based on material originally created by Dr. Harold Bligh, former managing editor of the Test Division of Harcourt, Brace, and World, Inc.

## WRITING SUPPLY AND COMPLETION QUESTIONS

Let us now turn our attention to specific item types and guidelines for their construction. Many of the suggestions for certain item types are applicable to the other types as well, and the suggestions given here were selected on the basis of practical applicability.

Supply items are generally of two types: simple direct questions (e.g., Who was the first American astronaut to fly in space?) and completion items (e.g., The name of the first American astronaut to fly in space was

**Table 7-2**  *Checklist of Achievement Item Writing Principles*

| Item Content | Yes | No |
|---|---|---|
| 1. Does item deal with content of sufficient importance and significance? | ___ | ___ |
| 2. Are various cognitive outcomes measured? | ___ | ___ |
| 3. Is content too specific? | ___ | ___ |
| 4. Is item content up-to-date? | ___ | ___ |
| 5. Is content unambiguous so that student does not have to make unwarranted interpretations? | ___ | ___ |
| 6. Are items grouped by content? | ___ | ___ |
| 7. Is content appropriate for grade and ability level? | ___ | ___ |
| 8. Are vocabulary and readability levels appropriate for examinees? | ___ | ___ |

| Item Structure | | |
|---|---|---|
| 9. Is problem statement clearly expressed? | ___ | ___ |
| 10. Is test free from interrelated items (items give answer to other items)? | ___ | ___ |
| 11. Is best question format used for given objective? | ___ | ___ |
| 12. Is item free from ambiguous wording? | ___ | ___ |
| 13. Is item free from irrelevant cues? | ___ | ___ |
| 14. Can answers to questions be objectively scored? | ___ | ___ |
| 15. Are multiple-choice answers mutually exclusive? | ___ | ___ |
| 16. Are multiple-choice answers plausible? | ___ | ___ |
| 17. Are multiple-choice answers grammatically parallel? | ___ | ___ |
| 18. Are multiple-choice answers of comparable length? | ___ | ___ |
| 19. Is test free from trick or catch questions? | ___ | ___ |

_____.). The chief advantage of the supply item is that it minimizes the effect of guessing. Because the student is required to construct his or her own response, supply items constitute one of the best ways of measuring objectives associated with the first level (knowledge dimension) of the *Revised Taxonomy of Educational Objectives.* Such an emphasis on memory, in moderation, is probably not unreasonable. Students must possess a certain amount of knowledge or factual information before they can do anything else. Thus an instructor's decision to check on specific facts, which are requisite to further work with supply items, is justified.

Another outstanding advantage of supply items, particularly for those teaching and testing in the early grades, is that they are "natural." Teaching in the elementary grades frequently employs the so-called Socratic question-and-answer format. In testing, then, the use of simple direct questions follows logically from the method of instruction. Supply items are also efficient from the instructor's standpoint, that is, they allow the student to summarize long and often complex problem-solving processes in a single, brief statement, thereby facilitating scoring.

One of the disadvantages of supply items is that scoring is not always completely objective. It is surprising how often students come up with correct but unanticipated answers. Unless the scoring key is revised in light of alternative correct answers, serious injustices may be perpetrated on students. Lack of objectivity can frequently be traced to the use of ambiguous words in the question. Because they are easily prepared, supply items too frequently become *only* a matter of identification and/or naming. For example, it would be far more meaningful to know what proved to be the weaknesses of the Articles of Confederation than to know in what year they were signed. It is unlikely that a test composed primarily of recall items would reflect all relevant instructional objectives.

It should be noted that the following specific guidelines are not "rules" in the strict sense of the word, but ways of asking questions that have been found useful. In many instances the choice of style depends on the personal preferences of the item writer and the intent in writing the item.

1. ***Require short, definite, clear-cut, and explicit answers.*** An indefinite statement is likely to lead to scoring problems for instructors and response problems for students.

   | | |
   |---|---|
   | Faulty: | Alice Walker wrote _____. |
   | Improved: | *The Color Purple* was written by _____. |
   | | Who wrote *The Color Purple?* |

   A correlated problem relates to the context of the item. Since test items, particularly completion/supply items, are dependent on context for meaning, they can be ambiguous. Context is used here in the sense that the examinee must have sufficient information to be able to respond intelligently to the question. The previous faulty item about Alice Walker does not give test takers sufficient clues as to what the questioner is asking.

2. ***Avoid multimutilated statements.*** Merely introducing blanks liberally into a statement—to form a test item, for example—can only lead to ambiguity. In addition, the instructor is not sure which portion of the

statement the student is responding to and therefore which objective is being measured. One can end up with a nonsensical sequence of blanks.

Faulty:      ____ pointed out in ____ that freedom of thought in America was seriously hampered by ____ ____ ____ ____.

Improved:   That freedom of thought in America was seriously hampered by social pressures toward conformity was pointed out in 1830 by (*De Tocqueville*).

3. *If several correct answers (e.g., synonyms) are possible, equal credit should be given to each one.*

4. *Specify and announce in advance whether scoring will take spelling and grammar into account.*

5. *In testing for comprehension of terms and knowledge of definitions, it is often better to supply the term and require a definition than to provide a definition and require the term.* The student is less likely to benefit from verbal association cues if this procedure is followed. In addition, asking the student to supply the definition is a better measure of his or her knowledge.

Faulty:      What is the general measurement term describing the consistency with which items in a test measure the same thing?

Improved:   Define "internal consistency reliability."

The item has been classified as "comprehension" as the examinee is required to state in his or her own words (paraphrase) the definition, and this equates to comprehension.

6. *It is generally recommended that in completion items the blanks come at the end of the statement.* Beginning an item with a blank is awkward for the student and may interfere with comprehension of the question. In general, the best approach is a simple and direct one.

Faulty:      A (an) (*intelligence quotient*) is the index obtained by dividing a mental age score by chronological age and multiplying by 100.

Improved:   The index obtained by dividing a mental age score by chronological age and multiplying by 100 is called a (an) (*intelligence quotient*).

In this instance perhaps a direct question format might be preferred.

Improved:   What is the term used to describe the index obtained by dividing a mental age score by chronological age and multiplying by 100?

7. *Minimize the use of textbook expressions and stereotyped language.*
When statements are taken out of context, they tend to become ambiguous. The use of paraphrased statements, however, will reduce the incidence of correct responses that represent meaningless verbal associations. In addition, it should reduce the temptation to memorize the exact wording of the test or lecture material.

Faulty:      The power to declare war is vested in _____.

Improved:   Which national legislative body has the authority to declare war?

Better yet, perhaps a true-false item could be used.

Improved:   Congress has the authority to declare war.

         True              False

8. *Specify the terms in which the response is to be given.*

Faulty:      Where is the most famous Sphinx located?

Improved:   In what country is the most famous Sphinx located?

A high degree of precision is particularly important in mathematics questions stated in free-response form. Otherwise, the student may be faced with the problem of trying to guess the degree of error to be tolerated. Is one decimal place accuracy sufficient? Two decimal place accuracy? Different students may come to different conclusions.

Faulty:      If a circle has a 4-inch diameter, its area is _____.

Improved:   A circle has a 4-inch diameter. Its area in square inches correct to two decimal places is _____.

9. *In general, direct questions are preferable to incomplete declarative sentences.*

Faulty:      Gold was discovered in California in the year _____.

Improved:   In what year was gold discovered in California? _____.

10. *Avoid extraneous clues to the correct answer.* The grammatical structure of an item may lead a student to the correct answer, independent of knowledge, particularly if the number of alternative answers is small.

Faulty:      A fraction whose denominator is greater than its numerator is a _____.

Improved:   Fractions whose denominators are greater than their numerators are called _____.

In the faulty item above, the article *a* functions as an irrelevant clue. Similarly, blanks should be of uniform length so as not to suggest the extensiveness of the expected response.

## WRITING TRUE-FALSE QUESTIONS

In responding to constant-alternative items, the examinee chooses one of two alternatives that remains the same throughout a series of items. The alternatives are usually true and false. Other forms might be: yes-no, right-wrong, true-false-depends, correct-incorrect, same-opposite, true-false and converse true or converse false, true-false with correction variety, and true-false-qualification. Because it is the most common representative constant-alternative type, the true-false item will be used as an example in this section.

Despite some difficulties in constructing such items, the true-false question is a potentially valuable data-gathering procedure. There are a number of advantages to the use of true-false items. Most prominent among these is efficiency. An instructor can present a large number of items per unit of testing time. This allows a survey of large content areas to obtain an estimate of students' knowledge. Scoring of true-false items and tests is, of course, rapid and easy. If great care is exercised in their construction, such items can be used to test understanding of principles and generalizations. In addition, they can profitably be used to assess persistence of popular misconceptions, fallacies, and superstitions (e.g., Swallowing watermelon seeds will result in appendicitis). As a footnote, it should be pointed out that the learning of significant amounts of misinformation from true-false items has *not* been demonstrated. What little mislearning does take place can be "washed out" if the test is reviewed by the students and instructor. This is, of course, a recommended class activity no matter what type of item is used. Finally, true-false items are well adapted to testing situations in which only two responses are possible (e.g., School emergency exits should open inwardly).

The disadvantages and limitations of true-false items may outweigh their merits unless thoughtful judgment and intelligence are exercised. Some experts say that, although seemingly easy to construct, meaningful and error-free constant-alternative items are the most difficult of all "objective" questions to write. Quality and precision of language are crucial to these items. Ambiguous terminology and reading ability probably have the greatest effect on true-false items, since a student must respond, in most instances, to a single, unqualified statement. Obviously, the smaller the stimulus, the greater the chance for misinterpretation. Guessing can also have a significant effect. On a 50-item, true-false test "blind guessing" is likely to result in a score of 25. The result, of course, is to reduce the usable range of scores from 50 (0 to 50) to 25 (25 to 50). It would, however, be a rare event for a student to respond blindly. Almost all students will have some information about an item. In addition, although the odds of a chance score of 25 on a 50-item test are 1 in 2, those of a chance score of 35 are 1 in 350. Once the indifference point (50-50) is passed, chance responses through guessing will work *against* the student. The solution is to increase test reliability by using a fairly large number of items, thereby reducing the overall effect of guessing. One final limitation of the true-false variety of constant-alternative items involves their susceptibility to "response sets." Response sets are tendencies to respond to test items on the basis of form rather than content. A response set labeled "acquiescence"—the reliable tendency to respond "true" when in doubt about a particular item—has been identified. This behavior, although constant and reliable, is unrelated to the purpose of the item and test, and therefore confounds the meaning of the scores. The best way to overcome this problem is to construct a reliable test to begin with. In addition, balancing the number of true and false items might help. There is some evidence, however, that false items discriminate better; perhaps a 60-40 split in favor of the false statements is the best recommendation.

Despite the seemingly overwhelming evidence of the limitations of true-false items, they can prove useful in classroom tests if used in moderation with upper-level students. One would not recommend a test entirely composed of constant-alternative items. Specific suggestions for improving true-false items follow.

1. ***Avoid the use of "specific determiners."*** Specific determiners are a class of words that function as irrelevant cues. For example, it has been found that, on most classroom tests, items that include the words *only, no, none, always, never,* and so forth, are generally false. On the other hand, items containing words like *could, might, can, may,* and *generally* will usually be true.

    Faulty:     A faulty "motherboard" may shut down a personal computer.

    Improved:     A faulty "motherboard" will shut down a personal computer.

    A test-wise but unknowledgeable student would be likely to decipher the correct answer in the imprecise wording of the item. If the number of true and false specific determiners is evenly balanced, their influence is reduced. There are, of course, situations in which an instructor may successfully use specific determiners in true-false items whose answers are the opposite of those suggested by the words in the question (e.g., The area of a rhombus is always equal to one half the product of its diagonals).

2. *Base true-false items upon statements that are absolutely true or false, without qualifications or exceptions.* This is a difficult requirement for the contents of some subject-matter areas (e.g., history, literature) where trends, generalizations, and principles are hard to demonstrate empirically. Statements that are not absolutely true or false are likely to perplex examinees, particularly the more knowledgeable, if an element of ambiguity can be introduced. Examinees may read different assumptions into the statement, and one can no longer be sure what the item is measuring.

Faulty:     World War II was fought in Europe and the Far East.

This appears to be an excellent item, but appearances can be deceiving. Responses to the item will depend upon one's interpretation of the item's content span. Did the test constructor wish to consider the location of all of World War II, or to focus on selected theaters of combat?

Improved:     The primary combat locations in terms of military personnel during World War II were Europe and the Far East.

3. *Avoid negatively stated items when possible and eliminate all double negatives.* Such phrasing may cause a student to miss an item because he or she does not comprehend the question. Double negatives are frequently interpreted as emphatically negative. Such items might be used to measure translating ability in an English course, but their general usefulness is negligible; they should be avoided.

Faulty:     It is not frequently observed that copper turns green as a result of oxidation.

Improved:     Copper will turn green upon oxidizing.

4. *Use quantitative and precise rather than qualitative language where possible.* Again, the specificity of word meanings comes into play in judging the effectiveness of an item. Such words as *few, many, young, long, short, large, small,* and *important,* unless accompanied by a standard of comparison, are open to interpretation and thus ambiguous.

Faulty:     Many people voted for Bill Clinton in the 1992 Presidential election.

Improved:     Bill Clinton received more than 60 percent of the popular vote in the presidential election of 1992.

5. *Avoid stereotypical and textbook statements.* Such statements, when taken out of context, are ambiguous and frequently meaningless and trivial.

| Faulty: | From time to time efforts have been made to explode the notion that there may be a cause-and-effect relationship between arboreal life and primate anatomy. |
|---|---|
| Improved: | There is a known relationship between primate anatomy and arboreal life. |

6. *Avoid making the true items consistently longer than the false items.* There is a tendency, particularly on the part of the beginning teacher and item writer, to write systematically longer true items. This phenomenon results from concern that all necessary qualifications be made, so that there can be no doubt that the item is, in fact, true.

7. *Avoid the use of unfamiliar or esoteric language.* Comprehension of an item is determined by its difficulty. It is always best to keep language simple and straightforward and not to confound the student with five-dollar words when fifty-cent ones will do.

| Faulty: | According to some peripatetic politicos, the *raison d'être* for capital punishment is retribution. |
|---|---|
| Improved: | According to some politicians, justification for the existence of capital punishment can be traced to the Biblical statement, "An eye for an eye." |

8. *Avoid complex sentences with many dependent clauses.* Highly involved sentences and compound statements tend to distract the examinee from the central idea of the item. It is a poor practice to make one of the dependent clauses in a true-false item false. It is likely that students will not focus on such seemingly unimportant parts of the statement, and the item becomes a "trick" or "catch" question. With compound statements, the student does not know which element is to be judged true or false.

| Faulty: | Jane Austen, an American novelist born in 1790, was a prolific writer and is best known for her novel *Pride and Prejudice*, which was published in 1820. |
|---|---|

There are so many details in this item that the student does not know on which one to focus. The item is false for many reasons (Austen was a British novelist, 1775–1817, and the book was published in 1813), and different students will get credit for different amounts of knowledge.

Improved:    Jane Austen is best known for her novel *Pride and Prejudice*.

9. ***It is suggested that the crucial elements of an item be placed at the end of the statement***. The function of the first part of a two-part statement is to "set the problem." To focus on the effect in a cause-and-effect relationship, for example, one should state the true cause in the first portion of the statement, and a false effect at the end. Conversely, to focus on the cause, one should state the true effect first, and a false cause at the end of the statement. This procedure is suggested because the student is likely to focus on the last portion of a statement she or he reads. Thus the instructor's objective and the student's attention will be synchronized. The following item is intended to focus on the effect.

Faulty:    Oxygen reduction occurs more readily because carbon monoxide combines with hemoglobin faster than oxygen does.

Improved:    Carbon monoxide poisoning occurs because carbon monoxide dissolves delicate lung tissue.

Obviously, "true" cause-and-effect items are also useful.

Often in education, and the behavioral sciences in general, there is a gap between theory and practice. Such may be the case in using short-answer and true-false items. These item types are frequently maligned as measuring nothing of importance. Sometimes in practice this happens, but it does not mean that significant educational outcomes cannot be measured. The method is there—use it intelligently.

## WRITING MULTIPLE-CHOICE QUESTIONS

Multiple-choice questions require the examinee to select an answer from among several alternatives (options, choices, foils) that change with each item. The selection may be made on any number of bases—for example, correct or best, most inclusive, cause or effect, most similar or dissimilar, and so on.

Each item is composed of a *stem* or *lead*, which sets the problem and alternative responses. The stem may be an incomplete statement (to be completed by the alternatives) or a direct question. Only one response is correct or best, and the others should be plausible but incorrect. Other formats may involve selecting the best from several correct answers, or a less desirable but sometimes used complex format where combinations may be correct (e.g., "a" and "c," but not "b" or "d"). For this reason the incorrect alternatives are sometimes referred to as "foils" or "distractors." They serve to distract the less knowledgeable and skillful student away from the correct answer.

The most common form of choice-type test item, and the one we concentrate on in this section, is the multiple-choice item. Probably the most flexible of all item types, it can be used to assess knowledge as well as such higher mental processes like application and analysis. Since alternative answers serve as a standard of comparison, these items are relatively free from ambiguity. This characteristic is one of their advantages over true-false items. Furthermore, the effect of guessing is markedly reduced, although not eliminated. In a 10-item four-alternative multiple-choice test, the probability of obtaining a score of 7 or more by chance alone is 1 in 1,000. To achieve freedom from guessing comparable to that of a four-alternative item multiple-choice test would require a true-false test of 200 items. The effectiveness of the multiple-choice item is, therefore, obvious. Multiple-choice items are generally preferable when the correct answer is long or can be expressed in a variety of ways. The use of plausible incorrect alternatives, therefore, can test fine discriminations and allow the test constructor easily to control the difficulty level of the items by varying the homogeneity of responses. The multiple-choice item is relatively free of "response sets" of the type described in connection with true-false items. As contrasted with true-false items, multiple-choice items can provide valuable diagnostic information if the alternatives are carefully constructed and if they represent different degrees of "correctness."

The primary limitation of multiple-choice items is that effective ones are difficult to construct. Plausible distractors are often difficult to find or construct (particularly that fourth or fifth incorrect option). One excellent source of alternatives is the pool of incorrect answers supplied when the stem of the multiple-choice item is administered as a free-response item. Multiple-choice items are subject to almost as many irrelevant cues as is any other type of short-answer question. The relatively greater amount of written stimulus material contributes to this situation, and also increases reading time and reduces the number of items (as compared with supply and selection items) than can be presented per unit of time. Their greater flexibility and reliability, however, more than compensate for this lessened efficiency. Some suggestions for writing multiple-choice items follow.

1. ***The stem should be a direct question.*** Although there is no research evidence to support the preferability of the direct question lead ("Who invented the first artificial heart?"), over the incomplete statement ("The first artificial heart was invented by"), it has been found in practice that the novice item writer will produce fewer weak and ambiguous items

if the direct question lead is used. One of the problems is that the use of the incomplete stem requires the examinee to recreate the question that was in the item writer's mind, which may waste the test taker's time and energy. There are many situations in which an incomplete statement stem would be acceptable or perhaps preferable. Just be sure that the incomplete statement stem unequivocally implies a single direct question.

2. ***The stem should pose a clear, definite, explicit, and singular problem.*** This suggestion follows from the preceding one. The major potential weakness of incomplete statement leads is that they are frequently too incomplete; in many instances the examinee must read the alternatives in order to determine what the question is. The direct question stem is more likely to make explicit the basis on which the correct response is to be chosen. It is generally easier for an item writer to express complex ideas with the direct question format. If the incomplete statement lead is used, it should be meaningful in itself and imply a direct question rather than leading into a collection of unrelated true-false statements.

Faulty:    Salvador Dali is

   a. a famous Indian statesman.

   b. important in international law.

   c. known for his surrealistic art.

   d. the author of many avant-garde plays.

Improved:    With which one of the fine arts is Salvador Dali associated?

   a. Surrealistic painting

   b. Avant-garde theater

   c. Polytonal symphonic music

   d. Impressionistic poetry

3. ***Include in the stem any words that might otherwise be repeated in each response.*** Streamlining an item in this way reduces reading time and makes for a more efficient question.

Faulty:    Milk can be pasteurized at home by

   a. heating it to a temperature of 130°.

   b. heating it to a temperature of 145°.

   c. heating it to a temperature of 160°.

   d. heating it to a temperature of 175°.

Improved:     The minimum temperature that can be used to pasteurize milk at home is:

         a. 130°.

         b. 145°.

         c. 160°.

         d. 175°.

4. *Items should be stated simply and understandably, excluding all nonfunctional words from the stem and alternatives.* The inclusion of extraneous words increases reading time and thereby reduces item efficiency. In addition, the central problem may become obscured, which leads to ambiguity.

Faulty:     Although the experimental research, particularly that by Fudrucker, must be considered equivocal and the assumptions viewed as too restrictive, most testing experts would recommend as the easiest method of significantly improving paper-and-pencil achievement test reliability to

         a. increase the size of the group being tested.

         b. increase the differential weighting of items.

         c. increase the objectivity of scoring.

         d. increase the number of items.

         e. increase the amount of testing time.

Improved:     Assume a 10-item, 10-minute paper-and-pencil multiple-choice achievement test has a reliability of .40. The **easiest** way of increasing the reliability to .80 would be to increase

         a. group size.

         b. scoring objectivity.

         c. differential item scoring weights.

         d. the number of items.

         e. testing time.

5. *Avoid interrelated items.* Instructors occasionally and unintentionally write items that overlap. That is, the stem or alternatives to one item give away the answer to other items. This is more likely to happen when the test is long. It may be necessary in some cases to index key words or concepts to check on overlap. Casual reading is rarely sufficient.

6. *Avoid negatively stated items.* Every attempt should be made to keep

the use of such items to a minimum, as they are frequently awkward and difficult to comprehend. If *not, no, never, none, except,* or a similar term is used, it should be highlighted for the student by underlining or capitalizing it. One is often better off rewriting the item positively.

Faulty:    None of the following cities is a South American capital except

a. Bogota.

b. Lima.

c. Rio de Janeiro.

d. Caracas.

e. La Paz.

Improved:    Which one of the following cities is a South American capital?

a. Bogota

b. Lima

c. Rio de Janeiro

d. Caracas

e. La Paz

There are, of course, situations where you might want to legitimately require the examinee to identify a "correct" negative instance or example.

7. ***Avoid making the correct alternative systematically different from other options.*** The usual example of a "systematically different correct alternative" is a correct answer that is obviously longer and more precisely stated than the distractors.

There is an unconscious tendency to include *all* relevant information so that the correct alternative will be unequivocally correct. A related error is the attempt to make the correct alternatives more technical than the foils.

8. ***If possible, the alternatives should be presented in some logical, numerical, or systematic order.*** Again, the purpose is to so structure the question so that responding to it will be facilitated. Alphabetizing single-word, concept, or phrase alternatives has *not* been shown to bias responses.

9. ***Response alternatives should be mutually exclusive.*** Overlapping or synonymous responses should be eliminated because they reduce the discrimination value of an item and allow examinees to eliminate two or more alternatives for the price of one.

Faulty:   If a test has a reliability of 0.78, what percentage of an observed score is attributable to errors of measurement?

    a. Over 5%

    b. Over 10%

    c. Over 20%

    d. Over 30%

The precise answer is 22% $[(.78 \times 100) - 100]$, but because of the way the alternatives are phrased, an examinee is likely to be unsure how to respond. The closest answer is "c," but alternatives "a" and "b" overlap "c" and must also be considered correct.

Improved:   If a test has a reliability of 0.50, what percentage of an observed score can be attributed to errors of measurement?

    a. 2.5%

    b. 5%

    c. 25%

    d. 50%

10. *Make all responses plausible and attractive to the less knowledgeable or skillful student.* The options to a multiple-choice item should include distractors that will attract the unprepared student. Foils should include the common misconceptions and/or errors. They should be familiar, natural, and reasonable.

Faulty:   Which of the following statements makes clear the meaning of the word *electron*?

    a. An electronic tool

    b. Neutral particles

    c. Negative particles

    d. A voting machine

    e. The nuclei of atoms

Improved:   Which of the following phrases is a description of an *electron*?

    a. Neutral particle

    b. Negative particle

    c. Neutralized proton

    d. Radiated particle

    e. Atom nucleus

11. *The response alternative "None of the above" should be used with caution, if at all.* Although some testing experts recommend the use of this
alternative, particularly with mathematics items, the author generally
does not recommend its use. When "None of the above" is the correct
answer, there is no assurance that the examinee does, in fact, know the
answer. Consider the following elementary example:

Faulty:     What is the area (in square inches) of a right triangle whose
            sides adjacent to the right angle are 4 inches and 3 inches long
            respectively?

            a. 7

            b. 12

            c. 25

            d. None of the above

The answer is 6 square inches, and the knowledgeable student would
select alternative "d." But a student who solved the problem incorrectly
(e.g., solving for the hypotenuse, which is 5), and came up with an
answer not found among the alternatives, would also select the correct
answer, "d," thereby getting the item right for the wrong reason. The
response "None of the above" may function very well as an alternative
if the correct answer is included among the preceding alternatives. In
such a situation, it would function as an all-inclusive incorrect alternative covering a multitude of sins.

Improved:   What is the area of a right triangle whose sides adjacent to the
            right angle are 4 inches and 3 inches respectively?

            a. 6 sq. inches

            b. 7 sq. inches

            c. 12 sq. inches

            d. 25 sq. inches

            e. None of the above

12. *Make options grammatically parallel to each other and consistent
with the stem.* Lack of parallelism makes for an awkward item and may
make it difficult for the examinee to grasp the meaning of the question
and of the relationships among the alternative answers.

Faulty:     As compared with the American factory worker in the early
            part of the nineteenth century, the American factory worker at
            the close of the century

            a. was working long hours.

            b. received greater social security benefits.

        c. was to receive lower money wages.

        d. was less likely to belong to a labor union.

        e. became less likely to have personal contact with employers.

Improved:    As compared with the American factory worker in the early part of the nineteenth century, the American factory worker at the close of the century

        a. worked longer hours.

        b. had more social security.

        c. received lower money wages.

        d. was less likely to belong to a labor union.

        e. had less personal contact with his employer.

Lack of parallelism between stem and alternatives may also lead to a "grammatical clue" to the correct answer.

Faulty:    A two-way grid summarizing the relationship between test scores and criterion scores is referred to as an

        a. correlation coefficient.

        b. expectancy table.

        c. probability histogram.

        d. bivariate frequency distribution.

The article *an* leads the student to the correct answer (b).

Improved:    Two-way grids summarizing test-criterion relationships are called

        a. correlation coefficients.

        b. expectancy tables.

        c. bivariate frequency distributions.

        d. probability histograms.

**13.** ***Avoid such irrelevant cues as "common elements" and "pat verbal associations."*** Because multiple-choice items require association between several options and a lead statement, any similarity between key words in the stem and alternatives may function as irrelevant cues. The term *irrelevant cue* describes an item fault that leads the examinee to the correct answer regardless of her or his knowledge of the topic under examination. Common elements in the stem and correct alternatives are the most obvious type of irrelevant cue.

Faulty: The "standard error of estimate" refers to

a. the objectivity of scoring.

b. the percentage of reduced error variance.

c. an absolute amount of possible error.

d. the amount of error in estimating criterion scores.

The test-wise but unknowledgeable student, seeing the terms *estimate* in the stem and *estimating* in the fourth option, would be led to the correct answer.

Faulty: The "standard error of estimate" refers to

a. scoring errors.

b. sampling errors.

c. standardization errors.

d. administration errors.

e. prediction errors.

Although we have made the alternative more homogeneous and eliminated the common elements, we are still left with a faulty item. The problem now is the verbal association between "estimate" and "prediction," which would again lead the student to the correct answer.

Improved: The "standard error of estimate" is most directly related to which of the following test characteristics?

a. Objectivity

b. Reliability

c. Validity

d. Usability

e. Specificity

14. *In testing for understanding of a term or concept, it is generally preferable to present the term in the stem and alternative definitions in the options.* The examinee is less likely to benefit from pat verbal associations, particularly if the correct answer is a paraphrase, rather than a verbatim extract from the text.

Faulty: What name is given to the group of complex organic compounds that occur in small quantities in natural foods that are essential to normal nutrition?

a. Calories

b. Minerals

> c. Nutrients
>
> d. Vitamins

Improved: Which one of the following statements is the best description of a vitamin?

> a. A complex substance necessary for normal animal development, which is found in small quantities in certain foods
>
> b. A complex substance prepared in biological laboratories to improve the nutrient qualities of ordinary foods
>
> c. A substance extracted from ordinary foods, which is useful in destroying disease germs in the body
>
> d. A highly concentrated form of food energy, which should be used only on a doctor's prescription

The *improved* item better focuses the task on determining whether or not the examinee "knows" the general definition of vitamin.

15. ***Use "objective" items.*** Use items on whose correct answers virtually all experts would agree. It is an interesting, humbling, and informative experience to have a colleague key one's tests. But it is perhaps of greater importance to go over each test with one's students, who are probably the best "test critics."

## Illustrative Multiple-choice Questions for the Cognitive Domain of the *Taxonomy of Educational Objectives* *

The *Taxonomy of Educational Objectives*, as we noted in Chapter 5, is a highly valuable source of ideas for achievement test items. The following items are presented to illustrate the variety of outcomes that can be measured using the *Taxonomy* as a guide. (See pages 115–118 for an overview of the *Taxonomy*.)

---

**Knowledge of Specific Facts**

---

1. The Monroe Doctrine was announced about 10 years after the
   a. Revolutionary War.
   b. War of 1812.
   c. Civil War.
   d. Spanish-American War.

---

*From the book *Taxonomy of Educational Objectives, Handbook II: The Cognitive Domain*, edited by B. Bloom. New York: David McKay Company, Inc., 1956. Reprinted by permission of the publisher.

**Knowledge of Principles and Generalizations**

2. Which of the following statements of the relationship between market price and normal price is true?

    a. Over a short period of time, market price varies directly with changes in normal price.

    b. Over a long period of time, market price tends to equal normal price.

    c. Market price is usually lower than normal price.

    d. Over a long period of time, market price determines normal price.

**Translation from Symbolic Form to Another Form, or Vice Versa**

3. Which of the above graphs best represents the supply situation where a monopolist maintains a uniform price regardless of the amounts which people buy?

    a.

    b.

    c.

    d.

**Application**

In the following items (4–11) you are to judge the effects of a particular policy on the distribution of income. In each case assume that there are no other changes in policy that would counteract the effect of the policy described in the item. Mark the item:

A. if the policy described would tend to *reduce* the existing degree of inequality in the distribution of income,

B. if the policy described would tend to *increase* the existing degree of inequality in the distribution of income, or

C. if the policy described would have *no effect*, or an indeterminate effect, on the distribution of income.

*Policy*

_____ 4. Increasingly progressive income taxes.

_____ 5. Confiscation of rent on unimproved urban land.

___ 6. Introduction of a national sales tax.

___ 7. Increasing the personal exemptions from income taxes.

___ 8. Distributing a subsidy to sharecroppers on Southern farms.

___ 9. Provision of educational and medical services, and low-cost public housing.

___ 10. Reduction in the degree of business monopoly.

___ 11. Increasing taxes in periods of prosperity and decreasing them in periods when depressions threaten.

---

### Analysis

---

12. An assumption basic to Lindsay's preference for voluntary associations rather than government orders ... is a belief
    a. that government is not organized to make the best use of experts.
    b. that freedom of speech, freedom of meeting, freedom of association, are possible only under a system of voluntary associations.
    c. in the value of experiment and initiative as a means of attaining an ever-improving society.
    d. in the benefits of competition.
13. The relation between the definition of sovereignty given in Paragraph 2 and that given in Paragraph 9 is best expressed as follows:
    a. There is no fundamental difference between them, only a difference in formulation.
    b. The definition given in Paragraph 2 includes that given in Paragraph 9 but in addition includes situations which are excluded by that given in Paragraph 9.
    c. The two definitions are incompatible with each other; the conditions of sovereignty implied in each exclude the other.

---

### Judgments in Terms of External Criteria: Given Possible Bases for Judgments about Accuracy, Recognize Criteria That Are Appropriate

---

For items 14–19, assume that in doing research for a paper about the English language you find a statement by Otto Jespersen that contradicts one point of view on language you have always accepted. Indicate which of the statements would be significant in determining the value of Jespersen's statement. For the purpose of these items, you may assume that these statements are accurate. Mark each item using the following key:

A. Significant positively—that is, might lead you to trust his statement and to revise your own opinion.

B. Significant negatively—that is, might lead you to distrust his statement.

C. Has no significance.

___ 14. Mr. Jespersen was Professor of English at Copenhagen University.

___ 15. The statement in question was taken from the very first article that Mr. Jespersen published.

___ 16. Mr. Jespersen's books are frequently referred to in other works that you consult.

____ 17. Mr. Jespersen's name is not included in the *Dictionary of American Scholars*.

____ 18. So far as you can find, Jespersen never lived in England or the United States for any considerable length of time.

____ 19. In your reading of other authors on the English language, you find that several of them went to Denmark to study under Jespersen.

## USING MULTIPLE-CHOICE QUESTIONS TO MEASURE PROBLEM SOLVING AND CRITICAL THINKING

Public schools are placing greater emphasis on problem-solving skills, and society is demanding individuals with significant skills in this area. Various terms have been used to describe the basic operations of application. Terms like *critical thinking* and *logical reasoning* are used as rubrics under which the basic processes of problem identification, specification of alternative solutions, evaluation of consequences, and solution selection are grouped. The actual process may be cognitive, as in playing bridge, or a combination of cognitive and psychomotor skills, as in the case of automobile engine diagnostics. One of the distinct advantages of paper-and-pencil problem-solving measures is that they can be used to simulate complex, expensive, and infrequently occurring situations.

A step-by-step procedure for creating problem-solving measures has been described by Dunning (1954), as cited in Adams (1964).

*Step 1.* Decide on the principle or principles to be tested. Criteria to be considered
  1. should be known principles but the situation in which the principles are to be applied should be new.
  2. should involve significantly important principles.
  3. should be pertinent to a problem or situation common to all students.
  4. should be within the range of comprehension of all students
  5. should use only valid and reliable sources from which to draw data.
  6. should be interesting to the students.

*Step 2.* Determine the phrasing of the problem situation so as to require the student in drawing conclusions to do one of the following:
  1. Make a prediction.
  2. Choose a course of action.
  3. Offer an explanation for an observed phenomenon.
  4. Criticize a prediction or explanation made by others.

*Step 3.* Set up the problem situation in which the principle or principles selected operate. Present the problem to a class with directions to draw a conclusion or conclusions and give several supporting reasons for their answer.

*Step 4.* Edit the students' responses, selecting those that are most representative of their thinking. These will include conclusions and supporting reasons that are both acceptable and unacceptable.

*Step 5.* To the conclusions and reasons obtained from the students, the teacher now adds any others that he or she feels are necessary to cover the salient points. The total number of items should be at least 50 percent more than is desired in the final form to allow for elimination of poor items. The following list is a guide to the type of statements that can be used.

1. True statements of principles and facts
2. False statements of principles and facts
3. Acceptable and unacceptable analogies
4. Appeal to acceptable or unacceptable authority
5. Ridicule
6. Assumption of the conclusion
7. Teleological explanations

*Step 6.* Submit test to other judges for criticisms. Revise test in view of criticisms.

*Step 7.* Administer test. Follow with thorough class discussion.

*Step 8.* Conduct an item analysis.

*Step 9.* In the light of steps 7 and 8, revise the test.

Norris and Ennis (1989) write about four kinds of critical thinking questions: deduction, credibility, induction, and assumption-identification. Following are examples of these types of items

---

### Deduction

1. "If these beings are from Earth, then another space ship must have landed on Nicoma. But no other space ship has landed on Nicoma."

   Suppose that what the speaker says is true. Then must this be true?

   These beings are not from Earth.

   A. Yes, it must be true.

   B. No, it cannot be true.

   C. We cannot tell for sure from the information given.

---

### Credibility

---

2. Which underlined statement is more believable?

    A. The health officer says, "<u>This water is safe to drink.</u>"

    B. Several others are soldiers. One of them says, "<u>This water supply is not safe.</u>"

    C. A and B are equally believable.

---

### Induction

---

Mr. Brown, who lives in the town of Salem, was brought before the Salem municipal court for the sixth time in the past month on a charge of keeping his pool hall open after 1 A.M. He again admitted his guilt and was fined the maximum, $500, as in each earlier instance.

3. On some nights it was to Mr. Brown's advantage to keep his pool hall open after 1 A.M., even at the risk of paying a $500 fine. This statement is

    A. True

    B. Probably true

    C. Probably false

    D. False

    E. Insufficient data

---

### Assumption Identification

---

4. "Since about half the villagers have very short hair, I think that at least half are male." Which is probably taken for granted?

    A. Half are female

    B. All males have short hair

    C. Only males have short hair

---

Frequently examinees will be asked to "justify" the answer they have selected to the item. This can be done in a multiple-choice or open-ended format.

Following are some sample problem-solving items (based in part on material developed by science educators at the University of Georgia: Drs. James R. O'Key, Russell Yeany, and Michael J. Padilla). These kinds of items can frequently be difficult and complex, but the range of application is considerable relative to both content and grade level.

1. Frank wanted to go to California. But Frank's father, who is quite strict with Frank, stated emphatically that he could not go unless he earned a B average for the year.

Frank's father always keeps his promises. When summer came, Frank went to California. If, from this information, you conclude that Frank earned a B average, you must be assuming that

   a. Frank had never made a B average before.

   b. Frank had no money of his own.

   c. Frank's father was justified in saying what he did.

   d. Frank went with his father's consent.

   e. Frank was sure he would be able to go.

2. Consider these facts about the coloring of animals:

   • Plant lice, which live on the stems of green plants, are green.

   • The grayish-mottled moth resembles the bark of the trees on which it lives.

   • Insects, birds, and mammals that live in the desert are usually sandy or gray in color.

   • Polar bears and other animals living in the Arctic region are white.

   • Jungle-dwelling tigers are yellowish in color and have parallel stripes which tend to camouflage them among the leaves and stems.

Which one of the following statements do these facts tend to support?

   a. Animals that prey on others use color as a disguise.

   b. Some animals imitate the color and shape of other natural objects for protection.

   c. The coloration of animals has little to do with their surroundings.

   d. Protective coloration is found more among insects and birds than among mammals.

   e. Many insects and animals have protective coloring.

Read the following paragraphs and then answer items 3 through 7.

In an area that had been moderately grazed, a steel tube 18 inches in diameter and 12 inches long was driven 9 inches into the ground. The part of the tube that was above ground, 3 inches deep and 18 inches in diameter, was filled with water. It took 11 minutes for all the water to soak into the ground. Another tube of the same size was similarly placed in a nearby ungrazed area. In this location the water soaked into the ground in one and one-half minutes.

When this experiment was reported to a high school class, a student said it showed that *water soaks into ungrazed land faster than it soaks into grazed land.*

Items 3 through 7 are statements that might be made in a discussion of this student's conclusion. Assuming that the information given in the first paragraph is accurate, decide which of the following answers best describes each statement.

Answers:

A. This statement tends to *support* the conclusion.

B. This statement tends to make the conclusion *doubtful.*

C. This statement *neither* supports the conclusion *nor* conflicts with it.

\_\_\_\_\_ 3. If *all* the grass had been grazed off the first area, the water would have taken longer than 11 minutes to soak in.

\_\_\_\_\_ 4. Grazing should be restricted by state laws.

\_\_\_\_\_ 5. Conserving water in the soil is more important than feeding cattle.

_____ 6. The second tube might have been made of a porous material, which itself absorbed a large amount of water.

_____ 7. The composition of the soil in the two areas was approximately the same.

---

Simulated observations or experiments can form a good context within which to measure problem-solving and logical-thinking skills. The following exercise illustrates one approach.

> A farmer observed the mice that live in his field. He found that the mice were either fat or thin. Also, the mice had either black tails or white tails.
>
> This made him wonder if there might be a relation between the size of a mouse and the color of its tail. So he decided to capture all of the mice in one part of his field and observe them. The mice that he captured are shown in Figure 7-1.

8. Do you think there is a relation between the size of the mice and the color of their tails (i.e., is one size of mouse more likely to have a certain color tail and vice versa)?

   a. Yes.

   b. No.

9. Reason

   a. 8/11 of the fat mice have black tails and 3/4 of the thin mice have white tails.

   b. Fat and thin mice can have either a black or a white tail.

   c. Not all fat mice have black tails. Not all thin mice have white tails.

   d. 18 mice have black tails and 12 have white tails.

   e. 22 mice are fat and 8 mice are thin.

---

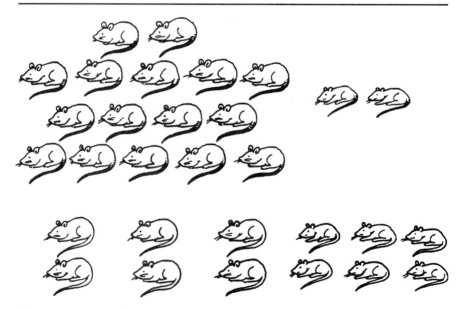

**Figure 7-1**

## WRITING MATCHING EXERCISES

The matching exercise is a variation of the multiple-choice question. While the multiple-choice question usually presents a single problem and several solutions, the matching exercise presents several problems and several solutions. The list of alternative solutions is constant for each new problem or stimulus. It is because of this constancy of alternatives that the quality and homogeneity of options so significantly influence the effectiveness of the entire exercise. Matching exercises may concentrate on form or content. Pictorial material can be used with success in these types of exercises. Content might be related to events, inventions, results, definitions, quotations, dates, or locations. At a more sophisticated level, matching (classification or key-list) items may concern cause-and-effect relationships, theoretical statements and experimental bases, or a phenomenon and its explanation in terms of principles, generalizations, or theories.

Most such exercises contain two columns, one on the left-hand side of the page containing the stimuli or premises, and one on the right side containing responses. Compound matching exercises (e.g., state-major industry-city or authors-novels-nationalities) are, of course, possible, but are used infrequently.

The matching exercise's chief advantage is efficiency in time and space. It uses the same set of response alternatives for a whole group of items. The matching exercise is, therefore, a compact and efficient method of rapidly surveying knowledges of the who, what, when, and where variety.

The matching exercise is not well adapted to the measurement of higher-order abilities. It is particularly susceptible to irrelevant cues, implausible alternatives, and the awkward arrangement of stimuli or responses; thus, great care is needed in development. Several suggestions for constructing or revising matching exercises follow:

1. *Matching exercises should be complete on a single page.* Splitting the exercise is confusing, distracting, and time-consuming for the student.

2. *Use response categories that are related but mutually exclusive.* If this suggestion is not followed, ambiguous items or items requiring multi-keying will result. Responses should be drawn from the same domain (e.g., do not mix dates and names of inventors in the same response list) but should not overlap. The degree of relatedness among stimuli and/or responses will, of course, dictate the degree of difficulty of the exercise.

3. *Keep the number of stimuli relatively small (e.g., 10 to 15), and let the number of possible responses exceed the number of stimuli by two or three.* This is, admittedly, an arbitrary suggestion but is related to a point well worth considering. If a matching exercise is too long, the task

becomes tedious (and perhaps even arduous) and the discriminations required too fine. A related problem is the possibility that the use of matching items might "overweight" the test. Because of their compactness, their weight in the test relative to the objectives and other item types may become disproportionate. One should also avoid matching the numbers of stimuli and responses, as this increases the likelihood that a student will benefit from guessing or from the process of elimination. In this regard the cautious use of the response "None of the above" may be recommended. One might include a statement in the test directions to the effect that the responses may be used once, more than once, or not at all.

4. *The directions should clearly specify the basis for matching stimuli and responses.* Although the basis for matching is usually obvious, sound testing practice suggests that the directions spell out the exact nature of the task. It is unreasonable to expect students to read through the stimulus and response lists in order to discern the intended basis for matching. It is also a good idea to include in the directions a statement to the effect that a response option may be used once, more than once, or not at all.

5. *Keep the statements in the response column short and list them in some logical order.* This suggestion is intended to facilitate response to the exercise. The responses should be so stated and arranged (e.g., alphabetically, chronologically, etc.) that the student can scan them quickly.

The following matching exercise does not embody the suggestions made above.

Faulty: Directions—Match List A with List B. You will be given one point for each correct match.

| List A | List B |
|--------|--------|
| a. cotton gin | a. Eli Whitney |
| b. reaper | b. Alexander Graham Bell |
| c. wheel | c. Walt Disney |
| d. TU54G tube | d. Louisa May Alcott |
| e. steamboat | e. None of these |

The primary shortcomings of this matching exercise may be summarized as follows:

1. The directions fail to specify the basis for matching or mechanics for responding.

2. The two lists are enumerated identically.

3. The responses are not listed logically—in this case, alphabetically.

4. Both lists lack homogeneity.

5. There are equal numbers of elements in both lists.

6. The use of "None of these" is questionable in this exercise, serving as a giveaway to List A elements "c" and "d." Furthermore, if a student uses it for element "e" of List A, it is not clear that he or she knows who did, in fact, invent the steamboat.

An improved version of the exercise follows:

Improved:     Directions—Famous inventions are listed in the left-hand column and inventors in the right-hand column below. Place the letter corresponding to the inventor in the space next to the invention for which he is famous. Each match is worth 1 point, and "*None of these*" may be the correct answer. Inventors may be used more than once.

| *Inventions* | *Inventors* |
|---|---|
| ___ 1. steamboat | a. Alexander Graham Bell |
| ___ 2. cotton gin | b. Robert Fulton |
| ___ 3. sewing machine | c. Elias Howe |
| ___ 4. reaper | d. Cyrus McCormick |
| | e. Eli Whitney |
| | f. None of these |

Many other types of short-answer items could be discussed. Such question forms as the rearrangement exercise (Cureton, 1960), interpretive exercise (Linn & Gronlund, 2000), analogies (Remmers, Gage, & Rummel, 1965, pp. 258–259), and problem-solving items (Adams, 1964, pp. 345–347) have been found useful in educational assessment. All methods discussed in this chapter could be adapted to an oral format. Space limitations will not allow us to consider these forms here, but the reader is referred to the above for additional treatments of item writing.

## CREATING ASSESSMENTS FOR ELEMENTARY AND MIDDLE SCHOOL STUDENTS[*]

The development of test items for young students is a difficult task. This is particularly true if the teacher has decided to use so-called objective or

---

[*]The material in this section is based on Dr. Clarence Nelson's monograph *Improving Objective Tests in Science* (1967), pp. 18–21. Sample items reproduced by permission of the National Science Teachers Association.

short-answer questions. Two of the main difficulties in writing items for the young involve (a) the development of comprehensible and appropriate stimulus materials, and (b) the development of a scheme for recording student responses efficiently.

At the kindergarten level, the best way to record answers is perhaps to have the youngsters draw an *X* on a picture. A series of pictures can be accompanied by a series of questions, as shown in Figures 7-2a, 7-2b, and 7-2c.

**Figure 7-2a**

1. Put an *X* on the picture of things that are alive.
2. Put a *Y* on the picture of each thing that is an animal.
3. Put a *Z* on the picture of each thing that is a mammal.
4. One of these three pictures is a kitty. Put an *X* on that picture.

**Figure 7-2b**

5. One of these three pictures shows what happens when something is heated or becomes warm. Put an X on that picture.

**Figure 7-2c**

To test for understanding of concepts, it is desirable to use a picture card illustrating objects similar but not identical to those discussed in class. If identical objects are used, one may be measuring recall rather than understanding.

A similar method of recording responses can be used at the first-grade level. Using pictorial material, the teacher may read the questions to the students. Two examples are seen in Figures 7-3a and 7-3b.

6. (The teacher demonstrates boiling, filtering, and straining of water, and then reads the test question.) Pure water can be taken out of salt water by:

**Figure 7-3a**

7. Salt has been mixed with chopped ice. If some of this chopped ice is packed around a container full of water, what will probably happen to the water in the container?

**Figure 7-3b**

Second- and third-graders can probably use a special answer sheet. The teacher may wish to make an answer sheet containing lettered or numbered squares as shown in Figure 7-4.

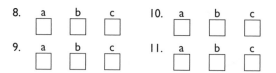

**Figure 7-4**

An alternative is to have the students circle the letters on an answer sheet. The questions could be handed out in duplicated form, and after the method for recording the answers is explained, the questions and answers could be read slowly to the students.

8. When a watch is laid flat on a table, if 12 on the dial represents north, then 9 on the dial represents
   a. south
   b. east.
   *c. west

9. If 12 on your watch dial represents north, which one of the following times represents southeast? (Use both the big and the little hand of the watch.)
   *a. 4:30
   b. 7:30
   c. 10:30

10. On a clear day a person standing at the seashore looking at a ship several miles from the shore can see the
   a. entire ship.
   *b. upper part of the ship only.
   c. lower part of the ship only.

11. The horizon would be farthest away
   a. if you were standing on the seashore and looking out over the ocean.
   b. if you were on top of the Empire State Building or the Washington Monument and looking straight ahead.
   *c. if you were looking out of an airplane window while flying four miles above the earth.

Middle school students can use commercially available (e.g., National Computer Systems [NCS]) answer sheets. Machine-scorable booklets can be successfully used with students beginning at the kindergarten level. A commercial scoring template may be used for hand scoring. If the answer sheet is teacher-made, a fan, strip, or cutout key (see Chapter 6) may be used. Following is a series of test items aimed at measuring the middle school student's understanding of land-feature diagrams. The test item should not be one previously studied in class.

Items 12–16 are middle school science items and refer to the cross-sectioned land-feature diagram in Figure 7-5. Formations are indicated by roman numerals.

12. Fossils would be least likely to occur in

   *a. III

   b. V

   c. VII

   d. VIII

   e. IX

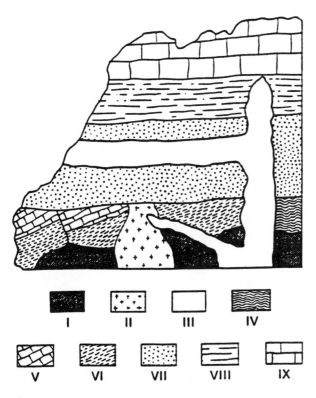

**Figure 7-5**

13. An unconformity exists between
    a. I and III
    b. III and VI
    *c. V and VII
    d. VII and VIII
    e. VIII and IX

14. The youngest formation is
    a. I
    b. II
    c. III
    d. V
    *e. IX

15. The oldest formation is
    *a. I
    b. II
    c. III
    d. V
    e. IX

16. Which formation is made up of igneous rock?
    *a. III
    b. V
    c. VII
    d. VIII
    e. IX

Similarly, the student's interpretation of a chemical formula not previously encountered can reveal whether or not he or she understands the symbols and conventions studied in class.

17. The number of atoms of oxygen in the formula $2A_2(SO_4)_3$ is
    a. 4
    b. 7
    c. 8
    d. 12
    *e. 24

Item writing is both art and science. Experience really helps improve the quality of items. One of the most enlightening things you can do to help improve your items and tests is to sit and *listen* to a student work through your questions out loud. You would be surprised what good critics students can be, plus it makes them feel part-ownership in the process. In architecture (for some), form follows function. This also may be the case in item writing. Some kinds of questions seem to lend themselves better to a direct question format—perhaps true-false, or when there are obviously a number of possible outcomes, as in multiple-choice. Sometimes extended samples of a student's own thinking are required; then we may move to the essay format (see Chapter 8). Trial and error, experience, and maybe a little formal study will help us make the best decisions.

## CASE STUDY

Following is an illustrative set of 24 items taken from the Reading Education midterm exam. Space does not permit reproduction of all 80 items from the exam. The items have been organized, for presentation purposes, by objectives. When administered, the test would have had items using the same format (e.g., supply, multiple-choice, true-false) grouped together for the convenience of student response. The intent here is to illustrate the item types discussed in Chapter 7. Readers are urged to try their own hands at creating items using a variety of formats with familiar content. One might write items about writing items—a good way to practice and study at the same time. Critique the following items from the standpoint of item-objective match and format. Do the items follow the guidelines? If not, then how can they be improved?

The items for this exam tend to cluster in three categories: knowledge, comprehension, and application. Other and higher-order outcomes—for example, synthesis (of an instructional plan) and evaluation (of student performance)—would come later and would probably require different approaches. For example, a checklist might be used to evaluate the instructional plan, and an observation schedule might be developed to evaluate implementation of instructional lesson plans.

Each item is keyed to one of the objectives presented in the Case Study Application for Chapter 5. The correct answers to each item are indicated with an asterisk(*).

OBJECTIVE: Associate different instructional practices with three conceptual frameworks (models) of the reading process (Objective 1).

LEVEL: Comprehension

1. Which of the following activities would you be *most* likely to observe in a classroom where the teacher had a *bottom-up orientation* to reading?
   a. Creative writing
   b. Storytelling
   *c. Letter-naming drills
   d. Round-robin reading

2. A child substitutes the word *puppy* for the word *dog*. If you were a teacher with a *top-down orientation* toward reading, what would you do?
   *a. Ignore the error.
   b. Ask the child to look at the word again and sound it out.
   c. Tell the child the word.

3. Mrs. Jones has a primarily *interactive orientation* toward the reading process. A student in her classroom comes to a word he or she cannot read. Which of the following suggestions would the teacher make to the child to help him or her decode the word?
   *a. Skip the word and try to figure out the word from the sentence meaning.
   b. Try to sound out the word by using the initial consonant and vowel sounds.
   c. Tell the child the word.

OBJECTIVE: Recognize the importance of automaticity in the reading process (objective 2).

LEVEL: Knowledge

4. Why is it important that readers decode words automatically?
   *a. Readers need to direct their attention to the meaning of the text.
   b. Readers need to read fast enough so that they will not lose their place.
   c. Readers need to consciously attend to the mechanics of decoding.

OBJECTIVE: Recognize instructional activities that emphasize the uses of language (objective 3).

LEVEL: Comprehension

5. Which of the following reading situations would *not* be recommended to enhance language meaning?

   a. Oral reading by the teacher
   b. Pretending to read a memorized story
   c. Rereading a favorite story
  *d. Reading a word list

OBJECTIVE: Identify ways to create a classroom environment where learning to read is supported (objective 5).

LEVEL: Knowledge

6. Dramatic activities and role play help children develop social skills and aid language development.
   *a. True
   b. False

OBJECTIVE: Recognize the characteristics of a particular language experience activity (objective 7).

LEVEL: Analysis

7. What is the *major* difference between a basal approach to reading instruction and a language experience approach to reading instruction?
   a. The language experience approach uses controlled vocabulary and the basal reader approach uses the children's natural language.
   b. The language experience approach uses more good literature than the basal reader approach.
   *c. The language experience approach uses stories dictated by the children and the basal reader approach uses "ready-made" stories.
   d. The language experience approach is more teacher-directed and the basal reader approach is more child-centered.

OBJECTIVE: Identify the goal of teaching students decoding strategies (objective 9).

LEVEL: Comprehension

8. Which of the following statements expresses the *primary* goal of decoding instruction?
   a. To provide students with various ways to figure out new words
   b. To help students identify individual words which results in comprehension

*c. To enhance independent usage of phonics skills, structural analysis, and context clue skills

d. To enable students to read more quickly

OBJECTIVE: Recognize three types of decoding strategies (objective 10).

LEVEL: Knowledge

9. What kind of decoding strategy would a student be using if he or she used words, phrases, and sentences surrounding an unknown word to decode the word?

*a. Context clues

b. Phonic principles

c. Structural analysis

d. Dictionary aids

OBJECTIVE: Apply phonics generalizations to decode nonsense words (objective 11).

LEVEL: Application

10. Which of the following words contains a consonant digraph?

a. Strip

b. Swipe

*c. Shell

d. Blimp

11. Which of the following words contains a vowel digraph?

a. Robe

*b. Bail

c. Stem

d. Stork

OBJECTIVE: Apply syllabication rules (objective 12).

LEVEL: Application

12. If "tiskal" were a word and "i" was short, where would it most likely be divided into syllables?

*a. tis kal

b. tisk al

c. ti skal

d. Not enough information

OBJECTIVE: Recognize the purpose of Informed Strategies for Learning (objective 13).

LEVEL: Knowledge

13. Informed Strategies for Learning (ISL) is focused on how to get information from a text rather than on learning the content of the text.
    *a. True
    b. False

OBJECTIVE: Recognize the characteristics of Informed Strategies for Learning (objective 14).

LEVEL: Knowledge

14. Students learn to use Informed Strategies for Learning without direct instruction because the strategies are automatic.
    a. True
    *b. False

OBJECTIVE: Identify three different kinds of discussion and recognize their characteristics (Objective 16).

LEVEL: Application

15. Which of the following discussions would be appropriate if you needed to determine an instructional approach to use with a child who was experiencing little success with basal instruction?
    a. Subject-mastery discussion
    b. Issue-oriented discussion
    *c. Problem-solving discussion

16. What is the *major* purpose of an *issue-oriented discussion?*
    a. To identify the major points of a textbook chapter
    *b. To identify student's beliefs/feelings about a particular topic
    c. To identify information students know about a subject before they read a textbook chapter

OBJECTIVE: Identify alternatives to round-robin reading (objective 21).

LEVEL: Knowledge

17. What is one way to overcome some of the negative aspects of "round-robin" reading?
    *a. Ask students to close their books if they are not reading.
    b. Have students take turns reading paragraphs.
    c. Ask students to follow along and assist each other with difficult words.
    d. Have students volunteer to read aloud and ask other students to follow along.

OBJECTIVE: Recognize reading instructional activities that are appropriate for exceptional children (both hard-to-teach and gifted) (objective 23).

LEVEL: Knowledge

18. Even though gifted readers generally have a high level of fluency, they still need reading instruction and guidance.
    *a. True
    b. False

19. The language experience approach is not an acceptable alternative to basal instruction for the "hard-to-teach" child.
    a. True
    *b. False

OBJECTIVE: Differentiate between characteristics of reliable versus valid tests (objective 29).

LEVEL: Comprehension

20. A reading test that assesses a child's use of phonics generalizations to decode words would be a valid measure of vocabulary meaning.
    a. True
    *b. False

OBJECTIVE: Recognize the purpose of question-answer relationships (objective 15).

LEVEL: Comprehension

21. What is the *primary* purpose of question-answer relationships?
    *a. Teach children how to find information when they have to answer questions
    b. Help teachers develop different types of questions
    c. Help children relate information they read about in the text with their personal information

OBJECTIVE: Recognize the place of alphabet instruction in early reading instruction.

LEVEL: Application

22. What activity would have the most impact on developing early reading skills in very young children? (Answer: Reading aloud frequently to the child)

OBJECTIVE: Identify activities that foster early literacy development before formal reading instruction begins.

LEVEL: Knowledge

23. What characteristic is most important in selecting reading material for early reading experience? (Answer: Realism)

OBJECTIVE: Associate different instructional practices with three conceptual frameworks (models) of the reading process.

LEVEL: Comprehension

24. The unit of instruction emphasized in the top-down model of reading is _____. (Answer: A sentence)

---

## CONTENT REVIEW STATEMENTS

1. The writing of test items, questions, or exercises basically involves finding the most suitable manner in which to pose problems to students.

2. A supply-type item requires the examinee to construct her or his own response to a direct question or incomplete statement.

3. A selection-type item requires the student to decide between two or more possible answers.

4. Common shortcomings of teacher-made tests include:
    a. too great a reliance on subjective but presumably absolute standards.
    b. hasty development and insufficient length.
    c. focusing on trivia and easily measured outcomes to the exclusion of important achievements.
    d. poor format, structure, and grammar.

5. Prerequisites for writing good achievement test items include:
    a. a rational philosophy of education.
    b. command of verbal and written communication skills.
    c. command of subject matter.
    d. command of item-writing techniques.
    e. knowledge about how students learn and develop.

6. General guidelines for writing "objective" items include:

   a. avoiding obvious, trivial, meaningless, obscure, or ambiguous content.

   b. following accepted rules of grammar.

   c. avoiding irrelevant or unintended clues or cues to the correct answer.

   d. avoiding interrelated items.

   e. using items whose scoring would be agreed upon by experts.

   f. stating questions in clear, explicit terms.

   g. providing equal credit for equally correct answers.

   h. specifying the terms in which the answer is to be stated.

   i. minimizing textbook expressions and stereotyped language.

   j. stating items in the form of direct questions.

   k. avoiding the use of "specific determiners" such as *only, all, none, always*, and *could, might, may*, or *generally*.

7. Supply items have the advantages of:

   a. minimizing the effect of guessing.

   b. being adaptable to actual classroom instructional practice (e.g., the Socratic method).

   c. providing good measures of knowledge.

8. The scoring of supply items is not always completely objective.

9. The use of true-false items is an objective and efficient method for surveying student knowledge.

10. False items tend to be more discriminating than true items and should probably comprise about 60 percent of the true-false items used.

11. There is no evidence that mislearning is stimulated by the use of true-false items, particularly if the test results are reviewed with students.

12. Although it influences scores to some extent, the effect of guessing on constant-alternative items is minor.

13. Multiple-choice or changing-alternative items provide a flexible method of measuring a great variety of outcomes, particularly at the higher levels of mental ability.

14. Multiple-choice items should include logically related and arranged alternatives, provide a correct or preferable answer, and list plausible, grammatically parallel, but incorrect answers.

**15.** "None of the Above" or "All of the Above" alternatives should be used cautiously, particularly when they are keyed as the correct answers.

**16.** The more similar (homogeneous) the alternatives in a multiple-choice item, the higher the likelihood of good discrimination between high- and low-achieving students.

**17.** Many useful ideas for achievement test items can be found in the *Taxonomy of Educational Objectives, Handbook 1: The Cognitive Domain.*

**18.** Graphic materials can provide a basis for measuring outcomes in a variety of subject-matter fields and levels of performance.

**19.** Selection items can be used effectively to measure problem solving and logical reasoning.

**20.** The matching item is a variation on the multiple-choice item and is useful in surveying knowledge of the who, what, when, and where variety.

**21.** Matching items should:
    a. include very detailed directions for responding.
    b. be limited to a single page.
    c. be limited to about 10 to 15 pairs.
    d. use mutually exclusive categories.
    e. present stimuli and responses in some logical order.

**22.** Great care must be taken in developing test materials for young children.

**23.** The stem or lead to a multiple-choice item should pose a clear, definite, explicit, and singular problem to be solved or questions to be answered.

**24.** Items where the stem(s) or alternative(s) of one question may give the answer to another question should be avoided.

**25.** Avoid making the correct alternative systematically different from the incorrect alternatives (e.g., longer).

**26.** Where relevant, present multiple-choice alternatives in some logical or systematic order (e.g., numerical).

**27.** Response alternatives should be mutually exclusive (e.g., nonoverlapping numerical answers).

**28.** Avoid using common language or terms in the stem of a multiple-choice item and the correct answer.

29. Require the examinee to select among alternative definitions if the objective is to measure comprehension of terms.

30. Measurements used with the very young should:

    a. have explicit directions, preferably read to the examinee.

    b. have practice exercises.

    c. be examined closely relative to the language used.

    d. use separate answer sheets only sparingly.

31. Critical thinking skills such as deduction, induction, and inference can be objectively assessed.

32. The five elements needed for creating effective criterion-referenced items are:

    a. detailed description of objective

    b. an illustrative item

    c. specification of stimulus attributes

    d. specification of response attributes

    e. specification of administration procedures

## SPECULATIONS

1. What are the advantages and disadvantages of using the supply and completion item format?

2. What are the major faults in writing supply and completion items?

3. What are the advantages and disadvantages of using the true-false item format?

4. What are the major pitfalls in writing true-false kinds of items?

5. Are specific determiners always bad?

6. Have you ever met a true-false item you didn't like? Why?

7. Why is it sometimes hard to complete a completion item?

8. What are the advantages and disadvantages of using the multiple-choice test item format? What are the major guidelines in writing these kinds of items?

9. What are the major faults to be avoided in constructing matching exercises?

**10.** What are the major advantages and disadvantages of using the matching exercise?

**11.** In what way are true-false and multiple-choice items alike?

**12.** What don't you like about multiple-choice items?

**13.** Is it possible to consistently measure higher-order educational outcomes with objective items?

**14.** What are some good sources of distractors for multiple-choice items?

---

## SUGGESTED READINGS

Cangelosi, J. S. (2000). *Assessment strategies for monitoring student learning.* New York: Longman.

Ebel, R. L., & Frisbie, D. A. (1991). *Essentials of educational measurement* (5th ed.). Englewood Cliffs, NJ: Prentice Hall. See Chapters 8, 9, and 10, respectively, for good discussions of item writing.

Gronlund, N. E., & Linn, R. L. (2000). *Measurement and evaluation in teaching* (8th ed.). New York: Macmillan. Chapter 7, "Constructing Objective Test Items: Simple Forms," and Chapter 8, "Constructing Objective Test Items: Multiple-Choice Forms," contain good advice and examples.

Haladyna, T. M., & Downing, S. M. (1989). A taxonomy of multiple-choice item-writing rules, and validity of a taxonomy of multiple-choice item-writing rules. *Applied Measurement in Education, 2*(1), 37–50, 51–78.

Kubiszyn, T., & Bôrich, G. (2000). *Educational testing and measurement* (6th ed.). New York: Wiley. Chapter 6 is a good overview of item writing in general.

Norris, S. P., & Ennis, R. H. (1989). *Evaluating critical thinking.* Pacific Grove, CA: Critical Thinking Press and Software. This paperback contains lots of valuable examples of how to create your own measures as well as commercially available instruments.

Roid, G. H., & Haladyna, T. M. (1982). *A technology for test-item writing.* New York: Academic Press.

# 8

# Writing Assessment

---

## FOCUS CONCEPTS AND KEY TERMS FOR STUDY

| | |
|---|---|
| **Analytic Scoring** | **Instrument Validity** |
| **Developmental Scoring Rubric** | **Modified Holistic Scoring** |
| **Extended Response Essay** | **Objectivity** |
| **Holistic Scoring** | **Reader Reliability** |
| **Instrument Reliability** | **Restricted Response Essay** |
| | **Writing Prompts** |

---

## STANDARDS ALERT

**Standard 2.10**          **Rater Reliability**

When subjective judgment enters into test scoring, evidence should be provided on both interrater consistency in scoring and within-examinee consistency over repeated measurements. A clear distinction should be made among reliability data based on (a) independent panels of raters scoring the same performances or products, (b) a single panel scoring successive performances on new products, and (c) independent panels scoring successive performance on new products.

## TAKING IT TO THE CLASSROOM

It is often a revealing (and sometimes humbling) experience to have a colleague score a set of your students' essays using your scoring rubric. The post-assessment discussion can be absolutely valuable!

---

Reprinted with permission from the *Standards for Educational and Psychological Testing*. Copyright © 1999 by the American Educational Research Association, the American Psychological Association, and the National Council on Measurement in Education.

Two general types of writing assessments will be considered in this chapter. The first is the traditional and still very useful "essay" piece, question, or exam that is used primarily by English and language arts teachers. Essay questions can of course be used whenever a teacher wants to tie communication skills to subject matter in the content areas, for example, in social studies, science, and even mathematics. The second type of writing assessment is that legislated by many states as part of their mandated student assessment program. These types of assessments tend to be limited in scope but administered to all students in a particular grade, typically fifth, eighth, and eleventh. Problems and procedures involved in constructing and administering essay items and tests, as well as scoring procedures, are discussed in this chapter. We first examine the traditional essay exam.

## GENERAL TYPES OF ESSAY QUESTIONS

Many instructors, particularly neophytes, believe that essay tests are the easiest type of measuring instrument to construct and score. Nothing could be further from the truth. Considerable time and effort is necessary if essay items and tests are to yield meaningful information. Essay questions and tests allow direct assessment of the attainment of a variety of objectives and goals. In contrast with traditional "objective" item types, essay questions demand less construction time per fixed unit of student time but they significantly increase labor and time for scoring. According to some investigators, using essay testing encourages more appropriate study habits.

### Extended Versus Restricted Response

Essay items can be classified by a number of different but relevant criteria. Two particularly useful categories are extended versus restricted response. No hard and fast rules determine when a "restricted response" essay becomes "extended," however. Three paragraphs? Five hundred words? The terms describe relative ends of a continuum.

One can differentiate the many types of essay items by the extensiveness of the student's response. The relative freedom of response has obvious practical implications for both instructor and student. From the instructor's standpoint, an extensive response to a few broadly based questions allows an in-depth sampling of a student's knowledge, thinking processes, and problem-solving behavior relative to a particular topic. The open-ended nature of the task posed by an instruction such as "Discuss essay and objective-type tests" is challenging to a student. To respond correctly, the student must recall specific information and organize, evaluate, and write an intelligible composition. On the other hand, because they are poorly structured, such free-response essay items tend to yield a variety of responses from examinees, in both content and organization, and thus inhibit reliable grading. The student is forced to guess what the instructor wants. The potential ambiguity of an essay task is probably the single most important contributor to unreliability. In addition, the more extensive the responses elicited, the fewer questions an instructor can ask—which, in turn, can lower the content validity of the test.

It follows, therefore, that a more restricted response essay question or test is preferable. An instruction such as "Discuss the relative advantages and disadvantages of essay and short-answer tests with respect to (1) reliability, (2) objectivity, (3) content validity, and (4) usability" presents a better-defined task more likely to lend itself to reliable scoring, yet allows students sufficient latitude to organize and express their thoughts creatively.

Complex learning outcomes can be measured effectively with essay questions. These are the abilities, for example, to

- explain cause-effect relationships
- describe applications of principles
- present relevant arguments
- formulate tenable hypotheses

- formulate valid conclusions
- state necessary assumptions
- describe the limitations of data
- explain methods and procedures
- produce, organize, and express ideas
- integrate learnings in different areas
- create original forms (e.g., design an experiment)
- evaluate the worth of ideas

This list is not exhaustive but should highlight some potential learning outcomes that can be assessed by essay questions and tests.

### Content Versus Mechanics of Expression

It is frequently claimed that the essay question or test allows the student to present his or her knowledge and understanding and to organize the material in a unique form and style. More often than not, such factors as expression, grammar, spelling, and the like are evaluated in conjunction with content. If the instructor has attempted to develop students' expressive skills, and if this learning outcome is included in his or her table of specifications, evaluating such skills is legitimate. If expressive skills are not part of the instructional program, it is unethical to evaluate them. If the score of each essay item includes an evaluation of the mechanics of English, this should, obviously, be brought to the student's attention. If possible, separate scores should be computed for content and expression. The decision to include either or both of these elements in a score, and the relative weighting of each, should be dictated by the table of specifications.

### Specific Types of Essay Questions

The following set of essay questions* illustrates how the phrasing of an essay item could be framed to elicit particular behaviors and levels of response.

---

**I. Recall**

---

    A. Simple recall

        1. What is the chemical formula for hydrogen peroxide?

        2. Who wrote "The Emergence of Lincoln"?

    B. Selective recall in which a basis for evaluation or judgment is suggested

        1. Which three individuals in the 19th century had the most profound effect on contemporary life?

---

*Reprinted and modified with permission from *Testing Bulletin No. 2*, "The Writing of Essay Questions" published by the Office of Evaluation Services, Michigan State University, September, 1967.

## II. Understanding

A. Comparison of two phenomena on a single designated basis

1. Compare the writers of the English Renaissance to those of the 19th century in their abilities to describe nature.

B. Comparison of two phenomena in general

1. Compare the French and Russian Revolutions.

C. Explanation of the use or exact meaning of a phrase or statement

1. The Book of John begins "In the beginning was the word . . ." From what philosophical system does this statement derive?

D. Summary of a text or some portion of it

1. State the central thesis of the *Communist Manifesto*.

E. Statement of an artist's purpose in the selection or organization of material

1. Why did Hemingway describe in detail the episode in which Gordon, lying wounded, engages the oncoming enemy?

2. What was Beethoven's purpose in deviating from the orthodox symphony form in *Symphony No. 6*?

## III. Application

It should be clearly understood that whether or not a question elicits application depends on the preceding educational experience. If a particular analysis has been taught explicitly, a question involving that analysis is a matter of simple recall.

A. Causes or effects

1. Why can too frequent reliance on penicillin for the treatment of minor ailments eventually result in its diminished effectiveness against major invasion of body tissues by infectious bacteria?

2. Why did fascism flourish in Italy and Germany but not in England and the United States?

B. Analysis (It is advisable not to use the word analysis in the question itself)

1. Why was Hamlet torn by conflicting desires?

2. Why is the simple existence of slavery an insufficient explanation for the outbreak of the American Civil War?

C. Statement of relationship

1. Intelligence is said to correlate with school achievement at about .65. Explain this relationship.

D. Illustrations or examples of principles

1. Name three examples of uses of the lever in typical American homes.

E. Application of rules or principles in specified situations

1. Would you weigh more or less on the moon? On the sun? Explain.

F. Reorganization of facts

1. Some writers have concluded that the American Revolution was not merely a

political revolution against England but also a social revolution, within the colonies, of the poor against the wealthy. Using the available evidence to support this assertion, what other conclusion is possible?

---

**IV. Judgment**

---

A. Decision for or against

1. Should members of the Communist Party be allowed to teach in American colleges? Why or why not?

2. Is nature or nurture more influential in determining human behavior? Why?

B. Discussion

1. Discuss the likelihood that four-year private liberal arts colleges will gradually be replaced by junior colleges and state universities.

C. Criticism of the adequacy, correctness, or relevance of a statement

1. The discovery of penicillin has often been called an accident. Comment on the adequacy of this explanation.

D. Formulation of new questions

1. What should one find out to explain why some students of high intelligence fail in school?

2. What questions should a scientist ask to determine why more smokers than non-smokers develop lung cancer?

---

# SPECIAL PROBLEM AREAS

Four specific sources of difficulty are likely to be encountered in the use of essay tests: question construction, reader reliability, instrument reliability, and instrument validity.

## Question Construction

Preparing the essay question is perhaps the most important step in the developmental process. Language usage and word choice are particularly important during task construction. The language dimension is critical not only because it controls the comprehension level of the item for the examinee, but also because it specifies the task parameters. You need to narrowly specify, explicate, define, or otherwise clarify what it is that you want from the respondent. Take, for example, the silly writing task, "Describe the origins of World War I." This recall knowledge item related to the complex events contributing to the outbreak of hostilities in 1914 would leave the examinee in a real quandary. Did the author want to focus on the multinational forces of nationalism, imperialism, or communism, political events, military events, or the assassination of Archduke Ferdinand of Austria? A more meaningful rephrasing of the question might be: "What were the principal diplomatic events in Europe between 1890 and 1913 that contributed directly to the outbreak of World War I?" This task is better defined and unequivocally demands the recall of specific selected information. What, if anything, is done with this information will depend on how the material was handled in the classroom. But sometimes specificity is not enough, as illustrated by my favorite essay item: "Describe the world and give two examples." The question must also have an answer that "experts" could agree upon, thereby rendering it **objective**. Here is another item that allows too much latitude in interpretation: "Comment on the significance of Darwin's *Origin of Species*." The intent is to provide sufficient range for the student to display his or her mastery of the material. Unfortunately, one could write for hours on the question and never address the intent of the instructor. An improved version follows: "Darwin, in his *Origin of Species*, emphasized that natural selection resulted in the survival of the fittest. To what extent has this been supported or refuted by subsequent biological research?" Limits have now been placed on the problematic situation.

Essay items are frequently disdained because it is claimed that they do not measure higher-order outcomes. This is perhaps a problem with how they are used rather than a legitimate comment on how they can be used. Following are two sample essay items taken from the *Taxonomy of Educational Objectives*. Depending on instructional background and the skill level of the student, this task to produce a plan or set of operations measures at least the analysis level of the *Taxonomy*.

Several authorities were asked to participate in a round-table discussion of juvenile delinquency. They were given the following data about City X and Communities A, B, and C within City X:

| | For City X as a Whole | For Community A | For Community B | For Community C |
|---|---|---|---|---|
| Juvenile Delinquency Rate (annual arrests per 100 persons ages 5–19) | 4.24 | 18.1 | 1.3 | 4.1 |
| Average Monthly Rental | $60.00 | $42.00 | $100.00 | $72.00 |
| Infant Death Rate (per 1000 births) | 52.3 | 76.0 | 32.1 | 56.7 |
| Birth Rate (per 1000 inhabitants) | 15.5 | 16.7 | 10.1 | 15.4 |

From *Taxonomy of Educational Objectives, Handbook I: The Cognitive Domain*, ed. by B. Bloom. New York: David McKay Company, Inc., 1956. Reprinted by permission of Longman Publishers, USA.

In addition, they were told that in Community A the crimes against property (burglary and so on) constituted a higher proportion of the total juvenile offenses than in Communities B and C, where crimes against persons (assault, and so on) were greater.

1. How would *you* explain the differences in these juvenile delinquency rates in light of the above data? (You can use any theory or material presented in the course.)

2. Following your explanation of the data, what proposals would you make for reducing the juvenile delinquency rate in each of the three communities?

### Reader Reliability

The classic studies of the reliability of grading free-response test items were undertaken in 1912 and 1913 (Starch & Elliott, 1912, 1913a, 1913b). In three studies focusing on high school English, history, and mathematics, researchers found tremendous variation in the independent gradings of a standard set of papers. They found discrepancies of as much as 48 points in English, 49 points in geometry, and 70 points in history. Even research, employing highly sophisticated designs and analysis procedures, has failed to demonstrate consistently satisfactory agreement among essay graders. A study undertaken by the College Entrance Examination Board (Myers, McConville, & Coffman, 1966) involving 145 readers, 80,000 essays, and a five-day reading period found average single-reader reliabilities of 0.41. When the number of readers was increased to four, the average reliability rose to 0.73. This significant increase in reliability was obtained under controlled conditions, with trained graders who read "holistically" and used a 4-point scale. The implication of this research is clear: several readers should participate in the grading of essay exams, and they should be trained in using the scoring rubric. The fallibility of human judgment cannot be underestimated as a source of unreliability in the scoring of essay examinations.

Research has shed light on some specific contributory factors to lack of reader reliability. Jon Marshall and Jerry Powers (1969), for example, experimentally demonstrated that pre-service teachers are influenced by such factors as quality of composition and penmanship, even when they are explicitly instructed to grade on content alone.

### Instrument Reliability

Even if an acceptable level of scoring reliability is attained, we have no guarantee that we are measuring consistently (see Chapter 14). There remains the issue of the sampling objectives or behaviors represented by the test. Although experienced readers can frequently agree on the scoring of two different forms of an essay test, the correlation between the forms can be quite low (e.g., 0.60). Thus it is possible for the reliability of scoring to exceed the reliability of the instrument itself.

Some experts have suggested that the essay test is less susceptible than the objective test to the effect of guessing. This may not be the case. If the examinee is torn between two or more responses to an open-ended question, he or she still must guess between them. Such guessing, if widespread, can contribute to increased error and decreased reliability. The only difference between guessing on essay tests and guessing on objective tests is that the essay writer devises her or his own alternatives, whereas the alternatives are provided on an objective test.

One way to increase the reliability of an essay test is to increase the number of questions and restrict the length of the answers. The more specific and narrowly defined the questions, the less likely they are to be ambiguous to the examinee. This procedure should result in more uniform comprehension and performance of the assigned task, and hence in the increased reliability of the instrument and scoring. It also helps ensure better coverage of the domain of objectives. Using multiple readers, and using a tie-breaker reader if necessary, can also help. Explicit scoring criteria or rubrics are critical.

**Instrument Validity**

The number of questions on the test influences validity as well as reliability. **Validity** is generally defined as a characteristic of the scores yielding desired and consistent results. The first step in developing an achievement test can be to summarize the instructional objectives as a table of specifications. As commonly constructed, an essay test contains a small number of items; thus, the sampling of desired behaviors represented in the table of specifications will be limited, and the test will suffer from lowered validity—specifically, decreased content validity. The limited sampling affects not only the behavior measured, but also the subject matter covered. Studies have shown that an essay exam elicits about half the knowledge an individual possesses about a particular topic, but requires twice as much time as a short-answer test.

The validity of an essay test may be questioned in another way. Theoretically, the essay allows examinees to construct a creative, organized, unique, and integrated communication. Very frequently, however, examinees spend most of their time simply recalling and assembling information, rather than integrating it. The behavior elicited by the test, then, is not that hoped for by the instructor or dictated by the table of specifications. Obviously, validity suffers in a situation such as this. Again, one way to handle the problem is to increase the number of items on the test, which provides a more comprehensive sample of the expected instructional outcomes.

## DEVELOPING AND CRITIQUING PROMPTS*

Just as the value of a set of multiple-choice questions rests on the quality of the questions, so the effectiveness of a writing assessment rests with the stimulus prompt. In creating prompts experience is the best teacher. One needs to write and try many prompts before a kind of personal style evolves and workable stimuli elicit the desired student behavior. Following are seven "keys" to effective prompt development to be used in sit-down writing experiences (versus term papers).

- Use the Writer's Own Experiences—Requesting opinions or stories about topics outside the student's experience will not allow for a quality assessment. The student must feel comfortable with the content, or psychological and cognitive blocks may inhibit expression. Finding universal material is not easy. Not every student has been to Disneyland, flown on a plane, or climbed Mount Everest.

- Allow Choice—Since you are not scoring for knowledge acquisition, but student ability to communicate, let students "fill in the blank." For example: Think of a time when you felt especially happy (frightened, nervous, surprised, etc.) And tell a story about it.

- Stimulate the Writer's Imagination—Writing about a favorite school subject may not excite the creativity of every schoolchild. Using a prompt that allows students to "imagine" and "create" will yield a much richer essay. For example: You have discovered an old shoe on the way home from school. Describe it in such a way that the reader will be able to "see" it and tell a story about how it came to rest where you found it.

  Trying to be too creative and cutesy can, however, get you into trouble, as in this example: Imagine that you woke up one day as a loaf of bread. How would you get through the day? One doesn't have to go into science fiction to find imaginative ideas. A little reality helps the young writer.

- Don't Do the Thinking for the Writer—Don't write the directions to your prompt in such excruciating detail that the essayist gets bogged down trying to fulfill your expectations. You don't want the student to have to make

---

*The ideas in this section were adapted from an undated publication entitled *Keys to Good Prompts* from the Northwest Regional Educational Laboratory of Portland, Oregon.

a literal response to your prompt. Following is a good example of a bad prompt: Think of a place that you have visited and that you would like to revisit someday. It could be near or far away, large or small, outside or inside a building. Recall the different smells, sights, and sounds that make it a place that you remember. Now describe it in such a way that the reader would like to go there with you and also find it memorable.

This wordy prompt calls for the student to fill in the blanks, not create an imaginative composition.

- Avoid Built-in Positives and Negatives—Allow the student to impose his or her own value judgments on the topic. Asking for the best, worst, favorite, or most delectable will generally not yield as meaningful an essay as "memorable" or "hard to forget" prompts. Freedom to determine direction and content makes for more honest expressions.

- Don't be Nosey—Real questions of privacy can be raised if a prompt inquires into the personal lives of students. If this guideline is not followed it can lead to potential bias. There are both legal and ethical reasons for avoiding prompts dealing with drugs, home, politics, or religion. Sometimes a situation can be posed that might allow the student to be creative. For example: You have been appointed as chairperson of a local government committee and asked to determine how to spend a $50,000 grant from a nonprofit charitable foundation. Write a letter to the mayor that would convince him or her of the wisdom of your recommendation(s).

- Make the Purpose Clear—It's a fine line between so structuring the prompt-task that students give what they think the examiner wants and leaving it so ambiguous that students don't know how to respond. There obviously needs to be sufficient freedom for students to impose their own ideas and structure on the task without restricting creativity. If the purpose is important to the teacher-examiner, then using appropriate stage-setting introductions such as "Tell what happened . . . ," "Explain how . . . ," "Persuade . . . ," or "Convince someone to agree with you" should both direct the response and allow creative freedom.

Good prompts are obviously a key to a good writing assessment program. The major ingredient is effective instruction and a high level of student motivation.

After you have created your prompts several teachers need to sit down together and critique the prompts. Following is a set of critical and insightful evaluative questions to be asked about prompts before use or, better yet, prior to tryout. The questions were developed by Dr. Belita Gordon (and her statewide advisors), director of the Writing Assessment Center at Test Scoring and Reporting Services at the University of Georgia.

**Creating, Reviewing, and Revising Writing Prompts**

- Is the topic a widely used classroom writing assignment?
- Is the topic a classroom writing assignment that requires scaffolding and pre-writing instructional activities that enable the students to write?
- Does the topic require knowledge and/or experiences that can be assumed for the complete examinee population?
- Is the topic accessible to a diverse student population?
- Does the topic provide a built-in advantage or disadvantage for one or more subgroups?
- Is the topic of intrinsic interest to student writers?
- Does the topic allow for a range of responses, thus satisfying both writer and reader interests?
- Does the topic promote negative thoughts or values?
- Does the prompt cue formulaic writing?
- Does the prompt cue the writer to produce a writing sample that "matches" the evaluative criteria?
- Does the prompt contain multiple messages about the expected response?
- Are the vocabulary and syntax appropriate for the grade level?
- Is the prompt complete?

**Sample Prompts**

Following are some sample prompts appropriate for eighth-grade students.

- Write about what you would do with $1 million. Pretend you received the money as a gift and could spend it any way you wished. You might want to spend part of your planning time thinking about how you would use the money to help yourself, another person, or the world. Think about information that will help your reader understand how you would use the million dollars and why you would use it in this way.
- Write about your favorite place. The place might be somewhere you imagined or it might be real. You might want to spend part of your planning time thinking about where your favorite place is, how you get there, and what you do when you are there. Think about information that will help your reader understand what your favorite place is like and why it is special to you.
- Write about a trip you want to take. It might be to a real place, such as the beach, mountains, city, or country. It might be make-believe, such as a trip to another planet. You might want to spend part of your plan-

ning time thinking about a place you want to visit, how you would get there, and what you would do once you arrived. Think about information that will help your reader understand where you want to go and why you want to take this trip.

- Write about a funny experience. It could be anything humorous that makes people smile or laugh. You might want to spend part of your planning time thinking about experiences that were funny to you or to someone else. Think about information that will help your reader understand why the experience was funny.

- Write about a character from a book, movie, or television show who reminds you of yourself. This character might be someone who had an experience similar to one that happened to you. The character might be someone who enjoys things you do. You might want to spend part of your planning time thinking about what you have in common with this character. Think about information that will help your reader understand how the character is like you.

- Write about an invention that is valuable to society. The invention could be something that was created a long time ago or recently. You might want to spend part of your planning time thinking about things that have made our lives safer, more interesting, or more enjoyable. Think about information that will help your reader understand what the invention is and how it changed our lives in a positive way.

To help the student before (and during) a writing assignment it would be worthwhile to remind him or her, as is done for the Georgia High School Graduation Test (at eleventh grade), that to create an effective writing sample the following guidelines should be followed:

---

**Prepare Yourself to Write**

---

- Read the topic carefully.
- Understand the purpose.
- Identify the audience.

---

**Make Your Paper Meaningful**

---

- State a clearly developed position.
- Use specific, convincing details.
- Present ideas in a clear order.

---

### Make Your Paper Interesting to Read

- Use effective word choice.
- Vary the sentence type, structure, and length.
- Use convincing and appealing supporting details.

---

### Make Your Paper Easy to Read

- Write effective paragraphs.
- Use effective transitions.
- Write in complete and correct sentences.
- Capitalize, spell, and punctuate correctly.

---

## MODELS FOR SCORING ESSAY QUESTIONS

Most instructors agree that scoring essay items and questions is one of the most time-consuming and frustrating tasks associated with conscientious classroom assessment. Instructors are frequently unwilling to set aside the large chunks of time necessary to score a stack of "blue books" carefully. It almost goes without saying that if reliable scoring is to be accomplished, an instructor must expend considerable time and effort. Reviewing the section in Chapter 10 on developing scoring rubrics may be helpful.

Before turning to specific methods of scoring, several general comments are in order. First, it is critical that the instructor prepare in advance a detailed "ideal" answer. This answer will serve as the criterion by which each student's answer is judged. If this is not done, the results could be disastrous. The instructor's subjectivity could seriously inhibit consistent scoring; it is also possible that student responses might themselves affect the evaluation of subsequent responses. Second, student papers should be scored anonymously. Third, all the answers to a given item should be scored at one time, rather than grading each student's total test separately.

The mechanics of scoring generally takes different forms, depending whether the focus is on content or subject matter or on delivery, that is, a unique communication consistent with accepted standards for expression, style, and grammar.

Table 8-1 outlines possible approaches to essay scoring for this measurement item type. The two foci are content (or subject matter), such as the Civil War or the anatomy of the human heart, and composition. Following is a brief description and discussion of these approaches.

**Table 8-1** *Combinations of Essay Scoring Methods and Focus Dimensions*

| | Focus Dimension | |
| --- | --- | --- |
| **Scoring Method** | **Content (Subject Matter)** | **Communication** |
| *Holistic* | Global overall evaluation | Global overall evaluation |
| *Modified Holistic* | Limited number of objectives | Limited number of dimensions |
| *Analytic* | Checklist point scoring of content | Detailed critique of essay |

### Holistic Scoring for Content Knowledge or Communication Effectiveness

Experienced readers make gross judgments about the quality of a given paper. The judgments are simply reported in two or more evaluation categories (e.g., acceptable/unacceptable; A/B/C/D/F; inadequate/minimal/good/very good). As many as eight categories can be used. Comments sometimes accompany the feedback to writers. Such a procedure, if not done anonymously, can be very susceptible to "halo" rating errors. As described here, the holistic scoring approach usually focuses on assessing writing effectiveness. The method could be applied in evaluating content achievement, but probably with considerably less reliability. The holistic approach also lacks detailed diagnostic value unless it contains extensive comments, in which case it almost becomes analytic.

### Modified Holistic Scoring for Communication Effectiveness

This method involves making overall evaluations of a limited number of components. Each component then gets a score from 1 to 4, 5, or 6. The modified holistic method is efficient when numerous papers must be scored and multiple readers are being used. Training in rubrics use is the key to success.

### Modified Holistic Scoring for Content Knowledge

In reality, the modified holistic approach to scoring essays for content knowledge is probably used very little. If applied in its fullest form, it would involve a rater making judgments about the adequacy of knowledge a student exhibited about a limited number of objectives. For example, the teacher of a human anatomy and physiology class might present an essay task requiring students to describe the following major systems: skeletal, reproductive, digestive, circulatory, and urinary. Judgments would be made about the adequacy of each description. The analysis of responses would be more detailed than holistic, but less than analytic scorings.

### Analytic Scoring for Communication Effectiveness

This method involves evaluating a number of specific categories—generally fewer than 10. Qualitative judgments are then made within categories. In general, this method emphasizes the totality or "wholeness" of the response and is used when the instructor is focusing on expression rather than content. Rating methods are generally efficient, but their reliabilities are very much tied to the number of categories and subdivisions within categories. The categories chosen are usually determined by the "ideal" answer constructed by the instructor. Another useful approach is to use a standard set of categories, particularly if one's primary interest is in evaluating English composition. A rating method found useful by Paul Diederich in his research on writing ability, and by many classroom teachers, is presented in Table 8-2. This scale weighs organization 50 percent, style 30 percent, and mechanics 20 percent. By using appropriate, if arbitrary, multiplications, the 40-point scale translates into a 100-point scale. Such a translation is useful if an instructor is disposed or required to report percentage grades.

The ultimate essay critique, however, is the detailed analysis paragraph by paragraph, line by line, and word by word, that is, the old "red pencil" approach. This type of analysis provides the maximum benefit to the student, but it obviously takes a great deal of time and effort. Such detailed analyses are impractical when composition is included as part of large-scale assessment, that is, on a statewide basis.

### Analytic Scoring for Content Achievement

The term *content achievement* as used here usually means knowledge and understanding. The analytic—or the checklist point score—method involves partitioning the "ideal" response into a series of points or features, each of which is specifically defined. This scoring technique is particularly useful when content is to be emphasized over expression. Each element in the answer is identified and a credit value is attached to it. If possible, the instructor's table of specifications should be used as a guide for determining credits.

Consider the following restricted response question: "What are the principal reasons that research in the social sciences has not progressed as far as has that in the biological and physical sciences?" The instructor's ideal answer might be, "Since the social scientist is himself part of what he is attempting to study, he cannot achieve the objectivity possible in the more precise sciences. Further, the conclusions he reaches frequently run

**Table 8-2**  *Diederich's Scale for Grading English Composition*

| | | | |
|---|---|---|---|
| Quality and development of ideas | 1 2 3 4 5 | | |
| Organization, relevance, movement | 1 2 3 4 5 | _____ x 5 = | _____ |
| | | Subtotal | |
| Style, flavor, individuality | 1 2 3 4 5 | | |
| Wording and phrasing | 1 2 3 4 5 | _____ x 3 = | _____ |
| | | Subtotal | |
| Grammar, sentence structure | 1 2 3 4 5 | | |
| Punctuation | 1 2 3 4 5 | | |
| Spelling | 1 2 3 4 5 | | |
| Manuscript form, legibility | 1 2 3 4 5 | _____ x 1 = | _____ |
| | | Subtotal | |
| | | Total grade | _____% |

1 = Poor   2 = Weak   3 = Average   4 = Good   5 = Excellent

*Source:* Adapted from "A Scale for Grading English Composition" by Paul B. Diederich. In *Improving English Composition,* Arno Jewett and Charles Buster, editors. Copyright © 1965. Washington, D.C.: National Education Association. Reprinted by permission of the National Education Association.

counter to deeply held prejudices and are therefore unacceptable. Feeling that many of the social affairs of men are not susceptible to scientific study, people have been less willing to subsidize social research than medicine, for example. Finally, the scientific study of nature has a much longer history than the scientific study of man. This history has provided a much larger body of data and theory from which to progress."

The essential elements in this ideal answer are identified and quantitative weights are assigned to each. The checklist point score sheet might look something like this:

| Element of Answer | Possible Points |
|---|---|
| 1. Scientist part of his subject | 2 |
| 2. Prejudice | 3 |
| 3. Lack of financial support | 2 |
| 4. Short history | 1 |
| 5. Small body of facts and theory | 1 |
| 6. Organization | 1 |
| 7. Language usage | 1 |

This approach to scoring has several advantages. It is objective and likely to be reliable. An analysis of the instructor's ideal response quite frequently reveals that the original question needs to be recast to elicit the desired response, which can result in time limit readjustment. A final advantage of the checklist point score method is its reliability. If used conscientiously, the analytic method can yield consistent scores on restricted response essay items for different graders.

The difference between analytic scoring and modified holistic scoring is perhaps more a matter of degree than kind because both involve making general judgments. Many of the suggestions for using essay items discussed in this chapter, as well as other recommendations by measurement authorities, are summarized in Table 8-3. All are self-explanatory with the exception of the eighth. Testing experts generally discourage the use of optional questions. Although appearing to be an inherently fair procedure, using optional questions results in essay tests that measure what the student knows, rather than what he or she doesn't know. If a test is to provide useful information about learning outcomes, negative as well as positive evidence should be gathered. We are emphasizing here the diagnostic use of essay tests. There can be situations in which it is legitimate to allow a student to select the questions he or she will answer. Such a situation might be a statewide testing pro gram with little control of the curriculum, in which an optional choice would probably constitute a fairer testing practice. But in a classroom testing situation, allowing a choice of questions is generally not recommended. If "choice" is to be permitted, the questions must be demonstrably equivalent.

## ASSESSING ELEMENTARY STUDENT WRITING SKILLS

Assessing the emerging language arts of the very young child can be a challenge to the elementary teacher. Tables 8-4 and 8-5 contain materials developed by the elementary teachers of Wilkes County, Georgia. It can be seen in Table 8-4 that foundational skills and content are included in the writing checklist of Table 8-5. It is also interesting that samples of artwork are tied to the total language experience, thereby enhancing students' ability to express themselves. As students move up the grade scale there is greater emphasis placed on quality of ideas, organization, and mechanics of expression (grammar).

**Table 8-3** *Suggestions for Constructing, Evaluating, and Using Essay Exams*

1. Limit the problem that the question poses so that it will have an unequivocal meaning to most students.

2. Use words that will convey clear meaning to the student.

3. Prepare enough questions to sample the material of the course broadly, within a reasonable time limit.

4. Use an essay question for the purposes it best serves, that is, organization, handling complicated ideas, and writing.

5. Prepare questions that require considerable thought, but that can be answered in relatively few words.

6. Determine in advance how much weight will be accorded each of the various elements expected in a complete answer.

7. Without knowledge of students' names, score each question for all students. Use several scores and scorers if possible.

8. Require all students to answer all questions on the test.

9. Write questions about materials immediately germane to the course.

10. Study past questions to determine how students performed.

11. Make gross judgments of the relative excellence of answers as a first step in grading.

12. Word a question as simply as possible to make the task clear.

13. Do *not* judge papers on the basis of external factors unless they have been clearly stipulated.

14. Do *not* make a generalized estimate of an entire paper's worth.

15. Do *not* construct a test that consists of only one question.

*Source:* Adapted with permission from *Testing Bulletin No. 1,* Essay Tests: General considerations. Published by the Office of Evaluation Services, Michigan State University, 1971.

## LARGE-SCALE ASSESSMENT OF WRITING PERFORMANCE

One of the most significant movements in public education is the large-scale assessment of writing performance* at selected grade levels. This is being done both informally at the local level and formally at the state level. State-level data gathered for accountability purposes can be very valuable. Such data give classroom teachers, schools, and systems important information about the students' progress in developing written communication skills.

**Table 8-4**  *Wilkes County (Georgia) Writing Sample Assessment Checklist Terminology. First Grade (See Table 8-5 for Checklist)*

**CONTENT**

**Picture Relates to Topic**—Picture drawn matches topic given.

**Appropriate Title**—Title matches topic given, is separate from story, is clearly identifiable as a title, and is the actual name given to the story.

**Words Relate to Topic**—Individual words child has written relate to topic.

**Sentence(s) Relate to Topic**—Sentence(s) child has written relate to topic.

**STYLE**

**Uses Descriptive Words**—Uses adjectives in story.

**GRAMMAR/MECHANICS**

**Punctuation (sentence ending marks)**—Child uses periods and other appropriate ending marks, clearly exhibiting understanding of the use of sentence ending marks.

**Beginning Sentence Capital Letters**—Child uses capital letters at the beginning of complete sentences, showing knowledge of capitalization. Sentences ended with periods, begun with lower case "and," and then the word "I," are not sentences begun with a capital letter.

**Complete Sentences**—Child writes sentences which include a subject, verb, and object, beginning capital letter, and correct ending punctuation.

**Correct Spelling of Basic Sight Words**—Child spells basic sight words common to first graders. If child spells any basic sight word correctly (even only two or three), a "1" must be recorded.

**Inventive Spelling**—Child uses inventive spelling of words not usually written by the average first grader. If no inventive spelling is present, a "0" must be recorded.

**PENMANSHIP**

**Correctly Formed Letters**—Letters in words written about the picture or topic are correctly formed.

**Correct Spacing Between Letters and Words**—Child uses correct spacing between the letters in words and correct spacing between the words.

**Marking Scale**—Assign a "0," "1," or "2" only to the paper you are assessing. Do not decide if it's "yes," "sometimes," or "no" based on how the child has progressed, or what the child is doing in your classroom.

**Developmental Stage**—Determine the developmental stage. Use the description of stages on the attached sheet. Put the month and year next to the stage (e.g., Stage 1 9/xx).

---

Each year we see an increase in the number of states implementing mass writing assessment programs. Public education is increasingly criticized by national commissions, reports, and surveys for its lack of attention to concerns of literacy, particularly to the development of writing skills. Teachers are said to be lax in their attention to the cultivation of such skills. From an instructional standpoint, teaching writing skills is very time-consuming and

**Table 8-5** *Wilkes County (Georgia) Grade One*
*Writing Sample Assessment Checklist*

**Directions:** Use the following Writing Benchmarks to assess the September & May writing assessment samples. Put a 0, 1, or 2 in each block. Remember, these Benchmarks reflect what a first grade student should be able to do at the end of the year.

Student Name _____ Teacher _____ Year _____

| Writing Topic: Narrative Essay | September | May |
|---|---|---|
| **CONTENT** | | |
| Picture Relates to Topic | | |
| Appropriate Title | | |
| Words Relate to Topic | | |
| Sentences Relate to Topic | | |
| **STYLE** | | |
| Uses Descriptive Words | | |
| **GRAMMAR/MECHANICS** | | |
| Punctuation (Sentence Ending Marks) | | |
| Beginning Sentence Capital Letters | | |
| Complete Sentences | | |
| Correct Spelling of Basic Sight Words | | |
| Inventive Spelling | | |
| **PENMANSHIP** | | |
| Correctly Formed Letters | | |
| Correct Spacing Between Letters and Words | | |
| **TOTAL** | | |

**Marking Scale:    0 No, Never    1 Sometimes    2 Most of the Time**

**DEVELOPMENTAL STAGES (See Figure 8-1 for description of each stage.)**

Stage 1 _____    Stage 2 _____    Stage 3 _____    Stage 4 _____    Stage 5 _____    Stage 6 _____

September Total _____    May Total ___    IMPROVEMENT    NO IMPROVEMENT
(Circle One)

Comments: _____

_____

must compete with other important objectives. A big problem is that evaluating writing samples requires considerable time and effort. Yet feedback is a critical element in the instructional process. The data needed are more than judgments of "acceptable" or "unacceptable" and should help direct the student toward areas requiring improvements.

In doing large-scale assessments, particularly in the elementary grades, a developmental variation of the modified holistic approach has been found useful. Figure 8-1 contains a description of the developmental scoring rubric for a fifth-grade statewide writing assessment. Note the logical progression of developmental cognitive skills as more detail and elaboration are added. Obviously not all writing samples from a statewide assessment are scorable. Among the unscorable paper types are blank responses, illustrations only (no text), not original text (e.g., copied from board or printed materials or other writers), not related to assigned writing tasks, illegible paper, or written in a language other than English. Figure 8-2 contains a learning aid for the visual learner. Again, the increasing focus, detail, and elaboration are evident.

## Rationale for Writing Assessment

Writing assessment is a natural outgrowth of classroom instruction in that it occurs as a process. Although the events in this process are not always agreed-upon, writing-as-a-process can be taught. The writing process should reflect the following characteristics:

- Is viewed as a developmental process that emerges as children experience language in a real, meaningful, and natural way.
- Is developmentally appropriate and authentic.
- Does not develop linearly. Shifts in skill level, rather than uninterrupted progress, are to be expected.
- Develops at varying rates.
- Is learned by doing it.
- Is taught as an ongoing process.
- Allows students to participate in the writing process by talking, reading, brainstorming, collaborating, planning, drafting, revising, proofing, responding, sharing, and revisiting.
- Is taught interactively with reading, listening, thinking, and speaking.
- Emphasizes the command of oral language as an integral part of writing.
- Is an integral part of the curriculum in all grades.
- Includes daily opportunities for students to write for various purposes and audiences.

**Developmental Stage/Scoring Guidelines • Georgia Writing Assessment for Grades 3 and 5**

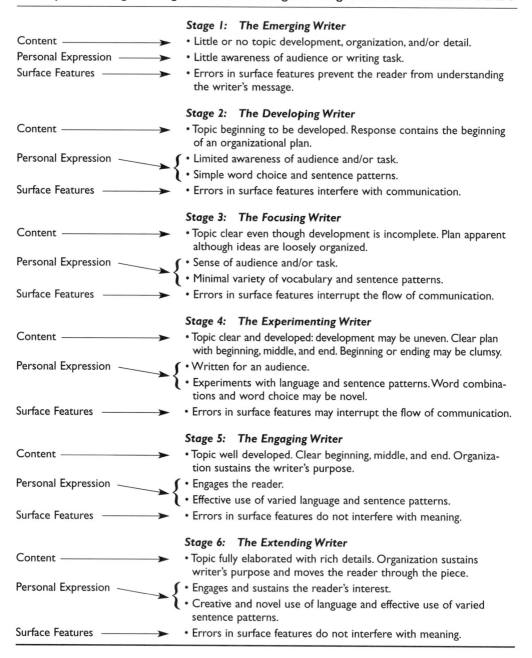

*Stage 1:   The Emerging Writer*

Content ⟶ • Little or no topic development, organization, and/or detail.

Personal Expression ⟶ • Little awareness of audience or writing task.

Surface Features ⟶ • Errors in surface features prevent the reader from understanding the writer's message.

*Stage 2:   The Developing Writer*

Content ⟶ • Topic beginning to be developed. Response contains the beginning of an organizational plan.

Personal Expression ⟶ { • Limited awareness of audience and/or task.
• Simple word choice and sentence patterns.

Surface Features ⟶ • Errors in surface features interfere with communication.

*Stage 3:   The Focusing Writer*

Content ⟶ • Topic clear even though development is incomplete. Plan apparent although ideas are loosely organized.

Personal Expression ⟶ { • Sense of audience and/or task.
• Minimal variety of vocabulary and sentence patterns.

Surface Features ⟶ • Errors in surface features interrupt the flow of communication.

*Stage 4:   The Experimenting Writer*

Content ⟶ • Topic clear and developed: development may be uneven. Clear plan with beginning, middle, and end. Beginning or ending may be clumsy.

Personal Expression ⟶ { • Written for an audience.
• Experiments with language and sentence patterns. Word combinations and word choice may be novel.

Surface Features ⟶ • Errors in surface features may interrupt the flow of communication.

*Stage 5:   The Engaging Writer*

Content ⟶ • Topic well developed. Clear beginning, middle, and end. Organization sustains the writer's purpose.

Personal Expression ⟶ { • Engages the reader.
• Effective use of varied language and sentence patterns.

Surface Features ⟶ • Errors in surface features do not interfere with meaning.

*Stage 6:   The Extending Writer*

Content ⟶ • Topic fully elaborated with rich details. Organization sustains writer's purpose and moves the reader through the piece.

Personal Expression ⟶ { • Engages and sustains the reader's interest.
• Creative and novel use of language and effective use of varied sentence patterns.

Surface Features ⟶ • Errors in surface features do not interfere with meaning.

**Figure 8-1** *Developmental scoring rubric for writing assessment*

Stage 1    The Emerging Writer

Stage 4    The Experimenting Writer

Stage 2    The Developing Writer

Stage 5    The Engaging Writer

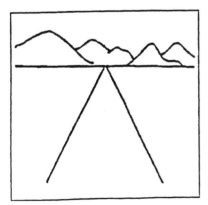

Stage 3    The Focusing Writer

Stage 6    The Extending Writer

**Figure 8-2** *Pictorial representation of developmental scoring rubric*

- Is practical in a classroom environment that supports risk-taking and experimentation with language.
- Takes place with teacher and student participating in a writing community.
- Enhances an appreciation of writing.
- Follows no prescribed sequence. Sequence can vary according to individual differences and task requirements.
- Allows students to work on more than one piece of writing at a time. Students should be able to select the piece of writing on which they want to work. One piece does not have to be completed before another can be started.
- Encourages students to use available resources during the different phases of the writing process. These resources include people, equipment, and materials.
- Applies to some but not all student writing. A piece of writing will be stronger if the writer has an investment in it and wants to continue working on it.
- Is best taught by modeling and demonstration along with the opportunity to practice.

The intimate association between instruction and assessment is fostered when the effective teacher is one who

- Builds a community of writers.
- Creates a classroom climate that encourages risk-taking and experimentation with language.
- Provides opportunities for writing.
- Writes along with the students.
- Plays an active role in all phases of writing instruction, including facilitating, directing, dialoguing, modeling, evaluating, and celebrating.
- Teaches the conventions of written language by using the following:
- Responding first and foremost to the writer's message in a piece of writing
- Asking questions that encourage the writer to revisit the piece
- Allowing the writer to maintain ownership of the piece
- Teaching students to see conventions as a courtesy to readers
- Using the writer's need to communicate with a reader to motivate the writer to learn the appropriate conventions.

## Evaluation of Writing in the Classroom

Classroom evaluation should inform instruction and, in turn, improve writing. Evaluation is an ongoing activity, involving both teachers and students. Students should be involved in evaluating their writing and selecting the pieces of writing that are to be kept. Classroom evaluation requires that

- Students' writing is collected over time.
- Students' writing is collected from writing samples that have been taken through many phases.
- Many different types of writing, written for many different purposes and under different conditions, are collected.
- The collections are stored in a manner that encourages students to revisit, reflect, rethink, and revise their writing.
- Students are involved in setting goals for strengthening writing skills.
- Progress that occurs over time is shared with students and parents.
- Procedures result in the improvement of writing *and* writing instruction.
- Conditions reflect a natural integration of the language arts.
- Conditions parallel, as closely as possible, the teaching of writing.
- Assessment occurs over a period of time, not in a single designated time period.

## Types of Writing

Typical of the types of writing found in the elementary grades are the following:

---

### Relating a Personal Experience

---

- Responses can include

    facts and events

    embellishments of facts and events
- Sources are based on

    personal, firsthand experiences

    personal experiences of people the writer knows

---

### Creating an Imaginative Story

---

- Imaginative writing encourages innovation and risk-taking. It is unusual, lively, and fun. It avoids retelling or writing plot summaries of someone else's imagination. Imaginative stories are based on the child's own imagination.

- Responses can include

| | |
|---|---|
| fables and tall tales | science fiction |
| myths and legends | space travel |
| mystery | new endings to existing stories |

---

### Responding to Literature

- Responses are based on published commercial literature or student writing. Responses include, but are not limited to
    - Character sketch
    - New ending
    - How the test makes the writer feel
    - Why the writer liked or disliked the text
    - Comparison of the writer's life to something in the text
    - Assuming the identity of a character in the text
    - Comparing/contrasting one text to another
- Sources include but are not limited to

| | |
|---|---|
| Autobiography | Biography |
| Classics | Fables, tall tales |
| Letters | Plays |
| Poetry, musical lyrics | Realistic fiction |
| Short stories | Wordless picture books |

---

### Scoring Statewide Writing Samples

Papers are read by at least two readers; if there is a significant disagreement the paper is rated by a third independent "master" rater who resolves the rating disagreement. "Model" papers are periodically inserted into the system to monitor reliability and accuracy. A reader can, on the average, score a paper in two minutes. Average agreement within one rating scale point within each of the six stages (see Figure 8-1) can be achieved in 90 percent of the cases.

Safeguards that are built into the system to help ensure highest quality, reliability and validity are the following:

- The use of a statewide advisory committee and the state curriculum to specify the assessment content and process
- Pilot testing
- Bias review
- Two independent scorings, examinee anonymity

- Extensive reader training
- Inserted pre-scored "validity" papers and check sets
- Daily monitoring with retraining as necessary

**Illustrative Writing Samples**

Figure 8-3 contains a fifth-grader's writing sample at the "focusing writer" level (see Figure 8-1). The reader can discern the topic of the grandmother's retirement party. The writer's plan is apparent but loose. The paper has no ending, development is incomplete, and the sequence of events is confusing to the reader. The writer is aware of an audience. Knowledge of minimal vocabulary and sentence patterns is evident throughout the paper. Surface feature errors interrupt but do not prevent communication.

A second writing sample is presented in Figure 8-4. This paper was taken from a student portfolio, written in response to the request to tell an imaginative story. This one is at the "extending writer" level (see Figure 8-1). The writer includes many details that build on each other to convey what happened and how much the writer enjoyed this adventure into invisibility. In addition to the fullness of detail, the writer uses a varied and colorful vocabulary ("farther than we ever had before," "beautiful sparkling stream," "sister *yelled*," "I *dodged*," "*sneak a swim*"). Although the attempt at an unexpected twist back to reality as a conclusion is less successful than the rest of the paper, it indicates the writer's effort to extend beyond what she or he does well toward new skills. (What more could we hope for?)

Although reading and assessing student writing samples can be a frustrating and laborious task, there are rewards. In addition to feeling good about a job well done and professional pride, readers are often tickled with quips such as these fifth-grade funnies:

- We had a normal relationship. We didn't expect anything from each other.

- Wiley wish that he had a cow so he can ride on it so he can be a cowboy.

- The wolf was in jail, the old lady would not show her face in public, the third pig morned the loss of his brothers, and the first two were left to answer a favorite of mine "is there a God?"

- My family went on a ten day weekend.

- The person who is special to me is my grandmother . . . she is the one I look up to because she is tall.

- . . . a huge Grizzly Bear started chasing us. He chased us for several hours. Then the bear shouted "hey Stop! I just want some grey poupon!"

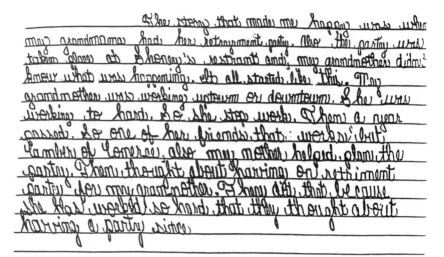

The story that made me happy was when my grandmama had her retirement party. The party was taken place at Shoney's restraunt and my grandmother didn't know what was happening. It all started like this. My grandmother was working uptown or downtown. She was working to hard. So she stop work. Then a year passed. So one of her friends that works... Chamber of Commerce, also my mother helped plan the party. Then thought about having on retirment party for my grandmother. They did that because she has worked so hard that they thought about having a party since.

**Figure 8-3** *Fifth grade writing sample at focusing writer level (Stage 3).* *(See Figure 8-1)*

Once upon a time, I was walking in the woods one day with my dogs Sigmund and Honey, my two hound dogs. Sigmund and Honey were ahead of me and started barking. We had gone farther then we ever had before. I rushed up to Sigmund and Honey and there in front of us was a beautiful sparkling stream. Me, Honey, and Sigmund were drinking when all of a sudden we were invisible. I walked out of the woods with Sigmund and Honey trailing behind me. Only the people or things that drank out of the stream could see each other. I started to ride my bike when my sister yelled out that there was an invisible ghost on my bike. She tried to stop me but I dodged her. Then I went out on the street. My dad was coming home when he saw my bike riding out in the street. He caught my bike and put it in the truck. Then I went to my friend's lake to sneak a swim. I got home just in time for me to be visible. The next day I went to the stream and to take a drink. And then I was invisible. This time I got a fishing pole and put it in the water. It turned invisible also. So I went to my friend's lake to go fishing. I got a worm but I didn't make it invisible. And I went fishing. I caught 10 catfish that day. Then I got home just in time for me to be visible. The next day I went to the stream. But it was gone. I told my mother about the stream and gave her the fish to sell. We made 20 bucks! Momma sent me to my room for punishment of drinking the water. The End

**Figure 8-4** *Fifth grade writing sample at extending writer level (Stage 6)* *(see Figure 8-1)*

We were pretty mad that we were running for hours, when all the bear wanted was some stupid mustard.

- I learned what responsibility means. I also learned a lesson never to buy a pregnant female dog.
- I'm proud of George Washington and General Custard.
- My horse was a black stallion named Missy. She was beautiful.
- Mrs. Smith was my science teacher, she was mean as a shark.
- The mall. How I love the mall.
- We played capture the Bad Girl in Blue . . . of course I was always the Bad Girl in Blue.
- I like Christmas because you will see relatives you have not seen in years. They bring gifts and the item they borrowed three years ago!
- Of all the holidays July the fourth is one of my favorites. I would have written about Christmas but everybody writes about Christmas. People who have to read these get tired of reading the same thing over and over again.
- I know you're thinking "not another phony essay about Christmas . . ."
- (At Christmas) When the relatives arrive, living agreements have to be made.
- I wish that Christmas lasted all year round, but I don't think people have that much niceness in them.

As we all know, children can be very creative.

### Feedback

In addition to indicating a student's developmental level in a report, commendations and recommendations are also communicated to the student and teacher to increase the instructional meaningfulness of the assessment. Following are samples of commendations and recommendations that raters select from a menu containing 10 of each type of statement.

---

**Commendations**

---

- Your skills as a writer are developing.
- The main idea of your paper is clear to your reader.
- The details you included helped me understand your ideas.
- Your great beginning made me want to hear more of your story.

---

**Recommendations**

---

- Your paper shows you are learning to put words together to make sense. Try to write in complete sentences.
- Your paper lists one idea after another. Try to concentrate on developing one main idea rather than writing one sentence about each different idea.
- Your writing loses focus because it strays from the topic. Try to say with the same topic.
- Organize your paper so the reader can follow your ideas. Try to rearrange your ideas so that you have a clear beginning, middle, and ending.

---

The emerging writer is really just getting started and therefore needs a different kind of nurturing. Following are suggestions made to the neophyte writer:

- Listen to stories and poems on tapes.
- Record your stories, letters, and poems on tape.
- Retell stories you read in your own words.
- Dictate stories and poems to someone.
- Use puppets to tell stories.
- Use computers and computer programs to write stories and poems.
- Use the visual arts to express your thoughts and feelings.
- Write a different ending to a story you have read.
- Write often and read widely.

Although the description and methods described here obviously meet the needs of language arts teachers, they apply in any of the content areas where communication in writing is to be assessed.

In summary it should be noted that the collecting and assessing of writing samples is one of the most flexible measurement methods available. It can be used to assess knowledge, the results of problem solving, and the students' ability to communicate and express themselves. Despite common misconceptions, creating essay questions or writing assessments is a time-consuming task. The phrasing of the question or prompt is critical. The poser of the questions must tread the line between *excessive generality*, where adequate answers cannot be compared in the available time, and *excessive specificity*, where all the examinee has time to do is recall and recount information. All these factors reflect the major problem of essay items: the reliability and validity of scoring. Sometimes we must make the effort and expend the time because this is the only way we can get the information that student and teacher need.

# CASE STUDY

Following is a brief short essay exercise aimed at measuring student knowledge about the use of the Language Experience Approach (LEA) to the teaching of reading. The LEA sometimes uses group-composed stories or compositions based on field trips, school activities, or personal experiences. Sometimes the chart summaries of these stimulus topics must include special words, observations, job assignments, questions to be answered, imaginative stories or poems, or class rules. In situations where the child's own language experiences are unique, such as a child who lives in the ghetto, the LEA may have some real benefits. A lot of the ideas contained in LEA served as a foundation for the development of the currently popular whole-language or integrated approaches to reading instruction and as an alternative to the basal-reader technique. The essay is aimed at achievement, and is *not* intended to measure the student's ability to communicate in the sense that a creative essay assignment might attempt to do. It is assumed that reasonable standards of grammar would, however, apply.

ESSAY: The Language Experience Approach is one of the most popular and serviceable approaches to the teaching of reading. Briefly describe in grammatically correct form three advantages and three disadvantages of this approach. Allow about 6 minutes for your response. This exercise is worth 20 points.

RESPONSE: The Language Experience Approach is one of the better approaches to use because teachers and kids like it. It lets them tell you what they know based on their life. Kids can use their motor and thinking skills. Learning makes them feel good because they can read and write about things they know. On the other side of the coin is the fact that charts of experiences can be boring and take a lot of class time. But anything worthwhile is going to take time.

## Criteria

The respondent could have selected from the following ideas in creating his or her answer. Each correctly identified element is worth 2 points, and 8 total points were allowed for grammar and spelling.

| *Pro* | *Con* |
|---|---|
| 1. Every child has some experience he or she can talk, read, or write about. | 1. There is a lack of sequential development. |

2. A variety of modalities are used.

3. Teacher and student work together.

4. Students' self-concept is enhanced.

2. Language experience charts can be boring.

3. Making charts is time-consuming.

4. It may lead to memorization.

5. There is a lack of vocabulary control.

With this information, assign a total score to the sample essay.

## CONTENT REVIEW STATEMENTS

**1.** Essay questions and tests can be used to assess a variety of learning outcomes, particularly those related to an individual's ability to organize, analyze, synthesize, and express evaluations of material, ideas, facts, and concepts.

**2.** The use of extended response essay questions allows examinees to express themselves freely and the instructor to explore in depth a sampling of student knowledge and skills.

**3.** The use of restricted response essay items allows an efficient survey of a moderately large content area.

**4.** The answer to an essay question can be strictly evaluated for either accuracy of content or clarity and mechanics of expression (including organization).

**5.** Reliability of grading is one major obstacle to the effective use of essay questions and tests.

**6.** Reliability of the sampling of student knowledge and skills is another potential problem area in essay testing.

**7.** The validity of essay items and tests for objectives must be a matter of great concern to the examiner.

**8.** An instructor should almost never rely exclusively on essay questions, or any single method for that matter, to assess the total learning outcomes of a unit or course of study.

**9.** The global or holistic rating of the components of an essay item—

such as organization, style, and mechanics of expression—is one approach to scoring essays for communication effectiveness.

**10.** Modified holistic scoring procedures can be efficiently and effectively used to assess large numbers of papers.

**11.** A developmental scoring rubric follows the logical skill progression of skill acquisition.

**12.** An analytic method should be applied in scoring essay items for content.

**13.** An instructor should write an "ideal" answer to a given essay question as a guide in evaluating individual student answers.

**14.** The checklist point score method allows each element of an essay answer to be objectively assessed when both content and expression are to be assessed.

**15.** Essay questions can be used to explore various affective learning outcomes.

**16.** Essay questions should
   a. be relevant and limited in scope.
   b. contain clearly defined tasks.
   c. be scored anonymously.
   d. be scored using the checklist point score method when knowledge is the focus.
   e. be the same for all students.

**17.** When attempting to maintain quality control in large-scale writing assessments, use safeguards such as the following:
   a. examinee anonymity
   b. cooperative or collegial instrument development
   c. multiple readings
   d. constant monitoring
   e. inserted "validity" papers

**18.** Following an assessment of a writing sample, suggestions should be made to students about how to improve their writing.

**19.** Writing assessments should be
   a. developmentally appropriate.
   b. collaborative between teachers and students.

    c. reflective of student creativity.

    d. focused on both content and process.

    e. integrated in all parts of the curriculum at all grades.

**20.** Types of writing include, but are not limited to

    a. relating of a personal experience.

    b. creating of an imaginative story.

    c. responding to literature.

## SPECULATIONS

**1.** Why is the topic statement "Is it true what they say about Dixie?" a bad essay task?

**2.** What are some procedures that can be used to help improve the scoring and grading of essay questions and tests?

**3.** What does it mean to score an essay using the "modified holistic method"?

**4.** When should the checklist point score method of evaluating essay items be used?

**5.** What are the advantages and disadvantages of allowing students to choose which essay items to answer?

**6.** Which is more important in an essay—content or grammar? Why?

**7.** Are there meaningful differences between extended and restricted essay tasks? If so, what are they?

**8.** What are some instructional and developmental assumptions that need to be made before a statewide writing assessment is undertaken?

**9.** How can large-scale writing assessment prove valuable to (a) the classroom teacher, (b) the system language arts coordinator, and (c) state superintendent of schools?

## SUGGESTED READINGS

Breland, H. E., Camp, R., Jones, R. J., Morris, M. M., & Rock, D. A. (1987). *Assessing writing skill* (Research Monograph No 11). New York: College Entrance Examination Board.

Coffman, W. E. (1971). Essay examinations. In R. L. Thorndike (Ed.), *Educational measurement* (2nd ed., pp. 271–302). Washington, DC: American Council on Education. This 32-page chapter contains a comprehensive and integrated survey of the research and practice of essay testing.

Greenberg, K. L., Wiener, H. S., & Donovan, R. A. (1986). *Writing assessment issues and strategies.* New York: Longman.

Hopkins, K. D., Stanley, J. C., & Hopkins, B. R. (1990). *Educational and psychological measurement and evaluation* (7th ed.). Englewood Cliffs, NJ: Prentice-Hall. Chapter 8, "Constructing and Using Essay Tests," begins with a very interesting historical overview (from before biblical times) that leads to a detailed consideration of modern-day practices.

Linn, R. L., & Gronlund, N. E. (2000). *Measurement and evaluation in teaching* (8th ed.). New York: Macmillan. Chapter 10, "Measuring Complex Achievement: The Essay Test," contains many excellent suggestions about how to phrase questions to elicit the desired student behavior.

Ruth, L., & Murphy, S. (1988). *Designing writing tasks for the assessment of writing.* Norwood, NJ: Ablex.

White, E. M. (1994). *Teaching and assessing writing* (2nd ed.). San Francisco: Jossey-Bass.

Williamson, M. M., & Huot, B. A. (Ed.). (1993). *Validating holistic scoring for writing assessment: Theoretical and empirical foundations.* Cresshill, NJ: Hampton Press.

# 9

# Analyzing and Refining Traditional Assessment Tasks

---

## FOCUS CONCEPTS AND KEY TERMS FOR STUDY

**Criterion Groups**

**Distractor Effectiveness**

**Negative Discrimination**

**Question Difficulty**

**Question Discrimination**

**Question File**

## STANDARDS ALERT

**Standard 3.9**        **Item Selection**

When a test developer evaluates the psychometric properties of items, the classical or item response theory (IRT) model used for evaluating the psychometric properties of items should be documented. The sample used for estimating item properties should be described and should be of adequate size and diversity for the procedure. The process by which items are selected and the data used for item selection, and/or item information, should also be documented. When IRT is used to estimate item parameters in test development, the item response model, estimation procedures, and evidence of model fit should be documented.

## TAKING IT TO THE CLASSROOM

Basically teachers want to know which items discriminate between those who know and can do relative to those who don't know or can't do a task. In addition, a teacher wants to know which tasks and what content were "mastered." Usually a simple examination of percent correct by item, question, or steps in a task will yield sufficient information.

Reprinted with permission from the *Standards for Educational and Psychological Testing*. Copyright © 1999 by the American Educational Research Association, the American Psychological Association, and the National Council on Measurement in Education.

Question or task analysis techniques are among the most valuable tools classroom teachers or test developers can apply when attempting to improve the quality of their measuring devices. The techniques are valuable for all types of measures, including achievement, aptitude, and personality. Even the most elementary analysis procedures can bring about a remarkable improvement of classroom instruments. In addition, question data have very valuable instructional applications. The methods discussed in this chapter are aimed primarily at improving traditional measures.

Question analyses are conducted for four general purposes: (1) to select the best available questions for the final form of an assessment; (2) to identify structural or content defects in the questions; (3) to detect learning difficulties of the class as a whole, identifying general content areas or skills that need to be reviewed by the instructor; and (4) to identify for individual students areas of weakness needing remediation.

A question analysis has three main elements. One is examining the

**difficulty** level of the items, that is, the percentage of students responding correctly to each question, item, or task in the assessment. Another is determining the **discriminating** power of each item. Item discrimination in its simplest form usually, but not always, refers to the relation of performance on each item to performance on the total test. For a classroom test, item discrimination is generally indexed by the number or percentage of high-scoring individuals (based on total score) responding correctly versus the number of low-scoring individuals responding correctly.

The third element in item analyses, if multiple-choice or matching items are used in the test, is examining the effectiveness of the **distractors** (foils, or alternative answers). Again, data derived from the high and low scorers are used. But now the complete response patterns associated with all the alternatives in each item are studied, rather than just the correct answer.

## PREPARING DATA FOR ANALYSIS

Preparing data for the item analysis of a classroom test generally involves counting the number of individuals responding correctly or in a particular direction. For norm-referenced measures, these individuals are in high- and low-scoring groups sometimes referred to as **criterion groups**. This count can be accomplished by a show of hands in class or by examining the answer sheets. In general, use the following steps to gather and record data for an analysis:

1. *Arrange the answer sheets in order from high to low.* This ranking is usually based on the individual's total score on the test. An item analysis of data derived from high and low scores (based on total score) is referred to as an *internal item analysis*. If an external criterion is used (e.g., another test that is supposed to measure the same thing as the one under analysis), the item analysis is referred to as an *external item analysis*. The total score on the test is the most satisfactory criterion on which to base a ranking of individuals for an analysis of a classroom test.

2. *High- and low-scoring groups are identified.* For purposes of item analysis, these two extreme sets of examination papers are called criterion groups. Each subgroup will generally contain from 25 percent to 50 percent of the total number of people who took the test. The goal is to include enough people in the criterion groups to justify confidence in the results, and yet keep the criterion groups distinct enough to

ensure that they represent different levels of ability. Truman Kelley (1939) has shown that maximally reliable item discrimination results will be obtained when each criterion group contains 27 percent of the total. Thus, in undertaking an item analysis on a classroom test, between 25 percent and 33 percent represents a reasonable size for the criterion groups. *The high and low groups, however, must contain the same number of individuals.*

3. ***Record separately the number of times each alternative was selected by individuals in the high and low groups.***

4. ***Add the number of correct answers to each item made by the combined high and low groups.***

5. ***Divide the total number of correct responses by the maximum possible, that is, the total number of students in the combined high and low groups, and multiply the result by 100.*** This percentage is an estimate of the *difficulty index*. Some test constructors allow items to be omitted, and students inadvertently omit items. If all individuals have not attempted all items, item difficulty indices should be obtained by dividing the total number of correct responses by the number of individuals who attempted the item. On timed tests, omitted items in the middle of the test should probably be considered wrong, while those at the end should be considered omitted.

6. ***Subtract the number of correct answers made by the low group from the number of correct answers made by the high group.***

7. ***Divide this number (the difference, H – L) by the number of individuals contained in the subgroup (that is, the number in the high [or low] group).*** This decimal number is the *discrimination index.*

Sample item data and the resulting indices derived from the procedures just described are presented in Table 9-1. These data refer to four hypothetical multiple-choice items answered by different classes (thus producing fluctuating numbers of cases in the high and low groups). The procedure for deriving indices of difficulty and discrimination can, of course, be used profitably with two-choice (e.g., true-false), matching, or any number of multiple-choice objective item types. Further, the concepts of difficulty and discrimination can be applied in evaluating more subjective item types, for example, completion and, with some difficulty, essay items.

The reader can now legitimately ask how these data can be used to improve the test. The following sections will consider how item analysis data can be used to improve the quality of a classroom test.

## USING INFORMATION ABOUT DIFFICULTY AND DISCRIMINATION

The exact use of information about difficulty and discrimination will, of course, depend on the intended use of the item, question, or task.

### Consideration of Question Difficulty

An item's difficulty level is important because it tells the instructor something meaningful about the comprehension of, or performance on, material or tasks contained in the item. Referring to Item 1 in Table 9-1, we can see that the item is easy (estimated difficulty index is = 83 percent). Note here an apparent paradox, namely, that the higher the value of the difficulty index, the easier the item is.

This paradox is comprehensible when we recall that the difficulty index represents the percentage of the total number of respondents answering the item correctly. In other words, an inverse relationship exists between the magnitude of the index and what it purports to represent. In any event, an instructor might be justified in concluding that nearly everyone had command of the material for Item 1. Extremely high difficulty indices, however, can indicate a structural defect in the item. The data for Item 1 could have been obtained from the following item:

*Item 1.* Among the major contributors to low reliability are
1. an appropriate time limit.
2. inadequate samplings of content and individuals. (Keyed as Correct)
3. lack of content heterogeneity in the test.
4. differential weighting of alternatives in scoring each item.
5. poor lighting in the testing room.

When we examine the content and structure of the test, it is obvious that a grammatical clue exists. The stem calls for a plural response, and the only plural response is "2"—which in this case happens to be the correct answer. A student who noticed this clue could respond correctly to the item without knowing the answer. This irrelevant clue could alone account for the high difficulty index, particularly where the low group is concerned. The lesson here is obvious. In selecting items for a test, considering content alone or item analysis data alone can be very misleading. Both factors need to be considered when you accept items for the final form of the test.

The difficulty index described in this chapter is only an estimate of the "real" difficulty level of an item and is based on the responses of only the high- and low-scoring groups. The middle groups, usually from 50 percent to 33 percent of the total, have been eliminated. It is assumed, and has been

**Table 9-1** *Sample Item-Analyses Data Derived from Four Hypothetical Multiple-Choice Items*

| | Group | Group Size | Response Alternatives[1] | | | | | Total No. Correct (H and L) | Difficulty Index | (H-L) | Discrimination Index |
|---|---|---|---|---|---|---|---|---|---|---|---|
| | | | **1** | **2** | **3** | **4** | **5** | | | | |
| Item 1 | High | 12 | 0 | 11 | 0 | 1 | 0 | 20 | 83% | 2 | +.17 |
| | Low | 12 | 2 | 9 | 1 | 0 | 0 | | | | |
| Item 2 | High | 25 | 2 | 2 | 20 | 1 | 0 | 26 | 52% | 14 | +.56 |
| | Low | 25 | 5 | 8 | 6 | 2 | 4 | | | | |
| Item 3 | High | 16 | 2 | 2 | 8 | 2 | 2 | 6 | 19% | −2 | −.13 |
| | Low | 16 | 4 | 3 | 4 | 1 | 4 | | | | |
| Item 4 | High | 30 | 20 | 3 | 2 | 1 | 4 | 28 | 47% | 12 | +.40 |
| | Low | 30 | 8 | 1 | 8 | 9 | 2 | | | | |

[1]Underlined numbers indicate correct answers.

found true in practice, that approximately half of the middle group will score like the high group and half like the low group. The index is only an estimate from another standpoint. Guessing can be a factor on any test item, particularly if the item is quite difficult. Each item should theoretically be corrected for guessing. For a classroom test, however, this scoring refinement is probably unnecessary. On the other hand, if the class is reasonably small, use *all* the students to estimate question difficulty.

A number of authorities have shown that if a test is comprised entirely of items at the 50 percent difficulty level, it is possible for the test to be maximally reliable or, more precisely, to evidence maximum internal consistency at least in the norm-referenced sense. In other words, items at the 50 percent level allow item discrimination indices to obtain their maximum possible value: unity. In a sense, median difficulty can be viewed as a necessity but not a sufficient condition for acceptable discrimination. It can be desirable, however, to include in the test items that are fairly easy (those at the beginning of the test for psychological reasons) or fairly difficult (those measuring highly complex learning outcomes). When these types of items are included in the test, generally lowered (internal consistency) reliability estimates will be obtained. Edward Cureton (1966) has shown this to be particularly crucial if the Kuder–Richardson formula 20 is used. (See Chapter 14 for a discussion of this approach to test reliability.) A paradox is evident. If an instructor uses the *Revised Taxonomy of Educational Objectives* as a framework for instruction and measurement, the resulting test will necessarily reflect a range of item difficulty indices. This results in lower Kuder–Richardson reliabilities, despite it representing a desired state of affairs. Two recommendations should help ameliorate the problem. First, limit the range of item difficulties, for example, to between 30 percent and 70 percent. Second, use caution when interpreting the Kuder–Richardson reliabilities derived from classroom tests. Whereas we generally desire Kuder–Richardson values above 0.85 for published tests of achievement, aptitude, and intelligence, on a single classroom test 0.70 might be considered acceptable. In addition, it is assumed that other data will be gathered, so that the reliability of the composite score used to make a final decision will reach a higher and more acceptable level.

Another paradox exists in interpreting the item difficulty indices. If a teacher has done a good job in teaching a particular concept skill or fact, students will perform well on items related to that topic. Item difficulty values will be high in numerical value, for example, 85, meaning that a large percentage of the students did well. If most everyone did well then there is no room for the item(s) to discriminate. An item is being penalized (persecuted) for doing a good job. The topic might be thrown out. Instead, we should look at discrimination by percentage passing before instruction compared with after instruction. (See sections on criterion-referenced measures later in this chapter for further discussion.)

A useful application of item analysis data is to develop a chart that relates student performance on each item (correct = +, incorrect = 0) and the content of the item. A sample chart for five students and four items is presented below. Obviously, the concept of reliability could be profitably reviewed.

| | Student | | | | |
| --- | --- | --- | --- | --- | --- |
| **Question Content** | $S_1$ | $S_2$ | $S_3$ | $S_4$ | $S_5$ |
| Use of table of specifications | + | + | 0 | 0 | + |
| Computing mean | + | 0 | 0 | + | + |
| Definition of reliability | + | 0 | + | 0 | 0 |
| Interpreting correlation coefficient | + | + | 0 | + | + |

In addition, several areas needing review for individual students have been highlighted by reproducing the responses of each examinee to each item. When the class and number of items are large, the sheer mechanics of recording responses can be quite laborious. The benefits that accrue to both student and instructor can, however, be substantial. In such cases, items with similar content could be grouped together. Another interesting variation is to refer back to the original table of specifications, particularly if the *Revised Taxonomy of Educational Objectives* was used to develop it, and use the corresponding behavior categories instead of content categories.

## Considerations of Question Discrimination

Item discrimination has been defined as the degree to which an item differentiates the high achievers from the low achievers. Actually, the term *differentiation* is probably more descriptive than *discrimination*, but we will stick with the latter term rather than trying to change many decades of psychometric history. A perfect positively discriminating item would be answered correctly by all of the high group and none of the low group; the discrimination index would then be +1.00. If all of the low group and none of the high group responded correctly, the index would be −1.00. In a sense, we might interpret the discrimination index as the correlation of the item with the total test score. Extreme values are almost never observed on a classroom test; rather, items in the middle range of positive discrimination are usually found.

The data reported in Table 9-1 for Item 2 were obtained from the following item:

Item 2. A teacher proposes the following objective for a course in fine arts:
"The students should be able to understand and appreciate good music."
The principal drawback to this objective, from a measurement standpoint, is that it is a

1. general objective.
2. student objective.
3. nonbehavioral objective. (Keyed as Correct)
4. teacher objective.
5. compound objective.

This item is "sound" from a number of standpoints. The "middle difficulty level" criterion has been met, with an index of 52 percent. In addition, it discriminates between the high and low groups, as indicated by the index of +0.56. The item is structurally sound and measures a desirable outcome, namely, the ability to apply knowledge about objectives in a new situation. Another possible explanation for the good discrimination is that the alternatives contain plausible but incorrect answers.

In general, all items in a test of relative achievement should discriminate positively. This assumes that we are striving for an additive scale, in which item scores are summed, that we want each item to make a positive contribution, and that we are interested in developing a test of relative achievement, as opposed to a mastery test, in which all items do not necessarily need to meet an internal discrimination criterion. In developing a classroom test, high positive total scores are assumed to be correlated with more knowledge and skill.

An instructor will occasionally find a **negatively discriminating** item such as the following (refer to Table 9-1 for appropriate item analysis data):

> *Item 3.* Which of the following alternatives best summarizes the limitations of the *Taxonomy of Educational Objectives?*
>
> 1. For the most part it is written in nonbehavioral terms.
> 2. It deals with "inferred" rather than "real" behavior.
> 3. It may restrict our thinking to only the categories of the *Taxonomy.*
> 4. The categories of the *Taxonomy* are not mutually exclusive.
> 5. All of the above are limitations of the *Taxonomy.* (Keyed as Correct)

This item, answered correctly by more of the low group than the high group is apparently ambiguous. One possible source of ambiguity is the nature of the task. In essence, the student is required to make a value judgment. Most students apparently do not possess enough information to make an appropriate judgment. The use of "all of the above," although correct in the instructor's eyes, may have contributed to the difficulty of the task (difficulty index = 19 percent) and made responding to the item easier for the low group than the high group. Students in the low group may have been able to identify correctly two of the "limitations" and therefore been drawn to answer 5. It is difficult to speculate about the line of thinking followed by the high group. The item obviously does not work well and should be rewritten or discarded.

Another point is raised by the data on Item 3. It was found that discrimination for this item was low, as was the difficulty index. In general, extremely difficult or extremely easy items will show very little discrimination.

An instructor will select items for the final or a future form of this test that have the highest discrimination indices and measure the desired outcomes of instruction. The late Robert Ebel (1965) suggested that items with discrimination indices below +0.40 could benefit from rewriting, and that those below +0.20 should be significantly improved or discarded.

## Examining Distractor Effectiveness

An *ideal* item, at least from a statistical item analysis standpoint, is one that all students in the high group answer correctly and all students in the low group miss. In addition, the responses of the low group should be evenly distributed among the incorrect alternatives. Again, however, this rarely happens in practice. The situation illustrated by Item 4 is frequently encountered.

> *Item 4.* The primary purpose of using a "table of specifications" in achievement test development is to
>
> 1. help ensure that each objective will be given the desired relative emphasis on the test. (Keyed as Correct)
> 2. show the students the content to be covered by the test.
> 3. translate statements of objectives from nonbehavioral to behavioral terms.
> 4. translate ultimate into immediate objectives.
> 5. show the students what to study for.

Again referring to the item analysis data in Table 9-1, we can see that, despite appropriate levels of difficulty and discrimination the item can be improved. First, the responses of the low group are not evenly distributed among the incorrect alternatives. Also, answers 2 and 5 have a particularly low frequency of selection and are therefore not contributing much to the item. They are actually making a negative contribution because more members of the high group than the low group are selecting them. The low frequency of selection of 2 and 5 might be accounted for by their content. They are similar and, relative to the stem, implausible. They should be replaced or eliminated because they just take up reading time. Incidentally, there is nothing sacred about the practice of providing four or five alternative answers for all multiple-choice items. Amos Tversky (1964) showed mathematically that the use of three alternatives per item will maximize the discriminability, power, and information yielded per unit of time. This makes intuitive sense; we all know how hard it is to invent consistently "good" fourth and fifth distractors. They frequently turn out to be merely space fillers.

## LIMITATIONS OF QUESTION ANALYSIS

In addition to the limitations of small sample size and the possibility of reduced content validity, several other cautions should be noted.

Some experts suggest that internal item analyses should be completed only on tests that measure essentially the same mental functions. For a classroom achievement test, which generally deals with heterogeneous learning outcomes, item analysis techniques like those described in this chapter should be considered crude devices for refining the test. If for no other reason, instructors should conduct an item analysis to force themselves to look critically at the measurements they are using to make important decisions about students.

The type of item, format, and reading level are among the many factors that can influence test and item difficulty. You should also be cautious about what damage is caused to the table of specifications when items not meeting minimum criteria are eliminated from the test. These items must be replaced or rewritten.

Item analysis techniques are less directly applicable to essay tests, although information related to mean performance on each item might have diagnostic significance for an instructor. In addition, we could contrast the mean performance on an essay item for a "high-achieving or -scoring" group with that of a "low-achieving or -scoring" group to see if the item differentiates levels of performance.

The items on rating scales—either self-rating or observational—can also be subjected to item analysis procedures. Chapter 12 contains a description of how Likert summated rating items can be item-analyzed.

Another limitation of item analysis data relates to its use in a diagnostic manner. By building a chart relating each student's response to each item, evaluations can be made of either individual or class strengths and weaknesses. We must be cautious that such evaluations are based on limited information that can question judgment reliability. Even when items are grouped by content or outcome (comprehension, recall of knowledge, application, and the like), only a few samples of behavior are available for analysis. Chance could therefore play an important role, at least for individual analyses, in determining the consistency and validity of a performance on a given item. As we increase the number of samples of behavior, we also increase the likelihood that we can have confidence in the results. The problem of attempting to base diagnoses on limited item information is not peculiar to classroom tests and practices. Many commercial test publishers erroneously encourage their clientele to make specific subject-matter judgments on the basis of item data. Decisions like these should be based on many sources of data, which can include the results of a diagnostic test (see Chapter 15) developed specifically to aid in guiding remediation.

## DEVELOPING A QUESTION FILE

Teachers are encouraged to develop a file of test items. Recording items on 3 × 5 or 5 × 8 cards and accumulating data on their difficulty and discrimination over several administrators allows the classroom tests to be refined and improved. Such a file has these advantages:

1. Encouraging the teacher to undertake an item analysis as often as is practical.

2. Allowing accumulated data to be used to make item analyses more reliable.

3. Providing a wider choice of item format and objectives—in other words, greater flexibility in test construction.

4. Facilitating item revision and suggesting ideas for new items.

5. Facilitating the relation of the test item and its objective to the table of specifications.

6. Facilitating the physical construction and reproduction of the test because each item is on a separate card.

7. Accumulating a large enough pool of items to allow some items to be shared with students for study purposes.

A test item file has these disadvantages:

1. Requiring a great deal of clerical time.

2. Inhibiting creative test construction efforts by the teacher because of access to ready-made items.

3. Providing the opportunity for the file of items to dictate the content of instruction.

These negative factors can influence a teacher's measurement practices, but the overall advantages of an item file certainly outweigh them.

A sample item analysis data card suitable for objective items from classroom tests is presented in Table 9-2 on page 276.

This chapter has only hinted at the many potential uses of item analysis data. Such data are particularly useful to a teacher in identifying instructional deficiencies in programs, for individual students, and for entire classes. Keep in mind, however, that a single test item in and of itself is quite unreliable and should be combined with other information.

# CASE STUDY

The item data for the *first* 21 items of the Reading Education midterm exam are summarized for the class of 18 students in Table 9-3 on page 277. An analysis of item difficulty, item discrimination (the relationship of each item with the total score on the test), and distractor effectiveness of the mul-

**Table 9-2** *Sample Item-Analysis Data Card*

---

**(Front)**

---

**Item No.:** 37
**Topic:.** Trade Barriers
**Level:** Comprehension–Middle School
**Ceil:** 14          **Objective:** 14

**Reference:** Dean's
*Introduction to
Economics*, rev. ed.,
2001, pp. 201–214.

---

*Item 3.* A tariff can be defined as a tax on
1. Imported goods.
2. Money brought into the country.
3. Exported goods.
4. Imported cats and dogs.

---

**(Back)**

---

**Item No.:** 37

**Test:** Midterm
**Class:** 7th

---

|  | First Use | | Second Use | | Third Use | |
|---|---|---|---|---|---|---|
| **Options** | **Upper Third** | **Lower Third** | **Upper Third** | **Lower Third** | **Upper Third** | **Lower Third** |
| *1 | 15 | 8 | | | | |
| 2 | 0 | 3 | | | | |
| 3 | 3 | 3 | | | | |
| 4 | 2 | 1 | | | | |
| 5 | | | | | | |
| Omits | 0 | 0 | | | | |
| Difficulty<br>Discrimination | 58%<br>.35 | | | | | |
| Date | 2/14/01 | | | | | |
| Class Size | 60 | | | | | |

Comments: Item discrimination and difficulty are good.
          Important objective is measured.

**Table 9-3** *Summary of Responses of 18 Students to 21 Items of Reading Education Midterm Test*

| Student | Total Score on 80 Item Midterm Exam | Item | | | | | | | | | | | | | | | | | | | | |
|---|---|---|---|---|---|---|---|---|---|---|---|---|---|---|---|---|---|---|---|---|---|---|
| | | 1 | 2 | 3 | 4 | 5 | 6 | 7 | 8 | 9 | 10 | 11 | 12 | 13 | 14 | 15 | 16 | 17 | 18 | 19 | 20 | 21 |
| $S_1$ | 58 | a | c | b | c | d | b | b | a | b | c | b | c | b | a | c | b | c | a | a | a | b |
| $S_2$ | 47 | c | a | c | c | b | a | b | a | a | b | b | a | a | b | a | a | a | a | b | b | c |
| $S_3$ | 58 | d | b | b | b | c | b | c | b | a | b | a | a | a | b | b | a | b | a | b | b | c |
| $S_4$ | 59 | c | a | a | a | d | a | c | a | a | c | b | a | b | b | b | b | a | a | b | b | a |
| $S_5$ | 68 | c | a | a | a | d | a | b | c | a | c | b | b | b | b | b | a | a | a | b | b | c |
| $S_6$ | 55 | a | b | c | a | b | a | b | c | a | b | b | a | a | a | c | c | c | a | a | a | a |
| $S_7$ | 58 | a | c | c | a | b | b | a | a | b | b | a | b | a | b | a | a | c | b | b | b | c |
| $S_8$ | 58 | a | b | c | c | b | c | a | a | a | b | b | b | b | b | a | b | c | a | b | a | a |
| $S_9$ | 55 | a | c | a | a | d | a | b | a | a | c | b | b | b | b | b | b | c | a | b | b | a |
| $S_{10}$ | 52 | c | a | c | a | b | a | c | a | a | c | c | a | a | a | a | c | c | a | b | b | c |
| $S_{11}$ | 62 | c | a | a | a | d | a | c | a | a | c | a | a | a | b | b | b | c | a | a | a | a |
| $S_{12}$ | 57 | c | c | a | c | a | c | b | a | a | c | b | a | b | b | a | b | a | b | b | b | a |
| $S_{13}$ | 62 | c | c | a | a | d | a | b | c | a | c | b | b | b | b | c | b | c | a | b | b | c |
| $S_{14}$ | 51 | c | a | a | a | b | a | c | a | a | c | b | a | a | a | b | b | a | a | b | b | a |
| $S_{15}$ | 65 | c | c | a | a | d | a | c | b | b | c | b | b | a | a | c | c | a | b | b | b | c |
| $S_{16}$ | 57 | b | a | b | b | d | b | c | c | a | c | b | b | b | b | b | b | c | a | b | a | b |
| $S_{17}$ | 62 | c | a | a | a | a | a | c | c | a | c | b | a | a | a | a | c | c | a | b | b | c |
| $S_{18}$ | 52 | a | c | c | a | d | a | b | a | a | c | b | a | a | b | a | a | c | a | b | b | c |

tiple-choice items should be undertaken. The data table contains a summary of (a) the total scores of each student on the total 80-item test, and (b) responses to the first 21 sample items presented in the case study materials for Chapter 7. These are real data. Your task, if you agree to do it, is to complete an item analysis of the sample 21 items using the high-low method with one-third of the scores in each group.

Following is the scoring key for the 21 items:

| | | |
|---|---|---|
| 1. c | 8. c | 15. c |
| 2. a | 9. a | 16. b |
| 3. a | 10. c | 17. a |
| 4. a | 11. b | 18. a |
| 5. d | 12. a | 19. b |
| 6. a | 13. a | 20. b |
| 7. c | 14. b | 21. a |

In determining which students are in the *high* and *low* groups, the reader should refer to the frequency distribution created for the Chapter 13 case study. Be sure to review the item analysis method and format described in Chapter 9.

---

## CONTENT REVIEW STATEMENTS

**1.** Question analysis techniques are among the most powerful tools a teacher can use to improve the quality of classroom assessment.

**2.** Question analyses are undertaken to select the best items, identify faulty items, and detect individual or class learning difficulties.

**3.** Question analysis generally involves examining item difficulty, item discrimination, and, if multiple-choice items are used, distractor effectiveness.

**4.** Question difficulty ($p$) can be indexed by the proportion of examinees who respond correctly or in a particular direction.

**5.** Question difficulty can be estimated from the proportion (or percentage) of the combined high-scoring and low-scoring thirds of the total distribution of scorers responding correctly to the item.

**6.** Question difficulties will range from 0 to 100 percent.

**7.** Question discrimination (D) can be indexed by subtracting the number of low-scoring students (the lower one-third of the total score distribution) from the number of high-scoring students (the upper one-third), and dividing the difference by the number that represents one-third of the total group.

**8.** The range of D is from −1.00 to 0.00 to +1.00.

**9.** To examine distractor effectiveness for multiple-choice items, the responses to each alternative for the high and low groups are inspected separately.

**10.** Question difficulty values should generally fall in the 30 percent to 70 percent range if the intent is to maximize the measured differences between individuals.

**11.** Question discrimination values should be as large as possible if the intent is to maximize the measured differences between individuals.

**12.** In general, the greater the number of items that have high discrimination values, the higher the internal consistency reliability of the test.

**13.** Questions with extremely high or low difficulty indices should be examined closely for possible structural or content defects or ambiguity.

**14.** Examining the mean scores on individual performance and essay items separately for high- and low-scoring students can provide useful information on discrimination.

**15.** Plotting the responses of each student to each item in terms of correctness (+ = right, − = wrong) can help identify individual student or class strengths and weaknesses.

**16.** If criterion-referenced performance measures are used, items with higher difficulty values are likely to be found.

**17.** The concept of within-group item discrimination has less value in the analysis of performance and other criterion-referenced measures.

**18.** If questions are eliminated from a test because of poor difficulty or discrimination indices they should be replaced with other items measuring the same objectives.

**19.** Developing a question file will assist the teacher in refining test items and provide considerable flexibility in test development.

**20.** Questions in the middle range of difficulty tend to yield better discrimination indices for norm-referenced measures.

## Speculations

1. What are the purposes of a question analysis?

2. Discuss how the concepts of test and item difficulty and discrimination can influence the meaning of an interpretation of test performances.

3. What are the characteristics of good alternative answers on a multiple-choice test item?

4. How are "discrimination" and "bias" different?

5. How can you use question analysis methods to examine and control possible sources of bias?

## Suggested Readings

Carey, L. M. (2001). *Measuring and evaluating school learning* (3rd ed.). Boston: Allyn & Bacon. Chapter 11, "Analyzing Objective Text Items and Tests," of this well-written text emphasizes instructional improvement through item analysis.

Henryssen, S. (1970). Gathering, analyzing, and using data on test items. In R. L. Thorndike (Ed.), *Educational measurement* (2nd ed.). Washington, DC: American Council on Education. Chapter 5 is a comprehensive overview of practical and technical issues for the intermediate student.

Katz, M. (1961). Improving classroom tests by means of item analysis. *Clearing House, 35,* 265–269. Presents detailed instructions for a useful method of analyzing classroom achievement test items.

Lange, A., Lehmann, I. J., & Mehrens, W. A. (1967). Using item analysis to improve tests. *Journal of Educational Measurement, 4,* 65–68. The procedures outlined in this chapter are illustrated in this brief article.

Sax, G. (1997). *Principles of educational psychological measurement and evaluation* (4th ed.). Belmont, CA: Wadsworth. Chapter 8 relates item data to norm- and criterion-referenced measures, item response theory, and the purposes of testing.

# PART Four

# Constructing Modern Assessments

*Beverly's Journal* ─────────────────────────────

Chelsea continues to call at odd times. That's what happens when you have a six-month-old. New challenges at home and at school. "What are these newfangled things called 'performance assessments'?" I guess if you want to find out what the students can do, you have to provide them with an opportunity to demonstrate it. But it does pose some problems in constructing and scoring the tasks. I told Chelsea that many teachers have bought into the reborn idea of constructivist teaching, where the student builds a structure for knowledge and skill development. Using real-life experiences helps that developmental process. We are then faced with the problem of how to assess how well they have honed those skills.

# 10

# Creating Performance, Product, and Observational Assessments

---

## FOCUS CONCEPTS AND KEY TERMS FOR STUDY

| | |
|---|---|
| **Anecdotal Records** | **Performance Assessment** |
| **Checklists** | **Portfolio Assessment** |
| **Graphic Scales** | **Product Assessment** |
| **Numerical Scales** | **Rating Errors** |
| **Observational Methods** | **Rating Scales** |
| | **Rubric** |

---

## STANDARDS ALERT

**Standard 5.9**          **Scoring Rubrics**

When test scoring involves human judgment, scoring rubrics should specify criteria for scoring. Adherence to established scoring criteria should be monitored and checked regularly.

## TAKING IT TO THE CLASSROOM

A four- or five-element rubric helps classify for both teacher and student the quality of the expected and observed performance.

**Standard 3.15**          **Behavior Samples**

When using a standardized testing format to collect structured behavior samples, the domain, test design, test specifications, and materials should be documented as for any other test. Such documentation should include a clear definition of the behavior expected of the test takers, the nature of the expected responses, and any materials or directions that are necessary to carry out the testing.

## TAKING IT TO THE CLASSROOM

In creating the assessment of a science lab performance water purity test, the conditions, materials, procedures, and scoring rubric(s) should be the same for all students.

---

Reprinted with permission from the *Standards for Educational and Psychological Testing*. Copyright © 1999 by the American Educational Research Association, the American Psychological Association, and the National Council on Measurement in Education.

Developing and refining performance assessment as an evaluation tool has been stimulated by a desire, particularly on the part of educational reformers, to more clearly align instruction and measurement. **Performance assessment** is a broad category that can involve creating a *product* or demonstrating a *process*. The closer the assessment approximates the teaching-learning situation, perhaps even considering the student's preferred learning style, the better the validity of the assessment. The essence of a performance is a sometimes complex, student-constructed response.

The obvious kinds of performance assessments are such things as essays, science experiments, physical demonstrations, and portfolios. Assessments might also include photographic collections, problem-solving games, audio-tapes or videotapes, computer shows, oral or written reports, drawings or diagrams, simulations, models, or constructed written responses to open-ended problems. The last type is likely to appear on some statewide or national assessments where very large numbers of students must be assessed at a single time. The classroom obviously affords a more convenient environment within which to complete more comprehensive and complex performance assessments. The availability of materials, reference resources, space, and time allow extended exploration of student problem-solving abilities. The characteristics of performance assessment are well discerned by Stiggins (1987). Table 10-1 is a summary of his analysis.

## DEVELOPING PERFORMANCE ASSESSMENTS

Much instructional time, particularly in the early grades, is devoted to developing specific performance skills. Examples are laboratory work, handwriting, physical skills, speaking, social skills, music, artistic and dramatic skills, essay writing, and a variety of vocational skills. We are, of course, interested in the products of learning, but we are also concerned with *how* the student arrives at his or her product. Often the technique or skill development can be considered an end in itself or so intimately tied to the product as to be inseparable.

The key to developing a performance assessment is simulation; most paper-and-pencil devices suffer from artificiality. Developmental situations in which an individual can exhibit real-life behaviors generally increase the relevance and accuracy of the assessment.

Performance assessment's advantage is that it can be both a teaching and a testing method. When presented in a game-like form, particularly to young children, simulations also have the motivational value of being fun. Performance assessments such as simulations allow data to be collected for events or situations that only occur rarely. Think, for example, of flight simulation used to train jet pilots. The simulation of an emergency such as the loss of an engine can be used to develop a pilot's skills. The dynamic functions of the human body and disease processes can be simulated to train and test doctors. Role playing is an effective and inexpensive method of examining interpersonal communication and counseling skills. Building a "city" in an elementary classroom (with post office, supermarket, bank, and so on) is another practical kind of simulation.

In educational settings, we must consider practical limitations; developing a simulation test involves compromises. Fitzpatrick and Morrison (1971) noted that in making these compromises we must

**Table 10-1** *Performance Assessment Characteristics*

| Characteristic | Example | Characteristic | Example |
| --- | --- | --- | --- |
| Purpose | Assess ability to translate knowledge and understanding into action | Potential sources of inaccurate assessment | Poor exercises<br>Too few samples of performance<br><br>Vague criteria<br><br>Poor rating procedures<br><br>Poor test conditions |
| Typical exercise | Written prompt or natural event framing the kind of performance required | Influence on learning | Emphasizes use of available skill and knowledge in relevant problem contexts |
| Student's response | Plan, construct, and deliver original response | Keys to success | Carefully prepared performance exercises<br><br>Clear performance expectations<br><br>Careful, thoughtful rating<br><br>Time to rate performance |
| Scoring | Check attributes present, rate proficiency demonstrated, or describe performance via anecdote | Major disability | Difficult and time-consuming to develop and score |
| Major advantages | Provide rich evidence of performance skills<br>Meaningful results | | Cost |
| Sources of error | Poorly written tasks<br>Too few tasks<br>Unreliable scoring<br>Limited content sample | | |

*Source: After Stiggins, 1987.*

1. Determine through careful analysis the critical aspects of the criterion situation to be assessed.
2. Determine the minimum accuracy or fidelity needed for each aspect and estimate the worth of increasing fidelity beyond the minimum.
3. Develop a scheme for representing a reasonably comprehensive set of tasks within the limits of available resources.

**4.** Adjust comprehensiveness and fidelity, compromising as necessary to achieve a balancing of considerations but paying primary attention to the aspects shown by analysis to be most critical for the purpose at hand.

The most important step in developing a performance exercise is identifying the criterion, which usually involves a task analysis. Some major aspects of a task analysis are the following:

**1.** Developing a simulation that represents the entire performance as accurately as possible.

**2.** Specifying those elements in the task that are most relevant to the quality of performance. Some of these elements might be

a. speed of performance

b. accuracy of performance

c. number and seriousness of procedural errors

d. errors in following instructions

e. discrimination in selecting appropriate tools or equipment

f. economy of effort (amount of "lost motion")

g. timing (in the use of machinery or physical performances such as gymnastics)

h. intensity or force (in sports)

i. coherence and appropriateness of the sequence of steps followed

**3.** Selecting elements for observation or performance in proportion to their emphasis in instruction or training.

**4.** Establishing criteria and standards.

**5.** Evaluating these elements considering the conditions necessary to be accurate, reliable, and valid.

**6.** Developing a reliable training program for rating and scoring.

**7.** Selecting those elements that require minimal time and expense.

**8.** Using results to (a) refine assessment and (b) improve the curriculum.

**9.** Providing feedback to relevant stakeholders in addition to students, such as parents, administrative personnel, and perhaps the community.

### Criteria for Task Selection

Selecting just the right task to assess the target behavior is absolutely crucial. Joan Herman, Pam Aschbacker, and Lynn Winters (1992) suggest six criteria that should be used to evaluate assessment tasks:

- Match specific instructional intentions.
- Represent content and skills students are expected to attain.
- Enable students to demonstrate their proficiencies and capabilities.
- Allow assessment of multiple goals.
- Reflect an authentic, real-world context.
- Allow an interdisciplinary approach.

All the criteria are important, but perhaps the greatest strength of performance assessment rests with the last two tasks. Integrating a variety of skills (e.g., completing a science experiment and then writing an essay about it) is obviously more desirable than focusing on a single lower-level outcome. Credibility, which in turn influences student motivation, will also be enhanced if the task has at least "face validity" for real-world challenges.

## DEVELOPING SCORING RUBRICS FOR PERFORMANCE ASSESSMENTS

Scoring rubrics can be generally classified into three general types: (a) holistic versus analytic, (b) developmental versus quantitative, and (c) generalizable versus specific. These terms can be generally defined as follows:

- *Holistic.* A general overall judgment is made about a performance. A limited number of categories is predefined. Holistic rubrics usually have competency labels associated with them—for example, proficient, advanced, and so on.
- *Analytic.* A relatively detailed set of criteria is applied, usually after a holistic evaluation has been made. A compromise between holistic and analytic scoring is sometimes termed *modified holistic.*
- *Developmental.* These rubrics are created to span grade levels or "distance" on a competency continuum.
- *Quantitative.* A rating scale, usually in the form of anchored or "defined" numbers, is applied either holistically or analytically.
- *Generalizable.* The same set of criteria categories is developed to be applied across different tasks. Holistic rubrics also tend to be generalizable.
- *Specific.* A rubric is created to score a single specific task. This approach is often used with open-ended supply and short-answer questions.

The most frequently used rubric types are holistic, generalizable, and modified holistic, which is developmental. The Wisconsin Student Assessment

System employs a holistic rubric, which in turn is modified slightly as it is applied to performance assessments in different subject areas. This system uses five categories: Advanced Response, Proficient Response, Nearly Proficient Response, Minimal Response, Attempted Response, and Not Scorable. Following is an example at the general level, then illustrations of it applied in mathematics. The guidelines are for a Proficient Response.

**General:** The response addresses all aspects of the task. It shows full application of appropriate knowledge and skills and uses methods of communication that are appropriate to the subject area and task. The response is conceptually and mechanically complete, although an occasional minor technical error may be present.

**Mathematics:** The response completely addresses all aspects of the task. It includes

— Appropriate application of mathematical concepts and structures
— Evidence of the use of appropriate mathematical procedures
— Coherent use of mathematical words, symbols, or other visual representations that are appropriate to the task
— Logical conclusions based upon known facts, properties, and relationships

Another sample scoring rubric, this time in language arts, comes from a basic skills writing test. It uses the modified holistic scoring procedure to assess communication effectiveness. This procedure, sometimes referred to as "primary trait," basically involves making gross judgments of worth, as is the case with total holistic scoring, but the communication value reporting of the writing sample is done through categories and scales like those included in Figure 10-1. Benchmark or "range finder" illustrative essays are usually identified. The holistic dimension is reflected because each "domain" (see Figure 10-1) is holistically scored. The modified holistic scoring approach (MHS) is considered a very efficient method for gaining a comprehensive picture of student writing ability. In addition, it is reliable and can be used by knowledgeable raters after approximately 20 to 24 hours of training. In most applications, the MHS approach is used: two readers are assigned to each paper and the results are combined. Sometimes weights reflecting differential importance are applied to the scores.

Questions or prompts selection is crucial. Content must not influence the ratings; keep it neutral so that the paper will only reflect true writing ability. A prompt such as "Describe your knowledge" won't be effective. The essay can be formulated as an autobiographical incident, memoir, business letter, story, problem solution, evaluation, or a simple reporting of information.

Creating scoring rubrics requires considerable time and energy. Collaboration among teachers during the developmental stages can be very

---

**Basic Skills Writing Test**

*Scoring Dimensions, Definitions, and Components*

**Content Organization:** The writer establishes the controlling idea through examples, illustrations, and facts or details. There is evidence of a sense of order that is clear and relevant.

- Clearly established controlling idea
- Clearly developed supporting ideas
- Sufficiently relevant supporting ideas
- Clearly discernible order of presentation
- Logical transitions and flow of ideas
- Sense of completeness

**Style:** The writer controls language to establish his or her individuality.

- Concrete images and descriptive language
- Easily readable
- Varied sentence patterns
- Appropriate tone for topic, audience, and purpose

**Sentence Formation:** The writer forms effective sentences.

- Appropriate end punctuation
- Complete sentences or functional fragments
- Appropriate coordination and/or subordination

**Usage:** The writer uses standard American English.

- Clear pronoun references
- Correct subject-verb agreement
- Standard form of verbs and nouns
- Correct word choice

**Mechanics:** The writer employs devices necessary in standard written American English.

- Appropriate capitalization
- Appropriate internal punctuation
- Appropriate formatting
- Correct spelling

**Score Point 1:** The writing is **Inadequate**. Very few if any of the components for the dimension are demonstrated.

**Score Point 2:** The writing is **Minimal**. Some of the components for the dimension are demonstrated.

**Score Point 3:** The writing is **Good**, yet not exceptional. Many of the components are demonstrated, and these are demonstrated successfully.

**Score Point 4:** The writing is **Very Good**. Most of the components are demonstrated, and these are demonstrated consistency.

---

**Figure 10-1** *Modified holistic scoring guide*

helpful. The kinds of dimensions of student work that can be included in scoring rubrics are suggested in Table 10-2, taken from the Illinois School and Student Assessment Program.

After those long hours developing your scoring rubric, one final task is to pass it through a "quality filter" such as that included in Table 10-3. Attention to these 18 criteria can help avoid problems during a tryout and training of scorers.

**Table 10-2** *Features of Student Work Commonly Included in Scoring Rubrics*

| Reading | Writing | Mathematics | Science | Social Science | Art | Phys Dev/Health |
|---|---|---|---|---|---|---|
| • Summarize<br>• Integrate<br>• Synthesize ideas within & between texts<br>• Use knowledge of test structure and genre to construct meaning:<br>—main ideas<br>—summaries<br>—themes<br>—interpretation<br>—literary devices<br>—multiple perspectives<br>• Identify and use reading strategies<br>• Apply and transfer to new situations, problems, text<br>• Identify text explicit<br>• Contributing skills:<br>—structural analysis<br>—study skills | • Purposes<br>—narrate<br>—persuade<br>—inform<br>• Features<br>—integration<br>—focus<br>—support/ elaboration<br>—organization<br>—conventions | • Problem solving strategies<br>—identify problems<br>—apply strategies<br>—use concepts, procedures, tools<br>• Representation<br>—charts<br>—graphs<br>• Reasoning<br>—interpret<br>—generalize<br>• Communication<br>—clear<br>—organized<br>—complete<br>—detailed<br>—mathematical language terminology, symbols, notations<br>• Content<br>—number concepts & skills<br>—percent/ratio proportion<br>—algebraic concepts & skills<br>—geometric concepts & skills | • Investigation<br>—hypotheses<br>—data<br>—observe<br>—use equipment<br>—draw inferences<br>• Concepts<br>—basic vocabulary of biological, physical & environmental sciences<br>—applications<br>• Social, environmental implications and limitations<br>• Communication<br>—language<br>—observational evidence<br>—conclusion/ interpretations | • Facts and concepts<br>• Critical thinking<br>—issues<br>—information<br>—conclusions<br>—alternative interpretations<br>—consequences<br>• Significant personalities, terms, events<br>• Relationships within and across disciplines<br>• Communication<br>—position<br>—support<br>—organization<br>—conclusions<br>—alternatives<br>• Group collaboration<br>—participation<br>—shared responsibility<br>—responsiveness<br>—forethought<br>—preparation | • Formal elements<br>—structure<br>—composition<br>• Technical elements<br>—techniques<br>—materials<br>• Sensory elements<br>• Expressive<br>—mood<br>—emotional quality<br>—energy quality<br>• Identify elements<br>• Integration of elements<br>• Impact of elements | • Human physical development & function<br>• Principles of<br>—nutrition<br>—stress management<br>—exercise<br>—self concept<br>—drug use and abuse<br>—illness prevention and treatment<br>• Apply to self<br>—as consumer<br>—as participant in sport and leisure activity<br>—as life saver |

Source: *Effective Scoring Rubrics—A Guide to Their Development and Use.* Springfield, IL: Illinois State Board of Education, School and Student Assessment Section (1995). Used by permission.

**Table 10-3** *Checklist for Effective Rubrics*

---

*Introduction:* An effective rubric is developmentally instructional; each level leads to the attainment of skills at the next level. Rubrics that have an impact on monitoring instruction and at the same time provide meaningful direction and feedback to the learner have many of the following characteristics.

### Structure

☐ 1. The levels in the rubric represent the full range of knowledge and skills that are the primary targets of instruction. (Checklists are not developmental. They can only indicate presence or absence of a specific feature or trait.)

☐ 2. Expectations for student performance are clear. The rubric is written in both student and parent language and avoids educational jargon.

☐ 3. The rubric has a minimum of four levels of performance to avoid results reflecting an artificial bell-shaped curve or being a measure of minimal competency.

☐ 4. An even number of levels is better for delineating proficiency unless a middle or equivocal position is desired. An even number of levels requires a decision between "almost there" and "barebones."

☐ 5. The rubric has *at least* one level above the standard to exemplify "distinguished" performance beyond the "barebones" level.

☐ 6. The rubric avoids using missing or implied levels that leave the user to interpret what degree and type of performance exist between the stated levels.

### Instruction & Training

☐ 7. The rubric is designed for continuous monitoring of progress rather than as a single sample of accountability.

☐ 8. The features being measured are clear and can be specifically defined from "least" developed to "most" developed.

☐ 9. Skills and traits are used consistently across each level of the rubric.

☐ 10. Each level of the rubric has examples aligned with it.

☐ 11. Lower levels of the rubric are not exclusively written in terms of missing skills (e.g., no speaking ability, lack of rhythm, not ready to dance, didn't show composure). The terms are developmental as opposed to pejorative.

☐ 12. The rubric is based on an absolute scale rather than a relative scale (e.g., criterion-referenced).

### Measurement

☐ 13. The type of measurement used in the rubric is clear and consistent across the levels (e.g., consistently measures change or improvement in the attainment of a standard).

☐ 14. Terms are stated in measurable constructs by avoiding words that are subjective and difficult to define or difficult to get consensus on what will be used to assess them (e.g., creativity, elegance, etc.). Terms are also avoided that have value-laden foundations, (e.g., lifelong learning, coping, good attitude, etc.).

☐ 15. Distinctive qualitative or quantitative (noticeable) differences exist between the levels in the middle of the rubric to effectively and reliably differentiate proficient from non-proficient performance (cut scores for the standard). See even-numbered reference under Structure.

☐ 16. The rubric avoids the use of terms that depict "averageness" (e.g., below average, intermediate, fair, usual, or above average; typical for this stage).

*(continued)*

☐ 17. The rubric avoids using adjectives attached to a feature continuum as a *sole* means of differentiating performance levels, (e.g., minimum, inadequate, inconsistent, and excellent understanding of . . . an excellent ability to . . . , etc.).

☐ 18. The distance between the rubric levels in terms of real-world performance is psychologically or perceptually equidistant; that is, to attain a performance score from one level to the next is equally easy or hard between each of the levels.

---

*Source: Effective Scoring Rubrics—A Guide to Their Development and Use.* Springfield, IL: Illinois State Board of Education, School and Student Assessment Section (1995). Used by permission.

## An Illustrative Middle School Instructional Technology Performance Assessment[1]

The following performance assessment was developed by Dr. Kevin Crabb of Georgia College and State University. It was pilot-tested at Indian Creek Middle School in Covington, Georgia. The assessment is based on an educational version of GIS (Geographic Information System) software called ArcVoyager. The following objectives were specified for the 10 day module:

*The students will be able to:*

1. **Know basic terms, component parts, mapping principles, and uses for a GIS.**

   a. Identify what each letter in GIS stands for.

   b. Define map theme.

   c. List four basic components of a GIS.

   d. Recognize point, line, and area data on a map.

   e. Identify one advantage GIS maps have over traditional (paper) maps.

   f. Cite one use for a GIS at the local, state, and national levels.

2. **Initiate the GIS ArcVoyager software program and successfully progress through the training sequence of activities of increasing difficulty.**

   a. Activate software by pointing and clicking mouse on appropriate desktop icon.

   b. Follow module directions to reach training tasks that build on the mastery of each preceding task.

   c. Recognize location and function of software tools that appear on the graphical user interface.

   d. Apply selected tools to module training tasks.

---

[1]The material in this section excerpted by permission from Crabb (2001).

**3. Apply ArcVoyager GIS software to perform basic spatial analysis.**

a. Utilize the measure, zoom, query, identify, and label tools correctly in various mapping scenarios.

b. Create a narrative "locate story" using a minimum of four thematic layers.

c. Determine the location for a nursing home in a Georgia county by executing appropriate tools to make site selection decision.

One can see the integration of knowledge and performance in these activities. The multidimensional nature of the tasks is characteristic of a performance assessment. Following is a sampling of the tasks included in the module.

## PERFORMANCE ASSESSMENT

**Directions:** You will answer # 1–7 using the GIS ArcVoyager software. The possible score for each question can be 0, 1, 3, or 5 points. The score you receive for each question will be determined by the teacher observing your selection and utilization of the software tools to address the performance requested. In addition, questions #1, 2, 3, and 6 require a fill-in-the-blank answer to complete the question.

You will be using the Georgia Reference Map for all questions in this portion of your GIS module post-test. Start the ArcVoyager GIS software from the computer desktop, then go to Level Three—*Designing Global Adventures: Point Me*. Click next on *Georgia*, then on the magnifying glass to the left of the heading *Georgia Reference Map*.

1. Use the **measure tool** to find the length (in miles) of Georgia's northern border.

    Answer: _____

2. Use the **identify tool** to find the 1990 population of Macon, Georgia.

    Answer: _____

Turn **off** Population 1990 Ga. Cities theme *and* Elevation Theme in the table of contents. Turn **on** County Outline Theme for the following questions.

3. Turn on the Medium Housing Value, 1990 theme and identify the county on the Atlantic Coast with the lowest 1990 median housing value.

    Answer: _____

4. Use the **label tool** and label on the map your answer to question 3.

5. Use the **pan tool** to make the state of Alabama appear in the center of the view window then return Georgia to the center of the view window.

6. Use the **query tool** and **identify tool** to find and name the Georgia County with a Hispanic population totaling 13 persons.

    Answer: _____

7. Use the **zoom tool** to create a map view where Athens and Augusta appear in your new zoomed in map view.

Now comes the challenging task of assessing the performances. Two scoring rubrics have been selected. The first relates to Task 4, where students must demonstrate a correct procedure, and Task 6 which, in addition to requiring demonstration of a skill, calls for the production of a product.

**Task 4 Rubric**

Score = 0; fails to initiate sequence to label county
Score = 1; selects label tool but fails to carry procedure to next step
Score = 3; selects label tool, fails to label correct county (McIntosh)
Score = 5; selects label tool, labels correct county (McIntosh)

**Task 6 Rubric**

Score = 0; fails to select query tool to begin sequence
Score = 1; selects query tool but does not know what to do from this point to get answer
Score = 3; selects query tool, requests correct data formula in tool, chooses new set, fails to use identify tool to find out name of county (Jenkins)
Score = 5; selects query tool, requests correct data formula in tool, chooses new set, uses identify tool to find out name of county (Jenkins)

An aggregate evaluative rubric could then be created covering performances contained in the entire module. Teachers might set standards as follows:

| Score on Assessment | Performance Category |
|---|---|
| 0–7 | Deficient in ability to use software; (should repeat entire module) |
| 8–14 | Needs development; (highly advised to repeat entire module; should repeat activities 6–9 in GIS module) |
| 15–21 | emerging proficiency; (should repeat activities 6–9 in GIS module) |
| 22–28 | proficient; meets basic requirements |
| 29–35 | exceptional; demonstrates software proficiency beyond basic requirements |

The assessment rubric contains implications for remediation as well as for grading.

In summary, developing a performance assessment is similar to developing any measurement, and includes the following steps:

1. Analyze the desired performance.
2. Identify crucial and representative elements for observation.
3. Select an appropriate simulation situation.
4. Specify the sequence of tasks that incorporate these crucial elements.
5. Specify the materials needed by the examinee to accomplish the tasks.
6. Prepare directions for examinee.

**7.** Develop methods for recording results of data collections.

**8.** Analyze reliability and validity.

Obviously, the item described here is not very complex because of administrative considerations. A classroom teacher can create meaningful tasks and more comprehensive and complex assessments by working with his or her colleagues to create reliable tasks and scoring rubrics.

An example of a complex and more involved performance assessment is contained in a collection of assessments aggregated by Educational Testing Service (1993) to illustrate how "national standards" might lead to relevant assessments. The following "Aquarium" task requires students to use mathematics to solve real-world problems, reason and problem-solve, measure, read, and write. It represents an interdisciplinary task involving math, science, and language arts. Students are given materials that describe (a) how to prepare an aquarium, and (b) the cost, size, and habits (e.g., who eats whom, do they go to "school," and so on) of eight freshwater fish. In two classroom periods the students are to respond to the following prompt:

**The Aquarium**

*Imagine that your school principal asks you to do a special job and gives you these written directions:*

Your class will be getting a 30 gallon aquarium. The class will have $25.00 to spend on fish. You will plan which fish to buy. Use the "Choosing Fish for Your Aquarium" brochure to help you choose the fish. The brochure tells you things you must know about the size of the fish, how much they cost, and their special needs.

Choose as many different kinds of fish as you can. Then write a letter to me explaining which fish you choose. In your letter,

   1. Tell me how many of each kind of fish to buy.

   2. Give the reasons you chose these fish.

   3. Show that you are not overspending and that the fish will not be too crowded in the aquarium.

This would probably be a good grade 4 exercise. Good assessment and instructional practice suggest a post-assessment debriefing with questions to the group concerning what they liked, didn't like, were surprised to learn, and want to share with the group. The task could be done collaboratively, but the letter task should be an individual effort.

## SELECTING QUESTIONS FOR PERFORMANCE ASSESSMENTS

The selection of any question for a performance assessment must be based on its match with the instructional objective. This is by far the most important criterion. A second criterion might be based on an examination of data from tryouts of the question or from previous applications.

### Summarizing Data from Performance Assessments

In a real sense, the data from a performance assessment would not be treated differently from that derived from a traditional multiquestion test. For example, consider a rating scale like the following:

Quality of Mousetrap          High        |___|___|___|___|        Low
                                          5    4    3    2    1

If everyone in the science class developed an experimental mousetrap, ratings could be made for each and then averaged for the class. Or perhaps several dimensions of the mousetrap were to be assessed such as

Quality of Mechanism          High        |___|___|___|___|        Low
                                          5    4    3    2    1

Practicality                  High        |___|___|___|___|        Low
                                          5    4    3    2    1

Attractiveness                High        |___|___|___|___|        Low
                                          5    4    3    2    1

A given student could then obtain multiple scores on the project. These could be aggregated for an individual student or the class.

If a teacher or group of teachers uses a rubric for scoring solutions to a math problem such as the following:

Advanced Response
Proficient Response
Nearly Proficient
Minimal Response

then using simple percentages of class (or school) students achieving at these levels could be used. You could also assign numerals to the categories—Advanced = 4, Proficient = 3, and so on—and average them for the class. The same approach could be used with portfolios, where the same rubric is employed over the course of a semester or year.

### Calculating Difficulty of Performance Tasks

Most performance tasks yield a continuous score. Using an earlier example with the quality of mousetrap rating scale, we might have the following data for a class of 25 students:

| | Sum of Scores | Mean | Difficulty (M/5) × 100 |
|---|---|---|---|
| Mechanism | 105 | 4.2 | 84% |
| Attractiveness | 40 | 1.6 | 32% |
| Practicality | 95 | 3.8 | 76% |

Expressing the mean as a percentage of the maximum possible rating, in this case, 5, yields a set of numbers representing, on an absolute scale, the "difficulty" of the task. Apparently the mousetrap project for this class tended to be reasonably effective and moderately practical, but truly ugly. Let it not be said that a better mousetrap could not be built.

Essay exams can be indexed in the same way. For example, the average (mean) score on a 35-point essay question for 25 students was 28.36. Expressing this mean as a percentage of the maximum possible score (35) yields a difficulty index of 81 percent. Apparently this was a fairly easy essay for this group.

## EVALUATING QUESTIONS FOR PERFORMANCE ASSESSMENTS

When performance measures are used in conjunction with mastery learning and individualized instruction programs, difficulty is encountered in selecting the "best" items for an assessment. If everyone masters the material and the test items are tied very closely to specific objectives, nearly everyone should do well on all the items. Therefore, it might be reasonable to expect and select items at about the 80 percent level of item difficulty, if instruction has been effective. It is imperative that students who participate in the item analysis of measures for use in performance assessment situations *have already worked through the material* being tested. Approaches that use data derived from performances at different times (pre- to post-) or between groups (masters versus nonmasters) can prove valuable in selecting questions or tasks.

Questions that do not discriminate between more and less knowledgeable or skillful students need not be eliminated from a performance- or criterion-referenced test if they reflect an important learning outcome (see Chapter 9). In a pre-/post-assessment situation, an index based on subtracting the percentage of those who passed the item on the pre-assessment from the percentage who passed it on the post-assessment provided information useful in identifying pre- items of diagnostic significance. Some of these items would have been overlooked if traditional item analysis methods had been used.

Following (see Table 10-4) are some possible pre-/post-instruction percentage scores that might arise under performance or criterion-referenced measuring (CRM) conditions for five questions. The question might be which questions should be retained.

Question 13 is obviously the "best" because it shows sensitivity to instruction by moving from 55 percent passing to 81 percent passing. Question 23 is insensitive and should be examined more closely. The instruction and objective associated with it might have to be revised. Even though Question 41 was easy pre- *and* post-instruction, we would keep it if it measures an important outcome. Question 57 is obviously bad as it reflects negative change, and the data should alert the teachers that something is wrong and reteaching is probably required. Finally, although the change is small, 21 percent to 36 percent, we would keep Question 69 because we can tolerate a lower level of sensitivity in a criterion-referenced measurement.

Because we hope that individuals will achieve instructional objectives as a result of their educational experiences, we might expect an item on a performance assessment to be answered correctly by a greater proportion of students after instruction than before it. If the instruction is successful, the proportion answering correctly should be high. Such indices of change in difficulty and absolute level of difficulty can be useful in assessing instructional effectiveness but should not be used to judge the adequacy of the item itself, as would be the case with norm-referenced tests. The quality of an item on a performance assessment is a function of the degree to which it matches the objective and is directly interpretable with reference to it. Panels of expert judges could be employed to help make these question-objective evaluations.

Finally, the instructor should be warned about being blinded by statistics. Item analysis data suggest the kinds of learning that have taken place and the items that need repair. The final decision about an item must be made by considering not only item analysis data but also the content and structure of the item and the nature of the group being tested.

## USING OBSERVATION TO GATHER PERFORMANCE DATA

Most of the myriad of possible achievement outcomes in schools and classrooms can be assessed with formal paper-and-pencil devices. This is particularly true of learning outcomes that involve knowledge, verbal and

**Table 10-4** *Possible Combinations of Pre-/Post-Instruction Item Percentage Scores*

| Item | Percent Passing (Pre) | Percent Passing (Post) | Decision to Retain for CRM |
|------|------|------|------|
| 13 | 55 | 81 | Yes |
| 23 | 15 | 19 | No |
| 41 | 86 | 91 | Yes |
| 57 | 73 | 47 | No |
| 69 | 21 | 36 | Yes |

thinking skill development, comprehension, and intellectual problem solving. In addition, it is becoming increasingly apparent that many affective outcomes can be assessed with paper-and-pencil measures, providing data useful for both student and teacher. But this is not the whole story. It is difficult at best to approach the assessment of proficiency in many skill areas and in situations in which personal-social development is emphasized. The best approach to assessing behavioral changes is direct observation. We need to know not only whether a student *knows* what to do, but also whether he or she *can* do it. Finally, we want to know if he or she *will* do it. The assessment of behaviors and outcomes in lifelike and realistic (as opposed to the classroom atmosphere) situations can supply us with some of the most valid data for decision making.

### Advantages of Observational Methods

The use of observational methods has been slighted in most school assessment situations, probably because of the difficulty of developing and applying the techniques. There are, however, many advantages to observation.

1. Observational and qualitative evaluation methods allow us to gather data, particularly about behavior and social-emotional-personal adjustment, in valid and reliable and precise ways not possible with more traditional methods.

2. Observational methods allow us to test an individual's ability to apply information in lifelike situations.

3. Because of the similarity between the testing situations and the setting in which the skills and knowledge are likely to be used, we find that observational measures tend to have higher predictive validity than do many other methods of predicting successful job performance.

4. Observational methods are easily adapted to a variety of settings, tasks, and kinds of individuals, at all ages and educational levels.

5. Observational data can serve as an invaluable supplement to achievement and ability data available from other sources.

6. Observation provides both qualitative and quantitative data.

7. Using data from a variety of sources results in a more reliable overall assessment.

8. The fact that observations take place in natural settings enhances their integration into the total instructional program and allows the instructor to use observation as part of the teaching process.

### Disadvantages and Difficulties in Using Observational Methods

Observing students is a difficult task. Many factors influence what a teacher perceives and how his or her observations are reported. Training and experience are the prime contributors to developing effective observational skills. Both experienced and inexperienced observers need to avoid a number of pitfalls:

1. *Faulty knowledge.* Armed with misinformation and mistaken ideas about human development and behavior, a teacher can distort observational records and the resulting interpretations.

2. *Uncritical acceptance of data.* Failure to distinguish between fact and opinion and the acceptance of rumors can lead to distortion of facts.

3. *Failure to pre-specify objectives.* Obviously, if we don't know what we are looking for, we may observe irrelevant behavior.

4. *Leaping to conclusions.* Drawing inferences from a single incident and failing to consider contradictory data can lead to faulty conclusions.

5. *Failure to consider situational modifiers.* Behaviors result from many influences, and observations must consider context. A single behavior can have two or more antecedents.

6. *Making false inferences from unreliable data.* The tendency to generalize from too limited a sampling of behaviors, and to make judgments on the basis of a few incidents, is a common pitfall.

7. *Failure to distinguish behaviors.* In most modern classrooms many activities take place simultaneously. It is difficult to distinguish relevant from irrelevant behavior.

8. *Failure to recognize personal expectations.* Teachers must realize that their observations will be colored by their own expectations, preferences, biases, and psychological needs.

9. *Failure to record observations accurately.* Observations should be recorded when they occur, or immediately afterward. Otherwise, selective forgetting can reduce the report's validity. We all have a tendency

to forget things that conflict with our own beliefs and expectations more readily than we do those that coincide with them.

10. *Excessive certainty.* Inferences from observations should be considered tentative and hypothetical until corroborative evidence is obtained.

11. *Oversimplification.* Guard against assigning a single cause to a single behavior; behavior has multiple determinants.

12. *Emotional thinking.* We tend to give disproportionate weight to incidents that have had a disturbing effect on us.

13. *Substitution fallacy.* There is a tendency to substitute an observed behavior for a desired objective—for example, substituting teacher behavior (process) for the criterion of student performance. Observing shop work or physical education, we can substitute "how students do something" for the quality of the product. This pitfall suggests the danger of giving such variables as "student-teacher interaction" or "group participation" the status of ultimate criteria.

## Applications of Observational Data

Despite the pitfalls to be avoided in collecting observational data, such data can make several very valuable contributions to the improvement of the teaching-learning situation. Observational data can be used to study:

1. group responsibility

2. group participation

3. attitudes toward subject matter

4. individual student interaction with the group

5. individual student and teacher interaction

6. teacher and class interaction

7. individual student achievement

8. class achievement

9. unanticipated but related outcomes

10. individual students in light of instructional hypotheses

11. teaching techniques

12. personal and academic problem areas

Observational methods are particularly useful when studying an individual's manipulative and psychomotor skills. In addition, opportunities to gather data in naturally occurring or contrived situations are limited only by teacher creativity. Interpersonal relationships can be observed and objectively summarized. Observation is a means of monitoring important outcomes, particularly those dealing with application skills, without encroaching on instructional time or disrupting the class. The presence of an outside observer can, however, inhibit the "naturalness" of the situation.

(Using observation data to assess interpersonal relationships and performance skills will be treated in detail later in this chapter.)

## USING RATING SCALES TO RECORD PERFORMANCE DATA

Rating scales are frequently used to record the results of observations. They can be easily applied in collecting self-observation self-report data. The three scales most frequently used in educational settings are numerical, graphic, and checklist. These types of scales are efficient both in terms of the amount of time required to complete them and in terms of the number of individuals who can be rated. Moreover, they do not require sophisticated raters and are relatively easily constructed. On the other hand, rating scales are all too often based on undifferentiated gross impressions and susceptible to conscious or unintentional distortion. "Anchored points," using descriptions, behaviors, products, illustrations, or samples, can enhance the usefulness of rating scales.

### Numerical Scales

Numerical scales generally take the form of a sequence of defined numbers. The definitions of the numbers might be in degree of favorableness, frequency, pleasantness, or agreement with a statement. Color or odor, for example, might be rated as

> 5 = Most pleasant
>
> 4 = Moderately pleasant
>
> 3 = Neutral
>
> 2 = Moderately unpleasant
>
> 1 = Most unpleasant

J. P. Guilford (1954) cautioned against using negative numbers or defining the end categories so extremely that no one will select them. It is probably a good idea to create more categories than you actually intend to use to maximize discrimination. You might, for example, use a scale like the following to gather the data:

> 4 = Always
>
> 3 = Usually

2 = Sometimes

1 = Never

Then, combine categories 1 and 2 with 3 and 4 for analysis purposes. Research seems to indicate that, depending upon the nature of the task and the sophistication of the rater, from seven to about 20 categories can be used. With checklists, as few as two categories (e.g., present-absent) can be used reliably.

The verbal definitions of the rating or numbers on a numerical scale can lead to semantic confusion. This problem is well illustrated by R. H. Simpson (1944), who asked a population of high school and college students to indicate what certain terms connoted for them. For example, does the term *often* mean 85 times in 100 or 65 times in 100 or less? A selected sample of Simpson's results is presented in Table 10-5. Obviously, individuals define terms very differently. The overlap in the range of the middle 50 percent for adjacent terms really introduces the ambiguity in measurement. Such differences undoubtedly lower both the validity and the reliability of ratings. Simpson did not, however, find appreciable differences between the sexes in the interpretation of frequency terms. One possible method of overcoming the problem of variable definitions is to specify the frequency to be assigned to each rating term. The following scheme might be used:

5 = Almost always (86 to 100 percent of the time)

4 = Generally (66 to 85 percent of the time)

3 = Frequently (36 to 65 percent of the time)

2 = Sometimes (16 to 35 percent of the time)

1 = Rarely (0 to 15 percent of the time)

This procedure allows some latitude in interpretation, but it provides raters with a common frame of reference.

## Graphic Scales

Another popular rating format is the graphic scale, which is ordinarily a straight line—sometimes vertical but usually horizontal—adorned with various verbal cues for the rater.

Guilford (1954) presents the following example of a graphic scale:

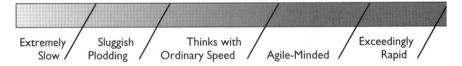

Extremely Slow / Sluggish Plodding / Thinks with Ordinary Speed / Agile-Minded / Exceedingly Rapid /

The rater is free to place a checkmark anywhere along the scale. In scoring, we might superimpose equal-interval categories (perhaps using a ruler)

**Table 10-5** *Meaning Assigned to Selected Frequency Terms Used in Rating Scales*

| Term | Average of Midpoint Ranges Assigned | Range of Middle 50% of Assignments |
|---|---|---|
| Always | 99 | 98–100 |
| Very Often | 88 | 80–93 |
| Usually | 85 | 70–90 |
| Often | 78 | 65–85 |
| Generally | 78 | 63–85 |
| Frequently | 73 | 40–80 |
| Rather Often | 65 | 45–80 |
| Sometimes | 20 | 13–35 |
| Occasionally | 20 | 10–33 |
| Seldom | 10 | 6–18 |
| Rarely | 5 | 3–10 |

*Source:* Adapted from Simpson (1944).

and assign numerical weights. For example, the midpoint between Agile-Minded and Exceedingly Rapid might be weighted 5, and so on. This procedure is similar to the scoring method suggested for the semantic differential technique described in Chapter 12. Another scoring approach involves using a ruler to measure the distance between one of the end categories and the checkmark. The suggestion of precision in such a procedure is probably not justified. Avoid using extremely long lines, which tend to produce a clustering of ratings; the resulting increase in reliability is so slight that the extra work involved is unjustified. It is probably also a good idea to determine the location of the "high" or "good" end of the scale randomly—for example, it might be on the right for one characteristic and on the left for another.

Graphic rating scales are simple and easy to administer and can be intrinsically interesting, although scoring can be time-consuming compared with other methods.

An illustration of some of the many forms that a graphic rating scale can take has been presented by Robert Guion (1965). The optimal number of rating points is probably seven to nine. Generally, you should provide more rating categories than you intend to measure to help spread ratings out, get more discrimination, and avoid "clumping" around a particular value. It is not unusual to select an odd number of points (e) so that the "average" will have a central position on the scale, yielding maximum discrimination. An even number of points can sometimes be used profitably, particularly if they are collapsed for scoring, for example, using a four-point scale (Never, Sometimes, Usually, and Always) to gather data, but scoring dichotomously. Some raters find it easier to make judgments when numerical point scales (b) are converted to verbal scales (c). An additional interpretation problem is thus introduced, however: the possibility that raters will read different meanings into the verbal scales. In any event, rating scales used with care and intelligence can yield meaningful data and are particularly adaptable to assessing products and performances.

### Checklists

Another popular method of recording the results of observations is the checklist. Even though the observer is checking categories, checklists are still considered ratings as we sum the number of or frequency with which behaviors occurred or characteristics were noted. Checklists can be used by relatively naive raters and tend to make complex judgments unnecessary. It is imperative, however, that the categories be as clear and precise as possible. The checklist developer would be well advised to use behavioral terms if at all possible. Checklists can be used to assess the following:

1. Which instructional objectives or skills have been met or mastered
2. Student interests, hobbies, problems, preferred reading material, radio or television programs, and the like
3. Student behavior in a variety of settings, especially problem behaviors in elementary school
4. Conformity to prescribed sequences of steps in task performance
5. Student products

Merl Bonney and Richard Hampleman (1962) cited the checklist example shown in Figure 10-2 used by an industrial arts teacher to identify the unsatisfactory items in a woodwork product before it goes to the finishing room.

An individual's "score" on the checklist can simply be the number of items checked or not checked or a standard for an acceptable product can be established. If some elements of the checklist are more important than others from an instructional standpoint, differential weights can be applied. A range of three possible values would probably suffice.

Some raters tend to use too many or too few items in a checklist. This response set can be combatted by requiring a fixed number of checks by the rater. Whether or not to use this technique will, of course, depend upon the nature and intended use of the checklist.

---

### Unsatisfactory Items in Woodwork Product

☐ 1. Knots      ☐ 11. Dimensions
☐ 2. Lack of Filling      ☐ 12. Operation Missing
☐ 3. Core or Glue      ☐ 13. Veneer Discolored
☐ 4. Joint Shrinkage      ☐ 14. Veneer Split
☐ 5. Veneer Sand-Through      ☐ 15. Rounded Edges
☐ 6. Glaze or Burnish      ☐ 16. Exposed Glue
☐ 7. Loose Veneer      ☐ 17. Coarse Sanding
☐ 8. Tear-Outs      ☐ 18. Grain and Color of Veneer
☐ 9. Rough Machinery      ☐ 19. Damage
☐ 10. Warpage      ☐ 20. Open Joints

---

**Figure 10-2** *Industrial arts checklist example*

The idea of a checklist and graphic scale are combined in the Superman Rating Scale in Figure 10-3. Note the continuum of prowess and the high standards needed to be a defender of the American way. There is no mention, however, of Kryptonite.

### Rating Errors

Despite the many advantages of using rating scales, several kinds of errors are associated with their application. Among them are the following:

- *Ambiguity.* The tendency to have different raters interpret rating terms in different ways. The previously summarized data of Simpson (1944) in Table 10-5 illustrate this well.

- *Leniency.* The tendency to rate or evaluate favorably those you know well higher than they should be rated. This kind of "generosity" can be offset somewhat by adjusting the scale to include a greater proportion of more positive points. For example:

*Physical Health*

Poor    Fair    Above Average    Average    Good    Very Good    Excellent

As one might expect, this kind of error is greatest when the rater must present the results to the ratee directly.

| Performance Factors | Far Exceeds Job Requirements | Exceeds Job Requirements | Meets Job Requirements | Needs Some Improvements | Does Not Meet Minimum Requirements |
|---|---|---|---|---|---|
| Quality | Leaps Tall Buildings with a Single Bound | Must Take Running Start to Leap Over Tall Buildings | Can Leap Over Short Buildings Only | Crashes Into Buildings When Attempting to Jump Over Them | Cannot Recognize Buildings At All |
| Timeliness | Is Faster Than a Speeding Bullet | Is As Fast As a Speeding Bullet | Not Quite As Fast As a Speeding Bullet | Would You Believe a Slow Bullet | Wounds Self With Bullet When Attempting To Shoot |
| Initiative | Is Stronger Than a Locomotive | Is Stronger Than a Bull Elephant | Is Stronger Than a Bull | Shoots the Bull | Smells Like a Bull |
| Adaptability | Walks on Water Consistently | Walks on Water in Emergencies | Washes With Water | Drinks Water | Does Not Recognize Water When Splashed |
| Communications | Talks to Heaven | Talks With The Angels | Talks to Himself | Argues With Himself | Loses These Arguments |

Note: Modified from original of unknown origin.

**Figure 10-3** *Superman's Performance Rating Scale*

- *Central Tendency.* The reluctance to give extreme ratings. Sometimes raters are reluctant to take extreme positions, either positive or negative. This tends to cause ratings to clump in the middle of the scale. You sometimes can counteract this by spacing descriptive phrases physically farther apart on the scale.

- *Halo.* A gross undifferentiated rating on a specific trait or behavior that is biased because it is based on an overall or total general attitude. "Michael Jordan is a great basketball player, therefore everything he does on the court is excellent—pass, shoot, play defense, and so on." Halo can be either positive or negative and can generalize across domains—for example, obnoxious personality = intellectual deficits.

- *Logical.* The tendency to give similar ratings to traits that seem to be logically related in the mind of the rater. If someone views "self-confidence" and "aggressiveness" to be part of the same personality dimension, then he or she might rate an individual similarly just on that basis rather than on the behavior being observed.

- *Contrast.* Some raters will evaluate or describe ratees in a direction opposite of themselves: "I am an extremely well-organized person; therefore, no one can be as organized as I am."

- *Proximity.* Nearness in time or location on a rating form. Traits to be rated on the same page tend to correlate higher than if they were rated on different pages.

Probably the best approach to reducing rating errors is through training and practice. Intelligence is only very modestly correlated with rating reliability. The dictum "know thyself" is good preparation for an observer/rater.

## THE DEVELOPMENT AND USE OF ANECDOTAL RECORDS

An anecdotal record is a description of what an individual does or says. It describes in concrete detail the situation in which the action or comment occurs, and what others present do or say. Randall (1936), who is credited with the development of the anecdotal record concept, defines it as a

> record of some significant item of conduct, a record of an episode in the life of the student, a word picture of the student in action; the teacher's best effort at taking a word snapshot at the moment of the incident; any narrative of events in which the student takes such part as to reveal something which may be significant about his personality.

The main thrust of the anecdotal record is to record social and emotional facets of a student's growth and adjustment. Records can also be made of other dimensions of relevant classroom or extra-classroom standing of individual students. Collected over a period of time, anecdotal material can provide a longitudinal view of a student's growth and patterns of change.

A sample anecdotal record is presented in Table 10-6. The kinds of information summarized in the anecdotal record could probably not be gathered in any other way.

1. Anecdotal records may supplement data gathered in other ways to assess progress toward a set of objectives.

2. Anecdotal records may suggest aspects of the curriculum that need to be reviewed or revised for particular students, or may suggest beneficial remedial activities.

3. Such data are useful in parent-teacher conferences to pinpoint specific areas of achievement or concern.

4. Anecdotal data can increase the teacher's insight into new students' strengths and weaknesses.

5. Many of the incidents reported in anecdotal form could be useful to school counselors, and teachers should make every effort to share them with counselors and other teachers to whom they are relevant.

6. Certain anecdotal records may have implications for vocational guidance and communication with educational and business personnel outside the school. Care should be taken to respect the security and confidentiality of such material.

## Suggestions for Generating and Improving Anecdotal Records

1. Determining in advance what is to be observed and being alert to unusual behavior.

2. Reporting only the "what" and "how" of the subject's actions and interactions with others.

3. Describing in detail the scene at the beginning of each period of observation.

4. Reporting in sequence each step in the course of every action taken by the subject.

5. Allowing no overlap between factual description and interpretation of the incident(s).

**Table 10-6** *Illustrative Anecdotal Record*

---

**Date:** 9/17/01                                    **Student's Name:** Cheddar

**Observer:** Chelsea (Student Teacher)

**Description of Incident:**

The fifth-grade class was working on a social studies display that involved the construction of models of many different kinds of homes common to different nationalities and countries. Cheddar was asked to work with Chloe, a black girl, to build, study, and make a class report on a typical South American home. At first Cheddar refused the assignment and asked to be allowed to work with one of her friends, another white girl. When the teacher insisted that she carry out the first assignment she began her project quite reluctantly. As her work progressed, her interest in the country and in working with Chloe became overtly enthusiastic.

**Comment:**

It appears that Cheddar has gained more than a knowledge of other lands and customs from this project. Cheddar has begun to work through some of her feelings regarding other races, and apparently may become more accepting and less fearful as a result of her experience.

---

6. Observing and recording sufficient material to make the report meaningful and reliable.

7. Recording the incident during or as soon after the observation as possible.

8. Restricting a given record to a single incident.

9. Recording both positive and negative incidents.

10. Collecting a number of anecdotes on a given student before attempting to make inferences.

11. Gaining practice in writing anecdotal records.

12. Establishing a plan for obtaining periodic systematic anecdotal samples.

## ILLUSTRATIVE PROCESS ASSESSMENTS

Following are examples of performance assessments in a variety of areas. Note that they are brief and easy to use, thus enhancing their practicality. Keeping the forms simple assists in data collection and getting reliable assessments.

### Skill in Using a Microscope

In this classic performance test, developed many years ago by Ralph Tyler, the instructor uses a checklist (see Table 10-7) to observe the sequence of actions required for properly identifying a specimen. The teacher is able to

**Table 10-7**  *Checklist of Student Reactions to an Object Under the Microscope*

| Student's Actions | Sequence of Actions | Student's Actions | Sequence of Actions |
|---|---|---|---|
| a. Takes slide | 1 | ad. With eye away from eyepiece turns down coarse adjustment | |
| b. Wipes slide with lens paper | 2 | | |
| c. Wipes slide with cloth | | ae. Turns up coarse adjustment a great distance segment | 13, 22 |
| d. Wipes slide with finger | | | |
| e. Moves bottle of culture along the table | | af. With eye at eyepiece turns down fine adjustment a great distance | 14, 23 |
| f. Places drop or two of culture on slide | 3 | ag. With eye away from eyepiece turns down fine adjustment a great distance | 15 |
| g. Adds more culture | | | |
| h. Adds few drops of water | | ah. Turns up fine adjustment screw a great distance | |
| i. Hunts for cover glasses | 4 | ai. Turns fine adjustment screw a few turns | |
| j. Wipes cover glass with lens paper | 5 | | |
| k. Wipes cover with cloth | | aj. Removes slide from stage | 16 |
| l. Wipes cover with finger | | ak. Wipes objective with lens paper | |
| m. Adjusts cover with finger | | al. Wipes objective with cloth | |
| n. Wipes off surplus fluid | | am. Wipes objective with finger | 17 |
| o. Places slide on stage | 6 | an. Wipes eyepiece with lens paper | |
| p. Looks through eyepiece with right eye | | ao. Wipes eyepiece with cloth | |
| q. Looks through eyepiece with left eye | 7 | ap. Wipes eyepiece with finger | 18 |
| | | aq. Makes another mount | |
| r. Turns to objective of lowest power | 9 | ar. Takes another microscope | |
| s. Turns to low-power objective | 21 | as. Finds object | |
| t. Turns to high-power objective | | at. Pauses for an interval | |
| u. Holds one eye closed | 8 | au. Asks, "What do you want me to do?" | |
| v. Looks for light | | av. Asks whether to use high power | |
| w. Adjusts concave mirror | | aw. Says, "I'm satisfied" | |
| x. Adjusts plane mirror | | ax. Says that the mount is all right for his eye | |
| y. Adjusts diaphragm | | | |
| z. Does not touch diaphragm | 10 | ay. Says he cannot do it | 19, 24 |
| aa. With eye at eyepiece turns down coarse adjustment | 11 | az. Told to start new mount | |
| | | aaa. Directed to find object under low power | 20 |
| ab. Breaks cover glass | 12 | | |
| ac. Breaks slide | | aab. Directed to find object under high power | |

*(continued)*

**Table 10-7** *(continued)*

| Noticeable Characteristics of Student's Behavior | Sequence of Actions | Characterization of the Student's Mount | Sequence of Actions |
|---|---|---|---|
| a. Awkward in movements | _____ | a. Poor light | X |
| b. Obviously dexterous in movements | _____ | b. Poor focus | _____ |
| c. Slow and deliberate | X | c. Excellent mount | _____ |
| d. Very rapid | _____ | d. Good mount | _____ |
| e. Fingers tremble | _____ | e. Fair mount | _____ |
| f. Obviously perturbed | _____ | f. Poor mount | _____ |
| g. Obviously angry | _____ | g. Very poor mount | _____ |
| h. Does not take work seriously | _____ | h. Nothing in view but a thread in his eyepiece | _____ |
| i. Unable to work without specific directions | X | i. Something on objective | _____ |
| j. Obviously satisfied with his unsuccessful efforts | X | j. Smeared lens | X |
| | | k. Unable to find object | X |

| Skills in Which Student Needs Further Training | Sequence of Actions |
|---|---|
| a. In cleaning objective | X |
| b. In cleaning eyepiece | X |
| c. In focusing low power | X |
| d. In focusing high power | X |
| e. In adjusting mirror | X |
| f. In using diaphragm | X |
| g. In keeping both eyes open | X |
| h. In protecting slide and objective from breaking by careless focusing | X |

*Source:* R.W. Tyler, "A Test of Skill in Using a Microscope," *Educational Research Bulletin,* 7, 1930, pp. 493–496.

note not only what the student does correctly, but also the kinds of errors he or she makes. Such data have diagnostic implications and can be used to correct the student's actions.

## Skill in Softball Batting

Many skills developed in physical education classes lend themselves to direct observation. A method of evaluating one of these skills is presented in Table 10-8. The use of such a checklist by an experienced observer can yield efficient and accurate results.

**Table 10-8** *Sample Checklist for Softball Batting Form*

| Date | Rater's Initials | Player's name _____ |
|------|------------------|-------------------------------|
| _____ | | Captain's name _____ |

*Instructions:* Rate the player each time he bats. Place a tally mark in the space which precedes the best description of player's form in each of six categories. Indicate your observation of errors in the right-hand half of the page, again with a tally mark. Write in any additional errors and add comments below.

1. *Grip*

_____ good

_____ fair

_____ poor

2. *Preliminary stance*

_____ good

_____ fair

_____ poor

3. *Stride or footwork*

_____ good

_____ fair

_____ poor

4. *Pivot or body twist*

_____ good

_____ fair

_____ poor

5. *Arm movement or swing*

_____ good

_____ fair

_____ poor

6. *General (Eyes on ball, judgment of pitcher, etc.)*

_____ good

_____ fair

_____ poor

*Errors*

_____ Hands too far apart

_____ Wrong hand on top

_____ Hands too far from end of bat

_____ Stands too near plate

_____ Stands too far away

_____ Rear foot closer to plate than forward foot

_____ Stands too far forward

_____ Stands too far backward

_____ Bat not in readiness position

_____ Fails to step forward

_____ Fails to transfer weight

_____ Lifts back foot from ground

_____ Fails to twist body

_____ Fails to wind up

_____ Has less than 90° of pivot

_____ Arms held too close to body

_____ Rear elbow held too far up

_____ Bat not held parallel to ground

_____ Jerky action

_____ Tries too hard

_____ Poor selection of bat

_____ Lacks confidence

*Source:* M. G. Scott and E. French, *Better teaching through testing* (New York: A. S. Barnes, 1945).

## ASSESSING STUDENT PRODUCTS

Many difficulties encountered in assessing interpersonal relationships and performances are also met when we attempt to measure the quality of student products. Such factors as the physical effort required to construct measures, complexity, administrative difficulties, and questions of validity and scoring are among the more prominent considerations. Although many products have physical dimensions that can be measured (e.g., size, weight, number of errors, color), more qualitative dimensions also need to be assessed. Such dimensions might be the flavor of a cake, the composition of a painting, or the neatness of handwriting. Aesthetic properties are more difficult to assess than physical attributes.

Process and product are intimately related. The decision to focus on product or process, or a combination of both, depends on the answers to the following questions:

**1.** Are the steps involved in arriving at the product either indeterminate or covert?

**2.** Are the important characteristics of the product apparent, and can they be measured objectively and accurately?

**3.** Is the effectiveness of the performance to be discerned in the product itself?

**4.** Is there a sample product available to use as a scale?

**5.** Is evaluation of the procedures leading to the product impractical?

If the answer to each of these five questions is "yes," the teacher may want to focus his or her assessment efforts on product evaluation.

Products can be readily assessed by carefully applying rating scales and checklists. Any product assessment's usefulness will depend on the accuracy with which its distinctive features have been delineated and defined. Assuming that the critical elements have been identified and appropriately weighted, observational scales like the ones in Tables 10-9 and 10-10 can be used to collect data.

### Assessing Woodshop Products

A variety of mechanical devices is available for measuring the quality of shop products, including gauges, rulers, T-squares, and calipers. Mechanical devices alone cannot measure all significant product characteristics, however. Almost any metal, plastic, or wood product has many qualitative dimensions. A rating scale useful in assessing the adequacy of nail fastenings has been developed by Dorothy C. Adkins and is presented in Table 10-9. The 10 categories may require overly fine discriminations, but the

**Table 10-9** *Sample Rating Scales for Nail-Fastening*

| 1. *Straightness* | 1 | 2 | 3 | 4 | 5 | 6 | 7 | 8 | 9 | 10 |
|---|---|---|---|---|---|---|---|---|---|---|
| | Are nails driven straight, heads square with wood, no evidence of bending? | | | | | | | | | |
| 2. *Hammer marks* | 1 | 2 | 3 | 4 | 5 | 6 | 7 | 8 | 9 | 10 |
| | Is wood free of hammer marks around nails? | | | | | | | | | |
| 3. *Splitting* | 1 | 2 | 3 | 4 | 5 | 6 | 7 | 8 | 9 | 10 |
| | Is wood free of splits radiating from nail holes? | | | | | | | | | |
| 4. *Depth* | 1 | 2 | 3 | 4 | 5 | 6 | 7 | 8 | 9 | 10 |
| | Are depths of nails uniform and of pleasing appearance? | | | | | | | | | |
| 5. *Spacing* | 1 | 2 | 3 | 4 | 5 | 6 | 7 | 8 | 9 | 10 |
| | Are nails spaced too close or too far apart? | | | | | | | | | |
| 6. *Utility* | 1 | 2 | 3 | 4 | 5 | 6 | 7 | 8 | 9 | 10 |
| | Will the nails hold? | | | | | | | | | |

Source: Dorothy C. Adkins, *Construction and analysis of achievement tests* (Washington: Government Printing Office, 1947), p. 231.

general analytic approach to rating this fairly simple skill has much to recommend it.

### Assessing Food Products

An efficient scale for evaluating a specific food product (waffles) is presented in Table 10-10. Note that both physical and aesthetic qualities are rated. The systematic summary of such data should be useful both for assessment and for teaching purposes. Go to your local waffle or pancake house and try this one out.

One trend in educational measurement is to use more observational or qualitative information. Such data can be used to confirm more traditional kinds of information, such as that derived from test scores. Looking at the same student or performance from different perspectives can be most revealing and confirm evaluations. Confirmation should lead to greater confidence in the validity of information, and better data should result in improved educational decisions. Rating scales help us summarize these observations and are particularly valuable if the "points" are described or illustrated.

## ORAL EXAMS

Oral exams are like oral supply or completion items, where the examinee completes or supplies an answer to a question or series of questions posed

**Table 10-10** *Food Score Card for Waffles*

| | | | Score |
|---|---|---|---|
| 1. Appearance | Irregular shape | Regular shape | 1. ___ |
| 2. Color | Dark brown or pale | Uniform, golden brown | 2. ___ |
| 3. Moisture Content | Soggy interior or too dry | Slightly moist interior | 3. ___ |
| 4. Lightness | Heavy | Light | 4. ___ |
| 5. Tenderness | Tough or hard | Tender; crisp crust | 5. ___ |
| 6. Taste and Flavor | Too sweet or flat or taste of leavening agent or fat | Pleasing flavor | 6. ___ |
| | | Total Score | ___ |

*Rate on a scale from 1 to 3.

*Source:* Clara M. Brown, Food Score Cards: Waffles, no. 53 (Minneapolis: University of Minnesota Press, 1940).

by an examiner. The oral exam is commonly used with elementary school students, graduate students, and students physically unable to take written tests. Although not used systematically in American education, the oral exam is a potentially useful technique. Certain measurement purposes can be better achieved with this technique than with any other technique.

The value of oral exams is readily apparent. Although written exams assume that the examinee understands the questions, the oral examiner can see if his or her question is understood. Further, the examiner can probe a student's understanding of a topic in more depth. Such probing also gives some indication of the thought processes used by the student. Not to be overlooked is the advantage of flexibility, that is, the variety of behaviors that can be sampled. The oral examination technique allows testing of both generalization and specific facts. In addition, the examiner(s) can observe a wide range of reactions to different stimulus questions. If a student hesitates in responding, fumbles for appropriate words, or manifests signs of stress, these reactions can be considered in appraising his or her degree of competence. Examiners of doctoral candidates are frequently concerned with these types of behavior. Examiners are interested not only in how much the candidate knows, but also in how he or she expresses and handles himself or herself in front of a group. In this respect, the oral examination is realistically related to contemporary life. Prospective teachers, for example, must be able to use their knowledge when speaking. In many other vocational activities, the spoken use of knowledge far exceeds its application in other ways.

Despite their potential advantages, several serious weaknesses of oral exams inhibit their use. Probably the oral examination's most thoroughly documented weakness is its unreliability. The difficulty of maintaining comparable standards of judgment, selective perceptions, and interpretation by different examiners and the limited sampling of the breadth of the student's knowledge potentially contribute to both unreliability and invalidity. Such factors as lack of precision in the conduct of an oral exam, failure to pre-plan the questions, and the relative inefficiency of the oral exam in faculty time detract from its usefulness. The technique requires careful planning. Another important disadvantage is the amount of time necessary to conduct a thorough oral exam. It is difficult, also, to know how to prepare for an oral exam. It is good for students to know that they will have an opportunity to exhibit their knowledge and reasoning ability, but how do they prepare for that? Probing questions can reveal a great deal, but there is always the danger that they can sidetrack or confuse the central issue(s). It is both an advantage and a disadvantage for this method that the response to questions will be spontaneous. The examiner likes this, but it can threaten the examinee. Extraneous factors such as the physical appearance and attractiveness of both parties can unfortunately influence the effectiveness of the oral exam. An overview of some factors that should be considered in the planning and use of oral exams is summarized in Table 10-11 on page 319. The exhibit on page 320 contains a bit of humor related to how *not* to use oral exams. The piece, of unknown origin, suggests many things to be avoided when oral questioning procedures are used. Graduate students in particular will appreciate the satirized guidelines.

In summary, there are two requisites if an examiner is interested in measuring and evaluating products or performances (behaviors): (a) a sample of the product or performance, and (b) a systematic guide for evaluating and recording the evaluation of that product or performance. The combination of observational data collection methods and rating scales can provide a useful approach to gathering data that cannot be gathered practically any other way.

# CASE STUDY

It is a rewarding and exciting experience to teach a skill or concept and then evaluate the hoped-for instructional effectiveness in a classroom setting. To assess whether or not that skill or concept transfers to an external performance situation can frequently be stressful for both student and instructor. Knowing what is expected and how it will be evaluated helps reduce the inherent ambiguity in the situation, which in turn lessens anxiety.

**Table 10-11** *Principles of Oral Examinations*

1. Use oral examinations only for the purposes for which they are best suited, i.e., to obtain information as to the depth of student's knowledge, where oral presentation is clearly a purpose of the course or program, or where other means are simply inappropriate.

2. Prepare in advance a detailed outline of materials to be sampled in the examination even to the extent of writing questions which will be asked.

3. Determine in advance how records of student performance will be kept and what weights will be assigned various factors.

4. Keep the questioning relevant to the purposes of the course or program.

5. Word questions in such a way that the students can see the point of the question with minimum difficulty.

6. Where several examiners are involved, make each one responsible for questions on a specified part of the full examination.

7. Judge students on the basis of their performance precisely defined—not in terms of a generalized impression of their total appearance.

8. Pose questions which students with the training which has preceded a particular examination can reasonably be expected to know. An examination is not the place for an instructor to demonstrate his own erudition.

9. Use both general and specific questions but do so in some logical order.

10. Do not spend a disproportionate time probing for the answer to one question. If the first several questions do not elicit the desired response, move on to some other matter.

11. Develop some facility with several basic techniques for successful oral examining, such as (a) creating a friendly atmosphere, (b) asking questions, and (c) recording responses.

12. Make a written record of the student's performance at the time it is given. However, do so without disturbing the student or disrupting the flow of the examination.

13. In most situations allow students ample time to think through and make responses to questions.

14. Avoid arguing with the student. It is his show—let him make the most of it.

*Source:* Reprinted and abridged from *Testing Bulletin No. 7*, published by the Office of Evaluation Services, Michigan State University, 1967.

This chapter has dealt with approaches to measuring academic skill and knowledge applications and performances in the sense that many kinds of educational outcomes need to be observed, reviewed, and/or rated. You now will have an opportunity to demonstrate your grasp of these methods by creating two measurement models: (a) an evaluation form for a sample Reading Education Lesson Plan, and (b) a brief observational schedule to be used during pre-practice teaching. First, evaluating a lesson plan.

Following is a description of the requirements for a teaching lesson plan. Use it as a basis for developing some systematic procedure that could

### What Not to Do in an Oral Exam Unless You Want to Scare the Examinee to Death

1. Before beginning the examination, make it clear to the examinee that his whole professional career may turn on his performance. Stress the importance and formality of the occasion. Put him in his proper place at the outset.

2. Throw out your hardest question first. (This is very important. If your first question is sufficiently difficult or involved, he will be too rattled to answer subsequent questions, no matter how simple they may be.)

3. Be reserved and stern in addressing the examinee. For contrast, be very jolly with the other examiners. A very effective device is to make humorous comments to the other examiners about the examinee's performance, comments which tend to exclude him and set him apart, as though he were not present in the room.

4. Make him answer each problem your way, especially if your way is esoteric. Constrain him. Impose many limitations and qualifications in each question. The idea is to complicate an otherwise simple problem.

5. Force him into a trivial error and then let him puzzle over it for as long as possible. Just after he sees his mistake but just before he has a chance to explain it, correct him yourself, disdainfully. This takes real perception and timing, which can only be acquired with some practice.

6. When he finds himself deep in a hole, never lead him out. Instead, sigh and shift to a new subject.

7. Ask him snide questions, such as "Didn't you learn that in Freshman Calculus?"

8. Do not permit him to ask you clarifying questions. Never repeat or clarify your own statement of the problem. Tell him not to think out loud, that what you want is the answer.

9. Every few minutes, ask him if he is nervous.

10. Station yourself and the other examiners so that the examinee cannot really face all of you at once. This enables you to bracket him with a sort of binaural crossfire. Wait until he turns away from you toward someone else, and then ask him a short direct question. With proper coordination among the examiners it is possible under favorable conditions to spin the examinee through several complete revolutions. This has the same general effect as item 2.

11. Wear dark glasses. Inscrutability is unnerving.

12. Terminate the examination by telling the examinee, "Don't call us; we will call you."

---

be applied in evaluating a set of such plans. The form should be as clear and precise as possible, as it will be shared with the students as they prepare their plans. The procedure could take many forms. It might be a simple checklist with an indication of satisfactory or unsatisfactory. That's probably not very discriminating. Perhaps a rating scale would be better. In any event, let your imagination run wild.

Another interesting experience would be to try your hand at an observational tool for describing and evaluating teaching performance (not effectiveness). Again, perhaps a checklist might be appropriate, or maybe a rating scale could be used to specify behaviors to be observed. Common sense and experience can suggest many more.

## Reading Education Lesson Plan Format

*Topic:* Brief description of topic.

*Grade:* The level for which you think the lesson is appropriate.

*Instructional Goal:* General statement concerning what you expect your students to gain from participating in the lesson.

*Purpose (Rationale):* Purpose includes general statement of *why* you are teaching this topic. This statement should be written and orally communicated to the students.

*Introduction (Focusing Event):* The introduction describes the way you will start the lesson. You should plan a stimulating, motivating introduction to help ensure students' attention to the lesson.

*Content (Curriculum):* List the specific facts and concepts you expect students to grasp after this lesson. Use this section to clarify your thinking about what is appropriate for the students to study. Think about whether you are planning to teach material that is too easy or too hard.

*Objectives:* Be sure objectives are stated in behavioral terms. When possible, include a description of the conditions under which the behavior is to be observed and the criteria for evaluating performance. Objectives should reflect depth of content and both higher and lower thinking skills.

*Activities (Procedures):* Activities must match objectives. Include at least one teacher-centered activity and one learner-centered activity. Label both activities. Be sure to include enough activities per objective to improve likelihood of mastery of objective. In addition, give consideration to the scheduling of activities/events.

*Materials:* List materials you will need for each activity. Be sure to plan interesting materials and media to illustrate concepts you are teaching. Materials must be referenced to each corresponding activity.

*Closure:* How will you summarize the lesson? Write this important step down and remember to *do* it. The teacher and/or the students can summarize the day's lesson. Sometimes closure can be done at the end of group work before the students begin work on individual projects.

*Enrichment/Remedial:* Plan as you would regular objectives. Specify who you are planning to use activities with.

*Evaluation:* Match evaluation procedures to the objectives checked. How will you know if your students have mastered the objectives? Evaluation is written in terms of what the teacher will do, while objectives are written about what the students will do. If your evaluation is teacher observation, you need to explain what you will be looking for.

## Content Review Statements

1. Performance assessments are useful in measuring and evaluating processes and products.

2. Developing a performance assessment involves the steps used in creating any assessment:
   a. identifying criterion behavior(s)
   b. constructing/selecting tasks
   c. specifying scoring rubric(s)
   d. collecting systematic and reliable data

3. A rubric represents a set of scoring guidelines for evaluating a performance assessment.

4. Rubrics can be described as holistic, analytic, developmental, quantitative, generalizable, or specific.

5. The use of rubrics builds in an evaluation of a measurement through criteria and standards.

6. Portfolio assessments allow student involvement in selection and self-evaluation of evidence achievements over time.

7. Portfolios can include a variety of evidence, such as essays, poetry, research papers, interviews, journal entries, posters, and self- or teacher comments.

8. Observational and simulation techniques can be used to assess a variety of learning outcomes, expressed as feelings, performances, or products.

9. The potential advantages of observational methods over paper-and-pencil measures are that they

    a. Are uniquely adaptable to certain learning outcomes.

    b. Are useful in assessing applications in real-life activities.

    c. Supplement other data sources.

    d. Can provide both quantitative and qualitative information.

**10.** The difficulties of making valid and reliable observations derive from

    a. Pre-observation knowledge and psychological set by the instructor.

    b. Failure to see isolated bits of behavior in the total context of the setting.

    c. Confusion of description and interpretation.

**11.** Observational methods can be used to study

    a. individual or group behavior.

    b. instructional procedures and their influences.

    c. student products and procedures.

    d. a variety of psychomotor and interpersonal behaviors.

**12.** Considerable care must be exercised in developing the wide variety of instruments—such as numerical and graphic rating scales and checklists—used to record the results of observations.

**13.** Rating scales should probably be limited to 10 points or less of gradation for each characteristic.

**14.** Rating errors include

    a. ambiguity

    b. leniency

    c. central tendency

    d. halo

    e. logical

    f. contrast

    g. proximity

**15.** The key to assessing student performances and skills is the simulation of the criterion behavior.

**16.** The development of performance tasks involves

    a. Analyzing the desired or criterion behavior.

    b. Identifying and selecting the most crucial elements to be observed.

    c. Providing directions and materials for the student.

    d. Recording the results of the simulation.

17. Performance, process, and procedure objectives can be considered ends in themselves.

18. The performances of students in such subject fields as music, vocational education, physical education, art, drama, public speaking, and science can be effectively studied by using rating scales and checklists.

19. Student products can be validly assessed through rating scales and checklists.

20. The key to the valid and reliable assessment of both performances and products is the specification of the expected criterion behavior.

21. Oral exams have the advantages of

    a. Allowing examinee comprehension of the task to be determined.

    b. Exploring examinee strengths and weaknesses.

    c. Being used with examinees who cannot respond in writing.

    d. Providing an opportunity to observe examinees "thinking on their feet."

    e. Testing for both generalization and fact.

22. Oral exams have the potential disadvantages of

    a. Unreliability of evaluation.

    b. Susceptibility to anxiety and stress.

    c. Lack of guidelines for examinee preparations.

23. The best performance- and criterion-referenced items tend to be those that show an increase in percentage passing as a function of instruction (pre- to post-) or those that differentiate proficient students from less proficient students.

## SPECULATIONS

1. What dimensions do observational methods contribute to educational measurement and evaluation?

2. What are the difficulties and problems in using observational methods?

3. Is it acceptable to observe a student without his or her knowledge?

4. What kinds of errors occur when rating scales are used, and what can be done to control the errors?

5. What are some ways that performance assessments can better be used as approaches in measurement and evaluation?

**6.** What evidence would you put in your portfolio for this class?

**7.** What might a product assessment for this book include?

**8.** How are methods used to select performance- and criterion-referenced tests different from those used to select norm-referenced items?

---

## SUGGESTED READINGS

Fitzpatrick, R., & Morrison, E. J. (1971). Performance and product evaluation. In R. L. Thorndike (Ed.), *Educational measurement* (2nd ed., pp. 237–270). Washington, DC: American Council on Education. Chapter 9 presents illustrations of methods that can be employed in measuring achievement performance tests. Suggestions for the development and scoring of such tests are also summarized.

Glatthorn, A. A. (1998). *Performance assessment and standards-based curricula: The achievement cycle*. Larchmont, NY: Eye on Education.

Guilford, J. P. (1954). *Psychometric methods* (2nd ed.). New York: McGraw-Hill. Chapter 11 is one of the most comprehensive descriptions of rating methods available. The chapter also surveys the relevant research findings.

Hoge, R. D. (1985). The validity of direct observations measures of pupil classroom behavior. *Review of Educational Research, 55*(4), 469–483. Data supporting the validity of broad measures of classroom behavior (e.g., on-task versus off-task).

Linn, R. L., & Gronlund, N. E. (2000). *Measurement and evaluation in teaching* (8th ed.). Columbus, OH: Merrill. Chapter 13, "Assessment Procedures: Observational Techniques, Peer Appraisal, and Self-Report," contains some excellent discussions and suggestions.

Moos, R. H. (1979). *Evaluating educational environments: Procedures, measures, findings, and policy implications*. San Francisco: Jossey-Bass. The climate is a very important moderator of the teaching-learning-testing process.

Stiggins, R. J. (1987). Design and development of performance assessments. *Educational Measurement: Issues and Practice, 6*(3), 33–42. An instructional module demonstrating how well-planned, systematic observations can be used to measure communication skills. Generalized step-by-step guidelines are presented. (See also Stiggins, R. J. *Evaluating students by classroom observation: Watching student effort*. Washington, DC: NEA, 1986.)

Webb, E. J., Campbell, D. T., Schwartz, R. O., Sechrest, L., & Grove, J. B. (1981). *Unobtrusive measures: Nonreactive research in the social sciences* (2nd ed.). Chicago: Rand McNally. This fascinating collection of methods is presented in a most appealing and understandable form.

Wortham, S. C. (1990). *Tests and measurement in early childhood education*. Columbus, OH: Merrill. Chapter 5, "Informal Evaluation Measures: Observations," and Chapter 6, "Informal Measures: Checklists and Rating Scales," are particularly useful for the primary and elementary school teacher.

# 11

## Creating and Using Portfolio Assessments

### FOCUS CONCEPTS AND KEY TERMS FOR STUDY

| | |
|---|---|
| **Advantages of Portfolios** | **Self-Evaluation** |
| **Artifact** | **Self-Reflection** |
| **Charrette Portfolio** | **Service-Learning** |
| **Disadvantages of Portfolios** | **Student-Led Conferences** |
| **Rubric** | |

**STANDARDS ALERT**

**Standard 3.14        Scoring Performance**

The criteria used for scoring test takers' performance on extended-response items should be documented. This documentation is especially important for performance assessment, such as scorable portfolios and essays, where the criteria for scoring may not be obvious to the user.

**TAKING IT TO THE CLASSROOM**

A group of teachers should work cooperatively to create a scoring rubric to be used in evaluating elementary student language arts portfolios. They should then check consistency in using the rubric by scoring a common set of portfolios.

Reprinted with permission from the *Standards for Educational and Psychological Testing.* Copyright © 1999 by the American Educational Research Association, the American Psychological Association, and the National Council on Measurement in Education.

A particularly useful type of performance assessment involves collecting and evaluating student work in a portfolio, not unlike that of a photographer or architect. Although used primarily in elementary school (especially in language arts), portfolios are employed in middle school math and high school social studies and science classes, among others. Portfolios are also used at the college and university level—for example, a teacher's performance portfolio is useful when the teacher is job seeking. Judith Arter and Vicki Spandel (1992) defined a student portfolio as a "purposeful collection of student work that tells the story of the student's efforts, progress, or achievement in (a) given area(s). This collection must include student participation in selection of portfolio content; the guidelines for selection; the criteria for judging merit; and evidence of student reflection" (p. 36). The *systematic* use of portfolios is a natural outgrowth of the educator's desire to perhaps cast a more humane perspective on how we evaluate and to diversify the methods so that we get a better match with instruction. Make no mistake, portfolios are messy to use, are at times expensive in terms of time and effort, and potentially suffer from a serious problem of reliability of scoring.

Ashelman and Lenhoff (1994) remind us that "portfolios" represent their most immediate educational value. The intersection is represented graphically in Figure 11-1. The commonalities in all three components are obvious. A video of a simulated teaching episode could be used as an

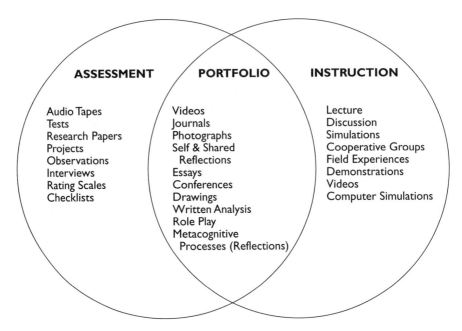

**Figure 11-1** *Intersection of Assessment and Instruction with Portfolios.*

instructional activity, as a method to gather assessment data, or as an artifact in a portfolio (an *artifact* being anything that the student wants to include in his or her portfolio). Artifacts may be tangible items that document the theme and meaningfulness to the student of the portfolio. Artifacts can be cognitive or affective. Theoretically, a portfolio could also be a collection of performance assessments.

## TYPES OF PORTFOLIOS

What kinds of materials should go into a portfolio? Literally anything that teacher and student together deem relevant is a candidate. A list of the specific documents and exhibits is not unlike one generated for performance assessments in general and would include the following:

- Art projects
- Essays
- Journal entries
- Parent/Teacher comments
- Posters
- Research papers

- Stories
- Attitude data
- Interviews
- Letters
- Poetry
- Problem solutions
- Self-Assessments
- Test results

The listing is practically endless, thanks to student and teacher creativity. Keep the requirements simple and share your criteria with the student.

## ADVANTAGES OF PORTFOLIO ASSESSMENT

Among the more important reasons for using portfolios are that the portfolio

- Is collected by the student in his or her own classroom, making it more natural.
- Provides a vehicle for the student to exhibit achievements that have relevance for him or her, teachers, and parents.
- Provides opportunity to track progress and growth over the semester or year, as well as the opportunity to demonstrate a final level of performance.
- Puts the student at the center of the instructional process.
- Stimulates teachers to confer with both students and parents.
- Enhances student self-evaluative skills and allows realistic assessment of proficiency.
- Provides an ongoing picture of performance with a series of snapshots that are spliced into a progress film.
- Represents tasks that are realistic approximations of everyday academic and real-world demands.
- Provides students the opportunity to "own" a piece of their learning: it is tangible evidence that, "I have accomplished something."

## DISADVANTAGES OF PORTFOLIO ASSESSMENT

Despite all the wonderful things about portfolio assessments, there are some drawbacks:

- The sometimes physical cumbersomeness of collecting and storing documents and other artifacts may inhibit their usefulness.
- Some students, teachers, and even parents are resistant to the implementation of this "new" approach.
- It is difficult to attain acceptable levels of reader/scorer/assessor reliability.
- Need for staff development may strain time and resources.
- Inappropriate and unfocused student selection of exhibits may lead to inaccurate generalizations.
- Failure to include a variety of selections leads to inaccurate generalizations.
- Failure to even create a scoring rubric.
- Efforts to create and field-test scoring rubrics are time-consuming.

## AN ILLUSTRATIVE PORTFOLIO— THE CHARRETTE*

Although traditional portfolios tend to focus on subject matter in the usual classroom descriptives such as language arts, mathematics, social studies, and science, other more focused and interdisciplinary collections are possible. The following portfolio resulted from the creative thinking of Dr. Elizabeth Pate of the Department of Elementary Education at the University of Georgia, and Dr. Katherine Thompson, a teacher at Clarke Middle School in Athens, Georgia. The portfolio came from a project, Community Context Curriculum Project (CCCP), whose short-term goal was to help middle school students learn about themselves, their community, and the workplace through curriculum. Four major questions were addressed:

- What was the impact of CCCP on the affective and cognitive domains of middle school students?
- What was the impact of CCCP on young adolescents' understanding of the community and their roles in it?
- What was the impact of CCCP on young adolescents' perceived world of work?

*The material in this section is based on documents generously made available by Dr. Elizabeth Pate, Associate Professor, College of Education, The University of Georgia.

- What is the nature of the relationship among academic community learning, curriculum integration, and contextual teaching and learning in the middle school curricula, and does this relationship lead to improved learning?

The rationale and framework for the project came from a group of scholars at the University of Georgia headed by Drs. Richard Lynch and Michael Padilla.[**] The characteristics of the framework, Context-Based Teaching and Learning, are as follows:

- Students are actively engaged.
- Students view learning as relevant.
- Students learn from one another through cooperation, discourse, teamwork, and self-reflection.
- Learning is related to "real-world" and/or simulated issues and meaningful problems.
- Students are encouraged to take responsibility for the monitoring and development of their own learning.
- Appreciating students' diverse life contexts and prior experiences is fundamental to learning.
- Students are encouraged to become active participants in the improvement of society.
- Student learning is assessed in multiple ways.
- The perspectives and opinions of students are valued and respected.
- The teacher acts as a facilitator of student learning.
- The teacher employs a variety of appropriate teaching techniques.
- The learning environment is dynamic and exciting.
- Higher-order thinking skills and problem solving are emphasized.
- Students and teachers are prepared to experiment with new approaches—creativity is encouraged.
- The process of learning is viewed as being as important as the content that is learned.
- Learning occurs in multiple settings and contexts.
- Knowledge is interdisciplinary and extends beyond the boundaries of conventional classrooms.

---

[**]Other major contributors included Professors Marty Carr, Stuart Foster, Richard Hayes, Elizabeth Pate, Julie Tallman, John Schell, and Carl Warren.

- The teacher accepts his or her role as a learner.
- Learning in multiple contexts allows students to identify and solve problems in new contexts (transfer) learning.

Portfolio assessment, obviously, should be seen as a natural component of this approach to learning. In addition, this framework is an extension of the "constructivist" theory of teaching-learning discussed in Chapter 3.

Students identified as average to low in reading and writing abilities collaborated with workplace workers from 19 different businesses, industries, and agencies, including the Chamber of Commerce, car dealerships, banks, telecommunications companies, sporting goods stores, veterinarians, department stores, the Department of Family and Children's Services, and hospitals.

After writing letters of introduction and requesting a "partnership," students engaged in a variety of activities, such as site visits, interviews, workplace observations, creating community concept maps, and writing definitions of critical terms and reflections. Students were urged to use cameras to document their experiences and the Internet to explore related concepts.

**Workplace Charrette**

The first type of portfolio to emerge from CCCP was a "charrette." In the nineteenth-century Parisian architectural studios at the Ecole des Beaux, students were instructed to toss their assignments into a cart, or charrette, while moving between worktables. The assignments were to be turned in whether complete or incomplete. The idea of a charrette has now become a device for visioning processes focused on solving a community problem.

The charrette that follows was developed by Shavoris and Ricardo in collaboration with a tire and rubber products manufacturing company. The charrette portfolio was to document the history, philosophy, products, and services of this organization, demonstrate language arts, mathematics, science, social studies, and technology knowledge and skills, and reflect workplace pride, responsibility, and accountability—quite a challenge for middle school students. The student's charrette included:

- A self-assessment, including results of a multiple intelligences survey, interest survey, work ethics survey, and technology survey
- A concept map showing the relationship of the industry to the community
- Photographs of the manufacturing site
- Personal resumes
- Summaries of research on the tire manufacturing industry
- Formal letters of inquiry and thank-you letters

- Summaries of interviews with workers

- Logs and journals of their activities and reflections

- Definitions of critical terms

What did Shavoris and Ricardo learn from their collaboration with the manufacturer? From their reports and portfolio the following facts, among many, were "discovered."

---

**What does a wage employee do?**

---

◆ takes measurements ◆ uses gauges ◆ writes directions ◆ reads micrometers ◆ understands machinery/equipment ◆ takes notes ◆ is cross-trained for other jobs ◆ solves problems ◆ follows directions ◆ analyzes products for quality control

---

**What makes a good employee?**

---

◆ "shows up for work and is on time" ◆ has successfully completed 60-day trial period ◆ works on job bid system ◆ uses team collaboration strategies ◆ is a team player ◆ is honest ◆ is self-directed ◆ participates in walk-abouts ◆ believes "work ethic is #1!"

---

**What content is needed?**

---

◆ social studies ◆ language arts ◆ science ◆ mathematics ◆ technology ◆ difference between synthetic and natural rubber ◆ where natural rubber comes from ◆ reading formulas ◆ following directions ◆ keeping logs ◆ communication skills ◆ use of computers

---

**What are the basic job requirements and wages?**

---

◆ $11.75 average hourly wage ◆ job positions depend on mathematics skills ◆ range of $16.00–$22.00 hourly wage if you have ability to maintain machinery ◆ completion of job application ◆ honesty on application a must ◆ high school diploma required ◆ successful passing of mathematics test on addition, subtraction, multiplication, division, percentages, conversion of units

---

This was obviously a very meaningful learning experience for these adolescents. They learned about the relationship between academics and the world of work, about their marketable skills and those that they might wish to develop, and about their community. A logical step for teachers from a workplace charrette would be into a **service-learning** program (Payne, 2000; Schine, 1997). Service-learning is a method of teaching through which students apply newly acquired academic skills and knowledge to address real-life needs in their own communities. Now that students and their corporate partners have established a collaborative relationship, the next logical step would be to do a needs assessment and identify a joint community project. Such projects can range from the revitalization of neighborhoods, to conserving and restoring public lands, building homes for the homeless, and recycling. A portfolio could be used to document both learning and service experiences.

## DECISION POINTS IN THE PORTFOLIO DEVELOPMENT PROCESS

As one begins to organize a portfolio system many preparatory decisions need to be made. Shaklee, Barber, Ambrose, and Hansford (1997) suggest that the developer address 10 critical decisions:

- What is the purpose in creating this portfolio?
- What will the portfolio look like?
- Who should be involved in creating the portfolio?
- What should be assessed?
- What is the time line for portfolio assembly and assessment?
- What kind of artifacts should be included in the portfolio?
- What decisions can I make from the portfolio?
- How will the portfolio be evaluated?
- How will evaluative data be summarized?
- How can I make the portfolio system an integral part of the teaching-learning process?

In order for the portfolio to be maximally relevant to both student and teacher it is imperative that the item/piece choices be linked to instructional objectives. These may be product or process in nature. A clear purpose is central as it helps provide a kind of framework and guide for student or joint student-teacher decision making. The ultimate value of the portfolio rests on how it can and is used to enhance learning. The random collection of "things" that the student likes will not likely benefit student learning.

## ORGANIZING AND IMPLEMENTING A PORTFOLIO SYSTEM

Portfolios are really not new. Like so many performance assessments described earlier, we have been using them since the beginning of humankind. Did not Moses, for example, have a stone portfolio? Jim Popham (2002, pp. 203–205) listed seven key elements in classroom portfolio assessment:

1. Develop student "ownership" in the portfolio by involving him or her in the selection and evaluation process.

2. Specify a variety of materials to be included.

3. Systematically collect and store the exhibits.

4. Identify the criteria for inclusion in the portfolio and evaluation of the contents.

5. Require students to periodically evaluate their portfolios, with special emphasis on change, growth, gain, and progress.

6. Systematically schedule student portfolio evaluation conferences.

7. Involve parents in the portfolio process by informing them of the purpose and content, and eventually, showing them examples and samples.

In summary, the major advantage in using portfolios as performance assessments is the involvement and investment of the student in a process that directly relates to instruction. The disadvantage is the time and effort needed to create scoring rubrics (see previous section) and applying these systematically so that reliable measurements will be obtained. Their primary application is in a classroom setting, whereas their use in large-scale (e.g., statewide) assessments in the service of accountability is currently problematic.

## PORTFOLIO-BASED STUDENT-LED PARENT (TEACHER) CONFERENCES

The availability of student portfolios provides an excellent opportunity to use them as centerpieces for student-led parent conferences. Having students conduct such conferences enhances their acceptance of responsibility for their own learning. The preparation alone is a learning experience. That learning is obviously related to content, but also to how the student can organize and manage his or her learning. The teacher may or may not be present at the conference. Usually in the early elementary grades, the teacher's role is that of observer and resource person. In addition to promoting responsibility for self-initiated learning, the student-led conference can help develop goal-setting behavior. Self-assessment as part of the preparation activity can be a powerful motivating force for learning and personal development.

Davis, Riss, and Flickinger (1996) suggest the following organizational plan for K–6 students:

| | |
|---|---|
| September: | Establish literacy goals and plans |
| | Review work samples |
| October: | Collect literacy samples for the portfolio |
| | Review work samples |
| | Metacognition, reflective thinking activities |
| November: | Three-way conferences |
| January: | Collect literacy samples for the portfolio (ongoing throughout the year) |
| | Metacognition, reflective thinking activities |
| March: | Role playing and rehearsal in preparation for the conferences |
| April: | Student-led conferences |

The role of the students will be to

- Prepare an agenda in consultation with the teacher.
- Discuss with parents activities that have led to the conference.
- Share portfolio samples to illustrate work quality, effort, and areas in need of improvement, and to set the stage for goal setting.

A key element in the process is reflection on the part of the student. Formal responses to the following kinds of questions would be discussed with teacher and parent:

What are some things I have studied this period?

What are some things I have learned this period?

Do I still have work that is overdue? Why?

What are some things I do well?

What are some things I do not do well?

How and what will I try to improve next period?

The student should obviously reflect on learning in general, but in addition should reflect on the items in the specific portfolio. Some questions that might lead to meaningful reflection about each item selected for inclusion by the student are (Arter & Spandel, 1992):

Why was each item/piece chosen?

Why is it better than others you have done?

What did you learn from creating it?

How can you improve this item/piece?

What are the strengths of your work?

Do you see some weaknesses in your work?

How does this item/piece cause you to think of a new item/piece?

## ASSESSING THE PORTFOLIO

Portfolios are usually evaluated by students and teachers, although other stakeholders in the student's progress might be involved to some degree. The portfolio (like any performance assessment) might be evaluated using any number of approaches, from checklists, to rating scales, to rubrics. The usual method is with a rubric. Pate, Homestead, and McGinnis (1999) remind us that a rubric is a set of scaled criteria that "clearly defines for the student and teacher what a range of acceptable and unacceptable performance looks like" (p. 25).

It will be recalled from Chapter 10 that we can consider two general categories of rubrics, holistic and analytic. Analytic rubrics employ a set of evaluative criteria, each of which are judged. Holistic scoring involves having a rater aggregate multiple criteria into a single overall score.

The most meaningful assessments of a student portfolio come from student and teacher. An interesting example of teacher portfolio assessment has been provided by Remmers and Londino (1994). They describe a public relations course offered at Kean College of New Jersey. The portfolio contains a variety of items, including news and feature releases, press advisories, speeches, video and slide-show scripts, brochure copy, and sample public service announcements. The portfolio is used to assess successful completion of the program of study and as a self-marketing tool during job searches. A very simple yet informative grading rubric is presented in Table 11-1.

Students have their portfolios evaluated by the instructor as well as by peers. It would add to objectivity to have two instructors evaluate the same set of portfolios and then check for interrater agreement. Results are meaningful to both students and instructors, as the data highlight areas where student and program goals can be accomplished.

It is usually recommended that students review their own portfolios before sharing them with teachers, parents, or peers. Table 11-2 contains a sample student self-evaluation form. The form itself should become part of the student portfolio.

Sometimes the "portfolio product" is less than acceptable. In such cases collecting additional information about requisite skills will be necessary. Such a "diagnostic self-evaluation" is presented in Table 11-3. The results of using this self-evaluation can help both student and teacher.

Portfolios have become a staple for the classroom teacher. They are flexible and provide a tremendous opportunity for learning. Authentic assessment lives!

**Table 11-1** *Illustrative Public Relations Portfolio Grading Rubric*

Student _____     Date _____

Evaluator _____

**On a scale from 1 to 5, how successfully does the work in this portfolio meet the following criteria:**

|  | Highest |  |  |  | Lowest |
|---|---|---|---|---|---|
| 1. Shows creativity | 1 | 2 | 3 | 4 | 5 |
| 2. Shows a variety of work | 1 | 2 | 3 | 4 | 5 |
| 3. Shows knowledge of correct style | 1 | 2 | 3 | 4 | 5 |
| 4. Is well-organized | 1 | 2 | 3 | 4 | 5 |
| 5. Shows clarity of writing | 1 | 2 | 3 | 4 | 5 |
| 6. Shows conciseness of writing | 1 | 2 | 3 | 4 | 5 |
| 7. Is adapted to audience | 1 | 2 | 3 | 4 | 5 |
| 8. Is persuasive | 1 | 2 | 3 | 4 | 5 |
| 9. Uses correct grammar | 1 | 2 | 3 | 4 | 5 |
| 10. Uses correct spelling | 1 | 2 | 3 | 4 | 5 |
| 11. Has good lead paragraphs | 1 | 2 | 3 | 4 | 5 |
| 12. Looks neat and professional | 1 | 2 | 3 | 4 | 5 |

Reprinted from Remmers, F. L., and Londino, C. (1994). The public relation portfolio (p. 32). In M. G. Knight & D. Gallaro, *Portfolio assessment*. Lanham, MD: University Press of America.

# CASE STUDY

Given that portfolios represent the intersection of instruction and assessment, you are hereby challenged with two tasks.

First, create a list of items for inclusion in a portfolio benefiting students in a "how to teach reading" course. What kinds of artifacts would be appropriate? Assume that the items will be dated. Second, create a rubric useful in assessing the quality of the portfolio.

## CONTENT REVIEW STATEMENTS

**1.** Portfolio assessments allow student involvement in selection and self-evaluation of evidence achievements over time.

**Table 11-2** *Student Self-evaluation Form for Reviewing Portfolios*

Name_____     Date _____

**When you can check yes for each box and have written down your list of artifacts, you are ready to have your teacher conference.**

| | | |
|---|---|---|
| Have I included an introduction to my portfolio? | ☐ Yes | ☐ No |
| Does my introduction explain what is in my portfolio? | ☐ Yes | ☐ No |
| The artifacts I chose to place in my portfolio were: | | |
| | | |
| Do the artifacts that I chose show my learning growth? | ☐ Yes | ☐ No |
| Have I explained why I chose each artifact? | ☐ Yes | ☐ No |
| Have I included self-evaluations that show my strengths? | ☐ Yes | ☐ No |
| Have I included self-evaluations that show areas that need improvement? | ☐ Yes | ☐ No |
| Have I included goals to improve my learning? | ☐ Yes | ☐ No |
| Are my goals ones I can reach and that challenge me? | ☐ Yes | ☐ No |
| Have I included a way to respond to my portfolio? | ☐ Yes | ☐ No |

Reprinted from Johnson, N. J., & Rose, L. M. (1997). *Portfolios: Classifying, constructing, and enhancing.* Lancaster, PA: Technomic (p. 252).

2. Portfolios can include a variety of evidence, such as essays, poetry, research papers, interviews, journal entries, posters, videos, and self- or teacher comments.

3. Rubrics are an efficient way to assess portfolios.

4. Portfolios are a meaningful way to link assessment and instruction.

5. Portfolio assessment can involve student, teacher, parents, and/or peers.

6. Portfolios are a valuable way for students to both learn and showcase their achievements.

7. Teacher summaries of portfolio assessments can aid in examining instructional activities.

8. Use of portfolios can be cumbersome, difficult to assess, time-consuming to create, and unfocused.

9. The charrette is a workplace student portfolio allowing for documentation of a student excursion.

**Table 11-3** *Student Self-Evaluation Rubric About Webpage Construction Skill*

| | |
|---|---|
| Level 1 | I cannot create a page which can be viewed with a web browser. |
| Level 2 | I can save text I've created as an html file with a command in my word processor. I know a few, simple html commands. |
| Level 3 | Using hand-coded html or a web page authoring tool, I can: |
| | —view web pages as source documents |
| | —create a formatted web page that uses background color, font styles and alignment, graphics, and tables |
| | —include links to other parts of my document or other Internet sites in my page |
| | —know basic guidelines for good web page construction and the district's web policies |
| Level 4 | I can use the web as an interface to databases. When appropriate, I can register my pages with search engine sites. I can help write web creation policies for design, content, and use. |

( Johnson, 1998).

10. Many decisions need to be made in developing a portfolio exercise, such as purpose, timeline, nature of artifacts, and how evaluation will take place.

11. Both student-parent and teacher-student-parent conferences benefit from using a student portfolio as the centerpiece.

12. Self-evaluation is a critical element in making the portfolio important in the learning process.

## SPECULATIONS

1. Why are portfolios considered examples of authentic, modern, or performance assessment?

2. How can the portfolio be used as a basis for (a) a student-teacher conference, (b) student-parent conference, or (c) a parent-teacher conference?

3. How can a student-led conference facilitate communication among parent, teacher, and student?

4. What is the relationship among instructional objectives, assessment, and portfolios?

**5.** What artifacts might you include in a portfolio for which this book is being used as the text?

## SUGGESTED READINGS

Arter, J. A., & Spandel, V. (1992). Using portfolios of student work in instruction and assessment. *Educational Measurement: Issues and Practice, 11*(1), 36–44. This instructional module, with excellent references, contains a valuable self-test checklist for portfolio users.

Farr, R., & Tone, B. (1998). *Portfolio and performance assessment (Helping students evaluate their progress as readers and writers* (2nd ed.). Orlando: Harcourt Brace College Publishers. Very comprehensive with a useful section on conferencing.

Grant, J. M., Heffler, B., & Meriwether, K. (1995). *Student-led conferences using portfolios to share learning with parents.* Markham, ON: Pembroke Publishers.

Johnson, N. J., & Rose, L. M. (1997). *Portfolios (Classifying, constructing, and enhancing).* Lancaster: Technomic Publishing. An excellent source of suggestions covering all aspects of portfolio development and application, with the theme being student self-assessment.

Knight, M. E., & Gallaro, D. (Eds.) (1994). *Portfolio assessment (Applications of portfolio analysis).* New York: Lanham. A collection of ideas from applications in higher education—for example, music, theater, visual arts, nursing, teaching, and occupational therapy.

Linn, R. L., & Gronlund, N. E. (2000). *Measurement and assessment in teaching* (8th ed.). Upper Saddle River, NJ: Merrill. Chapter 12, "Portfolios," contains insights into sound classroom practice.

Montgomery, K. (2001). *Authentic assessment (A guide for elementary teachers).* New York: Longman. See especially Chapter 8 on the purposes and content of portfolios.

Popham, W. J. (1995). *Classroom assessment—What teachers need to know.* Boston: Allyn & Bacon. Chapter 9 is a very practical and readable consideration of portfolio assessment. Both the positives and negatives are described.

Shaklee, B. D., Barbour, N. E., Ambrose, R., & Hansford, S. J. (1997). *Designing and using portfolios.* Boston: Allyn & Bacon. Very readable paperback, with concise overview of development process and good examples.

Tierney, R. J., Carter, M. A., & Desai, L. E. (1991). *Portfolio assessment in the reading-writing classroom.* Norwood, MA: Christopher Gordon Publishers.

# 12

## Assessing Attitudes

---

### FOCUS CONCEPTS AND KEY TERMS FOR STUDY

| | |
|---|---|
| **Affective** | **Likert Scales** |
| **Affective Assessment Methods** | **Opinionnaire Methods** |
| **Application of Affective Measures** | **Semantic Differential Technique** |
| **Diagnosis of Learning Difficulties** | |

---

## STANDARDS ALERT

**Standard 12.13          Informed Inference**

Those who select tests and draw inferences from test scores should be familiar with the relevant evidence of validity and reliability for tests and inventories used and should be prepared to articulate a logical analysis that supports all facets of the assessment and the inferences made from the assessment.

## TAKING IT TO THE CLASSROOM

It is incumbent upon any teacher, counselor, or administrator charged with the responsibility of selecting an instrument for class or school use, particularly if it is in the affective domain, to investigate the documentation to ensure that it is appropriate for the intended use.

---

Reprinted with permission from the *Standards for Educational and Psychological Testing*. Copyright © 1999 by the American Educational Research Association, the American Psychological Association, and the National Council on Measurement in Education.

Approaches to the assessment of affective variables are limited only by the developer's creativity and motivation. The term *affective* as used throughout this chapter refers to a tendency to be or not to be attracted to an idea, person, task, product, or activity. In general, *affective* relates to such characteristics as attitudes, interests, and values. Many methods have been developed by educators, psychologists, and sociologists in their studies of human behavior, but too few have been communicated to, or translated for use by, classroom teachers. It is not my intent nor is it possible in these few pages to develop the reader into a polished and accomplished creator of affective assessment instruments. Instead, I want to illustrate some useful methods that could be adopted for classroom use. Beyond that goal, however, I hope that you will come to appreciate the dramatic possibilities of affective outcomes exploration.

## SUGGESTED USES OF AFFECTIVE ASSESSMENTS

Applications of affective measures, particularly standardized measures, fall into five general categories: classroom applications, screening and selection, counseling, research, and program evaluation.

## Classroom Applications

The imaginative classroom teacher can create many situations in which affective measures contribute to the instructional program. An interest inventory, for example, could be used either before or after instruction to assess changes in work values associated with a unit on the "world of work," or it could be used as a starting point for exploring various occupations. It might be helpful to have students estimate their scores before taking the test, then compare these estimates with the test results. Individual student scores or class means could then be compared with selected normative data. The study of vocations could be stimulated by this method; discussion might revolve around known differences between occupational groups. It could be noted, for example, that psychiatrists score significantly higher than lawyers, CPAs, and engineers on Altruism and that teachers score higher than psychologists on Security. The entire class or small groups could examine in detail how various occupations relate to scores on the instrument.

If teachers are particularly concerned about the schoolwork habits of their students, a study habits inventory could be used to explore possible difficulties.

The personnel offices of businesses and industries frequently administer tests of various dimensions of personality to prospective employees, so classroom experience with an inventory should help students prepare for this experience. Practice on similar tests usually results in reduced anxiety in a formal assessment setting.

The largest classroom application area probably rests in examining attitudes toward subject matter on issues arising from units of instruction. The best way to know how students (or faculty or parents, for that matter) feel about what you have taught is to ask them. Systematically collected opinion data can be most revealing.

## Screening and Selection

The *School Interest Inventory* (Cottle, 1966) illustrates the sensible use of a standardized affective measure. The SII should be used on an intra-institutional basis, so that a student's scores are compared only with those of other individuals in the same school. The SII is used to identify potential dropouts. Students in the seventh or eighth grade could take the SII, and their scores could be ranked from highest to lowest within grade and sex. (Higher scores indicate a greater probability of the student's dropping out of school.) Using any number of criteria—for example, a cutoff score of 25 or above or selection of the top 20 percent—one could identify students who might benefit from counseling. Counselees could consider continuing in the same or another course of study, or explore vocational and social adjustments that do not require a high school diploma. The counselor or teacher could also set up "rap groups" in which personal, social, or vocational problems could be explored. Obviously, you should use other relevant data when you use a test as a screening instrument. School achievement records, attendance, teachers' opinions, and age relative to school grade should be considered.

Personnel managers frequently find that affective measures are useful in hiring and placing special classes of employees, and that scores may be related to job success. When an affective measure is used in this manner, its relevance must be demonstrable.

**Counseling**

Affective measures, particularly standardized ones, are often used for counseling, guidance, and psychotherapy. Such measures stimulate individuals to "look at themselves" and, in some cases, identify a variety of types of psychopathology. The usual application is personal development and career exploration. Such self-report devices can be used effectively as starting points or springboards to help establish rapport in an interview situation. Asking respondents to first predict their scores and then comparing predictions with actual results can be a very valuable experience for both students and counselors. This is particularly true when vocational interest inventories are used.

An example of a frequently used standardized affective measure in counseling and guidance is the *Study Attitude and Methods Survey* (Michael, Michael, & Zimmerman, 1988). In its current form, the SAMS is a 90-item survey that requires the respondent to select one of four responses: *Not At All Like Me or Different From Me*, *Seldom or Somewhat Like Me*, *Frequently or Much Like Me*, or *Almost Always or Very Much Like Me*. It is machine- or hand-scored and used for two purposes: (1) to identify students likely to have school difficulties because of poor study habits, and (2) to identify areas where counseling and guidance might help. Table 12-1 shows the six dimensions of the SAMS, together with sample items.

Reliability data consist primarily of internal consistency coefficients (all 0.80 or higher), and validity data are expressed as correlations with course grades and with other affective measures. Normative data are available for both high school and college populations.

A sample profile for a college student is presented in Figure 12-1. Note that raw scores are plotted on the profile sheet and can then be read as either normalized $T$-scores (with a mean of 50 and a standard deviation of 10) or percentile ranks. Refer to Chapter 13 for a discussion of these two

**Table 12-1** *Six Dimensions of the Study Attitude and Methods Survey*

| Dimensions | Interpretation | Sample Item |
|---|---|---|
| Academic Interest— Love of Learning | School excites students; high scores likely to get good grades. | Many courses are so interesting that I find myself doing more work than assigned. |
| Academic Drive | Determined to do well in school by doing what is expected. | I make every effort to do what the teacher expects of me. |
| Study Methods | Efficient use of time, review outline, budget effort. | I classify and organize facts and points as I am reading, studying, or rewriting notes. |
| Study Anxiety | Below T-50 score indicates concern about assignments and exams. Goal clarifications needed. | Examinations make me so nervous that I do not do nearly so well on them as I should. |
| Lack of Manipulation | Low scores indicate tendency to "play" up to teacher to gain favor. | I am convinced that one of the best ways to get ahead in school is to flatter and play up to the teacher. |
| Alienation Toward Authority | High score, 70 to 80 indicates comfort with rules, regulations, and requirements. Not trying to "beat the system." | It is my observation that teachers tend to require too much homework and other unimportant work. |

ways of expressing scores. Our hypothetical student scored high on Academic Interest (Love of Learning), Academic Drive, Lack of Manipulation, and Lack of Alienation Toward Authority. "High" in this case means a *T*-score of 50 or higher. The student has the drive and desire to do well in school and takes responsibility for her own behavior. It is not surprising, however, to find that this student is not doing well in school when we see the low scores on Study Methods and Lack of Study Anxiety, which exert a more direct effect on behavior. Both these factors can have a very detrimental effect on performance. The student should confer with a counselor or with teachers about ways to gain feelings of self-confidence and reduce feelings of tension and worry. Perhaps there is lack of communication between student and teacher. Study habits also need attention and, again, perhaps the teacher can provide suggestions on how to approach tasks. Commercial programs aimed at enhancing test-taking skills are available, such as Improving Test-Taking Skills (Riverside, 1983). A standardized measure used in this way is relatively nonthreatening, can be accomplished by any of a number of professional staff, and can yield quite valuable benefits

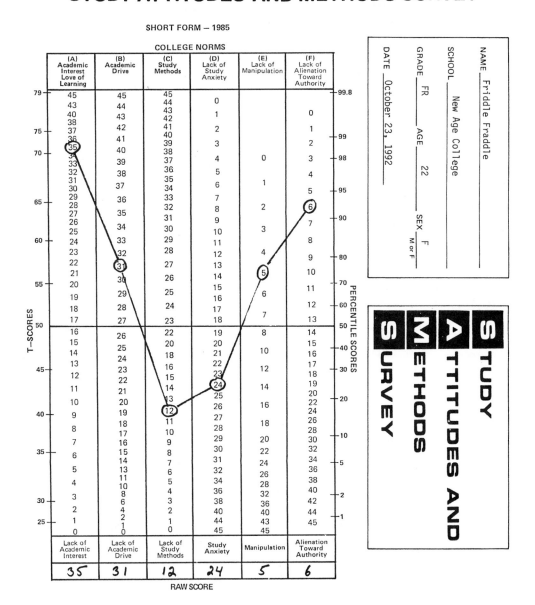

**Figure 12-1** *Study-Attitudes and Methods Survey*

Copyright © 1976/1985 by EDITS, San Diego, CA 92107. Reproduced by permission.

for the student. It should also be noted that with a multiscore instrument some considerations should be given to the standard error of measurement and the basic concepts of reliability as discussed in Chapter 14.

Readers interested in the use of tests in counseling are referred to books by Lewis Aiken (1988), Robert Kaplan and Dennis Saccuzzo (2001), and W. Bruce Walsh and Nancy Betz (1995).

### Research

Numerous research fields that use affective measures might also interest the educator. The authors of the *Study of Values* (Allport, Vernon, & Lindzey, 1970), for example, note that affective measures have been used to research the following topics:

1. Differences in the scores of those in various college majors and occupational, religious, ethnic, and nationality groups.

2. Changes in values over time and as functions of specific training and educational experiences.

3. Relationships with other attitude-style, interest-style, and cognitive-style measures.

4. Relationships between friendship choice and sociometric status.

More important might be student research projects exploring societal issues such as attitudes toward Social Security, health care, or foreign aid. Students learn a great deal of information about the topic and themselves during instrument development. Constructing a single open-ended questionnaire and carrying out analysis of the results can be a tremendous learning experience.

### Program Evaluation

Another area in which affective measures are achieving great popularity is program evaluation. Curriculum evaluation is receiving increased attention from educational measurement and assessment experts and consultants. Most state and federal educational programs require the assessment of affective variables, and local school systems are also becoming conscious of these important outcomes. Measures of such variables as attitude toward school, respect for self, and appreciation of artistic efforts illustrate educational product and process outcomes in a comprehensive evaluation system (Payne, 1994).

An illustration using a currently new popular school and classroom educational methodology is appropriate. There is a pervasive movement toward incorporating service-learning programs in the schools at all levels

(Payne, 2000). Such programs involve hands-on learning by taking classroom knowledge and skill into the community by providing a service. Examples might be science concepts related to water purity being applied to the monitoring of local ponds, creeks, and streams or the application of communication skills in helping develop oral histories in a retirement home. One dimension of the impact of such programs is the pre- and post-assessments of students with an affective measure. Such a measure is shown in Figure 12-2. The *Georgia Survey of Attitudes Toward Service* was developed by Dr. Michael McKenna of Georgia Southern University and has been used successfully with students in grades 4 through 12. It is highly reliable and can be machine-scored. An elementary school student version of a service-learning instrument is presented in Figure 12-3. It was created by a team of teachers at South Jackson Elementary School headed by Claudia Taxel. The "smiley" faces are an effective way to communicate with young students. This particular instrument was used successfully to evaluate the impact of a schoolwide recycling program.

## APPROACHES TO THE ASSESSMENT OF AFFECTIVE OUTCOMES

An extensive review of the literature and personal research have identified numerous methods that can be applied in the assessment of attitudes and sentiments, or, as they are sometimes called, "dynamic traits" (Cattell, Heist, & Stewart, 1950). Some of these methods are more useful in a classroom than others, but any of the techniques can be adapted to a variety of educational purposes. Selections from their list and some additional methods follow:

1. *Money.* The amount of money individuals spend on certain activities (or say they will spend) and courses of action are direct reflections of their attitudes and interests. In elementary school, simulation exercises involving purchases can be very revealing.

2. *Time.* The amount of time individuals devote to certain activities reflects, to some extent, their attitudes toward the activities. A survey of time students spend in various activities can reveal their relative interests.

3. *Verbal expressions.* A host of assessment methods use verbal expressions of attitudes. The Likert, semantic differential, and opinionnaire methods described later in this chapter are illustrative. The interview, either free-response or structured, can also be placed in this category.

School _____

Directions: Please fill in the bubble that is closest to how you feel about each statement. This is a scannable form, so please fill in the bubble completely.

| | Strongly Agree | Agree | In Between | Disagree | Strongly Disagree |
|---|---|---|---|---|---|
| 1. Everyone should give some of their time for the good of their town. | ⓈA | Ⓐ | Ⓑ | Ⓓ | ⓈD |
| 2. Kids should never help out for free if there are grown-ups who are paid to do the same job. | ⓈA | Ⓐ | Ⓑ | Ⓓ | ⓈD |
| 3. It is better for prisoners to pick up trash along the highway than for students to do it. | ⓈA | Ⓐ | Ⓑ | Ⓓ | ⓈD |
| 4. I feel bad when I don't finish a job I promised I would do. | ⓈA | Ⓐ | Ⓑ | Ⓓ | ⓈD |
| 5. Helping younger students with their schoolwork would be a waste of my time. | ⓈA | Ⓐ | Ⓑ | Ⓓ | ⓈD |
| 6. It might be fun to work as a volunteer for awhile in another country. | ⓈA | Ⓐ | Ⓑ | Ⓓ | ⓈD |
| 7. It would be embarrassing to ask strangers to give money to charity. | ⓈA | Ⓐ | Ⓑ | Ⓓ | ⓈD |
| 8. I would like to spend one Saturday a month collecting food for homeless people. | ⓈA | Ⓐ | Ⓑ | Ⓓ | ⓈD |
| 9. I would feel good about doing a chore for an elderly person. | ⓈA | Ⓐ | Ⓑ | Ⓓ | ⓈD |
| 10. It is my duty to help recycle paper and cans. | ⓈA | Ⓐ | Ⓑ | Ⓓ | ⓈD |
| 11. People who volunteer are usually trying to impress somebody. | ⓈA | Ⓐ | Ⓑ | Ⓓ | ⓈD |
| 12. If you do a good job helping others, you should be paid. | ⓈA | Ⓐ | Ⓑ | Ⓓ | ⓈD |
| 13. I would enjoy planting flowers or trees to make my school more beautiful. | ⓈA | Ⓐ | Ⓑ | Ⓓ | ⓈD |
| 14. It would make me feel good to give my old clothes to poor children. | ⓈA | Ⓐ | Ⓑ | Ⓓ | ⓈD |
| 15. I would enjoy listening to a younger student read. | ⓈA | Ⓐ | Ⓑ | Ⓓ | ⓈD |
| 16. I would like to deliver food baskets to poor families at Thanksgiving. | ⓈA | Ⓐ | Ⓑ | Ⓓ | ⓈD |
| 17. Needy people have no one but themselves to blame for their troubles. | ⓈA | Ⓐ | Ⓑ | Ⓓ | ⓈD |
| 18. Kids who do chores at home should be paid. | ⓈA | Ⓐ | Ⓑ | Ⓓ | ⓈD |

**Figure 12-2** *Georgia Survey of Attitudes Toward Service*

**Service Survey**

_____ Grade

_____ Boy _____ Girl

| Directions: | I am going to read some sentences about how people can help other people. Tell how you feel about each sentence by marking a smiley face (☺) if you agree with the sentence, or the frowny face (☹) if you disagree. If you can't decide use the face in the middle that looks like this (😐). |
|---|---|

Tell us how you really feel!

1. I like to help other people.

2. People should give money to help those who aren't as fortunate as they are.

3. It is my duty to help recycle paper and cans.

4. It would be O.K. if you didn't get paid for doing chores at home.

5. Making the school grounds look beautiful is everybody's job.

6. If parents can do a job, kids shouldn't have to do it.

7. I don't like doing chores for elderly people.

8. I would give up some playtime to help others.

9. People who help other people are just showing off.

10. Helping my friends is a lot of fun.

11. It makes me feel good about myself to help others.

12. Helping others in the community helps me think about what I want to do when I am an adult.

13. My parents are happy when I help others.

14. Teachers don't care if we help others.

15. I volunteer for special school projects.

**Figure 12-3** *Service Survey*

4. *Measures of attention or distraction.* Records of the length of time an individual attends to a stimulus, or a ranking of stimuli (e.g., pictorial) according to responsiveness to them, could profitably be used as measures of attitudes. Failure to respond to certain stimuli is also meaningful behavior. We know about the attention span of students, particularly very young ones. If we can capture students' attention and hold it, we at least have a chance to teach.

5. *Fund of information.* The amount or type of information an individual possesses about a certain object, individual, or issue to some extent reflects his or her attitude. There is a relationship between the cognitive and affective domains.

6. *Speed of decision (reaction time).* Decisions may be made more quickly about questions on which the subject has the strongest convictions.

7. *Written expressions (personal documents).* Analysis of such documents as biographies, diaries, records, letters, autobiographies, journals, and compositions can reveal an individual's attitudes. A personal document has been defined by Gordon Allport (1942) as any self-revealing record that intentionally or unintentionally yields information about the structure, dynamics, and functioning of the author's mental life. Student autobiographies reveal important facets of an individual's life and represent an opportunity to practice writing skills.

8. *Sociometric measures.* Analysis of friendship choices, social distances, preferences, and the general social structure of a classroom can provide information about attitudes.

9. *Misperception/apperception methods.* Provided with ambiguous stimuli, an individual may be tempted to perceive them in accordance with his or her own interests, attitudes, and desires. Many projective techniques (e.g., ink blots) have been based on this assumption.

10. *Activity level methods.* There are a number of measures of the individual's general excitement level in response to a stimulus, among them fluency (amount written), speed of reading, and work endurance.

11. *Observations.* Standardized reports systematically gathered by trained recorders operating within the limits of an explicitly stated frame of reference have provided extremely valuable data on attitudes and on how they operate within the individual. (The use of categorical observational systems was considered in Chapter 10.)

12. *Specific performances and behaviors.* An individual's behavior can illustrate his or her attitudes and their influences. Some argue that

behavioral measures are the most valid. The indirect methods we commonly use, however, can provide valid data if reasonable precautions are taken and stringent criteria are employed during the developmental stages. Eugene Webb and his colleagues (Webb, Campbell, Schwartz, Sechrest, & Grove, 1981) have written an extremely valuable reference work with examples of unobtrusive behavioral measures and observational methods.

13. *Physiological measures.* Autonomic and metabolic measures can provide useful data in controlled situations. Psychogalvanic response, pulse rate, pupillary response, muscle tension and pressure, and metabolic rate are some of the procedures employed.

14. *Memory measures.* Instructing an individual to learn given material, varying the controversial nature of the content, introducing an unrelated activity to distract the subject, and then asking him or her to recall all or part of the original material is one approach to the use of memory as an instrument of attitude assessment. The selective operation of memory in reminiscence, dream, or fantasy can also be analyzed.

15. *Simulations.* Contrived structured or unstructured activities can be used to stimulate and simulate affective responses. Role playing, for example, is useful as both an assessment and as an instructional technique. Gamelike activities provide particularly good opportunities to observe students under a variety of conditions, particularly for interpersonal relations.

## WRITING QUESTIONS FOR SELF-REPORT AFFECTIVE MEASURES

We have described many choices. Are there any general guidelines that might help when we try to create an instrument?

General guidelines and criteria are crucial to the development of statements for affective measures. Obviously, the questions or stimulus statements themselves are critically important. The most sophisticated analytic techniques will not overcome an inferior question that does not communicate. Allen Edwards (1957) provided a list of informal criteria for development and editing activities. Use statements that

1. Refer to the present rather than to the past or future.
2. Refer to affect not facts.
3. Can be interpreted in only one way.

4. Are relevant to the psychological object under consideration.

5. Would *not* be endorsed by everyone or anyone.

6. Reflect a wide range of affectivity.

7. Are written using precise, unambiguous, and direct language.

8. Contain less than 20 words.

9. Contain one complete thought.

10. Do *not* contain universals such as *all, always, none,* and *never* because these items often introduce ambiguity.

11. Do *not* use such ambiguous words such as *only, just,* and *nearly.*

12. Are simple sentences (as opposed to compound or complex ones).

13. Use vocabulary appropriate for level of respondent.

14. Do *not* include double negatives.

Most of these suggestions are common sense and are based on the need to communicate. Some of the suggestions—for example, numbers 3, 7, 9, 11, and 14—are similar to the suggestions for writing cognitive test questions, particularly true-false items.

## COREY'S SIMPLIFIED SCALE CONSTRUCTION TECHNIQUE

Steve Corey (1943) described a relatively efficient method for constructing an attitude scale. The instrument development process itself can serve as a learning experience for students and teachers. Its steps are as follows:

1. ***Collect a pool of statements.*** Each student, for example, might be asked to write three or four statements representing various attitudes toward cheating. Illustrative statements might be:

   Cheating is as bad as stealing.

   If a test isn't fair, cheating is all right.

   I won't copy, but I often let someone else look at my paper.

   A little cheating on daily tests doesn't hurt.

2. ***Select the best statements.*** Using the criteria for constructing attitude statements described in the previous section, about 50 items might be culled from the initial pool of 100 to 150 statements. Duplicates are eliminated, as are statements that are obviously ambiguous to the teacher or students. The students, for example, might be asked to indicate all those statements on the master list that represent opinions favoring cheating

(with a plus sign) and those representing negative opinions about cheating (with a minus sign). An agreement criterion of 80 percent is suggested; a show of hands is an efficient way to gather these data.

3. *Administer the inventory.* The following directions might be used:

   *Directions*: This is not a test in the sense that any particular statement is right or wrong. All these sentences represent opinions that some people hold about cheating on tests. Indicate whether you agree or disagree with the statements by putting a plus sign before all those with which you agree and a minus sign before all those with which you disagree. If you are uncertain, use a question mark. After you have gone through the entire list, go back and draw a circle around the plus signs next to the statements with which you agree very strongly, and a circle around the minus signs if you disagree very strongly.

   The inventory can be duplicated and distributed or administered orally. Discussion should be discouraged. Anonymous administration is preferable.

4. *Score the inventory.* Scoring can be accomplished by either teacher or student. The first step involves identifying those statements that were judged by the entire group (in step 2) as *favoring classroom cheating*. Next, the following score values are applied: a plus sign with a circle receives 5 points, a plus sign alone 4 points, a question mark 3 points, a minus sign 2 points, and a minus sign with a circle 1 point. Thus, when a person disagrees very strongly with a statement that favors classroom cheating, he or she earns 1 point; if a person agrees very strongly with the same statement, he or she gets 5 points.

   Those statements that express *opposition to cheating* are scored in the opposite fashion: a plus sign with a circle receives 1 point, a plus sign alone 2 points, a question mark 3 points, a minus sign 4 points, and a minus sign with a circle 5 points. In other words, a student who disagrees very strongly with a statement that opposes cheating actually has a very favorable attitude toward such a practice.

   If the inventory contains 50 items, the maximum score possible is 250, which indicates a favorable attitude. The minimum score possible is 50, and an indifference score is in the neighborhood of 150.

## THE SUMMATED RATINGS METHOD (LIKERT SCALES)

Beginning with a set of attitude statements representing both favorable and unfavorable attitudes, we can develop a scale using relatively uncomplicated procedures. Rensis Likert (1932) showed that assigning integer (whole-number) weights to a set of response categories yields scores that correlate very highly with those obtained from a Thurstone scale, which uses a very complex development method. The usual response categories are Strongly Agree, Agree, Undecided, Disagree, and Strongly Disagree. For those statements judged to be favorable toward the attitude object, weights of 5 for Strongly Agree, 4 for Agree, 3 for Undecided, 2 for Disagree, and 1 for Strongly Disagree are assigned. For unfavorable statements, weights of 1 for Strongly Agree, 2 for Agree, 3 for Undecided, 4 for Disagree, and 5 for Strongly Disagree are assigned. Thus, the higher the numerical score, the more positive the attitude.

### An Illustrative Problem

Following are seven statements that we can use in developing a scale of attitudes toward education (Glassey, 1945). Other subjects—for example, reading, science, or social studies—could be substituted.

1. I am intensely interested in education.
2. Education does far more good than harm.
3. Education enables us to live less monotonous lives.
4. Sometimes I feel that education is necessary and sometimes I doubt it.
5. If anything, I must admit a slight dislike for education.
6. I dislike education because it means that time has to be spent on home-work.
7. I go to school only because I am compelled to do so.

Gradations of favorableness are obviously reflected in these statements. We might even have a group of judges classify these statements as favorable, neutral, or unfavorable. If we can obtain, say, 80 percent agreement on their classification, we will have a basis for assigning scoring weights to the statements. We then administer the items to our target group and score according to the scheme outlined at the beginning of this section. We would assign high weights to agreement with favorable statements and to disagreement with unfavorable statements. The neutral statements would not be scored but would serve as buffers. This process would be undertaken for a large pool of items.

### Selecting Statements

The next step is to identify those statements that discriminate between individuals with very positive attitudes and those with unfavorable attitudes. The method used for selecting attitude statements is similar to the item analysis procedures used in refining achievement tests (see Chapter 9). The procedure involves obtaining a total score on the instrument for each individual in the group. The top third of the scores is called the high attitude group, and the bottom third is designated as the low attitude group. A good statement should, on the average, receive higher ratings from the high group than from the low group. A table like Table 12-2 should be developed for each statement, and a mean rating calculated for the two groups. The larger the mean difference, the better the item. Remember that the difference will sometimes favor the high group and sometimes the low group, depending on whether the statement is favorable or unfavorable. The final scale comprises those items with the greatest mean differences, keeping in mind that we want a full range of attitudes to be reflected, and would ideally include about 20 to 25 statements.

## FREE-RESPONSE AND OPINIONNAIRE METHODS

The opinionnaire is a frequently used polling method of gathering opinion and attitude data. The term *opinionnaire*, as opposed to *questionnaire*, is used intentionally, to suggest an emphasis on feelings rather than facts. A well-constructed opinionnaire tends to systematize the data-gathering process and ensure that the relevant questions are asked and all important aspects of the problem are surveyed.

### Advantages and Disadvantages of Questionnaire Methods

The questionnaire method, either open-ended or closed (structured), is frequently maligned. But often the user should be castigated for improper use, rather than the method itself. Questionnaires, if properly constructed and analyzed, can provide very valuable information about affective variables. They are, or can be, efficient in time for construction and obtaining responses from large or small groups of respondents, and are relatively inexpensive. Questionnaires do require carefully crafted questions. The unstructured free-response questionnaires will use large amounts of time for content analyses of the responses. A great deal of subjectivity is involved in interpreting responses. Respondents also can "wander around" in answering questions, so be prepared to separate the wheat from the chaff. Unfortunately, opinionnaires are often haphazardly constructed, without proper concern for question phrasing, the means of summarizing and analyzing data, or pilot testing or tryout of the schedule. Joseph Bledsoe (1972) suggested six criteria for a "good" opinionnaire:

**Table 12-2** *Determination of Mean Differences in Ratings of Hypothetical High and Low Attitude Groups for Statement on Attitude Toward Education*

| Response Categories | Low Group | | | High Group | | |
|---|---|---|---|---|---|---|
| | Weight | Frequency (f) | fX | Weight | Frequency (f) | fX |
| Strongly Agree | 5 | 4 | 20 | 5 | 12 | 60 |
| Agree | 4 | 8 | 32 | 4 | 20 | 80 |
| Uncertain | 3 | 16 | 48 | 3 | 10 | 30 |
| Disagree | 2 | 14 | 28 | 2 | 6 | 12 |
| Strongly Agree | 1 | 8 | 8 | 1 | 2 | 2 |
| Sums | | 50 | 136 | | 50 | 184 |
| Mean Rating | | $\frac{136}{50} = 2.72$ | | | $\frac{184}{50} = 3.68$ | |

1. Be brief.

2. Include items of sufficient interest and "face appeal" to attract the respondents and cause them to become involved in the task.

3. Allow depth of response to avoid superficial replies.

4. Word questions so they are neither too suggestive nor too unstimulating.

5. Phrase questions so they allay suspicions about hidden purposes and don't embarrass or threaten the respondent.

6. Phrase questions so that they are not too narrow in scope, allowing the respondent reasonable latitude in his or her responses.

Opinionnaires are generally of two types: the "closed" or precategorized type and the "open" or free-response type. Rating scales are also frequently associated with the structured opinionnaire (see Chapter 10 for further discussion of rating scales). The open-ended form of opinionnaire is recommended for classroom use. Such free-response questions allow the teacher to cover a wide variety of topics in an efficient manner. Analyzing the responses to free-response questions can, however, be quite time-consuming and difficult. In preparing opinionnaires, some general cautions should be observed (Payne, 1951):

1. Spell out in advance the objectives, purposes, and specifications for the instrument. This task should be undertaken *before* questions are written.

2. Try to limit the length of the questionnaire (e.g., 10 questions). If students become impatient to finish, they are likely not to consider their answers carefully enough.

3. Make sure students understand the purpose of the opinionnaire and are convinced of the importance of responding completely and candidly.

4. Use a sequence of questions if possible. John Green (1970) illustrated the advantages of this approach with a series of questions that could be used to stimulate attitudinal responses toward labor unions in a unit of a social studies course:

   a. How have labor-management relations been affected by unions?

   b. How have working conditions been affected by unions?

   c. What means, if any, should be used to control unions?

   d. What effects have unions had on the general economy of the country?

5. Make sure students are motivated to answer questions thoughtfully.

6. Control the administration of the opinionnaire so students are prevented from talking with one another about the questions before answering them.

7. Urge students to express their own thoughts, not give the responses they think the teacher wants.

8. Be sure the directions are clear, definite, and complete.

9. Urge students to ask about questions that are unclear to them.

10. If possible, try out the opinionnaire with other teachers or a couple of students to identify and clear up ambiguous questions, difficult terms, or unclear meanings.

### Content Analysis

A teacher (or student with guidance) will ordinarily undertake a content analysis of the responses to opinionnaire questions. Content analysis is a systematic, objective, and—ideally—quantitative examination of free-response material. In addition to examining opinionnaire responses, content analyses of textbooks, television broadcasts, essays, records of interpersonal interactions, plays, stories, dramas, newspaper articles, speeches, or propaganda materials can be undertaken. Several steps in completing the content analysis of a questionnaire are included below.

1. *Identify the units for the purpose of recording results.* The specification of units, which requires great care, can be undertaken before beginning the analysis if the teacher knows what to expect, or after a sample

of the responses has been examined. A unit is usually a single sentence, although any brief phrase that summarizes an idea, concept, feeling, or word will suffice.

2. *Identify the categories into which the units will be placed.* For example, the unit might be a sentence and the category a type of sentence, for example, declarative or interrogative.

3. *Analyze all the content (or a representative sample) relevant to the problem.* A piece of material could be sampled for a given student, or samples could be taken from a group of students.

4. *Seek a high degree of objectivity.* The teacher may want to complete an analysis or to put it aside and redo it (or a portion of it) later to check agreement of results. A comparison of the work of two teachers working independently could serve as another check on objectivity.

5. *Quantify the results, if at all possible.* The use of simple summary indices such as frequency counts and percents can be very helpful.

6. *Include a sufficiently large number of samples to ensure reasonable reliability.* The larger the sample of material(s) analyzed, in general, the greater the reliability.

### An Illustrative Content Analysis

In an effort to evaluate the impact of an eight-week summer enrichment program for academically and artistically talented students, I asked several questions such as the following on a participant follow-up opinionnaire:

1. What contribution, if any, did the program make toward your developing a positive attitude toward learning?

2. How suitable were the instructional methods?

3. To what degree did the program influence your desire to attend college?

4. What do you feel were the most beneficial dimensions of the program?

A content analysis of the last question yielded the following results (with a sample of 50 subjects):

|  | Frequency | Percent |
|---|---|---|
| a. Contact with individuals with both different and similar interests. | 34 | 68% |
| b. Freedom for independent and in-depth study. | 12 | 24% |
| c. The high quality of teachers. | 9 | 18% |
| d. The availability of cultural events, films, speakers, and the like. | 8 | 16% |
| e. Freedom to broaden interests. | 5 | 10% |

Not only were relevant dimensions of the program identified, but a ranking of the importance of these dimensions also became possible. The fact that this information came from the participants themselves helps ensure the validity of the responses. If pre-categorized responses had been used, we might have biased the respondents.

## AFFECTIVE MEASUREMENT AND THE DIAGNOSIS OF LEARNING DIFFICULTIES

Affective measurement can make meaningful contributions in five major use-categories: classroom applications, screening and selection, counseling, research, and program evaluation. Standardized affective measures are most frequently used in screening, research, and counseling. Commercially purchased measures of self-concept, general personality, and interests and values can provide meaningful information that helps us understand each student. These kinds of data are useful in counseling, particularly when coupled with relevant data from the "cognitive domain," for example, scores from ability, aptitude, or achievement tests. In a counseling situation a student may want to explore any or all of the areas in the following table.

| Area | Question Explored |
| --- | --- |
| Educational Planning | What educational plans are most realistic relative to my ability and resources? |
| | What can I do to maximize my likelihood of success in various kinds of training settings? |
| Career Planning | What are my vocationally relevant skills, competencies, and aptitudes? |
| | Where are my relative career interests, and are my interests similar to the ones of people who are successfully engaged in particular occupations or jobs? |
| Life Planning | As I begin to inventory my life goals, how would I allocate time, effort, and resources to a variety of roles such as student, marriage partner, parent, or citizen? |
| Personal Development | What are my feelings about myself and what attitudes do I value? |

In the classroom setting, with a little effort, teacher and student can work together to maximize student development and achievement. Lorin Anderson (1981) noted how the diagnostic process can be enhanced by affective measures. The process generally involves five steps as delineated in the table below:

| Steps in Diagnoses of Learning Difficulty | Process |
| --- | --- |
| Identification | Use data from relevant achievement measure (classroom or standardized) to locate area(s) of depressed performance. |
| Hypothesis Generation | Apply both measures of ability and affect to create a list of possible causes of difficulty. |
| Assessment | Assess area thought to be primary cause. |
| Diagnosis | Contrast data to lead to most likely cause(s). |
| Remediation | Apply relevant treatment. |

Assume a sixth-grade student is having difficulty in language arts, in particular, reading. A standardized achievement battery indicates the student is reading at a little below the fifth-grade level (grade equivalent = 4.8). Further evidence indicates scholastic ability equating to a percentile rank of 62. Any number of "home-made" measures can be used to examine the affective component of learning. Following are some examples.

### Forced-Choice Method

A paired-comparison scale could be devised to look at the "relative" interest the student has in reading. A series of items like the following could be devised:

I would like to
a. read a book.
b. visit the zoo.

I would like to
a. do some arithmetic problems.
b. have my teacher read us a story.

I would like to
a. do a science experiment.
b. get a book as a present.

I would like to
a. read a story to my classmates.
b. make a poster about health.

The student's "score" on such a device would be the number of times activities related to reading or books were preferred over other activities.

### Semantic Differential

A semantic differential using bipolar adjective pairs could be developed using either *book* or *reading* as the stimulus. The following example assumes that appropriate directions for responding have been presented.

*Reading*

| Good | ___ ___ ___ ___ ___ | Bad |
|------|---------------------|-----|
| Sweet | ___ ___ ___ ___ ___ | Sour |
| Fair | ___ ___ ___ ___ ___ | Unfair |
| Happy | ___ ___ ___ ___ ___ | Sad |
| Nice | ___ ___ ___ ___ ___ | Awful |

Using this approach a "score" would be derived by treating each adjective pair as a rating scale (1 to 5) and simply add the rating for the five pairs with "5" being at the positive (left) side. Maximum score = 25.

## Rating Scale

A pictorial variation on the Likert method could be used to "scale" attitude toward reading (Solley, 1989). For example, see Figure 12-4.

## Opinionnaire (Free Response)

A series of open-ended questions could be created and administered orally to a group of students. They write the answers on a form, or meet with the teacher in an individual interview, with the teacher recording the responses. After responses have been collected, a content analysis is undertaken and a scoring scheme devised. It might be economical from a labor standpoint to create a global scale for each question using specific responses as anchor points on a continuum.

Let's assume that in our hypothetical case, attitudes toward reading are found to be negative. Score interpretation by absolute or normative standards could be used, for example, "Had percentile rank of 35 in class of 22." Bases such as data from contrasted groups or identifying neutral points on a scale could also be used. Attitudes are learned, emotionally toned behavioral predispositions that can be changed and modified. If we can help students develop more positive affect about reading we assume that, because they have the ability, they can improve their performances. Changing attitudes and developing motivation are very difficult and challenging instructional tasks. Klausmeier (1985, p. 394) has outlined a series of steps that can be followed in changing attitudes in a classroom setting. (See Table 12-3.)

Affective assessments may indicate the need for additional information about a learning difficulty or behavior problem. Does this diagnostic path allow affect and cognition to go hand in hand? We want to strive to develop in the student feelings of competence and the freedom to be an independent learner.

---

**Directions Read to Student**

---

Each statement below describes a feeling toward writing. The Survey will help determine your attitudes toward writing. There is no right or wrong answer and you will not be given a grade. Answer each statement as honestly as you can by circling the puppy that best describes how you feel about the statement.

Puppy 1 = Very happy
Puppy 2 = Happy
Puppy 3 = Not happy or unhappy
Puppy 4 = Unhappy
Puppy 5 = Very unhappy

1. How do you feel when your teacher reads a story aloud?

2. How do you feel when you are asked to read aloud to your teacher?

3. How do you feel about reading books for fun at home?

The score would be the sum of the puppy ratings such that the higher the score the more positive the attitude (i.e., happiest puppy = "5" if statement is positive, or "1" if negative, vice versa, etc.).

**Figure 12-4** *Reading Attitude Survey*

**Table 12-3** *Changing Attitudes in a Classroom Setting*

| Step in Classroom Attitude Change Process | Activity |
|---|---|
| Identifying Attitude to be Taught or Changed | Targets might be broad, such as likes school, classmates, or teacher, or specific to a school subject such as reading, or very specifc such as grammar. Activities can be expanded to include values (e.g., equality, self-respect), as well as attitudes. |
| Provide Pleasant Emotional Experiences | Use shaping techniques such as praise and providing academic success. Avoid using fear and anxiety as motivators (e.g., don't drink and drive). |
| Provide Exemplary Models | Modeling is very effective, particularly with very young students (e.g., attractiveness of celebrity endorsements). |
| Extend Informative Experiences | Information and knowledge about object facilitates initial attitude acquisition (e.g., directed reading, observing). |
| Use Small-Group Instructional Techniques | Such techniques as (a) group discussion, (b) group decision making, (c) role playing, and (d) cooperative small-group activity have proved effective. |
| Encourage Deliberate Attitude Change | Student might be encouraged to actively recognize, then change, attitude through behavioral change (e.g., as in responding to those of other |

Many potential problems can arise from using these kinds of measuring instruments. William Cottle (1968) has identified the following cautions and concerns.

1. As is the case with standardized achievement and aptitude tests, one must be sure that the objectives, item content, and scores of the instrument are consistent with those of the user. Otherwise, gross misassessment can result.

2. The administration, scoring, and interpretation of such measures should be handled directly by, or under the guidance of, a trained and competent professional.

3. Respect for the privacy and integrity of the examinee is imperative. *Affective inventories should be voluntary.* The right of an individual to refuse should be honored.

4. The intent of a particular test must be explained in full to the student. The projected use of the results should also be described. Such a

description and the attendant discussion should help promote rapport, ensure seriousness of intent, and arouse examinee motivation.

**5.** It is generally advisable to encourage an examinee to record his or her initial response to an item. Such a procedure will tend to elicit "typical" reactions. Extended deliberations tend to confuse the respondent.

**6.** If possible, a graphic procedure (e.g., a profile) should be used to report the scores. This is a particularly informative approach when a multi-score instrument is being used.

**7.** Don't interpret responses to single items because they tend to lack reliability.

**8.** During interpretation, the respondent should be provided a copy of the description of the results from scoring the instrument.

**9.** Scoring services should return answer sheets with the reported scores or profiles. You should always spot-check for scoring errors.

**10.** The private nature of an affective inventory precludes discussion of a particular score or set of scores with anyone but the examinee. Summary statistics based on group data, in the form of means or standard deviations, are legitimate material for open discussion, however.

Is it worth the effort to address affective outcomes? If you value the developing student as a total person and want him or her to experience a quality life, then you must deal with affective issues.

Thus ends a treatise on all you wanted to know about developing affective measures but were afraid to ask. It's a lot of work! But aren't most things that are important?

## CONTENT REVIEW STATEMENTS

**1.** Affective measures can be used

    a. in the classroom as stimuli for learning units.

    b. for research purposes.

    c. for screening and selection.

    d. for counseling.

    e. for program evaluation.

**2.** The major standardized measures of affective learning outcomes that are useful to the classroom teacher focus on academic interests, motivation, attitudes, and values.

**3.** In using measures of affective learning outcomes, you should be careful to

    a. ensure that the instrument and instructional objectives are in harmony.

    b. have a qualified professional direct the administration, scoring, and interpretation.

    c. respect the privacy of individual students.

    d. explain to the students the reason for using a particular measure.

    e. ensure that all students receive an interpretation of their scores.

    f. respect the security and confidentiality of student scores.

    g. draw upon all relevant nontest information in interpreting a test score.

    h. exercise caution in interpreting out-of-date test scores.

    i. examine carefully the characteristics of any norm group selected for reference purposes.

    j. select a measure at an appropriate reading and experience level.

**4.** Profiling scores on multiscore affective inventories aids interpretation.

**5.** The critical reviews of standardized measures in Buros' *Mental Measurements Yearbooks* should be consulted when selecting a particular test.

**6.** Affective outcomes are hard to specify because it is difficult to identify appropriate overt behavioral evidence of the covert affect and because they are ever-changing.

**7.** Lack of attention to affective outcomes tends to result in their erosion in the classroom.

**8.** A teacher will probably need to specify fewer affective than cognitive outcomes.

**9.** Affective variables have a wide range of verbal and nonverbal measures; among them are the following:

    a. amount of time, money, and energy spent on a particular activity

    b. formal verbal responses to such scales as the semantic differential, Likert, and Thurstone scales

    c. reaction time

    d. amount of knowledge about a particular referent

    e. examination of personal documents

    f. sociometric measures

    g. projective techniques

    h. observational and performance measures

    i. physiological measures

    j. memory measures

    k. simulation

**10.** In building verbal measures of affective variables, use statements that are

    a. couched in the present tense.

    b. nonfactual.

    c. singularly relevant to the object.

    d. representative of a wide range of feelings.

    e. simple, clear, direct, and short.

**11.** Attitude statements and inventories can be developed from free-response questions submitted to students.

**12.** Most methods of developing affective measures initially involve identifying a series of statements that reflect gradations of favorableness or affect, from which a representative set is selected.

**13.** The Affective Domain Handbook of the *Taxonomy of Educational Objectives* contains excellent suggestions on the content and format of affective measures.

**14.** The method of summated ratings employs a 5-point scale (strongly agree, agree, undecided, disagree, strongly disagree) with statements reflecting positive (favorable) or negative (unfavorable) affect.

**15.** By the summated ratings method, statements that discriminate between individuals with high positive scores and those with high negative scores are selected for the final form of the instrument.

**16.** In developing affective measures, it is best to begin with at least three times as many items as the final form is expected to contain.

**17.** Judges should agree at least 80 percent of the time about whether a given statement is favorable or unfavorable.

**18.** In administering an affective inventory, one should urge subjects to express their initial reactions.

**19.** The opinionnaire and other free-response methods can be used to gather affective data effectively.

**20.** Opinionnaires should be brief, relevant, comprehensive, nonthreatening, and concise.

**21.** Content analysis is a valuable tool for examining the data gathered with an opinionnaire or the free-response method.

**22.** Standardized affective measures can be used to assist in educational, career, life planning, and personal development.

**23.** The diagnosis of a learning difficulty involves identifying, hypothesizing, assessing, diagnosing, and remediating.

**24.** Changing attitudes in the classroom involves identifying attitudes, creating a supporting emotional environment, modeling, informing, discussing, and encouraging.

**25.** There are similarities and differences in using standardized measures in the cognitive and affective domains.

## SPECULATIONS

**1.** Can we actually get students to respond meaningfully to instruments measuring affective outcomes? How?

**2.** Get three friends to write and discuss definitions for the following terms: neuroticism, depression, happiness, and rage. Describe how one might go about trying to measure the results of your deliberations.

**3.** What methods of assessing affective objectives do you prefer to use and why?

**4.** What are the advantages and disadvantages of using the following approaches to measure affective outcomes: (a) attitude scales, (b) semantic differential, and (c) opinionnaires?

**5.** How is writing achievement test items similar to writing attitude items?

**6.** How can affective measurement help diagnose learning difficulties?

## SUGGESTED READINGS

Aiken, L. R. (1996). *Rating scales and checklists.* (Evaluating behavior, personality and attitudes). New York: Wiley.

Anderson, L. W. (1981). *Assessing affective characteristics in the schools.* Boston: Allyn & Bacon. An easy-to-use reference with theory and method (and good examples).

Berdie, D. R., Anderson, J. F., & Niebuhr, M. A. (1986). *Questionnaire: Design and use* (2nd ed.). Metuchen, NJ: Scarecrow.

Bills, R. E. (1975). *A system for assessing affectivity.* University: The University of Alabama Press. Describes the development of a comprehensive system from planning through instrumentation.

Converse, J. M., & Presser, S. (1986). *Survey questions* (Handcrafting the standardized questionnaire). Beverly Hills, CA: Sage.

Gable, R. K., & Wolf, M. B. (1994). *Instrument development in the affective domain* (2nd ed.). Boston: Kluwer-Nijhoff. The authors have collected recent research and recommendations for instrument development in the affective domain. Very readable but not for the beginner.

Green, B. F. (1954). Attitude measurement. In G. Lindzey (Ed.), *Handbook of social psychology* (pp. 335–369). Reading, MA: Addison-Wesley.

Harmon, L. W. (1989). Counseling. In R. L. Linn (Ed.), *Educational measurement* (3rd ed.). New York: American Council on Education/Macmillan.

Mueller, D. J. (1986). *Measuring social attitudes.* New York: Teachers College Press.

Oppenheim, A. N. (1966). *Questionnaire design and attitude measurement.* New York: Basic.

Osgood, C. E., Suci, C. J., & Tannenbaum, P. H. (1957). *The measurement of meaning.* Urbana: University of Illinois Press. More than a description of a technique, this very important work also introduces the reader to psycholinguistics.

Payne, D. A. (Ed.). (1980). *Recent developments in affective measurement.* San Francisco: Jossey-Bass.

Spector, P. E. (1992). *Summated rating scale construction.* Newbury Park, CA: Sage.

Following are "collections" or compendia of instruments in the affective domain. Most instruments are "fugative," that is, they are not commercially available.

Chunn, K., Cobb, S., & French, R. P., Jr. (1975). *Measures for psychological assessment.* Ann Arbor: Survey Research Center, University of Michigan.

Educational Testing Service. (1991). *The ETS test collection catalog: Volume 5, attitude Tests.* Phoenix, AZ: Oryx. Abstracts of 1,275 attitude measures.

Lake, D. G., Miles, M. B., & Earle, R. B. (1973). *Measuring human behavior: Tools for the assessment of social functioning.* New York: Teachers College Press.

Robinson, J. P., Shaver, P. R., & Wrightsman, L. S. (1991). *Measures of personality and social psychological attitudes.* San Diego: Academic Press. Detailed psychometric information is presented, along with a copy of the instrument on 150 measures.

Shaw, M. E., & Wright, J. M. (1967). *Scales for the measurement of attitudes.* New York: McGraw-Hill.

Walker, D. K. (1973). *Socioemotional measures for preschool and kindergarten children.* San Francisco: Jossey-Bass.

# PART Five

# Summarizing Assessment Data

## Beverly's Journal

"Numbers, numbers everywhere, but what do they all say?" is the cry of most every teacher. We spend considerable amounts of time collecting data at the individual student, classroom, school, and district levels and then are faced with the daunting task of bringing meaning out of seeming chaos. Elementary statistical methods will help us do this, and over time I have found that simple descriptive indices such as the mean and standard deviation not only help me summarize information but interpret it as well. It doesn't have to be fancy, but one needs to "look" at the data and figuratively try to get a "feel" for it. Numbers can be our friends!

When you start to summarize assessment information, it is sometimes a good time to start looking at reliability and validity (not that we haven't been concerned about validity all along).

# 13

# Describing Measurement Data

## FOCUS CONCEPTS AND KEY TERMS FOR STUDY

| | |
|---|---|
| **Frequency Distribution** | **Positive Skewness** |
| **Interquartile Range** | **Range** |
| **Mean** | **Relationship/Correlation** |
| **Median** | **Scatter Diagram** |
| **Negative Skewness** | **Spearman-Rank Difference Correlation** |
| **Normal Curve Equivalent** | **Standard Deviation** |
| **Pearson Product-Moment Correlation** | **Standard Scores** |
| **Percentile** | **Stanine** |
| **Percentile Rank** | |

---

**STANDARDS ALERT**

**Standard 4.5**      **Relevant Norms**

Norms, if used, should refer to clearly described populations. These populations should include individuals or groups to whom test users will ordinarily wish to compare their own examinees.

**TAKING IT TO THE CLASSROOM**

Test publishers of commercial instruments should include norming descriptions in such detail that potential users can make informed decisions about applicability of the normative data in their local situation.

---

Reprinted with permission from the *Standards for Educational and Psychological Testing*. Copyright © 1999 by the American Educational Research Association, the American Psychological Association, and the National Council on Measurement in Education.

It is not my intent, nor is it possible, to develop the reader's statistical competencies to a high degree in this brief chapter. The statistical procedures to be described apply to such questions as "What is the typical score?", "What is the average score?", "How variable or 'spread out' are the scores?", "What methods are useful in summarizing individual student scores?", and "How can I describe the relationship of scores on my assessment to scores on a criterion measure that purports to assess the same variable?" In most instances, such topics as central tendency, variability, and correlation are presented by describing and illustrating the commonly used indices. Shortcut procedures, subject to some error but useful in analyzing classroom tests, are described. This should provide sufficient knowledge of and skill in elementary statistical procedures to facilitate the development, refinement, and interpretation of a variety of measuring devices.

The techniques and methods described in this chapter probably apply mostly to norm-referenced measures, but they can also be used with performance and criterion-referenced measures.

The study of statistics in relation to measurement is important for many reasons. First, and probably most important, the use of statistics greatly facilitates summarizing and describing large amounts of data about an individual student or group of students. Questions relating to average class performance and the spread of scores can be answered by applying appropriate statistical techniques.

Second, intelligent use of certain procedures can be very helpful in interpreting test scores. Raw scores, for example, scores indicating the number of correct responses on a test, are relatively meaningless in and of themselves. Raw scores must be summarized and related to some meaningful reference point (e.g., the average score on a particular test for a local or nationally representative group) to have meaning for studenst, school administrators, or parents. Certain kinds of "derived scores," some of which are described in this chapter, can communicate information about educational achievement.

Third, knowledge and comprehension of and skill in using certain statistical techniques are necessary for adequate analysis and evaluation of measuring instruments. Such test characteristics as reliability and validity can only be precisely assessed by statistical methods.

Fourth, certain numerical facts, summarized in statistical indices, aid in making decisions about, and evaluating, student achievement. Course mark assignment is an example of an area in which knowledge of typical or average performance and the variability of scores can significantly influence judgments about, and the system used to report, individual student performances.

Finally, as an "extra added attraction," the study of statistics allows serious students to read, with greater understanding, research in their discipline, research on testing and measurement, and test manuals.

## TABULATING DATA AND FREQUENCY DISTRIBUTIONS

The first step a test user ordinarily takes in analyzing the results of a test that has been administered is creating a **frequency distribution** of the scores. Such a distribution is obtained by relating each test score to a number that indicates the frequency with which it occurs. In an ordinary classroom situation, this can probably best be accomplished by listing the scores from high to low and tallying the number of times each occurs. It is sometimes desirable, when the class is very large and the **range** of scores is great, to group the scores into intervals of predetermined and uniform size. To determine the size interval to be used, figure out the range of scores (range = highest score minus lowest score plus 1) and divide the range by some number between 10 and 20. This procedure is recommended because most experts feel that 10 to 20 class intervals are sufficient to summarize the data efficiently without grossly misrepresenting the actual nature of the underlying distribution or introducing excessive grouping errors in the statistics to be computed. For most applications, particularly with classroom-size data sets, it is not necessary to group scores. Simply set the interval size equal to 1. A set of 30 hypothetical scores on a seventh-grade American

History test with a maximum of 50 points has been summarized in Table 13-1. The interval size used was 1. This distribution of scores would be described as slightly **negatively skewed**, that is, there is a relatively high frequency of high scores, and the scores decrease in frequency toward the low or negative end of the score scale. Conversely, if one found a relatively high frequency of low scores, with the frequencies trailing off at the high or positive end of the score scale, the frequency distribution would be described as **positively skewed**. See Figure 13-1 (a) and (b) for examples of both negatively and positively skewed distributions. Skewness, at a general level, is described by the "tail" of the distribution.

The frequency distribution provides a teacher with a graphic picture of the performance of the group as a whole on a given test. The degree of skewness, in turn, *can* indicate something about the general difficulty level of the test for a particular group of students. If the test is very easy, scores might clump at the high (or right) end of the scale and fall off to the left (negative skewness), or bunch up at the low (left) end of the scale and trail off to the high score side if the test were very difficult (positive skewness). We, of course, like to see scores bunched up at the high end, indicating everybody learned a lot!

For most classroom tests and small data sets ($N < 50$) it is usually *not* necessary to group the scores, that is, to use an interval size greater than 1.

## RELATIVE POSITION—PERCENTILE RANKS

Raw test scores have relatively little meaning by themselves. It is not generally recommended that an instructor interpret an individual student's performance by the proportion of the total number of test questions (items, points) answered correctly unless one is using criterion-referenced measures, that is, an absolute standard is used for interpretation. The primary difficulty here is that a test, being only a sample of behavior, could yield misleading interpretations if the "percent correct of total possible points" procedure was employed because other test samples might result in markedly different results and interpretations. Knowledge about the universe of behavior being sampled, the reliability of the test, and the difficulty levels of the items must be considered in making such an "absolute" type of test interpretation. We need, then, some method of deriving a score or number that will have meaning for an individual student, particularly if we are using norm-referenced measures. At the crudest level, rank in the group might be used, but the size of the group will obviously play a significant role in determining the meaning assigned to a particular rank (e.g., a

**Table 13-1**  *Illustration of Determination of Frequency Distribution and Calculation of Percentile Ranks for 30 Hypothetical Scores on American History Test*

**Raw Scores on American History Test**

| 49 | 33 | 25 | 37 | 41 | 39 | 44 | 21 | 37 | 35 |
|----|----|----|----|----|----|----|----|----|----|
| 35 | 42 | 33 | 38 | 36 | 36 | 36 | 28 | 34 | 31 |
| 38 | 29 | 24 | 37 | 40 | 31 | 38 | 38 | 27 | 38 |

| (1) Scores (X) | (2) Tally | (3) Frequency (f) | (4) Frequency X Score (f X) | (5) Cumulative Frequency (Cf) | (6) Percentile Rank (PR$_x$) | (7) Score Squared (X$^2$) | (8) Frequency X Score Squared (f X$^2$) |
|---|---|---|---|---|---|---|---|
| 49 | I | 1 | 49 | 30 | 100 | 2401 | 2401 |
| • | • | • | • | • | • | • | • |
| 44 | I | 1 | 44 | 29 | 97 | 1936 | 1936 |
| 43 | | | | | | | |
| 42 | I | 1 | 42 | 28 | 93 | 1764 | 1764 |
| 41 | I | 1 | 41 | 27 | 90 | 1681 | 1681 |
| 40 | I | 1 | 40 | 26 | 87 | 1600 | 1600 |
| 39 | I | 1 | 39 | 25 | 83 | 1521 | 1521 |
| 38 | THL | 5 | 190 | 24 | 80 | 1444 | 7220 |
| 37 | III | 3 | 111 | 19 | 63 | 1369 | 4107 |
| 36 | III | 3 | 108 | 16 | 53 | 1296 | 3888 |
| 35 | II | 2 | 70 | 13 | 43 | 1225 | 2450 |
| 34 | I | 1 | 34 | 11 | 37 | 1156 | 1156 |
| 33 | II | 2 | 66 | 10 | 33 | 1089 | 2178 |
| 32 | | | | | | | |
| 31 | II | 2 | 62 | 8 | 27 | 961 | 1922 |
| 30 | | | | | | | |
| 29 | I | 1 | 29 | 6 | 20 | 841 | 841 |
| 28 | I | 1 | 28 | 5 | 17 | 784 | 784 |
| 27 | I | 1 | 27 | 4 | 13 | 729 | 729 |
| 26 | | | | | | | |
| 25 | I | 1 | 25 | 3 | 10 | 625 | 625 |
| 24 | I | 1 | 24 | 2 | 7 | 576 | 576 |
| 23 | | | | | | | |
| 22 | | | | | | | |
| 21 | I | 1 | 21 | 1 | 3 | 441 | 441 |
| SUM | | 30 | 1050 | | | | 37820 |

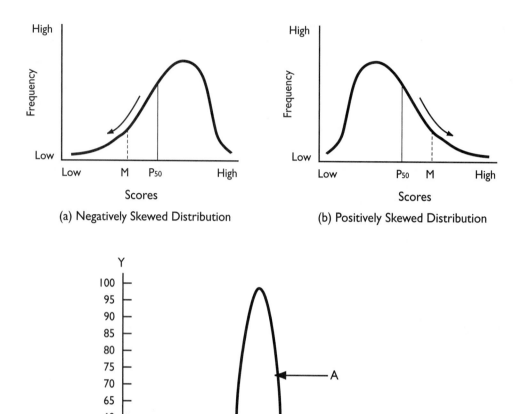

(a) Negatively Skewed Distribution

(b) Positively Skewed Distribution

(c) Two Normal Distributions with Equal Means
but Unequal Standard Deviations

**Figure 13-1** *Illustrative-frequency distributions*

rank of 3 in a group of 10 versus a rank of 3 in a group of 1,000). A derived score that has been found useful in describing individual student performance is the percentile rank (PR). A **percentile rank** is the percentage of scores at and below the given score point. To calculate a percentile rank, count the number of scores at and below the given score (the cumulative frequency, $Cf_i$), divide by the total number of students ($N$), and multiply by 100. Using the data in Table 13-1, we could determine the PR for a score of 29 as follows:

$$\text{Percentile Rank } = \frac{Cf_i}{N} \times 100, \qquad (13\text{-}1)$$

where $Cf_i$ = the number of cases at and below the interval containing the given score of interest (used when interval size is 1). The percentile rank for a score of 29 is

$$PR_{29} = \frac{6}{30} \times 100 = 20$$

Sometimes scores are grouped into intervals. In these cases this procedure would give a somewhat approximate value for the percentile rank (but close enough).

To facilitate the computation of percentile ranks, a *cumulative frequency* column can be included in a summary data table. Cumulative frequency is derived simply by adding successively the frequencies associated with each interval beginning with the bottom score and working up. Using this procedure, percentile ranks have been calculated for the hypothetical American History data and are listed in Table 13-1, Column 6. Interpretive problems sometimes arise because the highest score always gets a percentile rank of 100. Sometimes the mistake is made that the person with a percentile rank of 100 got all the items correct. Two procedures can help with this potential problem. One is to calculate percentile ranks from the midpoints; therefore there will be no 100. The other is simply to assign a percentile rank of "99" to the highest scores and a "1" to the lowest score.

What does our percentile rank of 20 mean? It means that if you got a score of 29 on this test in comparison with your classmates, you did as well as or better than 20 percent of the people in your group. There is obviously room for improvement.

(Another method for describing relative position by standard deviation units will be described later in this chapter in the section on "Standard Scores.")

## THE TOTAL DISTRIBUTION—PERCENTILES

If we want to describe how an individual student performed, percentile ranks are useful derived scores. But how can we describe the overall performance of the group? If our focus is on the total distribution, percentiles ($P_x$) constitute useful descriptive reference points. A **percentile** is a score point below which a given percent (x) of scores fall. The 50th percentile (usually referred to as the median and denoted $P_{50}$), for example, is that score point above which 50 percent of the scores fall and below which 50 percent of the scores fall. Although related to each other (e.g., the percentile rank of a score of 29 is 20, and the 20th percentile is 29), PRs and $P_x$s summarize different characteristics of a distribution of scores and the methods of calculation differ; more important, they are used for different purposes. Using PRs, you begin with a score point and end with a percent; using $P_x$s, you begin with a percent and end with a score point.

Complicated formulas can be used to calculate percentiles, but for most purposes, simple counting will suffice. For example, that very popular percentile, the **median**, $P_{50}$, can be approximated by simply counting one-half the scores (frequencies) and checking what raw score divides the distribution in half. Looking at the frequency distribution in Table 13-1, our best guesstimate of the median ($P_{50}$) would be around 35.5. That's close enough. We would estimate the $P_{25}$ to be about 30 (25 percent of the scores are below this point) and $P_{75}$ to be about 37.5 (75 percent of the scores are below this point). We have 50 percent of the scores within 7.5 points of each other (37.5 − 30 = 7.5). This suggests that the scores are scrunched up.

You should become familiar with the procedure for obtaining percentiles, not only because percentiles are useful in describing your own score distribution, but also because the norms of most standardized educational and psychological tests are reported in percentiles.

Selected percentile points are worthy of special mention because they are frequently referred to in test manuals and the measurement literature:

1. The nine percentile points that divide a distribution into 10 equal parts (sets of frequencies) are called *deciles* and are symbolized as follows: $D_1$, $D_2$, $D_3$, and so on.

2. The three percentile points that divide the distribution into four equal parts (sets of frequencies), are call *quartiles*, and are symbolized as follows: $Q_1$, $Q_2$, $Q_3$.

Identities such as the following should also be kept in mind:

$$\text{Median} = P_{50} = D_5 = Q_2$$
$$P_{25} = Q_1$$
$$P_{75} = Q_3$$

## AVERAGE OR TYPICAL PERFORMANCE

We have already discussed one index of average performance, the median. The median is useful because it is relatively unaffected by extreme scores and therefore useful with skewed distributions that are frequently encountered with classroom data. In many cases the best measure of "averageness" is the arithmetic **mean**, which is indexed by adding all scores and dividing the sum by the number of scores. Expressed as a formula:

$$M = \frac{\sum X}{N} \quad \text{or} \quad \frac{\sum fX}{N} \tag{13-2}$$

where

$M$ = the symbol for the arithmetic mean
$X$ = one observed score
$f$ = frequency of an observed score
$\sum$ = "the sum of"
$N$ = the total number of scores in the distribution

The resulting mean (see Table 13-1) would be as follows:

$$M = \frac{\sum fX}{N} = \frac{1050}{30} = 35$$

It is interesting to note the discrepancy between the mean ($M$ = 35) and the estimated median ($P_{50}$ = 35.5) of the distribution of hypothetical test scores. Recall that this frequency distribution is slightly negatively skewed. Because the mean is sensitive to every score in a distribution and because the median is essentially based on frequencies, we would expect a discrepancy between these two measures when the underlying distribution is skewed. Referring to Figure 13-1, we find the general expected trend, with the mean just a bit smaller than the median for our very slightly negatively skewed distribution. The more extreme the skewness, the greater the discrepancy between these two measures of central tendency.

## THE VARIABILITY OF PERFORMANCE

Measures of central tendency (e.g., the mean and median) describe only one important characteristic of a distribution of scores. It is often highly desirable to describe how "spread out" or variable the scores in a distribution are. Whereas the mean and median are points on the score scale, a measure of variability represents a distance along the score scale. Two reasonable reference points that describe distance along the score scale are the first quartile ($Q_1$, $P_{25}$) and the third quartile ($Q_3$, or $P_{75}$). The difference between these two score points, which describe the middle 50 percent of the scores, the **interquartile range** (IQR), can be used as a measure of variability.

$$IQR = Q_3 - Q_1 \tag{13-3}$$

If we take the interquartile range and divide by 2, we have a frequently referred-to statistic called, cleverly, the semi-interquartile range (Q):

$$Q = \frac{Q_3 - Q_1}{2} \tag{13-4}$$

In the previous section on percentiles $Q_1$ and $Q_3$ as $P_{25}$ and $P_{75}$ were identified. The values we obtained were 30 and 37.5, respectively. Q would therefore be

$$Q = \frac{37.5 - 30}{2} = 3.75$$

In a symmetrical distribution tending toward normality we usually find 25 percent of the score between $Q_2$ and 1Q and 25 percent between $Q_2$ and 1Q.

A more informative, refined, and sensitive statistic, useful in describing the variability of distributions of scores, is the **standard deviation** (S). The square of the standard deviation is called the **variance** ($S^2$). The standard deviation, in essence, represents the "average amount of variability" in a set of scores, using the mean as a reference point. Strictly speaking, the standard deviation is the positive square root of the average of the squared deviations about the mean. The most elementary form of the standard deviation formula is as follows:

$$S = \sqrt{\frac{\sum f(X - M)^2}{N}} \tag{13-5}$$

It can be seen that deviation about the mean ($X - M$) is the basic unit used to describe variability, and that the greater the variability the greater the standard deviation. Part c of Figure 13-1 shows two distributions in which the scores exhibit different degrees of variability. The magnitude of S will be larger for distribution B. Getting all these deviation ($X - M$) scores is a lot of work, and you really have to watch your decimals, so it's easier to use the raw scores. Probably the easiest raw score formula for standard deviation is the following:

$$S = \sqrt{\frac{\sum fX^2 - NM^2}{N}}$$  (13-6)

This is a good formula to use with a calculator. Note that we are using the raw scores squared and the mean squared. In this case the standard deviation using Equation 13-6 and the 30 raw scores of Table 13-1 would be

$$S = \sqrt{\frac{37820 - 30(1225)}{30}} = \sqrt{\frac{1070}{30}} = \sqrt{35.67} = 5.97 \quad \text{or} \quad 6$$

Why is the variability of a set of scores, and particularly the standard deviation of such scores, of interest? First, a measure of variability is descriptive. It reflects the degree of similarity in performances within groups of students. It can also be used to describe the variability between groups of students. Variability will influence the interpretation of the scores of both individual students and the total group. Second, variability is tied very closely to the concepts of reliability and validity. In general, the greater the variability of scores, the greater the reliability is, at least for norm-referenced measures. And again, in general, the greater the reliability, the greater the possibility that an acceptable level of validity can be obtained. Third, the standard deviation is used to derive standard scores, which are in turn useful in both interpreting scores of individual examinees and combining data for decision-making purposes, for example, assigning marks.

A frequently asked question is, "Is my standard deviation the right size, or is it too large or too small?" Standard deviations don't need reductions or enhancements. They are what they are, that is, they describe the data. The standard deviation might be an expected size or an unexpected size, depending somewhat on the number of cases. For large data sets ($N > 400$) we could expect a range of about 6 standard deviations; for small groups ($N < 15$ or 20), we might expect a range of only about 3.5 standard deviations.

A short-cut method for estimating the standard deviation was originally suggested by W. L. Jenkins of Lehigh University and presented by Paul Diederich (1964). This estimated standard deviation involves summing the raw scores in the upper one-sixth of the distribution, subtracting the sum of the raw scores for the lower one-sixth of the distribution, and dividing the result by half the total number of scores. Symbolically, the estimated standard deviation ($\hat{S}$) can be represented as follows:

$$\hat{S} = \frac{\sum X_U 1/6 - \sum X_L 1/6}{N/2} \qquad (13\text{-}7)$$

This formula has some intrinsic appeal for many because, of course, it does not involve extracting a square root. It should be noted, however, that this approximation formula theoretically assumes a normal distribution and is therefore subject to additional errors when the distribution is non-normal. Extensive use of this estimate, informally reported by teachers and instructors, and brief research reports by Robert Lathrop (1961) and Robert McMorris (1972), allow us to conclude that it is a robust statistic, that is, violations of the assumptions underlying its use do not seriously affect its accuracy. Lathrop found, for example, that even when used with small and non-normal distributions, $\hat{S}$ was a good approximation of $S$, with about a 3 percent to 5 percent error.

When we apply this formula to the data in Table 13-1 (where one-sixth of $N$ = 5) we find $\hat{S}$ to be 6.07, which corresponds favorably with the actual standard deviation of 5.97. For all practical purposes, we can simply round our standard deviation value to an even 6. What do we do if one-sixth turns out to be part of a person? If, for example, we have 40 scores, one-sixth of 40 (or 40/6) is about 6.7. To be accurate we should multiply 0.7 times the seventh score from the top and bottom and add it into the respective sum. In practice, because this procedure is an approximation, we can usually round to the next highest integer.

## RELATIVE POSITION—STANDARD SCORES

**Standard scores** are really nothing more than scores derived from the raw distribution expressed as deviations from the mean in standard deviation units. They are preferred by many as measures of relative position. Unlike percentile ranks, standard scores indicate an individual's position in a collection of scores compared with the mean of the original group. Both methods of reporting are important. Percentile ranks are sensitive to the shape of the distribution; standard scores are not. Standard scores arguably contain more information than PRs. The mean, however, describes just one important characteristic of a distribution, and we should also consider the variability of scores, which can significantly influence score interpretation. If, for example, a distribution of scores is quite homogeneous, the scores being very closely clustered about the hypothetical mean of 80, a score of

70 can represent an extremely low level of relative performance. On the other hand, a great deal of variability means that a few scores will likely fall below 70, which now represents fairly typical performance. Scores, then, whose distributions have standard deviations and means of some standard value, are known as standard scores. The operations by which raw scores are converted into standard scores are called *transformations*. Two kinds of standard score transformations that are frequently used in reporting test data will be discussed.

### Linear Transformations

The simplest type of standard score transformation is a linear one. A frequently used standard score system referred to in statistics is the z score system, which can be represented as follows:

$$z = \frac{X - M}{S} \tag{13-8}$$

Again referring to the American History data in Table 13-1, we can see that a score of 42 would have a z score of +1.17.

$$z = \frac{42 - 35}{5} = +1.17$$

What does this mean? Telling an individual that his z score was +1.17 indicates that his performance was above average—in fact, more than one standard deviation above the mean—which can be more meaningful and informative than telling him that he had a PR of 93. From Equation 13-8 we can see that if a student had a score equal to the mean, her z score would be 0; if it is one standard deviation above or below, her z score would be +1.00 or −1.00. Generally, plus and minus three z-score units (a range of 6 standard deviation units) will describe the full range of scores in any distribution. For a distribution of scores for a classroom test, the range can be considerably less.

Some individuals have trouble keeping track of the "sign" of z scores and working with decimals. The former problem, and to some extent the latter also, can be overcome by using the following standard score conversion:

$$Z = 10 \left( \frac{X - M}{S} \right) + 50 \tag{13-9}$$

or

$$Z = 10(z) + 50$$

We now have a new system of standard scores, where the "standard" mean is 50 and the "standard" standard deviation is 10. Our raw score of 42 would now have a $Z$ value of

$$Z = 10(+1.17) + 50 = 61.7 \quad \text{or} \quad 62$$

Both $z$ scores and $Z$ scores represent linear transformations. In other words, if the standard scores and corresponding raw scores were plotted as points that refer to a set of coordinate axes, the points would fall in a straight line. We have not changed the relationship of the scores or the shape of the underlying distribution. We have, in fact, subtracted a constant from each score and divided each difference by a constant.

**Nonlinear Transformations**

Classroom tests seldom yield so-called normal distributions. A normal distribution curve, as illustrated in Figure 13-2, is a graphic plot of a particular mathematical function. One cannot tell just by "looking at" a distribution whether or not it is normal. The normal curve, however, has certain characteristics that have proven useful in working with test data—for example, contrasting selected $z$ score values define fixed percentages of scores. A system of standard scores has therefore been derived from the normal curve. These scores are called $T$ scores. This system of standard scores is similar to $Z$ scores in that the mean is 50 and the standard deviation is 10. We would find that the PRs for $Z$ and $T$ scores are the same only in the case of a "normal distribution." The term "normal distribution" is in quotation marks because there is no single normal curve but, rather, a family or class of normal curves depending on the mean and standard deviation of the underlying raw scores. Figure 13-1 (c) shows two different normal curves. $T$ scores can be derived for non-normal distributions to allow us to project certain score interpretations based on the assumption of normality, for example, if we had 12,000 students instead of 120. One procedure involves actually changing the shape of the original raw score distribution by an area transformation using a table of the normal curve. We would check the normal distribution $z$ score for given percentile rank values, then use the transformation $T = 10(z) + 50$. Normalizing scores can be a reasonable thing to do if certain assumptions can be met. Many variables of education and psychology are normally distributed when they are based on large samples of individuals. Therefore, the normal curve can be a reasonable model for some kinds of measurements. In addition, because the normal curve has certain characteristics that facilitate test interpretation, a normal score transformation can be helpful. An individual with a $T$ score of 50 will not

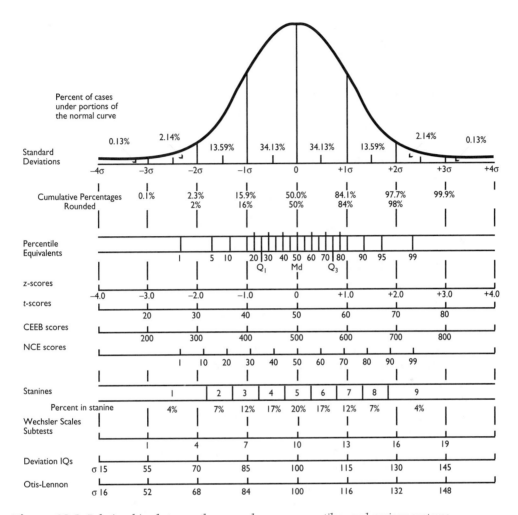

**Figure 13-2** *Relationships between the normal curve, percentiles, and various systems of standard scores.*

*Source: Test Service Bulletin 48* (January, 1980). Published by the Psychological Corporation, San Antonio, TX.

have a raw score equal to the mean if the underlying distribution is not normally distributed.

Figure 13-2 describes the relationship among many systems of standard scores and a normal curve. Note particularly the percentile equivalents for various standard deviation points along the score scale.

Appendix B shows the relationship between *T* and *z* scores and percentile ranks when the original distribution of scores is "normal."

Three standard-score systems in Figure 13-2 are worth brief mention.

The "standard nine" or **stanine** system of scores is increasing in popularity, particularly with publishers of standardized tests. It yields only nine possible values, which facilitates comprehension and interpretation, and is a normalized standard score. Its one drawback is that it groups together scores that might be quite different, assigning them the same stanine score, and therefore tends to mask individual differences. Stanines are actually defined in standard deviation units. For example, a stanine of 5 includes those individuals who are within plus and minus 0.25 standard deviations of the mean, which in a normal distribution includes the middle 20 percent of the observations.

College Entrance Examination Board (CEEB) scores are also a frequently used and encountered standard score type. This system, used with the widely known Scholastic Assessment Test and Graduate Record Exam, uses a score reporting system that avoids both negative numbers and decimals by arbitrarily setting the mean equal to 500 and the standard deviation equal to 100.

$$CEEB \text{ Scores} = 100(z) + 500 \qquad \text{(13-10)}$$

Another type of normalized standard score is the **normal curve equivalent** (NCE). Normal curve equivalents were developed in response to a demand for a standard score system where the unit of measurement approximated an equal-interval scale. If the assumption holds, differences between pairs of consecutive scores would be equal. Some psychometricians further argue that NCE scores can be used to compare scores on different tests. This is obviously a more refined method of reporting scores than percentile ranks.

The normal curve equivalent scale is a "normalized" scale, that is, it employs the normal curve as a mathematical model for its structure. To derive a NCE you (a) calculate percentile ranks for the scores in the distribution, (b) refer to a table of normal curve and identify the normal deviate $z$ score that corresponds to particular percentile ranks, and (c) multiply each $z$ by 21.06 and add 50. Appendix B illustrates the conversion.

Assume a percentile rank of 62, the normal $z$ score for which is 1.2. Multiplying by 21.06 and adding 50 gives us an NCE of 75.27, or 75 rounded. NCE conversion yields values from 1 to 99 and is similar to percentile ranks in that regard. Percentile ranks are based on an ordinal (or rank-ordered) scale whereas NCE values are based on an interval scale. This is an area transformation like those discussed earlier in the chapter and results in a change in the original distribution shape.

## DESCRIBING RELATIONSHIPS

In assessment we frequently need to describe the relationship between two sets of measures. The two measures might be scores by the same set of students on two different forms of the same test, thereby allowing us to describe reliability. Or they might be scores on a test, for example, the College Board Achievement Test in French, and a criterion measure such as final exam score in a first-year college French course, allowing us to describe the validity of the test or the scoring of a set of performance assessments by two different readers using the same rubrics.

Ideally, the first step in examining the relationship between two measures is to display the relationship or correlation graphically in the form of a **scatter diagram**. The procedure merely involves plotting the pairs of scores as dots on coordinate axes. Figure 13-3 is comprised of six scatter diagrams showing varying degrees of relationship. Diagram (a) shows a perfect positive correlation, where the highest $X$ value (30) is associated with the highest $Y$ value (22), the second highest $X$ value (27) is associated with the second highest $Y$ value (20), and so on down to the lowest $X$ value (3) and the lowest $Y$ value (4). Conversely, in diagram (b) we see a perfect inverse relationship between the scores, with the highest $X$ score (30) associated with the lowest $Y$ score (2) and so on. Both (a) and (b) represent perfect correlations; only the direction of the relationship is different, (a) being positive and (b) negative. Diagram (e) shows no consistent pattern between the measures. Two factors, then, are associated in correlation, magnitude (high to low) and direction (positive and negative), with the former generally being the more important. Scatter diagrams (a) through (d) represent linear relationships, that is, they have a tendency to follow a straight-line pattern. Curved-line relationships are, of course, possible (f). If we were examining the relationship between test anxiety and achievement-test performance, we might find that anxiety tended to be associated with increased performance to a certain point, at which an increase in anxiety would be associated with decreased performance. One reason for plotting scatter diagrams is to determine whether the relationship is linear or curvilinear and to get a "feel" for the data. The indices of correlation to be discussed in the rest of this chapter are appropriate for linear relationships only. The reader interested in curvilinear correlation procedures is referred to any number of standard texts (e.g., example, Guilford & Fruchter, 1978).

After graphically examining a relationship, we have the problem of describing it quantitatively. The most frequently used index of linear

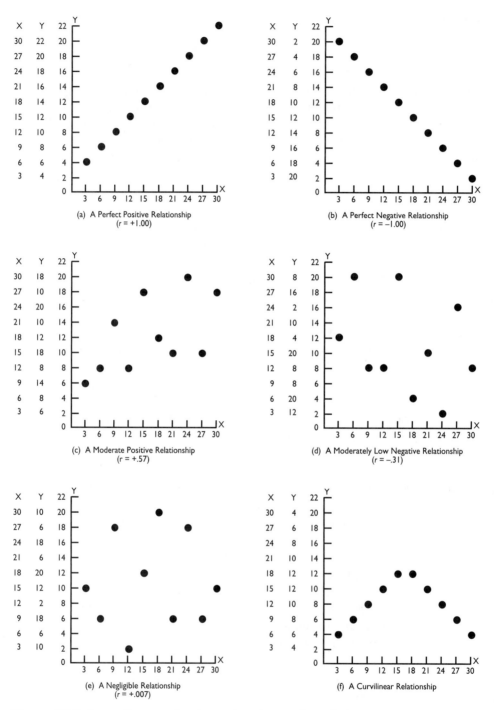

**Figure 13-3** *Scatter diagrams showing various degrees of correlation*

relationship is the **Pearson product-moment correlation coefficient** ($r$), which, in its simplest form, can be presented as follows:

$$r = \frac{\sum z_x z_y}{N} \tag{13-11}$$

where

$z_x$ and $z_y$ = standard scores of the form $(X{-}M)/S$
$\sum z_x z_y$ = the sum of the product of the $z$ scores
$N$ = the total number of pairs of observations

Using Equation 13-11 requires us to convert each $X$ and $Y$ score to a standard score, specifically a $z$ score, multiply the pairs of corresponding $z$ scores, sum the products, and divide by $N$. Table 13-2 illustrates the calculation of a product-moment correlation done in this manner. Ordinarily, the first step we would take in evaluating this relationship would be to look at a scatter diagram of the pairs of measures. This scatter diagram is presented in Figure 13-4. A good exercise might be to use the sample reference scatter diagrams in Figure 13-3 to guesstimate the range where we are likely to find our numerical value for the rank difference correlation coefficient. The correlation of 0.89 is quite strong, indicating that the CEEB test has good validity. If the French test were given in high school and the course exam were for a freshman year course, we would be looking at the predictive validity of the French test. If the test and exam data were gathered at approximately the same time, we would be investigating concurrent validity. In any event, we would be examining criterion-related validity. At no time is there any inference of cause or effect. Many factors can influence the magnitude of the relationship between sets of measures or scores. Among these are (a) the nature of the variables being measured, (b) the size and variability of the sets of scores, (c) the amount of time between the measurements, and (d) the reliability of either or both measurements.

A special case of the Pearson product-moment correlation called *biseral* is used frequently in item analysis. It is applied when one variable is continuous (e.g., the total score on the test) and the other is dichotomous (e.g., getting an item right or wrong).

The rationale for the method of calculating correlation coefficients is clear: scores (people, products, objects, and so forth) tend to rank themselves similarly on two different scales, the rankings must be related, or correlated, or the numbers are said to co-vary together. A third variable can also pull the two scores together. For example, let's say that scores on the Dean Test of Cognitive Reasoning Ability correlate 0.77 with grades in an introductory educational psychology course. Reading ability may be influencing

**Table 13-2** *Illustration of Calculation of Pearson Product-Moment Correlation Between College Board French Test (X) and Final Exam Scores (Y) Using Standard Scores (z)*

| Student | College Board Test (X) | Final Exam Score (Y) | $z_x$ | $z_y$ | $z_x z_y$ |
|---------|------------------------|----------------------|-------|-------|-----------|
| A | 448 | 70 | − .67 | −1.0 | .67 |
| B | 572 | 80 | .26 | .0 | .0 |
| C | 763 | 98 | 1.70 | 1.80 | 3.06 |
| D | 502 | 75 | − .26 | − .50 | .13 |
| E | 629 | 86 | .69 | .60 | .41 |
| F | 345 | 72 | −1.44 | − .80 | 1.15 |
| G | 525 | 68 | − .09 | −1.20 | .11 |
| H | 417 | 70 | − .90 | −1.00 | .90 |
| I | 327 | 66 | −1.58 | −1.40 | 2.21 |
| J | 518 | 84 | − .14 | .40 | − .06 |
| K | 654 | 94 | .88 | 1.40 | 1.23 |
| L | 780 | 97 | 1.83 | 1.70 | 3.11 |
| M | 528 | 85 | − .07 | .50 | − .04 |
| N | 409 | 78 | − .96 | − .20 | .19 |
| O | 644 | 83 | .80 | .30 | .24 |
| Σ | 8061 | 1206 | | | 13.31 |
| M | 537 | 80 | | | |
| S | 133 | 10 | | | |

Correlation Using z Scores

$$r = \frac{\sum z_x z_y}{N}$$

$$r = \frac{13.31}{15} = .89$$

the two measures to be highly correlated because reading is important both in the course and on the test. We could confirm this by administering the Allen Reading Test and looking at the correlation between the scores on it and our reasoning test and grades. Raw score formulas are also available, and any reasonably comprehensive hand calculator allows you to go directly from raw scores to the correlation. Following is the raw score formula for the Pearson product-moment correlation:

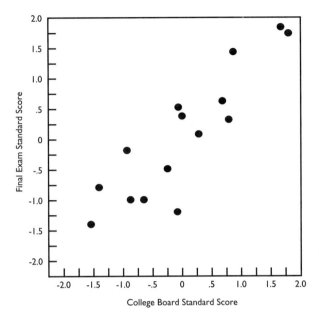

**Figure 13-4** *Scatter diagram for data in Table 13-2*

$$r = \frac{N \sum XY - (\sum X)(\sum Y)}{\sqrt{N \sum X^2 - (\sum X)^2} \sqrt{N \sum Y^2 - (\sum Y)^2}} \qquad (13\text{-}12)$$

Direct, inverse, and curvilinear (Equation 13-12) (see diagram f in Figure 13-3) relationships are all possible. For linearly related variables, a correlation of +1.00 represents a perfect positive relationship between two variables, and one of −1.00 indicates a perfect inverse or negative relationship. A correlation of 0.00 indicates the total absence of linear relationship between the scores. Note that a correlation of −0.68 indicates the same magnitude of relationship as does a correlation of +0.68, and that they would be equally useful in making predictions. It is not true, however, that a correlation of 0.60 indicates twice as strong a relationship as does a correlation of 0.30, that is, $r$ is not directly proportional to the degree of correlation.

In calculating a correlation using Equation 13-11 or 13-12, we were essentially describing the relationship between $X$ and $Y$ as an individual student's relative position on the two measures, expressed in standard score form. Correlation is invariant regardless of the linear units of measurement used. Earlier in this chapter we saw how ranks could also be used to represent relative position. An efficient procedure for correlating two sets of scores uses only ranks: the **Spearman rank difference** or **rank order correlation** ($r_s$):

$$r_s = 1 - \left( \frac{6 \left( \sum D^2 \right)}{N(N^2 - 1)} \right)$$

(13-13)

where

$\sum D^2$ = the sum of the squared differences in ranks (the number 6 is a constant value)

$N$ = the number of ranked pairs of scores

The procedure merely involves assigning a rank of "1" to the highest score on each variable, "2" to the next highest, and so on. Rankings are completed separately for the two variables being correlated. In the case of tied scores, averaged ranks are assigned. For example, if four examinees all had scores of 25 on the same test, and were tied for the ranks of 8, 9, 10, and 11, an average rank would be assigned—in this situation, 9.5 [(8 + 9 + 10 + 11)/4]. After the ranking has been completed (note that we cannot have more ranks than people and that the algebraic sum of the differences in ranks is 0), the differences in ranks are squared, summed, multiplied by 6, and substituted in Equation 13-13. This was accomplished on the same College Board and Exam scores of Table 13-2, and the calculations are summarized in Table 13-3. The rank difference correlation of 0.83 compares favorably with product-moment correlation of 0.89. The rank difference tends to be a more conservative (lower) estimate of relationship than the product-moment, unless a large number of ties tend to inflate the obtained coefficient. The Spearman correlation, because of its relative accuracy and computational ease, is recommended for use by classroom teachers as an adequate correlational index in analyzing their tests. (How correlational procedures can be applied in evaluating test reliability and validity is described in Chapter 14.)

Describing the central tendency and variability of scores, and their relationship with other scores, can be somewhat time-consuming and might be viewed as an arduous task. But these are necessary tasks; being able to describe this relationship allows us to begin to draw inferences and make interpretations of very important data. A wise man once said that only after data have been summarized and communicated do they become information, and rational decision making is based on information. That information should be as descriptive and accurate as possible.

**Table 13-3** *Illustration of Calculation of Spearman's Rank Order Correlation with Hypothetical College Board (X) and French Final Exam (Y) Scores from Table 2*

| Student | College Board Test (X) | Final Exam Score (Y) | Rank of x | Rank of y | D $R_x - R_y$ | D² $(R_x - R_y)^2$ |
|---------|------------------------|----------------------|-----------|-----------|---------------|--------------------|
| A | 448 | 70 | 11 | 12.5 | −1.5 | 2.25 |
| B | 572 | 80 | 6 | 8 | −2.0 | 4.0 |
| C | 763 | 98 | 2 | 1 | 1.0 | 1.0 |
| D | 502 | 75 | 10 | 10 | 0.0 | 0.0 |
| E | 629 | 86 | 5 | 4 | 1.0 | 1.0 |
| F | 345 | 72 | 14 | 11 | 3.0 | 9.0 |
| G | 525 | 68 | 8 | 14 | −6.0 | 36.0 |
| H | 417 | 70 | 12 | 12.5 | −0.5 | 0.25 |
| I | 327 | 66 | 15 | 15 | 0.0 | 0.0 |
| J | 518 | 84 | 9 | 6 | 3.0 | 9.0 |
| K | 654 | 94 | 3 | 3 | 0.0 | 0.0 |
| L | 780 | 97 | 1 | 2 | −1.0 | 1.0 |
| M | 528 | 85 | 7 | 5 | 2.0 | 4.0 |
| N | 409 | 78 | 13 | 9 | 4.0 | 16.0 |
| O | 644 | 83 | 4 | 7 | −3.0 | 9.0 |
| | | | | SUM | 0.0 | 92.5 |

$$r_s = 1 - \left( \frac{6\left(\sum D^2\right)}{N(N^2 - 1)} \right) = 1 - \left( \frac{6(92.5)}{15(15^2 - 1)} \right) = 1 - \frac{555}{3360} = .83$$

# CASE STUDY

## DESCRIBING MEASUREMENT AND ASSESSMENT DATA

The 80-item Reading Education midterm exam was administered to a class of 18 students approximately five weeks into the quarter, and a final exam (80 items) was administered one week before the end of the quarter. Following is a list of their raw scores:

| Midterm Exam | | | | | | Final Exam | | | | | |
|---|---|---|---|---|---|---|---|---|---|---|---|
| $S_1$ | 58 | $S_7$ | 58 | $S_{13}$ | 62 | $S_1$ | 65 | $S_7$ | 63 | $S_{13}$ | 67 |
| $S_2$ | 47 | $S_8$ | 58 | $S_{14}$ | 51 | $S_2$ | 51 | $S_8$ | 59 | $S_{14}$ | 52 |
| $S_3$ | 58 | $S_9$ | 55 | $S_{15}$ | 65 | $S_3$ | 61 | $S_9$ | 57 | $S_{15}$ | 69 |
| $S_4$ | 59 | $S_{10}$ | 52 | $S_{16}$ | 57 | $S_4$ | 67 | $S_{10}$ | 57 | $S_{16}$ | 56 |
| $S_5$ | 68 | $S_{11}$ | 62 | $S_{17}$ | 62 | $S_5$ | 74 | $S_{11}$ | 71 | $S_{17}$ | 67 |
| $S_6$ | 55 | $S_{12}$ | 57 | $S_{18}$ | 52 | $S_6$ | 53 | $S_{12}$ | 53 | $S_{18}$ | 63 |

In summarizing the performances of this group there are probably five activities that are important. They are (a) displaying the data in a meaningful way, (b) calculating indices of central tendency, (c) calculating indices of variability, (d) expressing individual performances, and (e) describing relationships. Complete these activities for the following statistics or diagrams on the midterm exam. Construct or calculate using the midterm data:

| Data Display | Central Tendency | Variability | Relative Position for a Score of 57 |
|---|---|---|---|
| (1) Frequency distribution | (1) Mean | (1) Range | (1) Percentile rank |
| (2) Frequency polygon | (2) Median | (2) Standard deviation | (2) Standard scores (z, Z, CEEB, and NCE) |
| | | (3) Estimated standard deviation (Lathrop) | |
| | | (4) Inter-quartile range | |
| | | (5) Semi-interquartile range | |

## Describing Relationships

1. Prepare a scatter diagram for the pairs of midterm and final exam scores.
2. "Guesstimate" the correlation using Figure 13-4 as a guide.
3. Calculate the spearman rank order correlation (Equation 13-13).

## CONTENT REVIEW STATEMENTS

1. The study of statistics is important because statistical methods do the following:

    a. Facilitate the summarization and description of data

    b. Assist in the interpretation of test scores

    c. Are necessary for an adequate analysis of measuring instruments

    d. Facilitate the decision making use of test data

2. A frequency distribution of test scores reveals the number of scores in each category along the score scale.

3. The frequency distribution facilitates examination of the shape of the distribution and, in particular, recognition of skewness or the tendency of scores to bunch at the extremes of a distribution.

4. A percentile rank, which describes the percentage of scores at or below a given score (or the midpoint of a set of scores), helps us interpret individual performances.

5. A percentile rank is calculated by dividing the total number of scores ($N$) into the cumulative frequency at and below a given score (or midpoint), and multiplying the result by 100.

6. A percentile is a score point that divides a score distribution into specified percentages or areas of the total distribution.

7. The median is that percentile (score point) that divides the total score distribution into two equal areas.

8. The first ($Q_1$), second ($Q_2$), and third ($Q_3$) quartiles divide the distribution into four equal areas.

9. A distribution of scores that is asymmetrical can be characterized as skewed.

10. A positively skewed distribution has a high frequency of low scores and trails off to a low frequency of high scores.

11. A negatively skewed distribution has a high frequency of high scores and trails off to a low frequency of low scores. Many achievement measures yield negatively skewed distributions.

12. The mean, or arithmetic average, is obtained by adding all the scores and dividing the sum by the total number of scores.

13. If the mean is larger than the median, it is likely that the distribution is positively skewed. Conversely, if the mean is less than the median, the distribution is likely to be negatively skewed.

14. The variability (or spread) of a distribution of measures can be described by the standard deviation, the interquartile or semi-interquartile range, or the range.

15. The variances of a set of scores are calculated by adding the squared deviations of the scores (from the mean of all the scores) and then dividing the total by the number of scores.

16. The standard deviation is the positive square root of the variance.

17. The standard deviation can be estimated by dividing half the number of scores into the difference between the sums of the upper one-sixth and lower one-sixth of the distribution of the scores.

18. In general, the greater the total number of scores, the greater the range is of scores in standard deviation units.

19. The variability of scores is likely to be positively related to total test reliability, and to some extent to validity.

20. Standard scores represent methods of expressing test scores that have fixed means and standard deviations.

21. The basic standard score is the $z$ score, which is calculated by dividing the standard deviation into the difference between a given raw score and the mean of all the scores.

22. A $Z$ score is obtained by multiplying a $z$ score by 10 and adding 50.

23. A $T$ score is the same as a $Z$ score when the scores are normally distributed.

24. The normal curve is an idealized theoretical (mathematical) bell-shaped curve that represents the distributions of some kinds of educational and psychological data, particularly when a large number of observations is involved.

25. The distribution of scores from classroom tests is rarely normal.

26. A College Board or CEEB standard score is obtained by multiplying the $z$ score by 100 and adding 500.

27. Non-normal distributions can be converted to normal distributions by transforming all raw scores to percentile ranks and then entering a normal curve table, which gives $z$-score equivalents of the percentile ranks (see Appendix B).

**28.** Stanine standard scores are usually normally distributed single-digit scores having a mean of approximately 5 and a standard deviation of approximately 2.

**29.** Normal curve equivalents are normalized standard scores arrayed across an equal-interval scale.

**30.** A correlation coefficient represents the degree of relation between a series of paired scores.

**31.** Correlation coefficients range from −1.00, indicating a perfect negative or inverse relationship, through 0.00, indicating the absence of relationship, to +1.00, indicating a perfect positive direct relationship.

**32.** When pairs of scores are expressed as *z* scores, the correlation coefficient is the average of the *z*-score products.

**33.** A correlation can be assessed using differences between ranks of paired scores (the Spearman rank difference method).

**34.** Examination of the degree and direction of relationship in a set of paired scores is facilitated by the plotting of the pairs on a two-way grid (scatter diagram).

**35.** The more closely the plots of pairs of scores fall on a diagonal, the higher the correlation; the diagonal running from the lower-left to upper-right corners is positive, and that running from the upper-left to lower-right corners is negative, assuming the scores have been plotted low to high, left to right, and bottom to top of the scatter diagram.

**36.** Correlation methods are useful in studying test reliability and validity.

---

## SPECULATIONS

**1.** What are the alternatives to using quantitative methods in assessment? What would be the consequences of using them?

**2.** Why is variability such an important concept?

**3.** How does the phrase "a picture is worth a thousand words" apply to statistical methods?

**4.** Try to orally describe to a friend the concepts of relative position, central tendency, variability, and relationship.

**5.** Why are there so many different ways to express test scores?

**6.** What is standard about a standard score?

**7.** Discuss how the concept of "averageness" makes logical sense, statistical sense, and educational sense.

## SUGGESTED READINGS

The following are standard textbooks in quantitative methods. The interested reader should examine primarily descriptive methods, paying particular attention to data display.

Guilford, J. P., & Fruchter, B. (1978). *Fundamental statistics in psychology and education* (6th ed.). New York: McGraw-Hill.

Moore, D. S. (1985). *Statistics: Concepts and controversies* (2nd ed.). New York: Freeman.

Mosteller, F., Fienberg, S. E., & Rourke, R. E. K. (1983). *Beginning statistics with data analysis*. Reading, MA: Addison-Wesley.

Sprinthall, R. C. (1994). *Basic statistical analysis*. Boston: Allyn & Bacon.

# 14

# Defining and Assessing Validity and Reliability

---

## FOCUS CONCEPTS AND KEY TERMS FOR STUDY

| | |
|---|---|
| **Consequential Validity** | **Reliability** |
| **Content Validity** | **Spearman–Brown Formula** |
| **Curricular Validity** | **Stability Reliability** |
| **Equivalence Reliability** | **Standard Error of Measurement** |
| **Expectancy Table** | **Systematic Measurement Errors** |
| **Instructional Validity** | **Unsystematic Measurement Errors** |
| **Internal Consistency** | **Validity** |
| **Kuder–Richardson Formula** | |

## STANDARDS ALERT

**Standard 2.5          Reliability Equivalence**

A reliability coefficient or standard error of measurement based on one approach should not be interpreted as interchangeable with another derived by a different technique unless their implicit definitions of measurement error are equivalent.

**Standard 1.16          Criterion Validity**

When validation relies on evidence that test scores are related to one or more criterion variables, information about suitability and technical quality of the criteria should be reported.

## TAKING IT TO THE CLASSROOM

There are different kinds of reliability for different uses. A classroom test should be relatively internally consistent so that the items are measuring the same or a related domain of objectives, whereas an assessment used to predict success in college would require a high degree of stability reliability. When predicting a criterion, it is important for both the predictor and the criterion to be related.

Reprinted with permission from the *Standards for Educational and Psychological Testing*. Copyright © 1999 by the American Educational Research Association, the American Psychological Association, and the National Council on Measurement in Education.

We have thus far considered some of the basic steps in developing assessments. The learning outcomes to be measured have been identified, data-gathering procedures specified, questions or tasks written or created and analyzed, the instrument administered, and scores summarized. Now let us step back and examine how well the job has been accomplished. We must seek answers to the questions, "Do the scores tell me what I want to know?" and "Are the assessments consistent?" The former question relates to *validity* and the latter to *reliability*. Most experts consider reliability an aspect of validity. Problems relating to the definitions, the methods of estimating, and the factors influencing validity and reliability are considered in this chapter. Although our discussion of these two highly important characteristics will be aimed at the individual who is actually engaged in instrument development, any person involved in selecting, administering, and interpreting measuring devices must be thoroughly familiar with these concepts to make intelligent and meaningful use of test results.

We have, of course, been considering questions of validity and reliability throughout the book. From Chapter 1 on we have tried to "build in" validity, to follow "best professional practice" as we created our assessments. At this point we are *formally* considering questions of validity and reliability. What evidence do we have (and what must we still gather) to support the interpretations we hope to make of the scores?

## THE CONCEPT OF ERRORS IN ASSESSMENT

Most tests, measurements, and assessments yield quantitative descriptions of individuals. In general, we are less concerned with the scores themselves than with what they represent, the characterizations they provide, and what the interpretations tell us about students, learning, curricula, teaching, or programs.

Assessment hopes, however, are rarely completely realized. For example, if we administer an assessment on two different occasions, it is highly unlikely that we would obtain the same score both times, people are just as fallible as measuring instruments are. Another example is a situation in which we are interested in predicting how well a particular high school student will perform in college. We have results from a scholastic aptitude test and we know how scores on it relate to grades during the first semester of the freshman year. On the basis of a test score we predict a C average, only to find that student achieves a B average. Errors are obviously involved in both situations—errors in measuring and errors in estimating (or predicting).

Two statistical indices useful in describing the variability of a set of scores are the standard deviation and the square of the standard deviation, the variance (refer back to Chapter 13). What contributes to these indices of variation? The primary contributors are true individual differences in the trait or skill measured by the test. Such factors as reading ability, memory, the physical condition of the examinee or testing room, and the form of the item can also differentially affect the individuals taking the test, causing their scores to be higher or lower than expected. These factors, because they do not represent what we want to measure, must be considered as errors. Some kinds of errors are more important than others. Guessing on a difficult test or the subjectivity sometimes encountered in evaluating essay questions can be the source of very significant errors. The physical condition of the examinee and the testing environment (within reasonable limits) do not represent sources of error that are likely to seriously distort the meaning of the scores. Whether a factor is a serious or less serious error depends on your intent in developing and using the measure.

For example, psychological change in an individual over time is not likely to be a serious error in assessing the equivalence of two forms of the same test; however, changes from the junior year in high school until the end of the freshman year in college could prove to be a serious source of error in predicting achievement from an academic ability test.

Errors can be meaningfully categorized as *unsystematic* or *systematic*. **Unsystematic** sources of variation are those factors whose effects are orderless, show no consistent pattern, and fluctuate from one occasion to the next. Perhaps the purest form of unsystematic error is guessing or inconsistent ratings of essays, changing from item to item, test to test, and examinee to examinee. Motivation to perform well on an achievement test, for example, could differentially influence individuals on the same or different occasions. In addition, such factors as variation in attention to the test task and guessing could act as unsystematic sources of error. **Systematic** effects are those whose influences are the same for an individual on different testing occasions, or for all examinees on the same occasion. If, for example, the test administrator does not rigidly adhere to the time limits specified in the directions for a speeded test and allows every examinee an extra five minutes, scores might be spuriously inflated. The extra time influences the scores in a way that, although constant in the situation, changes the meaning of the scores. Such factors as learning, training, forgetting, fatigue, and growth can function as systematic sources of errors, in some cases increasing and in others decreasing the scores that would have resulted under error-free conditions. One limitation of the systematic versus unsystematic classification is that it is not mutually exclusive. In other words, a given factor, such as, the physical condition of the testing room or anxiety, can be systematic in one situation (e.g., exposing all examinees to the same poor lighting conditions) and unsystematic in another (e.g., different testing room in a test-retest situation). In other words, a factor can influence either or both reliability and validity.

On the one hand, the problems associated with controlling and assessing the errors are problems of determining reliability. On the other hand, using a variety of experimental procedures to determine the extent to which a test is affected by constant errors affects the validity of a test.

## DEFINING VALIDITY

Exhibit 14-1 contains an excerpt from the *Standards* (Joint Committee, 1999) which captures the current thinking about what instrument validity is all about.

Validity refers to the degree to which evidence and theory support the interpretations of test scores entailed by proposed uses of tests. Validity is, therefore, the most fundamental consideration in developing and evaluating tests. The process of validation involves accumulating evidence to provide a sound scientific basis for the proposed score interpretations. It is the interpretations of test scores required by proposed uses that are evaluated, not the test itself. . . . Validation logically begins with an explicit statement of the proposed interpretation of test scores, along with a rationale for the relevance of the interpretation to the proposed use. The proposed interpretation refers to the construct or concepts the test is intended to measure. Examples of constructs are mathematics achievement, performance as a computer technician, depression, and self-esteem (p. 9).

**Exhibit 14-1**  *Excerpt about Validity from the* Standards *(Joint Committee, 1999)*

Validity is a very particularistic, specific, and individualistic concept. An assessment is not valid in general, but is valid for a particular interpretation in a specific application. We need, therefore, to test the test's validity before we can accept the inferences to be drawn from the test results.

This section describes various approaches to establishing the validity of measures commonly used in education and psychology. The ideas discussed could apply to any type of measuring device, multiple-choice format, supply or completion type questions, writing or other types of performance assessments. For classroom application, the material related to **content** and **criterion-related** evidence has the greatest application.

## SOURCES OF VALIDITY EVIDENCE

The concept of constant or systematic error was described in the previous section. The relationship of error to test validity implies that some standard or standards exist for evaluating the presence or absence of such errors. These errors usually are concerned with the accuracy of decisions made by teachers about students. Airasian (2001) has in fact defined validity as the ability to help the teacher make a correct decision. . . . it is the key to obtaining high-quality and meaningful assessment decisions" (p. 18). Criteria must be identified, constructed, or collected by the test developer, or sometimes by the user, so that judgments about validity of a test will in turn be dictated by the purposes of developing and using the test. Four rather broad sources of evidence have been identified (Joint Committee, 1999).

### Content-Based Evidence

*The test user wants to determine how an individual performs at present in a universe of situations that the test situation is claimed to represent.* For example, most achievement tests used in schools measure the student's performance on a sample of questions intended to represent certain educational achievements or educational objectives. The type of validity described here is generally referred to as *content validity*, which is of greatest concern to the classroom teacher.

### Response-Based Evidence

*The user seeks evidence that the examinee completes physical or mental tasks that are called for in the assessment.* A frequently used method to gather such data is to simply sit with examinees and listen to them as they respond to the tasks. A test of mathematical reasoning should elicit reasoning or problem-solving behavior, not recall.

### Internal Structure Evidence

*The test user wishes to make sure that the components (items) are related to each other in the predicted way such that the resulting score reveals what it is supposed to tell the user.* Reliability is an important dimension of internal structure. The user would ask questions about whether or not the structure of the test varies from subgroup to subgroup (e.g., males versus females).

In general, content validity is evaluated by a rational analysis of the question, task, or item content compared with the objectives and intent of developing the instrument. Take, for example, an educational achievement test. An instructor would assess validity by using professional judgments and considering the instructional objectives of a particular class or school. The instructor would seek an answer to this question: How adequately do the items of this test measure the objectives, both subject matter and cognitive skills, that I want them to measure? Content validity rests on specifying the universe of behavior to be sampled. For a standardized achievement test, this specification might take the form of a statement in the test manual summarizing the textbooks or subject-matter experts consulted or the course syllabi reviewed. For an informal classroom test, the universe might be defined as a table of specifications developed by the teacher. In either case, content validity is the match between a test item and the objective it is supposed to measure—sometimes also referred to as *relevance*.

With increasing frequency, commercial test publishers are providing extensive listings of the objectives on which their items were based. Descriptions include content specifications and can also delineate the mental operation necessary to perform successfully on the test, for example, application, analysis, and so forth.

### Evidence from External Relationships

*The test user wants to forecast an individual's future standing or estimate an individual's present standing on some variable of particular significance that is different from the test.* For example, an academic aptitude test can forecast grades, or a brief adjustment inventory can estimate what the outcome would be of a careful psychological examination. Validity defined in this way is sometimes called *criterion-related validity*. To establish a claim for criterion-related validity, however, one must draw upon statistical or experimental data. These data are usually presented as correlation coefficients. Means, standard deviations, or other descriptive indices derived from groups known to differ on the variable being measured are occasionally brought to bear on validity claims. The chief problem in using correlational techniques to establish validity involves identifying an acceptable criterion. The criterion must be external to the test and directly measure the variable in question. If we were interested in the variable "academic success during the freshman year in college," a criterion measure might be a grade point average or score on a comprehensive examination. A test estimating either of these criteria could be developed and experimentally administered to a group of high school seniors. Later their scores would be correlated with grade point averages or exam scores obtained at the end of their freshman year in college. If the correlation is high (e.g., example, +0.80), we would conclude that the test has a high degree of criterion-related validity and could be used with confidence to make predictions.

Following are some "typical"—if anything nowadays is typical—criterion-related validity coefficients.

1. It was found in a preschool program for at-risk 4-year-olds that the *Developmental Indicators for the Assessment of Learning—Revised* correlated +0.48 with the *Peabody Picture Vocabulary Test—Revised* (Payne, McGee-Brown, Taylor, & Dukes, 1993).

2. The 35-item *Opinions About Deaf People* scale correlated +0.75 with Cowen's *Attitudes to Deafness* scale for 290 university undergraduates (Berkay, Gardner, & Smith, 1995).

3. College grade point average was moderately predictable from the *Scholastic Aptitude (Assessment) Test* as indicated by a correlation of

+ 0.49. The SAT correlated 0.47 with high school grades alone, and high school grades correlated 0.58 with college grades (Wesley, 1994).

In addition to correlation indices, a useful way of summarizing criterion-related validity data is in an **expectancy table**. An expectancy table is a two-way grid that relates test and criterion scores. A sample expectancy table relating scores on the sentences subtest of the Differential Aptitude Test and grades in a rhetoric course for 100 freshman females is presented in Table 14-1. The left portion of the table summarizes the entries from a bivariate frequency distribution or scatter diagram similar to those described in Chapter 11. In the right portion of the table, each cell frequency has been converted to a percentage based on the total number of tallies in its row. These data might be interpreted as follows: of the 23 freshman women who took the course in rhetoric and had test scores between 50 and 59, 39 percent (or nine individuals) received a grade of C, 35 percent (eight women) received a grade of B, and 26 percent (six women) received a grade of A. Not one of the students with a score of 50 or more obtained a grade lower than C. We might, then, use this expectancy-table information to predict the performance of women who take this course in the future.

The situation can be applied to either the predictive or concurrent use of tests, depending on the amount of time elapsed between the collection of test scores and criterion data and the purpose for which the scores are intended. For the concurrent use of criterion-related validity data, we might be interested in answering a general question such as: "Can I substitute this test score for a more elaborate and expensive criterion measure?" Here the test scores and criterion data would be gathered at the same time and correlated.

In addition to looking for evidence of positive relationships (consequence) a developer/user would be interested in whether the measure in question is not correlated with variables that are not logically or theoretically related (divergence). A scholastic aptitude measure *should* be related to grade point average, but not to anxiety or depression. For a discussion, not for a beginner, see Campbell and Fisk (1959) for an excellent discussion of the concept of convergence and discriminant validity.

Finally, evidence must be obtained about how well the instrument functions with different subgroups or populations. Such data would be evidence of validity generalization. Does the Scholastic Assessment Test operate in the same way at Hope College as it does at Michigan State University?

**Table 14-1** *Expectancy Table Relating DAT Sentences Scores to Grades in Rhetoric for 100 College Freshman Females\**

| Total No. | Number Receiving Each Grade | | | | | Test Scores | Percent Receiving Each Grade | | | | | Total Percent |
|---|---|---|---|---|---|---|---|---|---|---|---|---|
| | F | D | C | B | A | | F | D | C | B | A | |
| 1 | | | | | 1 | 80–89 | | | | | 100 | 100 |
| 5 | | | | 1 | 4 | 70–79 | | | | 20 | 80 | 100 |
| 22 | | | 3 | 14 | 5 | 60–69 | | | 14 | 63 | 23 | 100 |
| 23 | | | 9 | 8 | 6 | 50–59 | | | 39 | 35 | 26 | 100 |
| 22 | | 3 | 13 | 6 | | 40–49 | | 14 | 59 | 27 | | 100 |
| 16 | 1 | 3 | 9 | 3 | | 30–39 | 6 | 19 | 56 | 19 | | 100 |
| 8 | 1 | 4 | 3 | | | 20–29 | 13 | 50 | 37 | | | 100 |
| 2 | | 2 | | | | 10–19 | | 100 | | | | 100 |
| 1 | | 1 | | | | 0–9 | | 100 | | | | 100 |
| 100 | 2 | 13 | 37 | 32 | 16 | $M = 48.58$ | | | | | | |
| | | | | | | $S = 15.20$ | | | | | | |

Correlation = 0.71

*Source:* Reprinted from Alexander G. Wesman, Expectancy tables: A way of interpreting test validity. *Test Service Bulletin, 38* (1949): 12. Published by the Psychological Corporation, San Antonio, TX.

## Evidence of Consequential Validity

*The user is interested not only whether the data provide evidence that the intended outcomes are achieved, but also whether there are unintended outcomes.* This type of evidence is particularly important where educational and psychological tests are used to make selection, promotion, or placement decisions. We must be assured, as test users, that the claims for a particular instrument are the only ones likely to be realized. Is a test of ability to use selected electronic devices a measure only of those skills and not of reading ability? Other examples of consequential validity concerns might be as follows:

Don't use an aptitude test with a group that has not been included in the standardization. Don't use an achievement test to make inferences about an individual's intelligence. Don't use an aptitude test to make grade-to-grade promotion decisions. Don't use a comprehensive student achievement battery to make teacher salary decisions.

This dimension of validity has a strong element of ethics that reflects the potential for biased test use. Use a measure for the purpose for which it was developed. You must be prepared to justify application of the results such that the consequences are positive and appropriate.

### Integrating Validity Evidence

Putting all the evidence together to draw inferences is an ongoing process. When new information becomes available and users have experience in administering and interpreting the scores, new insights into the meaningfulness of scores become evident. The relative weights given to the sources of data just described will be different depending on the user's intent and intended interpretation. Table 14-2 contains a brief outline of what a validation study might look like. Our hypothetical measure of motivation for academic achievement would have to be based on some theory, such as, David McClelland's need for achievement (Atkinson, 1958). Items would have to be based on theory and then data gathered. This requires a great deal of work, but consider what we are trying to do—confirm that the interpretation of the scores says something meaningful about the examinee and that the scores are about a characteristic that we can't actually see or touch. We *infer* its presence. For an expanded discussion of integrating validity evidence, see Cronbach and Meehl (1955). Their discussion of construct validity is the standard for measurement professionals. See also Messick (1989).

## OTHER FACES OF VALIDITY

### Curricular Validity

As stated previously, the validity of a test or item depends on its matching the objective. Objectives are operationalized in many different ways. In other words, a variety of instructional materials could be used to address a particular objective. To tell whether a test or item matches the curriculum materials, you should map the relations of these two elements. For example, use a table of specifications (a two-way grid with content along one dimension and expected behavior along the other) to cross-reference the test and materials (Schmidt, 1983). Curricular validity relates directly to the extent to which the curriculum materials are addressed in the assessment.

### Instructional Validity

The ultimate test of a test or item is whether or not it represents a reasonable sample of what actually went on in the classroom. The test must measure what was taught, and students must have had an "opportunity to learn." Theoretically, objectives, curriculum, and instruction correspond almost perfectly. But many factors can disturb this perfection. Students don't always behave in predicted ways, and therefore teachers must sometimes

**Table 14-2** *Hypothetical Construct Validation of a Measure of Motivation for Academic Achievement*

| Type of Validity Evidence | Example |
| --- | --- |
| Group Differences | Ability of items to discriminate between under- and overachieving students. |
| Changes in Performance | Study of scores on motivation instrument over time to see if fluctuations are related to academic performance differences or score sensitivity by instructional intervention. |
| Correlations | Correlations with other motivation measures, teacher estimates of effort, grades, and achievement test scores. |
| Internal Consistency | Calculation of Kuder–Richardson formula 20, and factor analyses. |
| Studies of Test-Taking Process | What is motivation *not* correlated with, for example, socially desirable responses, aptitude, anxiety. Relate scores to original theory. |

adjust or modify instruction. For the test to be instructionally valid, the test must sample relevant instructional outcomes. Ideally, evaluation of instructional validity should come from an independent observer. Usually instructional validity, however, rests on the subjective judgment of the teacher. Legal challenges have confirmed the legitimacy of this type of validity.

Some in the testing profession support the positions taken by E. S. Yalow and James Popham (1983) regarding curricular and instructional validity. Yalow and Popham claim that these are really not kinds of *test* validity but, rather, that curriculum and instructional validity reflect the opportunities that students have had to become prepared to perform on the test. But correct interpretation of test scores should consider as many factors as possible that can affect scores. Therefore, we should accept curricular and instructional validity as components in assessing the overall "validity" of the intended purpose in gathering and interpreting the scores.

It is a law of measurement that test scores must be reliable before they can be valid. In a very real sense, however, validity is not strictly a characteristic of the instrument but of the *inference* that is to be made from the test scores derived from the instrument. We need primarily to be concerned with the validity of the interpretation we make from test results.

## COMMONSENSE APPROACHES TO ESTABLISHING CLASSROOM ACHIEVEMENT TEST VALIDITY

Validity is not something added at the end of test development but, rather, should be built into the instrument while it is being created and assembled.

After the test is developed, we can check how good a job we did by examining the test results against accepted criteria. We want to answer affirmatively the question, "Are the scores on this test telling us what we want to know about this student?"

Certain steps—some formative, some summative, some formal, some informal—can help build validity. Most of these apply to assessing achievement, but many of the procedures could be generalized for any educational or psychological measuring instrument. Among the steps are the following:

1. *Use objectives as a basis for question development.* This strikes at the heart of content validity, namely, the *relevance* of the items compared with *intent*. Value judgments are involved, but we hope those are based on experience and knowledge and an overview of what actually went on in the classroom.

2. *Use accepted question development principles*. Make sure that the items, tasks, and questions are free from cues and ambiguity and meet the highest communicative standards.

3. *If multiple behaviors are being sampled, they should be in proper proportion*. For an achievement test this means using a table of specifications or test blueprint.

4. *Extraneous sources of influence on test responses need to be eliminated or controlled.* Possible bias (e.g., gender, racial, commonality of experience) should be investigated empirically and eliminated or adjusted (e.g., using separate norms by sex). Such response tendencies as social desirability and test anxiety are some of the many that must be controlled.

5. *Extraneous sources of distraction during test administration must be controlled.* Every examinee is entitled to demonstrate his or her maximum performance and respond in a quiet and disturbance-free environment.

6. *Verify correctness, appropriateness, and accuracy of answers to items and scoring of tasks.* Objectivity is a major contributor to validity. Use fellow teachers periodically to look at what and how you are assessing.

7. *Assessment materials must be appropriate to the level of functioning and experience.* One example of this commonsense guideline is that the readability of verbal items must be within the comprehension range of the examinee.

8. *Check the reliability of the measures used.* The old adage that a test cannot be valid without being reliable is true.

9. ***Where possible, check test scores against external criteria.*** It seems logical that achievement test scores should relate to such external measures as teachers' grades, performance during future educational experiences, and scores on other relevant informal or standardized measures.

10. ***Test items that are related to change during instruction should be retained for future use.*** Training or instruction should have an impact on test scores or task performance.

11. ***Use the most appropriate format***. Sometimes performance tasks are preferable. Sometimes an efficient multiple-choice format can be used. Question type should be dictated by what you are trying to measure.

Validity is the keystone of an effective and meaningful assessment. It must rest on a reliable foundation.

## DEFINING RELIABILITY

The determination of reliability concerns the problem of the influence of unsystematic errors in measurement. We define the reliability of a test as the degree to which the test and its scores reflect true or nonerror variance. In other words, we can define the reliability of a test and its scores as the degree to which they are influenced by unsystematic factors. That's a fancy way of saying that if a test has reliability it should produce *consistent* results. Reliability will be represented symbolically as $r_{tt}$. In a real sense this symbolizes the correlation of the test with itself.

The two basic methodological considerations in assessing reliability are *time* and *content*. We can take samplings of test performance over time to check on stability reliability and over content by using different forms of the test to check on equivalence. The relationship between these two dimensions is seen in Figure 14-1. Because it is obviously more economical to estimate reliability from a single administration of a test, there are many formulas and "quickie" methods. Equivalence reliability is particularly important when we are making inferences about a student's performance on a "domain" of tasks.

Building two forms of a test also can be a revealing experience for test constructors and item writers because the process allows them to check themselves as architects and builders. Stability reliability is important in examining criterion-related validity, particularly when we want to predict future performance criteria or behavior with the test. For some kinds of tests—for example, intelligence and personality—we are concerned with

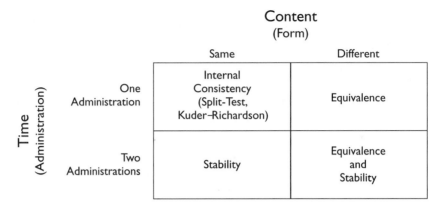

**Figure 14-1** *Relationship of time and content in assessing reliability*

both equivalence and stability. Reliability does limit validity, sometimes mathematically and sometimes conceptually. We always consider the reliability of our primary measure, for example, the achievement test, but when we use it to predict future behavior or a score on another test or criterion, we also must consider the reliability of the criterion. For example, it doesn't make much sense to try to predict success in first-year college French if we don't have a reliable (or valid for that matter) measure of that language competency.

Let's use this information about test theory and type of application to outline some specific procedures that can be applied in estimating reliability. Reliability changes every time a test is used, whether with the same or different examinees. But we can make some very good estimates of what the reliability will be based on what it was.

### Reliability Determined from Repetition of the Same Test (Stability)

This technique simply involves administering the same form of a test to the same examinees on two or more occasions and correlating the scores. There is usually a significant delay between administrations, for example, a week. This method has the advantage of requiring only one form of a test and the potential disadvantage of being significantly influenced by practice and memory. In addition, the test-retest method can cause an interaction between the test and examinee, particularly when used with personality inventories. Having taken the inventory once may have caused the examinee to introspect, which might result in significant score changes the second time the inventory is administered. Some testing experts claim that the test-retest method is an estimate of the reliability not of the instrument but of the examinee. Nevertheless, such information is useful within a specific testing situation. We could not expect, for example, to estimate future behavior if scores on the prediction test did not hold up over time.

## Reliability Determined from Two Forms of the Same Test (Equivalence)

To determine reliability in this way we must, of course, have two forms of the test. The items on each form must be parallel in terms of content and the mental operations required to respond to the items. In developing equivalent forms, the test developer must begin with a complete and detailed set of specifications. Such a blueprint would ideally specify item type, difficulty level, content coverage, and the like. In a real sense, the correlation of equivalent forms monitors the consistency and ability of the item writer. More important, however, this correlation serves as a check on the sampling from the universe of behaviors in question. There is no particular reason to believe that any given set of 35 vocabulary items is superior or inferior to any other set. If we find a high degree of response consistency over forms of the test, however, we will have greater confidence in the sampling of items, that is, greater confidence that the samples of items accurately represent the universe from which they were drawn. Applying this reliability-estimating procedure merely involves administering two forms of the same test to the same group and correlating the scores. If there is a significant time delay between administration of the two forms, we have an estimate of equivalence and stability (see Figure 14-1).

## Reliability of Ratings

When assessing the reliability of performance assessments, it is often desirable to compare the ratings of the same set of performances or papers by two different raters, or have one rater do a repeat rating on that same set of scores. Another variation is to have a rater score two comparable performances for the same set of students. In these cases, simply calculating the correlation between the pairs of scores would actually be the reliability (see Equation 13-13). That correlation coefficient is the reliability coefficient as it comes out of the equation. The process is almost identical with equivalent forms of reliability, but the forms now become raters.

## Reliability Determined from Comparable Parts of a Test (Internal Consistency)

Both reliability-estimating techniques described require two test administrations of the measuring device. This can take considerable time and effort. Several methods have been devised to estimate reliability from a single administration of a test. Although practical, single-administration estimating procedures probably yield an inflated estimate of reliability compared with equivalent forms. The procedures usually involve splitting a test in half and using information derived from the half-tests, for either a correlation or variance, to estimate the reliability of the full-length test. The four bases used most frequently for splitting a test in half are (a) random halves, (b) top and bottom halves, (c) "equivalent" halves, and (d) odd and even halves. The last two methods are worth special consideration. The "equivalent halves" approach is probably the most desirable of the split-test procedures for estimating reliability. In a sense, it parallels the equivalent-forms method. Determining equivalence requires matching of pairs of items, guided by the original test blueprints or table of specifications. After the test is administered, a score for each of the equivalent halves is derived. A more efficient procedure that yields very similar results, at least for a teacher-made test, is the odd-even method. Here again, two scores are derived for each examinee, one from the odd-numbered items and one from the even-numbered items. This procedure has been followed with sample data from a 10-item test administered to 25 students; results are summarized in Table 14-3.

At this point the determination of reliability can take one of two directions. Let us look first at a correlational procedure for estimating reliability from half-test scores. We first determine the Pearson product-movement or Spearman rank-order correlation between the scores on the odd and even halves of the test. (Readers may refresh their memories about rank-order correlation by referring to Table 13-4.) For our example, the rank-order correlation was found to be 0.752. This correlation describes the relationship between scores on the halves of the test, but we are interested in the full-test reliability. We must, therefore, put the test, like Humpty Dumpty, back together again. The **Spearman–Brown formula** allows us to estimate the full-length test reliability. The Spearman–Brown formula is a succinct summary of the relationship of the number of items on a test and reliability. We can see that relationship in Figure 14-2. You can see that as the test is lengthened, the reliability increases. The lower the initial reliability, the greater the effect of lengthening the test. If the beginning reliability is good, for example, around 0.80, increasing length would not be necessary or probably practical. Other means to increase reliability are also available, such as removing "bad" items (refer to Chapter 9).

The general form of the Spearman–Brown formula is as follows:

$$r_{tt} = \frac{nr}{1 + (n - 1)r} \qquad (14\text{-}1)$$

**Table 14-3**  *Hypothetical Data Used in Estimating Reliability from the Single Administration of a Test*

| Student | Odd Items | | | | | Even Items | | | | | Odd Score | Even Score | Total Score |
|---|---|---|---|---|---|---|---|---|---|---|---|---|---|
| | 1 | 3 | 5 | 7 | 9 | 2 | 4 | 6 | 8 | 10 | | | |
| A | + | 0 | + | 0 | + | + | 0 | + | + | 0 | 3 | 3 | 6 |
| B | + | 0 | 0 | 0 | 0 | + | 0 | + | 0 | 0 | 1 | 2 | 3 |
| C | + | + | + | + | 0 | + | + | + | + | + | 4 | 5 | 9 |
| D | 0 | + | + | 0 | 0 | 0 | + | 0 | + | 0 | 2 | 2 | 4 |
| E | 0 | + | + | + | 0 | + | + | 0 | 0 | 0 | 3 | 2 | 5 |
| F | + | 0 | 0 | 0 | 0 | 0 | 0 | 0 | 0 | 0 | 1 | 0 | 1 |
| G | + | + | + | + | 0 | + | + | 0 | + | 0 | 4 | 3 | 7 |
| H | + | 0 | + | + | 0 | 0 | + | + | 0 | 0 | 3 | 2 | 5 |
| I | + | 0 | 0 | 0 | 0 | 0 | + | 0 | 0 | 0 | 1 | 1 | 2 |
| J | + | + | + | + | + | + | + | + | + | + | 5 | 5 | 10 |
| K | + | 0 | + | 0 | 0 | + | + | 0 | + | + | 2 | 4 | 6 |
| L | + | + | + | 0 | + | + | + | + | 0 | + | 4 | 4 | 8 |
| M | 0 | 0 | + | + | + | + | + | + | + | + | 0 | 0 | 0 |
| N | + | + | 0 | + | 0 | 0 | + | + | + | + | 3 | 4 | 7 |
| O | + | + | + | + | + | + | + | + | + | 0 | 5 | 4 | 9 |
| P | + | + | 0 | 0 | 0 | + | + | + | + | + | 2 | 5 | 7 |
| Q | + | + | + | 0 | 0 | + | + | 0 | 0 | 0 | 3 | 2 | 5 |
| R | + | 0 | 0 | + | 0 | + | 0 | + | 0 | 0 | 2 | 2 | 4 |
| S | + | 0 | 0 | 0 | + | + | 0 | 0 | 0 | 0 | 2 | 1 | 3 |
| T | 0 | 0 | 0 | 0 | 0 | + | 0 | 0 | 0 | 0 | 0 | 1 | 1 |
| U | + | + | 0 | + | + | + | + | + | 0 | 0 | 4 | 3 | 7 |
| V | + | + | 0 | 0 | 0 | + | + | + | 0 | 0 | 2 | 3 | 5 |
| W | 0 | + | 0 | 0 | 0 | + | 0 | 0 | 0 | 0 | 1 | 1 | 2 |
| X | + | + | 0 | 0 | + | + | 0 | + | 0 | + | 3 | 3 | 6 |
| Y | 0 | + | 0 | + | 0 | 0 | + | 0 | 0 | + | 2 | 2 | 4 |
| Nc | 19 | 15 | 11 | 10 | 7 | 18 | 16 | 13 | 9 | 8 | | | |
| $p$ | .76 | .60 | .44 | .40 | .28 | .72 | .64 | .52 | .26 | .21 | | | |
| $q$ | .24 | .40 | .56 | .60 | .72 | .28 | .36 | .48 | .64 | .68 | | | |
| $pq$ | .18 | .24 | .25 | .24 | .20 | .20 | .23 | .25 | .23 | .22 | | | |

$M_o = 2.48$    $M_e = 2.56$    $M_x = 5.04$    $\Sigma pq = 2.24$

$S_o^2 = 1.85$    $S_e^2 = 2.09$    $S_x^2 = 6.84$

$S_o = 1.36$    $S_e = 1.45$    $S_x = 2.62$

where

$n$ = the number of times the test is to be lengthened
$r$ = the original test reliability or correlation

In our example, we are trying to determine the full-test reliability if the length of the test was *doubled*. Equation 14-1 could be written as follows:

$$r_{tt} = \frac{2r_{oe}}{1 = r_{oe}} \tag{14-2}$$

where

$r_{oe}$ = the correlation between the odd and even halves of the test
$r_{oe}$ = 0.752

with

$$r_{tt} = \frac{2(0.752)}{1 = (0.752)} = \frac{1.504}{1.752} = 0.86$$

Obviously 0.86 is larger than 0.75. What does this tell us about which variable has a greater influence on test reliability? The length or number of items on the test is a very important factor. Assuming that most reliability coefficients over 0.70 are within an acceptable range, our obtained estimate of 0.86 would allow us to use this hypothetical test with a relatively high degree of confidence. The Spearman-Brown formula could also be used to estimate the effect of reducing the length of the test—for example, if we had a 100-item test with a reliability of 0.90. Responding to a 100-item test takes a long time. What would be our best estimate of the reliability if we dropped 50 items? The symbol $n$ in Equation 14-1 now becomes a decimal, in this case 0.50 because we are reducing the length of the test by 50 percent. Substituting in Equation 14-1, we would find that eliminating 50 items (being careful not to distort the content coverage) would yield a new reliability estimate of 0.82—quite a savings in student testing time. The Spearman–Brown is only an estimate of what is likely to happen, but empirical research strongly supports its usefulness and accuracy.

The Spearman–Brown formula—as expressed in Equations 14-1 and 14-2—really describes the effect of lengthening the test on reliability. Generally, as we increase the number of items we increase reliability. This assumes that the items added are equivalent to the original items in functions measured, difficulty level, and the like. One additional assumption of Equation 14-2 is that the standard deviations of the two halves of the test are about equal. Violating this assumption will lead to an overestimate of reliability. Although the overestimation is not extremely large—not more than 5 percent when one variance is 50 percent as large as the other—some

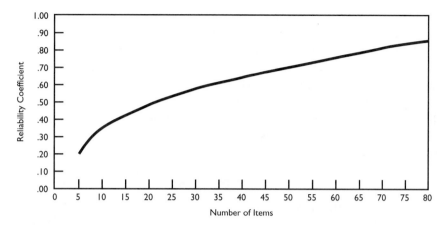

**Figure 14-2** *Relationship between test length and reliability*

error is introduced. Because of this tendency to overestimate, the relative inefficiency of rank-order correlation procedures with large groups, and the need to use the Spearman–Brown formula, a more direct method of estimating reliability from the halves of a test is suggested.

The following calculating formula, first described by John Flanagan (1937), should be used:

$$r_{tt} = 2\left(1 - \frac{S_o^2 + S_e^2}{S_x^2}\right) \tag{14-3}$$

where

$S_o^2$ and $S_e^2$ = the raw score variance on the odd and even halves of the test respectively,

and

$S_x^2$ = the variance of total test raw scores

Applying this formula to the data in Table 14-3 yields the following results:

$$r_{tt} = 2\left(1 - \frac{1.85 + 2.09}{6.84}\right) = 0.85$$

Our reliability estimate is almost identical to that derived by Equation 14-2, because the variances are not very discrepant. Equation 14-3 is really an estimate of the degree of equivalence between the two full-length tests, which are as similar as the two halves of one test are. Some test experts believe this represents a very reasonable estimate of reliability. Equation 14-3 is useful not only because of the less restrictive assumptions underlying its use but also because the variances involved in the formula can be estimated using the approximation formula of a standard deviation presented in Chapter 13 (see Equation 13-9 and Table 13-2). Another plus for this method is that it can be used with two test halves that have a mix of item types. For example, we might have taken our hypothetical final exam test and randomly divided it into two halves, each of which contained a 15-point essay question, four 3-point problems, 20 multiple-choice, 10 true-false, and 5 completion items. We could calculate two half-test scores and use Equation 14-3.

### Reliability Determined from Item Data (Internal Consistency)

Intuition suggests that if we want to determine whether or not the items in a test measure the same thing, we should examine item scores as well as examinee scores. A reliability-estimating procedure developed a long time ago by G. Frederic Kuder and Marion Richardson (1937) does just this. The usual **Kuder–Richardson formula** assumes, however, that the items in the test (a) are scored right or wrong, (b) are not significantly influenced by speed, and (c) measure a common factor. The last assumption may be critically important when we estimate the reliability of a classroom test, although recent research suggests that the method is quite robust, that is, violations of its assumptions do not seriously distort the results (Feldt & Qualls, 1996). In many instances, such tests are not homogeneous in content or learning outcome measured. Therefore, we must exercise some caution when applying either of the two following Kuder–Richardson formulas. The most frequently used Kuder–Richardson formula, number 20 (this is the same as Cronbach's Alpha [Cronbach, 1951], when items are scored dichotomously), can be expressed as follows:
where

$$r_{tt} = \left( \frac{k}{k-1} \right) \left( \frac{S_x^2 - \sum pq}{S_x^2} \right) \qquad ( \qquad (14\text{-}4)$$

$k$ = the number of items in the test
$p$ = proportion of examinees answering item correctly (or the proportion responding in a specified direction)
$q$ = $1 - p$
$S_x^2$ = the variance of the total test raw scores

Calculation of the term $pq$ can be facilitated by using columns 1 and 3 of the table in Appendix A. The term $p$ or $q$ can be entered in column 1 and the term $pq$ read directly from column 3. The term $pq$ represents the variance of an item. The items that measure the same thing are assumed to have fairly homogeneous difficulty levels and, therefore, variances. If items on a norm-referenced test all have difficulty levels of about 50 percent, a test will tend to be maximally reliable. The correction factor $(k/k-1)$ must be accepted on faith. Note, however, that if we have a small number of items, say 10, the correction can be relatively large compared with a situation in which we have 80 items. Applying Equation 14-4 to the hypothetical data in Table 14-3, we find that:

$$r_{tt} = \left( \frac{10}{10-1} \right) \left( \frac{6.84 - 2.24}{6.84} \right) = (1.11)(0.67) = 0.74$$

This value is noticeably lower than any other we have seen thus far. The discrepancy might be attributed to overestimation by the other methods or underestimation by $KR_{20}$ because of failure to meet assumptions. Inasmuch as $KR_{20}$ is a very precise method, that is, it considers actual item variances, it will be the accepted value. The item variances of classroom tests tend to be relatively similar, so we may be able to shortcut the actual calculation of the item variances. This can be done by using Kuder–Richardson formula 21. This formula assumes that the items all have the same difficulty level. $KR_{21}$ is written:

$$r_{tt} = \left( \frac{k}{k-1} \right) \left( 1 - \frac{M(k-M)}{kS_x^2} \right) \qquad ( \quad (14\text{-}5)$$

where

$k$ = the number of items on the test
$M$ = the mean of the total test raw scores
$S_x^2$ = the variance of the total test raw scores

Knowing only the number of items, mean, and variance (which can be approximated from Equation 13-9), we can calculate a reasonably precise estimate of reliability. Again using the data in Table 14-3, we find that:

$$r_{tt} = \left( \frac{10}{10-1} \right) \left( \frac{5.04(10 - 5.04)}{10(6.84)} \right) = 0.70$$

This reliability estimate, although close, is smaller than that derived from Equation 14-4 ($KR_{20}$). Such will be the case unless all of the test items are of the same difficulty level.

Joe Saupe (1961) has derived some very efficient estimates of $KR_{20}$ reliability. One of these, which he labels $R_{20}'$, can be expressed as follows:

$$R'_{20} = \left( \frac{k}{k-1} \right) \left( 1 - \frac{0.20k}{S_x^2} \right) \qquad (14\text{-}6)$$

Now all we need to know is the number of items and variance and we can estimate reliability with a high degree of efficiency and accuracy—if the number of items and the variance are reasonably large. This brief formula yields an estimate of reliability very close to those made previously:

$$R'_{20} = \left( \frac{10}{10-1} \right) \left( 1 - \frac{0.20(10)}{6.84} \right) = 0.79$$

Edward Cureton, Joseph Cook, Raymond Fischer, Stephen Laser, Norman Rockwell, and Jack Simmons (1973) provided another method of estimating internal consistency reliability that is useful to the classroom teacher. Their formula reads as follows:

$$r_{tt} = 1 - 0.043k \left( \frac{N}{\sum X_{U1/6} - \sum X_{L1/6}} \right)^2 \qquad (14\text{-}7)$$

where

| | |
|---|---|
| $k$ | = the total number of dichotomously scored items on the test |
| $N$ | = total number of subjects about whom we have data |
| $\sum X_{U1/6}$ | = the sum of the total scores for individuals in the upper one-sixth of the distribution |
| $\sum X_{L1/6}$ | = the sum of the total scores for individuals in the lower one-sixth of the distribution |

Recall that we used the terms $\sum X_{U1/6}$ and $\sum X_{L1/6}$ when estimating standard deviation in Chapter 13.

Using the data in Table 14-3, we find that Equation 14-7 gives us an estimate close to the others we have calculated:

$$r_u = 1 - 0.43(10) \left( \frac{20}{36-6} \right)^2 = 0.81$$

One-sixth of $N$ is 3.3, but because this is too few individuals on which to base an estimate we rounded to 4.

Faced with all these formulas, which one should a teacher select to analyze his or her tests? Most of the formulas presented in this section on reliability have been shown to yield highly similar results, so the decision will probably be based on familiarity with the formulas, computational ease, form of the data, or nature of the test. Taking all these factors into account, I recommend Flanagan's formula (Equation 14-3). The advantages are relative ease of calculation and the fact that items need *not* be scored right or wrong to justify its use, that is, you can use it with rating scales and essay items, or combinations of items with different point values. If you can meet the assumption, $KR_{21}$ is also a good bet.

## RELIABILITY OF CRITERION-REFERENCED MASTERY TESTS

Criterion-referenced or mastery tests are different than the usual objectives-based tests in that success is usually defined by whether or not a student met a particular performance standard (or criterion) or not. The decision is usually absolute: pass/fail, graduate/not graduate, promoted/not promoted, or met cutoff score/did not meet cutoff score.

The methods available to assess the reliability of such tests are cumbersome and require computer hardware and complex software. A simple "percent agreement" can suffice.

Consider the data in the 2 × 2 table in Figure 14-3. The letters in the cells represent the frequency of people so classified. The consistency of classification (A) is simply the proportion of examinees classified the same way on two administrations (see Equation 14-9).

$$A = (a + d)/N \qquad (14\text{-}9)$$

Reliability based on two administrations or forms can be approximated by two halves of the test or two different raters. If we look back at our table we can think of it now not as administration one and two, but as Half One and Half Two. A master or nonmaster classification requires a criterion—for example, the examinee must get 80 percent correct. In our half-test example, to be *consistently* classified as a master, a student would have had to gather 80 percent on Half One and 80 percent on Half Two. The halves could be equivalent or odd-even splits. The proportion $A = (a + d)/N$ is descriptively useful in and of itself.

Let's look at an example. But first we have to have a criterion. Using the data of Table 14-3 we will be generous and say that mastery equates to 60 percent (three of five correct) on each half. A student must get 60 percent on *both* halves of the test to get into cell "a," and less than 60 percent on *both* halves to get into cell "d." Classifying all 25 students in Table 14-3 yields the results in Table 14-4.

Summarizing our classifications we find the information in Figure 14-4. The proportion of agreements (Equation 14-9) $A = 19/25 = 0.76$. That's not too bad. Obviously, the higher the percentage, the better the consistency.

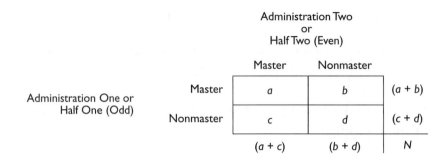

**Figure 14-3** *Two × two table*

**Table 14-4** *Classification of Half-Test Data of Table 14-3*

| | **Mastery Classification** | | | | **Mastery Classification** | | |
|---|---|---|---|---|---|---|---|
| **Student** | **Odd** | **Even** | **Cell** | **Student** | **Odd** | **Even** | **Cell** |
| A | Y | Y | a | N | Y | Y | a |
| B | N | N | d | O | Y | Y | a |
| C | Y | Y | a | P | N | Y | c |
| D | N | N | d | Q | Y | N | b |
| E | Y | N | b | R | N | N | d |
| F | N | N | d | S | N | N | d |
| G | Y | Y | a | T | N | N | d |
| H | Y | N | b | U | Y | Y | a |
| I | N | N | d | V | N | Y | c |
| J | Y | Y | a | W | N | N | d |
| K | N | Y | c | X | Y | Y | a |
| L | Y | Y | a | Y | N | N | d |
| M | N | N | d | | | | |

# RELIABILITY OF PERFORMANCE ASSESSMENTS

The reader is urged to review the section dealing with the scoring reliability and instrument reliability of writing samples in Chapter 8 as the problems presented with this type of assessment would generalize to almost any performance assessment. If the scoring of the performance assessment yields continuous scores (e.g., rating scale 1–5 over several dimensions), using a simple correlation between two scorers would suffice, such as, Spearman-rank or Pearson product-moment correlations (see Chapter 13). If a rubric is used for scoring, then looking at some percent of agreement

Even Half

|  | Master | Nonmaster | |
|---|---|---|---|
| **Odd Half** Master | 9 | 3 | 12 |
| Nonmaster | 3 | 10 | 13 |
| | 12 | 13 | 25 |

**Figure 14-4** *Classification summary in a two × two table*

Observer A

| | VG | MTS | MS | U | |
|---|---|---|---|---|---|
| **Observer B** VG | 7 | | | | 7 |
| MTS | | 5 | | | 5 |
| MS | | | 5 | | 5 |
| U | | 4 | 4 | 3 | 11 |
| | 7 | 9 | 9 | 3 | 28 Total |

would yield useful information. Following is an example for an analysis of collaborative group work in a speech class (Glatthorn, 1998, p. 56) using two observers, A and B.

| *Criterion Level* | *Behavior* |
|---|---|
| Very Good (VG) | Makes many useful contributions; facilitates group work |
| More Than Satisfactory (MTS) | Makes several contributions; no disruptions |
| Minimally Satisfactory (MS) | Makes a few contributions; disrupts occasionally |
| Unsatisfactory (U) | Does not contribute; often disrupts |

The frequency of agreement data from two observers is compared for a class of 28 students as follows:

The overall agreement seems to be pretty good at 71 percent (20/28), but Observer B seems to be a little hard and suggests that the two observers might want to review the criteria together. There are some very sophisticated statistical methods that can be used to examine reliability (e.g., generalizability theory), but they are outside the purview of this book. Suffice it to say that a classroom teacher can learn a lot about his or her scoring consistency by working with a colleague. It also is a good way to improve the scoring rubric.

# FACTORS INFLUENCING THE INTERPRETATION OF VALIDITY AND RELIABILITY

Actually, we can interpret validity and reliability coefficients at face value. We might say that a reliability coefficient of 0.80 can be loosely interpreted as meaning that 80 percent of a given score represents true "something"— that "something" is a question of validity. The other 20 percent is error. What kind of error depends on the reliability estimation method. If a teacher creates a test with reliability of 0.45, should it be thrown out? No! It can be added to other measures, thereby probably making the total quite reliable. We can also throw out some of the bad items as a result of item analysis (Chapter 9) and improve reliability.

If the coefficient were the correlation between a test and a criterion (criterion-related validity) we could again interpret it at face value. The larger the value, the stronger the relationship. Sometimes the correlation (validity) coefficient is squared and multiplied by 100, yielding a coefficient of determination. The correlation reflects the amount of common variance shared by the two measures. Obviously, the larger the common variance is, the stronger the relationship.

### Item Analysis

Research suggests that items in the middle range of difficulty on norm-referenced measures that show a high degree of discrimination should be selected for the final form of a test. Such a procedure helps ensure that the test has a high degree of internal-consistency reliability because items that are highly correlated with the total score are likely to be highly correlated with each other. This procedure assumes that an instructor has the opportunity to pre-test the items. Very frequently, however, this opportunity does not present itself. Two alternatives are available.

The first requires rescoring of the test *after* the item analysis has been completed. Although bad items cannot be rewritten, poor items can be eliminated. The analyzed and rescored test should be more reliable than the original. A large number of items cannot, of course, be eliminated. If this were allowed to happen, many important learning outcomes would not be measured, and the content validity of the test would be lowered. The rescoring procedure must be used with caution. My informal studies have indicated, in addition, that the correlations between original and rescored tests run in the high +0.90s, suggesting essentially unchanged ranking.

The second and more desirable alternative to pre-testing is to select items from a file set up over a period of time. When a particular item is used, the resulting item analysis data are recorded on a card. Such data are accumulated until the instructor has weeded out most of the poor items and can select items with a greater degree of confidence. The availability of an item file provides a great deal of flexibility for an instructor. The instructor can, for example, assemble parallel forms of a test with comparative ease. Another justification for developing an item file is that a teacher usually has small samples of students on whom to try each item. This limitation can be overcome by accumulating information on each item. The comparability of the groups and testing conditions is important in accumulating data. Such a subtle factor as the position of an item on a test can also be significant. Item analysis data, then, must be considered "relative," meaning that an instructor cannot expect an item to function in exactly the same way on two or more occasions.

### Variability of Scores

Heterogeneity refers to the range of talent or individual differences represented in the group with which validity or reliability study is undertaken. In general, heterogeneity has a greater effect on reliability than on validity. A great range of talent, however, increases the likelihood of detecting validity if it exists.

If a standard deviation is small, logically we will not be able to discriminate reliably among members of a homogeneous group. We have described reliability as the influence of error. Assume a specified amount of unsystematic error, and assume further that with error constant we find that Group A has a large standard deviation and Group B has a small standard deviation. If we estimate reliability by correlating two forms of a test, we would find that Group A has the larger reliability coefficient, whereas the amount of error is the same for both groups. Another example would be selecting only the top 20 percent of applicants based on a test score and the correlation of these scores with some job proficiency criterion (e.g., supervisor's ratings). The resulting validity coefficient would, of necessity, be low because of the restricted range of individual differences represented in the group. We need a method of expressing the reliability of a test independent of variability. This can be accomplished by using the standard error of measurement ($S_{em}$):

$$S_{em} = S_x\sqrt{1 - r_{tt}} \qquad (14\text{-}8)$$

The standard error of measurement theoretically represents an estimate of the standard deviation of the (unsystematic) errors obtained in repeated sampling with parallel forms of a test with the same subjects. In addition to serving as an index of reliability independent of group variability, the $S_{em}$ can be used to assist in interpreting test scores. The individual's score can then be conceived of as a band or interval rather than a point. A frequently used procedure is to establish "reasonable limits" (plus and minus), corresponding to two or three times the $S_{em}$, around an observed score. Let us consider a practical situation in which the use of the standard error of measurement can facilitate decision making with a test.

As a college admissions officer, you have required all applicants to take the Goetz Aptitude Test. You intend to select the freshman class, other things being equal, from the top half of the ability distribution. The "cutoff score" corresponds to a score of 70. Cheddar has a score of 65. On the basis of her academic record and recommendations, she appears to be someone who would greatly benefit from a college education. Because her test score did not equal or exceed the cutoff score, should she be rejected? No! We know that tests are fallible, that is, not perfectly accurate. Some errors of measurement are always present, and these errors sometimes cause scores to be higher or lower than they should be. We need to consider, then, the error of measurement in interpreting Cheddar's score. We might ask, "Is it possible that Cheddar's *true* score is higher than the cutoff point on the admissions test?" Such a question assumes that an observed test score comprises some true ability plus some error. Our task is to specify and evaluate the error component of the test score.

Let us assume that our Goetz Aptitude Test has a standard deviation of 20 and a reliability of 0.75. Using Equation 14-8 we find that $S_{em}$ is equal to 10. If we establish reasonable limits of $1S_{em}$ around Cheddar's observed score (65 plus and minus 10), we note that it would be quite possible for her to obtain a score above the cutoff score if tested again. We are, therefore, justified in including Cheddar in the pool of applicants from which we want to select the freshman class. A useful reference is presented in Table 14-5. This table, from an article by James Ricks (1956), presents the standard errors of measurement (Equation 14-8) for selected combinations of standard deviation values and reliability coefficients. For most purposes, it will be sufficiently accurate if the table is entered with values nearest the actual ones.

The standard error of measurement is useful not only for describing measurement consistency, but also for interpreting different scores for the same individual on different tests, or for different individuals on the same test.

### Speededness

One basis that can be used to classify a test is the extent to which speed influences scores. At one extreme are pure speed tests, whose items are easy and all of approximately equal difficulty. At the other extreme are power tests. The items in a power test are generally arranged in increasing

**Table 14-5** *Standard Errors of Measurement for Given Values of Reliability Coefficient and Standard Deviation*

| SD | Reliability Coefficient | | | | | |
|----|------|------|------|------|------|------|
|    | .95 | .90 | .85 | .80 | .75 | .70 |
| 30 | 6.7 | 9.5 | 11.6 | 13.4 | 15.0 | 16.4 |
| 28 | 6.3 | 8.9 | 10.8 | 12.5 | 14.0 | 15.3 |
| 26 | 5.8 | 8.2 | 10.1 | 11.6 | 13.0 | 14.2 |
| 24 | 5.4 | 7.6 | 9.3 | 10.7 | 12.0 | 13.1 |
| 22 | 4.9 | 7.0 | 8.5 | 9.8 | 11.0 | 12.0 |
| 20 | 4.5 | 6.3 | 7.7 | 8.9 | 10.0 | 11.0 |
| 18 | 4.0 | 5.7 | 7.0 | 8.0 | 9.0 | 9.9 |
| 16 | 3.6 | 5.1 | 6.2 | 7.2 | 8.0 | 8.8 |
| 14 | 3.1 | 4.4 | 5.4 | 6.3 | 7.0 | 7.7 |
| 12 | 2.7 | 3.8 | 4.6 | 5.4 | 6.0 | 6.6 |
| 10 | 2.2 | 3.2 | 3.9 | 4.5 | 5.0 | 5.6 |
| 8 | 1.8 | 2.5 | 3.1 | 3.6 | 4.0 | 4.4 |
| 6 | 1.3 | 1.9 | 2.3 | 2.7 | 3.0 | 3.3 |
| 4 | .9 | 1.3 | 1.5 | 1.8 | 2.0 | 2.2 |
| 2 | .4 | .6 | .8 | .9 | 1.0 | 1.1 |

*Source: Test Service Bulletin 50* (1956). Published by the Psychological Corporation, San Antonio, TX.

order of difficulty. Perfect scores on power tests are unlikely even with the most generous time limits. The selection of a reliability-estimating technique will be influenced by the extent to which speed affects the scores. A test user or developer must first decide whether he or she wants speed of response to have a significant influence on the scores, and then select an appropriate reliability-estimating technique with a pure speed test. The maximum difference between the odd and even scores would be one, assuming that if an item is attempted there is a very high likelihood that it will be answered correctly. The half-test scores would obviously be highly correlated and an overestimate of reliability would result. The appropriate procedure is to use equivalent forms, or perhaps separately timed halves.

**Guessing**

Guessing was used at the beginning of this chapter as an example of unsystematic error that could adversely affect any assessment's reliability, and if reliability is adversely influenced validity will be as well because the scores and the interpretation of those scores will be distorted relative to the original intent. Students tend to guess on questions or tasks that are difficult.

The questions can be difficult because the student doesn't have the requisite knowledge or skill or can't understand or misunderstands the question because of structural flaws in the question. If the question is free of faults, then a guess can be acceptable. A less knowledgeable or skillful student responding on a reliable measure will not artificially inflate his or her score by guessing. The bottom line is to make sure you have a high-quality instrument. Then guessing won't be a problem.

### Objectivity of Scoring

It's a simple notion, but if two raters or scorers can't agree on the value or correctness of a response, then how can the assessment mean much to either the student or teacher? Using collaboratively created scoring rubrics, for example, in a writing assessment, together with practice or training can yield reliable evaluations. But the only way to know if you have objectivity among raters is to examine interrater agreement.

Another dimension of objectivity relates to the "correctness" of the answers. If we can't agree that "this" answer is the correct or best one or that this is the process to be followed, then we don't have *objectivity*, and reliability and validity have been distorted, if not destroyed.

### Commonality of Examinee Experiences

If students have not had an equal opportunity to learn or if they did not bring a similar experiential background with them to the assessment, then the scores won't mean the same thing for all individuals. An example is that fall assessments with standardized achievement batteries (before instruction) are less reliable than spring assessments (after instruction). The opportunity-to-learn variable is central to establishing instructional validity. We should start systematically investigating it rather than assuming its presence. Think of the commonality variable in conjunction with the norms on a standardized test. If students making up the norms group did not have that common experience then the normative data will be less meaningful. Again, in the context of standardized testing, if the importance of the results is not the same for all examinees, motivation to perform well has a differential effect and the scores will have differential meaning.

### Quality of Instruments

Obviously, poor-quality information-collecting devices will yield inferior data. Failure to adhere to technical and commonsense standards in instrument development and application can result in misleading inferences being made about students, schools, and systems. These standards can range from simple subject-predicate agreement or irrelevant cues in test questions to failure to find interrater agreement in scoring a performance assessment. Awkward arrangement of questions, poor directions for administration, and inappropriate level vocabulary are additional factors that can distort the meaning of information.

### Assessment Environment

The physical and psychological state of the examinee can have powerful effects on performance. Distractions might differentially affect students. Failure to adhere to time limits on a standardized measure will compromise not only the applicability of the norms about the raw meaning of resulting scores themselves. Whenever we have a "differential" effect on some variable (i.e., it affects different students in different ways), we may have a reliability and validity problem.

If students don't know how to record their answers or what they should do about guessing, this can adversely affect results. A good example is "guessers" versus "omitters." A complete record of answers would be available for individuals who attempted every item, whereas only a partial picture would be reflected from the omitters. You then would be looking at incomplete pictures, and you cannot be sure what the blanks mean.

## VALIDITY AND RELIABILITY KNOWLEDGES AND SKILLS NEEDED BY CLASSROOM TEACHERS

What do I as a classroom teacher need to know about validity and reliability—just enough to "appreciate" their importance? Everyone should have some growth experiences—for example, marriage, being a parent, angioplasty, and so on. Calculating a reliability coefficient on your own test and having a colleague "key" the questions on one of your tests represent two other growth experiences. It really doesn't take that much effort to calculate an internal consistency coefficient (split-half or Kuder–Richardson formula 21). The process itself should give you insight into what it means to measure consistently and what kinds of questions seem to work best. It is also enlightening to grapple with the problem of content validity. This can be done several ways. You could ask a colleague to match your questions with your objectives or place them in your table of specifications. Another approach is to pre- and post-test and find which items (and objectives) seem most sensitive to instruction. Sitting and listening to students critique assessments can, however, be the best source of information about how good evaluations really are. *Reliability and validity are concerned with the consistency and accuracy of the inferences we make about students from our assessment data.*

You may have perceived this chapter as a bit overwhelming. But give it a chance. Read and study it a couple more times. Outline the major points. The content is *that* important, just as the content of any test is *that* important.

# CASE STUDY

## Validity

The assessment of validity is not really something that's left to a late date in instrument development. It is an ongoing process and begins with the very first objective. But sometimes it is useful to periodically stop and take a formal look at validity.

The items of a test must measure the intended instructional objectives. We call this test characteristic *relevance*, and it is directly related to test validity. It is also hoped that the intended objectives are, in fact, the ones implemented in the classroom. Test constructors must use their best professional judgment in evaluating the match between item and objective. For a classroom test the teacher is by far the most credible judge. Other teachers who are responsible for a particular course could serve as "expert witnesses" relative to *relevance*.

Another important dimension of content validity relates to the sampling of outcomes or behaviors for a unit or course. To a great extent the parameters of these outcomes are described by the test blueprint or table of specifications.

Having another teacher try to classify your items into your table of specifications (or "key" the items) can be a most enlightening and humbling experience. As an exercise in investigating content validity, figure out some way to compare the classifications of our sample 21 Reading Education midterm exam questions in Table 14-6, and those by a colleague-expert judge. The original items were presented in the case study applications for Chapter 7. Colleague classifications were in terms of one of the 40 cells ($C_1 - C_{40}$) in the table of specifications. The colleague classifications were as follows:

| Item | Cell | Item | Cell |
|------|------|------|------|
| 1 | 1 | 12 | 24 |
| 2 | 1 | 13 | 5 |
| 3 | 11 | 14 | 5 |
| 4 | 4 | 15 | 26 |
| 5 | 12 | 16 | 16 |
| 6 | 2 | 17 | 7 |
| 7 | 23 | 18 | 8 |
| 8 | 14 | 19 | 8 |
| 9 | 4 | 20 | 20 |
| 10 | 24 | 21 | 13 |
| 11 | 24 | | |

**Table 14-6** *Original Classification of 21 Reading Education Midterm Exam Questions*

| Content | Knowledge | Behavioral Outcome Comprehension | Application | Analysis | Total |
|---|---|---|---|---|---|
| Reflection | 4 $C_1$ | 1 2 3 $C_{11}$ | $C_{21}$ | $C_{31}$ | 4 |
| Emerging Literacy | 6 $C_2$ | 5 $C_{12}$ | $C_{22}$ | $C_{32}$ | 2 |
| LEA | $C_3$ | $C_{13}$ | $C_{23}$ | 7 $C_{33}$ | 1 |
| Decoding Strategies | 9 $C_4$ | 8 $C_{14}$ | 10 11 12 $C_{24}$ | $C_{34}$ | 5 |
| Comprehension Strategies | 13 14 $C_5$ | 21 $C_{15}$ | $C_{25}$ | $C_{35}$ | 3 |
| Discussion Strategies | $C_6$ | $C_{16}$ | 15 16 $C_{26}$ | $C_{36}$ | 2 |
| Basal Reader | 17 $C_7$ | $C_{17}$ | $C_{27}$ | $C_{37}$ | 1 |
| Exceptional Children | 18 19 $C_8$ | $C_{18}$ | $C_{28}$ | $C_{38}$ | 2 |
| Bilingual Learners | $C_9$ | $C_{19}$ | $C_{29}$ | $C_{39}$ | 0 |
| Evaluation | $C_{10}$ | 20 $C_{20}$ | $C_{30}$ | $C_{40}$ | 1 |
| Total | 8 | 7 | 5 | 1 | 21 |

The resulting analysis reflects on the content validity of the assessment.

One of the methods for assessing test validity requires correlating test scores with some relevant external criterion. It would be hoped that scores on our Reading Education midterm exam (and final exam and lesson plan evaluation as well) would be related to classroom teaching performance. The form in Table 14-7 was completed by a trained student-teaching supervisor for each of our 18 reading education students midway through their student teaching experience. The form is an adaptation of the *Teacher Performance Assessment Instrument* used with beginning teachers in the state of Georgia. There was a timeframe of approximately 18 months between when the midterm exam was administered and the teaching performance assessments were made. To check on criterion-related validity, correlate the following pairs of scores. Use the rank-order correlation method. The Assessment of Teaching Performance (ATP) total scores were derived using the following scheme: Unacceptable = 0 points, Needs Improvement = 1 point, Acceptable = 2 points, and Excellent = 3 points. See Millman and Darling-Hammond (1990) for an excellent collection of readings about teacher evaluation.

| Student | Midterm Exam | ATP |
|---|---|---|
| 1 | 47 | 30 |
| 2 | 58 | 48 |
| 3 | 58 | 51 |
| 4 | 52 | 28 |
| 5 | 51 | 53 |
| 6 | 55 | 49 |
| 7 | 58 | 45 |
| 8 | 58 | 57 |
| 9 | 55 | 52 |
| 10 | 59 | 54 |
| 11 | 57 | 54 |
| 12 | 62 | 55 |
| 13 | 68 | 71 |
| 14 | 52 | 46 |
| 15 | 57 | 61 |
| 16 | 62 | 52 |
| 17 | 65 | 65 |
| 18 | 62 | 59 |

## Reliability

We have now progressed from objectives to a table of specifications to item construction to administration and data summary and, finally, to item analysis. We next need to assess the reliability of the Reading Education midterm exam before we can have any confidence in using the results. Since a reliability estimate based on multiple administrations of our midterm is not practical, the focus must be on one of the single administration internal consistency estimating methods. Kuder–Richardson formula 20 is the most accurate and frequently reported index of internal consistency. It will be used in this exercise. Refer back to the item data contained in the table in the case study application of Chapter 9. Let us assume that these 21 items represent an intact test. Use the data from *all* 18 examinees for these 21 items to calculate $KR_{20}$ (Equation 14-4). In addition, for fun and comparative purposes, also calculate $KR_{21}$ (Equation 14-5). *Hint:* You will obviously have to score the 21-item test for each student; therefore, refer back to the beginning of the Chapter 9 case study application for the scoring key. In that same regard you also will need the $p$ (difficulty) values generated for those 21 items in the case study for Chapter 9.

**Table 14-7** *Assessment of Teaching Performance*

| | Evaluation | | | |
|---|---|---|---|---|
| Task | Unacceptable | Needs Improvement | Acceptable | Excellent |
| 1. Specifies or selects learner objectives for lessons. | U | NI | A | E |
| 2. Creates or selects learner activities. | U | NI | A | E |
| 3. Creates or selects material and/or media. | U | NI | A | E |
| 4. Plans activities and/or assignments which take into account learner differences. | U | NI | A | E |
| 5. Creates or selects procedures or materials for assessing learner performance on objectives. | U | NI | A | E |
| 6. Uses instructional time effectively. | U | NI | A | E |
| 7. Provides a physical environment that is conducive to learning. | U | NI | A | E |
| 8. Uses acceptable written expression with learners. | U | NI | A | E |
| 9. Uses acceptable oral expression. | U | NI | A | E |
| 10. Demonstrates command of subject matter on reading education. | U | NI | A | E |
| 11. Uses instructional methods acceptably. | U | NI | A | E |
| 12. Matches instruction to learners. | U | NI | A | E |
| 13. Uses instructional aids and materials during the lesson observed. | U | NI | A | E |
| 14. Implements activities in a logical sequence. | U | NI | A | E |
| 15. Gives or clarifies explanations related to lesson content. | U | NI | A | E |
| 16. Uses learner responses or questions regarding lesson content. | U | NI | A | E |
| 17. Provides information to learners about their progress throughout the lesson. | U | NI | A | E |
| 18. Communicates personal enthusiasm. | U | NI | A | E |

**Table 14-7** *Continued*

| Task | Unacceptable | Needs Improvement | Acceptable | Excellent |
|------|:------------:|:-----------------:|:----------:|:---------:|
| | | **Evaluation** | | |
| 19. Stimulates learner interest. | U | NI | A | E |
| 20. Demonstrates warmth and friendliness. | U | NI | A | E |
| 21. Helps learners develop positive self-concepts. | U | NI | A | E |
| 22. Maintains learner involvement in instruction. | U | NI | A | E |
| 23. Redirects learners who are off-task. | U | NI | A | E |
| 24. Communicates clear expectations about behavior. | U | NI | A | E |
| 25. Manages disruptive behavior. | U | NI | A | E |

Now for the ultimate measure of total commitment to the exploration of single administration test reliability alternatives. Apply Equations 14-2, 14-3, 14-6, and 14-7. When all the data have been collected, try your hand at an interpretive synthesis of these coefficients.

## Content Review Statements

**1.** Test validity should be evaluated by the intent of testing and the use(s) to which the data are to be put.

**2.** A test is not valid or invalid in general but, rather, is valid or invalid for a particular criterion in a particular situation with a particular group for a particular interpretation.

**3.** Content validity involves how well the items on a test sample a defined universe of tasks.

**4.** A chief problem in establishing validity is defining and securing a reliable measure of a relevant criterion.

5. External evidence of validity involves the ability of a test to estimate, usually through the use of correlational procedures, an individual's status in relation to some relevant criterion.

6. Correlations between test and criterion data that were gathered at about the same time or later are called *validity coefficients*.

7. Validity involves the degree to which we can infer from a test score whether or not an individual possesses some hypothetical trait or characteristic.

8. Content validity relies on the proper delineation of the behaviors to be assessed and can be judged by the table of specifications.

9. Establishing validity is a process of gathering evidence.

10. Expectancy tables are useful ways of interpreting validity.

11. Evidence of instrument validity can be examined by noting
    a. Differences between groups assumed or known to differ in relation to the construct or trait in question.
    b. Changes in performances as a result of treatment related to the construct.
    c. Correlations with other reliable and valid measures of the construct.
    d. The degree to which the items on the test tend to measure the same thing.
    e. The factors that influence the test-taking performance itself.
    f. Examining the consequences of using the instrument.

12. Curricular validity can be established by correlating the instructional objectives and instructional materials.

13. Instructional validity of a test must rest on the demonstrated implementation of objectives-based teaching.

14. Educational and psychological tests must always be considered fallible measuring instruments because of the influence of many kinds of errors, primarily involving sampling of behaviors, examinee instability, and scoring.

15. Unsystematic errors—for example, guessing—fluctuate both within and between testing situations and primarily tend to reduce test reliability.

16. Systematic errors—for example, extending test administration time, yielding inflated scores—are consistent and primarily tend to affect test validity.

17. Test reliability generally involves consistency in measurement with different sets of items, examinees, examiners, occasions, or scorers.

18. In general, if a test is valid, it is also reliable; however, the converse is not always true.

19. Test-retest reliability requires administering the same test on two different occasions and correlating the results.

20. Equivalent-forms reliability is established by correlating scores on two forms of a test constructed from the same table of specifications.

21. Internal-consistency reliability can be estimated by correlating the score on two halves of a test and applying the Spearman–Brown formula, one of the Kuder–Richardson formulas, or one of a number of other estimating formulas.

22. Length, objectivity, and mental functions measured are three factors that significantly influence test reliability.

23. Kuder–Richardson reliability coefficients estimated from speeded tests tend to be spuriously inflated.

24. Estimating internal-consistency reliability with Kuder–Richardson formula 21 requires only knowledge of the mean, variance, and number of items, if the items are dichotomously scored.

25. If the range of item difficulties on a test is large, Kuder–Richardson formula 21 can yield a low reliability estimate reflecting lack of item homogeneity.

26. The standard error of measurement is a general estimate of the magnitude of unsystematic errors expressed in actual test-score units.

27. Multiplying the standard deviation of test scores by the square root of the difference between the reliability coefficient and unity will provide an estimate of the standard error of measurement.

28. In general, tests composed of items that measure similar content or mental functions tend to have higher reliabilities than those that measure dissimilar functions.

29. Validity is like having all your shots hit the *center of the target*.

30. Reliability is like having all your shots hit in *about the same area*.

31. Reliability and validity factors influencing the interpretations of scores as performances include the

    a. range of talent in the group.

    b. guessing.

    c. nature and "goodness" of the items.

    d. length of the assessment.

    e. quality of the instrument.

    f. influence of speed of response.

    g. opportunity to learn and commonality of background of students.

    h. objectivity of scoring.

    i. quality of the assessment environment.

---

## SPECULATIONS

1. Why are there so many different ways to estimate test validity?

2. Is one kind of validity more important than another?

3. How would you demonstrate the validity of a test you had developed?

4. What are some reasons why a test and a criterion may *not* be related?

5. Describe ways in which an "expectancy table" could be used in this class.

6. Why is it logical that a test can be reliable without being valid, but not vice versa?

7. What is the relationship of item analysis to reliability?

8. Would you use different procedures to determine the validity of a criterion-referenced test versus a norm-referenced test? If yes, how would the methods be different?

9. Are the phrases "valid test" and "valid interpretation" equivalent? Why or why not?

10. If a commercial test publisher said their scholastic ability test had high validity, what kinds of questions would you ask? What questions would you ask in response to the same claim for an achievement battery?

**11.** What are some ways that you might demonstrate instructional, curricular, and consequential validity?

**12.** Why are there so many different ways to estimate test reliability?

**13.** What are the factors that can influence measurement reliability?

**14.** How would you demonstrate the reliability of a test you had developed?

**15.** Describe the many different ways the concept of "error" influences tests and measurements.

**16.** Do the reliability coefficient and standard error of measurement tell us different things about a test? If yes, what? If no, why?

**17.** Why can humans not live by reliability alone?

**18.** What do Humpty Dumpty and uncorrected split-half reliability coefficients have in common?

**19.** How does item analysis influence reliability?

**20.** What are some possible interpretations of the statement, "My mother-in-law is 99 percent reliable"?

## Suggested Readings

American Educational Research Association, American Psychological Association, & National Council on Measurement in Education. (1999). *Standards for educational and psychological testing.* Washington, DC: American Psychological Association. Chapter 1, "Validity," provides an overview of the primary and secondary technical validity standards for published tests. Chapter 2, "Reliability and Errors in Measurement," contains a discussion of the primary and secondary standards for test reliability.

Crocker, L., & Algina, J. (1986). *Introduction to classical and modern test theory.* New York: Holt, Rinehart, & Winston.

Cronbach, L. J. (1971). Test validation. In R. L. Thorndike (Ed.), *Educational measurement* (2nd ed). Washington, DC: American Council on Education. See Chapter 14. Intended for intermediate and advanced students, this chapter contains the seminal thinking on the topic of validity of one of the nation's foremost experts. Rather than approaching the validation of the test per se, Cronbach describes methods useful in validating interpretations of data arising from specified procedures.

Glatthorn, A. A. (1998). *Performance assessment and standards-based curricula: The achievement cycle.* Larchmont, N.Y.: Eye on Education.

Helmstadter, G. C. (1964). *Principles of psychological measurement.* New York: Appleton-Century-Crofts. Chapters 4, 5, and 6 contain some of the most readable discussions of content, criterion-related, and construct validity available. The presentations are simultaneously brief and technically correct.

Mehrens, W. A., & Lehmann, I. J. (1987). *Using standardized tests in education* (4th ed.). New York: Longman. Chapter 3, "Reliability," introduces a little elementary classical test theory.

Messick, S. (1989). Validity. In R. L. Linn (Ed.), *Educational measurement* (3rd ed.). New York: Macmillan. Lots of philosophy and theory. Excellent for the advanced student in search of an understanding of construct validity.

Sax, G. (1997). *Principles of educational psychological measurement and evaluation* (4th ed.). Belmont, CA: Wadsworth. Chapter 9, "The Reliability of Measurements," is current, comprehensive, and readable.

# PART Six

# Applications of Assessment Data

*Beverly's Journal* _____

It seems that the newspaper every night and my professional journals every issue carry articles about standardized testing. They are everywhere! They can be useful, but we probably overdo it a little. Let's not let the testing get in the way of teaching and learning.

I don't know how many grades I have given over the years, but it's been a bunch. Although there is a strong element of subjectivity in grading, and one is called upon to make value judgments (that's part of what we get paid to do), the process can be quite objective.

Over 26 years of teaching! I know I'm older, but hopefully wiser.

# 15

# Standardized Norm- and Criterion-Referenced Measures

## FOCUS CONCEPTS AND KEY TERMS FOR STUDY

**Achievement Test**

**Aptitude Test**

**Diagnostic Test**

*Mental Measurements Yearbook*

**NAEP**

**Non-Standardized Test**

**Out-of-Level Testing**

**Readiness Test**

**Specific Subject Test**

**Standardized Test**

**Survey-Battery Test**

**Test Purchaser Qualifications**

---

## STANDARDS ALERT

### Standard 13.1    Consequences of Testing

When educational testing programs are mandated by school, district, state or other authorities, the ways in which test results are intended to be used should be clearly described. It is the responsibility of those who mandate the use of tests to monitor their impact and to identify and minimize potential negative consequences. Consequences resulting from the uses of the test, both intended and unintended, should also be examined by the test user.

### Taking It to the Classroom

There are potential negative consequences unless school- or systemwide assessment programs are in place. These include (a) narrowing the curriculum, (b) overemphasis and inappropriate emphasis on test-taking practices to the exclusion of instructionally relevant practice, and (c) excluding qualified students from programs or graduation.

---

Reprinted with permission from the *Standards for Educational and Psychological Testing*. Copyright © 1999 by the American Educational Research Association, the American Psychological Association, and the National Council on Measurement in Education.

Standardized tests have maintained their popularity over many decades because of their convenience and generally high technical quality. Standardized tests are constructed by measurement and content experts. These kinds of measurements provide methods for obtaining samples of behaviors under uniform conditions, that is, a fixed set of questions is administered with the same set of directions and timing constraints. In addition, the scoring procedure is carefully delineated, monitored, and controlled. In most cases scoring is done by the publisher using optical scoring hardware and software. A standardized test usually has been administered to a norm or standardization group so that a person's performance can be interpreted by comparing it to the performance of others. The test is then considered norm-referenced. Criterion-referenced tests can also be standardized.

## CLASSIFICATION OF STANDARDIZED TESTS

Standardized tests can be classified in many ways. In Chapter 6 we noted that we could use the method of administration as a basis for classifying tests. Tests, therefore, can be considered oral, written, or behavioral. Tests can be administered to large groups by a single administrator or on a one-examinee/one-examiner basis. Educational measures can also be used to gather data on an individual's maximum performance or typical performance—maximum efforts being expected on achievement and aptitude tests and typical responses on personality measures. Think about the purposes or uses to which the information is to be put rather than cogitate about the methods of classifying tests.

A typical set of "use categories" has been presented by Bill Mehrens and Irv Lehmann (1987). They describe how tests can be used to assist in making *instructional, guidance, administrative*, and *research* decisions (see Table 15-1).

Different kinds of tests can be used to provide relevant information for making these four kinds of decisions. Achievement tests or assessments of an individual's status compared with a particular set of instructional, training, or educational objectives can be relevant for all four purposes. Achievement tests can be classified as diagnostic, single-subject, or battery. A diagnostic test is administered to isolate specific weaknesses in a restricted range of achievement and skill development in a subject area. Single-subject tests measure specialized areas included in the curriculum. Separate tests are available in nearly every subject at appropriate grade levels. In some respects, a battery is a collection of single-subject tests. Achievement tests measure the effects of formal educational experiences.

A clear distinction between aptitude (especially academic aptitude) tests and achievement tests is sometimes difficult to make because both can be influenced by formal educational experience, but aptitude measures (including readiness tests) are administered after the fact. There are differences in what each type of test asks students to do, however. According to Charles Hopkins and Richard Antes (1990), **achievement tests** measure (a) the effects of special programs, (b) the effects of a relatively standardized set of experiences, (c) the effects of learning that occur under partially known and controlled conditions, and (d) what the individual student can do at a given point in time. **Aptitude tests**, on the other hand, tend to measure or predict (a) the effects of the cumulative influence of experiences, (b) the effects of learning under relatively uncontrolled and unknown conditions, and (c) the future behavior, achievements, or performance of individuals or groups. Aptitude tests include scholastic aptitude tests, general mental ability tests, intelligence tests, multi-aptitude tests, or specific aptitude tests used to predict success in general academics, a subject, or a special occupational area. They measure students' out-of-school abilities, problem-solving skills, and abilities developed as a result of general experience. Aptitude batteries sometimes include combinations and paper-and-pencil cognitive items along with psychomotor tasks such as assessments of finger dexterity and hand-eye coordination. Scholastic aptitude tests are often contrasted with group or individual intelligence tests (e.g., *Wechsler Intelligence Scale for Children*, Third Edition) (Wechsler, 1991). There are similarities in form and content, but the major difference between these tests is the greater variety of abilities sampled by intelligence tests.

Affective, interest, personality, and attitude inventories generally survey affective variables related to mental health, self-esteem, life adjustment, and career, vocational, and academic interests and orientations.

### Types of Tests and Decision Making

The relationship between type of test and decision-making purpose is also summarized in Table 15-1, taken from a book on standardization testing authored by Bill Mehrens and Irv Lehmann (1987). One of the first things you will note is that in many instances the jury is still out on the applicability of certain kinds of tests in certain situations. Information requirements must be based on the requirements of the decision to be made. The interest, personality, and attitude measures could logically be combined into an "affective" category (see Chapter 12). The greatest proportion of test uses relates to individual student evaluation, the diagnosis of strengths and weaknesses, instructional program planning, and the measurement of growth.

The rest of this chapter focuses on achievement tests because these represent the major kinds of tests that local school personnel are most likely to use. Those readers interested in a more comprehensive overview of standardized tests are referred to Lee J. Cronbach (1990), Anne Anastasi (1988), or Gilbert Sax (1997).

## APPLICATIONS OF STANDARDIZED ACHIEVEMENT TESTS

Educational achievement has been defined as the extent to which specified instructional objectives are attained. Achievement tests, then, provide evidence about a student's status or level of learning. They may deal with knowledge of facts and principles and the ability to apply these facts and principles in complex and usually lifelike situations.

Achievement tests hold a relatively unique position among the many types of educational and psychological tests. Measures of intelligence, personality, and the like deal with "constructs." We hypothesize and infer the presence of the construct from the responses to the instrument. Thus we have only one indirect evidence of its nature. In assessing an achievement

**Table 15-1**  *Purposes of Standardized Tests\**

| Purposes | Aptitude | Achievement | Interest | Personality | Attitude |
|---|---|---|---|---|---|
| **Instructional** | | | | | |
| Evaluation of learning outcomes | x | x | ? | ? | |
| Evaluation of teaching | x | x | | | |
| Evaluation of curriculum | x | x | ? | | ? |
| Learning diagnosis | x | x | | | |
| Differential assignments within class | x | x | ? | ? | ? |
| Grading | ? | ? | | | |
| Motivation | | ? | | | x |
| **Guidance** | | | | | |
| Occupational | x | x | x | x | x |
| Educational | x | x | ? | ? | x |
| Personal | ? | ? | x | x | x |
| **Administrative** | | | | | |
| Selection | x | x | ? | | |
| Classification | x | x | x | | |
| Placement | x | x | ? | | |
| Public relations (information) | x | x | ? | | |
| Curriculum planning and evaluation | x | x | | | |
| Evaluating teachers | ? | ? | | ? | |
| Providing information for outside agencies | x | x | | | |
| Grading | ? | ? | | | |
| **Research** | x | x | x | x | x |

\* "x" indicates that a test can and should be used for that purpose. "?" indicates that there is some debate about whether or not a test can serve that purpose.

*Source: Using Standardized Tests in Education* by William A. Mehrens & Irvin J. Lehmann. Copyright © 1987 by Longman Publishing Group. Used by permission of the authors.

behavior, we attempt to measure a sample of the behavior itself; the evidence is therefore more direct.

Achievement test data can be applied in a variety of ways by teachers, principals, and other administrative and supervisory personnel. The late Walter W. Cook identified 15 major functions served by achievement tests (Cook, 1951, p. 36). According to Cook, achievement tests direct curriculum emphasis by

1. Focusing attention on as many of the important ultimate objectives of education as possible.
2. Clarifying educational objectives to teachers and students.
3. Determining elements of strength and weakness in the instructional program of the school.
4. Discovering inadequacies in curriculum content and organization.

Achievement tests also, according to Cook, provide for educational guidance of students by

5. Providing a basis for predicting individual student achievement in each learning area.
6. Serving as a basis for the preliminary grouping of all students in each learning area.
7. Discovering special aptitudes and disabilities.
8. Determining the difficulty of material a student can profitably read.
9. Determining the level of problem-solving ability in various areas.
10. Enabling students to think of their achievements in objective terms.
11. Giving students satisfaction for the progress they make, rather than for the relative level of achievement they attain.
12. Enabling students to compete with their past performance records.
13. Measuring achievement objectively by accepted educational standards, rather than by the subjective appraisal of teachers.
14. Enabling teachers to discover the areas in which they need supervisory aid.
15. Providing the administrative and supervisory staff an overall measure of the effectiveness of the school organization and of the prevailing administrative and supervisory policies.

The foregoing functions are those primarily served by comprehensive batteries. Such batteries have limited value in planning the instructional programs of individual students or identifying individual strengths and weaknesses. They are useful in making intraindividual and interindividual comparisons across broad subject-matter areas and identifying areas in which more focused testing would prove informative. Although the lack of curriculum detail is a drawback, norm-referenced interpretations of strengths and weaknesses are a potential positive contribution of batteries.

With increasing frequency, test publishers are offering custom-made tests created to the specifications of a local or state school system. Often, however, custom-made tests tend to be reconfigurations of the company's already existing tests or a selection of questions from their item banks.

# TYPES OF STANDARDIZED ACHIEVEMENT TESTS

There are three general types of standardized achievement tests. The first is the *survey battery*, which consists of a group of individual subject-matter tests designated for use at particular levels. The second category is the *specific subject or area test*. The third category is the *diagnostic test*, which is usually administered when a survey battery or specific subject test indicates substandard performance. Its purpose is to diagnose the area or areas of weakness so that remedial instruction can be instituted. Following are brief discussions of these three categories of standardized achievement tests, accompanied by descriptions of representative tests of each type.

### Survey Batteries

Comprehensive survey achievement batteries are the mainstay of school testing, providing valuable information about the effectiveness of various instructional programs. During the past two or three decades, the quality of achievement batteries has significantly improved, particularly in the learning outcomes measured and the quality of normative data made available to facilitate interpretation.

The content of a battery will, of course, vary according to the level of student achievement being measured. Despite being fairly broad in coverage, they are still significantly narrower than most school curricula. We teach many more things than the tests test. In addition, commercial test publishers are in the business of making money and they must therefore market instruments that have the greatest appeal to potential purchasers. One way of increasing that general appeal is to include items that tap objectives common to a large number of curricula. Using a "common denominator" guideline for objectives tested obviously narrows the range of outcomes assessed. Let the potential user beware of tests claiming to measure every relevant educational outcome. This is a very serious limitation when such measures are used to evaluate schools, teaching, or teachers. Relevance is the construct in test validity. The breadth-of-curriculum problem is probably greater at the secondary school level than at the elementary school level. There is a general trend toward an increase in the range of content coverage as one moves up the grade scale, and a tendency throughout to measure comprehension rather than recall of specific facts. Most survey batteries also evidence extensive and comprehensive coverage of a variety of abilities. The articulation over grade levels provides a basis for tracking student progress, which also reflects school effectiveness. The term *articulation* as used here refers to the development of a score-reporting scale that has comparable meaning over different levels of a test. Some school systems are opting to build their own system-level tests and testing programs. This is an extensive proposition but has the advantage of having maximally relevant tests in consideration of the curriculum. Such system testing programs tend to be criterion-referenced in nature and cover less content areas at fewer grade levels.

A distinct advantage of the survey battery over a series of individual subject-matter tests from different publishers is its simultaneous standardization of all subtests. Scores on individual subtests can thus be considered comparable, because the normative data were derived from the same population.

The *Stanford Achievement Test Series*, Ninth Edition (*Stanford 9*) (Kelley et al., 1996) is an illustrative survey battery. Many other high-quality batteries are also commercially available, for example, the *Iowa Tests of Basic Skills, Comprehensive Tests of Basic Skills, Metropolitan Achievement Tests*, and the *Science Research Associates Achievement Series*. The *Stanford 9* is selected only for illustrative purposes.

The *Stanford 9* has three components: the *Stanford Early School Achievement Test* (grades K–1.5), the Primary, Intermediate, and Advanced batteries (grades 1.5–9.9), and the *Stanford Test of Academic Skills* (grades 9.0–13.0). The *Stanford* was originally published in 1923 and is now in its ninth edition. Changes in school curricula and the need to update normative data make periodic revision and restandardization necessary. Normative data (fall and spring) were gathered using a sampling plan that considered such demographic variables as size of school district, ethnicity, region of the country, and density of student population. The total standardization and research sample consisted of between 500,000 and 600,000 students. That's a lot! Items were revised by content experts, copy editors, measurement specialists, teachers, and an independent panel of educators whose job it was to control for potential racial, gender, or ethnic bias. One valuable feature of the *Stanford 9* is the dual standardization of the batteries together with the *Otis-Lennon School Ability Test*, Seventh Edition. This dual standardization of achievement and ability measures helps ensure comparability across all levels and forms of the battery. Most major publishers of survey batteries now provide dual standardization with a school or mental ability test.

The *Stanford 9* allows an adopter to customize the battery for local use. Traditional multiple-choice and open-ended questions can be combined in any of four general areas: reading, mathematics, science, and social science. The structure of the *Stanford 9* is aligned with national standards projects and models, such as the National Council of Teachers of Mathematics standards and the National Science Education standards.

Recent editions of achievement survey batteries contain questions that require the student to understand and apply thinking and reasoning skills. These newer kinds of tasks are included in the Ninth Edition of the *Stanford Achievement Series*. Figure 15-1 contains two sample items from the *Stanford 9*. These items were based on the National Standards for Civics and Government and are aimed at assessing the student's understanding of key concepts in social science disciplines.

The variety of educational outcomes that can be measured using the multiple-choice format is amazing. It takes time to gather good information. The complete battery of Form 5 of the *Stanford 9* Intermediate 1 level (grades 4.5–5.5) survey, for example, requires 5 hours and 20 minutes.

### Specific Subject Tests

Individual tests on special topics do not differ significantly from the kinds of subtests found in most survey batteries. They do differ in depth of coverage. The specific subject test contains more items and covers more aspects of a topic than does a subtest from a battery purporting to measure the same material. There are, in addition, many specialized tests on topics not commonly covered by batteries, for example, economics, trigonometry, physics, chemistry, and computer programming.

The primary reason for using individual tests, compared with battery subtests, is that they provide detailed accounting. In some cases single-subject tests can be individually administered—for example, the *Woodstock Reading Mastery Tests - Revised* (Woodcock, 1987)—thereby allowing flexibility in administration and observation of test performance in a face-to-face situation. Specific tests are generally administered after an unusual student performance is noted on one or more subtests of a survey battery or to explore a subject area in depth. Such tests are being used with less frequency because of already-crowded testing schedules. In any event, test batteries generally cover the desired topics. Currently available single-subject tests tend to be in mathematics and reading.

A typical comprehensive system is the *Gates-MacGinitie Reading Test* (G-MRT) (MacGinitie & MacGinitie, 1989). The *Gates-MacGinitie* is a group-administered measure of beginning reading skills and language concepts for grade 1. In grades 2 through 12, the test includes vocabulary and comprehension. The G-MRT has normative data available for fall, winter, spring, or out-of-level testing. **Out-of-level testing** takes place when students

DIRECTIONS
Read the question and choose the best answer.
Then mark the space for the answer you have
chosen.

A. **The passage of the 13th Amendment to the United States Constitution in 1865 resulted in**

○ lowering of the legal voting age

○ establishment of the federal income tax

○ end of slavery

○ end of Prohibition

In the United States there are three levels of government. The first level is local, or community government. Then there is state government. Finally there is
the federal or national government.

B. **Which action can be taken only by the national government?**

○ Building a new library

○ Printing money

○ Testing people who want drivers' licenses

○ Building new parks

**Figure 15-1** *Sample Social Science Items from Stanford Achievement Test: Ninth Edition. Copyright* © *1996 by Harcourt, Inc. Reproduced by permission. All rights reserved.*

are tested at their functional level rather than at their grade or age placement. This practice is sometimes followed when the test content is too difficult or inappropriate. An examinee is then assessed with a "lower" level test. Out-of-level testing could also be undertaken at the high end of the ability scale, for example, with academically gifted students. Vocabulary reference lists, for example, Dale's List of 3000 Words Known by Students in Grade Four, were used to balance nouns, verbs, adjectives, and other parts of speech. Comprehension subject matter focused on fictional story material in the early grades and on poetry, natural and social sciences, and the arts at the upper grades. An innovation in reporting G-MRT performances is the use of *Extended Score Scales* (ESS). The ESS were developed so that student progress could be continuously monitored over time. The standard score ESS are assumed to allow equivalent interpretations of score differences at different levels. For example, a difference of 25 ESS units anywhere on the scales represents the difference between the achievement of beginning grade 5 and beginning grade 6 students (at the time of standardization). Robert Aaron and C. Gillespie (1990) noted that "The tests are an excellent first screening for large groups of students and can also be used to identify pupils at the beginning reading stage who need additional specific skills evaluation. The discussion of evaluation procedures and recommendations for mediation are excellent and are a strong feature of the testing program."

### Diagnostic Tests

Diagnostic tests are usually administered after an extended period of instruction, sometimes to a group but usually to individuals, to identify learning weaknesses in a detailed and analytical way, with a view to remediation. The initial use of an achievement battery to identify students who demonstrate inadequate learning is generally recommended. Diagnostic tests are intended for use with students who are observed or known to be having problems. The diagnostic process might involve the following sequence: (1) informal assessment by teacher, (2) survey battery, (3) group diagnostic test, and (4) individual diagnostic test. Individual diagnostic tests are usually administered by testing experts. A standardized diagnostic test can be used to (a) identify for the student and instructor the types of errors being made, (b) make the instructor aware of the important elements, difficulties, and subject and skill sequences in the learning process, and (c) suggest remedial procedures. A substantial amount of diagnostic testing to obtain even more detailed information about student difficulties uses informal teacher-made devices and direct observation of behavior.

In addition to exhibiting the usual characteristics required of a test (e.g., high reliability, validity, and objectivity), diagnostic tests should (a) be tied to specific curricular objectives and expected learning outcomes, (b) include items that directly measure and analyze specific functions or emphasize selected mechanical aspects of learning, (c) suggest specific remedial procedures for the errors indicated by responses to specific items, and (d) cover reasonably broad integrated learning sequences. Three critical questions should be asked when you select a diagnostic reading test. These questions are generalizable to any diagnostic test:

1. Does the test measure the necessary component skills, and do the subscores represent meaningful areas for providing remedial instruction?

2. Are the subscore reliabilities sufficiently high (above 0.90) for individual application?

**3.** Are the intercorrelations among the subscores sufficiently low (below 0.65) to warrant differential diagnosis?

Unfortunately, most diagnostic tests available do not meet even minimal criteria. There is a lack of efficient high-quality instruments that can be used diagnostically in program planning. Many achievement batteries attempt to serve as *both* survey instruments and diagnostic tests. The general procedure is to provide between five and 10 subject scores and an item-by-item or objective-by-objective breakdown of the individual student scores. Such a breakdown is too general and based on too few items to be considered a reliable procedure. It is difficult to state just how many items are necessary. This should be determined empirically. Studies have shown that we can get acceptable reliability with as few as six to 10 items. The procedure can be of some value when used as an initial screening, but such an analysis should not form the basis for instruction. It might be fairer to say that diagnostic tests differ from survey and specific subject-matter tests in the degree of refinement with which they measure achievement than to say that they measure different kinds of achievement. Another way of viewing the distinction between survey and single-subject tests, on the one hand, and diagnostic tests, on the other, is that the former tend to focus on and sample common curricular content, whereas the latter tests sample typical errors or mistakes.

Diagnostic tests usually cover either arithmetic or reading skills. A brief description of two representative diagnostic tests should illustrate the general approach to developing diagnostic tests and the kinds of information they yield.

The *Stanford Diagnostic Mathematics Test* (SDMT) (Beatty, Madden, Gardner, & Karlsen, 1984) is one of the best available diagnostic mathematics tests. The SDMT's two equivalent forms can be used with students in grades 1.5 through 12. The fall/spring standardization has normative data reported in five forms: percentile ranks, stanines, scaled scores, grade equivalents, and normal curve equivalents. The number of items ranges from 90 to 117; administration time is from 85 to 100 minutes, depending on level; and tests can be hand- or machine-scored. Reports are available for individual students and at the class, building, and system levels. Following is a list of the separate reliable scores available with Form G at the 10th-grade level.

1.0 Number System and Numeration
  1.1 Whole Number and Decimal Place Value
  1.2 Rational Numbers and Numeration
  1.3 Operations and Properties

2.0  Computation

    2.1  Addition with Whole Numbers

    2.2  Subtraction with Whole Numbers

    2.3  Multiplication with Whole Numbers

    2.4  Division with Whole Numbers

    2.5  Fractions

    2.6  Decimals

    2.7  Percent

    2.8  Equations

3.0  Applications

    3.1  Problem Solving

    3.2  Read and Interpret Tables and Graphs

    3.3  Geometry and Measurement

SDMT items are keyed to Content/Skill Progress Indicators that focus on starting points for instruction.

Another representative diagnostic test is the *California Diagnostic Reading Test* (CTB/McGraw-Hill, 1988). This instrument provides information in six overlapping level batteries for students in grades 1.1 through high school. It can be hand- or machine-scored and can be used with the publisher's TESTMATE, a microcomputer software system that enables users to report both norm-referenced and objectives-mastery information. The test is also linked with the extensive *Comprehensive Tests of Basic Skills* (CTB/McGraw-Hill, 1987).

Following is a list of the domains sampled.

1.0  Word Attack

    1.1  Visual Discrimination

    1.2  Auditory Discrimination

    1.3  Word Analysis

2.0  Vocabulary

3.0  Reading Comprehension

4.0  Reading Applications

    4.1  Skimming and Scanning

    4.2  Reading Rate

    4.3  Reference Skills

    4.4  Life Skills

As with the *Stanford*, an attempt was made to control for possible bias by content examination and empirical means.

These tests are typical and representative of their type. Adoption of one or the other would depend on a detailed analysis of the skills measured, type of information likely to result, and ease of administration in addition to technical information on reliability, validity, and adequacy of normative data.

## EARLY CHILDHOOD AND READINESS TESTING

It is difficult to decide whether early childhood tests and readiness tests like those used at kindergarten and first grade levels are achievement or ability tests. Perhaps the search for the "correct" classification is nothing more than an academic exercise. We generally think of an achievement test as being a device to assess the impact of a specified curriculum, whereas a readiness test is used to measure whether a child has acquired the basic knowledge and skills necessary to move into more formal and structured learning experiences. Readiness tests typically include measures of auditory memory, beginning consonants, letter and visual matching, and basic number concepts. With increasing frequency kindergarten programs are using structured curricula aimed at testing these basic skills and knowledge. Given this typical application we should probably think of the readiness test as an ability test—at least ability as influenced by preschool, kindergarten, and home experiences. It is unacceptable to make a decision about placement or promotion on the basis of a single test score. Therefore, if standardized tests are used at the kindergarten level, they should be used along with teachers' assessments and observations. We must consider the developmental level and needs of the child.

There appears to be a movement toward the use of structured formal assessments as well as informal assessments in the early grades, particularly at the end of kindergarten. The potential user must be alerted to the fact that assessment (group or individual) with any device at these early age levels can be unreliable. Abilities are not yet fully developed and children vary greatly in the developmental processes. Typical of these end-of-kindergarten assessments is the *Georgia Kindergarten Assessment Program—Revised* (GKAP-R). GKAP-R is not a test in the usual sense but, rather, is basically a formative instructional device that requires each kindergarten teacher to assess each student in three activity areas which include basic competencies needed for academic survival up the grade scale. The assessment is administered and data used by the teacher for remediation until every child is successful. The three activity areas and associated skills are as follows:

Literacy Activities

L1.     Prints name

L2.     Holds print materials in correct position (left-right, top-bottom)

L3.     Draws pictures and/or uses letters and phonetically spelled words to write about experiences/people/events

L4.     Identifies upper- and lower-case letters out of sequence

L5.     Blends sounds orally to make words (Parts 1–2)

L6.     Distinguishes between letters, words, and sentences

L7.     Responds to literal, inferential, and evaluative questions

L8.     Sequences pictures to tell a story/interprets pictures to predict logical outcomes

L9.     Recognizes rhyming words

L10.    Verbalizes consonant sounds when shown letter

L11.    Associates sounds with letters

L12.    Blends sounds orally to make words (Part 3)

L13.    Reads selected sight words

L14.    Copies letters


Mathematics Activities

M1.     Counts by rote, 0 to 10

M2.     Recognizes and selects the numerals for 0 to 10

M3.     Identifies six basic geometric shapes (circle, square, triangle, rectangle, oval, diamond)

M4.     Uses words indicating physical relationships (top, bottom, inside, outside, in front of, behind)

M5.     Sorts geometric shapes

M6.     Continues simple pattern

M7.     Uses words indicating physical relationships (above, below, under, in, on, out of, between, left, right)

M8.     Determines equivalence using physical models by establishing one-to-one correspondence

M9.     Compares and describes lengths (longer, shorter, same as)

M10.    Counts the elements in a set and writes numerals (0–10)

M11.    Constructs/interprets simple graphs using objects/pictures

M12.    Names coins (penny, nickel, dime, quarter) and dollar bill

M13.    Uses ordinal number to indicate first through fifth

M14.    Models, acts out, uses pictures to solve simple problems


Social/Emotional Activities

SE1.    Follows teacher's directions

SE2.    Treats others with respect

SE3.    Follows classroom rules

SE4.    Stays on task

Teacher judgments are made about each competency and are recorded as NE = No Evidence of Accomplishment, IP = In Progress, and AC = Accomplished. Descriptors are used to clarify each judgment. Based on a statewide standard setting, decisions are made about a student needing instructional assistance in first grade or that a student is ready for first grade.

# NATIONAL ASSESSMENT OF EDUCATIONAL PROGRESS

The kinds of external tests and testing systems described so far have for the most part originated from local or state requirements. The federal government is also involved in testing via the National Assessment of Educational Progress (NAEP).

The ever-increasing cost of public education is a matter of growing concern to professional educators, laypersons, and government personnel. The concept of accountability is being implemented in a variety of ways to make the educational process more effective and efficient. Efficiency, of course, influences cost. Billions of dollars are spent in the United States each year on buildings, salaries, and curricula, with minimal attention paid to the effectiveness of these expenditures. The purpose of the National Assessment of Educational Progress is to collect information that can be used in rational decision making about schools. The resulting data have implications both for curricula and for the allocation of funds.

The NAEP is a congressionally mandated project of the National Center for Education Statistics in the U.S. Department of Education. It is a census-like survey of the knowledge, skills, understanding, and attitudes of certain groups of young Americans. It focuses on growth and decline in selected educational attainments of young Americans. Subject areas such as citizenship, science, writing, music, mathematics, literature, social studies, reading, art, and career and occupational development are examined cyclically. The first assessment cycle began in 1969, with coverage of science, writing, and citizenship. Repeated assessments reveal whether change has occurred. Extreme care is exercised to avoid identifying any individual, student, school, city, or state, although there now exists a voluntary state component. A given student will respond to only a portion of the exercises.

There are two major types of NAEP administration: Main and Long-Term Trend. The Main NAEP reports results for grade samples (4, 8, 12). In 2000 Main NAEP assessed mathematics and science at grades 4, 8, and 12, and reading at grade 4. Long-Term NAEP measures students' achievements in mathematics, science, reading, and writing. All assessments are voluntary and also are implemented periodically by state. A variety of reports are produced to facilitate communication about and dissemination of results. Among these are Report Cards, Instructional Reports, Cross-State Data Compendia, Trend Reports, and Technical Reports, among others.

Approximately half the exercises administered during any given year are reported. Results in the form of Report Cards are reported as percentages of various groups that respond correctly (and incorrectly) to the exercises. The groups comprise individuals representing various combinations of the following categories:

1. Ages: 9, 13, and 17, and young adults (ages 26 to 35).

2. Geographic region: Northeast, Southeast, Central, and West.

3. Size of community: big cities, urban fringes, medium-size cities, and less populated places.

4. Type of community: impoverished inner cities, affluent suburbs, and rural areas.

5. Sex.

6. Color: black, non-black, and total.

7. Socioeducational background.

Scholars, school personnel, and representatives of the public expended extensive efforts to identify the most relevant objectives of U.S. education. The resulting objectives were then translated, mostly under contract with commercial test developers, into a variety of tasks—some paper-and-pencil, some group activities, and a variety of other formats.

Currently available NAEP data suggest that U.S. education is at a crossroad. Although long-term gains are reflected in the major subject areas of reading, mathematics, and science, and the gap between white and non-white students is decreasing, desired absolute levels of performance still are not being approached. In particular, there is a deficiency in the development of higher-level cognitive problem-solving skills. Major overhauls of curriculum and instruction may be needed to bring about substantive changes. Data from NAEP suggest the likelihood that success can result if changes are made. It was found, for example, that students who reported participatory and varied instructional practices in science and literature classes tended to have higher performance than those students who were exposed to traditional approaches, such as textbook reading, completion of individual exercises in workbooks or on the board, and teacher "explanations." The interplay of instruction and assessment is obvious. Test data can help us see what we are doing in the schools and with students.

To facilitate interpretation of results and comparisons across assessment years for age groups and subpopulations, a five-level proficiency scale was devised. The NAEP mathematics scale was computed as a weighted composite over five content areas: (a) knowledge and skills, (b) higher-level applications, (c) measurement, (d) geometry, and (e) algebra. Following is a set of definitions and items illustrating the levels of proficiency concept.

### Level 150—Simple Arithmetic Facts

Learners at this level know some basic addition and subtraction facts, and most can add two-digit numbers without regrouping. They recognize situations in which addition and subtraction apply. They also are developing rudimentary classifications skills.

Which of these numbers is closest to 30?

20

*28

34

40

### Level 200—Beginning Skills and Understanding

Learners at this level have considerable understanding of two-digit numbers. They can add two-digit numbers, but are still developing an ability to regroup in subtraction. They know some basic multiplication and division facts, recognize relations among coins, can read information from charts and graphs, and use simple measurement instruments. They are developing some reasoning skills. Following is a sample question.

### Level 250—Basic Operations and Beginning Problem Solving

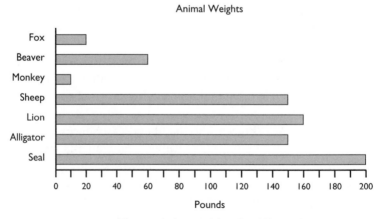

Animal Weights

The animals that weigh less than 100 pounds are

- ○ alligator, sheep, lion
- ○ monkey, sheep, lion
- ● fox, beaver, monkey
- ○ fox, lion, seal

Learners at this level have an initial understanding of the four basic operations. They can apply whole number addition and subtraction skills to one-step word problems and money situations. In multiplication, they can find the product of a two-digit and a one-digit number. They can also compare information from graphs and charts, and are developing an ability to analyze simple logical relations.

Sam has **68** baseball cards. Juanita has 127. Which number sentence could be used to find how many more cards Juanita has than Sam?

- ● $127 - 68 = q$
- ○ $127 + q = 68$
- ○ $68 - q = 127$
- ○ $68 + 127 = q$
- ○ I don't know

## Level 300—Moderately Complex Procedures and Reasoning

Learners at this level are developing an understanding of number systems. They can compute with decimals, simple fractions, and commonly encountered percents. They can identify geometric figures, measure lengths and angles, and calculate areas of rectangles. These students can also interpret simple inequalities, evaluate formulas, and solve simple linear equations. They can find averages, make decisions on information drawn from graphs,

Refer to the following graph. This graph shows how far a typical car travels after the brakes are applied.

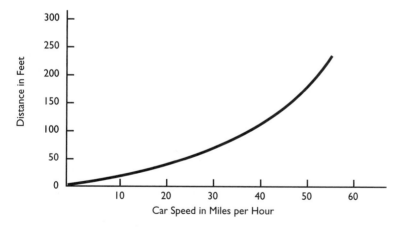

A car is travelling 55 miles per hour. About how far will it travel after applying the brakes?

- ○ 25 feet
- ○ 200 feet
- ● 240 feet
- ○ 350 feet
- ○ I don't know

and use logical reasoning to solve problems. They are developing the skills to operate with signed numbers, exponents, and square roots.

### Level 350—Multistep Problem Solving and Algebra

Learners at this level can apply a range of reasoning skills to solve multistep problems. They can solve routine problems involving fractions and percents, recognize properties of basic geometric figures, and work with exponents and square roots. They can solve a variety of two-step problems using variables, identify equivalent algebraic expressions, and solve linear equations and inequalities. They are developing an understanding of functions and coordinate systems.

> Christine borrowed $850 for one year from the Friendly Finance Company. If she paid 23% simple interest on the loan, what was the total amount she repaid?
>
> ANSWER $1045.50

A typical report of mathematics achievement might look like the data display in Table 15-2.

It is distressing to note that more than a quarter of middle school students (representing more than three-quarters of a million students) had not mastered skills in whole-number addition, subtraction, multiplication, and division necessary to perform everyday tasks. One might have expected higher percentages of students at ages 13 and 14 demonstrating success in dealing with decimals, fractions, percents, and basic geometry and algebra, given the emphasis on those topics in middle/junior high school. The fact that nearly 50 percent of 17-year-olds do not possess these skills has serious implications for these individuals as they approach graduation and the world of work or, for some, higher education. These are "life support" mathematical skills.

Up-to-date information on and data from NAEP can be found at http://nces.ed.gov/nationsreportcard/guide/2000456.html.

## INTERNATIONAL ASSESSMENTS

Results from the Third (1998) International Math and Science Study (TIMSS) revealed less than outstanding performance by U.S. students. U.S. student scores were not significantly different from those of seven other countries. U.S. students outperformed those from only two other countries. These results were used to renew a plea for higher standards in our schools. Used as one example of depressed performance was the following question for advanced physics students:

> A car moving at a constant speed with a siren sounding comes toward you and then passes by. Describe how the frequency of sound you hear changes.

**Table 15-2** *Percentages of Students at or Above Proficiency Levels on NAEP Scales—1986: Ages 9, 13, and 17*

| Level/Description | | Elementary School (Age 9) | Middle School (Age 13) | High School (Age 17) |
|---|---|:---:|:---:|:---:|
| 350 | Can solve multistep problems and use basic algebra | 0 | 0 | 6 |
| 300 | Can compute with decimals, fractions, and percents; recognizes geometric figures, and solves problems | 1 | 16 | 51 |
| 250 | Can add, subtract, multiply, and divide using whole numbers | 21 | 73 | 96 |
| 200 | Can add and subtract two-digit numbers and recognize relationships among coins | 74 | 99 | 100 |
| 150 | Knows some basic addition and subtraction facts | 98 | 100 | 100 |

*Source:* Applebee, Langer, and Mullis (1989).

The international average was only 37 percent, but the U.S. average was 12 percent. Figures 15-2 and 15-3 contain two other items from the TIMSS assessment.

> Kelly went for a drive in her car. During the drive, a cat ran in front of the car. Kelly slammed on the brakes and missed the cat.

> Slightly shaken, Kelly decided to return home by a shorter route. The graph below is a record of the car's speed during the drive.

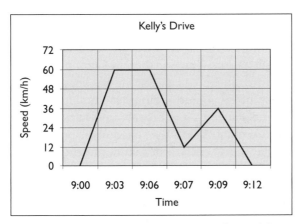

What was the maximum speed, in kilometers per hour, of the car during the drive?

*Correct Answer: 60 km/h*     *U.S. Average:* **85 percent**     *International Average:* **74 percent**

**SOURCE:** Third International Mathematics and Science Study, 1994–1995.

**Figure 15-2** *Sample Mathematics General Knowledge Items from TIMSS*

Experts say that 25 percent of all serious bicycle accidents involve head injuries and that, of all head injuries, 80 percent are fatal.

What percent of all serious bicycle accidents involve fatal head injuries?

A. 16%

B. 20%

C. 55%

D. 105%

Correct Answer: B U.S. Average: **57 percent**     International Average: **64 percent**

**SOURCE:** Third International Mathematics and Science Study, 1994–1995.

**Figure 15-3** *Sample Mathematics General Knowledge Item from TIMSS*

TIMSS is surely not a definitive source of information about the overall health of U.S. education, but it does provide a valuable perspective on some potential areas in need of examination if not remediation. For more information on TIMSS, see www.timss@bc.edu.

## ESTABLISHING A SCHOOLWIDE ASSESSMENT SYSTEM

If educators are truly concerned with the "total student," it is imperative that a comprehensive assessment system be established. The term *assessment* is used intentionally, in preference to *testing*, because most schools have testing programs to meet accreditation requirements. The data from such programs are all too often filed away and never benefit student, teacher, or administration. The backbone of an assessment system can, however, be the testing program. It should be supplemented with periodic assessments of such nontraditional variables as student attitudes toward school and learning, classroom environment, parental attitudes, and teacher values. The cost of a schoolwide program is not inconsequential and can be many dollars per student per year, but the potential benefit to the student, school, and society justifies the cost. Data from a comprehensive program can be used to (a) improve the instructional program, (b) facilitate curriculum revision, (c) assist in educational vocational counseling, (d) help the administrative staff appraise the overall impact and effectiveness of the educational program, and, most important, (e) help the individual examine his or her progress and strengths.

### Designing a Program

A schoolwide program design has at least nine major phases:

1. Examine the school's educational philosophy and purpose in establishing the system. Answers are sought to the question, "What information is desired and why?"
2. Solicit staff cooperation and involvement in program development.
3. Communicate to all faculty the nature, extent, and purpose of the assessment.
4. Designate those who will use and have access to the information.
5. Determine the manner in which information will be used.
6. Designate responsibilities for the program execution.
7. Stimulate financial and moral support for the program.
8. Provide for the administrative machinery for reevaluation of the program.
9. Interpret the program to the community. The last phase is particularly critical as the general public becomes increasingly involved in setting school policies and monitoring the educational process.

These phases and the following criteria would apply generally to county programs as well.

### Criteria for an Effective Program

Following is a set of 15 criteria, in the form of "critical questions," which can be used to examine the effectiveness of an assessment system:

1. Is the program comprehensive?
2. Does the program include all the students in the school?
3. Are the tests given at regular intervals?
4. Are the tests administered at times of the year that maximize their usefulness?
5. Are the tests in the school's testing program comparable?
6. Do the tests used agree with the objectives and the curriculum of the school?
7. Are the specific tests carefully chosen?
8. Are the tests carefully administered to each group?
9. Are the tests scored accurately?
10. Are the test results interpreted in terms of appropriate norms?
11. Are the test results quickly disseminated to teachers and counselors in understandable terms?

**12.** Are the test results recorded on individual cumulative record forms?

**13.** Is a definite attempt made to relate the test scores to other kinds of information?

**14.** In addition to the regular testing program, is there provision for special testing as needed?

**15.** Does the school have an in-service program for educating teachers in the use of test results?

This list of criteria suggests some very important requirements for an effective assessment system. Among the most important is, of course, the match between the school curricular objectives and the test items and information available relative to their interpretation. Technical adequacy and security are also major considerations. The final criterion worth noting is the need to see that all users of the test data, decision makers and audiences, receive the information in a timely and understandable form.

### A Hypothetical Assessment Program

The following assessment program is considered "hypothetical" as each school system (and, to some extent, school) has unique curricular and instructional requirements for the nature and timing of information needed for a variety of decision-making applications, Table 15-3 contains an outline of a possible K–12 student assessment system.

The criterion-referenced measures are usually of basic reading and math skills. The criterion-referenced measure might be from a commercial publisher or locally developed by the school system or a state agency. At the 10th-grade level, reading and math skills are assessed together with writing. The assessment of writing is increasingly becoming a major event in all testing programs. The ability to communicate in written form reflects on the application of these very important language skills. It is usual for a state or a system to select grades in which to test rather than testing in all grades. The program might be a split between state-mandated assessment and local information needs.

Tests useful for guidance purposes can be employed at almost any point during the schooling process. Data from scholastic aptitude or school ability tests, multiple-aptitude batteries, and interest inventories can provide an extremely valuable starting point for educational and vocational counseling. Personality inventories also can be used as part of the guidance and counseling program. Graduation tests are sometimes required at 11th or 12th grade.

**Table 15-3** *Hypothetical School Testing Program*

| Grade | Kind of Test |
|---|---|
| Kindergarten | Readiness |
| One | Achievement (usually criterion-referenced) |
| Two | Norm-referenced achievement battery/school ability test |
| Three | Achievement (usually criterion-referenced) |
| Four | Norm-referenced achievement battery/school ability test |
| Five | Optional (achievement or ability) |
| Six | Achievement (usually criterion-referenced), writing sample |
| Seven | Norm-referenced achievement battery |
| Eight | Achievement (usually criterion-referenced), writing sample |
| Nine | Norm-referenced achievement battery |
| Ten | Survey of basic skills (usually criterion-referenced) |
| Eleven | Scholastic aptitude (optional) |
| Nine-Twelve | Vocational aptitude/interest inventories (as needed) |

Scheduling nonclassroom testing during the school year represents a dilemma. Data derived from a fall test administration should have maximum usefulness throughout the school year, if for no other reason than they are recent relative to the start of school. Such data are less likely to be used for teacher evaluation or student promotion decisions. Fall data would have maximum value in planning instructional programs. The results of spring testing are likely to have their maximum value in program evaluation and in assessing school effectiveness.

## LOCATING INFORMATION ABOUT TESTS

It would be impossible to list, let alone critically evaluate, all those tests that might interest a particular instructor or administrator. A potential user needs answers to such questions as the following: (a) What types of tests are available that will yield the kinds of information I am interested in? (b) What do the "experts" say about the tests I am interested in? (c) What research has been undertaken on this test? (d) What statistical data relating to validity and reliability are available for examination? (e) With what groups can I legitimately use this test? Answers to these and many other relevant questions can be found in one or more of the following resources:

1. *Mental Measurements Yearbook.*

2. Test reviews in professional journals.

3. Test manuals and specimen sets.

4. Textbooks and reference books on testing.

5. Bibliographies of tests and testing literature.

6. Educational and psychological abstract indexes.

7. Publishers' test catalogs.

8. Test critiques (e.g., Keyser & Sweetland, 1988).

Any competent librarian can help you access other sources of information, such as *Tests in Print*, *Directory of Selected National Testing Programs*, Educational Testing Service Test Collection catalogs, *Index to Tests Used in Educational Dissertations*, test critiques, *Education Index*, *Dissertation Abstracts International*, *Psychological Abstracts*, and the Educational Resources Information Center (especially the one in Tests and Measurements), which publishes *Resources in Education* and *Current Index to Journals in Education*. Computer searches of these and other databases (DIALOG) can greatly facilitate information gathering.

Of the resources listed, the first three are probably the most immediately informative. These three sources will be discussed in turn, with the types of information that each provides.

### The *Mental Measurements Yearbook*

Probably the most useful sources of evaluative information about commercial tests is the *Mental Measurements Yearbook* (MMY). Originated by the late Dr. Oscar K. Buros, the *Yearbook* is now the province of the Buros Institute of Mental Measurements at the University of Nebraska. Up-to-date and comprehensive bibliographies, test reviews, and book reviews are published in the *Yearbook*. Buros' goal was to develop in the potential user and publisher a critical attitude toward tests and testing, to facilitate communication, and in general to significantly increase the quality of published tests. Specifically, Buros wanted the *Yearbook* "(a) to provide information about tests published as separates throughout the English-speaking world; (b) to present frankly critical test reviews written by testing and subject specialists representing various viewpoints; (c) to provide extensive bibliographies of verified references on the construction, use, and validity of specific tests; (d) to make readily available the critical portions of test reviews appearing in professional journals; and (e) to present fairly exhaustive listings of new and revised books on testing, along with evaluative excerpts from representative reviews which these books receive in professional journals." The *Yearbooks* have made a significant and lasting contribution toward these ends.

There also exists an easily computer-searchable database for the MMY. Based on the MMY classification schemes, users can access the MMY database with a variety of algorithms to isolate tests for specific variables, populations, price, publication date, and so forth. Between editions of the *Yearbook*, the Buros Institute publishes a softback *MMY Supplement* with the most recent test reviews.

## Test Reviews in Journals

Despite the availability of such authoritative comprehensive sources as the *Yearbook*, it is often difficult to locate recent data on either new or old tests. Research data or questions related to reliability, validity, and usability, and occasional test reviews are periodically carried in the journals of professional organizations, especially teacher organizations. An excellent source of validity studies is the quarterly publication *Education and Psychological Measurement*.

## Test Manuals and Specimen Sets

After preliminary decisions have narrowed the field, a potential user should probably obtain specimen sets from publishers. Such a set usually contains a copy of the test questions, scoring key, answer sheets, examiner's manual, and occasionally a technical manual. The sets, available at a nominal cost, should be ordered on official school or institution letterhead stationery because most publishers attempt to ensure that their materials are distributed to qualified individuals only for security reasons. If there is any question about the qualifications required for the purchase of a particular test, consult the publisher's catalog. Following are some excerpts from the Qualifications for Test Purchase for Harcourt Educational Measurement. Adherence to the *Standards* is required.

> The tests listed in this catalog are carefully developed assessment devices that require specialized training to ensure their appropriate professional use. Eligibility to purchase these tests is therefore restricted to individuals with specific training and experience in a relevant area of assessment. These standards are consistent with the *1999 Standards for Educational and Psychological Testing* and with the professional and ethical standards of a variety of professional organizations.

Tests are categorized as being:

*Level A:* Purchase orders will be filled promptly. Registration is *not* required. [An illustrative Level A instrument is an occupational interest inventory called the *Self-Directed Search*.]

*Level B:* These tests are available to firms having a staff member who has completed an advanced level course in testing from an accredited college or university, or equivalent training under the direction of a qualified supervisor or consultant. Registration *is* required. [Examples of tests at this level are the *Watson-Galser Critical Thinking Appraisal* and the *Metropolitan Achievement Tests* (Sixth Edition).]

*Level C:* These tests are available only to firms for use under the supervision of qualified professionals, defined as persons with at least a master's degree in psychology or a related discipline and appropriate training in the field of personnel testing. The qualified person may be either a staff member or a consultant. Registration *is* required. [An example of a Level C test is the *Weschler Intelligence Scale for Children—Revised*.]

Once a user has been granted access to a particular test, additional guidelines must be followed. These relate to test security. Following is an excerpt of such test security precautions.

Purchaser agrees to comply with these basic principles of test security:

1. Test taker must not receive test answers before beginning the test.

2. Test questions are not to be reproduced or paraphrased in any way by a school, college, or any organization or person.

3. Access to test materials is limited to persons with a responsible, professional interest who will safeguard their use.

4. Test materials and scores are to be released only to persons qualified to interpret and use them properly.

5. If a test taker or the parent of a child who has taken the test wishes to examine responses or results, the parent or test taker is permitted to read a copy of the test and the test answers of the test taker in the presence of a representative of the school, college, or institution that administered the test.

The test manual is the most informative and readily accessible source of information about a specific test. Directions for administering and scoring the test, brief statistical information about validity, reliability, and norms, a description of the test's development, and suggestions for interpreting and using the test results constitute the usual content of the manual. The reviewer should remember, however, that the publisher has a vested interest, and all tests should be evaluated critically. Most Level B and C tests also have technical manuals that contain extensive data on the development of the tests.

# SELECTING AN ACHIEVEMENT TEST

After informally reviewing several tests in a particular area and making a preliminary decision about the purpose of testing and the projected uses of the test data, the instructor would profit from a detailed examination of two or three tests. A set of evaluative questions that have been found useful in judging a test for possible use in schools is reprinted below. The first eight categories are essentially descriptive, but nevertheless important. For example, such factors as the affiliation of the author and the copyright data affect such significant criteria as credibility, authenticity, and recency. The outline presented here is an adaptation and expansion of one originally developed by Lee J. Cronbach (1960, pp. 147–153).

In undertaking a "critical analysis," you will consult many sources. (Refer to earlier pages in this chapter for information on identifying references.) In addition, it would be worthwhile for the test evaluator to refer to *Standards for Educational and Psychological Testing* (Joint Committee, 1999) for assistance in identifying minimally acceptable criteria for many of the variables described in this outline. It is usually a good idea to record the comments, evaluations, and sources consulted during the review process.

### Outline for Critical Analysis of a Standardized Achievement Test

1. *Title:* Note complete and exact title of test.
2. *Author:* A brief summary of professional affiliations and credentials would be informative.
3. *Publisher:* Some publishers are more reputable than others. Check with experts in testing.
4. *Copyright Date:* Note dates of first publication and each revision.
5. *Level or Group for Whom Test Is Intended:* Such factors as age, grade, and ability level should be considered. What background does the author presuppose for examinees? Is the test available at different levels? If so, which ones?
6. *Forms of the Test:* What forms of the test are available? If the forms are not essentially the same, major differences should be mentioned and evaluated. What evidence is presented on equivalence of forms?
7. *Purpose and Recommended Use:* Summarize the use of the test recommended by the author.
8. *Dimensions of Areas that the Test Purports to Measure:* Give a brief definition or description of the variables involved. If the test has numerous scales (or scores) it may be necessary simply to mention the sub-

scores and highlight only the group or distinctive scores. If at this point there is no match with local objectives or intents, you should probably terminate the review of this particular instrument.

9. *Administration:* Describe briefly. The median time required to complete the test should be indicated. If parts of the test are timed separately, note how many starting points are necessary. Are the directions easy for the test administrator to follow and the test takers to comprehend? Is special training required for valid administration: Is the test largely self-administering? Are there objectionable features?

10. *Scoring:* Scoring procedures should be described very briefly. Is the test planned and organized so that machine-scored answer sheets can or must be used? Is a correction for guessing justified or applied? (Refer to the discussion of guessing in Chapter 6.)

11. *Source of Items:* Where did the author get the items? What criteria were used in item selection? Are some items taken from other tests? If so, which ones?

12. *Description of Items (Format and Content):* Briefly describe the major types of items used. Attention should be given to *item form* (e.g., multiple-choice, analogy, forced-choice) and *item content* (e.g., culture-free symbols, nonsense syllables, food preferences, occupational titles). How many response categories are there? Note a typical example of the major type(s) of items used. It is imperative that the actual items be evaluated in light of questions a teacher would ask of the data.

13. *Statistical Item Analysis:* Was an item analysis made to determine item discrimination and difficulty? What were the results? What criteria were used to select items for the final form(s) of the instrument? What analytic techniques were used?

14. *Method and Results of Validation Reported by Publisher and Author:* For most tests this topic is related to categories 11, 12, and 13. You must ask, "What was done to make the test valid and useful?" Some tests are validated by expert judgment, some by an external criterion, and so on. What has the author done to demonstrate the validity of the test? What correlations with other tests are presented? Has an external criterion been used to evaluate the usefulness of the scores? This section should deal with data other than those obtained in the construction of the test. What specific "predictions" could you make from an individual's test score on the basis of the validity data presented?

15. *Validity as Determined by Others:* This is in many respects *the* crucial evaluative criterion. The recent literature should be consulted, and studies briefly summarized.

16. **Reliability:** State briefly how reliability was determined. Report interesting or unusual data on reliability. Was reliability computed separately for each subgroup or part of the test?

17. **Norm Group(s):** How many were involved? How were they selected? Are separate norms available for each group with whom you want to compare an individual's score, that is, norms for each sex, age level, curriculum major, occupation?

18. **Interpretation of Scores:** How are scores expressed? (Percentile ranks, standard scores, grades scores?) What is considered a "high" score? A "low" score? How are these scores interpreted?

19. **Major Evaluations by Experts:** What assumptions are examined and what questions are raised in the *Mental Measurements Yearbook*? What do measurement experts and the journals say about the test?

20. **Cost Factors:** The initial cost of booklets and answer sheets should be considered, as well as such factors as cost of scoring, reusability of booklets, and availability of summary and research services.

21. **Distinguishing Characteristics:** What are the outstanding features of this test, its construction, and its use? Note both desirable and undesirable features.

22. **Overall Evaluation:** How well do such factors as validity, reliability, standardization, and item content coincide with the intended use of the test?

How should the information in these 22 categories be weighted? No universal answer can be given because the selection of a particular test or battery depends on the individual needs of specific instructors or schools. The purpose of testing must be foremost in the mind of the test evaluator. Such questions as "What specific information is needed?" and "How will the test data be interpreted and used?" are highly significant. Questions relating to validity, reliability, and the representativeness of the normative data should be critically reviewed and heavily weighted in the final decisions if the test is to be used in a norm-referenced way.

The critical evaluation of any standardized test is a time-consuming and involved process. But considering the kinds of decisions that will be made about students and programs as a result of such tests, the expenditure of effort is more than justified.

Standardized tests, particularly achievement and ability tests, represent valuable tools to be used to help realize human potential. They are sources of information, but they are not the *only* source of information. Legal and professional efforts are being made to ensure fair and equitable use of tests, but we should ascribe any shortcomings of use to the user rather than to the tool. Education and training are the major avenue to more informed test use and decision making.

Let us not forget the admonition of Walter S. Monroe who wrote in his 1924 text, *Educational Tests and Measurements*, "Standardized tests and scales are not 'playthings.'"

---

## CONTENT REVIEW STATEMENTS

1. Standardized tests used in the schools are classified by the domain sampled: aptitude, achievement, or affective.

2. Standardized tests are carefully developed and tested on usually large and representative populations.

3. The term *standardization* refers to the uniform and controlled conditions required for administration and scoring and sometimes to the availability of normative data.

4. Standardized achievement tests are usually based on extensive analyses of common educational outcomes.

5. Refined item-selection procedures and test analyses characterize standardized measures.

6. Standardized achievement tests are used to

    a. direct curricular emphases.

    b. provide educational guidance.

    c. stimulate learning activities.

    d. direct and motivate administrative and supervisory efforts.

7. Achievement survey batteries provide an overview of the major instructional thrusts in primary, elementary, and secondary schools and colleges in such areas as language arts, mathematics, social studies, science, reading, and study skills.

8. Survey battery subtests have the advantage of being standardized on the same populations.

9. Specific subject or area tests provide detailed coverage of limited topics in such areas as chemistry, history, economics, foreign languages, and the like.

10. The diagnostic achievement tests usually applied in the fields of elementary reading and arithmetic
    a. provide very detailed analyses of student strengths and weaknesses.
    b. have items that are tied to specific instructional objectives.
    c. have scores with direct implications for actual remedial procedures.

11. Readiness tests sample fundamental skills such as auditory memory, visual memory, and letter and number concepts.

12. Scholastic aptitude tests, unlike achievement tests, tend to measure factors less influenced by formal educational experiences.

13. Information about standardized tests can be secured primarily from:
    a. Buros' *Mental Measurements Yearbooks*.
    b. test reviews in professional journals.
    c. test manuals, specimen sets, and publishers' catalogs.

14. In establishing a schoolwide assessment system, we must consider the following factors:
    a. school educational philosophy and objectives.
    b. the uses to which the data are to be put.
    c. communication and security of results.
    d. scheduling of tests.
    e. evaluation of the testing program.
    f. cooperation from teachers, administrators, students, and members of the community.

15. Schoolwide assessment systems must be responsive to the needs of students, teachers, and society.

16. Among the factors that must be considered in selecting a standardized achievement test for possible use are
    a. level and appropriateness of content.
    b. cost.
    c. copyright date.
    d. adequacy of administration and scoring directions.
    e. adequacy of reliability and validity data.
    f. adequacy of suggested interpretive guides and normative data.

**17.** The National Assessment of Educational Progress (NAEP) is an attempt to provide censuslike survey data on the growth of knowledge, skills, understanding, and attitudes among educational subgroups.

**18.** NAEP is concerned with performance differences in a variety of subject areas, four age groups, various geographic regions, and community sizes and types, but not individual students, schools, or systems.

## SPECULATIONS

**1.** What kinds of information are you likely to obtain from the *Mental Measurements Yearbook*?

**2.** On what basis is the use of comprehensive achievement test batteries justified or not justified in schools?

**3.** Are measures of academic achievement and academic aptitude really different? If so, in what way?

**4.** What are the contributions of the National Assessment of Educational Process?

**5.** Why should or should not standardized achievement test results be used to assess teaching effectiveness?

**6.** Compare and contrast standardized and nonstandardized achievement tests.

**7.** What is "diagnostic" about a diagnostic achievement test?

## SUGGESTED READINGS

Bauernfeind, R. H. (1963). *Building a school testing program*. Boston: Houghton Mifflin. Even though dated, this book provides an overall picture of the processes involved in developing a comprehensive and integrated testing program and presents informative discussions of basic measurement principles and factors in test interpretation.

Wilson, S. M., & Hiscox, M. D. (1984). Using standardized tests for assessing local learning objectives. *Educational Measurement: Issues and Practice, 3*(3), 19–22. A step-by-step procedure is described.

The following books have both educational and psychological orientations and are primarily concerned with commercially available standardized tests.

Aiken, L. R. (1988). *Psychological testing and assessment* (6th ed.). Boston: Allyn & Bacon.

Anastasi, A. (1988). *Psychological testing* (6th ed.). New York: Macmillan.

Cronbach, L. J. (1990). *Essentials of psychological testing* (5th ed.). New York: Harper & Row.

Cunningham, G. K. (1986). *Educational and psychological measurement*. New York: Macmillan.

Kaplan, R. M., & Saccuzzo, D. P. (2001). *Psychological testing* (5th ed.). Pacific Grove, CA: Brooks/Cole.

Sax, G. (1997). *Principles of educational and psychological measurement and evaluation* (4th ed.). Belmont, CA: Wadsworth.

Walsh, W. B., & Betz, N. E. (1985). *Tests and assessment*. Englewood Cliffs, NJ: Prentice-Hall.

# 16

## Interpreting the Meaning of Standardized Norm-referenced Test Scores

---

### FOCUS CONCEPTS AND KEY TERMS FOR STUDY

**Absolute Derived Scores**

**Age Norms**

**Derived Scores**

**Developmental Standard Score Norms**

**Expectancy Norms**

**Extrapolated Scores**

**Grade-Equivalent Norms**

**High-Stakes Test**

**Interpolated Scores**

**Lake Woebegon Effect**

**Local Norms**

**Norms**

**Percentile Rank Norms**

**Relative Derived Scores**

**Standard Score Norms**

**Standard Setting**

**User Norms**

## STANDARDS ALERT

**Standard 2.11**           **Reliability**

If there are generally accepted theoretical or empirical reasons for expecting that reliability coefficients, standard errors of measurement, or test information functions will differ substantially for various subpopulations, publishers should provide reliability data as soon as feasible for each major population for which the test is recommended.

## TAKING IT TO THE CLASSROOM

Although aimed primarily at standardized measures, this Standard has the implication that classroom assessments are not equally reliable for all students. This fact should be taken into account in interpreting results. The Standard does require publishers of commercial tests to publish meaningful data disaggregated by subgroup.

Reprinted with permission from the *Standards for Educational and Psychological Testing.* Copyright © 1999 by the American Educational Research Association, the American Psychological Association, and the National Council on Measurement in Education.

This chapter focuses on the problem of deriving meanings from scores on standardized tests. Many of the ideas and suggestions can, however, be applied by classroom teachers to their own tests.

## METHODS OF EXPRESSING TEST SCORES

In the beginning there was a test score. This raw score is derived from a measurement, be it the total number of correct answers, the ratings of some attitude items, or the amount of time needed to complete a task. A raw score needs some referent to help with interpretation. Scores that are modifications or transformations of the raw scores are called **derived scores**. There are generally two classes of referents: *absolute* and *relative*. We might use a procedure where a score is expressed in terms of a maximum possible, for example, score of 75 correct answers on a 90-item test where each item is worth 1 point would receive a score, a *percent*, or an **absolute derived score** of 83. We can also talk of the percentage of objectives mastered. These kinds of derived scores are generally associated with criterion-referenced and mastery tests. It is easy to confuse percentage scores and percentile ranks. Parents in particular are likely to erroneously equate a percentile rank of 82 with getting 82 percent of the items correct or getting 82 percent of the possible points. Everybody can think in terms of 100 units. But where do the units come from? The key is the denominator. For a *percent* score the denominator is the number of items or number of points. When calculating a *percentile rank* the denominator is the number of students at and below the one for which we were calculating the percentile rank.

**Relative derived scores** use a group or groups of test takers as a basis for scaling. Such data, when collected over large groups of test takers, are called *norms*. H. D. Hoover (1984) distinguished between two types of score scales: status and developmental. The notion of status and developmental scales follows logically from the discussion of mastery and developmental objectives presented in Chapter 5. Status scales describe relative performance of individual students in a single comparison group. This group can simply be an individual teacher's class, a school, a system, or a national sample. The scales used to express performance under these conditions simply reflect a simple rank-ordering of individuals, compared with other individuals, whereas percent scores provide a rank-ordering of scores compared with a standard. Developmental scale scores describe performances with a series of different comparison groups such as grade level or age groups. Sometimes scores are simply expressed as linear or one-to-one transformations or, for percentile ranks, as $z$ scores. Other times, depending on the intended use and the audience for the score, an area transformation is undertaken. The model frequently used for the area transformation is the normal curve. Users of standardized tests should examine very carefully the technical description of the derivation of the score scales used with their measures.

The combination of the status and developmental scale categories and linear and area transformation derivation categories yields four different families of score scales. These are summarized in Figure 16-1. The methods used to derive most of these scores have been described in Chapter 13. The only new score is the expanded standard score, which employs sophisticated statistical techniques and usually requires the within group (usually grade) distribution to be normal. Some testing people assume that "normalizing" a distribution makes it into an equal-interval scale. It does not!

Other kinds of status standard scores, such as the College Entrance Examination Board Scores, are used to report performance on the Scholastic Assessment Test and the American College Testing program tests. A variety of developmental scores are also created and used by different test publishers for different kinds of tests.

The collections of derived scores that are formed into distributions for specified groups are referred to as norms. Norms are used for making rela-

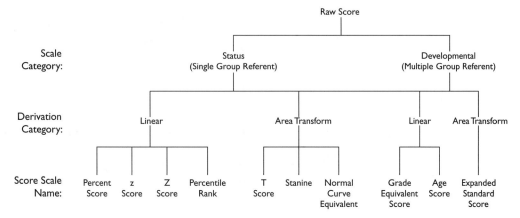

**Figure 16-1** *Types of derived score scales*

tive interpretations of scores. In the following section the major kinds of norms and some of their strengths and weaknesses are described.

### Percentile Rank Norms

Percentile ranks can be used to express local or national normative data and are also particularly useful with classroom tests. The process merely requires developing a frequency distribution and calculating a percentile rank for each raw score according to the procedures outlined in Chapter 13. Given that an individual has a raw score equivalent to a percentile rank of 64, we can say that a performance is as good as or better than 64 percent of the people with whom we are contrasting it. The use of percentile ranks is recommended because they are readily understood by almost everyone and can be used with many types of tests and distributions of scores. The fact that percentile ranks depend on the frequency distribution creates a potential danger in interpretation: the units used to express percentile ranks are not equal to raw score units (except in the unlikely occurrence of a rectangular distribution, that is, a distribution in which each observed score has the same frequency of occurrence). The difference in raw score units between percentile ranks of 84 and 88 is *not* equal to the differences between the percentile ranks of 50 and 54. We have, then, an interpretation based only on a ranking of individuals, without considering differences between ranks. Because of the unequal units, percentile ranks should not be averaged (unless you want to describe average percentile ranks). The point is that the mean percentile rank is not equal to the percentile rank of the mean.

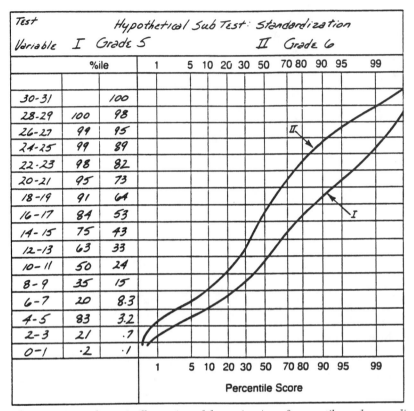

**Figure 16-2** *Schematic illustration of determination of percentile rank norm lines for grades 5 and 6 on hypothetical mathematics test*

An illustration of the method used to determine percentile ranks from norm tables for a hypothetical mathematics test is presented in Figure 16-2. The procedure is relatively straightforward. Each raw score distribution (for grade 5 and grade 6 separately) was plotted on normal percentile paper, a smooth curve was fitted to the points, and the percentile rank corresponding to each score was read. For grade 5, a raw score of about 11 has a percentile rank of 50, but for grade 6 a raw score of about 17 is needed for the same percentile rank. In other words, the 50th percentile for grade 5 is 11 and for grade 6 is 17.

**Standard Score Norms**

As with percentile ranks, standard scores can be used to express either local or national normative data. They are very effective with classroom tests. Standard scores have an advantage over percentile ranks because the raw score directly reflects the size of the measurement unit. In addition, the scores are on a "standard scale" with fixed mean and standard deviation, which allows us to manipulate them mathematically with greater confidence. Refer to Appendix B for a table showing the relationship between $T$ and $z$ scores, and percentile ranks when the underlying distribution is normally distributed. Another frequently used type of standard score is the normal curve equivalent (see Chapter 13).

There are some disadvantages in using standard scores. Standard scores are insensitive to the shape of the distribution. This relates to a problem of interpretation. Suppose an individual student had taken two tests, say a math and a science test. He achieved a standard score of $+1.2$ on each test. Could we conclude that his performance was *equivalent* on both tests? No! His performance might correspond to quite different percentile ranks depending on the shape of the individual distributions, and of course the fact that the tests measured different content and had different numbers of items, means, and standard deviations. Equivalent standard scores do not mean equivalent interpretation on different measures or at different grade levels.

### Grade-Equivalent Norms

A grade equivalent (GE) for a given raw score is the grade level of those students whose median (or mean) is the same as that particular raw score. If the median score of a group of seventh-graders at the beginning of the school year is 54, all raw scores of 54 would have grade equivalents of 7.0. Decimal numbers are usually used, the first digit representing the school year and the second representing the month in a 10-month school year.

A sample of grade-equivalent norms from the *Stanford Achievement Test* is presented in Table 16-1. These norms are for the Social Science subtest (Grade 5, Forms S and T, Intermediate 2 level). Scores are expressed as raw scores, percentile ranks, stanines, and scaled scores. Referring to Table 16-1 it can be seen that a raw score of 21 on the Social Science subtest translates to a scaled score of 645, which in turn converts to a percentile rank of 93 and a stanine of 8—a good performance!

Because they are expressed in terms of the units around which schools are organized, grade equivalents are assumed to be easily understood. In addition, they lend themselves to the plotting of achievement profiles in various subject areas, thus allowing examination of a given pupil's strengths and weaknesses.

A number of potential problems can be encountered in interpreting grade equivalents:

**Table 16-1** *Sample Scaled Scores, Percentile Ranks and Stanines for the Standard Achievement Test—Social Science for Students Tested on Forms S and T in the Spring of Grade 5 (Open Ended) (Norms Table Modified From Original).*

| SOCIAL SCIENCE (OE) | | | Sta-nine | %-lie Rank | SOCIAL SCIENCE (OE) | %-lie Rank |
|---|---|---|---|---|---|---|
| **Raw Score** | **Scaled score** | | | | | |
| | **Fm S** | | | | | |
| | | | **9** | 99 | ABOVE 669 | 99 |
| | | | | 98 | 663–669 | 98 |
| | | | | 97 | 657–662 | 97 |
| 27 | 768 | | | 96 | 653–656 | 97 |
| 26 | 717 | | **8** | 95 | 650–652 | 95 |
| 25 | 691 | | | 94 | 647–649 | 94 |
| 24 | 675 | | | 93 | 644–646 | 93 |
| 23 | 663 | | | 92 | 642–643 | 92 |
| 22 | 653 | | | 91 | 640–641 | 91 |
| 21 | 645 | | | 90 | 638–639 | 90 |
| 20 | 637 | | | 89 | 636–637 | 89 |
| 19 | 631 | | **7** | 88 | 635 | 88 |
| 18 | 624 | | | 87 | 633–634 | 87 |
| 17 | 619 | | | 86 | 632 | 86 |
| 16 | 613 | | | 85 | 630–631 | 85 |
| 15 | 608 | | | 84 | 629 | 84 |
| 14 | 602 | | | 83 | 628 | 83 |
| 13 | 597 | | | 82 | 626–627 | 82 |
| 12 | 592 | | | 81 | 625 | 81 |
| 11 | 587 | | | 80 | 624 | 80 |
| 10 | 582 | | | 79 | 623 | 79 |
| 9 | 577 | | | 78 | 622 | 78 |
| 8 | 572 | | | 77 | 621 | 77 |
| 7 | 567 | | **6** | 76 | 620 | 76 |
| 6 | 561 | | | 75 | 619 | 75 |
| 5 | 554 | | | 74 | 618 | 74 |
| 4 | 547 | | | 73 | 617 | 73 |
| 3 | 538 | | | 72 | 616 | 72 |
| 2 | 525 | | | 71 | 615 | 71 |
| 1 | 503 | | | 70 | 614 | 70 |
| | | | | 69 | 613 | 69 |
| | | | | 68 | 612 | 68 |
| | | | | 67 | 611 | 67 |
| | | | | 66 | 610 | 66 |
| | | | | 65 | 609 | 65 |
| | | | | 64 | 608 | 64 |
| | | | | 63 | 607 | 63 |
| | | | | 62 | 606 | 62 |
| | | | | 61 | 605 | 61 |
| | | | | 60 | 604 | 60 |

*Source: Stanford Achievement Test:* Ninth Edition. Copyright © 1996 by Harcourt, Inc. Reproduced by permission. All rights reserved.

1. It is incorrect to say, for example, that a sixth-grader who achieves a grade equivalent of 8 on a test is performing at an eighth-grade level. She has been taught and tested on sixth-grade material, not eighth-grade material. Rather, she performs as would the typical eighth-grader taking *her* test.

2. Grade-equivalent norms assume uniform growth throughout the year, which is not the case within or across subject areas or grades. Students don't all learn at the same rate! A grade score of 3.0 might yield a percentile rank of 40 on a reading subtest and a percentile rank of 20 on a math subtest of a survey achievement battery. The units of measurement are ambiguous. This lack of uniformity in scaling is illustrated in Figure 16-3. The curve represents a plot of grade-equivalent scores and raw scores, which obviously departs from a straight-line relationship. Caution, then, must be used when interpreting a given individual's score on different subtests and on assessing growth. In other words, a change of 3 score points can result in a variable change in grade scores, depending on raw scores involved. Again, *students learn different subjects at different rates*.

3. It is impossible to test all grade levels. Therefore, a great many grade equivalents are based on extrapolated or interpolated values, which tend to be nothing more than statistical guesses. **Extrapolated** grade equivalents are estimates *beyond* the actual database, and **interpolated** values are *between* actual data points.

4. The procedures used to determine grade equivalents tend to exaggerate the significance of small differences in raw scores because of customarily large within-grade variability.

5. There is a danger that, because of the correspondence between the label *grade equivalent* and the way the schools are organized, teachers will consider the grade equivalent a *standard* for performance. Such a misinterpretation attests to lack of knowledge of local objectives and individual differences.

6. A score on any achievement test is a function of the treatment of the subject matter in the curriculum. An assumption of uniformity for test standardization is unwarranted.

7. Extremely high or low grade equivalents are difficult to interpret because of the lack of reliable measurement at the extremes of any score scale.

8. Most norms tables are based on a 10-month school year and thus ignore the gains or losses of proficiency that occur during the summer months.

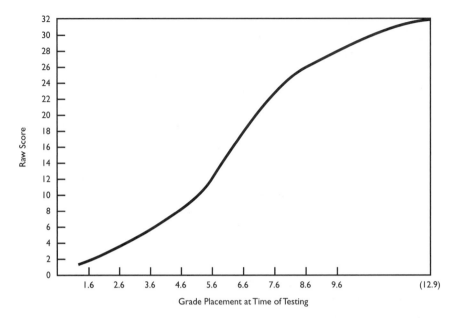

**Figure 16-3** *Hypothetical relationship between raw score and grade placement used to establish grade-equivalents*

Because of these shortcomings, grade equivalents are frequently and ferociously attacked by members of the testing profession and the general public. H. D. Hoover (1984), however, suggested that, as so often is the case, it is not an inherent weakness of the grade-equivalent concept that is the problem; rather, it is the user who faults the interpretation. Hoover also presented strong evidence that grade equivalents can be averaged and the grade equivalents below grade placement are fairly accurate indicators of level performance.

Grade-equivalent scores should not be interpreted literally. They are useful, particularly for interpreting elementary school performances and in areas characterized by continual development, but should only be used as rough guides to level of performance.

### Age Norms

Similar to grade norms, age norms are based on average test performances at various age levels. The units are also unequal, that is, equal age units do not correspond to equal score units. They are useful for expressing growth in mental ability, reading ability, and other phenomena characterized by fairly consistent growth patterns and treatment in the instructional program. Age norms are probably underused. They can be useful in monitoring development and growth.

## Local Norms

Local norms are valuable for many purposes besides those stated by test publishers. Because of the idiosyncrasies of the local curriculum, student body, community needs, and teacher characteristics, national norms may not be representative of the local instructional situation. Local school personnel must then develop their own reference data. Generating test data and summarizing them in the form of percentile ranks and standard scores would be most helpful, particularly for achievement test results. Some test manuals provide guidelines for the development of local norms. In addition, many test publishers will provide a norming service for a nominal fee.

## Expectancy Norms

It is unreasonable to interpret performance on a test without considering other relevant variables. For an achievement test, one relevant variable is student ability. Many test publishers therefore provide for the dual standardization of achievement and scholastic aptitude (or intelligence) tests. The correlation between achievement and aptitude measures is determined and, using the aptitude score, an expected achievement performance can be predicted. In this manner, a student can be judged to be under- or overachieving in a particular subject. The expectancy table is one form in which these data are expressed (see Chapter 14 for a description of expectancy tables).

## "User" Norms

To keep their norms as current as possible, test publishers occasionally accumulate data from systems who buy their tests and services. These current files of scores can be used to build tables of norms. Obvious bias exists in such so-called normative data as only the self-selected users of that particular test or battery are included in the database, but perhaps such data can be used to gauge fluctuations in performance over the life of the current edition. An enlightened system test coordinator can, in fact, accumulate or have the publisher accumulate data so that local norms can be established.

## Developmental Standard Score Norms

A continuous developmental scale is desirable if we are to describe developmental level and measure growth. Expanded standard score scale norms are used for this purpose. Instruction is usually organized around grade groupings. Most developmental scales are therefore derived from grade-referenced groups. The intended use of a developmental or standard score system is to facilitate comparison of performances for the same individual on different forms or at different levels of the test, thereby allowing for the study of change in performance over time. The Ninth Edition of the *Stanford Achievement Test*, for example, reports its normative scores in the form of raw scores, scaled scores (ranging from the 300s to 800s, depending on level and form of the battery), individual percentile ranks, stanines, normal curve equivalents and grade equivalents, achievement/ability comparisons, small ($N < 50$) and large ($N > 50$) group percentile ranks and stanines, content cluster performance categories, skill groups, and item difficulty ($p$) values. Relationships among the stanines, percentile ranks, normal curve equivalents, and performance classifications are shown in Figure 16-4.

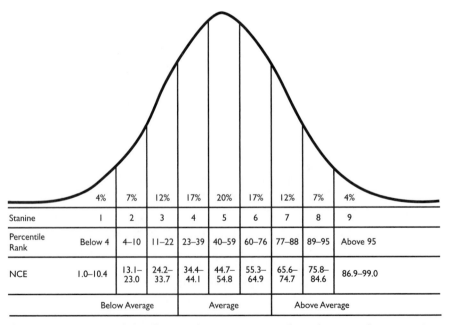

**Figure 16-4** *A normal distribution of stanines, percentile ranks, normal curve equivalents, and performance classifications*

**Table 16-2**  *Scaled Scores for Selected Percentile Ranks Across Grades for Hypothetical Reading Comprehension Test*

| Percentile Rank | Grade | | | | | | | | | | | | |
|---|---|---|---|---|---|---|---|---|---|---|---|---|---|
| | K | I | 2 | 3 | 4 | 5 | 6 | 7 | 8 | 9 | 10 | II | 12 |
| 90 | 469 | 608 | 643 | 667 | 679 | 695 | 704 | 711 | 720 | 726 | 732 | 735 | 739 |
| 75 | 445 | 563 | 617 | 640 | 656 | 672 | 681 | 688 | 697 | 703 | 709 | 712 | 715 |
| 50 | 427 | 516 | 584 | 609 | 626 | 646 | 653 | 663 | 672 | 678 | 682 | 686 | 688 |
| 25 | 415 | 482 | 550 | 579 | 595 | 616 | 625 | 636 | 646 | 652 | 655 | 659 | 661 |
| 10 | 402 | 463 | 523 | 555 | 569 | 591 | 601 | 613 | 623 | 628 | 631 | 634 | 637 |

The large and small group data are based on averages and are therefore less variable. The broad performance categories that might be used for instructional grouping are Below Average (stanines 1, 2, and 3), Average (stanines 4, 5, and 6), and Above Average (stanines 7, 8, and 9). Table 16-2 contains scaled scores for selected percentile ranks across grades K to 12 for a hypothetical reading comprehension test. Note the proportional increase in standard score as one moves from the kindergarten to the 10th percentile rank (402) to the 90th (469), and from the 90th of kindergarten (469) to the 90th level at 12th (739). The continuous nature of the scaling is graphically reflected in Figure 16-5.

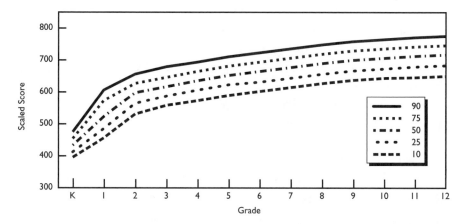

**Figure 16-5** *Plot of scaled scores for selected percentile ranks across grades for hypothetical reading comprehension test (data from Table 16-2)*

## CRITERIA FOR PUBLISHED NORMS AND MANUALS

A test manual should provide a comprehensive description of the procedures used in collecting normative data. Among the essential and desirable characteristics of normative data are the following (American Psychological Association, et al., 1985; American Educational Research Association, American Psychological Association, & National Council on Measurement in Education, 1999):

1. The nature, rationale, and derivation of the scales used to report scores should be spelled out early in test publications.

2. Normative data should be described clearly so that a potential user can readily judge the relevance of the norms for particular testing purposes.

3. Normative data should be reported in the form of standard scores and percentile ranks.

4. If grade norms are provided, provision should be made for converting grade equivalents to standard scores and percentile ranks.

5. With each test revision or renorming, relationships between new and old norms should be described and equivalency tables provided, particularly for content.

6. Normative data and technical manuals should be published at the same time as the test.

7. The publisher should make every effort to keep norms as current as possible.

8. The publisher should point out the importance of establishing local norms as well as procedures useful for doing so.

9. Descriptive data (e.g., measures of central tendency and variability) should be reported for the normative sample(s).

10. In addition to norms, tables should be provided showing the expectation a person who achieves a given test score has of attaining or exceeding some relevant criterion score (expectancy tables).

11. Sufficient information should be provided on such variables as number of schools, sex, number of cases, geographic location, age, educational level, and the like, so that it can be determined whether a set of norms are in fact representative of the population they claim to represent.

12. Sampling procedures should be spelled out in detail.

13. Normative data should be reported only if the associated reliability and validity data are also available, and they should be related to score interpretation.

**14.** The testing conditions under which the normative data were obtained should be specified.

**15.** If profiling of different subtests is suggested, the relevant normative data should be comparable, that is, gathered on the same population(s).

**16.** If an anchor test was used to equate test forms, its parameters should be described in detail.

**17.** Equivalence of alternative test administration modes should be documented (e.g., computer administration).

**18.** Test manuals should (a) describe rationale for uses of test, (b) summarize relevant research, (c) list qualifications needed by users, (d) describe alternate response recording modes, (e) explain interpretation guidelines in detail, and in general (f) describe all norming studies.

**19.** Promotional material should be accurate and honest.

**20.** Empirical data and acceptable standard-setting methods should be used to establish "cut" scores.

## TEACHER RESPONSIBILITIES

Examinees feel tension and anxiety before, during, and after a testing experience. This is particularly true if the test is of great consequence to the examinee, for example, with **high-stakes tests**. Midterms and finals, college entrance exams, and scholarship qualifying exams are examples of tests likely to evoke considerable test anxiety potentially harmful to student performance. In the classroom situation, improper uses of tests can damage the teacher-student relationship. The misuse of tests stems primarily from two sources: (1) misunderstanding of the proper role of tests, and (2) failure to appreciate the emotional problems posed for some children by an ego-threatening evaluation procedure. Eight kinds of problems can be noted:

**1.** If teachers think of the norm on a standardized test as a goal to be reached by all students and if they criticize those who fail to meet this rigid standard, students will quite naturally think of tests as hurdles rather than as stepping stones to development.

**2.** If teachers, in interpreting test results, fail to consider other relevant information—ability differences, health status, home background, and the like—they are likely to render an unjust appraisal of a child's work, which may well discourage or antagonize the child.

**3.** If teachers overemphasize tests in the evaluation program and fail to realize that they cover only a part of the desired outcomes, they run the risk of placing undue emphasis on certain objectives and confusing students about what they are supposed to be learning.

**4.** If teachers habitually use test results as bases for invidious comparisons among students, not only is the student-teacher relationship damaged, but also the relationships among the students are damaged.

**5.** If teachers berate or scold children because of poor performance on a test, children may develop unfavorable attitudes toward future testing and learning.

**6.** If teachers fail to let students know how they did on a test, or give any indication of how the testing is related to educational purposes, it is hard for students to make sense of the procedure.

**7.** If a teacher is insecure, and feels threatened by the tests, it is almost certain that this attitude will be communicated to the children. If a school-wide or systemwide testing program is in operation, and the teachers have had no part in planning nor do they understand the purposes, they are obviously in no position to make clear to the students how the testing is likely to do them any good. If the test results are used as a means of appraising teacher competence, the temptation becomes very strong for the teacher to teach for the tests.

**8.** If teachers are unsympathetic to a testing program in which they must participate, and make sarcastic references to "these tests that we have to give again," they are certainly engendering a poor attitude among students; even young children are shrewd enough to sense, however vaguely, that by such behavior the teacher is abdicating this rightful position.

Teachers, of course, are not the only users of tests. Anyone administering or using test information must be sensitive to the issues just raised.

Such commonsense procedures as returning test papers as soon as possible, discussing test items with the entire class, and demonstrating to the class how test information is used will help develop proper student attitudes and a healthy perspective on the place and value of testing in the instructional program. There is no substitute for respect for individual students and their needs and desires.

## INTERPRETING AND REPORTING TEST RESULTS TO THE PUBLIC

Because of their considerable interest and investment in education, members of the general public need to be appraised of student progress and achievement. One of the most efficient ways of communicating information on performance is probably the use of standardized test scores. Despite their shortcomings, the results derived from standardized tests constitute an immediately understandable summary of student performances. Public reports of test scores must be carefully presented and explained. Gene Hawes (1972) summarized several guidelines for reporting test results to the public:

1. *Prepare the public and press for the impending report.* A briefing session should be held to discuss the intent of administering the tests and their use.

2. *Introduce the results with an explanation of test content.* A series of scores is relatively meaningless by itself. A description of the tests' content will help communicate their value to individual students, the schools, and the public.

3. *Prepare a tabular summary of the results for general release.* Breakdowns accompanied by descriptions of such factors as full score ranges, medians, socioeconomic background of the school population, and sex differences will help convey a clearer picture of the results. Consider ways of reporting results for special samples and comparative and growth data.

4. *Avoid the use of composite scores for each school.* Composite scores invite invidious comparisons between schools and are open to misinterpretation and misuse. The use of composite scores in-house is, however, defensible.

5. *Avoid reporting grade equivalents.* The danger of using grade equivalents has been discussed. If possible, report percentiles by grade.

6. *Avoid implying that norms are standards.* Emphasize that normative data are references and benchmarks. A more informative approach is to cite growth data over time (assuming the same tests are involved).

7. *For school-by-school release, report factors influencing test score meaning.* There are many relevant "input factors." Ability level of the student body, teacher turnover rate, per-student cost factors, socioeconomic base of the school population, average class size, student-teacher ratios, teacher salaries, minority enrollment, student mobility, average daily attendance, average years' teaching experience, and teachers' educational level are some variables that help account for a school's test results. Any innovative approach—a large number of open classrooms, for example—should be acknowledged, because it influences curriculum and, in turn, affects test results.

8. *Provide an overall summary of the results.* It is better for the local educational agency to prepare the summary than to allow those less

informed about tests to make possibly damaging interpretations. Emphasis should be on the broad significance of the results for the community, particularly on planning and the need for innovative programs.

## STANDARD SETTING FOR HIGH-STAKES TESTS

Technological innovations and public and private demand for knowledge about school effectiveness have resulted in many changes in type of data collected and how those data are transmitted and interpreted. Following is a discussion of major issues that have arisen in the past decade.

Evaluation is just that—the making of a value judgment. The use of criteria and standards in evaluating outcomes of an assessment sets it apart from most other scientific activities. As most experts note, there must be "worth determination." Historically, "worth" has been defined in statistical terms, for example, whether data fit a particular mathematical model. Recent trends focus on involving the stakeholders or evaluators or both in the process of setting outcome-based standards (e.g., 50 percent of the students must master 75 percent of the outcomes).

There are vocal opponents and proponents of standard setting, particularly for determining student competence with high-stakes tests (e.g., high school graduation). Opponents argue that virtually all methods of establishing standards are arbitrary and that it is difficult, if not impossible, to get judges to agree on applicable standards. Proponents cite research supporting good consistency in specifying standards, particularly when there is training involved and pilot test data are available to help guide decisions.

A useful classification scheme for organizing some 38 different standard-setting methods has been proposed by Ron Berk (1986) and modified by the late Richard Jaeger (1989). An initial dichotomy is proposed: state versus continuum. A *state* model assumes that competency is an all-or-nothing condition, and therefore to be categorized as a "master," the examinee must have a perfect test performance. The procedure calls for adjusting backward from 100 percent (e.g., to 90 percent) to set the standard. A *continuum* model assumes that mastery or competence is continuously distributed. The standard-setting task is to search for all meaningful boundaries to establish categories. Continuum models can be test-centered or examinee-centered. All standard-setting methods involve making judgments. This activity is implicit in all standard-setting procedures. Table 16-3 contains a summary of three approaches to standard setting.

An example of the test-centered approach should help illustrate the process. In this case it will be Angoff's modified procedure (Angoff, 1971).

**Table 16-3**  *Summary of Categories of Standard-Setting Methods*

| Category | Description | Example |
|---|---|---|
| State | Adjustments down from 100 percent performance criterion are made based on judgments about fallibility of test and characteristics of examinees. | Child will have demonstrated mastery of specified knowledge, ability, or skill when he performs correctly 85 percent of time (Tyler, 1973). |
| Test-Centered Continuum | Population of judges makes probability estimates about item performances of borderline or minimally competent examinees. | Minimum standards were researched based on the National Teacher Examination (Cross, Impara, Frary, & Jaeger, 1984). |
| Examinee-Centered Continuum | Judges familiar with examinees categorize them (e.g., master, borderline, nonmaster), test is administered, overlap in distributions is assessed. | Second-grade basic skills tests (language arts, mathematics) were used to compare teacher judgments and examinee performance (Mills, 1983). |

*Source:* After Jaeger (1989).

Assume an instructor wants to set a basic passing score for a midterm exam in an introductory statistics course. The exam is composed of 40 items.

Sample Item: A student obtains a raw score of 23 in a unimodel, moderately skewed distribution of test scores with a median of 23. What would be the student's z score?

(a) Exactly zero

(b) Greater or less than zero, depending on value of the standard deviation

(c) Greater or less than zero, depending on the direction of the skewness (answer)

A group of experts (instructors and advanced doctoral students) were asked to make judgments about each item. The judging directions were as follows:

What percentage of minimally competent introductory statistics students will correctly respond to this item?

Judges (experts) were to select from one of the following percentages:

5%, 20%, 40%, 60%, 75%, 90%, 95%

Each judge's estimates were summed across items, thus yielding an "expected score" for a hypothetical minimally competent student. The expected scores were then averaged across judges. We can readily see some interesting variations on this approach. Data on previous students' performance on the item could be provided to the judges. Instead of a dichotomous decision, data about multiple-competency categories could be gathered. Groups of students who had been previously classified on bases other than the test could have been administered the test and actual and expected results compared.

### Training for Setting Standards

For the collective judgment approach to work effectively, some preparation and training must occur. This is particularly crucial when high-stakes standards are involved (e.g., setting grade promotion score standards). W. J. Popham (1987b) suggested several guidelines for preparing judges. Among the information necessary for *informed judgment* is the following:

1. Delineation of consequences of decision: What are potential effects on the individual and society?

2. Description of examination: If possible, have decision makers take exams to assess difficulty level.

3. Provision of information on reliability and validity of exam: In particular, questions of bias should be addressed.

4. Overview of phase-in time for exam and system: Shorter time perhaps calls for more relaxed standards.

5. Description of examinee instructional preparation for exam: Was it adequate and sufficiently comprehensive?

6. Overview of audiences with interest in results of application of standard: An examination of possible vested interests in higher or lower standards.

7. Description of experts' recommendations: Formal review of test by expert groups should be part of process.

8. Overview of field-test results and actual data on subgroups: Data should be examined.

9. Assess standard-setting time-line alternatives relative to objectives of exercise: Standards can be elevated or lowered depending on phase-in and preparation time.

10. Inform interested audiences about the process and products of standard setting: Media representatives, in particular, need to be prepared.

Standard setting is a very important, if complex and sensitive, task that needs to be taken seriously by policy makers and testing experts alike. If taken seriously, standard setting will require a great deal of preparation, planning, organization of data, and—above all—patience.

## THE LAKE WOEBEGON EFFECT

The ever-present influence of the "accountability" movement in education usually has a positive impact, but perverse reactions can also result. The improvement of the quality of curriculum, instruction, and school administrative practices is the most frequent outcome of demands for reform. Occasionally teachers will teach test material or deviate from proper test-taking procedures to inflate outcome measures. This reaction may be one underlying cause of J. J. Cannell's description of the so-called Lake Woebegon Effect—so named because of National Public Radio's Garrison Keillor's characterization of fantasized Lake Woebegon, Minnesota, children as all being above average (Cannell, 1988). Cannell's survey of 50 states revealed that no state had a mean that was below the 50th percentile for national elementary school norm groups. His data were derived from six different commercially available standardized tests. We must be cautious in interpreting the 100 percent above median finding because only a *sample* of the elementary students are included within each state. In addition to teaching for or to the test, probably the major source of the normal problems is the likelihood of bias or lack of representativeness in the original standardizations.

Despite the extreme care that test publishers take in collecting data from representative school systems, schools, and classes, bias does creep in. Participation in the norming process is voluntary. Publishers do provide "free" goods and services to participating schools. If a school has a restricted budget, these services might look very appealing. Because of the phenomenal costs, test publishers only renorm their large batteries every six to nine years. This also means that norms are "time-bound," that is, the lag between revision and restandardization is behind current use. This implies that current performances are probably better than the norms. Research also shows that the students in systems using a particular test service do better than nonusers, including those in the standardization.

> [I]f a state's average score in reading is at the 54th percentile, the proper interpretation of this score is that the average or typical *student* in the state performed better than 54% of the norming sample. It is not appropriate to conclude that all students in the state are above average in reading, that the state as a whole is above average in reading relative to other states, or that the state as a whole is above average in reading relative to the national norm. (Lenke & Keene, 1988).

This caution again underscores the potential danger of viewing norms on standardized tests as "standards" to be achieved by all students.

Following are some measures that are being used to guard against distortion in norms' relevant interpretation: (a) better test security, (b) more frequent renorming, (c) less frequent testing that might also employ some matrix sampling scheme, (d) improved information for test users on interpretation of the meaning of scores, and (e) possible use of National Assessment of Educational Progress data to make normative interpretations. Based on his in-depth analysis of the problems (Mehrens & Kaminski, 1989) and remarks made before the Georgia Educational Research Association and School Test Coordinators in Atlanta on October 13, 1989, Dr. William A. Mehrens noted,

1. The desire for accountability and test-curriculum match increases the tendency to teach toward specific objectives, skills, subskills, and maybe even items.

2. Teaching toward the test can be either helpful or harmful.

3. Inferences to a domain only sampled by the objectives will necessarily be incorrect if the preceding instruction was limited to only the objectives sampled.

4. Inferences from tests used to (a) inform the public about educational quality, or (b) inform parents and students about how the education of the student is progressing will almost always be to a domain that is greater than the objectives tested.

5. We are misleading the public, students, and perhaps ourselves when we limit instruction to the objectives tested.

6. It is inappropriate to use study guides or practice tests that encourage such limited instruction.

7. School districts and states must seriously consider and establish policies regarding:

   a. the appropriate test/curriculum match and what constitutes inappropriate teaching to the test.

   b. legitimate and illegitimate study guides.

8. Test security must be maintained.

What this phenomena really means is that the testing industry must redouble its efforts to evaluate and inform the test-using community not only about the advantages of standardized testing but also about the potential negatives as well.

Interpreting test scores—whether to individual students, colleagues, parents, or members of the community in general—requires careful preparation and a thorough understanding of what test scores mean, what influences them, and how they can be used. It is a demanding task.

## CASE STUDY

Our Reading Education midterm exam was administered to the class of Ms. Dot Com with the following results.

Mean = 57.56          Standard Deviation = 5.1
Reliability = 0.79     Number of items = 80

Using these data, write out interpretations for the following scores. Readers may wish to refer back to Chapter 13 to refresh their memories about the meaning of basic formulas. Basic data on the class performance are also contained in the case study application associated with Chapter 13.

1. Red got a raw score of 64 on the test. What would be (a) an absolute and (b) a relative interpretation of his performance?
2. Chelsea got a raw score of 69 on the test. Is it likely that her score is meaningfully different from that of Red?
3. Assume that Chelsea's score translates to a grade equivalent of 13.3. What interpretation could be made of her performance?
4. Red's score is equivalent to a percentile rank of ____? What does that mean?

## CONTENT REVIEW STATEMENTS

1. Test performances can be interpreted in light of absolute standards, relative averages, or test content.

2. Norms will generally reference performances to a single group (status) or multiple groups (developmental).

3. Normative scores will either be linear (take the shape of the underlying raw score distribution) or reflect area transformation (usually to a normal distribution).

4. Normative data can be expressed in the form of raw scores, standard scores ($z$, $Z$, $T$, CEEB score, or stanines), percentile ranks, age scores, or grade scores.

**5.** The value of any set of normative data rests primarily on the nature, representatives, and number of students and schools included.

**6.** Percentile rank and standard score norms have direct interpretability if the national sample matches the local group in relevant demographic and educational characteristics.

**7.** A grade equivalent is the average raw test score for a particular grade.

**8.** Among other problems, grade-equivalent forms suffer from the following shortcomings:

    a. A given grade equivalent does not mean the same thing for each student who receives it, whether the student is in the same class or grade or is above or below it.

    b. Most grade norms are based on the untenable assumption of uniform growth throughout the year and therefore use ambiguous units of measure.

    c. Most grade norms discount the learning or loss of learning that occurs over the summer months.

    d. Extrapolated (estimated) grade norms are open to many misinterpretations.

    e. Grade norms should not be considered standards.

    f. The value of grade norms depends on the match between curriculum and test content.

    g. Extreme grade equivalents are difficult to interpret.

**9.** Age norms are based on average test scores at various age levels.

**10.** It is highly desirable to develop local test norms.

**11.** Expectancy norms for achievement tests can be developed by relating test scores to ability measures or other relevant external criteria.

**12.** Developmental standard score norms allow for the tracking of growth.

**13.** Published test norms should be

    a. Clearly described.

    b. Expressed as standard scores and percentile ranks.

    c. As up-to-date as possible.

**14.** In interpreting test scores to students, consider the potential psychological impact of such scores and the many related factors that affect meaning.

**15.** A student has a right to an interpretation of his or her score on any test.

**16.** In interpreting and reporting scores to the public, take care to

    a. Explain the purpose of the tests.

    b. Avoid the use of composite scores for each school.

    c. Prepare a tabular and narrative summary.

    d. Avoid implying that norms are standards.

    e. Consider the many economic and demographic variables that influence test scores.

**17.** The Lake Woebegon Effect describes the phenomena of the appearance of all students being at or above the 50th percentile (above average).

**18.** Computer-generated test interpretations need to be considered with caution.

**19.** Setting standards for interpreting scores involves collecting "informed judgments."

**20.** Judges can be trained to reliably set standards.

**21.** Teachers can develop a supportive assessment environment that will allow students to maximize their performances.

---

## SPECULATIONS

**1.** What are the most important characteristics of test norms?

**2.** What are "local norms"?

**3.** What are the advantages and disadvantages of grade-equivalent scores used as norms?

**4.** Are there any conditions under which it is acceptable to "teach for the test"?

**5.** Is it likely that a test-wise student can successfully guess his or her way through a test?

**6.** What are the pros and cons of having separate norms tables for subsamples of school populations (e.g., ethnic or gender groups)?

**7.** Is it possible for everybody to be above average?

## SUGGESTED READINGS

Carey, L. M. (2001). *Measuring and evaluating school learning* (3rd ed.). Boston: Allyn & Bacon. Chapter 15 is a very readable summary of approaches to interpreting standardized test results.

Hopkins, K. D., Stanley, J. C., & Hopkins, B. R. (1990). *Educational and psychological measurement and evaluation.* Englewood Cliffs, NJ: Prentice Hall. Chapter 3 focuses on the types of and interpretation of test scores and use of norms.

Linn, R. L., & Gronlund, N. (2000). *Measurement and evaluation in teaching* (8th ed.). New York: Macmillan. Chapter 19 contains an educationally oriented discussion of the interpretation of test scores and use of norms.

Lyman, H. B. (1978). *Test scores and what they mean* (3rd ed.). Englewood Cliffs, NJ: Prentice Hall. An excellent overview of the many ways in which test scores can be reported. The emphasis on score interpretation is a strong unit of the book.

Miller, D. M. (1972). *Interpreting test scores.* New York: Wiley. This self-study programmed book contains most of the basic information necessary for initial approaches to test interpretation.

# 17

# Reporting Student Progress

---

## FOCUS CONCEPTS AND KEY TERMS FOR STUDY

| | |
|---|---|
| **Absolute Marks** | **Parent Conferences** |
| **Adjusted Raw Scores** | **Purposes of Marking** |
| **Dishonest Marking** | **Relative Marks** |
| **Goal Card** | **Standard Scores** |
| **Models for Marking** | **Student-Led Conferences** |

---

## STANDARDS ALERT

**Standard 13.7          Decision-making**

In educational settings, a decision or characterization that will have a major impact on a student should not be made on the basis of a single test score. Other relevant information should be taken into account if it will enhance the overall validity of the decision.

**Taking It to the Classroom**

Multiple data sources (e.g., formal assessments, observations, papers, products, performances) should be used in making any evaluation about student achievement, whether a progress report, final grade, or diagnostic decision. Multiple data collection aids reliability and validity.

---

Reprinted with permission from the *Standards for Educational and Psychological Testing.* Copyright © 1999 by the American Educational Research Association, the American Psychological Association, and the National Council on Measurement in Education.

The need for informative reporting and marking procedures may be more acute today than at any time in the history of U.S. schools. Increased experimentation with innovative teaching methods and organizational systems is accompanied by a demand for effective communication among those engaged in the educational enterprise. Obviously, students should be appraised of their progress. In addition, data are needed to help teachers plan for effective instructional experiences. This need becomes increasingly important as more and more schools implement individualized instruction and mastery learning programs, which require the continuous monitoring and feedback of progress information. Parents, too, are taking an increased interest in schools. Their need to be informed should be met with the best techniques available.

## ON THE PHILOSOPHY OF MARKING

It is incumbent on all teachers, at every level of instruction, to spell out for their students the basis on which marks will be assigned. The practice of marking, regardless of the problems of accuracy and reliability, will likely continue for many years. Despite instructors' disagreements with the whole notion of marking, they have obligations to assign the most valid and reliable marks possible.

The many and important decisions that are made about students every day, and throughout their educational and occupational careers, dictate such a recommendation. Instructors who pursue a "no-grade" philosophy abrogate their responsibility as educators to communicate with each student about his or her progress.

Teachers, particularly at the elementary levels, are perhaps in an awkward position as they are special support friends as well as standard setters. Unfortunately, too often a mark becomes an indication of justice tempered by mercy. Only if the mark is a valid representation of what the student knows and can do will it be used in the best interest of the student and others. Anything less is a disservice to all.

There is no solution to the marking problem that will prove satisfactory to all concerned. Suffice it to say that the assignment of marks constitutes a powerful system of reward and punishment, which can be used to bring about some highly desirable behavioral changes. Such a point of view implies expending a significant amount of time and effort in arriving at student marks. But preoccupation with marks, on the part of either teacher or student, must be considered unhealthy. Keeping in mind the limitations of marks, the basis of their assignment, and that many significant outcomes of education are neither subject to marking nor markable (e.g., attitudes, values, interests) should lead to a proper perspective. Marks represent an integral, fallible, potentially meaningful, although perhaps irritating, element in the educational process.

## PURPOSES OF MARKING AND REPORTING

Many educators decry the use of marks (or grades—these terms will be used interchangeably) for any purpose. They claim that grades do not motivate but, rather, are quite detrimental to the student psyche and actually have a negative impact. Grades may be perceived as punishment. If grades are reliable, valid, and represent the degree of success achieved in working toward important goals, then information about progress in developing competencies (knowledge and skills) is related to future academic, occupational/vocational, and "life" success. Yes, grades do represent extrinsic rewards, but so do most other recognitions of achievement—from salary increases to ribbons, plaques, and trophies.

Students and teachers, and to some extent parents, exhibit a noticeable degree of tension as marking time rolls around. This tension is especially characteristic of beginning teachers and can generally be attributed to their lack of experience in assigning marks and reporting student progress. The summation of complex human behavior into a simple index, in the form of a letter or number mark, may be presumptuous. If, in addition, marks are *not* based on a rational philosophy of education and a set of operational definitions of expected learning outcomes, their meaning will be obscure and ambiguous, and their purpose(s) will be subverted.

### Communicating with Students and Parents

Marks provide useful and efficient data that can be used to communicate with students and their parents. Marking and reporting are essentially information-processing activities and can be likened to elements in a communications network. Marks are merely the means by which a teacher communicates his or her evaluation of the progress each student has made toward a specified set of educational goals. As in any communications system, the message, that is, information about achievement, may be incorrectly transmitted to the receiver because of faulty encoding or decoding or because of "noise" or "static" in the network.

Students have a right and a need to learn about their progress. In addition to achievement data such as rank in class, grade equivalents, standard scores, and percentile ranks, students seem to desire more "subjective" and criterion-referenced evaluations of their performances. They want to know if their work is outstanding, good, acceptable, or unacceptable. The teacher is probably in a better position than anyone else to integrate the many factors in learning and achievement and to communicate his or her summary to the student.

Parents, too, have a right and need to learn the educational progress of their progeny. Marks are sensible summarizing appraisals that parents can use to counsel their children about their schoolwork and future educational and vocational plans.

### Communicating with Present and Future School Personnel

Just as the results of standardized achievement tests can be used to evaluate the overall progress of a particular instructional program and school, so can distributions of marks indicate trends related to progress. Such data are useful when you are making decisions about promotion, graduation, transfer, and future education.

Indices of past achievement are probably the best single indication of future achievement. College admissions personnel, therefore, view marks as generally indicative of the performance level to be achieved by individual students admitted to the institution. Marks serve as academic currency in the college marketplace, although their exchange and conversion properties are limited.

Promotional decisions should, of course, never be made on the basis of marks alone. Tom Holmes (1989) has shown that requiring a student to repeat a grade results in very little improvement in achievement and only compounds "social" promotion. A summary (meta-analysis) of 63 studies found that, on the average, retained children are worse off than their promoted counterparts using both academic and personal adjustment criteria. Little research has focused, however, on the effect of retention *plus* intensive remediation. Retention usually just means "doing it over again."

### Motivating Student Learning

The research literature reveals evidence that marks can reinforce or inhibit learning. Although we would ideally like learning to result from intrinsic motivation, the gross extrinsic force exerted by marks must be acknowledged.

In considering the motivational function of marks, it is important to define the basis on which marks are assigned. If a mark simply indicates status at a particular point in time, most students are unlikely to feel challenged to work for higher marks. If, however, marks reflect improvement or achievement relative to ability, students may be spurred to greater efforts.

### Guiding Future Instruction

Past achievement is the best predictor and prognosticator of future achievement. Information about skills and knowledge already acquired and developed, then, is immensely helpful in designing future educational programs for individual students, groups, or classes. Data about important affective educational outcomes can also serve as a basis for planning meaningful student experiences. The data from criterion-referenced assessment and "goal cards" can be extremely helpful if it is carefully examined.

## RECENT DEVELOPMENTS AND ISSUES IN MARKING AND REPORTING PROCEDURES

There have been many changes in the grading and reporting practices prevalent in schools during the past several decades (Geisinger, 1982; Marzano, 2000; Natriello & Dornbusch, 1984; Terwilliger, 1971). Among the changes are the following:

1. Reporting progress rather than just status.
2. Including character traits as well as achievement (e.g., work habits, personal development).

3. Selectively applying pass/fail systems.

4. Detailed reporting of competencies or skills (especially at the elementary school level) rather than simple letter grades in subject areas.

5. Considering student ability in assigning grades.

6. Expanding the size of grade scale.

7. Encouraging more comments back and forth between teacher and parent.

8. Developing "contracting" grade systems where individual teacher and student pairs negotiate objectives, methods, evaluation, and standards.

Some of these practices were tried and found deficient or of limited applicability. The late Bob Ebel (1965), for example, proposed an ability-adjusted mark distribution model that turned out to be a basic variation on the normal-curve model; it simply results in a higher percentage of higher grades in higher-ability classes and a low percentage of low grades in low-ability classes. Some teachers have philosophical problems with this.

Another system of limited applicability is the pass/fail approach. Although perhaps useful when the only intent is to evaluate the attainment of *minimal* objectives or standards, it may not be advantageous for developmental objectives (greater range of difficulty and complexity) (Terwilliger, 1989). There is some evidence that students do not maximize their efforts under the pass/fail system and that student achievement levels may actually decline (Gold, Reilly, Silberman, & Lehr, 1971).

Individual grade/work contracts seem like an inherently fair way to approach teaching-learning-assessment tasks. There are some distinct advantages of using this approach to manage instruction through the use and clarification of objectives. It can foster positive relations between student and teacher and clarifies expectations. On the negative side is the considerable amount of paperwork required and the loss of data for comparative ranking purposes. The method probably should not be used in public school settings; if it is, it should be on a limited basis. Application of contracts is better used at professional levels for personnel evaluation and supervision (Swanicki, 1981).

A contemporary problem in grading is "inflation." This is primarily a function of assigning a limited number (usually two) of high grades (usually A and B) (Millman, Slovarek, Kulick, & Mitchell, 1983). Reliability tends to suffer if grade inflation is present. The causes of inflation are many. Among these are (a) a shift from norm-referenced to individually referenced performance standards, (b) administrator's increased use of instructional effectiveness ratings about faculty made by students, and (c) general shifts to less rigorous grading standards. In general, grades have become less of an incentive in a motivational sense, and the focus has been retargeted on performance and what individuals can do and what they know. This has caused more testing and the "certification" by exam.

An example of an improved and informative report/progress card is displayed in Figure 17-1. Note in particular the flexibility that allows traditional grades as well as specification of factors contributing to that grade. In addition to cognitive outcomes, some attention is given to the student's affective development.

Another reporting device is the **goal card** objectives or checklist. A goal card, primarily useful at the elementary school level, is simply a listing of skills, knowledges, or competencies with a place to indicate mastery or progress. The unique feature of goal cards is their specificity (e.g., the examinee can construct simple plane figure with straight edge and compass, can set up word problems, can use facts in two-digit columns addition [no carrying], and so forth). Robert Bauernfeind (1967) noted six major advantages of using goal cards:

1. Goal cards help students "see" their progress as they acquire information and develop skills.

2. Goal cards help the teacher specify objectives and arrange them in a logical way.

3. Goal cards are an effective way to communicate with parents and the general public. They serve as an excellent basis for a parent-teacher conference.

4. Goal cards can contribute to planning for instruction, particularly if individualized programs are desired.

5. Goal cards facilitate communication among educators, for example, the grade 1 arithmetic teacher with Grade 2 teachers, or the regular teacher with a substitute teacher.

6. Because they emphasize important objectives, preferably specified in behavioral terms, goal cards can serve as a sound basis for classroom assessment.

See Figure 17-2 for a sample grade 2 mathematics goal card.

An interesting variation of the goal card is being used by the Tucson (Arizona) Unified School District. A prototype elementary school progress report has been piloted with success. Rather than relying on percentages, letter grades, or checked objectives, the system uses "performance narra-

| | First Quarter | | | Second Quarter | | | Third Quarter | | | Fourth Quarter | | |
|---|---|---|---|---|---|---|---|---|---|---|---|---|
| | Excellent Achievement | Work is Satis-factory | Improvement Needed | Excellent Achievement | Work is Satis-factory | Improvement Needed | Excellent Achievement | Work is Satis-factory | Improvement Needed | Excellent Achievement | Work is Satis-factory | Improvement Needed |

## LANGUAGE ARTS

**READING**

| | | | | | | | | | | | | |
|---|---|---|---|---|---|---|---|---|---|---|---|---|
| Working in readiness activities | | | | | | | | | | | | |
| Shows growth in vocabulary | | | | | | | | | | | | |
| Reads with understanding | | | | | | | | | | | | |
| Using word attack skills | | | | | | | | | | | | |
| Reads orally with expression and meaning | | | | | | | | | | | | |
| Reads for enjoyment | | | | | | | | | | | | |
| READING | | | | | | | | | | | | |

**PENMANSHIP**

| | | | | | | | | | | | | |
|---|---|---|---|---|---|---|---|---|---|---|---|---|
| Manuscript _____ Cursive _____ | | | | | | | | | | | | |
| Working in readiness activities | | | | | | | | | | | | |
| Forms letters correctly | | | | | | | | | | | | |
| Spaces properly | | | | | | | | | | | | |
| Writes neatly | | | | | | | | | | | | |
| PENMANSHIP | | | | | | | | | | | | |

**ENGLISH**

| | | | | | | | | | | | | |
|---|---|---|---|---|---|---|---|---|---|---|---|---|
| Applies basic rules of grammar | | | | | | | | | | | | |
| Spells correctly in written work | | | | | | | | | | | | |
| Shows growth in creative expression | | | | | | | | | | | | |
| ENGLISH | | | | | | | | | | | | |

**SPEAKING AND LISTENING**

| | | | | | | | | | | | | |
|---|---|---|---|---|---|---|---|---|---|---|---|---|
| Speaks clearly and distinctly | | | | | | | | | | | | |
| Expresses ideas well | | | | | | | | | | | | |
| Listens attentively | | | | | | | | | | | | |
| Recalls with accuracy | | | | | | | | | | | | |

## MATHEMATICS

| | | | | | | | | | | | | |
|---|---|---|---|---|---|---|---|---|---|---|---|---|
| Working in readiness activities | | | | | | | | | | | | |
| Forms numerals correctly | | | | | | | | | | | | |
| Understands the meanings of numbers | | | | | | | | | | | | |
| Counts and writes in more than one sequence | | | | | | | | | | | | |
| Uses symbols and terms correctly | | | | | | | | | | | | |
| Reads, writes, and solves equations | | | | | | | | | | | | |
| Reasons well in solving problems | | | | | | | | | | | | |
| Knows and understands number facts | | | | | | | | | | | | |
| MATHEMATICS | | | | | | | | | | | | |

## SCIENCE

| | | | | | | | | | | | | |
|---|---|---|---|---|---|---|---|---|---|---|---|---|
| Shows curiosity | | | | | | | | | | | | |
| Applies observation techniques | | | | | | | | | | | | |
| Demonstrates understanding & makes application | | | | | | | | | | | | |
| Bases conclusions on facts and experiences | | | | | | | | | | | | |
| SCIENCE | | | | | | | | | | | | |

**Figure 17-1** *Representative elementary school report form*

| | First Quarter | | | Second Quarter | | | Third Quarter | | | Fourth Quarter | | |
|---|---|---|---|---|---|---|---|---|---|---|---|---|
| | Excellent Achievement | Work is Satisfactory | Improvement Needed | Excellent Achievement | Work is Satisfactory | Improvement Needed | Excellent Achievement | Work is Satisfactory | Improvement Needed | Excellent Achievement | Work is Satisfactory | Improvement Needed |

**SOCIAL STUDIES**

| | | | | | | | | | | | | |
|---|---|---|---|---|---|---|---|---|---|---|---|---|
| Contributes to activities and discussions | | | | | | | | | | | | |
| Has interest in current events | | | | | | | | | | | | |
| Shows growth in understanding of people | | | | | | | | | | | | |
| Understands charts, maps, and graphs | | | | | | | | | | | | |
| Reports information accurately and effectively | | | | | | | | | | | | |
| SOCIAL STUDIES | | | | | | | | | | | | |

ACHIEVEMENT IN SUBJECT AREAS:
A – Excellent
B – Good
C – Fair
D – Poor

**MUSIC AND ART**

| | | | | | | | | | | | | |
|---|---|---|---|---|---|---|---|---|---|---|---|---|
| Participates in music | | | | | | | | | | | | |
| Participates in art | | | | | | | | | | | | |

**HEALTH AND PHYSICAL EDUCATION**

| | | | | | | | | | | | | |
|---|---|---|---|---|---|---|---|---|---|---|---|---|
| Practices good health habits | | | | | | | | | | | | |
| Participates in organized games and free play | | | | | | | | | | | | |

**WORK AND STUDY HABITS**

| | | | | | | | | | | | | |
|---|---|---|---|---|---|---|---|---|---|---|---|---|
| Works independently – uses time wisely | | | | | | | | | | | | |
| Uses materials wisely | | | | | | | | | | | | |
| Works well with the group | | | | | | | | | | | | |
| Takes pride in work | | | | | | | | | | | | |
| Follows directions | | | | | | | | | | | | |

**PERSONAL GROWTH**

| | | | | | | | | | | | | |
|---|---|---|---|---|---|---|---|---|---|---|---|---|
| Accepts responsibilities | | | | | | | | | | | | |
| Practices self-discipline | | | | | | | | | | | | |
| Practices good sportsmanship | | | | | | | | | | | | |
| Respects the rights and property of others | | | | | | | | | | | | |
| Shows courtesy and consideration | | | | | | | | | | | | |
| Shows growth in self-confidence | | | | | | | | | | | | |

**ATTENDANCE**

| | | | | |
|---|---|---|---|---|
| Date of Report | | | | |
| Days Present | | | | |
| Days Absent | | | | |
| Days Tardy | | | | |

**Figure 17-1** *Representative elementary school report form (continued)*

MATHEMATICS GOAL RECORD CARD 2

Pupil _____ Teacher _____ Year _____

Check

Addition combinations 10 and under (automatic response) ......... _____
Subtraction combinations 10 and under (automatic response) ....... _____
Can count to 200 ........................................ _____
Can understand zero as a number ........................... _____
Can understand place value to tens ......................... _____
Can read and write numerals to 200 ......................... _____
Can read and write numeral words to 10 ...................... _____
Can read and write number words to 20 ...................... _____
Use facts in 2-digit column addition (no carrying) ............... _____
Roman numerals to XII .................................... _____
Can tell time:
    Half hour ........................................... _____
    Quarter hour ........................................ _____
Calendar (months, days of week, dates) ...................... _____
Coins and their equivalent value to 25¢ ...................... _____
Recognition of 50¢ coin and $1.00 .......................... _____
Recognize and use ½, ¼, ⅓ of a whole ...................... _____
Addition facts to 18 (aim for mastery) ....................... _____
Subtraction facts to 18 (aim for mastery) ..................... _____
*Can identify simple plane figures:
    Quadrilateral ........................................ _____
    Pentagon ........................................... _____
    Hexagon ............................................ _____
    Octagon ............................................ _____
*Can use compass to bisect line segment, construct triangles, and
    construct perpendiculars ............................... _____
Word problems: (check one)
    1. Can set the problem up ............................. _____
    2. Can understand process involved ..................... _____
    3. Can notate work problems ........................... _____
*(Goals starred are not essential for all students)

Comments:

**Figure 17-2** *Sample grade two mathematics goal card*

tives" similar to the scoring rubrics described in Chapters 8 and 10. Based on "State Essential Skills," a core curriculum was produced. Two general categories of student outcomes are addressed in a report: Learner Qualities and Content Areas. The concepts and skills under Learner Qualities are those of a Self-Directed Learner, Collaborative Worker, Problem Solver, Responsible Citizen, and Quality Producer. The Content Areas are reading, writing, listening and speaking, mathematics, social studies, science, health, and fine arts. An example of the four category rubrics under Self-Directed Learner is as follows:

**4** Student regularly sets achievable goals, considers risks and makes choices about what to do and in what order to do them, reviews progress, and takes responsibility for own actions.

**3** Student often sets achievable goals, considers risks and makes some choices about what to do and in what order to do them, usually reviews the progress being made, and often takes responsibility for own actions.

**2** Student rarely sets achievable goals, has difficulty making choices about what to do and in what order to do them, needs help to review progress, and seldom takes responsibility for own actions.

**1** Student requires help setting goals, completing tasks, and making choices; does not yet take responsibility for own actions.

Parent, student, and teacher have a description of progress each marking period. The report could be used profitably when mixed method assessment procedures are used and integrated into one of four rubrics. A similar and comprehensive approach to grading using rubrics as they relate to "standards" has been proposed by Marzano (2000).

## FACTORS INFLUENCING TEACHER GRADING

The importance of grades in the academic marketplace and the increasing concern with complex learning outcomes (e.g., higher-order problem solving and performance assessment) places great demands on teachers to report student learning outcomes in a valid and reliable manner (Brookhart, 1994). The issue of grade inflation further complicates the meaning of marks.

Many factors influence the marking and grading practices of teachers. A recent survey of secondary teachers (Padgett-Harrison, 2000) identified the following nine influences (together with percent of time mentioned):

Colleagues (95)    Central Office (57)

Board Policies (83)    Graduate Courses (55)

School Administrators (76)    Parents (54)

Students (69)    Undergraduate Courses (53)

Staff Development (64)

It is not surprising to find that colleagues and boards of education carry the most weight in deciding on the content and methods of grading. The relatively small influence of college coursework seems to identify a deficiency in teacher training programs. Further findings by Padgett-Harrison (2000) revealed the relative importance of 11 variables in determining student grades. They were:

Classwork (98)    Ability Level (51)

Homework (88)    Preparedness (45)

Reports (73)    Progress (44)

Effort (68)    Attendance (40)

Participation (66)    Attitude (40)

Notebooks (55)

It was heartening to see that the three most important contributors to student grades were cognitive in nature. If grades are to be used as a kind of "certification" for knowledge and skill acquisition, then those grades must be embedded in a framework of academic performance.

## RECOMMENDATIONS FOR MARKING PRACTICES

After an extensive review of the available but sparse research literature on grading and marking, expert suggestions, and current best practice, Richard Stiggins, David Frisbie, and Philip Griswold (1989) made the following recommendations for assigning grades.

| Recommendation | Reason |
|---|---|
| 1. Students should be informed of procedures and standards to be used. | Professional (ethical) obligations, perhaps even logical requirement. |
| 2. Acquisition of knowledge and skills should be basis for grade. | Teacher and student agree on clear basis for grade. |
| 3. Attitude should not be used as basis for grade. | Trait difficult to define and assess. |

| | |
|---|---|
| 4. Learning ability should not be used as basis for assigning grades. | No fair or universal way to factor ability into grade. |
| 5. Motivation and effort should not be used as basis for grade. | Not primary academic objective. Effort does not equate to knowledge or skill. |
| 6. Interest in subject matter should not be used as basis for grade. | Difficult to define and of questionable legitimacy. |
| 7. Personality (temperament, disposition, character) should not be used as basis for grade. | Not evaluatable traits relative to curriculum. |
| 8. Do not use formative assignments for grades. | These are part of instructional process. |
| 9. Rely primarily on summative measures as basis for grade determination. | Frequent data give most reliable picture of progress. |
| 10. Paper-and-pencil exams can provide valid and reliable bases for grades. | Permit measurement of variety of learning outcomes. |
| 11. Oral exams should be used very sparingly. | Method is of questionable reliability. |
| 12. Performance observations can be reliably employed as partial basis for grade. | Some instructional outcomes can only be assessed through observation. |
| 13. Collect data frequently in concise units. | Frequency is positively related to reliability. |
| 14. Data should be gathered that is maximally valid, reliable, and cost-effective. | Self-monitoring of quality control seldom done. |
| 15. Weight components in accordance with announced specifications. | If weights are not controlled by grader, grades will not be valid. |
| 16. District, school, and teacher grading policies need to be communicated. | Everyone should be held accountable for adherence to the same standards. |
| 17. The normal curve model should not be used to assign grades. | Life is not normally distributed. |
| 18. "Fixed percentages" grades are acceptable if there is a link between percentage and material to be required. | Reference should be on percentage of material, not percentage of individuals obtaining a particular grade. |
| 19. Do not simply aggregate raw score points for assigning grades. | Related to number 15, which suggests that different outcomes have different weighted values. |
| 20. Borderline grade cases should be reviewed in light of additional achievement information. | Graders are fallible. |

Most of these recommendations reflect commonsense approaches, but common sense is frequently overlooked when we engage in the often-emotional task of assigning grades.

# DECISION POINTS IN ESTABLISHING MARKING SYSTEMS

Despite tremendous technical and theoretical advances in education and psychology during the past century, particularly in quantitative methods, we are still unable to recommend a perfectly viable system for assigning marks that will satisfy the majority of educators. This is true partly because most people consider marking a philosophical decision-making process, rather than a statistical one. This view leads to the treatment of marks as "evaluations" representing value judgments about students' learning and achievement. Others resolve the problem by considering grades as "measurements." Information about a student's progress toward a specified set of instructional objectives is gathered, combined in appropriate ways, and summarized as a mark, usually a letter (A through E) or number (1 through 100). Such marks are viewed as summarizations of data, rather than value judgments. This view of marking has some intrinsic appeal because it seems to relieve the teacher of the burden of making subjective judgments. Teachers can say, "Look, I'm just reporting how well my students achieved. I'm not making judgments about them." Despite the psychological comfort that can be derived from such a philosophy, the problem has really not been resolved. The teacher continually makes value judgments about what to teach, how to teach, and the like, and how "measurement" will be reported unavoidably rests on a subjective decision by the teacher.

Failure by an instructor, department, school, or school system to specify the basis on which marks are assigned can only result in chaos. Look, for example, at interschool differences in marking practices. A survey of 129 high schools completed by the Educational Testing Service indicates the diversity of marking policies and practices in effect: (a) 22 percent of the schools in the survey had no fixed policy governing the assignment of marks, (b) 27 percent reported that an absolute standard of achievement was used, (c) 29 percent marked students on achievement in relation to ability, and (d) 16 percent said that marks represented achievement compared with others in the class. Apparently marks mean different things to different people. The purpose of assigning marks is obscured if uniform policies are not adopted. Among the more important decisions that must be confronted in developing policy statements on marking are the following questions.

## Should an Absolute or Relative Standard Be Used?

Because most of the data of education and psychology do *not* conform to the requirement of a ratio scale—that is, a zero on the scale has an absolute meaning—use an absolute scale to assign grades with caution. Even if a student responds correctly to every item on a test, this does not mean that he or she knows all there is to know about a particular subject. Such a score does not represent 100 percent comprehension. Tests are only samples of behavior, and a percentage of the total number of items on a test, or of the raw total number of points it is possible to obtain over a semester's work, should be used with some caution as a basis for assigning marks.

An allied problem is that a fixed method of marking is frequently imposed by school administrators and boards of education. The usual method requires specifying a fixed percentage, for example, 65 percent, as a passing grade. Furthermore, an instructor is frequently limited in the percentage of certain grades he or she can assign. Such limitations actually require the instructor to predict the difficulty level of the items on his or her tests and predetermine the shape of the final distribution of scores, so that a specified number of students will fall into each achievement category. Such a task is almost impossible, even for the most highly trained professional test developer. Such an imposition of fixed percentages requires the teacher to play "catch-up" at the end of the semester. The teacher can provide bonus points for projects or construct very difficult or very easy tests (without considering what the tests are supposed to measure) until the "correct" number of marks has been achieved.

The ability levels of classes as a whole do vary, and it therefore seems reasonable to allow the class performance to determine the distribution of marks. A reference point, however, is needed. We can use a measure of central tendency—either the mean or the median—as a starting point for assigning marks. The former, however, being an arithmetic average, is unduly affected by extreme scores, and because classroom tests frequently yield asymmetrical distributions, the mean is probably an unwise choice. The median is generally considered the most representative measure of central tendency of all the scores in a distribution, and its selection makes sense, at least from a logical standpoint. If you assign marks on a relative basis, a more logical starting point than the mean or median is needed. Such a starting point could be derived from the table of specifications and list of objectives for the course. Minimal requirements and competencies to be achieved could be identified, translated into expected scores, and then used to assign marks.

### Should Level of Achievement or Effort Form the Basis of Marks?

Even under the most ideal conditions, marks are ambiguous. It seems, then, that expanding the content base of a mark to include such variables as effort, perseverance, and assiduousness could only further cloud already murky waters. Is it reasonable for us to assign a higher mark to a student who "tried harder" but attained the same level of achievement as several of her or his peers? Probably not. Effort should be rewarded, both formally and informally. The teacher can positively reinforce a student's efforts to learn. That a student is working hard should be communicated to parents. A marking and reporting system that treats achievement and effort separately is recommended. Within the achievement domain, do not overlook the significant weight that can be given to homework.

## Should Growth or Status at a Particular Point Form the Basis for Marks?

Assigning marks on the basis of improvement over the semester has great intrinsic appeal, and intuitively appears to be a fair and unbiased approach. Consider, for example, two students, X and Y. Both have shown a growth of 35 points, according to a pre- and post-test, in a course in American History. Student X, however, was below $Q_1$ to begin with, whereas student Y was above $Q_3$. Does the growth of these two students represent the same thing? Obviously not, either relative to content and skills resulting from instruction as measured on the tests, or in final level achieved. In addition, gain or growth scores tend to be quite statistically unreliable.

Marking on the basis of final status, particularly when measured by a comprehensive terminal examination, has much to recommend it. A final-status index is responsive to individual differences in learning rate and is more reliable than growth scores.

## Should a Letter or Number Marking System Be Used?

Both letter and number systems of marking have enjoyed wide popularity, and each has its strengths and weaknesses. The letter system, which usually uses the symbols A through E, theoretically emphasizes the distinction between marks as measurements and as evaluations. The letter grade represents a translation from a number base, resulting from a combination of test scores, ratings, and the like, and the degree of excellence achieved is assumed to be better represented by a letter. Letter marks have a common meaning for most people, and for this reason should probably be retained. One disadvantage of letter marks is that they must be converted to numbers if they are to be added or averaged. In addition, the use of only five categories of marks to some extent masks individual differences, that is, we lose information. The Bs received by five different students may not mean the same thing, in either level (there are high and low Bs) or content and proficiencies.

The number system of marking appeals to many people. It allows a greater range of marks than is provided by five letters. One possible source of interpretive error is that the number system implies a greater degree of precision in measuring educational achievement than is warranted by the data. Does the use of a wide range of number marks really mean that fine discriminations among individuals are possible? No! We can probably do a reasonably good job of ranking individuals in the class, but differences of two or three points are not very meaningful. In summary, a grading or marking system that embodies the following is recommended:

ABSOLUTE STANDARDS

+

ACHIEVEMENT

+

STATUS

+

LETTER MARKS

## COMBINING AND WEIGHTING DATA

The process of assigning marks, like the tests that make up the major database for grades, can be norm-referenced or criterion-referenced. Norm-referenced marks are **relative** and criterion-referenced marks are **absolute**. A relative mark is based on a student's standing in the group and tends to be based on fixed percentages of grades assigned. Compared with the relative approach, the absolute method sets performance standards for each grade category. In either system it is necessary to consider the relative importance of the various outcomes in a course. Perhaps a project that requires integrating a large amount of knowledge and skills (e.g., a map construction) or a major research paper should receive considerably more weight in an achievement composite than several quizzes. Some method to account for these different weights should be applied.

To assign marks, it is generally desirable to derive a composite score distribution weighting individual measurements obtained over, for example, a semester's work, in the appropriate proportions. Several problems relate to combining separate measures into a single composite measure for each individual student, not the least of which is that test scores tend to weight by their variabilities. For example, if an instructor wants to combine scores on the midterm exam with those on the final exam to form a composite, he or she is likely simply to add the two scores. Let us further assume that the instructor wants each exam to contribute 50 percent to the composite score. If, however, the standard deviation of the final exam is 20, and that of the midterm is 10, the final exam contributes *twice* as much as the midterm to the composite. A related problem is a logical dilemma: Are we justified in combining scores from a number of sources, representing different learning outcomes, into a composite? Strong arguments can be made both pro and con. Assuming an underlying variable called "achievement in such and such a course," we are probably justified in ranking students by overall performance. On the other hand, most methods of combining data assume that the measures to be combined are independent of each other—a tenuous assumption at best. If for no other reason than the practical exigencies of the educational assessment situation, deriving composite scores is justified.

Four methods of deriving composite scores will be described in this section. The first three apply primarily to assigning norm-referenced grades. Many methods have been investigated and they have been found to yield similar results. Keep in mind that the pooled appraisal of competence represented by the composite is a *relative* measurement, not an absolute one. It permits comparisons among individuals and judgments involving "more" or "less." But the real or absolute meaning of the scores is often obscured in a composite score.

### Weighting with Standard Scores

A relatively straightforward method of combining scores is through the use of **standard scores**. The reader will recall from Chapter 13 that standard score use is advocated because it allows a legitimate comparison of an individual's scores on different tests. This is an acceptable procedure because the use of a standard transformation puts all tests on a common score base. The standard score system suggested here is the $Z$ transformation, which can be expressed as follows:

$$Z = 10 \left( \frac{X - M}{S} \right) + 50$$

(11-9)

where

$X$ = an individual's raw score

$M$ = the raw score mean

$S$ = the raw score standard deviation

The mean of the $Z$ scores is 50, and the standard deviation is 10. Converting all the measures that we want to combine into standard scores equates their means to an arbitrary value of 50, but, more important, adjusts the individual scores by the standard deviation. Note that deriving a composite score requires that we work with the variabilities of the distributions because weights are proportional to the variabilities. In this regard, the means are irrelevant in obtaining weighted scores.

How are these standard scores used to obtain composite scores? Refer to the data in Table 17-1. Assume that an instructor wants to combine two quizzes and a final exam, and also wants to weight the final exam three times as heavily as the two quizzes. The first step is to determine the means and standard deviations for the three sets of scores (see columns 1, 2, and 3 of Table 17-1). The estimated standard deviations ($\hat{S}$) derived from the scores of the high- and low-scoring one-sixth of the distribution are very good estimates of the actual standard deviations. Next, Equation 13–9 is used to determine $Z$ scores for every student on every test (see columns 4, 5, and 6 of Table 17-1). Finally, after applying the appropriate weight to $Z_F$, the composite scores are determined by addition. At this point, any of the marking procedures described in the next section can be applied. Note that in addition to providing a convenient method of eventually combining scores, standard scores themselves can be useful in test interpretation.

### Weighting with Adjusted Raw Scores

An efficient method of equating the standard deviations of several measures is to divide each raw score in a particular distribution by its own standard deviation. Such a procedure automatically adjusts each raw score in relation to the variability of the total distribution. The **adjusted raw scores** for the three exams represented in Table 17-1 are summarized in Table 17-2.

The mere fact that the adjusted raw score procedure bypasses computation of the raw score mean and standard scores may be enough to recommend it. The results obtained through the standard score use or adjusted raw scores yield the identical ranking of students.

### Weighting by Common Denominator

Test scores weight by their variabilities. If the variabilities are approximately equal, then the importance-weights can be applied directly to the scores. What does it mean to be approximately equal? One rule of thumb suggests that if one standard deviation is less than one and a half times as large as another then we can probably treat them as equals. Consider the standard deviations of Table 17-1: 5.6, 9.6, and 13.2. The standard deviations of 9.6 and 13.2 are more than 1.5 times as large as the 5.6 for Quiz 1. A reasonable adjustment to make the distributions more or less equal in variability would be to multiply Quiz 1 by 2 and leave the Quiz 2 and Final Exam scores alone. We could then apply the importance weights of one and three, respectively. The conversion equation to get an appropriate weight composite is:

**Table 17-1** *Hypothetical Test Data Illustrating Derivation of Composite Scores Using Standard Scores*

| Student | Raw Scores | | | Standard Scores | | | Composite[a] | Rank of Composite |
|---|---|---|---|---|---|---|---|---|
| | Quiz 1 | Quiz 2 | Final Exam | $Z_1$ | $Z_2$ | $Z_F$ | $Z_c$ | |
| $S_1$ | 38 | 48 | 93 | 69 | 62 | 65 | 326 | 2 |
| $S_2$ | 36 | 53 | 98 | 66 | 68 | 68 | 338 | 1 |
| $S_3$ | 34 | 47 | 94 | 62 | 61 | 65 | 318 | 3 |
| $S_4$ | 33 | 53 | 89 | 61 | 68 | 62 | 315 | 4 |
| $S_5$ | 32 | 42 | 82 | 59 | 56 | 56 | 283 | 6 |
| $S_6$ | 31 | 45 | 85 | 57 | 59 | 59 | 293 | 5 |
| $S_7$ | 30 | 38 | 77 | 55 | 52 | 53 | 266 | 8 |
| $S_8$ | 29 | 40 | 74 | 53 | 54 | 50 | 257 | 9 |
| $S_9$ | 27 | 43 | 79 | 50 | 57 | 54 | 269 | 7 |
| $S_{10}$ | 26 | 34 | 72 | 48 | 48 | 49 | 243 | 11 |
| $S_{11}$ | 26 | 35 | 72 | 49 | 48 | 49 | 244 | 10 |
| $S_{12}$ | 26 | 34 | 69 | 48 | 48 | 46 | 234 | 12 |
| $S_{13}$ | 25 | 32 | 70 | 46 | 46 | 47 | 233 | 13 |
| $S_{14}$ | 25 | 30 | 68 | 46 | 44 | 46 | 228 | 14 |
| $S_{15}$ | 24 | 29 | 65 | 44 | 42 | 43 | 215 | 15 |
| $S_{16}$ | 23 | 26 | 60 | 43 | 39 | 40 | 202 | 17 |
| $S_{17}$ | 22 | 28 | 63 | 41 | 41 | 42 | 208 | 16 |
| $S_{18}$ | 20 | 22 | 61 | 37 | 35 | 40 | 192 | 18 |
| $S_{19}$ | 19 | 24 | 55 | 36 | 37 | 36 | 181 | 19 |
| $S_{20}$ | 16 | 22 | 48 | 30 | 35 | 31 | 158 | 20 |
| M = | 27.1 | 36.2 | 73.7 | | | | | |
| S = | 5.6 | 9.6 | 13.2 | | | | | |
| $\hat{S}$[b] = | 5.7 | 9.3 | 13.2 | | | | | |

[a] Composite obtained with following expression, $Z_c = Z_1 + Z_2 + 3(Z_F)$.
[b] $\hat{S}$ = Sum of scores for the highest scoring one-sixth of the distribution, minus the sum of the scores for the lowest scoring one-sixth of the distribution, divided by one-half the number of students.

$$C = 4(Q_1) + (Q_2) + 3(FE)$$

The "4" for $Q_1$ comes from the "2" variability adjustment and the "2" importance weight. The advantage of this method is that it does not require calculating standard scores and we can work directly with the raw scores.

Everything considered, however, using adjusted (by the standard deviation) raw scores is probably the easiest, given the ultimate intent of weighting.

**Table 17-2**  *Derivation of Composite Scores Through Use of Adjusted Raw Scores (Based on Actual Raw Scores and Standard Deviations of Table 17-1)*

| Student | Adjusted Raw Scores ($\frac{X}{S}$) (1) Quiz 1 | (2) Quiz 2 | (3) Final Exam[1] | Composite[2] (4) | Rank of Composite (5) | Mark[3] (6) |
|---|---|---|---|---|---|---|
| $S_1$ | 6.79 | 5.00 | 21.13 | 32.92 | 2 | B |
| $S_2$ | 6.43 | 5.52 | 22.27 | 34.22 | 1 | A |
| $S_3$ | 6.07 | 4.90 | 21.36 | 32.33 | 3 | B |
| $S_4$ | 5.89 | 5.52 | 20.22 | 31.63 | 4 | B |
| $S_5$ | 5.71 | 4.38 | 18.63 | 28.72 | 6 | B |
| $S_6$ | 5.54 | 4.69 | 19.31 | 29.54 | 5 | B |
| $S_7$ | 5.36 | 3.96 | 17.49 | 26.81 | 8 | C |
| $S_8$ | 5.18 | 4.17 | 16.81 | 26.16 | 9 | C |
| $S_9$ | 4.82 | 4.48 | 17.95 | 27.27 | 7 | C |
| $S_{10}$ | 4.64 | 3.54 | 16.36 | 24.54 | 11 | C |
| $S_{11}$ | 4.64 | 3.65 | 16.36 | 24.65 | 10 | C |
| $S_{12}$ | 4.64 | 3.54 | 15.68 | 23.86 | 12 | C |
| $S_{13}$ | 4.46 | 3.33 | 15.90 | 23.69 | 13 | C |
| $S_{14}$ | 4.46 | 3.13 | 15.45 | 23.04 | 14 | C |
| $S_{15}$ | 4.29 | 3.02 | 14.77 | 22.08 | 15 | D |
| $S_{16}$ | 4.11 | 2.71 | 13.63 | 20.45 | 17 | D |
| $S_{17}$ | 3.93 | 2.92 | 14.31 | 21.16 | 16 | D |
| $S_{18}$ | 3.57 | 2.29 | 13.86 | 19.72 | 18 | D |
| $S_{19}$ | 3.39 | 2.50 | 12.50 | 18.39 | 19 | D |
| $S_{20}$ | 2.86 | 2.29 | 10.91 | 16.06 | 20 | F |

[1] Final exam adjusted raw obtained by dividing each raw score by the standard deviation, and multiplying by 3.

[2] Composite obtained by summing entries across columns.

[3] Mark determined by relative approach: 7% A, 24% B, 38% C, 24% D, and 7% F.

## Weighting with Absolute Scores

If performance or achievement is expressed as a percentage of the maximum possible, we still need to weight the various elements in a program of study. Criterion-referenced or absolute scores all have a base of 100. For example, a raw midterm exam score of 35 on an 80-item exam where each item was worth 1 point is 44 percent, and a quiz comprising six 3-point credit completion items converts a raw score of 11 to an absolute score of 61 percent. Tony Nitko (1983) suggested that absolute or criterion-referenced scores can be weighted simply by (a) multiplying each percent score by the desired weight, (b) adding the adjusted weights for each student individually, and (c) dividing by the total of the combined weights.

This procedure is illustrated in Table 17-3. Each of the three components is converted to a percentage, weighted by a multiplier, added together, and then averaged by dividing by 5, the sum of the weights. Using this method assumes that the absolute scores are based on individually representative sampling from well-defined and homogeneous domains. In addition, the question of variability is not directly addressed because the focus is on mastery, not on how one student compares with another.

## THREE MARKING MODELS: A DON'T, A MAYBE, AND A DO

Before discussing the assignment of marks, several words of caution are in order. First, the use of quantitative procedures does not eliminate the human factor from marking. Marking decisions are still basically philosophical, evaluative, and judgmental; they can and do engender guilt. Second, the meaning ascribed to marks, be they letters or numbers, really rests on arbitrary conventions. The measures we use to assign marks must have meaning for the expected changes in students if the resulting marks are to have any meaning. Finally, the very act of condensing a multidimensional performance into one of five categories results in the loss of information and reliability.

### The Inspection Model (A Don't)

A method of assigning grades that is perhaps more widely used than acknowledged is the inspection method. It generally involves examining the distribution of composite scores in the hopes of finding "natural breaks" or "cutoff points" and represents the zenith of marking on a relative curve. The observed distribution of scores, then, in a sense determines the percentage of marks to be assigned. Some experts argue that these "natural breaks" in distribution are unreliable. Because so many arbitrary decisions are made and a sound interpretive base is lacking, it is not a recommended procedure.

### The Norm-Referenced or Relative Model (A Maybe)

In using the so-called norm-referenced (group or relative) model for assigning marks, several assumptions of varying degrees of credibility are involved. First, the distribution is based on some arbitrary model or curve (sometimes, unfortunately, a normal curve) and assumes that achievement

**Table 17-3**   *Illustration of Assigning Absolute Marks*

| Student | Quiz 1 | Quiz 2 | Final Exam | Quiz 1 | Quiz 2 | Final Exam | Composite[2] | Composite Percent[3] | Mark[4] |
|---|---|---|---|---|---|---|---|---|---|
| | **Raw Scores** | | | **Percent Scores[1]** | | | | | |
| $S_1$ | 38 | 48 | 93 | 76 | 87 | 93 | 442 | 88 | B |
| $S_2$ | 36 | 53 | 98 | 72 | 96 | 98 | 462 | 92 | A |
| $S_3$ | 34 | 47 | 94 | 68 | 85 | 94 | 435 | 87 | B |
| $S_4$ | 33 | 53 | 89 | 66 | 96 | 89 | 429 | 86 | B |
| $S_5$ | 32 | 42 | 82 | 64 | 76 | 82 | 386 | 77 | C |
| $S_6$ | 31 | 45 | 85 | 62 | 82 | 85 | 399 | 80 | C |
| $S_7$ | 30 | 38 | 77 | 60 | 69 | 77 | 360 | 72 | C |
| $S_8$ | 29 | 40 | 74 | 58 | 73 | 74 | 353 | 71 | C |
| $S_9$ | 27 | 43 | 79 | 54 | 78 | 79 | 369 | 74 | C |
| $S_{10}$ | 26 | 34 | 72 | 52 | 62 | 72 | 330 | 66 | D |
| $S_{11}$ | 26 | 35 | 72 | 52 | 64 | 72 | 332 | 66 | D |
| $S_{12}$ | 26 | 34 | 69 | 52 | 62 | 69 | 321 | 64 | D |
| $S_{13}$ | 25 | 32 | 70 | 50 | 58 | 70 | 318 | 64 | D |
| $S_{14}$ | 25 | 30 | 68 | 50 | 55 | 68 | 309 | 62 | D |
| $S_{15}$ | 24 | 29 | 75 | 48 | 53 | 65 | 296 | 59 | F |
| $S_{16}$ | 23 | 26 | 60 | 46 | 47 | 60 | 273 | 55 | F |
| $S_{17}$ | 22 | 28 | 63 | 44 | 51 | 63 | 284 | 57 | F |
| $S_{18}$ | 20 | 22 | 61 | 40 | 40 | 61 | 263 | 53 | F |
| $S_{19}$ | 19 | 24 | 55 | 38 | 44 | 55 | 247 | 49 | F |
| $S_{20}$ | 16 | 22 | 48 | 32 | 40 | 48 | 216 | 43 | F |

[1] Based on points: $Q_1 = 50, Q_2 = 55$, FE $= 100$
[2] Weighted $Q_1 = 1, Q_2 = 1$, FE $= 3$ (Total points possible $= 5 \times 100$)
[3] Composite Percent $=$ Composite/5
[4] Using the percentages from page 531.

is distributed in a fixed way and that if the resulting distribution does not match the model, it is a result of sampling error. Second, the sample means and standard deviations are assumed to be the best estimates of the means and standard deviations of the population of which this particular class is a sample. These assumptions involve about as much subjective judgment as any teacher must make to mark.

A typical relative model in the "normal curve" distribution of marks is presented in Figure 17-3. This curve can be used in at least two ways to assign marks. First, the instructor can mark off appropriate standard deviation units

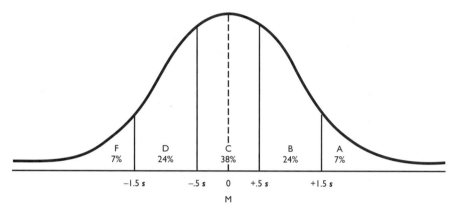

**Figure 17-3** *Hypothetical distribution of marks based on standard deviations*

along the score scale and assign marks to them. Second, the percentage of marks dictated by the normal curve can be assigned to the class. Will either procedure ensure that the normal curve assumptions have been met? Yes— but if and only if the underlying class distribution is normally distributed, which is an unlikely event.

The usual "relative" model involves simply assigning a fixed and arbitrary percentage of grades. Typically, the percentage does not follow a normal curve. The school board, in consultation with parents, teachers, and school administrators, should set the guidelines for establishing marks. Bob Linn and Norman Gronlund (1995) have suggested, based on no scientific data and making no assumption about the distribution shape, that perhaps for an introductory course the following flexible distribution (percent of students receiving grade) could be used to begin development of a relative marking system (academics are known for making giant intuitive leaps with no provocation):

A = 10–20%
B = 20–30%
C = 40–50%
D = 10–20%
F = 0–10%

Consideration must be given to school educational philosophy, ability level of student body, performance level, and the purpose of assigning the grades.

To illustrate a normal curve, model marks have been assigned to the students in Table 17-2 using the grade distribution of Figure 17-2. No matter what the level of performance, the same distribution of marks is made.

## The Absolute Standard Grading Model (A Do)

Basically, the idea is to assign marks on the basis of proportions of objectives mastered or points earned. The percentage can be arbitrary, as it is in most systems, or based on an examination of content, objectives, skills, knowledge, or competencies. The question always is, "Does 80 percent mean that the individual has mastered 80 percent of the requirements?" This is a difficult measurement question to answer. The teacher should set standards and specify outcomes that will equate to particular grades. It is virtually impossible to dictate uniform meaning to marks at the school or system level across subject areas and marks. In a real sense, each mark is a case study, the meaning of which is the result of the interaction among student, teacher, and instructional program.

One problem in using the absolute approach in the public schools is when administrators require fixed percentages for grades, the teacher is being asked to equate or fix percentages of outcomes, that is, to build instruments that will equate to the percentages previously specified. Building instrumentation to meet this requirement is a very challenging task, even for a very skilled measurement professional.

Using the so-called absolute system involves pre-specified criteria (expressed as the percentage of points achieved) to student performance data. For example:

| Mark | Percent Correct |
|------|-----------------|
| A | 91–100 |
| B | 81–90 |
| C | 71–80 |
| D | 61–70 |
| F | 60 and below |

The percentages are usually fixed by boards of education, but with input from teachers, school administrators, and parents. We can also apply a variety of standard-setting procedures (Jaeger, 1989). These procedures are similar to those involved in establishing standards for criterion-referenced and mastery tests.

Determining the composite on which to base an absolute mark is easier than assigning a relative mark. Because the focus is on absolute levels of individual performance, percent scores (score points possible) only have to be aggregated in appropriate proportions. If, for example, you simply want to have each of four bits of information contribute an equal amount, simply add them. If, however, you want the first bit to contribute twice as much, simply multiply it by 2. If mixed percentages are desired, reduce the proportion to a common denominator and apply the weights. For example, 35%: 25%: 40%: 10% translates to 3.5: 2.5: 4: 1. For five measures that are desired to be weighted 30%: 20%: 10%: 20%: 20%, that translates to 3: 2: 1: 2: 2.

An illustration of the "absolute assignment of marks" is present in Table 17-3. The group did not fare particularly well—six Fs were assigned. Is this bad? Mastering only 60 percent of the content surely does not reflect a high level of performance or competency. The absolute system does represent an approach to maintaining standards, yet still allows *everyone* to achieve high marks with hard work.

In comparing the distribution of marks in Tables 17-2 and 17-3, we find the following:

| Mark | Relative (Table 17-2) | Absolute (Table 17-3) |
|------|-----------------------|------------------------|
| A | 1 | 1 |
| B | 5 | 3 |
| C | 8 | 5 |
| D | 5 | 5 |
| F | 1 | 6 |

The discrepancy is now apparent at the low end of the achievement scale. How can we change the distribution of marks? Maintain the marking standards but make the tests easier, change the standards, get the students to work harder, or do a better job of teaching?

The last two approaches make the most sense.

## DISHONEST WAYS OF MARKING

We cannot leave the topic of marking without pointing out some pitfalls that await the unwary, unthinking, or unmotivated grader. Orvile Palmer (1962) has provided seven danger signs that should be heeded if we are to grade successfully.

Do not fall victim to grading by any of the following:

1. **Abdication.** Don't, because of overwork or lack of effort, tailor courses to tests or rely on tests developed by other teachers or textbook publishers.

2. ***Employing the carrots and clubbing system.*** Don't add bonus credit for good behavior or avoidance of the teacher's prejudices.

3. ***Default.*** Don't base a final grade on a single exam because of a deep-seated hatred of grading and testing in which a single misstep could spell disaster.

4. ***Becoming a zealot.*** Do not set the students racing with a vengeance and make the course an ordeal, endurance contest, or problem in survival in which you measure everything short of classroom posture.

5. ***Changing rules in midgame.*** Don't strew the line of march with booby traps and obstacles aimed at tightening up the standards after the game has started.

If you do suddenly change the rules, beware of possible confusion and consequences as shown in the following story:

The Big Bad Wolf disguised as Grandmother met Little Red Riding Hood disguised as a wolf in the midst of a forest glade. However, the wolf disguised as Grandmother was very surprised to see Little Red Riding Hood in wolf's clothing. He was very confused, especially when the wolf said, "Why, hello, Grandmother, I was just coming to see you." The wolf didn't know what to say and in the pause the Grandmother walked up disguised as Little Red Riding Hood.

Immediately everyone became suspicious and uneasy. Little Red Riding Hood, disguised as a wolf, knew that *she* was Little Red Riding Hood and thinking that she was protecting the Grandmother who was really the wolf, pounced on the Grandmother disguised as Little Red Riding Hood and killed her. At this the Big Bad Wolf disguised as the Grandmother became so confused, because he knew he was really the wolf, that he turned tail and ran. Little Red Riding Hood thought that the Big Bad Wolf was really her Grandmother and started chasing after him into the woods. A nearby hunter seeing a wolf chasing an old lady shot and killed the wolf who was really Little Red Riding Hood.

The Big Bad Wolf, still disguised as the Grandmother, fled into the woods, where he was attacked and killed by his fellow wolves because they thought he was a little old lady.

6. ***Becoming a psychic grader.*** Don't believe you have powers inaccessible to ordinary humans, allowing only you to "see" how much a student has learned without using any measurements.

7. ***Anchoring everyone in a system of impossible perfection.*** Don't overlook the fallibility of human-as-student or set yourself up as guardian of standards.

## REPORTING STUDENT TEST SCORES

Reporting student test scores, particularly those derived from system or state assessment programs, provides an opportunity to see many applied concepts, methods of expressing performance, and describing and using information discussed through this book.

To be meaningful score reports must communicate. After examining state reports and conducting a national survey of test users and coordinators, Aschbacker and Herman (1991) created a useful checklist for effective score reporting. Reputable test developers will adhere to these guidelines as they work with test users and professional organizations.

**1.** Know the audience and the purpose.

    a. Use their expectations to enhance credibility and utility of the report.

    b. Use their expertise and background knowledge to guide expectations and details.

    c. Use language appropriate to the audience; avoid jargon.

**2.** Keep it simple.

    a. Present information in a small number of categories.

    b. Use summaries.

    c. Be straightforward.

**3.** Be clear, accurate, comprehensive, and balanced.

    a. Interpret statistics clearly and provide explanations.

    b. Provide as rich a picture as appropriate for the audience and purpose.

    c. Apportion space according to the importance of the ideas.

**4.** Use techniques to direct reader's attention.

    a. Use visual techniques (e.g., graphics, colors).

    b. Use effective headings.

    c. Use negative wording for special effect.

**5.** Suit format to purpose.

    a. Use numeric and adjectival descriptions of data.

    b. Be consistent.

    c. Select graphic format to suit purpose.

    d. Follow guidelines for effective graphs and tables.

Let's look at an example of where these guidelines were applied.

In 1991, the Georgia General Assembly passed legislation that required a criterion-referenced graduation test (HSGT) to be administered in the spring of the 11th grade. This test was to be based on the state's Quality Core Curriculum. The content of the HSGT is described in Figure 17-4. The four content areas are supplemented by a 90-minute writing task. Two days are required for the test (one hour per student test) with each administration including 10 field test items in each of four areas, Language Arts, Mathematics, Science and Social Studies. Graduation requirements have been set for Science and Social Studies, but have not yet been implemented. Figure 17-5 contains a sample printout for Norman Conquest, a rising senior.

Norman's report includes several features discussed in previous chapters. These include

- the use of percentile ranks for reporting
- application of a pass/fail "cut-score" derived from a statewide standard setting
- the use of standard scores for reporting
- indication of where (a) student could profitably put his study efforts and (b) areas where the school instructors might profitably focus their efforts if the lowered curricular and instructional performances appeared to be widespread.

School, system, and state summary reports are also provided.

Norman did well in Language Arts but has a long way to go in Science, Mathematics, and Social Studies. His writing performance was reported separately, and he passed so he is en route to graduation. He failed Science, but passed Mathematics and Social Studies, so he would have "banked" the Language Arts and would have had four more chances to reverse his failures. The sample report speaks to the informational needs of students, parents, teachers, school, system, and state.

## PARENT CONFERENCES

Conferencing with parents or guardians concerning student progress is both a responsibility and an opportunity. Parents have a right to know what

# The Georgia High School Graduation Tests

## Content of the Tests

The Georgia High School Graduation Tests cover only a sample of the knowledge and skills that constitute a complete high school education. A Georgia high school graduate will have had opportunities to learn – and is expected to have mastered – much more than these tests can address. The knowledge and skills assessed on the graduation tests were selected by Georgia educators and curriculum specialists. These tests are based on the standards specified in the Quality Core Curriculum as established by the State Board of Education and revised in November 1997.

The Georgia Department of Education has published a detailed Test Content Description for each of the content area tests and a Georgia High School Writing Test Instructional Guide for the Writing Test. The Test Content Descriptions are also available on the Department's web site (http://www.doe.k12.ga.us).

Following are brief descriptions of the range of knowledge and skills covered in the content area tests. The percentage figures indicate how much weight is given to each subarea or strand of the total test.

## Social Studies
### (Pass Plus = 526)

**World Studies (18-20%)** Items test major themes of world history and world geography. World history topics include exploration, change, and world wars. World geography topics include cultural and physical geography and the relationship between geography and human activity.

**U.S. History to 1865 (18-20%)** Items test information related to early inhabitants of North America and exploration of the New World, Colonial America, the Revolutionary Era, the Constitutional Era, the growth of the nation, the Civil War, and Reconstruction.

**U. S. History Since 1865 (18-20%)** Items test expansion and development of the nation, the nation becoming a world power, and the modern nation. The American economic system, organized labor, the banking system, and command and market economies are also included.

**Civics/Citizenship (12-14%)** Items in this strand, known as Citizenship/Government in earlier forms of the tests, assess the structure and functions of government (local, state, and national), the role of the citizen, legal issues, individual rights and responsibilities, and Constitutional amendments.

**Map and Globe Skills (15%)** Items test map features such as scale, direction, grids, keys, and legends. Various types of maps are used in current and historical settings to assess students' abilities to gather and interpret information and relate that information to events.

**Information Processing Skills (15%)** Items test several skills including identifying the main idea in a passage, separating fact and opinion, interpreting charts and tables, recognizing different types of information sources, and using information from multiple sources to solve a problem.

## English/Language Arts
### (Pass Plus = 538)

**Reading/Literature (47-49%)** Items test students' ability to read and respond to literature and other written material. Skills include literal and inferential comprehension. Also tested are such literary concepts as point of view, tone, figurative language, plot, and historical aspects of American literature.

**Critical Thinking (37-39%)** Items test the use of thinking skills in English and other academic areas. Examples include drawing conclusions, generalizing, recognizing fallacies, separating fact from opinion, and understanding logical relationships.

**Writing/Usage/Grammar (14-16%)** Items test knowledge of grammar and mechanics of standard American English as well as levels of usage. Other language/writing skills are assessed in the Writing test.

## Mathematics
### (Pass Plus = 535)

**Number & Computation (17-19%)** Items test uses and properties of numbers, operations, computing with integers, decimals, fractions, percents, and proportions. Real-world applications include various aspects of using money as well as estimation and problem solving (which operation to use).

**Data Analysis (19-21%)** Items test use of exact and approximate numbers, probability, and reading and interpreting graphs, charts, and tables. Statistical measures such as mean, median, mode, and range are also assessed.

**Measurement and Geometry (32-34%)** Items test estimation and determination of length, area, volume, weight, time, and temperature. Similar and congruent figures, use of proportions to find missing sides of figures, and use of scale drawings are also assessed. The coordinate plane is tested, as well as geometric properties and figures, solving problems with angles, and use of the Pythagorean theorem.

**Algebra (28-30%)** Items test algebraic principles such as evaluating and simplifying algebraic expressions, solving equations, and ratios and proportions.

## Science Test
### (Pass Plus = 531)

**Process/Research Skills (30-32%)** Items test processes and skills common to all areas of science: use of resources, experimental design, and reading and interpreting data presented in tables, charts, or other formats.

**Physical Science (33-35%)** Items test all areas of physical science, including chemical concepts. Specific topics include properties of matter, electricity, acids and bases, pH, force, work, wave motion, and energy transfer. Most items present physical concepts in real-world situations.

**Biology (33-35%)** Items test knowledge of the cellular basis of life, animal and plant systems, reproduction, genetics, classification schemes, ecology, and principles of environmental conservation.

**Figure 17-4**

## Student Content Area Summary

**GEORGIA HIGH SCHOOL GRADUATION TESTS**

Student: NORMAN CONQUEST
Date of Birth: 1/84
System: STRICKLAND COUNTY
School: CRAMER HIGH SCHOOL

Student ID: 123456789
Date Tested: Spring, 2001
System Code: 345
School Code: 6789

Date Printed: 02APR01

| Content Area/ Strand | Scaled Score | 400 | 450 | 500 | 550 | 600 |
|---|---|---|---|---|---|---|
| **English Lang Arts** | | | | | | |
| Percentile rank | 55 | | | | | |
| Reading/Literature | 559 | | | | | |
| Critical Thinking | 560 | | | | | |
| Language/Writing | 540 | | | | | |

You PASSED the English Language Arts test.
Your score was 538.
Congratulations! You have earned the Pass Plus level of distinction.

| Content Area/ Strand | Scaled Score | 400 | 450 | 500 | 550 | 600 |
|---|---|---|---|---|---|---|
| **Mathematics** | | | | | | |
| Percentile rank | 41 | | | | | |
| Number & Computation | 538 | | | | | |
| Data Analysis | 530 | | | | | |
| Measurement & Geom | 517 | | | | | |
| Algebra | 554 | | | | | |

You PASSED the Mathematics test.
Your score was 523.
Congratulations!

| Content Area/ Strand | Scaled Score | 400 | 450 | 500 | 550 | 600 |
|---|---|---|---|---|---|---|
| **Social Studies** | | | | | | |
| Percentile rank | 46 | | | | | |
| World Studies | 524 | | | | | |
| US Hist to 1865 | 539 | | | | | |
| US Hist since 1865 | 527 | | | | | |
| Citizenship/Govt | 538 | | | | | |
| Map Skills | 506 | | | | | |
| Info Proc Skills | 468* | | | | | |

You PASSED the Social Studies test.
Your score was 514.
Congratulations!

| Content Area/ Strand | Scaled Score | 400 | 450 | 500 | 550 | 600 |
|---|---|---|---|---|---|---|
| **Science** | | | | | | |
| Percentile rank | 32 | | | | | |
| Process/Res Skills | 512 | | | | | |
| Physical Science | 488* | | | | | |
| Biology | 487* | | | | | |

You FAILED the Science test.
Your score was 497.
You must take this test again. Please see your guidance counselor for information about remedial help and about re-taking the test.

- The Passing Score is 500 for all tests.
- Content Area scores are not simple averages of strand scores because strands have different numbers of items.
- Percentile rank indicates the percentage of students who scored lower than you.
- See the back of this report for important information.
- *--Your performance was low in these strands.

**Figure 17-5**

students are doing in school, what they have accomplished (e.g., with a portfolio of student work), and how they might improve. Helpful hints to parents about what they can do to assist student learning may be one of the most useful outcomes of a parent conference. The opportunity to have face-to-face contact with parents is another valuable reason for the conference. The face-to-face nature of the meeting enhances communication and adds a human dimension to the interaction. Notes, letters or newsletters sent home are important and can be informative, but nothing matches personal contact. Parents are becoming more and more involved in school affairs and governance.

In conducting a parent conference, common sense and courtesy can accomplish as much as any specific method.

- *Be positive.* Emphasize what the child has accomplished and the progress she or he has made.
- *Be prepared.* Let the parent know that this conference was important enough for you to plan and organize so that all important topics might be addressed.
- *Discuss areas where improvement can be made.* The parent should feel ownership in the child's education.
- *Be sensitive to parent situation.* If parent job situation does not allow much instructional input, explore alternatives, such as tutors, after-school programs, or perhaps a school volunteer program.
- *Control your emotions.* Parents are not present at school to see all the pressures on students and teachers.
- *Be honest and objective.* Not all students were born to be rocket scientists. Be realistic about the student's objectives.
- *Don't use educationaleze.* Plain talk, good English and appropriate vocabulary will go a long way to helping establish a warm, friendly, and accepting relationship.
- *Be punctual.* Parent time is as valuable to them as yours is to you.
- *Be a good listener.* It's wonderful what you can learn about your students from their parents. Be alert to both what is said and what is not said.
- *Make suggestions.* Don't give advice.
- *Don't talk about other parents, students, and teachers.* The focus should be on this particular parent-teacher-child triangle.

Above all, remember you are attempting to build a cooperative relationship for the best interests of the student, teacher, parent, and community.

## STUDENT-LED CONFERENCES

A recent innovation related to maintaining the invaluable communication between parent and school is the student-led conference (Austin, 1994; Benson & Barnett, 1999). Basically, students take responsibility, in a 20- to 40-minute meeting, for describing and showing to parents or caregivers (or other significant adults) the results of their learning. The focus is on a student portfolio (see Chapter 11). Selections included in the portfolio might also be accompanied by a "student reflection" about why each choice was made. Emphasis is on goal setting together with student self-appraisal of strengths and weaknesses. Teachers model the session prior to implementation.

There are many advantages to the student-led conference. Among these are

- student acceptance of responsibility for learning

- opportunity for student and parent to connect

- enhanced student feelings of self-confidence

- student pride in his or her work

- motivation for productive future goal-directed behavior

- enhancement of parent-teacher relationship

- enhancement of shared responsibility for child's learning

- student practice in organizational and oral communication skills

## CASE STUDY

Among the most stressful times of the teaching quarter, semester, or year is marking or grading time. Whatever approach an instructor takes to the assignment of marks, it should be rational and based on reliable data. Let us review for just a moment.

It was noted earlier that there are two basic approaches to the assignment of marks: *absolute* and *relative*. The absolute approach specifies the percentage of "points" or credits that must be achieved to receive a certain mark. It represents a "percent of perfection." The following absolute system is typical:

| Mark | % Points Needed | Meaning |
|------|-----------------|---------|
| A | 91–100 | Excellent/Outstanding |
| B | 81–90 | Very Good |
| C | 71–80 | Average to Good |
| D | 61–70 | Below Average |
| F | 60 and below | Failing |

This represents a 10-point range for each grade category. Other sizes are obviously possible, for example, an 8-point range where A = 93–100, B = 85–92, and so forth. Nowhere is it chiseled in stone that all grade categories have to be the same size. Decisions relating to grading standards should be joint ventures among teacher, school administrators, the board of education, and parents. It is important that if the "absolute" approach to marking is taken, that it be in the context of a criterion-referenced or at least objectives-referenced instruction-measurement system.

The *relative* approach employs standards that relate to percentages of people rather than percentages of points. For example:

| Mark | % of Students Receiving Mark |
|------|------------------------------|
| A | 7 |
| B | 24 |
| C | 38 |
| D | 24 |
| F | 7 |

These percentages are assigned regardless of the distribution or level of performance. As was the case with the *absolute* method, these percentages can be changed by committee decision. The data used to assign **relative marks** must be appropriately weighted, which means they could be made-up standard scores or adjusted raw scores.

Following are data from our reading education course.

| | Midterm Exam | Final Exam | Lesson Plan |
|--|--------------|------------|-------------|
| Total Possible Points | 80 | 80 | 40 |
| *Student* | | | |
| 1. Cheddar Dean | 47 | 35 | 23 |

| | Midterm Exam | Final Exam | Lesson Plan |
|---|---|---|---|
| 2. Chloe Ball | 58 | 74 | 38 |
| 3. Chelsea Black | 58 | 74 | 38 |
| 4. Big Guy | 52 | 39 | 33 |
| 5. Jim Nastike | 51 | 52 | 26 |
| 6. C. J. Huberty | 55 | 56 | 35 |
| 7. Seymour Clearly | 58 | 40 | 30 |
| 8. Allen Carlyle | 58 | 76 | 39 |
| 9. Dixie Smith | 55 | 76 | 38 |
| 10. Dean Creighton | 59 | 62 | 31 |
| 11. Michael Allen | 57 | 58 | 32 |
| 12. Jeffrey Allen | 62 | 65 | 34 |
| 13. Karen Ann | 68 | 80 | 37 |
| 14. Dee Pressed | 52 | 53 | 24 |
| 15. Lawayne Chaplin | 57 | 61 | 29 |
| 16. Joe Lynn | 62 | 68 | 27 |
| 17. Jarred David | 65 | 78 | 37 |
| 18. Pam Lynn | 62 | 69 | 33 |

There are obviously other kinds of data that might be included in the final course evaluation. Perhaps a term paper or project grade, quizzes, or the results of practice teaching. The 18 scores will need to be converted in some way so that they can be weighted in the specified way for the relative mark part of the exercise. Converting the scores to Z scores (Mean = 50, SD = 10) is probably the easiest. Rounding to the nearest whole number is suggested.

Assign marks to all 18 students using both the absolute and relative methods, and compare the results. For the absolute system use the 10-point range, and for the relative grades use the 7-24-38-24-7 percent distribution.

Following are scores from three measures that will be used to make up the final mark in our reading education course. Weight them in such a way that the contribution will be as follows:

| Midterm Exam | Final Exam | Lesson Plan |
|---|---|---|
| 40% | 40% | 20% |

Compare the grades assigned by the two methods.

## CONTENT REVIEW STATEMENTS

1. Students have a need and a right to be apprised of their progress in school.

2. It is the responsibility of every teacher to develop valid and informative marking and reporting procedures.

3. The advent of individualized instruction and mastery learning programs intensifies demand for the development of viable reporting systems.

4. Marking and reporting systems should be based on sound and integrated philosophies of education and on defensible technical procedures.

5. Marking and reporting programs serve the following broad purposes:
   a. communicating to students and parents.
   b. communicating to present and future school personnel.
   c. motivating student learning.
   d. guiding future instruction.

6. Recent developments in reporting procedures can be characterized as increasingly concerned with
   a. student behavior.
   b. affective outcomes.
   c. student needs at various levels.
   d. student achievement relative to ability.
   e. free-response instruction questions.
   f. the involvement of all those concerned with students in developing the reporting system.
   g. computer processing of reports, allowing more, and more detailed, information to be communicated.

7. Issues related to marking and reporting include
   a. the development of pass/fail systems.
   b. the evaluations of contract plans.
   c. grade inflation.

8. A goal card, listing instructional objectives, can be used effectively as part of the reporting system.

9. Current recommendations for marking practices emphasize frequently gathered multiple summative measures of cognitive achievement.

10. Decisions about marking procedures focus on the issues of
    a. absolute versus relative standards.
    b. level of achievement versus effort.
    c. growth versus status.
    d. letter versus numerical marks.

11. It is generally recommended that an absolute system of marks, using a limited number of categories and relying on an individual's level of achievement, be applied.

12. Marks lack meaning unless reasonable procedural uniformity is achieved within and across classes, departments, and schools.

13. A mark should reflect a variety of areas of achievement, for example, test scores, class contributions, homework, projects, and similar data.

14. The weight of each component in a composite mark is determined by the variability of the separate component scores.

15. The "inspection model" of marking relies on the instructor to identify naturally occurring breaks in the distribution of composite scores; it tends to be unreliable and is therefore not recommended.

16. The "relative model" of marking defines fixed percentages of students to receive specified marks, and sometimes assumes a normal distribution of achievement that rarely occurs.

17. An absolute system of marks holds the student responsible for specified levels of mastery.

18. Marks represent an integral, fallible, potentially meaningful, although perhaps irritating, element in the educational process.

19. Performance narratives and rubrics can form the basis for a meaningful achievement report.

20. Parent conferences are an obligation and an opportunity.

21. When holding a parent conference be
    a. positive.
    b. prepared.
    c. punctual.
    d. courteous.
    e. informative.

22. Student-led conferences have the advantages of
    a. Giving the student a leadership role.
    b. Developing student self-confidence and pride.
    c. Allowing the student to practice organizational and communication skills.
    d. Enhancing school/community relations.
    e. Allowing the student to display the fruits of learning.

## SPECULATIONS

1. Do you think marks and achievement reports can be used to help involve parents in the education process of their children? How?

2. How should effort and attitude be treated as part of school reports?

3. What are the comparative advantages and disadvantages of absolute and relative marking systems?

4. Are relative and absolute marks compatible in the same school system? Under what conditions?

5. What are the comparative advantages and disadvantages of alphabetical and numerical marking systems?

6. What would school be like without marks?

7. On what basis do you decide to fail a student?

8. What suggestions can you make for improving the basis and process of assigning grades?

9. How do you decide the weights for the different components of a mark?

10. Should the distribution of grades be about the same in all the sections of classes taught by (a) the same teacher, and (b) different teachers in the same department? Why or why not?

11. How would you combine traditional and performance assessments effectively into a reporting system?

## SUGGESTED READINGS

Anderson, R. S., & Speck, B. W. (1998, Summer). Changing the way we grade student performance: Classroom assessment and the new learning paradigm. *New Directions for Teaching and Learning*, 74. San Francisco: Jossey-Bass.

Carey, L. M. (2001). *Measuring and evaluating school learning* (3rd ed.). Boston: Allyn & Bacon. Chapter 14, "Grading and Reporting Student Progress," contains an excellent description of how to create recording systems for day-to-day achievement indicators and how to format and summarize the results.

Falk, B. (2000). *The heart of the matter (Using standards and assessment to learn)*. Portsmouth, NH: Heinemann.

Geisinger, K. F. (1982). Marking systems. In H. J. Mitzell (Ed.), *Encyclopedia of educational research* (5th ed.). New York: Macmillan. An excellent summary of the limited research that has been completed on its grading process, as well as an overview of the variety of systems used in the schools.

Grant, J. M., Hefflea, B., & Mereweather, K. (1995). *Student-led conferences using portfolios to share learning with parents*. Markham, ON: Pembroke Publishers.

Guskey, T. R., & Bailey, J. M. (2001). *Developing and reporting systems for student learning*. Thousand Oaks, CA: Corwin Press.

Kubiszyn, T., & Borich, G. (2000). *Educational testing and measurement*. (6th ed.). New York: HarperCollins. Chapter 11, "Marks and Marking Systems," is a very readable overview of the basics.

Linn, R. L., & Gronlund, N. E. (2000). *Measurement and evaluation in teaching* (8th ed.). Englewood Cliffs, NJ: Prentice-Hall. Chapter 15, "Grading and Reporting," is a good how-to-do-it introduction. The chapter also addresses parent conferences.

Marzano, R. J. (2000). *Transforming classroom grading*. Alexandria, VA: Association for Supervision and Curriculum Development.

Oosterhof, A. C. (1987). Obtaining intended weights when combining student scores. *Educational Measurement: Issues and Practice, 6*(4), 29–37.

Terwilliger, J. S. (1971). *Assigning grades to students*. Glenview, IL: Scott, Foresman. An excellent overview of both practical and technical issues in the marking process.

# 18

# Assessing Educational Materials

## FOCUS CONCEPTS AND KEY TERMS FOR STUDY

| | |
|---|---|
| **Accuracy** | **Instructional Text Effectiveness** |
| **Appropriateness** | **Presentation** |
| **CD-ROM** | **Quality** |
| **Content Criteria** | **Scope** |
| **Courseware Evaluation** | **Teacher Support** |
| **Documentation** | **Technical Adequacy** |
| **Educational/Instructional Materials** | **Videodisc** |
| **Educational Software** | |

---

## STANDARDS ALERT

**Standard 3.22**　　　　　　**Rating Scales**

Procedures for scoring and, if relevant, scoring criteria should be presented by the test developer in sufficient detail and clarity to maximize the accuracy of scoring. Instructions for using rating scales or for deriving scores obtained by coding, scaling, or classifying constructed responses should be clear. This is especially critical if tests can be scored locally.

## TAKING IT TO THE CLASSROOM

In evaluating a piece of instructional material, the teacher needs to be as detailed as possible. It is not sufficient to simply say that the technical documentation for mathematics computer software was inadequate. Elaboration about what content was missing or how instructions were inadequate needs to be made.

---

Reprinted with permission from the *Standards for Educational and Psychological Testing.* Copyright © 1999 by the American Educational Research Association, the American Psychological Association, and the National Council on Measurement in Education.

Educational materials come in all shapes, colors, and sizes. A teacher will frequently be called upon to assess or assist in selecting instructional materials. There usually will not be time to do a full-blown systematic comparative evaluation study. Teachers must rely on best professional judgments, usually using accepted absolute standards.

The term *educational materials* is used interchangeably with *instructional materials* in this chapter. The terms are probably not identical. The broader term *educational* could include storybooks and videos that simply present information. Materials considered *instructional* have specific objectives and methodologies built into them that are focused on bringing about behavioral or cognitive change.

## GENERAL CRITERIA FOR ASSESSING EDUCATIONAL MATERIALS

What are some general criteria that need to be addressed in evaluating educational materials, particularly instructional materials?

One need only briefly peruse the professional journals or wander around the exhibits at national conventions to develop a sense of being overwhelmed by the crush of "new" instructional materials, procedures, devices, and Web sites. Theoretically, publishers and developers should field-test their products before they are offered for professional consumption. Unfortunately, this does not happen in the majority of cases. Most procedures for evaluating instructional materials must be tailormade for the objectives, uses, and situation. One may wish to focus on a primary or payoff evaluation, where data on the impact of the materials are of greatest concern, or on secondary evaluation, where the attributes or characteristics of the materials themselves are of greater interest. There are probably four major attributes of the secondary type that need to be addressed (Eash, 1972):

- *Objectives*: Are there actual objectives, stated in operational form and aimed at the use of the materials? In addition, both general and instructional objectives should be available. The objectives should flow from some relevant conceptual framework or theory. Are relevant problem-solving and creative skills addressed?

- *Scope and Sequence*: The organization of the material should be such that it follows some conceptually developed pattern, which was based on a task analysis or other relevant research. Is a recommended sequence specified that is responsive to a variety of individual or system needs?

- *Methodology*: Are a variety of approaches and media used? Is the mode that is used based on a rational match of instructional intent and student readiness in the sequence? Is the methodology relatively straightforward, not requiring extensive, complicated preparation?

- *Student Evaluation*: Are procedures provided whereby student progress and achievement can be assessed? Are the procedures available at different levels? Are the evaluation procedures compatible with the objectives and methodology?

The Southern Regional Education Board (www.SREB.org) has collected a set of criteria useful in evaluating audiovisual materials, computer courseware, videodiscs, Web sites, and CD-ROMs. The evaluative criteria were developed by the Educational Resources Evaluation unit of the North Carolina Department of Public Instruction. The criteria can be grouped under three general headings: Content, Technical Aspects, and Documentation. The assessment of the five categories of instructional resources noted above share some common criteria. The criteria presented here are in edited form and would be adjusted depending on which instructional materials you require.

## Content

- Accuracy

    Error-free information

    Current information

    Objective, balanced presentation

    Bias-free viewpoints and images

    Balanced cultural, racial, and ethnic representations

    Correct use of grammar, spelling, and sentence structure

- Appropriateness

    Concepts and vocabulary relevant to student ability

    Relevant to curriculum

    Interaction compatible with audience capability

- Scope

    Information of sufficient scope to adequately cover topic for intended audience

    Logical progression/sequence of topics with relevant outlinks

    Variety of topics

## Technical Aspects

- Presentation

    Uncluttered and concise screen displays

    Information stimulates imagination and curiosity

    Follows good graphic design and labeling principles

- Quality

    Appropriate and sufficient quantity, and high-quality visuals

    Sound that is clearly understandable

    Sound and music that are clearly relevant to the images

## Documentation

- Technical Information

    Adequate description of hardware requirements

    Instructions for installation and operation

    Toll-free technical support telephone number

- Teacher's Guide

    Description of target audience

Summary of contents

Instructional and/or behavioral objectives

Suggestions for classroom use, lesson plans, related activities

Ancillary materials for student and teacher use (e.g., worksheets, activity pages, reference and other resources, tests, vocabulary lists)

With regard to CD-ROMs and to some extent Web sites and computer courseware, additional characteristics would be many features related to navigation, such as rapid retrieval, menus, controllable pacing, search options, bookmarking, intuitive icons, internal and external linking, save and record keeping features, and printing/downloading options. To the foregoing attributes we might add cost, appearance, attractiveness to student and teacher, and durability.Instructional materials may be "things of beauty and joys forever," but if they do not efficiently and effectively relate to the instructional task(s) at hand, they serve as no more than time and space fillers.

Evaluations of materials can be informal and take place on a small scale. Teachers do it every day when they try out an activity with a student or class focused on a particular problem. Or evaluations might be as extensive as the National Assessment of Educational Progress, the giant federal program aimed at assessing U.S. educational effectiveness. No matter the size or cost, evaluations of text materials, if conducted efficiently and professionally, can yield results that will help improve the educational process.

## EVALUATING INSTRUCTIONAL TEXT

Educational (instructional) materials may be locally developed or purchased from a commercial vendor. Today's schools reflect, with increasing frequency, a greater variety of instructional materials in the classroom. The availability of an array of materials places great decision demands on teachers and administrators. In addition to the usual textbooks and other written materials, we may now find personal computers, videodisc and VCR players, participating-games, manipulatives, and a variety of multimedia devices. The most frequently used instructional mode, however, is still the written text.

Lipscombe (1992) has made a significant contribution to the literature with the development of a theory-based text evaluation form. Her intent was to develop a system for evaluating medical text materials although her approach generalizes to any type of text material. The particular theory used to serve as a foundation for instrument development was Gagné's events of instruction (Gagné, Wages, & Rojar, 1981). The six events used were: (1) inform learner of objectives, (2) stimulate recall of prerequisite material, (3) present stimulus material, (4) provide learning guidance, (5) elicit performance, and (6) provide feedback. Criterion questions were written for each event. These questions were critiqued by instructional and content experts. The content experts in this case were instructors in a variety of medical settings since the first application of the instrument was to evaluate instructional materials in medical science. A total of 32 questions were positively reviewed and grouped for convenience under four general headings: Purpose and Objectives, Content, Structure, and Helping Features. Readability and up-to-dateness (vintage) were also assessed. The "vintage" index (Pittinger, 1978, p. 279) is the difference between the latest copyright date and the cube root of the product of the mean, median, and mode reference dates. An agreement index of 0.92 was found among the judgments of instructional experts, and 0.95 among medical experts in evaluating the appropriateness of the criteria. The instrument, *Lipscombe Textbook Evaluation Form* (LTEF), was found to differentiate reliably among three microbiology and seven general medical textbooks (e.g., hematology, immunology). Readability ranged (in a grade level metric) from 19 to 24, and vintage from 4 to 6 years.

Following is a copy of the LTEF. As one can see, the questions are generic and could be used effectively with virtually any text material.

In using the Lipscombe form one could weight the responses (Yes = 2, Sometimes = 1, No = 0) and attain a "score," which in turn could be subjected to some absolute standard-setting procedure or used to make comparative judgments among competing texts. The user may also want to employ a text-selection committee to help make the judgments. At either the local or state level, such textbook selection activities can prove to be very interesting indeed. The interaction of politics, budget, community awareness, and instructional integrity can prove to be a volatile brew.

## EVALUATING COMPUTER EDUCATIONAL SOFTWARE

Virtually every teacher and classroom in today's schools has access to a personal computer. As budgets are enhanced, more complex, comprehensive, and creative multimedia installations will be evident. The original applications of computers as *tool* and *tutor* has given way to the more meaningful use as *tutee*. It is in this later area of application where real "learning" can take place, by having the student create programs that teach. Well-conceived

# LIPSCOMBE TEXTBOOK EVALUATION FORM

Title _____

Author _____

Copyright _____

Select the response which best represents your evaluation of this specific text with regard to each of the criteria. Read each criterion carefully and place it in the context of an instructional setting. If you do not feel a particular criterion is relevant, simply indicate that by checking Not Relevant. Be sure to respond to each criterion.

| | Yes | Sometimes | No | Not Relevant |
|---|---|---|---|---|
| **PURPOSE AND OBJECTIVES** | | | | |
| 1. Does the preface and/or introduction clearly state the purpose of the text? | ____ | ____ | ____ | ____ |
| 2. Are objectives clearly stated or at least implied by the use of an advance organizer or an overview of each chapter? | ____ | ____ | ____ | ____ |
| **CONTENT** | | | | |
| 3. Are the sources of current research findings and other information properly identified? | ____ | ____ | ____ | ____ |
| 4. Does the author follow through in developing ideas specified in the introduction? | ____ | ____ | ____ | ____ |
| 5. At the end of each chapter or section, does the author summarize the essential concepts covered? | ____ | ____ | ____ | ____ |
| 6. Is the material presented to the reader logically through successive levels of difficulty? | ____ | ____ | ____ | ____ |
| 7. Does the information reflect the current status of the field? | ____ | ____ | ____ | ____ |
| 8. Is the difficulty level of the text appropriate for the intended audience or use? | ____ | ____ | ____ | ____ |

|  | Yes | Sometimes | No | Not Relevant |
|---|---|---|---|---|
| 9. Does the table of contents clearly reflect the organization of the text? | ___ | ___ | ___ | ___ |
| 10. Is a bibliography included with each chapter or section? | ___ | ___ | ___ | ___ |
| 11. Are a variety of sources listed in the bibliography? | ___ | ___ | ___ | ___ |
| 12. Is there a glossary which defines terms new to the students using this level of text? | ___ | ___ | ___ | ___ |
| 13. Does the index list both major and minor topics? | ___ | ___ | ___ | ___ |
| 14. Does the index provide multiple cross listings? | ___ | ___ | ___ | ___ |
| 15. Is the context of each citation in the index listed? | ___ | ___ | ___ | ___ |
| 16. Are there one or more appendices which contain useful data to facilitate independent work? | ___ | ___ | ___ | ___ |
| 17. Is illustrative material such as graphs, tables, charts, and pictures placed appropriately in the text? | ___ | ___ | ___ | ___ |
| 18. Are graphs and charts easily read and interpreted? | ___ | ___ | ___ | ___ |
| 19. Are key concepts and terms emphasized by the use of italics or boldface type? | ___ | ___ | ___ | ___ |
| 20. Are headings and subheadings used frequently and clearly? | ___ | ___ | ___ | ___ |
| 21. Does the physical layout of the text clearly set off subsections? | ___ | ___ | ___ | ___ |
| 22. Is color used effectively throughout the book? | ___ | ___ | ___ | ___ |

**HELPING FEATURES**

| 23. Is there a statement describing the knowledge and prerequisite skills needed before mastery of the text material? | ___ | ___ | ___ | ___ |

| | Yes | Sometimes | No | Not Relevant |
|---|---|---|---|---|
| 24. Is there a preface at the beginning of each chapter or section which relates new material to previously learned material? | _____ | _____ | _____ | _____ |
| 25. Does the text guide the learner to sources outside the text for further information if needed? | _____ | _____ | _____ | _____ |
| 26. Are all new terms and concepts defined when they are used or presented? | _____ | _____ | _____ | _____ |
| 27. Are an adequate number of examples provided to illustrate the concepts presented? | _____ | _____ | _____ | _____ |
| 28. Are intratextual clues used such as: | | | | |
| a. first, second, etc., to indicate sequencing of ideas? | _____ | _____ | _____ | _____ |
| b. most of all, a key factor, etc., to emphasize important concepts? | _____ | _____ | _____ | _____ |
| c. however, on the other hand, etc., to emphasize comparisons? | _____ | _____ | _____ | _____ |
| d. for example, such as, etc., for illustration? | _____ | _____ | _____ | _____ |
| e. therefore, as a result, etc., to signal a conclusion? | _____ | _____ | _____ | _____ |
| 29. Are there problems or questions representative of the principles and concepts covered at the end of each chapter or section? | _____ | _____ | _____ | _____ |
| 30. Do the questions require the student to evaluate and analyze data? | _____ | _____ | _____ | _____ |
| 31. Are answers provided for the previous questions and problems? | _____ | _____ | _____ | _____ |
| 32. Are these answers explained so that the student can understand how they were derived? | _____ | _____ | _____ | _____ |

computer software stimulates the use to interact truly with the system. When the software is enhanced by access to the World Wide Web, some truly meaningful experiences are possible.

Traditional computer software evaluation approaches focus on the expected kinds of secondary characteristics such as content, user-friendliness, and nature, extent, and appeal of the graphics. The terms *software*, *educational computer program*, and *courseware* will be used here interchangeably. The *appeal* dimension should not be treated lightly since the program should attract and maintain the user's attention if meaningful interaction is to take place. Different kinds of courseware will have different requirements. Ideally, each different kind of intended-use-courseware should have a custom-made evaluation form (Cohen, 1983). Criteria for evaluating computer software aimed at educational applications should (1) be responsive to what research suggests is sound educational practice, (2) focus on a specific knowledge or skill, and (3) exploit the full potential of the microcomputer environment (e.g., tracking progress).

The development of criteria for evaluating computer educational software should address at least two important dimensions of use, namely, instructional and technical. The instructional or content criteria should focus on how well the objectives to be accomplished (both cognitive and affective) are achieved, the generalizability of accuracy and up-to-datedness, skills developed, and appropriateness of approach relative to the objectives addressed. As with the selection of any instructional device, the match of software objectives and curriculum objectives is critical. The use of enhancements, be they graphics, color, or sound, are also of concern. Are these enhancements simply window dressings or gimmicks that could prove distracting, or do they utilize principles of good mirage design? Technical criteria would involve consideration of ease of interaction and activity level of uses, increments in complexity and skill development, nature of reinforcement and feedback (provision for review), and a whole host of "user-friendly" characteristics. The screen format should be relevant, and the user should be able to "navigate" with ease through the program.

Personnel at the Northwest Regional Educational Laboratory in Portland, Oregon, have created a useful courseware evaluation form, which is reproduced in Figure 18-1. This relatively brief but efficient form could be used by a single evaluator or a committee. Absolute standards could be established, again using some standard-setting procedure. The best *evaluators* are, of course, the users. The dictum of sitting with users as they go through the program is very good advice. Nothing can substitute for hands-on experience. It would also be nice to be able to document whether learning took place as a result of using the program. In that regard, vendor support materials are

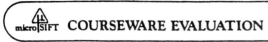

**COURSEWARE EVALUATION**

NORTHWEST REGIONAL
EDUCATIONAL LABORATORY

Package title_____ Producer _____

Evaluator name _____ Organization _____

Date _____ ☐ Check this box if this evaluation is based partly on your observation of student use
of this package.

SA - Strongly Agree  A - Agree  D - Disagree  SD - Strongly Disagree  NA- Not applicable
Please include comments on individual items on the reverse page.

**CONTENT CHARACTERISTICS**
(1) SA  A  D  SD  NA     The content is accurate.
(2) SA  A  D  SD  NA     The content has educational value.
(3) SA  A  D  SD  NA     The content is free of race, ethnic, sex and other stereotypes.

**INSTRUCTIONAL CHARACTERISTICS**
(4) SA  A  D  SD  NA     The purpose of the package is well defined.
(5) SA  A  D  SD  NA     The package achieves its defined purpose.
(6) SA  A  D  SD  NA     Presentation of content is clear and logical.
(7) SA  A  D  SD  NA     The level of difficulty is appropriate for the target audience.
(8) SA  A  D  SD  NA     Graphics/color/sound are used for appropriate instructional reasons.
(9) SA  A  D  SD  NA     Use of the package is motivational.
(10) SA  A  D  SD  NA    The package effectively stimulates student creativity.
(11) SA  A  D  SD  NA    Feedback on student responses is effectively employed.
(12) SA  A  D  SD  NA    The learner controls the rate and sequence of presentation and review.
(13) SA  A  D  SD  NA    Instruction is integrated with previous student experience.
(14) SA  A  D  SD  NA    Learning can be generalized to an appropriate range of situations.

**TECHNICAL CHARACTERISTICS**
(15) SA  A  D  SD  NA    The user support materials are comprehensive.
(16) SA  A  D  SD  NA    The user support materials are effective.
(17) SA  A  D  SD  NA    Information displays are effective.
(18) SA  A  D  SD  NA    Intended users can easily and independently operate the program.
(19) SA  A  D  SD  NA    Teachers can easily employ the package.
(20) SA  A  D  SD  NA    The program appropriately uses relevant computer capabilities.
(21) SA  A  D  SD  NA    The program is reliable in normal use.

**QUALITY**
Write a number from 1 (low) to 5 (high) which represents your judgment of the quality of the package in
each division:

_____ Content Instructional

_____ Characteristics

_____ Technical Characteristics

Describe the potential use of the package in classroom settings.

_____

_____

---

**RECOMMENDATIONS**

☐     I highly recommend this package.

☐     I would use or recommend use of this package with little or no change. (Note suggestions
for effective use below.)

☐     I would use or recommend use of this package only if certain changes were made. (Note changes under weaknesses or other comments.)

☐     I would not use or recommend this package. (Note reasons under weaknesses.)

Estimate the amount of time a student would need to work with the package in order to achieve the objectives: (Can be total time, time per day, time range or other indicator.)

_____

Strengths/Weaknesses/Other Comments

_____

_____

_Source:_ Reprinted by permission. Developed by the Northwest Regional Laboratory under contract No. 400-83-0005 with the National Institute of Education.

---

**Figure 18-1** _Northwest Regional Educational Laboratory Courseware Evaluation Form_

important. Are criterion measures built into the programs, or are they available as separates?

The evaluation forms presented in this chapter, although extremely useful at the outset of a systematic examination of effectiveness, have tended to focus narrowly on the instructional rationale of the programs and operational characteristics. Instructional effectiveness will, however, be the ultimate criterion. Assessing that will require an actual field test.

## CONTENT REVIEW STATEMENTS

1. General assessments of educational materials involve evaluative consideration of

    a. objectives

    b. scope and sequence

    c. methodology

    d. student evaluation

2. Effective instructional materials should be

    a. error-free

    b. up-to-date

    c. unbiased

    d. relevant to the curriculum

    e. appealing

    f. easy to use

    g. provided with support resources

    h. presented in standard communication form

**3.** In addition, computer-based instructional materials should provide for

    a. ease of navigation

    b. rapid retrieval of information

    c. bookmarking

    d. internal and external links

    e. menus

    f. controllable pacing

**4.** Instructional text should provide relevant

    a. objectives

    b. content

    c. structure

    d. helping features

**5.** All instructional materials should be expressed in proper grammar with vocabulary appropriate to the intended audience.

## SPECULATIONS

**1.** What should be the relative importance ranking in evaluating instructional materials: Content relevance, documentation, cost, appropriateness, appearance? Why did you order them in this way?

**2.** What are three of your favorite instructional materials? Why are they your favorites?

**3.** How would you go about evaluating a new instructional computer program?

**4.** Should you evaluate text and computer software with different criteria? Why or why not?

**5.** How does the nature of the instructional material interact with how we assess student learning?

## SUGGESTED READINGS

Eash, M. J. (1972). Developing an instrument for assessing instructional materials. In J. Weiss (Ed.), *Curriculum evaluation: Potentiality and reality* (pp. 193–205). Ontario, Canada: The Ontario Institute for Studies in Education.

Flagg, B. N. (1990). *Formative evaluations for educational technologies*. Hillsdale, NJ: Erlbaum.

Merrill, P. F., Hammons, K., Tolman, M. N., Christensen, L., Vincent, B. R., & Reynolds, P. L. (1992). *Computers in education*. Boston: Allyn & Bacon. Chapter 7 addresses the major instructional and presentation criteria, helpful in evaluating educational software.

Siegel, M. A., & Davis, D. M. (1986). *Understanding computer-based education*. New York: Random House. See particularly Chapter 9, "The Computer in the Classroom," for a discussion of criteria for evaluating educational software.

Tuckman, B. W. (1985). *Evaluating instructional programs* (2nd ed.). Boston: Allyn & Bacon. See in particular Chapter 6, "Surveying the Inputs and Processes from the Classroom."

# Appendix *A*

*Normal Deviates (z) Corresponding to Proportions (p) and Products (pq) of a Dichotomized Unit Normal Distribution*

| Proportion (p)* | Deviate (z) | pq | Proportion (p)* | Deviate (z) | pq |
|---|---|---|---|---|---|
| .99 | 2.326 | .0099 | .49 | - .025 | .2499 |
| .98 | 2.054 | .0196 | .48 | - .050 | .2496 |
| .97 | 1.881 | .0291 | .47 | - .075 | .2491 |
| .96 | 1.751 | .0384 | .46 | - .100 | .2484 |
| .95 | 1.645 | .0977 | .45 | - .126 | .2475 |
| .94 | 1.555 | .0564 | .44 | - .151 | .2464 |
| .93 | 1.476 | .0651 | .43 | - .176 | .2451 |
| .92 | 1.405 | .0736 | .42 | - .202 | .2436 |
| .91 | 1.341 | .0819 | .41 | - .228 | .2419 |
| .90 | 1.282 | .0900 | .40 | - .253 | .2400 |
| .89 | 1.227 | .0979 | .39 | - .279 | .2379 |
| .88 | 1.175 | .1056 | .38 | - .305 | .2356 |
| .87 | 1.126 | .1131 | .37 | - .332 | .2331 |
| .86 | 1.080 | .1204 | .36 | - .358 | .2304 |
| .85 | 1.036 | .1275 | .35 | - .385 | .2275 |
| .84 | .994 | .1344 | .34 | - .412 | .2244 |
| .83 | .954 | .1411 | .33 | - .440 | .2211 |
| .82 | .915 | .1476 | .32 | - .468 | .2176 |
| .81 | .878 | .1539 | .31 | - .496 | .2139 |
| .80 | .842 | .1600 | .30 | - .524 | .2100 |
| .79 | .806 | .1659 | .29 | - .553 | .2059 |
| .78 | .772 | .1716 | .28 | - .583 | .2016 |
| .77 | .739 | .1771 | .27 | - .613 | .1971 |
| .76 | .706 | .1824 | .26 | - .643 | .1924 |
| .75 | .674 | .1875 | .25 | - .674 | .1875 |
| .74 | .643 | .1924 | .24 | - .706 | .1824 |
| .73 | .613 | .1971 | .23 | - .739 | .1771 |
| .72 | .583 | .2016 | .22 | - .772 | .1716 |
| .71 | .553 | .2059 | .21 | - .806 | .1659 |
| .70 | .524 | .2100 | .20 | - .842 | .1600 |
| .69 | .496 | .2139 | .19 | - .878 | .1539 |
| .68 | .468 | .2176 | .18 | - .915 | .1476 |

| Proportion (p)* | Deviate (z) | pq | Proportion (p)* | Deviate (z) | pq |
|---|---|---|---|---|---|
| .67 | .440 | .2211 | .17 | - .954 | .1411 |
| .66 | .412 | .2244 | .16 | - .994 | .1344 |
| .65 | .385 | .2275 | .15 | -1.036 | .1275 |
| .64 | .358 | .2304 | .14 | -1.080 | .1204 |
| .63 | .332 | .2331 | .13 | -1.126 | .1131 |
| .62 | .305 | .2356 | .12 | -1.175 | .1056 |
| .61 | .279 | .2379 | .11 | -1.227 | .0979 |
| .60 | .253 | .2400 | .10 | -1.282 | .0900 |
| .59 | .228 | .2419 | .09 | -1.341 | .0819 |
| .58 | .202 | .2436 | .08 | -1.405 | .0736 |
| .57 | .176 | .2451 | .07 | -1.476 | .0651 |
| .56 | .151 | .2464 | .06 | -1.555 | .0564 |
| .55 | .126 | .2475 | .05 | -1.645 | .0475 |
| .54 | .100 | .2484 | .04 | -1.751 | .0384 |
| .53 | .075 | .2491 | .03 | -1.881 | .0291 |
| .52 | .050 | .2496 | .02 | -2.054 | .0196 |
| .51 | .025 | .2499 | .01 | -2.326 | .0096 |
| .50 | .000 | .2500 | .00 | 0.000 | .0000 |

*Can also be read as $q$, where $q = 1 - p$.

# Appendix *β*

*Relationships Among T Scores, z Scores, and Percentile Ranks When Raw Scores Are Normally Distributed*

| z Score | T Score | Percentile Rank | z Score | T Score | Percentile Rank |
|---------|---------|-----------------|---------|---------|-----------------|
| 3.0 | 80 | 99.9 | -3.0 | 20 | 0.1 |
| 2.9 | 79 | 99.8 | -2.9 | 21 | 0.2 |
| 2.8 | 78 | 99.7 | -2.8 | 22 | 0.3 |
| 2.7 | 77 | 99.6 | -2.7 | 23 | 0.4 |
| 2.6 | 76 | 99.5 | -2.6 | 24 | 0.5 |
| 2.5 | 75 | 99.4 | -2.5 | 25 | 0.6 |
| 2.4 | 74 | 99.2 | -2.4 | 26 | 0.8 |
| 2.3 | 73 | 99 | -2.3 | 27 | 1 |
| 2.2 | 72 | 99 | -2.2 | 28 | 1 |
| 2.1 | 71 | 98 | -2.1 | 29 | 2 |
| 2.0 | 70 | 98 | -2.0 | 30 | 2 |
| 1.9 | 69 | 97 | -1.9 | 31 | 3 |
| 1.8 | 68 | 96 | -1.8 | 32 | 4 |
| 1.7 | 67 | 96 | -1.7 | 33 | 4 |
| 1.6 | 66 | 95 | -1.6 | 34 | 5 |
| 1.5 | 65 | 93 | -1.5 | 35 | 7 |
| 1.4 | 64 | 92 | -1.4 | 36 | 8 |
| 1.3 | 63 | 90 | -1.3 | 37 | 10 |
| 1.2 | 62 | 88 | -1.2 | 38 | 12 |
| 1.1 | 61 | 86 | -1.1 | 39 | 14 |
| 1.0 | 60 | 84 | -1.0 | 40 | 16 |
| 0.9 | 59 | 82 | -0.9 | 41 | 18 |
| 0.8 | 58 | 79 | -0.8 | 42 | 21 |
| 0.7 | 57 | 76 | -0.7 | 43 | 24 |
| 0.6 | 56 | 73 | -0.6 | 44 | 27 |
| 0.5 | 55 | 69 | -0.5 | 45 | 31 |
| 0.4 | 54 | 66 | -0.4 | 46 | 34 |
| 0.3 | 53 | 62 | -0.3 | 47 | 38 |
| 0.2 | 52 | 58 | -0.2 | 48 | 42 |
| 0.1 | 51 | 54 | -0.1 | 49 | 46 |
| 0.0 | 50 | 50 | 0.0 | 50 | 50 |

# Glossary

***Academic Aptitude Test***  A measure of the native and acquired abilities needed for schoolwork.

***Accountability***  Documenting the acceptability of agreed-upon criteria.

***Achievement Test***  A test that measures the extent to which an individual has "achieved" something—acquired certain information or mastered certain skills—usually as a result of specific instruction or general schooling.

***Acquiescence***  The tendency to "agree" with true items on a true-false test. An individual's personality interacts with the test to produce a response style and results in invalidity. Also the tendency to select central or middle values on a rating scale.

***Adaptive Testing***  Computer-assisted test administration where the presentation of items is dictated by examinee's responses to previous items or ability.

***Affective***  Pertaining to attitudes, interests, values, feelings, preferences, likes, pleasures, confidence, pride, and satisfaction.

***Age Norm***  Values or scores representing typical or average performance of individuals classified according to chronological age.

***Alternate-Form Reliability***  A measure of the extent to which two equivalent or parallel forms of a test correlate in measuring whatever they measure.

***Alternative***  See *distractor*.

***Ambiguity Error***  Rating error introduced when different raters interpret the same rating form term differently, for example, what is "average" or how frequently is "sometimes."

***Analytic Scoring***  Breaking down a communication, for example, an essay, into component parts, such as grammar with a differentially weighted scoring guide.

***Anecdotal Record***  Summary written description of student observation.

**Anticipated Achievement**  Expected or predicted performance or achievement based on past performance or aptitude/ability measures.

**Aptitude**  A combination of abilities and other characteristics, native or acquired, known or believed to be indicative of an individual's ability to learn in a given particular area. Thus, "musical aptitude" refers to that combination of physical and mental characteristics, motivational factors, knowledge, and other characteristics that is conducive to achieving proficiency in the field of music. Motivational factors, including interests, are sometimes distinguished from aptitude, but the more comprehensive definition seems preferable.

**Aptitude Test**  A measure, usually cognitive or psychomotor, of the likelihood of an individual's benefiting from a training program.

**Arithmetic Mean**  The sum of a set of scores divided by the number of scores (commonly called *average* or *mean*).

**Articulated Tests**  A series of tests that provides different levels for different ages or grades, constructed and standardized so that the same or comparable elements or objectives are measured at all levels. Well-articulated tests are characterized by considerable interlevel overlap to test the wide ranges of abilities and achievements in any given grade or class. On a well-articulated series of test batteries, a given grade group achieves the same derived scores whether a lower or higher level of the test is used.

**Assessment**  The systematic evaluative appraisal of an individual's ability and performance in a particular environment or context. Characterized by synthesis of a variety of data.

**Average**  A general term applied to measures of central tendency. The three most widely used averages are the *arithmetic mean*, the *median*, and the *mode*.

**Balance**  The degree to which the proportion of items measuring particular outcomes corresponds to the "ideal" test or to that suggested by the table of specifications.

**Battery**  A group of tests standardized on the same population, so that results on the several tests are comparable (integrated norms). Sometimes loosely applied to any group of tests administered together.

**Behavioral Objectives**  Statements of intended educational outcomes defined as criteria for student performance, sometimes specifying the conditions under which the behavior is to be observed. Akin to "performance" and "competence" objectives.

**Bias**  Systematic, but invalid, advantage or disadvantage for a particular group or subgroup based on irregularities in test content, administration, or interpretation. Controlled by judgmental or empirical methods.

**Bimodal Distribution**  The tendency of a frequency distribution to reflect two identifiable scores or regions along the score scale.

**Biserial Correlation**  A frequently used method of expressing the relationship between an artificial dichotomy (e.g., example, high/low) and a continuous variable. Often used to correlate responses to items and total test scores.

**Ceiling**  The upper limit of ability that can be measured by a test. Individuals are said to have reached the ceiling of a test when their abilities exceed the highest performance level at which the test can make reliable discriminations.

**Centile** A value on the scoring scale below which a given percentage of cases is located. Any of 99 values that divide a distribution into 100 equal units. The synonym *percentile* is regarded by some statisticians as superfluous. (See *percentile*.)

**Central Tendency Error** The reluctance to give extreme ratings, either positive or negative.

**Chance Score** The most likely score to result from guessing. (See *correction for guessing*.)

**Coaching** Instruction and practice on test tasks like those to be encountered on a criterion measure (e.g., Scholastic Assessment Test). Also included general practice on test-taking strategies.

**Coefficient Alpha** A generalized measure of internal consistency for items on a continuous response scale. Specifically, the average degree of interitem correlation. (See *internal consistency*.)

**Coefficient of Determination** The square of the correlation coefficient (times 100) reflecting the overlap or common variance. Usually between predictor and criterion measures.

**Cognitive** Pertaining to such mental abilities as recall, comprehension, problem solving, and synthesis, and the sensing and processing of information.

**Completion Item** A test question calling for the completion of a phrase or sentence one or more parts of which have been omitted; a question for which the examinee must supply (rather than select) the correct response.

**Concurrent Validity** See *criterion-related validity*.

**Consistency** See *reliability*.

**Construct Validity** The degree to which a test measures given psychological qualities. By both logical and empirical methods the theory underlying the test is validated. Arguments for construct validity must be based on theory and empirical evidence. Examples of such methods are correlations of the test score with other test scores, factor analysis, study of the effect of speed on test scores.

**Content Validity** The degree to which the content of the test samples the subject matter, behaviors, or situations about which conclusions are to be drawn. Content validity is especially important in an achievement test and is determined by using the table of specifications and objectives. Examples of procedures to measure content validity are textbook analysis, description of the universe of items, judgment of the adequacy of the sample, review of representative illustrations of test content, intercorrelations of subscores, and solicitation of the opinions of a jury of experts.

**Contrast Error** The tendency of a rater to judge a ratee in a direction opposite that of the rater, for example, "Nobody is as neat and clean as I am."

**Convergent Validity** The extent to which two different measures of the same criterion are correlated. (See *discriminate validity*.)

**Correction for Attenuation** An estimate of the effect of lack of perfect test and criterion reliability on validity or the correlation between the test and the criterion.

**Correction for Guessing** A reduction in score for wrong answers, sometimes applied in scoring true-false or multiple-choice questions. Many doubt the validity or usefulness of this device, which is intended to discourage guessing and yield more accurate measures of examinees' true knowledge. It is assumed that if an examinee guesses on an objective test, the number of resulting wrong answers will be proportional to the number of alternative responses to each item.

**Correlation**  The relationship or "going-togetherness" between two sets of scores or measures; the tendency of scores on one variable to vary concomitantly with those of another, for example, the tendency of students with high IQs to be above average in reading ability. The existence of a strong relationship—that is, a high correlation—between two variables does not necessarily indicate a causal relationship. (See *correlation coefficient*.)

**Correlation Coefficient (r)**  The most commonly used index of relationship between paired facts or numbers, indicating the tendency of two or more variables or attributes to rank themselves, or individuals measured on them, in the same way. A correlation coefficient (r) can range in value from –1.00 for a perfect negative relationship, through 0.00 for a none or pure chance to +1.00 for a perfect positive relationship, and summarizes the degree and direction of the relationship.

**Criterion**  A standard by which a test can be judged or evaluated; a set of scores or ratings that a test is designed to correlate with or to predict. (See *validity*.)

**Criterion-Referenced Test**  A test whose items are tied to specific objectives. Usually used when mastery learning is involved. Variability of scores is of little consequence. Emphasis is on an individual's performance relative to an absolute rather than a normative standard, that is, an individual's performance is compared with a prior criterion instead of with the performance of other people.

**Criterion-Related Validity**  The degree to which test scores correlate with measures of criterion performance. Measures of criteria can be gathered concurrently (concurrent validity)—for example, correlation of the distribution of scores for men in a given occupation with those for men-in-general, correlation of personality test scores with estimates of adjustments made in counseling interviews, or correlation of end-of-course achievement or ability test scores with school marks—or at a later time—for example, correlation of intelligence test scores with course grades, or correlation of test scores obtained at beginning of the year with marks earned at the end of the year.

**Cross-Validation**  The process of determining whether a decision derived from one set of data is truly effective by applying the decision process (or strategy) to an independent but relevant set of data.

**Culture-Fair Test**  An idealized test where the influence of such potentially biasing factors as sex, race, or religion has been attenuated. Examinees should not be penalized because of the lack of uniform sociocultural experiences.

**Curricular Validity**  The strength of the match and link among objectives, curriculum, and assessment.

**Curriculum Evaluation**  The process of collecting and processing data for decision making about the merit of an educational program. Such data can include (1) objective descriptions of goals, environments, personnel, methods, content, and results, and (2) recorded personal judgments of the quality and appropriateness of goals, inputs, and outcomes.

**Decile**  Any of the nine percentile points (scores) in a distribution that divide it into 10 equal parts; every 10th percentile. The first decile is the 10th percentile, the ninth decile is the 90th percentile, and so on.

**Derived Score**  A score that has been converted from a qualitative or quantitative mark on one scale into the units of another scale (e.g., standard score, percentile rank, intelligence quotient).

**Deviation**  The amount by which a score differs from some reference value, such as the mean, norm, or score on another test.

**Deviation IQ**  A measure of intelligence or "brightness" based on the extent to which an individual's score deviates from a score that is typical for the individual's age. Usually expressed as a standard score. (See *intelligence quotient*.)

**Diagnostic Test**  A test used to identify specific areas of weakness or strength and to determine the nature of deficiencies; it yields measures of the components of larger areas of knowledge and skills. Diagnostic achievement tests are most commonly developed for the skill subjects: reading, arithmetic, and spelling.

**Difference Score**  The difference between two test scores. When the difference scores are from pre- and post-measures, the gain or change scores tend to be unreliable.

**Differential Prediction**  Prediction among populations or subpopulations (or subsamples) with combinations of predictors and criteria.

**Differential Weighting**  The elements of a composite are differentially weighted according to empirically determined weights or on the basis of presumed importance, for example, items on a test or subscore in a battery.

**Difficulty Index**  The percentage of some specified group, such as students of a given age or grade, who answer an item correctly or score in a particular direction.

**Direct Instruction**  An approach to education that involves prescribed objectives, a high degree of teacher control, frequent reviews and assessments, and active student participation.

**Discriminate Validity**  If a test is in fact not correlated with a measure with which it is hypothesized not to correlate, it is said to have discriminate validity.

**Discrimination Index**  The ability of a test item to differentiate between individuals who possess a given characteristic (skill, knowledge, attitude) in abundance, and those who possess little of it.

**Distractor**  Any of the plausible but incorrect choices provided in a multiple-choice or matching item. Sometimes called a foil, alternative, or option. The choice is "distracting" and appears attractive to the less knowledgeable or skillful examinee, thereby reducing the efficacy of guessing.

**Distribution**  An ordered tabulation of scores showing the number of individuals who obtain each score or fall within each score interval. (See *frequency distribution*.)

**Diversity**  Any number of human or cultural characteristics that can place variable demands on the teaching-learning process (e.g., ethnicity, age).

**Domain**  The specifications for a population of expected outcomes, behaviors, or learning.

**Domain Referenced**   Scores are based on a percentage correct of a sample of items correlated with a specified universe of objectives.

**Dual Standardization**   The procedure of norming or standardizing two tests, for example, a group intelligence test and an achievement battery, simultaneously on one sample, thereby integrating the two instruments.

**Educational Assessment**   The evaluation and application of instruction data on or from students gathered by a variety of measurement methods.

**Error of Estimate**   See *standard error of estimate*.

**Error of Measurement**   Inconsistent or random error (e.g., effect of guessing) that decreases the reliability of measurement. Technically or theoretically the difference between an individual's "true" score and an obtained score. (See *standard error of measurement*.)

**Equivalent Forms**   Any of two or more forms of a test whose content and difficulty are similar, and that yield very similar average scores and measures of variability for a given group.

**Evaluation**   The process by which quantitative and qualitative data are processed to arrive at a judgment of value, worth, merit, or effectiveness.

**Expectancy Table**   Usually a two-way grid or bivariate table expressing the relationship between two (or more) variables by stating the probability that individuals who belong to each of a set of subgroups defined on the basis of another variable will perform at a specified level or exhibit certain characteristics. A method of expressing the validity of a test, if one of the variables is the predictor and the other the criterion.

**External Test**   Usually a standardized achievement or aptitude test the control of which rests with an agency outside the school, for example, the state or national college application organization. The primary audience for results is outside the school.

**Extrapolation**   As applied to test norms, the process of extending a norm line beyond the limits of the data to permit interpretation of extreme scores. This extension can be accomplished mathematically by fitting a curve to the obtained data or by less rigorous graphic methods. (See *interpolation*.)

**Face Validity**   The acceptability of the test and test situation by the examinee and, to some extent, the user, in light of the apparent uses to which the test is to be put. A test has face validity when it appears to measure what it purports to test.

**Factor**   A hypothetical trait, ability, or component of ability that underlies and influences performance on two or more tests, and hence causes scores on the tests to be correlated. Strictly defined, the term *factor* refers to a theoretical variable derived by a process of factor analysis from a table of intercorrelations among tests, but it is also commonly used to denote the psychological interpretation given to the variable—that is, the mental trait assumed to be represented by the variable, such as verbal or numerical ability.

**Field Dependence-Independence**   Ability to differentially perceive patterns in figure-ground relationships.

**Foil**   See *distractor*.

**Forced-Choice Item**   Broadly, any multiple-choice item that requires the examinee to select one or more of the given choices. The term is best used to denote a special type of multiple-choice item in which the options are (1) of equal "preference value"—that is, chosen equally often by a typical group—but (2) of differential discriminating ability—that is, such that one and only one of the options discriminates between persons high and low on the factor that this option measures.

**Formative Evaluation**   The use of evaluation data to modify, revise, and generally improve an educational program during its developmental stages. (See *summative evaluation*.)

**Free-Response Item**   Examinees construct or supply the answer or response. Response can be very brief, for example, word or numeral, or somewhat extended, for example, sentence or paragraph.

**Frequency Distribution**   An ordered tabulation of scores showing the number of individuals who obtain each score or fall within each score interval.

**Generalizability**   The extent to which a test produces comparable results over situations, populations, administrators, or locations. The key is the search for the relationship between a sample of scores relative to a universe of scores. Intricate statistical procedures may be applied.

**Generosity Error**   See *leniency error*.

**Grade Equivalent**   The grade level for which a given score is the real or estimated average. A grade equivalent of 6.4 is theoretically the average score obtained by students in the fourth month of the sixth grade. Grade-equivalent score units are subject to much distortion because of variations in curriculum, individual aptitude, and learning.

**Graphic Rating Scale**   A scale that presents the rater with a continuum of phrases describing degrees of a particular trait. The rater makes a judgment about an individual or object with reference to the trait and indicates his or her opinion by placing a mark on a line.

**Group Test**   A test that can be administered to a number of individuals simultaneously by a single examiner.

**Guessing**   See *correction for guessing*.

**Halo Rating Error**   The biased effect of a gross or global overall general impression of an individual on the rating of specific traits. The effect in practice is usually positive.

**High-Stakes Test**   A measurement the results of which will have a significant impact on a student, for example, promotion, graduation, or receipt of a scholarship.

**Histogram**   A graphic representation of a frequency distribution using vertical bars to represent the different frequencies for scores or groups of scores.

**Incremental Validity**   The increase in relationship between the predictor(s) and the criterion measure when another predictor is added to the set.

**Individual Test**   A test that can be administered to only one person at a time.

**Instructional Validity**   The strength of the match and link between instruction and assessment.

**Intelligence Quotient**   A now-outmoded index representing the ratio of a person's mental age to his or her chronological age (MA/CA) or, more precisely, especially for older persons, the ratio of mental age to the mental age typical of chronological age (in both cases multiplied by 100 to eliminate the decimal). More generally, IQ is a measure of "brightness" that considers both the score on an intelligence test and age. (See *deviation IQ.*)

**Internal Consistency** The extent to which items on a test are correlated with each other, implying the measurement of a common content skill, behavior, or other factor.

**Interpolation** In general, any process of estimating intermediate values between two known points. As applied to test norms, the term usually refers to the procedure used in assigning values (e.g., grade or age equivalents) to scores between the successive average scores actually obtained in the standardization process. In reading norm tables, it is necessary to interpolate to obtain a norm value for a score between the scores given in a table. (See *extrapolation.*)

**Interquartile Range** The score difference corresponding to the difference between the third and first quartile (75th and 25th percentiles).

**Ipsative Measurement** Intraindividual comparison in which a given variable score is limited by scores on the other variables; the sum of scores across all scales is the same for all examinees. A forced-choice format is used.

**Item** A single question or exercise in a test.

**Item Analysis** Any of several methods used in test development and refinement to determine how well a given test item discriminates among individuals differing in some characteristic. The effectiveness of a test item depends upon three factors: (1) the validity of the item measured against an outside criterion, curriculum content, or educational objective; (2) the discriminating power of the item for validity and internal consistency; and (3) the difficulty of the item.

**Item Response Theory** See *latent trait theory.*

**Item Sampling** A procedure used in standardization of tests and curriculum evaluation. Instead of requiring all individuals to respond to all items, subgroups take subsets of items. For example, instead of requiring 100 individuals to answer 70 items, 10 groups of 10 individuals each answer 7 items.

**Key** See *scoring key.*

**Kuder–Richardson Formula(s)** Formulas for estimating the reliability—specifically, the internal consistency—of a test from (1) information about the individual items in the test, or (2) the mean score, standard deviation, and number of items in the test. Because the Kuder–Richardson formulas permit estimation of reliability from a single administration of a test, without dividing the test into halves, their use has become common in test development. The Kuder-Richardson formulas are not appropriate for estimating the reliability of speeded tests.

**Latent Trait Theory** Statistical procedures are used to relate an individual examinee's score to an estimated hypothetical latent trait. Several models are used in item analysis, calibration, and test scaling as part of the standardization process.

**Learning Style** A student-preferred mode or medium of instruction (e.g., lecture, visual).

**Leniency Error** The tendency to rate more favorably those whom one knows best.

**Likert Scale** A method of scaling attitudes in which a respondent indicates her or his degree of agreement to disagreement to a series of propositions about people, places, ideas, activities, concepts, or objects.

**Logical Error** The tendency to give similar ratings to those traits that appear to the rater to be logically related to each other, for example, assertiveness versus aggressiveness.

**Mastery Test** A test of the extent to which a student has mastered a specified set of objectives or met minimum requirements set by a teacher or examining agency. Usually a criterion-referenced measure. (See *criterion-referenced test*.)

**Matching Item** A test item calling for the correct association of each entry in one list with an entry in a second list.

**Mean** The sum of a set of scores divided by the number of scores.

**Measurement** The process of quantifying according to a standard. The assignment of numerals to represent objects, individuals, or phenomena.

**Measurement-Driven Instruction** The use of criterion-reference measures to dictate nature of instructional experiences, especially in high-stakes situations.

**Median** The 50th percentile; the point that divides a group into two equal parts. Half of a group of scores fall below the median and half above it.

**Mental Age (MA)** The age for which a given score on an intelligence test is average or normal. If a score of 55 on an intelligence test corresponds to a mental age of 6 years 10 months, 55 is presumed to be the average score that would be achieved by an unselected group of children 6 years 10 months of age.

**Minimum Competency Test** Measures of basic skill and competencies in subject areas (and writing) used to make graduation, certification, and promotion decisions.

**Mode** The score or value that occurs most frequently in a distribution.

**Multicultural Assessment** Concern with classroom diversity during assessment. (See *pluralistic assessment*.)

**Multicultural Education** The adaptation or modification of instructional practices to accommodate classroom diversity.

**Multicultural Validity** The inclusion of elements in the assessment process (construction, administration) which results in fairer and more valid data.

**Multiple-Choice Item** A test item for which the examinee's task is to choose the correct or best answer from several given options.

**Multiple Correlation** The relationship between one variable and the weighted sum of two or more other variables.

**Multiple Regression** A method of combining two or more predictors to estimate a single criterion measure. For example, freshman grade point average may be predicted from a combination of high school rank, intelligence test score, and interest inventory scores.

**Multiple-Response Item** A type of multiple-choice item in which two or more of the given choices may be correct.

**N** The symbol commonly used to represent the number of cases in a distribution, study, or other sampling. The sum of the frequencies = $N$ for population and $n$ for a sample.

**Normal Curve Equivalent** A normalized standard score with a mean of 50 and a standard deviation of 21.06.

***Normal Distribution*** A derived curve based on the assumption that variations from the mean occur by chance. The curve is bell-shaped and is accepted as a representational model because of its repeated recurrence in measurements of human characteristics in psychology and education. It has many useful mathematical properties. In a normal distribution curve, scores are distributed symmetrically about the mean, thickly concentrated near it and decreasing in frequency as the distance from it increases. One cannot tell if a particular distribution is "normal" simply by looking at it, but must determine whether the data fit a particular mathematical function.

***Normalized Standard Score*** Normalized standard scores are made to conform to standard score values of a normal distribution curve by use of percentile equivalents for the normal curve. Most frequently expressed with a mean equated to 50 and a standard deviation equated to 10. (See *T* scores.)

***Norm-Referenced Measure*** A measure used to distinguish among members of a group by comparing an individual's performance with the performance of others in the group.

***Norms*** Statistics that describe the test performance of specified subgroups, such as students of various ages or grades, in the standardization group for a test. Norms are often assumed to represent some larger population, such as students in the country as a whole. Norms are descriptive of average or typical performance; they are not to be regarded as standards or desirable levels of attainment. Grade, age, percentile, and standard score are the most common types of norms.

***Objectivity*** Consistency in scoring. Objectivity is a characteristic of a test that precludes differences of opinion among scorers as to whether responses are to be scored right or wrong. Such a test is contrasted with a "subjective" test—for example, the usual essay examination to which different scorers can assign different scores, ratings, or grades. Objectivity is a characteristic of the scoring of the test, not its form. An objective test is one in which the method of gathering data does not distort the phenomenon being measured.

***Ogive*** A smooth curve resulting from the plot of cumulative frequency or cumulative frequency expressed as a percentage of the total against individual scores.

***Omnibus Test*** A test (1) in which items measuring a variety of mental operations are combined into a single sequence rather than grouped together by type of operation, and (2) from which only a single score is derived. Omnibus tests make for simplicity of administration: one set of directions and one overall time limit usually suffice.

***Option*** See *distractor*.

***Percentile*** One of the 99 point scores that divide a ranked distribution into groups each of which is composed of 1/100 of the scores. Also, a point below which a certain percentage of the scores fall. For example, the median (the 50th percentile) is the point in a distribution below which 50 percent of the scores fall. Sometimes called *centile*.

***Percentile Rank*** The percentage of scores in a distribution equal to or lower than the score in question. If a person obtains a percentile rank of 70, his or her standing is regarded as equaling or surpassing that of 70 percent of the normative group on which the test was standardized.

**Performance Test**   A test usually requiring motor or manual response on the examinee's part and generally but not always involving manipulation of concrete equipment or materials, as contrasted with a paper-and-pencil test. The term is also used to denote a work-sample test, which simulates the behavior about which information is desired. A work-sample instrument can use paper-and-pencil to test skills such as accounting, shorthand, and proofreading. Also used to designate any "applied" task where prior training or instruction is used in problem solving.

**Pluralistic Assessment**   A philosophy and approach to educational assessment that attempts to be responsive to cultural diversity in the classroom and school. Usually involves performance assessments.

**Point-Biserial Correlation**   Used to describe the relationship between a true dichotomous variable (e.g., sex) and a continuous variable. Also used in item analysis.

**Portfolio Assessment**   The collection and evaluation of student created performances according to expected criteria.

**Power Test**   A test intended to measure level of performance and to sample the range of an examinee's capacity, rather than the speed of response; hence a power test has either no time limit or a very generous one.

**Practice Effect**   The influence of previous experience with a test on a later administration of the same or a similar test, usually resulting in an increase in score. Practice effect is greatest when the time interval between testing is small, the content of the two tests is very similar, and the initial test administration represents a relatively novel experience for the subject.

**Predictive Validity**   See *criterion-related validity*.

**Product-Moment Coefficient**   See *correlation coefficient*.

**Profile**   A graphic representation of an individual's or a group's scores on several tests, expressed in uniform or comparable terms. This method of presentation permits easy identification of areas of strength or weakness.

**Proximity Error**   A rating error that results in inflated correlations between traits just because they are rated at about the same time or are adjacent to one another on a response form.

**Q-Sort**   A technique used to measure personality, requiring the subject to sort a large number of statements into piles representing the degrees to which they apply to her or him.

**Quartile**   One of three points that divide the cases in a distribution into four equal groups. The first quartile is the 25th percentile, the second quartile is the 50th percentile or median, and the third quartile is the 75th percentile.

**Range**   The difference between the highest and lowest scores, plus 1, obtained on a test by a particular group.

**Rating Scale**   A data-gathering method involving the use of numerals or phrases in conjunction with points along a continuum. A given instrument can include several such scales.

*Raw Score*   The first quantitative result obtained in scoring a test. Usually the number of right answers, the time required for performance, the number of errors, or a similar direct, unconverted, uninterpreted measure.

*Readiness Test*   A test that measures the extent to which an individual has achieved the degree of maturity or acquired the skills or information necessary to undertake some new learning activity successfully. Thus a *reading readiness test* indicates the extent to which a child has reached the appropriate developmental stage and acquired the prerequisite skills to profitably begin a formal instructional program in reading.

*Recall Item*   An item that requires the examinee to supply the correct answer from his or her own memory, as contrasted with a *recognition item*, which requires the examinee to select or identify the correct answer.

*Recognition Item*   An item requiring the examinee to recognize or select the correct answer from among two or more given answers.

*Regression Effect*   The tendency for a predicted score to be relatively nearer the mean of its series than is the score from which it was predicted to the mean of its series. For example, if we predict school marks from an intelligence test, we will find that the mean of the predicted school marks for all students who have IQs 2 standard deviations above the mean will be less than 2 standard deviations from the mean of the school marks. There is a regression effect whenever the correlation between two measures is less than perfect.

*Relevance*   The extent to which specific items are actually measures of specific objectives. In a real sense, relevance is a function of item validity usually demonstrated by professional judgment.

*Reliability*   The extent to which a test is accurate or consistent in measuring whatever it measures; dependability, stability, and relative freedom from errors of measurement. Estimation of reliability generally involves examination of internal consistency, equivalence of forms, or stability of scores over time.

*Reliability of Difference*   The extent to which a difference between scores is consistent, for example, the extent to which differences between pre- and post-test scores on one form of a test are related to pre- and post-differences on another form of the test.

*Representative Sample*   A sample that accurately represents the population from which it is selected for characteristics relevant to the issue under investigation—for example, in an achievement-test norm sample, representation might be according to students from each state, various regions, segregated and nonsegregated schools, and so on.

*Response Set*   A test-taking attitude whereby examinees want to present a particular picture of themselves, for example, faking good or bad.

*Response Style*   Predisposition to respond in a particular manner as a function of the *form* rather than the *content* of the question. For example, when in doubt on a true-false test the tendency is to agree when guessing, thereby agreeing with authority. (See *acquiescence.*)

*Responsive Assessment*   An approach to assessment that (a) begins with a student learning problem, and (b) ends with a negotiated solution.

*Rubric*   A differentially graded scoring guide for performance assessments.

**Scaled Score**   A unit in a system of equated scores corresponding to the raw scores of a test in such a way that the scaled score values can be interpreted as representing the mean performance of certain reference groups. The intervals between any pair of scales scores can be interpreted as differences in the characteristics of the reference group.

**Scatter Diagram**   A bivariate frequency distribution where pairs of scores are plotted on coordinate axes. A graphical representation of relationship.

**Scholastic Aptitude**   See *academic aptitude test.*

**Scoring Key**   The standard against which examinee responses are compared. A list of correct or expected answers.

**Selection Item**   See *recognition item* and *multiple-choice item.*

**Semantic Differential Technique**   A method requiring individuals to express their feelings about a concept by rating it on a series of bipolar adjectives, for example, good-bad, strong-weak, or fast-slow. The format is usually a seven-interval scale, and three major dimensions are generally measured: evaluation, potency, and activity.

**Semi-Interquartile Range**   One-half of the difference between the third and first quartile (75th and 25th percentiles).

**Skewness**   The tendency of a distribution to depart from symmetry or balance around the mean. For example, a positively skewed distribution may have more extreme low scores than high scores, causing the mean to be higher than the median.

**Social Desirability**   A source of invalidity on self-report affective measures whereby the respondent answers in a predominantly socially desirable way, for example, always saying "No" to items like "I have never stolen anything in my life," although desirable, are rarely true.

**Sociogram**   A diagram of interpersonal relationships within a group showing friendship choices and rejections.

**Sociometry**   Measurement of the interpersonal relationships prevailing among the members of a group by means of sociometric devices, for example, the *sociogram.* An attempt is made to discover the patterns of choice and rejection, to identify the individuals most often chosen as friends or leaders ("stars") or rejected by others ("isolates"), and to determine how the group subdivides into clusters or cliques.

**Specific Determiners**   Two classes of ambiguous words that invalidate test items, particularly true-false items. One set (*some, might, could, sometimes*) tend to call for a True response. The other set (*never, always*) tend to call for a False response.

**Spiral Omnibus Test**   Test where different kinds of item formats are used with different content throughout the test and the items increase in difficulty level as the examinee progresses through the test.

**Stability**   As applied to the examination of reliability, the method involves administering the same test to the same group on two different occasions and correlating the scores. (See *reliability.*)

**Standard Deviation**   A measure of the variability of dispersion of a set of scores. The more the scores cluster around the mean, the smaller the standard deviation.

**Standard Error of Estimate**  An expression of the degree to which predictions or estimates of criterion scores are likely to correspond to actual values (standard deviation of the criterion times the square root of the quantity, 1 minus the correlation coefficient squared). A method of expressing the validity of the test. All other things being equal, the smaller the standard error, the better the validity is.

**Standard Error of Measurement**  A measure of the estimated difference between the observed test score and the hypothetical "true score," that is, errorless score (standard deviation of the test times the square root of one minus the reliability coefficient). A method of expressing the reliability of a test. All other things being equal, the smaller the error of measurement, the higher the reliability is. Used in estimating the true score.

**Standard Score**  A general term referring to any of a variety of "transformed" scores; raw scores can be expressed for reasons of convenience, comparability, ease of interpretation, and the like. The simplest type of standard score expresses the deviation of an individual's raw score from the average score of his or her group in relation to the standard deviation of the scores of the group. Thus:

Standard score $(z)$ = raw score $(x)$—mean $(m)$ ÷ standard deviation $(s)$

Standard scores do not affect the relative standing of the individuals in the group or change the shape of the original distribution. More complicated types of standard scores may yield distributions differing in shape from the original distribution; in fact, they are sometimes used for precisely this purpose.

**Standardization Sample**  The reference sample of those individuals, schools, or other units selected for use in norming a test. This sample should be representative of the target population in essential characteristics such as geographical representation, age, and grade.

**Standardized Test**  A systematic sample of performance obtained under prescribed conditions, scored according to definite rules, and capable of evaluation by reference to normative information. Some writers restrict the term to tests possessing the above properties whose items have been experimentally evaluated or for which evidence of validity and reliability is provided.

**Stanine**  A unit that divides the norm population into nine groups. Except for Stanines 1 and 9, the groups are spaced in half-sigma units, with the mean at Stanine 5 and those scoring the highest at Stanine 9. Stanines are usually normalized standard scores.

| Stanine | 1 | 2 | 3 | 4 | 5 | 6 | 7 | 8 | 9 |
|---|---|---|---|---|---|---|---|---|---|
| % in stanine | 4 | 7 | 12 | 17 | 10 | 17 | 12 | 7 | 4 |

**Stencil Key**  A scoring key which, when positioned over an examinee's responses in a test booklet or on an answer sheet, permits rapid identification and tabulation of correct answers. Stencil keys can be perforated in positions corresponding to those of the correct answers, so that only correct answers show through, or they can be transparent, with the positions of the correct answers identified by circles or boxes printed on the key.

**Strip Key**  A scoring key on which the answers to items on any page or column of the test appear in a strip or column that can be placed beside the examinee's responses.

*Subtest*   A collection of items in a battery or test that have distinct similar characteristics or functions. A separate score is usually provided.

*Summative Evaluation*   The use of evaluation data to determine the effectiveness of a unit, course, or program after it has been completed. (See *formative evaluation*.)

*Supply Item*   See *free-response item* and *completion item*.

*Survey Test*   A test that measures general achievement in a given subject or area, usually with the understanding that the test is intended to measure group, rather than individual, status.

*T Score*   A derived (normalized) standard score based on the equivalence of percentile values to standard scores, which avoids the effects of skewed distributions, and usually having a mean equated to 50 and a standard deviation equated to 10.

*Table of Specifications*   Usually a two-way grid summarizing the behavioral outcomes and content of a course or unit of instruction. Percentages in the cells of the table indicate the importance of subtopics dictated by value judgments, instructional time spent, and the like. Used to guide achievement test development and selection. The specifications may also call for particular types of items, behaviors, and the like. Tables of specification are also used in the development of tests other than proficiency measures.

*Tailored Testing*   See *adaptive testing*.

*Test*   A systematic procedure for gathering data to make intra- or interindividual comparisons.

*Test-Wiseness*   Competency in test-taking skills and ability to outwit inept test constructors, for example, ability to spot *specific determiners* and respond appropriately.

*Test-Retest Reliability Coefficient*   A type of reliability coefficient obtained by administering a test to the same sample a second time after an interval and correlating the two sets of scores. (See *stability*.)

*True Score*   The average score on an infinite series of administrations of the same or exactly equivalent tests, assuming no practice effect or change in the examinee during the testings. A score for which errors of measurement have been averaged.

*Validity*   The extent to which a test does the job for which it is used. Thus defined, validity has different connotations for various kinds of tests and, accordingly, different kinds of evidence are appropriate: (1) the validity of an achievement test is the extent to which the content of the test represents a balanced and adequate sampling of the outcomes of the course or instructional program in question (content, face, or curricular validity). It is best determined by a comparison of the test content with courses of study, instructional materials, and statements of instructional goals, and by critical analysis of the processes required to respond to the items. (2) The validity of an aptitude, prognostic, or readiness test is the extent to which it accurately indicates future learning success in the area in question. It is manifested by correlations between test scores and measures of later success. (3) The validity of a personality test is the extent to which the test yields an accurate description of an individual's personality traits or personality organization. It can be manifested by agreement between test results and other types of evaluation, such as rating or clinical classification, but only to the extent that such criteria are themselves valid. The traditional definition of validity—"the extent to which a test measures what it is supposed to measure"—fails to acknowledge that validity is always specific to the purposes for which the test is used, that different kinds of evidence are appropriate to different types of tests, and that final responsibility for validation rests with the test interpreter and user. (See *content, construct,* and *criterion-related validity.*)

**Variance**  The aggregate amount of variability in a set of scores. The square of the standard deviation or the average of the squared deviations about the mean.

# References

Aaron, R. L., & Gillespie, C. (1990). Gates-MacGinitie reading tests. In R. B. Cuder, Jr. (Ed.), *The teacher's guide to reading tests* (3rd ed.). Scottsdale, AZ: Gorsuch Scarisbrick.

Adams, G. S. (1964). *Measurement and evaluation in education, psychology, and guidance.* New York: Holt, Rinehart & Winston.

Aiken, L. R. (1988). *Psychological testing and assessment* (6th ed.). Boston: Allyn & Bacon.

Airasian, P. W. (2001). *Classroom assessment* (4th ed.). New York: McGraw-Hill.

Alderman, D. L., & Powers, D. E. (1979). *The effects of special preparation on SAT–Verbal scores.* Research Report RR-79-1. Princeton, NJ: College Entrance Examination Board.

Alkin, M. C. (1972). Accountability defined. *Evaluation Comment, 3*(3), 1–5. Los Angeles: University of California at Los Angeles Center for the Study of Evaluation.

Allport, G. W. (1942). *The use of personal documents in psychological science.* New York: Social Science Research Council.

Allport, G. W., Vernon, P. E., & Lindzey, G. (1970). *A study of values.* Boston: Houghton Mifflin.

American Psychological Association. (1992). *Ethical principles of psychologists and code of conduct.* Washington, DC: Author.

American Educational Research Association, American Psychological Association, & National Council on Measurement in Education (1999). *Standards for educational and psychological testing.* Washington, D.C.: American Educational Research Association.

Anastasi, A. (1988). *Psychological testing* (6th ed.). New York: Macmillan.

Anderson, L. W. (1981). *Assessing affective characteristics in the schools.* Boston: Allyn & Bacon.

Anderson, L. W., & Krathwohl, D. R. (2001). *A taxonomy for learning, teaching and assessing* (A revision of Bloom's Taxonomy of Educational Objectives). New York: Longman.

Anderson, R. D., et al. (1994). *Issues of curriculum reform in science, mathematics and higher order thinking across the disciplines.* Washington, DC: U.S. Department of Education, Office of Research, OR 94-3408.

Angoff, W. H. (1971). Scales, norms and equivalent scores. In R. L. Thorndike (Ed.), *Educational measurement* (2nd ed., pp. 508–600). Washington, DC: American Council on Education.

Angoff, W. H., & Anderson, S. B. (1963, February). The standardization of educational and psychological tests. *Illinois Journal of Education,* 19–23.

Anrig, G. R. (1987). ETS on "Golden Rule." *Educational Measurement: Issues and Practice, 6*(3), 24–27.

Applebee, A. N., Langer, J. A., & Mullis, I. V. S. (1989). *Crossroads in American education.* Princeton, NJ: Educational Testing Service.

Arter, J. A., & Spandel, V. (1992). Using portfolios of student work in instruction and assessment. *Educational Measurement: Issues and Practice, 11*(1), 36–44.

Ashbacker, P. R., & Herman, J. L. (1991). *Guidelines for effective score reporting.* CSE Technical Report 326. Los Angeles: University of California at Los Angeles Center for Research on Evaluation, Standards and Student Testing.

Ashelman, P., & Lenhoff, R. (Eds.). (1994). *Portfolio assessment* (Applications of portfolio analysis). New York: Lanham.

Atkinson, J. W. (1958). Towards experimental analysis of human motivation in terms of motives, expectancies, and incentives. In J. W. Atkinson (Ed.), *Motives in fantasy, action, and society* (pp. 288–305). Princeton, NJ: D. Van Nostrand.

Austin, T. (1994). *Changing the view: Student-led parent conferences.* Portsmouth, NH: Heinemann.

*Baker v. Columbus Municipal Separate School District* (1971). 329 F. Supp. 706 (N.D. Miss).

Bangert-Downs, R. L., Kulik, J. A., & Kulik, C. C. (1983). Effects of coaching programs on achievement performance. *Review of Educational Research, 53*(4), 571–585.

Banks, J. A., & Banks, C. A. M. (Eds.). (1995). *Handbook of research on multicultural education.* New York: Macmillan.

Baruth, L. G., & Manning, M. L. (1992). *Multicultural education of children and adolescents.* Boston: Allyn & Bacon.

Bass, R. K., & Dills, C. R. (Eds.). (1984). *Instructional development: The state of the art II.* Dubuque, IA: Kendall/Hunt.

Bauernfeind, R. H. (1967). Goal cards and future developments in achievement testing. *Proceedings of the 1966 Invitational Conference on Testing Problems.* Princeton, NJ: Educational Testing Service.

Beatty, L. S., Madden, R., Gardner, E. F., & Karlsen, B. (1984). *Stanford diagnostic mathematics test* (3rd ed.). San Antonio, TX: The Psychological Corporation.

Becker, L. D., Bender, N. N., & Morrison, G. (1978). Measuring impulsivity—reflection: A critical review. *Journal of Learning Disabilities, 11*(10), 626–632.

Bennett, R. E. (2001). How the Internet will help large-scale assessment reinvent itself. *Education Policy Analysis Archives, 9*(5), 20 (retrievable from http://epaa.asu.edu/epaa/v9n5.html).

Benson, B., & Barnett, B. (1999). *Student-led conferencing using showcase portfolios.* Thousand Oaks, CA: Corwin Press.

Berk, R. A. (1986). A consumer's guide to setting performance standards on criterion-referenced tests. *Review of Educational Research, 56*(1), 137–172.

Berk, R. A. (Ed.). (1982). *Handbook of methods for detecting test bias*. Baltimore: Johns Hopkins University Press.

Berkay, P. J., Gardner, E., & Smith, P. L. (1995). The development of the opinions about deaf people scale: A scale to measure learning adults' beliefs about the capabilities of deaf adults. *Educational and Psychological Measurement, 55,* 105–114.

Blaha, J. (1982). Predicting reading and arithmetic achievement with measures of reading attitudes and cognitive styles. *Perceptual and Motor Skills, 55,* 107–114.

Bledsoe, J. C. (1972). *Essentials of educational research* (2nd ed.). Athens, GA: Optima House.

Bloom, B. S. (Ed.). (1956). *Taxonomy of educational objectives*. Handbook I: *The cognitive domain*. New York: David McKay.

Bloom, B. S. (1970). Toward a theory of testing which includes measurement-evaluation-assessment. In M. C. Wittrock & D. E. Wiley (Eds.), *The evaluation of instruction: Issues and problems* (pp. 25–69). New York: Holt, Rinehart & Winston.

Bond, L. (1981). Bias in mental tests. In B. F. Green (Ed.), *New directions for testing and measurement: Issues in testing—coaching, disclosure and ethnic bias* (No. 11, pp. 55–77). San Francisco: Jossey-Bass.

Bonney, M. E., & Hampleman, R. S. (1962). *Personal-social evaluation techniques*. Washington, DC: Center for Applied Research in Education.

Brookhart, S. M. (1994). Teachers' grading. Practice and theory. *Applied Measurement in Education, 7*(4), 279–301.

*Brookhart v. Illinois State Board of Education*. 697F.2d 179 (7th Cir. 1983).

Brophy, J. E., & Good, T. L. (1986). Teacher behavior and student achievement. In M. C. Wittrock (Ed.), *Handbook of research on teaching* (3rd ed., pp. 328–375). New York: Macmillan.

Bunderson, C. V., Inouye, D. K., & Olsen, J. B. (1989). The four generations of computerized educational measurement. In R. L. Linn (Ed.), *Educational measurement* (3rd ed., pp. 367–407). Washington, DC: American Council on Education/Macmillan.

Campbell, D. T., & Fiske, D. W. (1959). Convergent and discriminant validation by the multitrait-multimethod matrix. *Psychological Bulletin, 56,* 81–105.

Cannell, J. J. (1988). Nationally normed achievement testing in America's public schools: How all 50 states are above the national average. *Educational Measurement: Issues and Practice, 7*(2), 5–9.

Cattell, R. B., Heist, A. B., & Stewart, R. G. (1950). The objective measurement of dynamic traits. *Educational and Psychological Measurement, 10,* 224–248.

Chivdo, J. J. (1987). The effects of exam anxiety on grandma's health. *The Education Digest, 52,* 45–47.

Cizek, G. J. (1999). *Cheating on tests (How to do it, detect it, and prevent it)*. Mahwah, NJ: Erlbaum.

Clark, L., DeWolf, S., & Clark, C. (1992). Teaching teachers to avoid having culturally assaultive classrooms. *Young Children, 47*(5), 4–9.

Cohen, V. B. (1983). Criteria for the evaluation of microcomputer courseware. *Educational Technology, 23*(1), 9–14.

Cole, N. S., & Moss, P. A. (1989). Bias in test use. In R. L. Linn (Ed.), *Educational measurement* (3rd ed., pp. 201–219). New York: Macmillan.

Cook, W. W. (1951). The functions of measurement in the facilitation of learning. In E. F. Lindquist (Ed.), *Educational measurement*. Washington, DC: American Council on Education.

Corey, S. M. (1943). Measuring attitudes in the classroom. *Elementary School Journal, 43,* 437–461.

Cottle, W. C. (1966). *School interest inventory.* Boston: Houghton Mifflin.

Cottle, W. C. (1968). *Interest and personality inventories.* Boston: Houghton Mifflin.

Crabb, K. D. (2001). *Case study of GIS integration in a world geography classroom.* Unpublished doctoral dissertation, University of Georgia, Athens, GA.

Cronbach, L. J. (1951). Coefficient alpha and the internal structure of tests. *Psychometrika, 16,* 297–334.

Cronbach, L. J. (1960). *Essentials of psychological testing* (2nd ed.). New York: Harper & Row.

Cronbach, L. J. (1990). *Essentials of psychological testing,* (5th ed.). New York: Harper & Row.

Cronbach, L. J., & Meehl, P. E. (1955). Construct validity in psychological tests. *Psychological Bulletin, 52,* 281–302.

Cross, L. H., Impara, J. C., Frary, R. B., & Jaeger, R. M. (1984). A comparison of three methods for establishing minimum standards on the National Teacher Examination. *Journal of Educational Measurement, 21,* 113–130.

CTB/McGraw-Hill (1987). *Comprehensive tests of basic skills.* Monterey, CA: CTB/McGraw-Hill.

CTB/McGraw-Hill (1988). *California diagnostic reading tests.* Monterey, CA: CTB/McGraw-Hill.

Culkins, L., Montgomery, K., & Santman, D. (1998). *A teacher's guide to standardized reading tests: Knowledge is power.* Portsmouth, NH: Heinemann.

Cureton, E. E. (1960). The rearrangement test. *Educational and Psychological Measurement, 20,* 31–35.

Cureton, E. E. (1966). Kuder-Richardson reliabilities of classroom tests. *Educational and Psychological Measurement, 26,* 13–14.

Cureton, E. E., Cook, J. A., Fischer, R. T., Laser, S. A., Rockwell, N. J., & Simmons, J. W., Jr. (1973). Length of test and standard error of measurement. *Educational and Psychological Measurement, 33,* 63–68.

Cushner, K., McClelland, A., & Safford, P. (1992). *Human diversity in education.* New York: McGraw-Hill.

Dana, R. H. (1993). *Multicultural assessment perspectives for professional psychology.* Boston: Allyn & Bacon.

Davis, S. L., Riss, M., & Flickinger, G. (1996, April). Honoring student self-evaluation in the classroom community. *Primary Voices K–6, 4* (2), 24–32.

*Debra P. v. Turlington* (1979). 474 F. Supp. 244 (M.D. Fla.).

*Debra P. v. Turlington* (1984). F. Suppl. No. 83–3326.

Dewey, J. (1916). *Democracy and education.* New York: The Free Press.

Dick, W., & Carey, L. (1990). *The systematic design of instruction* (3rd ed.). Glenview, IL: Scott, Foresman/Little, Brown.

Diederich, P. B. (1964). *Short-cut statistics for teacher-made tests* (2nd ed.). Evaluation and Advisory Service Series, Pamphlet no. 5. Princeton, NJ: Educational Testing Service.

Domino, G. (1971). Interactive effects of achievement orientation and teaching style on academic achievement. *Journal of Educational Psychology, 62,* 427–431.

Dunn, R., & Dunn, K. (1978). *Teaching students through their individual learning styles: A practical approach.* Reston, VA: Reston Publishing Co.

Dunn, R., Dunn, K., & Price, G. E. (1978). *Learning style inventory*. Lawrence, KS: Price Systems.

Dunning, G. M. (1954). Evaluation of critical thinking. *Science Education, 38*, 191–193.

Dyer, H. S. (1967). The discovery and development of educational goals. In *Proceedings of the 1966 Invitational Conference on Testing Problems* (pp. 12–24). Princeton, NJ: Educational Testing Service.

Eash, M. J. (1972). Developing an instrument for assessing instructional materials. In J. Weiss (Ed.), *Curriculum evaluation: Potentiality and reality* (pp. 193–205). Ontario, Canada: The Ontario Institute for Studies in Education.

Ebel, R. L. (1965). *Measuring educational achievement*. Englewood Cliffs, NJ: Prentice Hall.

Ebel, R. L., & Frisbie, D. (1991). Essentials of educational measurement (5th ed.). Englewood Cliffs, NJ: Prentice Hall.

Educational Testing Service. (1993). *Performance assessment samples*. Princeton, NJ: Educational Testing Service.

Edwards, A. L. (1957). *Techniques of attitude scale construction*. New York: Appleton-Century-Crofts.

English, H. B., & English, A. (1958). *A comprehensive dictionary of psychological and psychoanalytical terms*. New York: Longman.

Equal Employment Opportunity Commission (EEOC). (1966, 1970, 1978). Washington, DC: Author.

Feldt, L. S., & Qualls, A. L. (1996). Bias in coefficient alpha arising from heterogeneity of test content. *Applied Measurement in Education, 9*(3), 277–285.

Fitzpatrick, R., & Morrison, E. J. (1971). Performance and product evaluation. In E. L. Thorndike (Ed.), *Educational measurement* (2nd ed., pp. 237–270). Washington, DC: American Council on Education.

Flanagan, J. C. (1937). A proposed procedure for increasing the efficiency of objective tests. *Journal of Educational Psychology, 28*, 17–21.

Fosnot, C. T. (1996). *Constructivism: Theory, perspectives and practice*. New York: Teachers College Press.

Gage, R., Wages, W., & Rojar, A. (1981). Planning and authoring computer-assisted instruction lessons. *Educational Technology, 21*(9), 17–21.

Gagné, R. M. (1985). *The conditions of learning*. New York: Holt, Rinehart & Winston.

Gagné, R. M., & Briggs, L. J. (1979). *Principles of instructional design* (2nd ed.). New York: Holt, Rinehart & Winston.

Gagné, R., Wager, W., & Rojar, A. (1981). Planning and authoring computer-assisted instruction lessons. *Educational Technology, 27*(9), 17–21.

Garcia, G. E., & Pearson, P. D. (1994). Assessment and diversity. In L. Darling-Hammond (Ed.), *Review of Research in Education 20*, 337–391.

Gardner, H. (1983). *Frames of mind: The theory of multiple intelligences*. New York: Basic Books.

Geisinger, K. F. (1982). Marking systems. In H. E. Mitzel (Ed.), *Encyclopedia of educational research* (5th ed., pp. 1135–1149). New York: Macmillan.

Glaser, R. W. (1963). Instructional technology and the measurement of learning outcomes: Some questions. *American Psychologist, 18*, 519–521.

Glassey, W. (1945). The attitude of grammar school pupils and their parents to education, religion, and sport. *British Journal of Educational Psychology, 15*, 101–104.

Gold, R. M., Reilly, A., Silberman, R., & Lehr, R. (1971). Academic achievement declines under pass-fail grading. *Journal of Experimental Education, 39*, 17–21.

*Golden Rule Insurance Co. et al. v. Washburn et al.* (1984). No. 419–476 (Ill, 7th Jud. Cir.).

Green, J. L. (1970). *Introduction to measurement and evaluation.* New York: Dodd, Mead.

*Griggs v. Duke Power Co.* (1968). 292 F. Supp. 243 (MD NC).

Guerin, G. R., & Maier, A. S. (1983). *Informal assessment in education.* Palo Alto, CA: Mayfield.

Guilford, J. P. (1954). *Psychometric methods* (2nd ed.). New York: McGraw-Hill.

Guilford, J. P., & Fruchter, B. (1978). *Fundamental statistics in psychology and education* (6th ed.). New York: McGraw-Hill.

Hawes, G. R. (1972, April). Twelve sound ways to announce test results. *Nations Schools, 89*(4), 45–52.

Heath, D. H. (1972). Aesthetics and discipline. *School Review, 80*(3), 353–371.

Henning-Stout, M. (1994). *Responsive assessment.* San Francisco: Jossey-Bass.

Herman, J. L., Aschbacker, P. R., & Winters, L. (1992). *A practical guide to alternative assessment.* Alexandria, VA: Association for Supervision and Curriculum Development.

Heubert, J. P., & Houser, R. M. (1999). High stakes (testing for tracking, promotion, and graduation). Washington, DC: National Academy Press.

Hollinger, R. C., & Lanza-Kaduce, L. (1996). Academic dishonesty and the perceived effectiveness of countermeasures: An empirical survey of cheating at a major public university. *NASPA Journal, 33*(4), 292–306.

Holmes, C. T. (1989). Grade level retention effects: A meta-analysis of research studies. In L. A. Shepard & M. L. Smith (Eds.), *Flunking grades: Research and policies on retention* (pp. 16–33). London: Falmer Press.

Hoover, H. D. (1984). The most appropriate scores for measuring educational development in the elementary schools: GE's. *Educational Measurement: Issues and Practice, 3*(4), 8–14.

Hopkins, C. D., & Antes, R. L. (1990). *Classroom measurement and evaluation* (3rd ed.). Itasca, IL: Peacock.

Irvine, J. J., & York, D. E. (1995). Learning styles and culturally diverse students: A literature review. In J. A. Banks & C. A. M. Banks (Eds.), *Handbook of research on multicultural education* (pp. 484–497). New York: Macmillan.

Jaeger, R. M. (1989). Certification of student competence. In R. L. Linn (Ed.), *Educational measurement* (3rd ed., pp. 485–514. New York: Macmillan.

Johnson, D. (1998). *The indispensable teacher's guide to computer skills: A staff development guide.* Columbus, OH: Linworth Publishing.

Joint Committee, American Psychological Association, American Educational Research Association, & National Council on Measurement in Education. (1999). *Standards for educational and psychological testing.* Washington, DC: American Psychological Association.

Joyce, B., & Weil, M. (1986). *Models of teaching* (3rd ed.). Englewood Cliffs, NJ: Prentice-Hall.

Kahl, J. A. (1965). Some measurements of achievement orientation. *American Journal of Sociology, 4*, 669–681.

Kaplan, R. M., & Saccuzzo, D. P. (2001). *Psychological testing* (5th ed.). Pacific Grove, CA: Brooks/Cole.

Kelley, T. L. (1939). The selection of upper and lower groups for the validation of test items. *Journal of Educational Psychology, 30,* 17–24.

Kelley, T. L., et al. (1988). *Stanford achievement test series.* San Antonio, TX: The Psychological Corporation.

Kelley, T. L., et al. (1996). *Stanford achievement test series.* San Antonio, TX: Harcourt Educational Measurement.

Keyser, D. J., & Sweetland, R. C. (Eds.). (1988). *Test critiques* (2nd ed.). Kansas City, MO: Test Corporation of America.

Kirkhart, K. E. (1995). Seeking multicultural validity: A postcard from the road. *Evaluation Practice, 16*(1), 1–12.

Klausmeier, H. J. (1985). *Educational psychology* (5th ed.). New York: Harper & Row.

Krathwohl, D. R., Bloom, B. S., & Masia, B. B. (1964). *Taxonomy of educational objectives.* Handbook II: *The affective domain.* New York: David McKay.

Kuder, G. F., & Richardson, M. W. (1937). The theory of estimation of test reliability. *Psychometrika, 2,* 151–160.

Kulik, C. C., Kulik, J. A., & Bangert-Downs, R. L. (1990). Effectiveness of mastery learning programs: A meta-analysis. *Review of Educational Research, 60*(2), 265–299.

*Larry P. v. Riles et al.* (1979). 495 F. Supp. 926 (N. D. Cal.) *appeal docketed* No. 80-4027 (9th cir., Jan. 17, 1980).

Lathrop, R. L. (1961). A quick but accurate approximation to the standard deviation of a distribution. *Journal of Experimental Education, 29,* 319–321.

Lenke, J. M., & Keene, J. M. (1988). A response to John J. Cannell. *Educational Measurement: Issues and Practice, 7*(2), 16–18.

Likert, R. (1932). A technique for the measurement of attitudes. *Archives of Psychology,* no. 140.

Linn, R. L., & Drasgow, F. (1987). Implication of the Golden Rule settlement for test construction. *Educational Measurement: Issues and Practice, 6*(2), 13–17.

Linn, R. L., & Gronlund, N. E. (2000). *Measurement and assessment in teaching* (8th ed.). Upper Saddle River, NJ: Prentice-Hall.

Linn, R. L., & Gronlund, N. E. (1995). *Measurement and evaluation in teaching* (7th ed.). New York: Macmillan.

Lipscombe, M. J. (1992). The use of instructional analysis in the development and application of an instrument to assist in the selection of textbooks used in the training of medical professionals. Unpublished paper, Athens, GA: University of Georgia.

Lu, C., & Suen, H. K. (1995). Assessment approaches and cognitive styles. *Journal of Educational Measurement, 32*(1), 1–17.

MacGinitie, W. H., & MacGinitie, R. K. (1989). *Gates-MacGinitie reading tests* (3rd ed.). Chicago: Riverside.

Mager, R. F. (1962). *Preparing objectives for programmed instruction.* San Francisco: Fearon.

Mantel, N., & Haenszel, W. (1959). Statistical aspects of the analysis of data from retrospective studies of disease. *Journal of the National Cancer Institute, 22,* 719–748.

Marshall, J. C., & Powers, J. M. (1969). Writing neatness, composition errors, and essay grades. *Journal of Educational Measurement, 67,* 97–101.

Marzano, R. J. (2000). *Transforming classroom grading.* Alexandria, VA: Association for Supervision and Curriculum Development.

Matsumoto-Grah, K. (1992). Diversity in the classroom: A checklist. In D. A. Byrnes & G. Kiger (Eds.), *Common bonds—Anti-bias teaching in a diverse society* (pp. 105–108). Wheaton, MD: Association for Childhood Education International.

McColskey, W., & McMunn, N. (2000, October). Strategies for dealing with high-stakes state tests. *Phi Delta Kappan, 81*, 115–120.

McMorris, R. F. (1972). Evidence on the quality of several approximations for commonly used measurement statistics. *Journal of Educational Measurement, 9*(2), 113–122.

McMorris, R. F., & Boothroyd, R. A. (1993). Tests that teachers build: An analysis of classroom tests in science and mathematics. *Applied Measurement in Education, 6*(4), 321–342.

Mead, A. D., & Drasgow, F. (1993). Equivalence of computerized and paper-and-pencil cognitive ability tests: A meta-analysis. *Psychological Bulletin, 114*(3), 449–458.

Mehrens, W. A., & Kaminski, J. (1989). Methods for improving standardized test scores: Fruitful, fruitless or fraudulent? *Educational Measurement: Issues and Practice, 8*(1), 14–22.

Mehrens, W. A., & Lehmann, I. J. (1987). *Using standardized tests in education* (4th ed.). New York: Longman.

Mehrens, W. A., & Popham, W. J. (1992). How to evaluate the legal defensibility of high-stakes tests. *Applied Measurement in Education, 5*(3), 265–283.

Mehrens, W. A., & Lehmann, I. J. (1991). *Using standardized tests in education* (4th ed.). New York: Longman.

Messick, S. (1989). Validity. In R. L. Linn (Ed.), *Educational measurement* (3rd ed.). New York: Macmillan.

Messick, S., & Jungeblut, A. (1981). Time and method in coaching for the SAT. *Psychological Bulletin, 89*, 191–216.

Metfessel, W. S., Michael, W. B., & Kirsner, D. A. (1969). Instrumentation of Bloom's and Krathwohl's taxonomies for the writing of educational objectives. *Psychology in the Schools, 6*, 227–231.

Michael, W. B., Michael, J. J., & Zimmerman, W. S. (1988). *Study attitude and methods survey.* San Diego: Edits.

Millman, J., & Darling-Hammond, L. (1990). *The new handbook of teacher evaluation (Assessing elementary and secondary school teachers).* Newbury Park, CA: Sage.

Millman, J., & Greene, J. (1989). The specification and development of tests and achievement and ability. In R. L. Linn (Ed.), *Educational measurement* (3rd ed., pp. 335–366). New York: American Council on Education/Macmillan.

Millman, J., Slovarek, S. P., Kulick, E., & Mitchell, K. J. (1983). Does grade inflation affect the reliability of grades? *Research in Higher Education, 19*(4), 423–429.

Mills, C. M. (1983). A comparison of three methods of establishing cut-off scores on criterion-referenced tests. *Journal of Educational Measurement, 20*(3), 283–292.

Monroe, W. S. (1924). *Educational tests and measurements.* Boston: Houghton Mifflin.

Mullis, I. V. S., & Jenkins, L. B. (1988). *The science report card.* Princeton, NJ: Educational Testing Service.

Myers, A. E., McConville, C., & Coffman, W. E. (1966). Simplex structure in the grading of essay tests. *Educational and Psychological Measurement, 26*, 41–54.

Myers, I. B., & Briggs, K. C. (1976). *Myers-Briggs type indicator.* Palo Alto, CA: Consulting Psychologists Press.

National Council on Measurement in Education. (1990). *Standards for teacher competence in educational assessment of students.* Washington, DC: Author.

National Council on Measurement in Education. (1994). Competency standards in student assessment for educational administrators. *Educational Measurement: Issues and Practice, 13*(1), 44–47.

National Council on Measurement in Education. (1995). *Code of professional responsibilities in educational measurement.* Washington, DC: Author.

National Commission on Testing and Public Policy. (1990). *From gatekeeper to gateway: Transforming testing in America.* (Executive summary). Chestnut Hill, MA: Boston College.

Natriello, G. (1987). The impact of evaluation processes on students. *Educational Psychologist, 22*(2), 155–175.

Natriello, G., & Dornbusch, S. M. (1984). *Teacher evaluative standards and student effort.* New York: Longman.

Nitko, A. J. (1983). *Educational tests and measurement: An introduction.* New York: Harcourt Brace Jovanovich.

Norris, S. P., & Ennis, R. H. (1989). *Evaluating critical thinking.* Pacific Grove, CA: Critical Thinking Press and Software.

Nowicki, S., Jr., & Strickland, B. R. (1973). A locus of control scale for children. *Journal of Consulting and Clinical Psychology, 40*, 148–154.

Olson, J. F., Bond, L., & Andrews, C. (1999). *Annual survey of state student assessment programs—A summary report.* Washington, DC: Council of Chief State School Officers.

Orlich, D. C., Harder, R. J., Callahan, R. C., & Gibson, H. W. (1998). *Teaching strategies: A guide to better instruction.* Boston: Houghton Mifflin.

Otis, A. S., & Lennon, R. T. (1988). *Otis-Lennon school ability test.* San Antonio: The Psychological Corporation/Harcourt Educational Measurement.

Padgett-Harrison, S. K. (2000). *Influences on secondary teacher grading practices.* Unpublished doctoral dissertation. University of Georgia, Athens, GA.

Palmer, O. (1962). Seven classic ways of grading dishonestly. *The English Journal, 51*, 464–467.

*Parents in Action on Special Education v. Hannon* (1980). 506 F. Supp. 831 (N.D. Ill.).

Pate, P. E., Homestead, E., & McGinnis, K. (1993, November). Designing rubrics for authentic assessment. *Middle School Journal*, 25–27.

Payne, B. D. (1984). The relationship of test anxiety and answer-changing behavior: An analysis by race and sex. *Measurement and Evaluation in Guidance, 16*(4), 205–210.

Payne, D. A. (1994). *Designing educational project and program evaluations.* Boston: Kluwer.

Payne, D. A. (2000). *Evaluating service-learning activities and programs.* Lanham, MA: Scarecrow Press/Technomic Books.

Payne, D. A., McGee-Brown, M. J., Taylor, P., & Dukes, M. (1993). Development and validation of a family environment checklist for use in selecting at-risk participants for innovative educational preschool programs. *Educational and Psychological Measurement, 53*, 1079–1084.

Payne, J. A. (2002). New approaches to the assessment of perpetrator intelligence. *Georgia Journal of Law Enforcement, 1*(1), 1–11.

Payne, K. A. (1996). Plant life as revelation of truth. *Australian Journal of Ecological Exploration 19*(3), 19–65.

Payne, M. A. (2002). Multiple approaches to the diagnosis of DAD disease. *Newsletter of the American Association of Veterinary Offspring, 2*(3), 59–66.

Payne, S. L. (1951). *The art of asking questions*. Princeton, NJ: Princeton University Press.

Phillips, S. E. (1994). High-stakes testing accommodations: Validity versus disabled rights. *Applied Measurement in Education, 7*(2), 93–120.

Piaget, J. (1970). *The science of education and the psychology of the child*. New York: Orion Press.

Pike, L. W. (1978). *Short-term instruction, testwiseness, and the Scholastic Aptitude Test: A literature review with research recommendations* (ETS RB 78-2 and CB RDR 66-7, No. 1). Princeton, NJ: Educational Testing Service.

Pittinger, C. B. (1978). How up-to-date are current anesthesia and related textbooks? *Anesthesiology, 49*, 278–281.

Popham, W. J. (1975). *Educational evaluation*. Englewood Cliffs, NJ: Prentice-Hall.

Popham, W. J. (1987a). The merits of measurement-driven instruction. *Phi Delta Kappan, 68*(9), 679–682.

Popham, W. J. (1987b). Preparing policymakers for standard setting on high-stakes tests. *Educational Evaluation and Policy Analysis, 9*(1), 77–82.

Popham, W. J. (1991). Appropriateness of teachers' test-preparation practices. *Educational Measurement: Issues and Practice, 10*(4), 12–15.

Popham, W. J. (2002). *Classroom assessment: What teachers need to know* (3rd ed.). Boston: Allyn & Bacon.

Popham, W. J., Cruse, K. L., Smart, C. R., Sandifer, P. D., & Williams, P. L. (1985). Measurement-driven instruction: It's on the road. *Phi Delta Kappan, 66*(9), 628–634.

Powers, D. E. (1993). Coaching for the SAT: A summary of the summaries and an update. *Educational Measurement: Issues and Practice, 12*(2), 24–30.

Prediger, D. J. (1993). *Multicultural assessment standards: A compilation for counselors*. Alexandria, VA: American Counseling Association (Association for Assessment in Counseling Division).

Randall, J. A. (1936). The anecdotal behavior journal. *Progressive Education, 13*, 21–26.

Reiff, J. (1992). What research says to teachers: Learning styles. Washington, DC: National Education Association.

Reiff, J. (1993). *At-risk middle grade students or field dependent learners?* Paper presented at the annual meeting of the American Association for Childhood Education International, Phoenix, AZ.

Reigeluth, C. M. (Ed.). (1983). *Instructional design theories and models: An overview of their current status*. Hillsdale, NJ: Erlbaum.

Reisman, F. K., & Payne, B. D. (1987). *Elementary education: A basic text*. Columbus, OH: Charles E. Merrill.

Remmers, F. L., & Londino, C. (1994). The public relations portfolio. In M. E. Knight & D. Gallaro (Eds.), *Portfolio assessment (Applications of portfolio analysis)* (pp. 27–35). Lanham, MA: University Press of America.

Remmers, H. H., Gage, N. L., & Rummel, J. F. (1965). *A practical introduction to measurement and evaluation* (2nd ed.). New York: Harper & Row.

Renzulli, J. S., & Smith, L. H. (1978). *The learning styles inventory: A measure of student preferences for instructional techniques*. Mansfield Center, CT: Creative Learning Press.

Research Concepts. (1978). *Country school examinations: Fall term examinations, 1914*. Muskegon, MI: Test Maker, Inc.

Reynolds, C. R., & Brown, R. T. (1984). Bias in mental testing: An introduction to the issues. In C. R. Reynolds & R. T. Brown (Eds.), *Perspectives on bias in mental testing* (pp. 1–40). New York: Plenum.

Ricks, J. H. (1956). How accurate is a test score? *Test Service Bulletin 50*. New York: Psychological Corporation.

Ripple, R. E. (1965). Affective factors influence classroom learning. *Educational Leadership, 22*(7), 476–480.

Riverside Publishing Co. (1983). *Improving test-taking skills.* Iowa City: Riverside.

Rosenshine, B. (1985). Teaching functions in instructional programs. *The Elementary School Journal, 83*(4), 335–351.

Saupe, J. L. (1961). Some useful estimates of the Kuder–Richardson Formula Number 20 reliability coefficient. *Educational and Psychological Measurement, 21*, 63–71.

Sax, G. (1997). *Principles of educational and psychological measurement and evaluation* (4th ed.). Belmont, CA: Wadsworth.

Schine, J. (Ed.). (1997). *Service-learning* (Ninety-sixth Yearbook of the National Society for the Study of Education). Chicago: University of Chicago Press.

Schmidt, W. H. (1983). Content biases in achievement tests. *Journal of Educational Measurement, 20*(2), 165–178.

Schurr, S. L. (1992). *The abc's of evaluation* (26 alternative ways to assess student progress). Columbus, OH: National Middle School Association.

Scriven, M. (1967). The methodology of evaluation. *Perspectives of Curriculum Evaluation.* Monograph No. 1. Chicago: Rand McNally.

Scriven, M. (1972). Pros and cons about goal-free evaluation. *Evaluation Comment, 3*(4), 1–7.

Sheppard, L. (2000). The role of assessment in a learning culture. *Educational Researcher, 29*(7), 4–14.

Simpson, R. H. (1944). The specific meanings of certain terms indicating different degrees of frequency. *Quarterly Journal of Speech, 30*, 328–330.

Slavin, R. E. (1987). Cooperative learning and the education of black students. In D. S. Strickland & E. J. Cooper (Eds.), *Educating black children: America's challenge* (pp. 63–68). Washington, DC: Howard University Press.

Sleeter, C. E., & Grant, C. A. (1987). An analysis of multicultural education in the United States. *Harvard Educational Review, 57*(4), 421–444.

Smith, G. P. (1995). *Toward defining culturally responsible and responsive teacher education: The knowledge bases for educating teachers of minority and culturally diverse students.* Paper/Institute presented at the Fifth Annual Conference of the National Association for Multicultural Education, Washington, DC.

Snelbecker, G. E. (1985). *Learning theory, instructional theory, and psychoeducational design.* New York: University Press of America.

Solley, B. A. (1989). *The effects of cognitive monitoring strategies on fifth grade children's narrative writing.* Unpublished doctoral dissertation, University of Georgia, Athens, GA.

Spielberger, C. D., & Vagg, P. R. (Eds.). (1995). *Test anxiety: Theory, assessment and treatment.* Washington, DC: Taylor & Francis.

Stake, R. (1967). The countenance of educational evaluation. *Teachers College Record, 68*(7), 523–540.

Stake, R. (1975). *Evaluating the arts in education: A responsive approach.* Columbus, OH: Charles E. Merrill.

Starch, D., & Elliott, E. C. (1912). Reliability of grading high school work in English. *School Review, 20*, 442–457.

Starch, D., & Elliott, E. C. (1913a). Reliability of grading work in history. *School Review, 21*, 676–681.

Starch, D., & Elliott, E. C. (1913b). Reliability of grading work in mathematics. *School Review, 21,* 254–257.

Sternberg, R. J. (1988). *The triarchic mind: A new theory of human intelligence.* New York: Viking.

Stiggins, R. J. (1987). Design and development of performance assessments. *Educational Measurement: Issues and Practice, 6*(3), 33–42.

Stiggins, R. J., Frisbie, D. A., & Griswold, P. A. (1989). Inside high school grading practices: Building a research agenda. *Educational measurement: Issues and Practice, 8*(2), 5–14.

Swanicki, E. F. (1981). Contract plans: A professional growth-oriented approach to evaluating teacher performance. In J. Millman (Ed.), *Handbook of teacher evaluation.* Beverly Hills, CA: Sage.

Terwilliger, J. S. (1971). *Assigning grades to students.* Glenview, IL: Scott, Foresman.

Terwilliger, J. S. (1989). Classroom standard setting and grading practices. *Educational measurement: Issues and Practice, 8*(2), 15–19.

Trueba, H. T., Cheng, L. R. L., & Ima, K. (1993). *Myth or reality (Adaptive strategies of Asian Americans in California).* Washington, DC: Falmer.

Tversky, A. (1964). On the optimal number of alternatives at a choice point. *Journal of Mathematical Psychology, 1,* 386–391.

Tyler, R. W. (1933). Permanence of learning. *Journal of Higher Education, 4,* 203–204.

Tyler, R. W. (1973). Testing for accountability. In A. C. Ornstein (Ed.), *Accountability for teachers and school administrators.* Belmont, CA: Feardon Publishers.

*United States v. State of South Carolina* (1977). 445 F. Supp. 1094 (DSC).

Wall, J., & Summerlin, L. (1972). Choosing the right test. *The Science Teacher, 39,* 32–36.

Walsh, W. B., & Betz, N. E. (1995). *Tests and assessment* (3rd ed.). Englewood Cliffs, NJ: Prentice Hall.

Webb, E. J., Campbell, D. T., Schwartz, R. O., Sechrest, L., & Grove, J. B. (1981). *Nonreactive measures in the social sciences* (2nd ed.). Boston: Houghton Mifflin.

Wechsler, D. (1991). *Wechsler intelligence scale for children—Third Edition.* San Antonio: The Psychological Corporation/Harcourt Brace Jovanovich.

Wesley, J. C. (1994). Effects of ability, high school achievement, and procrastinatory behavior on college performance. *Educational and Psychological Measurement, 54*(2), 404–408.

Witkin, H. A. (1971). *Group embedded figures test.* Palo Alto, CA: Consulting Psychologists Press.

Witkin, H. A., & Goodenough, D. R. (1981). *Cognitive styles: Essence and origins.* New York: International Universities Press.

Woodcock, R. W. (1987). *Woodcock reading mastery tests—Revised.* Circle Pines, MN: American Guidance Service.

Wren, D. G. (2000). *The development and validation of an instrument for measuring children's test anxiety.* Unpublished doctoral dissertation, University of Georgia, Athens, GA.

Yalow, E. S., & Popham, W. J. (1983). Content validity at the crossroads. *Educational Researcher, 12*(8), 10–14, 21.

Yelon, S. L., & Scott, R. O. (1970). *A strategy for writing objectives.* Dubuque, IA: Kendall/Hunt.

# Name and Title Index

# Subject Index

Edu.Cur. Coll. LB 3051 .P334
Payne, David A.      2003
Applied educational
  assessment      + CD in
                    pocket

LIBRARY
UNIVERSITY OF NEW HAVEN

DATE DUE

| | | | |
|---|---|---|---|
| MAY 18 2011 | | | |
| | | | |
| | | | |
| | | | |
| | | | |
| | | | |
| | | | |
| | | | |

DEMCO 128-5046

DEMCO